Macrosociology

Macrosociology

AN INTRODUCTION TO HUMAN SOCIETIES

Fourth Edition

Stephen K. Sanderson
Indiana University of Pennsylvania

An Imprint of Addison Wesley Longman, Inc.

New York • Reading, Massachusetts • Menlo Park, California • Harlow, England
Don Mills, Ontario • Sydney • Mexico City • Madrid • Amsterdam

Editor-in-Chief: Priscilla McGeehon
Acquisitions Editor: Alan McClare
Marketing Manager: Megan Galvin
Supplements Editor: Lisa Ziccardi
Project Coordination and Text Design: Electronic Publishing Services, Inc., NYC
Cover Designer/Manager: Nancy Danahy
Cover Photo: PhotoDisc, Inc.
Full Service Production Manager: Valerie Zaborski
Print Buyer: Denise Sandler
Electronic Page Makeup: Heather A. Peres
Printer and Binder: The Maple-Vail Book Manufacturing Group
Cover Printer: Coral Graphic Services, Inc.

For permission to use copyrighted material, grateful acknowledgment is made to the copyright holders on p. 455, which are hereby made part of this copyright page.

Library of Congress Cataloging-in-Publication Data
Sanderson, Stephen K.
    Macrosociology: an introduction to human societies/Stephen K. Sanderson. --4th ed.
    p.   cm.
  Includes bibliograhical references and index.
  ISBN 0-321-01846-X
  1. Macrosociology.   I. Title.
HM51.S26   1998
301--dc21   98-22973
                                                                                        CIP

Please visit our website at http://longman.awl.com

ISBN 0-321-01846-X

12345678910—MA—01009998

For Ruth, Derek, and Sarah

No description can even begin to lead to a valid explanation
if it does not effectively encompass the whole world.

—Fernand Braudel

Contents

Preface

Macrosociology is intended for use as a textbook in introductory sociology courses taught by instructors who wish to take a comparative, historical, and evolutionary perspective on human societies. It treats not only modern industrial societies, but also the full range of preindustrial societies—hunter-gatherers, horticulturalists, pastoralists, and agrarian societies. It also looks at how these societies have emerged one from the other in the long span of human history and prehistory, especially the past 10,000 years. In my view there are several important advantages to this broad perspective: enhanced scientific rigor, because comparison is the essence of science; an enhanced ability to combat ethnocentrism; a strong focus on the extremely important issue of social change; and an enhanced ability to prepare students for the global social order in which we now live. A comparative and evolutionary perspective provides a fascinating learning experience that is capable of giving us more insight into the nature of our own society than would otherwise be possible. I have gained enormous pleasure over the years from the comparative analysis of human behavior and human societies, and I am delighted to be able to share what I have learned with others.

In this fourth edition of *Macrosociology* I have concentrated mainly on shortening, streamlining, and to some extent simplifying the text. The first edition of this book was approximately 500 pages in length, but the next two editions grew to 565 and 600 pages, respectively. In all honesty, that is a little too long, and so it was decided to shorten this edition to approximately the length of the first edition. I have done this by condensing some longer discussions and also by eliminating less essential sections. The basic core of the book, however, remains unchanged. Additional chapter-by-chapter changes are indicated below.

- *Chapter 1:* Revised discussion of the idealist and conflict strategies; new special topic, Why Americans Prefer Beef.

- *Chapter 2:* Revised and highly streamlined discussion of human evolution; revised and updated discussion of language; updated discussion of research on ape language; revised discussion of the special topic on sociobiology.
- *Chapter 3:* Simplified discussion of adaptation.
- *Chapter 4:* Updated discussion of hunter-gatherers as the "original affluent society."
- *Chapter 5:* New special topic, The Potlatch.
- *Chapter 7:* Revised discussion of early capitalism.
- *Chapter 8:* Updated discussion of the contemporary situation in postsocialist societies.
- *Chapter 9:* Updated statistical data; updated discussion of empirical research on dependency theory; new section on globalization.
- *Chapter 10:* Revised discussion of stratification under state socialism; updated discussion of stratification and the postsocialist transition; new special topic on stratification and the welfare state.
- *Chapter 12:* Simplified discussion of the emergence of early modern states; new special topic on revolutions and state breakdowns.
- *Chapter 13:* New definition of racism; expanded discussion of racism, especially concerning whether it existed in the ancient and medieval worlds.
- *Chapter 14:* Updated statistical data; updated discussion of the sociobiological interpretation of gender.
- *Chapter 15:* This chapter and old Chapter 16 on the modern Western family have been condensed and merged into one chapter; expanded discussion of monogamy, polygyny, and polyandry.
- *Chapter 16:* More logical organization of the chapter; expanded discussion of the nature of educational expansion; updated statistical data.
- *Chapter 17:* New section on the Axial Age and the rise of Christianity; new special topic on revitalization and millenarian movements.
- *Chapter 18:* Updated discussion of environmental depletion.

I recognize that the organization of *Macrosociology* may not be the preferred one for everyone. It is organized thematically, because that is the way most instructors approach the introductory course, but some instructors may prefer a more chronological or historical organization. That can easily be achieved by reordering the chapters approximately as follows:

- *Conceptual and Theoretical Foundations:* Chapters 1, 2, and 3.
- *Preindustrial and Precapitalist Societies:* Chapters 4, 5, 6, 11, and 15, and appropriate parts of 14, 16, and 17.
- *The Capitalist World-Economy and Industrial Capitalist and Socialist Societies:* Chapters 7, 8, 10, 12, and 13, and appropriate parts of 14, 15, 16, and 17.
- *The Third World:* Chapter 9 and appropriate parts of 12, 14, and 16.
- *The Future:* Chapter 18.

I am grateful to Arthur S. Alderson of Indiana University–Bloomington for his useful suggestions for improvements in this new edition. Margaret Dornfeld of Electronic Publishing Services, Inc., served as the project editor and helped move the book smoothly through the production process. I would also like to thank the reviewers for the current edition: Garrett Olmsted, Bluefield State College; David L. Harvey, University of Nevada–Reno; John Teddy Ambenge, University of Connecticut; David J. Maume, Jr., University of Cincinnati; Peggy A. Lovell, University of Pittsburgh; Christopher Chase-Dunn, Johns Hopkins University; Brian C. Aldrich, Winona State University; and Jack Sattel, Minneapolis Community College. As in all previous editions of this book, I dedicate it to my wife Ruth, and my children, Derek and Sarah, who were unborn when I first started writing the book and wee tots when I finished the first edition, but who have now grown old enough to read it and understand it—not that they are necessarily so inclined!

Stephen K. Sanderson

Chapter

1

Sociology and the Scientific Study of Human Societies

The degree of diversity in human social life is quite remarkable. Some societies are small and simple in organization; others are large and extremely complex. Some societies depend for their livelihood on the hunting of wild animals and the collecting of wild plants, others depend upon agriculture, and still others depend upon modern industry. Among those dependent upon industry, some have capitalist economies while others have established socialism. Democratic governments prevail in many modern societies, authoritarian governments in a number of others. Many societies of the past had no formal governments at all, a situation that persists even in some present-day societies. Warfare has been a chronic feature of a large number of societies, yet among some groups it is virtually unknown. Men in most of the world's cultures have preferred to take more than one wife, yet in modern industrial societies this practice is prohibited by law. People in some societies value individual ambition and competition, while the members of other groups emphasize instead intensive forms of cooperation and sharing. Women in many cultures are regarded as inferior and treated as such by men, while numerous other cultures regard women as more or less the equals of men and treat them accordingly. The list could go on almost endlessly.

Despite the great range of variation in human thought and action, however, there are a number of characteristics common to all or most societies.

All societies have economic systems, modes of marriage and family life, means of maintaining law and order, and forms of religious belief and ritual. All societies prohibit or discourage incest. No society is governed by women, nor does any society give women primary responsibility for the conduct of war. In short, human societies have common as well as variable features, similarities as well as differences.

Another noteworthy feature of human social life is the degree to which societies change. Contemporary Americans, for instance, live in a society that has changed enormously over the past 200 years and is currently undergoing dramatic social change. The changes that have occurred have been not only deep but rapid as well, and the speed of change is constantly increasing. Yet some societies change very little, even over long periods of time. One can find even today a few groups still dependent upon the hunting of wild animals and the collection of wild plants. These groups perpetuate a lifestyle that differs little from that carried on by their ancestors thousands of years ago.

What accounts for these phenomena? Why are societies similar in certain broad respects? Why do they differ from one another in important ways? Why do some change with great magnitude and speed while others change so little and so slowly? These questions and others are the central focus of this book, which is an introduction to that science of social life known as **sociology.**

THE NATURE OF SOCIOLOGY

Microsociology Versus Macrosociology

Sociology is the scientific study of human social life. Sociologists inquire into the nature and causes of regularized and repeatable *patterns* of human thought and conduct. Unlike psychologists, who focus on the thoughts and actions characteristic of distinctive individuals, sociologists are interested only in those thoughts and actions that are shared by persons as members of groups or societies. Yet sociology is a broad and diverse discipline, and there are different kinds of sociologists who study different things with different aims in mind.

It is conventional to distinguish between two major types of sociology, known as microsociology and macrosociology. **Microsociology** investigates the patterns of thought and behavior that occur in relatively small-scale social groups. Persons identifying themselves as microsociologists are interested in such things as styles of verbal and nonverbal communication in face-to-face social relationships, the process of decision making by juries, the formation and disintegration of friendship groups, and the influence of individuals' group memberships on their outlook on the world.

Macrosociology, by contrast, devotes itself to the study of large-scale social patterns. It focuses on total societies and their major elements, such as the economy, the political system, the mode of family life, and the nature of the religious system. It also has an abiding concern with world networks of interacting societies. Many macrosociologists limit themselves to the study of a single society in a single historical period. Macrosociologists in the United States, for example, frequently restrict their research to the broad social patterns characteristic of contemporary American society. Other macrosociologists have somewhat broader fields of inquiry; they expand their interests to include the comparative study of many different contemporary societies. Some macrosociologists go much further still and focus on the comparative study of the entire range of human societies, both past and present.

This book is exclusively concerned with macrosociology, and it is macrosociological in the broadest sense. It is devoted to the systematic examination of the major similarities and differences between societies, and it is concerned as well with the nature of the changes that societies undergo.

The version of macrosociology presented in this book is one that overlaps extensively with and draws heavily upon the concepts, theories, and findings of two other social sciences: anthropology and history.

Anthropology is a very broad field devoted to the study of humankind. It is actually a composite discipline consisting of four separate yet closely related subfields. **Cultural anthropology** aims at understanding the patterns of organized social life among preindustrial or primitive peoples. A major concern of cultural anthropologists is the construction of **ethnographies,** or detailed descriptive accounts of the ways of life of contemporary primitive peoples. Cultural anthropologists are, however, concerned with more than just descriptions of different cultures. Many of them spend much of their time attempting to build coherent theories about why different cultural patterns exist. Therefore, cultural anthropologists engage in explanatory as well as descriptive endeavors. **Biological anthropology** is principally devoted to understanding the course of human biological evolution through a detailed examination of the record of the fossilized remains of earlier human beings. **Anthropological linguistics** studies the nature and formation of human languages and the relationship between these languages and patterns of social life. **Archaeology** is that branch of anthropology that is concerned with the remains of ancient societies. By studying these remains,

archaeologists hope to learn about patterns of social life, as well as about some of the major social changes that occurred in the past. These subfields of anthropology are intimately related to each other, and the practitioners of one subfield frequently draw upon the findings of one or more of the other subfields.

History is a large and varied field of study concerned with describing and explaining what happened in the past, and a large number of historians study various aspects of social life characteristic of societies of earlier times.

Many of the findings and theories of history and anthropology (particularly cultural anthropology and archaeology) form an important part of this book. These findings and theories are connected with those produced by sociologists on the nature of contemporary industrial societies. The result is a very broad-based comparative and historical macrosociology. It is only through this sort of broad-based approach that the nature and causes of human social life can be properly understood. And that, indeed, is the primary aim of sociological investigation.

The Role of Science in the Study of Social Life

As indicated earlier, sociology is the **scientific** study of human social life. The most distinctive characteristic of science is its **empirical** approach. Scientists require that all claims to truth be submitted to rigorous scrutiny and tested against the facts derived from observation of the world. A claim to truth is valid in the scientific sense not because it has an intuitive plausibility or because a person or group with prestige or authority proclaims it. It is valid only to the extent to which it is in agreement with known facts.

Many scientists spend much of their time doing basic descriptive work: identifying, characterizing, and classifying the phenomena they are concerned with. However, description alone is not the aim of science, and it is in fact only a preliminary stage of scientific investigation. The ultimate aim of science is *explanation:* the identification of the basic causes of the phenomena under investigation. Scientific explanation in sociology proceeds through the construction of **theoretical strategies** and **theories.** Theoretical strategies are highly global sets of basic assumptions, concepts, and orienting principles (cf. M. Harris, 1979). They are designed to apply to social phenomena in the broadest possible sense. Their purpose is to generate specific theories and initiate lines of research to test those theories. A theory is a specific statement or interrelated set of statements designed to explain some particular phenomenon. A theory is thus much narrower and more specific than a theoretical strategy. A theoretical strategy applies broadly to a great range of phenomena and is composed of a great many interrelated theories. While these interrelated theories apply to different phenomena, they have much in common, for they all proceed from the same global set of assumptions, concepts, and principles.

Sociologists engage in the empirical testing of both theoretical strategies and theories. A theoretical strategy is a good one only to the extent that it generates specific theories that hold up under empirical scrutiny. We can have great confidence in a theoretical strategy that has generated and continues to generate many well-supported theories. By contrast, a theoretical strategy that contains few well-supported theories and many theories known to be false is judged to be inadequate. It inspires little confidence and is a poor guide to further theorizing and research.

It is important to note that all theoretical strategies contain at least some theories that must be rejected as false. But the rejection of any particular theory is not a sufficient basis for the rejection of an entire theoretical strategy. So long as a theoretical strategy contains many well-supported theories, continued reliance on it is justified, regardless of the fact that some of its theories are unacceptable.

A number of diverse theoretical strategies currently exist within contemporary macrosociology. All of these strategies have, of course, their proponents and their detractors. Following is a discussion of the general nature of these strategies and an indication of the ones that provide the orienting framework for this book.

THE MAJOR THEORETICAL STRATEGIES IN CONTEMPORARY MACROSOCIOLOGY

Materialist Versus Idealist Strategies

The Idealist Strategy Sociologists have long debated the relative merits of **idealist** versus **materialist** approaches to the study of human social life. Idealist approaches—and there are several varieties of these—attempt to explain the basic features of social life by reference to the creative capacity of the human mind. Idealists believe that human uniqueness lies in the fact that humans attach symbolic meanings to their actions. Humans create elaborate networks of ideas and ideals and use these mental constructs to guide their patterns of behavior. Different behavior patterns characteristic of different societies are seen as the result of different sets of ideas and ideals. However, idealists usually give little attention to the problem of how different sets of ideas and ideals originate in the first place, a serious weakness in their theories.

One of the most prominent idealist theoretical strategies in contemporary sociology is an approach known as **social constructionism.** This is really a family of theories that consists of two main branches, called respectively symbolic interactionism and ethnomethodology. These are usually thought of as micro- rather than macrolevel approaches, but they have significant implications for macrosociology and are sometimes applied at that level. **Symbolic interactionism** originated as an American sociological approach in the early part of this century and has continued to be an influential perspective. It emphasizes the capacity of individuals to interact through the use of symbols and to impose their own subjective definitions of reality onto social situations that they confront. An early symbolic interactionist, William Isaac Thomas, coined the term *definition of the situation*, which he explained by the phrase, "If men define situations as real they are real in their consequences." Thomas was stressing that people's subjective definitions of reality can be so powerful that they bring about objective consequences that conform to those subjective definitions regardless of whether the definitions were originally objectively true. Two contemporary symbolic interactionists are Herbert Blumer and Howard Becker. Blumer (1969) took a rather extreme position that emphasized the almost limitless ability of individuals to define situations in their own way and to act accordingly. Becker took a less extreme position, but he also made the social definition of reality the linchpin of his theoretical position. For example, he wrote a famous essay (1963) in which he claimed that the experience of smoking marijuana was due at least as much to the social definitions surrounding the drug's effects as to their actual physiological consequences for the body. To experience marijuana smoking as a pleasurable experience, he argued, one had to be part of a group that defined it as pleasurable. Otherwise, the effects could be very different.

Ethnomethodology is a recent strategy that carries symbolic interactionism's emphasis on the subjective definition of reality to a greater extreme. The key phrase in this perspective is "the social construction of reality" (Berger and Luckmann, 1966). In its most extreme form, this means that society or social life does not exist in an objective form—that is, in actuality. Rather, it exists only in people's minds as a set of perceptions, definitions, and ways of talking. Ethnomethodology's "founding father" was Harold Garfinkel (1967). Garfinkel and the many students he has influenced have been interested in the same problem that has preoccupied sociological functionalists (see below): the problem of social order, or social continuity and stability through time. However, whereas the functionalists have seen this order as an objective one, the ethnomethodologists have viewed it as a distinctively subjective one. For the latter, social order is merely definitional, and it persists the way it does because of people's attachments to their subjective definitions. Ethnomethodologists claim to be most interested in finding out just how it is that people construct reality, and how and why they come to be so attached to the particular definitions that they develop.

Another version of idealism is found in the writings of the late contemporary American sociologist Talcott Parsons (1937, 1966). Parsons holds that the core of every society is a network of socially shared meanings, beliefs, and values. The beliefs and values that the members of a society are able to create structure the basic ways in which they organize their social life. For instance, Parsons sees modern Western societies as strongly organized around fundamental values associated with Christianity and liberal democracy. He believes that because Westerners have developed these systems of religious and political values they have been able to solve certain societal problems that still plague other societies, whose members live according to very different beliefs and values.

The Materialist Strategy Materialists strongly reject the kinds of theories just mentioned. Rather than giving ideas and ideals causal priority, they attempt to explain the basic features of social life in terms of the practical, material conditions of human existence. These conditions involve such things as the nature of the physical environment, the level of technology, and the organization of the economic system. Materialists see these factors as constituting the basic prerequisites of human existence. The first concern of human life is adaptation to the natural environment, and this must be done by constructing a technological and economic system. Once certain technologies and economies are created, they constrain the nature of the other social patterns that humans will create. Different kinds of technologies and economies give rise to different kinds of social patterns. Furthermore, materialists generally see human ideas and ideals as arising from previously created social patterns. Like idealists, they recognize the creative capacity of the human mind. Unlike idealists, however, materialists hold that ideas and ideals are not self-generating, but arise as responses to the material and social conditions already established.

The materialist approach to social life began with the work of the famous nineteenth-century German social theorists Karl Marx (1818–1883) and Friedrich Engels (1820–1895). Marx and Engels (1970; orig. 1846) developed what they referred to as the "materialist conception of history," and what has since come to be known as **historical materialism** (sometimes called **dialectical materialism**). This was a theoretical approach to social life developed in direct opposition to the current of idealism that prevailed at that time in German philosophy. Although historical materialism was constructed primarily as a means of understanding modern capitalist societies, Marx and Engels understood it to be applicable as well to the whole range of human societies in both the past and the present.

Marx and Engels divided human societies into two major components. One of these they referred to as the *infrastructure* or *base,* sometimes also called the **mode of production.** The base was in turn divided into two categories: the *forces of production* and the *relations of production.* The forces of production consisted of the raw materials and social creations necessary for a society to engage in economic production: the available level of technology and the specific nature of natural resources, such as the quality of the land. The relations of production referred to the ownership of the forces of production. Marx and Engels noted that in some societies the forces of production were owned communally (by the entire group), but in other societies private ownership of the productive forces had emerged. The group that acquired ownership of the productive forces was able to compel other groups to work for it. Marx and Engels noted that several different forms of private relations of production existed in different societies.

The other major component of human societies identified by Marx and Engels was the *superstructure.* This component consisted of all those aspects of a society not included in the base, such as politics, law, family life, religion, and ideas and ideals.

Marx and Engels held that a society's base and its superstructure were directly related. Although they noted that the superstructure could occasionally influence the base, they argued that the primary direction of causation ran from the base to the superstructure. They believed, in other words, that the patterns of human thought and action found within a society's superstructure were largely shaped by the features of the society's base. They also thought that social changes within the superstructure were brought about mainly by changes that had already occurred within the base. This was the essence of their materialism.

The materialism of Marx and Engels was long rejected by most sociologists as an inadequate strategy for studying social life. In recent decades, however, it has been significantly revived, and many contemporary sociologists adhere to the basic principle of materialistic causation that Marx and Engels advocated. However, many other contemporary sociologists continue to reject this principle, either in whole or in part. Contemporary idealists generally reject it entirely, preferring instead to reverse the direction of causation specified in the Marxian strategy. Yet others reject it only in part, claiming that it has some validity but that by itself it greatly oversimplifies the nature of social reality. Such sociologists frequently advocate combining materialist and idealist strategies. They argue that social life is the joint product of both material conditions and ideas and ideals.

This book takes an explicitly materialist approach to the study of social life. It accepts as fundamentally valid the basic principle of causation put forth by Marx and Engels. However, the materialist approach of this book is a revised and updated version of classical historical materialism.

Functionalism

The theoretical strategy known as **functionalism** came to be a part of sociological analysis during the 1940s. It reached its peak level of influence during the 1950s; during this time, functionalism became the standard theoretical strategy of the majority of sociologists, and it received little theoretical opposition. Beginning in the 1960s, however, functionalism's theoretical dominance came to be severely challenged, and its adequacy was called increasingly into question. It entered a period of rapid decline. Nonetheless, even though a majority of sociologists today do not seem to advocate a functionalist approach to the study of social life, functionalism is still seriously endorsed by a significant sociological minority (Sanderson and Ellis, 1992). In fact, since the early 1980s a notable functionalist revival has occurred (J. C. Alexander, 1982, 1984, 1985).

Functionalism's basic principles are essentially as follows:

- Societies are complex systems of interrelated and interdependent parts, each of which significantly influences the others.
- Each part of a society exists because it has an important function to perform in maintaining the existence or well-being of the society as a whole.
- The existence of any part of a society is explained when its function for the whole society is identified.
- All societies have mechanisms that integrate them or allow them to hold together, one of the most important of which is the commitment of a society's members to a common set of beliefs and values.
- Societies tend toward a state of equilibrium or homeostasis, and disturbances in any part of a society tend to bring about adjustments elsewhere in the society designed to restore the equilibrium.
- Social change is a much less common occurrence in societies than social stability, but when change does occur it generally leads to beneficial consequences for society as a whole.

Functionalists have shown interest in the debate between materialists and idealists, yet few of them have explicitly chosen one side or the other in this debate. Although a few functionalists have leaned strongly toward the idealist side, most have opted for a middle-ground position, arguing that both material factors and ideas and ideals are crucial influences on the nature of social patterns. This position is consistent with the typical functionalist claim that societies are systems of interdependent parts in which each one vitally affects the others.

As indicated earlier, functionalism came under severe criticism during the 1960s. The major criticisms that were leveled against the functionalists may be summarized as follows (Dahrendorf, 1958; P. Cohen, 1968; Zeitlin, 1973):

- Functionalists tend to overemphasize the degree to which human societies are harmonious, stable, and well-integrated systems.
- Because of this overemphasis on harmony and stability, functionalists tend to neglect or underemphasize the extent to which social conflict is a basic feature of most societies.
- With their exaggeration of harmony and underemphasis of conflict, functionalists tend to encourage a conservative bias in the study of social life; that is, they appear to argue for the necessity of preserving whatever social arrangements exist in a society.
- Functionalists generally limit themselves to the study of a society at only a single point in time (the present), and thus apply a remarkably ahistorical approach to the study of social life.
- Since functionalists ignore the historical dimension to social life, they have considerable difficulty accounting for social change.
- Functionalists treat societies as if they are entities with their own existence quite apart from the individuals who make them up, and thus engage in a dramatic **reification** of social life; that is, they assign a level of reality to society that it cannot logically possess.

An important distinction must be made between functionalism and **functional analysis** (G. A. Cohen, 1978). This distinc-

tion explains the charge of reification noted above. Functionalism involves the basic substantive principles set forth earlier. Functional analysis, however, is distinctively different. Rather than being based on a set of substantive principles, it represents the basic methodological tactic of assuming that certain phenomena should be analyzed and understood from the point of view of their adaptive significance, that is, from the vantage point of their usefulness in fulfilling some aim or objective. Functional analysis is widely used in the social sciences quite apart from the functionalist principles just mentioned. In fact, social theorists who disagree strongly with functionalism often use forms of functional analysis in developing their theories. Karl Marx, for instance, would have been repelled by modern functionalism, but he frequently engaged in a type of functional analysis. When he argued that a society's ideas and ideals should be understood in terms of the purposes they serve for the members of powerful social groups, he was undoubtedly engaging in functional analysis. For another example, a number of modern social theorists have attempted to explain why the ancient Israelites placed a taboo on the eating of pork, a taboo that is still respected by Orthodox Jews. Some of these theorists have approached this problem by attempting to discern the ways in which this taboo may have been useful for the ancient Israelites—how it may have assisted them in solving certain basic problems of living they confronted (M. Harris, 1974, 1977). This kind of approach is a classic instance of what is meant by functional analysis.

Another way of thinking about the distinction between functionalism and functional analysis is to deal with the level of analysis at which each operates. A major feature of functionalism is the idea of **societal needs.** Functionalists believe that societies are much like biological organisms in that they have fundamental needs that must be met for the society to continue to exist or at least to function smoothly. The basic features of social life—the structures of society—emerge in order to fulfill these societal needs. Although the notion of societal needs may appear at first sight to be entirely reasonable, on closer inspection it is revealed to be troublesome if not downright mystical. Careful thought will show that societies cannot have needs in any meaningful sense; only individual persons can. While it is true that people develop particular needs as a result of living together, these are still the needs of concrete, flesh-and-blood persons rather than of some abstraction called "society." Functional analysis recognizes this crucial distinction and makes it basic to its mode of inquiry. Those who engage in functional analysis (but not functionalism) propose that the aims or objectives fulfilled by specific social phenomena are always the aims or objectives of concrete persons. Functional analysts recognize that what we call "society" does not exist as an entity in and of itself; rather, it is simply a word that we use for a collectivity of people who interact in certain ways in order to satisfy their needs and desires.

The major criticisms of functionalism are more or less valid; however, these criticisms do not apply to functional analysis. Although this book does not advocate or make use of functionalist principles, it does make frequent use of functional analysis. It does so, however, largely in the context of a materialist perspective and, moreover, in conjunction with what is often referred to as a conflict approach.

The Conflict Strategy

What is usually called **conflict theory** began to emerge in American sociology during the 1960s. Actually, the emergence of conflict theory was a revival of many of the ideas set forth much earlier by Karl Marx and another famous early German sociologist by the name of Max Weber (1864–1920). Although both Marx and Weber were conflict theorists, and thus agreed with each other in important ways, they nonetheless developed rather different versions of conflict theory. Modern conflict theory is therefore split into two main types: neo-Marxian and neo-Weberian conflict theory. The neo-Marxian version is the better known and more influential of the two.

What all conflict theories have in common, and thus what Marx and Weber agreed on, is the rejection of the idea that societies tend toward some basic consensus or harmony in which the features of society work for everyone's good. Conflict theorists see **conflict** and struggle—the opposing interests and concerns of different individuals and groups—as the prime determinants of the organization of social life. In other words, the basic structure of society is mainly determined by the efforts made by individuals and groups to acquire scarce resources that will satisfy their needs and wants. Since these resources are always, to one degree or another, in short supply, conflict over access to them is always occurring. Marx and Weber applied this general notion to their sociological theories from different vantage points.

Marx held that structured forms of conflict between individuals and groups arose primarily through the establishment of private relations of production. At a certain point in the evolution of human social life, private relations of production began to supplant communal ownership of the forces of production. Societies were thus split into groups that owned and groups that did not own the productive forces—into social classes. In any given class-divided society, the social class that owned the productive forces was able to subordinate other social classes and to compel them to work to satisfy its particular interests. The dominant class was therefore related to subordinate classes through a process of economic exploitation. Naturally enough, subordinate classes came to resent being exploited and threatened to rebel against the dominant class and to take away its privileges. But the dominant class, sensing the possibility of rebellion from below, created a powerful political apparatus—the state—capable of suppressing any such rebellion by force.

Marx therefore saw the *class struggle* as the most fundamental form of conflict in human societies. This struggle reverberated throughout society. It led to other forms of social conflict and played a major role in shaping noneconomic social patterns, such as politics and religion. Marx was most concerned with the role of class struggle in modern capitalist society. In historical forms of society, Marx said, class divisions between masters and slaves or landlords and peasants were prominent, but in capitalist society the main class division was that between *capitalists* and *workers*. The capitalists owned the forces of production in the form of capital (land, buildings, machinery, raw materials, money) and sought to produce goods that could be sold for a profit. The means to profit lay fundamentally in exploiting the working class by paying it less than the full value of the products it was producing. It was this exploitative relationship between capitalists and workers that was at the root of capitalist society, and the nature of capitalist society as a whole could only be properly understood by giving that class relationship center stage.

The modern Marxian conflict strategy is mainly a formalization and elaboration of the ideas just discussed. The major principles of this strategy are as follows:

• Social life is primarily an arena of conflict and struggle between and among opposing individuals and groups.

• Conflict and struggle occur over many valued resources, but economic resources and social power are the primary things over which individuals and groups struggle.

• The typical outcome of the struggle among individuals and groups is the division of a society into economically dominant and subordinate groups.

• The basic social patterns of a society are heavily determined by the disproportionate social influence of economically dominant groups.

• Social conflict and struggle within and between societies constitute powerful agents of social change.

• Since conflict and struggle are basic features of social life, social change is common and frequent.

It should be obvious that the Marxian conflict strategy is essentially a materialist rather than an idealist one. This is not surprising in view of the fact that Marx was the originator of both materialist and conflict theoretical ideas. Marxian conflict theorists see social conflict as primarily arising over access to the material conditions that sustain life, and they see both of these phenomena as crucial determinants of the basic social patterns characteristic of a society.

One important disagreement between Marx and Max Weber concerned Marx's materialism. Weber believed that conflict occurred in a much broader way than simply in regard to basic material conditions (R. Collins, 1985a). Weber recognized that conflict over economic resources was a basic feature of social life, but he thought that many other types of conflict occurred as well. Of these types, Weber tended to emphasize two. He regarded conflicts in the political arena as very fundamental. For him, social life was to a large extent a struggle for power and domination of some individuals and groups over others, and he did not regard this struggle for power as simply motivated by the desire for economic gain. On the contrary, he saw it to a large extent as an end in itself. Weber thought that the struggle for power was not confined to formal political organizations, but occurred within all types of groups, such as religious or educational organizations.

A second type of conflict Weber frequently emphasized was conflict over ideas and ideals. He thought that people often struggled to gain dominance for their own view of the world, whether it be a type of religious doctrine, a social philosophy, or a conception of the best sort of cultural lifestyle. Furthermore, not only were ideas and ideals things that people struggled over, but these ideas and ideals could be used as weapons or tools in other kinds of struggle, such as political struggles. That is, people could fight for power while at the same time trying to convince one another that it wasn't really power that they were after, but the victory of the right ethical or philosophical principles.

It is clear that Weber was neither a materialist nor an idealist. In fact, he is usually referred to by modern sociologists as a major example of a thinker who combined both materialist and idealist modes of explanation within his general sociological approach. Thus Weber thought that ideas were not mere results of underlying material conditions, but that they frequently had causal significance in their own right.

There were two other basic disagreements between Weber and Marx. One of these concerned the origins of self-interested behavior. Marx assumed that at birth individuals had no natural inclination toward selfish or unselfish behavior. They could just as easily be highly cooperative and altruistic (self-sacrificial) as selfish, and it was the nature of society that determined

which kind of behavior they displayed. If people behaved selfishly, it was because they were conditioned by their society to do so. Although he rarely if ever said so explicitly, Weber, by contrast, seemed to assume that humans were self-interested by nature, and that self-interested behavior was to be expected in all societies. Society determined how self-interest manifested itself, but the self-interest was there all along.

This disagreement led to another: Could social conflict be resolved in a future society? Marx said yes, Weber no. Marx held that once control over the forces of production was returned to the entire society, basic social conflict would be eliminated. Once socialism replaced capitalism, classes would be abolished and class struggle would cease. A new kind of socialist personality, one concerned with the well-being of humanity as a whole, would replace the selfish and greedy personality characteristic of capitalist society. Weber took a much more pessimistic (some would say more realistic) view. He believed that struggle was one of the great, ineradicable principles of social life. In any type of future society, whether socialist, capitalist, or something else, people would always struggle over some types of resources. Weber therefore expected social divisions or cleavages to be a permanent feature of all complex societies, although the particular forms these might take, as well as their degree of severity, could vary substantially.

Although both Marxian and Weberian conflict approaches have been embraced by many modern sociologists, these approaches have by no means achieved universal endorsement. However, this book argues for the great usefulness of the conflict ideas set forth by Marx and by Weber and thus makes extensive use of many of them. It leans on the Marxian side in its advocacy of a materialist version of conflict theory, but on the

Weberian side, in its view that humans are naturally self-interested and that social conflict is a permanent feature of human society.

Evolutionary Strategies

An **evolutionary theoretical strategy** is one that attempts to describe and explain sequences of long-term social change. Evolutionists generally argue that many societies have undergone broadly similar changes from earliest times to the present, and they are concerned with identifying the nature of these changes and explaining why they have occurred.

Erik Olin Wright (1983) has given us a more precise conception of an evolutionary theory. He suggests that all evolutionary theories share the following characteristics:

- They organize history into a typology of stages.
- They assume that this stage ordering represents a direction along which societies tend to evolve.
- They postulate that the probability of movement to a later (or "higher") stage exceeds the probability of movement back to an earlier (or "lower") stage.
- They identify a mechanism or set of mechanisms that is said to explain the movement from one stage to another.

As Wright is at pains to point out, evolutionary theories need not assume that the sequence of stages through which societies move is a rigid one that is the same for all societies, or that social evolution is some sort of automatic process of the unfolding of latent tendencies or potentialities inherent in the nature of societies. They do not even need to assume that forward movement always occurs. Regression is acknowledged as a possible (and sometimes actual) occurrence, and it is fully recognized that for many societies and at many times in history

long-term steady states (rather than social transformation) may be the normal order of things. It is important that these points be established and well understood, because there are still many misconceptions concerning the nature of evolutionary theories.

Evolutionary approaches to social life were extremely popular among both sociologists and anthropologists in the second half of the nineteenth century. In fact, evolutionary theorizing dominated these two disciplines at that time. One of the most famous of the nineteenth-century evolutionists was the English philosopher and sociologist Herbert Spencer (1820–1903), who developed a theory of social evolution that was similar in some ways to Darwin's theory of biological evolution. Spencer attempted to understand the operation of all things in the universe by reducing them to a single universal principle that he called the "Law of Evolution." According to this law, all things in the universe have a tendency to "evolve from a state of indefinite, incoherent, homogeneity to a state of definite, coherent, heterogeneity." What Spencer meant was that all things tend to develop from simple and unspecialized forms into more complex and specialized forms. Spencer saw this universal tendency as the master key to unlocking all the great riddles of the universe. He considered the evolution of human societies as but a special instance of a great cosmological tendency inherent in the nature of the universe itself.

Another well-known nineteenth-century evolutionist was the American anthropologist Lewis Henry Morgan (1818–1881). Morgan was much concerned with the evolution of technology. He divided human history into three great stages, each of which was associated with a different level of technological development: Savagery, Barbarism, and Civilization. The stage of Savagery was characteristic of peoples who subsisted primarily by hunting wild animals and gathering wild plants. The transition to Barbarism was marked by the domestication of plants and animals and the development of additional improvements in overall technology. The emergence of Civilization marked the transition from "primitive society" (what Morgan called *societas*) to "civil society" (what Morgan called *civitas*). Morgan saw the development of the phonetic alphabet and writing as a major characteristic of this stage.

Although the ideas of these and other early evolutionists were provocative, they contained a number of serious flaws. One of these was the tendency to pass off mere descriptions of evolutionary transformations as explanations for those transformations. This tendency was especially characteristic of the work of Spencer. Spencer held that social evolution was inherent in the very nature of things, and he seemed to regard this observation as sufficient to explain why social evolution occurred. But merely to note that evolution tends to occur says nothing about why it does so. Another flaw in the thinking of the nineteenth-century evolutionists was their **ethnocentrism.** They viewed their own society (Western civilization) as superior to all others, holding that societies at earlier evolutionary stages represented various gradations of inferiority to their own. They therefore claimed that social evolution was indicative of **progress,** of a general improvement in human rationality, happiness, and morality. They tended to see Western civilization as the end point of social evolution, as the culmination of millennia of human progress. These are views that are sharply rejected today by many modern sociologists and anthropologists, as Chapter 3 will show more thoroughly.

Because of these and other flaws, evolutionary thinking came under severe criticism beginning near the end of the nineteenth century. As the criticisms mounted against it, evolutionism was ultimately abandoned by most social scientists. Throughout the early decades of the twentieth century, social scientists turned their attention to questions and problems other than those dealing with long-term social change. But evolutionism was not dead; it was only dormant. Beginning in the 1940s, it staged a significant revival, and the whole problem of long-term evolutionary change began once again to preoccupy the minds of many social scientists. Today evolutionary approaches to the study of social life are embraced by many sociologists and anthropologists.

However, there is currently no single evolutionary strategy for the study of human societies. Many different evolutionary theories exist, most of which can be placed in one of two distinct evolutionary strategies: a *functionalist evolutionary* strategy and a *materialist evolutionary* strategy. Although these two strategies are both evolutionary in the sense identified earlier, in many ways they are more different than similar. The assumptions they make about which evolutionary events are most important, and how these events should be explained, differ markedly.

The functionalist evolutionary strategy involves the application of a functionalist approach to the study of social evolution (A. D. Smith, 1973). In this strategy, social evolution is viewed primarily as a process of **social differentiation,** of increasing societal complexity. As societies evolve, they develop an increasing diversity of parts, and these parts come to be related to each other in complicated ways. Increasing differentiation is held to lead to greater adaptive capacity: By developing increasing internal diversity, societies become more and more capable of making successful adaptations to their environments. The implication is clearly that more complex societies are "superior" to less complex ones.

Functionalist evolutionary thinkers generally see social evolution as resulting from the functional needs of societies as whole systems. Evolutionary changes are presumed, therefore, to lead to beneficial consequences for entire societies. This notion is a very prominent feature of the work of Talcott Parsons (1966), the best known of all the functionalist evolutionary theorists. Parsons claims, for example, that the evolution of social stratification—of inequalities in wealth and power—was a major achievement in social evolution having beneficial consequences for the members of society in general. He believes that the unequal rewarding of the members of a society is a means of motivating some individuals to assume important positions of responsibility and authority. Privileged individuals and groups will use their positions of authority to undertake activities that will benefit the other members of society. Parsons therefore sees the emergence of social stratification as an important evolutionary "breakthrough."

The functionalist evolutionary approach is scarcely an improvement on the leading ideas of the nineteenth-century evolutionary theorists, and it tends to share the same flaws. For example, the functionalist evolutionary strategy tends to view contemporary Western society as the most highly adapted of all societies, and it generally holds that small-scale, simple societies have low adaptive capacity. This view is ethnocentric in the extreme. Furthermore, the functionalist evolutionary approach is obviously subject to the same criticisms as functionalism in general, since it merely represents the application of functionalism to the study of evolutionary processes. Like other functionalists, functionalist evolutionists overemphasize societal harmony, underemphasize the degree and importance of social conflict, and argue that the features of any society exist out of functional necessity. Inasmuch as functionalism represents an inadequate approach to societies in general, functionalist

evolutionism represents an inadequate approach to the study of long-term social change.

The evolutionary materialist strategy is strikingly different. This approach involves the application of a general materialist strategy to an understanding of social evolution. It assumes that social changes are most likely to begin in the material conditions that sustain life. These changes, once they occur, set off corresponding changes in a society's social patterns and in its ideas and ideals. Unlike functionalist evolutionists, evolutionary materialists make no assumption that evolutionary changes lead to improved forms of societal adaptation. They do not assume that evolutionary changes necessarily lead to increasing benefits for entire societies. On the contrary, they emphasize that such changes are just as likely, if not more likely, to lead to a deterioration in the quality of life for a great many members of societies. Evolutionary materialists hold that conflict and struggle are crucially important elements in human social life, and they believe that these phenomena are closely related to processes of evolutionary change. They argue that conflict and struggle are both causes and consequences of social evolution. There is thus a strong affinity between the evolutionary materialist strategy and the Marxian conflict strategy.

THE THEORETICAL STRATEGY OF THIS BOOK

This book is committed to an evolutionary materialist view of human social life. This view is evolutionary in the sense that it focuses on patterns of long-term social change. Attention is given to how and why the major similarities and differences among human societies originate, persist, and change. It is materialist in the sense that it holds that the material conditions of human existence are the principal causes of social similarities and differences. Inasmuch as evolutionary materialists share many of the principles of the conflict theoretical strategy, these principles also play a very significant role in the book. Although the conflict and evolutionary materialist strategies are not identical, they overlap extensively, and their similarities greatly outweigh their differences.

The evolutionary materialist and conflict strategy of this book stands sharply opposed to both functionalism and idealism. The main difficulties with functionalism have already been discussed. The major difficulty with an idealist approach is that it consistently leaves unanswered a crucial set of questions: Where do different ideas and ideals come from, and how and why do they change? An answer to such questions is imperative when it is claimed that ideas and ideals are the leading causes of social life. Thus, failure to answer these questions all but invalidates the idealist approach. (As later chapters will show, materialists *can* answer questions concerning where different sets of material conditions come from and how and why they change.)

The evolutionary materialist strategy is discussed in much greater detail in Chapter 3. There its main principles are formally stated, and a justification for the claim that it is a superior theoretical approach is provided.

SUMMARY

1. Sociology is the scientific study of human societies. Microsociologists specialize in the study of social behavior in relatively small groups and social settings. Macrosociology, by contrast, focuses on large-scale social patterns, such as total societies and the larger global networks within which societies are placed. Macrosociologists commonly emphasize a comparative and historical perspective.

2. Sociological investigation requires theoretical strategies and theories. Theoretical strategies are highly abstract sets of concepts and principles, whereas theories represent the application of these concepts and principles to specific phenomena. Theoretical strategies consist of networks of mutually interpenetrating theories.

3. Modern sociology, macrosociology included, is a highly divided discipline characterized by great theoretical diversity and disagreement. Thus, numerous theoretical strategies compete for the allegiance of contemporary macrosociologists. These include materialism, idealism, functionalism, neo-Marxian and neo-Weberian conflict strategies, and functionalist and materialist versions of social evolutionism. Summaries of the basic features of these strategies, and of the role they play in *Macrosociology*, are to be found in Table 1.1.

Table 1.1 MACROSOCIOLOGICAL THEORETICAL STRATEGIES

Theoretical Strategy	Major Characteristics	Role in this Book
Materialism	Assumes that the material conditions of human existence —such things as the level of technology, the mode of economic life, and the features of the natural environment— are the leading causes of the organization of human societies and the major changes that occur within them.	This book is consistently materialist throughout.
Idealism	Argues for the significance of the human mind and its creations —thoughts, ideas, symbolic codes, language, and so on—in determining social organization and social change.	Idealist theories are consistently criticized and rejected throughout.

continued

Table 1.1   (Continued)

Theoretical Strategy	Major Characteristics	Role in this Book
Functionalism	Attempts to explain the basic features of human social life as responses to the needs and demands of societies as ongoing social systems. Assumes that existing social traits contribute in important ways to the survival and well-being of whole societies or their major subsystems.	Numerous functionalist theories are discussed throughout, but are consistently criticized as wrong or strongly overstated.
Conflict strategies	View societies as arenas in which individuals and groups struggle for and against each other for the satisfaction of their needs and desires. Conflict and struggle lead to domination and subordination, and dominant groups use their power to structure society for their own benefit. Marxian conflict theories are materialist and emphasize class struggle, whereas Weberian conflict theories are broader and stress the multidimensional nature of conflict and domination.	This book consistently employs a conflict perspective that makes use of the insights of both Marx and Weber.
Evolutionary strategies	Focus on describing and explaining long-term social transformations, which are assumed to exhibit an overall directionality. Functionalist evolutionary theories concentrate on growing societal complexity, which is taken to indicate increased functional efficiency and social progress. Materialist evolutionary theories stress that social evolution is a response to changing material conditions, and are skeptical of equating evolution and progress.	This book employs a materialist (and conflict-oriented) version of evolutionism as a unifying perspective throughout.

SPECIAL TOPIC: WHY AMERICANS PREFER BEEF

In recent years one particular focus of the debate between materialists and idealists has centered around why societies have particular food preferences and dietary habits. In Chapter 3 materialist theories of two well-known food taboos will be examined: the Hindu taboo on the eating of beef and the ancient Jewish taboo on pork. Here, however, the discussion will deal with something closer to home: the American preference for beef.

   The emphasis on beef in the American diet is well known. After all, what could be more American than the hamburger? Although it was not invented in this country, the hamburger is probably more closely associated with the United States than with any other society. Moreover, throughout the twentieth century beef has been the meat of choice to serve dinner guests. It thus seems that beef is the meat of highest prestige in American culinary habits. How is this preference to be explained?

An idealist explanation of this phenomenon has been offered by Marshall Sahlins (1976a), who views the emphasis on beef in American culture as deriving from an ancient Indo-European cultural code that associates cattle with virility. Yet this explanation scarcely seems convincing, and there seem to be some very obvious reasons for rejecting it. As Eric Ross (1980:182) points out, inasmuch as "the same vague Indo-European ideological heritage culminated in a taboo, rather than a preference, on beef in India, it is obvious that ideology alone cannot explain American beef consumption." Ross himself has set forth a radically different interpretation. His theory stresses ecological, technological, and economic factors as the leading causes of the evolution of this American dietary practice.

The American diet has not always stressed beef. Until well into the second half of the nineteenth century pork rather than beef was the most important meat consumed. Pigs seemed to be especially well suited to the woodlands of colonial and early postcolonial America, and thus pig raising was widely practiced. Although cattle were raised, their flesh constituted only a small fraction of all the meat that was consumed, and they were scarcely a threat to hogs.

Besides the fact that the pig was very well suited to the woodland environment of eighteenth- and nineteenth-century America, the popularity of pork at this time can also be understood in terms of the technology of meat packing. As Ross notes, until the second half of the nineteenth century little fresh meat was consumed. Both hogs and cattle were sometimes driven to market and slaughtered and their meat consumed fresh, at least when they had to be driven only short distances. Hogs, though, were more difficult to drive and they died more frequently in the process. Therefore, emphasis tended to be placed on processing pork by smoking or curing it in order to preserve it. Since smoked or cured pork generally tasted better than beef processed in this manner, pork naturally was a much more popular meat.

Beginning approximately in the 1870s the emphasis began to shift from pork to beef. This transition can be understood, Ross argues, as the result of a combination of changing material circumstances: the opening of the grasslands of the Great Plains for cattle raising, the invention of refrigerated railway boxcars, and the expansion of American capitalism into the Western frontier. By about 1870 the buffalo, whose systematic destruction had begun around 1830, was being extensively eliminated from the Great Plains grasslands. This made these grazing lands available for cattle breeding, and cattle ranchers began to spread into them in greater and greater numbers. The real shift from pork to beef was made when cattle ranching in the Great Plains was combined with the expansion of the railroads and the invention of refrigerated boxcars. As Ross explains (1980:201–202):

> What was especially decisive in the centralization of a high-volume system of beef production, however, was the development of new refrigeration technology which "made it possible to utilize to the fullest extent the supply of livestock and . . . made the distribution system of meats nation-wide and world-wide. It prevented decay of perishable products. As it lengthened the period of consumption it led to greatly increased demand [Clemen 1923:8]." While this gave a certain stimulus to the trade in fresh pork, it was principally beef that refrigeration advanced, since it made practicable the centralized slaughter and mass production of fresh (dressed) beef, a form in which beef could effectively compete with pork in taste and especially in price. . . .

Moreover, American swine were immediately placed at a severe disadvantage because they had never been bred to produce fresh meat, but rather to yield flesh which was ideally suited to salting and curing and which was fairly soft and fatty.... Thus, after the 1870s, meat packing—although still heavily involved in pork—shifted its focus, as it entered the era of corporate capitalism.

The great emphasis on beef in the twentieth century has to be understood in terms of the development of American capitalism. The major meat-packing companies have been absorbed into giant capitalist conglomerates, and these conglomerates have contributed significantly to the decline in the small family farm, the kind of farm most commonly associated with the raising of hogs. Moreover, the rise in beef consumption since about 1960 has been an integral part of American capitalism (Ross, 1980:213):

Beef consumption was actively and profitably promoted by supermarket chains which were, in fact, often closely associated with beef producers. Thus, the Kern County Land Company of California, with 2 million acres of grazing land in Arizona, New Mexico, and California and its own feed lots in Kern County, was developed as a major beef producer in the 1950s by the former marketing vice president of Safeway, Inc.; in 1967, Kern was taken over by Tenneco Corporation.

Much of the rise in beef consumption in the United States since 1960 has involved the growing popularity of hamburger. Close to half of the beef currently consumed is ground beef. Fast-food hamburger franchises have become one of the most prominent aspects of American popular culture. As Ross notes, the increasing popularity of fast-food hamburgers has resulted from such factors as increased suburban growth and a major rise in the number of working women. Yet this phenomenon cannot be understood apart from American, indeed, international, capitalism. Much of the beef that American meat-packing companies now process has been produced in the grasslands of Central and South America. Thus, as Ross points out, the high level of beef consumption in the United States "continues to rest upon the availability of grassland—but, now, as part of a process of international capitalist [production] in which arable land is actually being converted to cattle pasture . . . and being withdrawn from local subsistence production" (1980:214).

FOR FURTHER READING

Collins, Randall. *Theoretical Sociology.* San Diego: Harcourt Brace Jovanovich, 1988. Easily the best textbook on contemporary sociological theory. Well written and loaded with insightful analyses by one of the leading sociological theorists in the United States.

Collins, Randall. *Four Sociological Traditions.* New York: Oxford University Press, 1994. An extremely clear overview of conflict theory, functionalism, and social constructionism. Shorter and more accessible than Collins's full-scale textbook.

Harris, Marvin. *The Rise of Anthropological Theory.* New York: Harper & Row, 1968. An excellent and highly comprehensive treatment of the development of competing theoretical strategies within cultural anthropology. Much of the discussion is organized around the opposition between materialist and idealist approaches.

Harris, Marvin. *Cultural Materialism: The Struggle for a Science of Culture.* New York: Random House, 1979. Sets forth the major elements of the theoretical strategy that Harris calls *cultural materialism,* an approach that is broadly the same as the evolutionary materialist strategy of the present book. Also discusses and severely criticizes a range of alternative theoretical strategies currently advocated by different groups of cultural anthropologists and sociologists.

Ritzer, George. *Sociological Theory.* Third edition. New York: Knopf, 1992. Probably the best textbook available that covers the entire range of social theory from the classical thinkers to contemporary currents.

Sanderson, Stephen K. *Social Evolutionism: A Critical History.* Oxford: Blackwell, 1990. Compares, contrasts, and evaluates evolutionary theories in the social sciences from the middle of the nineteenth century to the present. Also includes a systematic comparison of social and biological evolutionism.

Sanderson, Stephen K., and Lee Ellis. "Theoretical and political perspectives of American sociologists in the 1990s." *The American Sociologist* 23(2):26–42, 1992. A national survey showing the current popularity of various theoretical perspectives among American sociologists.

Sociological Theory. A leading journal devoted to the latest contributions, debates, and controversies in social theory. Appears three times annually. Available in many libraries.

Theory and Society. Another leading journal devoted to issues in modern social theory. Appears six times a year. Also available in many libraries.

Tucker, Robert C. (ed.). *The Marx-Engels Reader.* Second edition. New York: Norton, 1978. A collection of excerpts from the major writings of Marx and Engels. Provides a good introduction to the leading ideas propounded by these two great thinkers.

Zeitlin, Irving M. *Rethinking Sociology: A Critique of Contemporary Theory.* Englewood Cliffs, N.J.: Prentice-Hall, 1973. A critical discussion of several of the leading theoretical strategies in contemporary sociology. Provides an excellent critique of functionalism and functionalist evolutionism.

Chapter
2

Biological Evolution and the Emergence of Human Society and Culture

The human animal is a very special kind of creature. Like all other organisms, humans have a biological structure that has evolved over a very long period of time. This biological structure helps to determine how human beings act and think. It opens up a vast range of possibilities for variation in human thought and action, but it also sets definite limits to how humans are likely to think and act. Like many other creatures, humans are social animals. They live in groups and societies and depend upon each other for survival and satisfaction in life. But unlike all other creatures, humans are cultural animals. They and they alone create and transmit learned and shared traditions of thought and behavior. Only humans manufacture complex tools, devise monetary systems, appoint or elect political leaders, marry one another, engage in religious ritual, or attach specific symbolic values and beliefs to any of these activities. In short, humans are a lot like other creatures, but they are also unique.

This chapter explores the nature of the human animal as a biological, social, and cultural creature. It examines the general process of biological evolution and shows how humans evolved from an apelike ancestor several million years ago. It discusses the implications of calling humans unique, culture-bearing animals, and it delineates those physical traits that have allowed humans to invent, transmit, and modify culture.

THE BASIC PRINCIPLES OF BIOLOGICAL EVOLUTION

The Development of Evolutionary Biology

The idea of **evolution**—the notion that life forms have arisen from one another in an unbroken chain of transformation and modification—was not, as is often assumed, first expressed by Charles Darwin. Several of Darwin's immediate forerunners, including his own grandfather, Erasmus Darwin, accounted for the variety and diversity of life by the hypothesis of evolutionary modification. Darwin was therefore hardly alone in his belief in evolution. The distinctiveness of his contribution to evolutionary thinking lay in the mechanism he held to be responsible for evolution. This mechanism he called **natural selection.** The idea of evolution through natural selection is the leading idea in his great book *On the Origin of Species*, published originally in 1859, and this theoretical principle is accepted today by the vast majority of modern biologists and biological anthropologists as the key to explaining evolutionary processes.

Darwin's theory of natural selection was disarmingly simple. In every generation, he argued, any population of organisms produces more offspring than can survive. There thus emerges a struggle for survival among these organisms, and those that have the characteristics that best suit them for success in the struggle for existence have an advantage over others. They are more likely to grow to reproductive age, leave offspring, and pass along their genes to the next generation. Their genetic characteristics come to characterize the population's gene pool.

Darwin achieved a coherent, though incomplete, understanding of evolution despite his unfamiliarity with the processes of heredity. In fact, when he published *On the Origin of Species* in 1859 the science of genetics did not yet exist, and Darwin's own theory of heredity was wholly inadequate. It remained for Gregor Mendel to establish the principles governing the inheritance of characters, which he did in a series of experiments on garden peas, publishing his findings in 1865. The results of his work passed without any real notice, however, and Darwin and those scholars who championed his case were forced to defend his theory of natural selection against its hostile critics without an adequate knowledge of the processes of heredity. This left the theory in a vulnerable position throughout the remainder of the nineteenth century and prevented it from gaining widespread intellectual support. Most biologists were willing to accept the notion of evolution itself, but there was great resistance to natural selection as the mechanism of evolution (Mayr, 1982, 1988).

Yet all this was soon to change. At the turn of the twentieth century, the principles of heredity established earlier by Mendel were rediscovered and applied toward gaining a more definitive understanding of how natural selection actually worked. By the early 1930s the science of genetics had been extended to the study of heredity in whole populations, and the science of population genetics was born. It was soon realized that not only was the new population genetics compatible with Darwinian natural selection, but that the two could be synthesized into a new comprehensive theory of evolution. This theory, known generally as the modern synthetic theory of evolution, was formalized in the 1940s under the leadership of such eminent biologists as Theodosius Dobzhansky (1962), Julian Huxley (1942), George Gaylord Simpson (1949, 1953), and Ernst Mayr (1942, 1963; cf. Mayr, 1982, 1988, 1991).

The basic principles of the modern synthetic theory may be stated in approximately the following way (Futuyma, 1986; Mayr, 1982, 1988, 1991):

• Evolution is an adaptive process, or one in which the characteristics of organisms arise as means of adjustment to the environments in which those organisms are found.

- Genetic variation, which arises through both genetic recombination and genetic mutation, provides the raw material on which evolution works.
- Genetic variation arises randomly, that is, without regard to whether or not it is useful to an organism.
- Evolution occurs when a process of natural selection operates on genetic variation, retaining and elaborating useful genes and eliminating harmful ones; natural selection is the very antithesis of the process of genetic variation; that is, it is systematic rather than random.
- Evolution is gradual; that is, it occurs through the step-by-step accumulation of small genetic variations over long periods of time.
- Evolution is a creative process that produces elaborate biological designs, but it operates without any "designer"; design is merely the end product of the accumulation of small adaptive traits.
- Evolution is not a goal-directed process, but rather one that strives only for local adaptation.
- Evolution is opportunistic; that is, it can only work on the genetic materials available at any given time.
- The evidence for evolution is so overwhelming that it cannot be seriously doubted; this evidence comes from paleontology (the fossil record), experimentation, and naturalistic observation of species in their local habitats.

The modern synthetic theory, or neo-Darwinism as it is sometimes called, remains the leading intellectual framework from which contemporary evolutionary biologists understand the evolutionary process.

However, beginning in the early 1970s some evolutionists began to challenge some of this framework's assumptions. For example, Niles Eldredge and Stephen Jay Gould (1972; Gould and Eldredge, 1977) have challenged the key neo-Darwinist premise that evolution is the gradual accumulation of small-scale changes—that macroevolution is simply accumulated microevolution. Eldredge and Gould have proposed instead a theory they call the *theory of punctuated equilibria*. This theory holds that evolution occurs in rapid and sudden bursts that occasionally interrupt ("punctuate") long periods of evolutionary stasis or continuity.

This challenge to the modern synthesis, though, as well as other challenges, is still highly controversial and has won the acceptance of only a minority of evolutionary biologists (cf. Stebbins and Ayala, 1981; Futuyma, 1986). Indeed, it may not be that much of a challenge at all, for something like punctuated equilibria was actually referred to by Darwin and may be fully compatible with the modern synthetic emphasis on the gradualness of evolution (Dawkins, 1986).

In any event, some of the basic assumptions of the modern synthetic theory stated above require elaboration and further explanation.

Heredity and Genetic Variability

Knowledge of a few principles of genetics is essential for a proper understanding of how evolution by natural selection occurs.

The basic unit of heredity is the *gene*, a unit of biochemical information. Genes are composed of the fundamental building block of all life, deoxyribonucleic acid, or, for short, DNA. DNA has the unique capacity of making a perfect replica of itself. Since genes consist of DNA, they are capable of making exact replicas of themselves from one generation to the next and thus of perpetuating themselves indefinitely.

Most of the time, genes replicate themselves perfectly in succeeding generations. Occasionally, however, something goes wrong with the replicating mechanism, and a gene fails to copy itself exactly. This occurrence is known as a *gene mutation*. In any population of animals, such mutations are always arising; at least a few occur in each new generation. Because of the constant production of mutant genes, new genetic variability is always arising in animal populations. The overwhelming majority of these mutant genes are harmful to the organisms in which they arise. From time to time, however, a mutant gene may confer some benefit on the organism that contains it.

Genetic mutation is one of two main sources of genetic variability in populations of organisms. The other is genetic recombination, which results from sexual reproduction, or the fact that organisms inherit genes from two parents. The variability produced by recombination and mutation is constantly acted upon by a selective force that systematically eliminates harmful variants and preserves and perpetuates useful variants. This force is called *natural selection*. Although natural selection acts on both sources of genetic variability, the variability that arises through mutation is necessary for the production of large-scale biological transformations.

Adaptation and Natural Selection

Natural selection is that process whereby nature selects those particular genetic materials that allow an animal to adjust to the environment in which it lives. By allowing an animal to survive and prosper in a particular environment, natural selection is an **adaptive** process. If a species is highly adapted to its habitat, and if that habitat is largely stable or unchanging, we may presume that no further evolution (of any substantial sort) is being undergone by the species. (Natural selection is still occurring, however, for in each generation there is always a struggle for survival. It is just that natural selection is not producing evolutionary modifications.)

If major changes in the environment begin to take place, however, the species may no longer be well suited for survival. In order to readapt to the changed conditions, the species will have to undergo some degree of evolutionary modification or else be threatened with extinction. Whether or not it will be able to change depends on many factors. In a hypothetical case, an animal species confronted with a changing environment may produce a number of mutant genes in its next generation of offspring. Since most of these will be harmful to the organisms that contain them, most are likely to be eliminated by the next generation (or at least within a few generations), because the organisms containing them are not well designed to survive and prosper and thus to reproduce and leave their genes in future generations. Natural selection has therefore operated selectively to weed out and minimize these harmful mutants.

But if a mutant gene that arises confers some benefit on the organism and assists it in adapting to the changing environment, the organism is likely to prosper and grow to reproductive age. It will then reproduce itself by leaving copies of its genes—including the beneficial mutant gene—in the next generation. The mutant gene will now be contained in several organisms, and these organisms in turn will have a slight adaptive edge over those without the beneficial mutant. These organisms with the beneficial gene in turn prosper, reproduce, and leave yet more copies of the once-mutant gene. The original mutant gene will begin to spread throughout the total gene pool of the species, and it may eventually characterize the species as a whole. If so, then a small bit of evolutionary modification has occurred in this species of animal.

Of course, other beneficial mutants may also arise in this species in due time; if so, they are likely to be preserved and to spread throughout the species by natural selection. Over a considerable period of time, such genetic modifications may accumulate to a point at which the species will have a substantially different genetic structure. It may even come to be so different from what it once was that it constitutes a new species.

The process of genetic mutation is vitally important to evolution. It provides the most important form of new genetic variability on which natural selection can operate, and without which major evolutionary modifications could not occur (Dobzhansky, 1962). Large-scale evolution is therefore the result of the interaction between natural selection and genetic mutation.

In the scenario given above, the species confronting environmental change was successful in adapting to the new environment through evolutionary modification. This evolutionary process led to the "survival of the fit"; fit genes were preserved and proliferated, and unfit genes were gradually eliminated. Fit genes are simply those that confer adaptive advantage on an organism in a particular environment; likewise, unfit genes are those that are maladaptive with respect to the environment. The fitness of a gene is entirely relative, and it is the environment that determines whether or not a gene is fit. The fitness of an organism must be defined in terms of *differential reproductive success*. An organism that is able to leave more offspring in future generations than another organism has superior fitness.

In the nineteenth century, and even in the early twentieth century, many non-Darwinian theories of evolution survived alongside Darwinian natural selection, and these theories were generally **teleological** in nature (Bowler, 1983, 1988). They saw evolution as a goal-directed process, or one in which "lower" organisms were striving toward "higher" forms. Evolution was viewed as a process of increasing improvement or even perfection, the pinnacle of which was humankind. Darwin's theory of natural selection did not depend on—indeed, strongly opposed—such teleological assumptions, and its triumph with the emergence of the modern synthetic theory has banished teleology from the realm of nature. Evolution by natural selection is not goal-directed at all. Indeed, it cannot be, for the raw material natural selection depends on, genetic variability, arises in an entirely random and unsystematic way. As pointed out earlier, evolution is opportunistic, able to work only with what it has available, and it cannot determine what will be available at any given time. As Darwin emphasized, it is this naturalistic process that has been responsible for the existence of all the diverse varieties of life that have appeared on the earth over the past three and a half billion years, including, of course, all species of humankind.

HUMAN EVOLUTION

The story of the evolution of hominids—of members of the human family—spans at least the past four million years. The earliest hominids arose in southern and eastern Africa. They probably looked more apelike than human, but they had two of the characteristics that biological anthropologists view as quintessentially human, upright posture and bipedal (two-footed) locomotion. These individuals, known collectively as the australopithecines, were small both in stature and in brain size. After some two million years or so, they gave way to two other human species, *Homo habilis*, and, slightly later, *Homo erectus*. These species were much larger and had much bigger brains, although they were still a long way from modern humans intellectually. About 500,000 years ago an archaic or early version of our species, *Homo sapiens*, arose. Like its two immediate predecessors—*H. habilis* and *H. erectus* it was found throughout Africa, Europe, and Asia.

The last acknowledged species before the emergence of fully modern humans was that known as the Neanderthals, which lived throughout Europe and the Middle East between about 200,000 and 30,000 years ago. They were much like fully modern humans in many respects (intelligence being one), but had especially stocky builds and a large brow ridge over the eyes, characteristics that have been interpreted as adaptations to the extremely cold climate in which they lived. It used to be thought that the Neanderthals were the immediate ancestors of our own species, but this notion has lost favor in recent years among many scholars. In the 1980s an alternative theory, known variously as the "Out of Africa" or "Eve" hypothesis, was formulated. This theory holds that the ancestry of all modern humans is African (Stringer and Andrews, 1988; Cann, 1987; Cann, Stoneking, and Wilson, 1987; Klein, 1989). The basic idea is that anatomically modern humans evolved in Africa perhaps as early as 200,000 years ago, and that some of them migrated to Europe and Asia no later than 40,000–60,000 years ago (and perhaps as early as 100,000 year ago). Once they got to Europe and Asia, modern humans encountered the Neanderthals (in Europe and the Middle East) and archaic *H. sapiens* (elsewhere in Asia), and because of their superior adaptive capacity they drove these other species to extinction. This could have happened through superior survival skills (superior technology, better foraging techniques, and so on), warfare, or a combination of the two.

This argument for a single origin of modern humans, although supported by a good deal of hard evidence, remains extremely controversial and has been seriously challenged by a group of scholars advocating an alternative theory known as the "multiregional evolution" theory (Frayer et al., 1993; Wolpoff, 1989). This theory holds that modern humans evolved along somewhat independent lines in Africa, Europe, and Asia. The evolution of modern humans on each continent, though, was not a completely independent process, because for hundreds of thousands of years there was considerable migration and gene exchange between human populations on all three continents.

It is impossible in a macrosociology textbook to adjudicate this extremely complex and technical controversy, which only biological anthropologists and molecular biologists are competent to resolve. However, at present the single origin or "Out of Africa" theorists seem to have gained the upper hand and I suspect that their interpretation will eventually win out over its rival (Stringer and Gamble, 1993; Shreeve, 1995). In any event, this will certainly be a fascinating debate to follow.

What were the main developments in human evolution, the main benchmarks of change? A crucial development was the transition to an upright posture and bipedalism. Indeed, these are major characteristics that we associate with being human. The development of upright posture and bipedalism was of great importance because these characteristics freed the hands, which would otherwise have been needed for locomotion. The hands, being freed, became available for other ends, the most important of which was tool use. Other primates besides humans have been known to make and use very crude tools, but only in humans has tool use been extensive. Without the development of upright, bipedal locomotion, it is doubtful that tool use could ever have emerged in any significant way, and it is doubtful that culture-creating hominids would ever have evolved.

The great advantage of tools is that they allow for a highly advantageous exploitation of the environment. The emergence of tool use among humans allowed them eventually to develop complex technologies that in turn allowed for the increasing development of culture. But other factors were also important for the development of culture. Chief among these was the gradual increase in the size and complexity of the brain. This increase gave human beings a tremendous capacity for learning. Humans began to gain an enormous flexibility in their capacity to adapt to nature in ways other than that simply dictated by their genes; and as they began to do so, they began to live successfully in wider and more varied environments.

THE EVOLUTIONARY UNIQUENESS OF HUMANS

The most important development in hominid evolution was the development of culture, the existence of which sets humans apart from all other animals. The emergence of culture clearly had a great deal to do with the evolution of the brain and the expansion of learning capacity. More specifically, however, culture was made possible by the development of a unique mode of human communication: *symbolic communication.* While all animals communicate—that is, transmit behaviorally relevant information—only humans do so through the use of **symbols.**

Symbolic Communication and Language

Nonhuman communication systems take a wide variety of forms involving a range of sensory organs. Like human communica-tion, much animal communication contains both vocal and nonvocal elements. At the nonvocal level, communication can take place through the use of the senses of smell, touch, and sight. Honeybees communicate information about a new food source by performing a "waggle dance" resembling a figure eight (E. O. Wilson, 1975). Many primates and other mammals indicate their territorial space by marking it with urine to discourage would-be transgressors. Chimpanzees pat each others' hands and faces and kiss in affection (Jolly, 1972). At the vocal level, the primates and many other mammals produce a variety of sounds, each of which transmits some bit of information.

Although enormously variable, all nonhuman communication systems share one fundamental feature: All are based on the use of *signs* or *signals.* The distinctive quality of a sign is that the relationship between it and the meaning it is intended to convey is genetically fixed. The honeybee's "dance," the chimpanzee's grunt, and the hyena's cry are all genetically programmed acts of communication in which there is a strictly limited, one-to-one relationship between the act and its meaning. Signs are thus *closed,* or *nonproductive,* mechanisms of communication; their meaning is rigidly predetermined, and there is no possibility of new meanings being added.

Human communication is distinctive in that it is based on symbols. Symbols differ from signs in that *their meanings are arbitrary.* The meaning of a symbol is determined by those who make use of it in a certain way, and thus symbols lack the rigidity or restrictiveness of signs. In contrast to signs, symbols are *open,* or *productive:* they are capable of attaining new or different meanings (or even several different meanings simultaneously) depending on the use to which their users put them. Both signs and symbols transmit information, but because of their open, or productive, quality, symbols can do so in an enormously more efficient way. Symbols not only make communication more efficient; they are also capable of communicating information of much greater quantity and complexity than is possible with signs.

Individual symbols provide the building blocks for that distinctive human accomplishment, *language.* Language may in fact be defined as a complex arrangement of symbols. With the development of language, humans crossed a kind of evolutionary threshold.

Charles Hockett and Robert Ascher (1964) have specified four primary characteristics of true language. First, language has the quality of *openness.* The symbols out of which language is built can take on new and varied meanings, as opposed to the predetermination of meaning characteristic of sign systems. In addition, speakers can emit new utterances that have never been heard or said before. This makes language *productive* in that it is capable of producing new utterances, new meanings, and new combinations of utterance and meaning. Second, language is characterized by the feature known as *displacement.* Displacement refers to the ability to speak of things that are out of sight, in the past or future, or even nonexistent. By contrast, signs are confined to those situations in which their expression is relevant. Hockett and Ascher note, for instance, that gibbons do not emit their food call unless they have found food. Third, *duality of patterning* is a distinctive characteristic of language. Language has, on the one hand, a patterning of a basic set of elementary sound units, themselves meaningless in isolation, and, on the other hand, a patterning that combines these individual sound units into prescribed sequences that render them meaningful. Sign systems lack such duality, and each vocalization carries a single, predetermined meaning. Finally, language is *transmitted by learning.* This transmission contrasts sharply with the genetic transmission of sign systems.

The Origin of Language

Exactly when and how language first arose is still the subject of much debate. Linguists are in sharp disagreement as to how old language may actually be. Some see it as a relatively recent evolutionary development, perhaps no more than 100,000 years old (Bickerton, 1990; Noble and Davidson, 1996), whereas others believe that it may have evolved as early as a million years ago (Hockett and Ascher, 1964) or even two million years ago or earlier (Pinker, 1994).

One important effort to understand the origin of language is that of Derek Bickerton (1990). Bickerton argues that humans could not have gone directly from a prelinguistic state to language. He therefore posits the existence of an intermediate communication system, what he calls *protolanguage,* which he believes paved the way for the development of true language. Bickerton claims that protolanguage is characteristic of four categories of speakers: apes trained to use so-called sign language, children under the age of two, adults deprived of language use in their early years, and speakers of pidgin languages.

Bickerton relates the story of Genie, a thirteen-year-old girl who had been locked alone in her bedroom by her father and prevented from having any exposure to language. When she attempted to learn language at age thirteen, she was only able to produce something like the following (Bickerton, 1990:116):

Want milk.

Mike paint.

Big elephant, long trunk.

Applesauce buy store.

At school wash face.

Tell door lock.

Very sad, climb mountain.

I want Curtiss play piano.

Father take piece wood. Hit. Cry.

Genie's speech is highly characteristic of children under age two, but here is a normally developing child named Seth a little past the age of two (Bickerton, 1990:166):

I want to put the squeaky shoes some more, Daddy.

Let's get a piece of rock and make it go ding.

Where'd the ball go? Where's the ball?

There's Geoffrey. There's ya cookie monster. There's the nother cookie monster.

According to Bickerton, the critical difference between protolanguage and language is the absence of both syntax—the ability to form complex sentences—and grammatical items in protolanguage. Bickerton believes that Genie was only able to acquire protolanguage because the acquisition of language cannot occur outside of a critical developmental period early in life.

When did protolanguage first emerge? Bickerton suggests that it might have appeared with *Homo habilis*, but if not then almost certainly with *Homo erectus* about one and a half million years ago. However, he argues that it was not until the emergence of fully modern humans that true language emerged, and he suggests that this transition probably occurred very abruptly. He suspects that the emergence of true language was made possible by a particular internal reorganization within the brain that was the result of a single genetic mutation in a single individual. The abrupt transition to language is indicated, he argues, by changes in technological and conceptual development that accompany fully modern humans (Bickerton, 1990:172):

Perhaps the most forceful evidence in this respect is the fossil record. One of the few undisputed facts about that record is that, until almost the end of the *erectus* period, there was relatively little development in the species's tool kit; in particular, very few new types of artifact were developed. Only with the emergence of our own species did there appear bladed tools, cave paintings, stone figurines, moon calendars, and a rich variety of other artifacts.

William Noble and Iain Davidson (1996), although rejecting Bickerton's argument for a stage of protolanguage that mediated the evolution from prelanguage to language, agree with him that language is a relatively recent development. They argue that language probably emerged at the earliest 100,000 years ago, and possibly no earlier than 70,000 years ago. Their reasoning for this late date is essentially the same as Bickerton's. The archaeological evidence for modern human behavior that indicates foresight and planning—consciousness or "minded" behavior—does not go back, they claim, more than 100,000 years at the most, and they hold that language would have been required for such behavior.

Yet a third view of language origins has been developed by Steven Pinker in his book *The Language Instinct* (1994). Pinker accepts Bickerton's argument that the emergence of language logically must have been preceded by some sort of protolanguage. However, he is incredulous at Bickerton's suggestion that language emerged suddenly as the result of a single genetic mutation, opting for a much more gradualist interpretation. Pinker would also extend the date for the origin of language much farther back in time. He suggests that *Homo habilis* and *Homo erectus* may have had some form of language, and even suggests that the first traces of language may have emerged with the australopithecines!

Although it may be preliminary to try to adjudicate these various disagreements concerning language origins, it is likely that language is a relatively recent phenomenon, and for the reasons indicated by Bickerton and Noble and Davidson. The existence of language suggests the kinds of conceptual abilities and behavioral styles associated only with fully modern humans. Language implies the ability to see ahead and to plan, and there is no reliable evidence that *Homo habilis* and *Homo erectus*, let alone the australopithecines, had such capacities.

Language as an Evolutionary Adaptation

Despite the disagreement between Bickerton and Pinker concerning how rapidly and how early language may have evolved, they firmly agree that the evolution of language was of critical significance for humankind. What, then, was its importance? The answer is that it permitted enormous increases in the efficiency and effectiveness of human communication, and such increases would have had a major impact on the likelihood of survival. Pinker explains (1994:367–368):

> If contemporary hunter-gatherers are any guide, our ancestors were not grunting cave men with little more to talk about than which mastodon to avoid. Hunter-gatherers are accomplished toolmakers and superb amateur biologists with detailed knowledge of the life cycles, ecology, and behavior of the plants and animals they depend on. Language would surely have been useful in anything resembling such a lifestyle. . . . There is a fantastic payoff in trading hard-won knowledge with kin and friends, and language is obviously a major means of doing so.
>
> And grammatical devices designed for communicating precise information about time, space, objects, and who did what to whom are not like the proverbial thermonuclear flyswatter. Recursion in particular is extremely useful. . . . With this ability a speaker can pick out an object to an arbitrarily fine level of precision. These abilities can make a big difference. It makes a difference whether a far-off region is reached by taking the trail that is in front of the large tree or the trail that the large tree is in front of. It makes a

difference whether that region has animals that you can eat or animals that can eat you. It makes a difference whether it has fruit that is ripe or fruit that was ripe or fruit that will be ripe. It makes a difference whether you can get there if you walk for three days or whether you can get there and walk for three days.

The tremendous usefulness of language suggests to Pinker that it was an evolutionary adaptation perhaps equal in importance to the overall increase in the size and capacity of the brain. Language has evolved as a fundamental human instinct, he claims, by which he means that the logical structure of language is wired into the human brain. The content of language—the particular words and specific grammatical features of a language—of course, is learned, but the brain comes equipped with a kind of "language organ." This is a compelling argument, and Pinker marshalls a great deal of evidence to support it. One of the most important lines of evidence is the remarkable speed at which children acquire language and their ability to create an infinite number of phrases and sentences that they have never heard before.

Putting it more sociologically, we can say that the great significance of language is that it paved the way for the development of *culture*, that complex system of tools, thoughts, and actions that has provided humans with their uniquely effective means of adaptation. Languages are complex symbol systems, and culture requires symbolization capacity because it intimately depends on a means for storing and transmitting vast quantities of socially learned information. Only language provides such a means.

Is Symbolic Communication Uniquely Human?

The results of recent attempts to teach apes the rudiments of language have cast doubt on the uniqueness of human symbolization capacity. Many scholars have concluded from these results that symbolic communication is not a human monopoly, and therefore that the gulf between humans and other animals is less wide than once believed.

David Premack (1970) taught a young chimpanzee named Sarah a kind of symbol system. Sarah was required to place a variety of plastic chips on a magnetized board, with each chip representing a word and a sequence of chips representing a phrase. Sarah apparently acquired the use of about 130 "words." Using a system of rewards and direct guidance, Gardner and Gardner (1969) taught the chimp Washoe to understand American Sign Language for the Deaf (ASL). Washoe was ultimately able to attain a vocabulary of well over 100 words, and the Gardners claimed that she strung many of these words together into short sentences. Francine Patterson (1978) has been successful in teaching ASL to Koko, a young female gorilla. Koko was able to use some 300 words and, allegedly, combine these words into sentences. Sue Savage-Rumbaugh (1986) taught two young male chimpanzees, Sherman and Austin, a symbolic communication system in which they made responses on a computerized keyboard. Savage-Rumbaugh succeeded in getting Sherman and Austin to communicate not only with her and other teachers, but also with each other.

By far the greatest success, however, has been with the bonobo or pygmy chimpanzee (Pan paniscus). Savage-Rumbaugh, Rumbaugh, and McDonald (1985) worked with Kanzi, a male bonobo, using the same method employed with Sherman and Austin. Kanzi went far beyond these other two chimps. He could use symbols representationally (i.e., to stand for absent objects or events) at an earlier age than Sherman and Austin, and he was much more likely than Sherman and Austin to make spontaneous rather than prompted or imi-

tated utterances. In marked contrast to Sherman and Austin and all other apes used in symbolic communication experiments, Kanzi has shown a capacity to understand spoken English, even seeming to understand conversations between two people that did not involve him at all.

These experiments were initially met with great enthusiasm, but enthusiasm dimmed significantly after the publication in 1979 of two articles by Herbert Terrace and his colleagues (Terrace, 1979; Terrace, Petitto, Sanders, and Bever, 1979; cf. Terrace, 1985). After a detailed analysis of videotapes they had made of their experiments with Nim Chimpsky, a young male chimpanzee, they concluded that he wasn't really learning language as we ordinarily understand it. Terrace claimed that Nim's utterances were prompted and imitated rather than spontaneous, and that he could not engage in the naming of objects, which Terrace regarded as a crucial feature of language. Moreover, it was said that Nim's combined utterances revealed no evidence of true grammar or syntax. Terrace extended these conclusions to all other apes involved in language-teaching experiments (except for Kanzi, as experiments with him came later).

Terrace's conclusions have been strongly challenged by Savage-Rumbaugh (1986), who holds that Terrace's criteria for language are too stringent. She claims that language exists when meanings are communicated, and that this was clearly happening in her work with Sherman and Austin and in other ape language-teaching work. She also claims that apes make many of their utterances spontaneously and representationally. Of course apes do not have the full language competence of humans, she notes, but it is absurd to think they would. Nevertheless, they are capable of many of the facets of language.

What do we make of this line of research? One plausible conclusion is that apes are capable of protolanguage in Bickerton's sense, but not of true language, which clearly remains a unique human trait. That is, they can communicate symbolically in the sense that they can share arbitrarily represented meanings. However, two key ingredients of language, grammatical rules and syntax, are entirely absent. And more can be said. I hate to sound like a spoilsport, but I have had difficulty mustering much enthusiasm for all the research on teaching language to apes. Despite their protolanguage competence, this competence was completely unrealized in the wild. Moreover, even their protolanguage is highly limited, and would fall terribly short of the protolanguage of a young child.

Steven Pinker is even more negative. He claims that the apes were not learning true sign language at all, instead relying on their own natural repertoire of gestures. He also claims that the apes' abilities at anything like grammar were virtually nil; that they did not take turns in conversation but rather signed along with their partner; and that they seldom signed spontaneously, thus having to be drilled and molded. Pinker (1994:342) concludes that the linguistic failures of these apes were certainly "no shame on them; a human would surely do no better if trained to hoot and shriek like a chimp, a symmetrical project that makes about as much scientific sense."

SOCIETY, CULTURE, AND HUMAN ADAPTATION

The Societal Mode of Organization

A species of animals is social when its members live together, interact, and depend upon one another for their survival. Human beings are social animals because they live together in organized groups that we call *societies*. Yet this scarcely makes humans unique, for a great many animal species live in societies, and the societal mode of organization is not confined to the so-called higher species. Many insects live in rather elaborate and complex social groups, the individual members of which intimately depend upon one another for survival. In short, social life is a widespread phenomenon in the animal world.

Nevertheless, social life is not randomly distributed among animal species. The evolutionary status of a species bears a direct relationship to the prevalence of the societal mode of organization. The higher a species stands on the phylogenetic scale of life, the greater the likelihood of its exhibiting organized social life. Thus, while only some insects live in societies, most mammals are social and all primates carry on their lives within a societal framework.

It would be a serious error, however, to assume that the respective societies of bees, chimpanzees, and human beings are fundamentally similar. The specific nature of and basis for societal existence are strikingly different in each instance. The social life of bees, ants, and wasps is complex and elaborate, but the social behavior of such species is wholly regulated by instinctual mechanisms. The social insects come preprogrammed with a ready-made set of behavioral responses. Learning plays virtually no part in their actions.

Such a description of the basis for social behavior does not apply to nonhuman primates. For instance, while much of chimpanzee social life is genetically determined, recent research now makes it clear that learning plays a significant role in their social behavior. The role of learning in this case is one illustration of the general principle that the greater the evolutionary complexity of an organism, the greater the influence of learning (van den Berghe, 1978).

This principle is helpful in understanding the basis for human social life, for it is only in the human species that the role of learning exceeds the part played by biological factors in the shaping of social behavior. But it is not sufficient merely to claim that human social behavior is highly subject to learning. It is essential to point out that human behavior is learned through culture, and thus that human societies, as opposed to all other animal societies, are *culturally ordered* or *culturally regulated* systems.

Culture and Human Adaptation

The concept of culture is indispensable for the study of human behavior and human societies. Unfortunately, there is no universal agreement as to the meaning of this concept. Some social scientists use it to refer solely to the symbolic meanings that individuals attach to their behavior, thereby excluding behavior itself from consideration as a part of culture (cf. Goodenough, 1969; D. M. Schneider, 1968). This book takes the position that such a conceptualization of culture is much too narrow, since it is limited to only one of many relevant aspects of human social life. Accordingly, we shall define **culture** in a much broader way as *the total lifeways characteristic of the members of a society, including tools, knowledge, and patterned ways of thinking and acting, that are learned and shared and transmitted from one generation to the next by means of langauge.* This definition of culture stresses that it is a complex totality consisting of three interrelated sets of phenomena: the tools and techniques—in short, the technologies—that humans have invented to adapt to their environments; the patterns of behavior that individuals engage in as members of society; and the shared beliefs, values, and rules that humans create as a means of defining their relationships to one another and to their natural environments.

There are four primary characteristics of culture. First, culture *rests on symbols.* Symbols are essential to culture in that they are the mechanisms necessary for the storage and transmission of the large quantities of information that constitute culture. Second, culture is *learned* and does not depend upon biological inheritance for its transmission. (However, this does not mean that human biology is irrelevant to the nature of culture. Indeed, all human culture rests upon a biological foundation, and human biology therefore partly determines the nature of the cultures that humans develop.) Third, culture is a system that is *shared* by the members of a society; that is, it is representative of the members of a society considered collectively rather than individually. While there are differences in the degree to which various individuals accept or conform to the patterns of their culture, a culture by definition is representative of the members of a society considered collectively. Finally, culture tends to be *integrated.* The various parts or components of culture tend to fit together in such a way that they are consistent with one another, despite the conflicts, frictions, or contradictions that are also present.

Considerable attention has been given by both sociologists and anthropologists to distinguishing between the concept of society and that of culture. *Society* is generally used to refer to the "patterned relationships obtaining between people," while *culture* is often regarded as "the products of such patterned relationships" (i.e., the technology, beliefs, values, and rules that both serve as guides to, and result from, such patterned relationships). While this distinction may be a useful one for various analytical purposes, it is highly artificial and is sharply divorced from the concrete reality of the lives of human beings. The distinction therefore has little to commend it, and it has probably done more harm than good. Accordingly, to avoid this distinction it is useful to follow those who have used the hybrid term *sociocultural system* (M. Harris, 1985b; Lenski and Lenski, 1987). The real advantage of this term is that it brings into relief the full range of factors constituting the "systems" in which individuals conduct their lives. The nature of sociocultural systems, and the way in which they may be appropriately compartmentalized, is the subject of Chapter 3.

The real significance of culture is its adaptive nature. Culture has created for human beings a new means of adaptation to the conditions of their existence, and this mode of adaptation is one that has been vastly superior to biological adaptation. At a lower phylogenetic level, societies themselves were adaptive mechanisms developing out of a long process of biological evolution. As societies evolved to higher levels of complexity, and as the conditions were developed for the emergence of symbol systems out of sign systems, culture itself came about as an evolutionary product. As all of this happened, the stage was set for the development of sociocultural systems in which culture rivaled, and eventually replaced, biology as the prime basis for human adaptation.

Is Culture Uniquely Human?

The recent discovery that some nonhuman primates frequently engage in rudimentary forms of tool use has led a number of observers to challenge the conventional wisdom that culture is uniquely human. Chimpanzees, for example, have been shown to use blades of grass as crude tools for withdrawing termites from their holes. Furthermore, the chimps actually shape or fashion these tools before using them (Jolly, 1972). It has been discovered that groups of Japanese macaque monkeys have developed the practice of washing sweet potatoes and wheat before eating them. These practices are learned by other members of the group, although by observation and not by direct teaching (Jolly, 1972). Baboons have used stones as weapons, and chimpanzees actually seem to aim at targets and club with objects (Jolly, 1972).

These crude forms of tool use clearly must be regarded as a rudimentary form of culture.* They vary from one group of the same species to another, and therefore they are learned and shared behavior patterns that cannot be accounted for in terms of biological inheritance. Nevertheless, it is inappropriate to draw dramatic conclusions about nonhuman "culture." While nonhuman primates have a few rudimentary elements of culture, and thus while the distinction between humans and other primates must be regarded as quantitative, this quantitative difference is so large that it seems feasible to argue that culture is a uniquely human product for all practical purposes. In a technical sense humans are not the only creatures with culture, but they are certainly extraordinarily better at creating it than any other animal. No investigator has ever discovered a group of chimpanzees who worshiped gods, transferred bride payments, or painted murals on the walls of caves.

Ethnocentrism and Cultural Relativism

A basic feature of human life that quickly comes to be realized by any aspiring anthropologist or sociologist is the extraordinary degree of diversity in sociocultural systems. Social scientists frequently find themselves confronted by cultures that differ dramatically from their own. The sense of horror and shock that is often experienced by anthropological field-workers when first confronting a vastly different culture is vividly described by Napoleon Chagnon upon his first meeting with the Yanomama Indians of South America (Chagnon, 1983:10–11):

> I looked up and gasped when I saw a dozen burly, naked, sweaty, hideous men staring at us down the shafts of their drawn arrows!

*Some social scientists now use the term *proto-culture* to refer to this sort of crude infrahuman tool use, reserving the term *culture* for human achievements alone.

Immense wads of green tobacco were stuck between their lower teeth and lips making them look even more hideous, and strands of dark-green slime dripped or hung from their nostrils—strands so long that they clung to their pectoral muscles or drizzled down their chins. We arrived at the village while the men were blowing a hallucinogenic drug up their noses. One of the side effects of the drug is a runny nose. The mucus is always saturated with the green powder and they usually let it run freely from their nostrils. . . . My next discovery was that there were a dozen or so vicious, underfed dogs snapping at my legs, circling me as if I were to be their next meal. I just stood there holding my notebook, helpless and pathetic. Then the stench of the decaying vegetation and filth hit me and I almost got sick. I was horrified. What kind of welcome was this for the person who came here to live with you and learn your way of life, to become friends with you? . . .

    As we walked down the path to the boat, I pondered the wisdom of having decided to spend a year and a half with this tribe before I had even seen what they were like. I am not ashamed to admit that had there been a diplomatic way out, I would have ended my fieldwork then and there.

    The extreme culture shock experienced by Chagnon is not limited to professional social scientists. It can be, and has been, experienced by virtually all persons suddenly encountering a way of life remarkably different from their own. This reaction results from the phenomenon known as ethnocentrism: the tendency for individuals to view their own way of life as superior to all others. Thus, Chagnon was horrified by what he saw since Western industrial culture had hardly prepared him for such phenomena as drawn bows, nakedness, green slime dripping from the nose, and filthiness when he approached the tribe as a visitor. To a very substantial degree, we are products of our own culture, and virtually all of us are inclined to think of our own way of life as the most desirable and other cultures as representing various gradations of less desirable lifestyles. Ethnocentrism is a universal human phenomenon. The Yanomama themselves are no exception to this rule. Chagnon reports that, since he was a non-Yanomama, they tended to regard him as less than human. The Yanomama are one of the world's most hostile and warlike societies, yet when Chagnon described to them the conduct of Americans in the Vietnam War, they were morally repelled and regarded such behavior as savage and inhumane!

    Ethnocentrism creates a special problem for research in other cultures since, if powerful enough, it represents a severe barrier to any sort of objective (and hence accurate) study. Had Chagnon been unable to overcome his ethnocentrism, he could never have carried out even a remotely successful research project. Anthropologists and sociologists have combated this problem through the development of a counter doctrine known as **cultural relativism.** Cultural relativism is the doctrine that no culture is inherently superior or inferior to others, but that, since every culture represents an adaptive solution to fundamental human problems, all cultures are "equally valid." Cultural relativists believe that the standards of one culture cannot be used to evaluate another, and therefore that the standards for the evaluation of a culture can only be those of that culture itself. If we were to apply this doctrine in judging the propriety of female infanticide (the selective killing of female infants) among the Yanomama, all we could really say would be something like "while it's wrong for us, it's right for them, and cannot be categorically condemned." And we would say this through recognition of the fact that infanticide "is right" for the Yanomama since it represents an adaptive solution to a problem of human existence.

As a moral or ethical perspective, cultural relativism has been subjected to severe criticism, and it does not constitute a satisfactory system of ethics (Kohlberg, 1971; O. Patterson, 1977). The problems with it are fairly well known. For one thing, it can quickly collapse into "the disease of which it is the cure" (Kohlberg, 1971). That is, "it leads to the approval of practices that are patently inhumane" (Hatch, 1983:81). For example, a strict cultural relativist perspective would have us endorse such practices as the Nazi effort to exterminate the Jews, Soviet forced labor camps, Roman slavery or black slavery in the New World, Yanomama gang rape of women, and countless other cultural phenomena that seem morally repulsive by most reasonable standards—all in the name of tolerance toward other ways of life. In addition, cultural relativism seems to perpetuate a kind of "tyranny of custom" by leaving little or no room for the autonomy of the individual (Hatch, 1983).

In fact, the limitations of cultural relativism have appeared obvious even to many of the cultural relativists themselves, some of whom have actually violated their own principles in practice despite formally enunciating them. For instance, Ruth Benedict, one of the major architects of cultural relativism in the early decades of this century, has consistently undermined her own relativist stance when she has discussed cultural differences (Hatch, 1983). In her well-known book *Patterns of Culture* (1934), Benedict clearly shows a preference for certain cultural traits over others, displaying, for example, a particular dislike for cultures in which force plays a major role.

Elvin Hatch (1983) has suggested a way around cultural relativism that overcomes its basic deficiencies while at the same time retaining what seems to be of value in it: its general plea for tolerance. Hatch proposes what he calls a "humanistic principle" as a means of judging other cultures. This principle holds that cultures can be evaluated in terms of whether or not they harm persons by such means as torture, sacrifice, war, political repression, exploitation, and so on. It also judges them in terms of how well they provide for the material existence of their members, that is, the extent to which people are free from poverty, malnutrition, disease, and the like. Beyond this consideration, cultures cannot really be meaningfully evaluated (Hatch, 1983:138):

> Relativism prevails in relation to the institutions that fall outside the orbit of the humanistic principle, for here a genuine diversity of values is found and there are no suitable cross-cultural standards for evaluating them. The finest reasoning that we or anyone else can achieve will not point decisively to the superiority of Western marriage patterns, eating habits, legal institutions, and the like. We ought to show tolerance with respect to these institutions in other societies on the grounds that people ought to be free to live as they choose.

While Hatch's proposal does seem to improve considerably on cultural relativism, such complex ethical questions unfortunately cannot be settled quite so easily. It is highly doubtful that even Hatch's strongly modified version of cultural relativism can be taken as a truly acceptable ethical philosophy. Yet despite our objections to either of these versions of relativism, we must recognize that cultural relativism is useful and necessary as a sort of practical guiding premise in exploring the nature of sociocultural systems. It therefore has *methodological,* if not ethical, value. It has methodological value because it compels the examination of cultural patterns in terms of their adaptive character. Without cultural relativism as a methodological tool, we would confront other cultures wearing a set of cultural blinders, the result of which would undoubtedly be the perpetuation of ignorance rather than the illumination of the basic workings of sociocultural systems.

Culture, Subculture, and Counterculture

The term *culture* is usually applied to the total way of life of a society considered as a whole. However, in sociocultural systems of great complexity, such as Western industrial societies, it is essential to recognize the nature of diverse cultural patternings that exist within such societies. For this reason sociologists have developed the concepts of **subculture** and **counterculture.**

A subculture is a smaller culture existing within the framework of a larger culture. The members of a subculture share specific cultural patterns that are in some way different from those that prevail in the larger culture, while at the same time generally accepting and sharing in the patterns of the larger culture. American college students, for example, constitute a subculture in the sense that they act and think in ways that are in some respects distinct from American culture as a whole. Diverse ethnic groups in complex industrial societies— groups that are distinguished on the basis of cultural or national origin—display rather distinctive subcultural patterns in that they carry on ways of thinking and acting that are in some way unique. College professors, doctors, coal miners, and professional athletes also embody certain subcultural differences, the differences in these cases arising from distinctive occupations. Many other subcultures exist in complex societies, of course, with such factors as race, religion, regionalism, and social class serving as important criteria for subcultural distinctions.

Like subcultures, countercultures contain distinctive cultural patterns existing within some larger culture. Unlike subcultures, however, the members of countercultures generally do not share in the dominant cultural patterns. Instead, countercultures tend to be based on hostility to, and rejection of, such dominant patterns. Some countercultures are genuinely revolutionary in that they are predicated upon an attempt to make a fundamental alteration in the dominant culture. Most countercultures, however, are not imbued with such revolutionary intentions; instead, they are generally organized around a withdrawal from the mainstream of cultural life. In this category would fall such groups as the "beatniks" of the 1950s and the "hippies" of the 1960s. One of the most recent countercultures to appear in Western society is that of the "punkers" of the 1980s.

SUMMARY

1. Biological evolution is a process whereby organisms acquire those characteristics that allow them to be highly adapted to particular environments. Evolution occurs through the selective effect of the environment on genetic variation, especially mutations. Most mutations are negative in their effect on the organism and are selectively eliminated through the death or sterility of the organisms containing them. Beneficial mutations, though, are selectively preserved because the organisms containing them are differentially favored for survival. The unequal survival of favored and unfavored organisms is a process known as natural selection.

2. Human biological evolution spans the past four million years. Our earliest ancestors were the australopithecines, who lived on the savannas of eastern and southern Africa between two and four million years ago. They gave way in time to *Homo habilis* and *Homo erectus*, who were bigger and brainier. After about 500,000 years ago various forms of archaic *Homo sapiens* evolved in Africa, Asia, and Europe from *Homo erectus* populations. In Europe and the Middle East archaic *Homo sapiens* was replaced by the Nean-

derthals after about 200,000 years ago. The origin of our current species, *Homo sapiens*, is hotly debated. One group of scholars holds that fully modern humans evolved in Africa around 200,000 years ago and eventually migrated to Europe and Asia, where they drove the human populations in those regions to extinction. Another group claims that humans evolved somewhat independently on all three continents over the past several hundred thousand years. The former group claims that the Neanderthals were an evolutionary dead end, whereas the latter claims that they were our immediate ancestors.

3. The most important developments in human evolution have been the transition to an upright posture and bipedal means of locomotion, the acquisition of tool use, and the enormous increase in the size and complexity of the brain.

4. Another great achievement in human evolution was the development of symbolic communication and language. Whereas all other animals communicate through the use of signs, humans communicate by using symbols, or sounds and gestures that are arbitrary, learned, and shared. Complex systems of symbols constitute languages.

5. Language was an evolutionary adaptation of enormous significance, but there is still wide disagreement as to just when and how it may have evolved from earlier sign systems. Derek Bickerton has described a process involving the shift from protolanguage to language, which he believes occurred abruptly sometime after about 200,000 years ago. William Noble and Iain Davidson also see language as a relatively modern development, emerging no earlier than 100,000 years ago. Steven Pinker sees language emerging much more slowly and much earlier. He theorizes that *Homo habilis* and *Homo erectus* probably had some sort of language, and that the very beginnings of language may have occurred in the days of the australopithecines.

6. Although many experiments have been conducted over the past thirty years attempting to teach apes the rudiments of language, the real accomplishments of these experiments fall far short of the claims usually made for them. Apes show, at best, an extremely limited capacity for the use of symbols, and the communicative gulf between them and humans is huge.

7. The great significance of language for humans is that it makes culture possible. While some other animals have rudimentary forms of culture known as protoculture, only humans have true culture, or complex systems of tools, knowledge, and learned and shared patterns of thought and action. Many animal species live in societies, but only humans live in sociocultural systems, or societies organized culturally.

8. Culture is a human achievement with enormous adaptive significance. It allows humans to cope with a great number and variety of survival problems. Culture has now replaced biology as the prime means of human adaptation.

9. Cultures differ enormously, and most humans in all cultures respond to cultural differences ethnocentrically, or by assuming their own way of life to be superior to all others. Social scientists generally agree that ethnocentrism is an unfortunate human trait, and it certainly constitutes an obstacle to meaningful sociological understanding. Many social scientists have adopted the doctrine known as cultural relativism as a means of counteracting ethnocentrism. This doctrine advocates tolerance for cultural diversity and suggests that all cultural traits have value in their own contexts. While this doctrine may be methodologically useful to social scientists, it does not seem to constitute an adequate ethical philosophy. Indeed, many social scientists, including those who otherwise defend cultural relativism, are sharply critical of such cultural practices as oppression, exploitation, slavery, and various forms of human brutality.

10. In complex societies, there are almost always subpopulations having cultural traits distinct in some ways from the dominant culture. These smaller cultures within a larger culture are known as subcultures and countercultures. Subcultures generally accept the dominant culture, whereas countercultures generally reject it to one extent or another.

SPECIAL TOPIC: THE SOCIOBIOLOGY CONTROVERSY

One of the newest theoretical strategies in sociology is known as sociobiology. As this strategy began to emerge in the middle of the 1970s, it generated one of the more heated of recent controversies in the social sciences. Although the heat has now dissipated considerably, the controversy has not gone away and the issues it addresses are crucial ones.

Sociobiologists attempt to discover the extent to which human social behavior is the result of genetic traits characteristic of the entire human species. In other words, they are interested in identifying the basic features of **human nature**. They base their assumptions on the Darwinian model of biological evolution through natural selection. They believe that as humans evolved from their primate ancestors they inherited certain biological traits from those ancestors that continue to exist in modern humans. These traits are held to have a direct influence on many patterns of social behavior. Sociobiologists do not claim that human social behavior is merely the product of our genetic programming; they recognize that most human activities result from specific forms of learning in particular social and cultural environments. Nevertheless, they argue that human behavior is not entirely learned, and that many aspects of it may be under genetic control.

A well-known example of sociobiological reasoning is found in the work of Lionel Tiger and Robin Fox (1971). Tiger and Fox argue that humans come equipped with a *biogrammar*: a basic set of biological instructions predisposing them to act in certain ways. They do not regard these instructions as constituting fixed, immutable instincts. Rather, they view them as general behavioral tendencies that are subject to being modified or even neutralized by certain learning experiences. They see the following as the most essential elements of the human biogrammar:

- The tendency of humans to form strongly hierarchical groups and societies in which the competition for status is of paramount importance.
- The tendency of males to bond together in political coalitions in which they exercise political dominance and control over females.
- The tendency of mother and child to form a strong mutual attachment.
- The predisposition of humans (especially males) to engage in various forms of aggression and violence.
- The tendency of humans to defend territorial space against intrusions by outsiders.

Tiger and Fox reach these conclusions by drawing analogies between human behavior and the behavior of contemporary nonhuman primates. They note that most nonhuman primates are organized into societies based on status hierarchies with dominance of males over females, and they infer from this that a basic primate biogram has been retained throughout human evolutionary history. The tendency for modern humans to form hierarchical, competitive, and male-dominated social systems is therefore seen as resting essentially in our genes. The same kind of bioevolutionary reasoning is applied by Tiger and Fox in reaching the conclusion that mother-child bonding and the predisposition toward aggression and territoriality are rooted in our biological nature.

Tiger and Fox's arguments are illustrative of one particular version of sociobiological theorizing. Other sociobiologists employ the **theory of kin selection** as the guiding principle in their thinking (E. O. Wilson, 1975; Symons, 1979; Trivers, 1985). This theory is based on the recent assumption made by many evolutionary biologists that the gene, rather than the organism or species, is the unit on which natural selection operates (cf. Dawkins, 1976). Evolutionary biologists who maintain this assumption claim that natural selection operates to preserve certain genes and maximize their representation in future generations.

Kin selection theory (it might more appropriately be labeled a strategic principle) posits that many forms of behavior result from the attempts of individuals to maximize their **inclusive fitness.** Inclusive fitness is the sum of an individual's own fitness *plus* the fitness present in the genes of all its relatives. A major application of kin selection theory has been to the commonly observed phenomenon of altruism among closely related individuals. For example, the theory holds that when a parent behaves in a self-sacrificial manner toward its offspring it is assisting them to survive and reproduce and therefore leave more copies of its genes in future generations. Such altruistic behavior, then, serves to maximize the parent's inclusive fitness.

The theory of kin selection has been highly successful in explaining many features of animal behavior. It successfully explains, for instance, the extreme altruism characteristic of the social insects (W. D. Hamilton, 1964), as well as altruistic behavior in other animal species (cf. Barash, 1977; van den Berghe, 1978). Some social scientists believe that it can adequately account for several features of human social behavior. Since the theory successfully explains the importance of kinship bonds in many animal species, it has been proposed that it helps to explain the universality of human kinship systems and the great significance that is attached to kinship in so many societies (van den Berghe, 1979). It has also been suggested that it is a promising way of explaining widespread patterns of human gender role behavior (Daly and Wilson, 1978).

Most sociologists have reacted negatively to sociobiology. They insist that the vast majority of human behavior is learned through culture, and that the most basic feature of human nature is its flexibility and capacity for learning. Such things as status competition, male domination, or mother-child bonding are viewed as cultural creations that vary greatly from one society, or one segment of society, to another. A good deal of the negative reaction has been rooted in political considerations. Many sociologists feel that sociobiology is a new form of social conservatism that wants to turn back the clock on important social changes. Sociobiology has often been called sexist and racist, and one of its founders, zoologist Edward O. Wilson, has been harrassed at scientific conferences (Pines, 1978).

Among psychologists and anthropologists sociobiology seems to have been much better received, and so sociologists may be unique in the extent of their disparagement of this approach. In a survey of American sociologists (Sanderson and Ellis, 1992), it was found that only about three percent identified sociobiology as one of their preferred theoretical perspectives, and sociologists gave biological factors an extremely limited role in explaining a wide range of human behavior. A more recent study of sociological theorists (Lord and Sanderson, 1997) obtained very similar results. Yet a study of cultural anthropologists conducted in the late 1980s (Lieberman, 1989) found many of them to be quite receptive to sociobiology, and psychologists are often prominently represented as authors of sociobiological works.

Even if sociobiology can be defended against its critics, it is still very much an open question the extent to which it holds promise as a *general* strategy for the study of human social life. Many sociobiologists readily admit that the basic differences among human societies are more the result of social and cultural factors than of biological ones, and for this reason they expend more effort studying the universal or highly similar features of societies. In addition, sociobiology probably has little light to shed on the major historical transformations that interest macrosociologists and that play such an important role in this book.

Nevertheless, despite sociobiology's obvious limitations, it does seem to have an important contribution to make. It is hard to dismiss such widespread forms of human behavior as male domination, status competition, and social hierarchies as having nothing to do with human biology. Moreover, considerable evidence has accumulated in recent years to show that such phenomena as homicide (Daly and Wilson, 1988), ethnicity and ethnocentrism (van den Berghe,

1981; Reynolds, Falger, and Vine, 1986), mental and emotional disorder (Gazzaniga, 1992), incest avoidance (Shepher, 1983), and homosexuality (Ellis and Ames, 1987) have important biological roots. Sociobiology seems to have an especially important contribution to make in dealing with human sexuality (Symons, 1979) and those phenomena that closely revolve around it, such as gender roles, kinship, and marriage, as Chapters 14 and 15 of this book will show. This is unsurprising in view of sociobiology's emphasis on inclusive fitness and reproductive success.

The cold reception sociology has given sociobiology stems, unfortunately, more from ideological factors than from any hard assessment of sociobiology's scientific validity. My previous reference to the political overtones of the sociobiology controversy has perhaps already made this apparent. Sociologists' strong humanistic stance and social reformist tendencies often lead them to feel threatened by many of sociobiology's pronouncements, which sociologists have (erroneously) taken to mean that the status quo cannot be changed. Sociologists also seem to feel that their disciplinary identity—which rests, they seem to think, on the basic premise that social life must be explained in terms of social and cultural factors—is threatened by an approach that makes biology a prominent explanatory factor.

But sociologists' fears are groundless. That biology matters does not mean that society cannot be changed in ways that we desire. In fact, social change can be undertaken far more intelligently with the recognition of the various ways in which biology impinges on human behavior. Certainly, putting our heads in the sand won't make biological factors, if they are important, go away. If they are important and we ignore them, then our efforts at social change will most surely fail. And as for biology threatening our disciplinary identity, this fear is groundless too. Even the sociobiologists themselves admit that there is enormous room for explanation in terms of social and cultural factors. The trick is to see how these interact with biology to produce particular behavior patterns, and sociologists (and anthropologists too) are best skilled at doing that.

Again, sociobiology plays only a limited role in this book, because its highly macrosociological character, especially its concern with general patterns of long-term social evolution, brings other kinds of factors sharply into play.

FOR FURTHER READING

Bickerton, Derek. *Language and Species.* Chicago: University of Chicago Press, 1990. An excellent analysis of the nature and origin of language.

Chagnon, Napoleon. *Yanomamö: The Last Days of Eden.* San Diego: Harcourt Brace Jovanovich, 1992. The latest version of a well-known ethnography that provides insight into the nature of culture and vividly depicts the kinds of obstacles that must be overcome in order to gain a scientifically valid understanding of other cultures.

Dawkins, Richard. *The Blind Watchmaker.* New York: Norton, 1986. A first-rate articulation and defense of the modern synthetic theory of evolution. Extremely well written and intended for a broad audience.

Degler, Carl N. *In Search of Human Nature: The Decline and Revival of Darwinism in American Social Thought.* New York: Oxford University Press, 1991. Documents the rejection of biological explanations of human behavior and the rise of environmentalism in American social science in the 1930s, and shows that this intellectual development was rooted more in political ideology than in science.

Futuyma, Douglas J. *Evolutionary Biology.* Second edition. Sunderland, Mass.: Sinauer, 1986. A first-rate textbook of evolutionary biology by a leading scholar. Contains excellent discussions of numerous theoretical and empirical questions.

Hatch, Elvin. *Culture and Morality: The Relativity of Values in Anthropology.* New York: Columbia University Press, 1983. An excellent discussion of cultural relativism in social science, with reference to its origins, its proponents and detractors, its strengths and weaknesses, and its current status.

Klein, Richard G. *The Human Career: Human Biological and Cultural Origins.* Chicago: University of Chicago Press, 1989. A good treatment of human biological evolution.

Mayr, Ernst. *One Long Argument: Charles Darwin and the Genesis of Modern Evolutionary Thought.* Cambridge, Mass.: Harvard University Press, 1991. An outstanding overview of the emergence of Darwin's theory and its ultimate triumph in the modern synthetic theory. Mayr was a major contributor to the modern evolutionary synthesis and has no peer as an interpreter and expositor of Darwin's thinking.

Pinker, Steven. *The Language Instinct: How the Mind Creates Language.* New York: William Morrow and Co., 1994. A beautifully written and extremely compelling analysis of the biological foundations of language.

Trivers, Robert. *Social Evolution.* Menlo Park, Calif.: Benjamin/Cummings, 1985. A leading textbook on sociobiology by a major sociobiologist. The title, which is unfortunately chosen, refers to the evolution of human social behavior under the impact of natural selection, not to the evolution of human society and culture.

Chapter

3

Sociocultural Systems and the Nature of Sociocultural Evolution

This chapter establishes some conceptual and theoretical foundations essential to the study of human social life. It further explores the concept of a sociocultural system by offering a tripartite scheme for classifying the basic components of sociocultural systems. The chapter also begins the study of sociocultural evolution. It discusses the general nature of this process and the various ways in which it may occur. The evolutionary materialist approach to the study of social life, touched on in Chapter 1, is explored more fully. The basic principles of this theoretical strategy are formally stated and discussed, and an attempt is made to demonstrate their usefulness as general theoretical tools.

THE BASIC COMPONENTS OF SOCIOCULTURAL SYSTEMS

The basic unit of macrosociological analysis is a **sociocultural system:** a collection of people who make use of various means of adapting to their physical environment, who engage in patterned forms of social conduct, and who create shared beliefs and values designed to make sense of their collective actions. However, as a starting point for systematic inquiry, it is necessary to break sociocultural systems down into their most essential components. This makes it possible to inquire into the relationships among the components, to see how one or more components may affect the others. Only in this way is it possible to see how sociocultural systems actually work as single functioning wholes.

Numerous ways of compartmentalizing sociocultural systems have been proposed by social scientists. The procedure offered in this book is quite similar to that developed by Marvin Harris (1979), who has presented a compartmentalizing scheme that elaborates on Marx's famous distinction between base and superstructure (see Table 3.1). This scheme is an extremely useful analytic device for understanding the structure and functioning of sociocultural systems.

Material Infrastructure

The **material infrastructure** consists of the basic raw materials and social forms pertinent to human survival and adaptation. A society's infrastructure is its most basic component in the sense that without it physical survival is literally impossible. The infrastructure is itself composed of four fundamental subunits:

- *Technology.* **Technology** consists of the information, tools, and techniques with which humans adapt to their physical environment (Lenski, 1970). It consists not merely of physical or concrete tools or objects, but also of knowledge that humans can apply in particular ways. Thus, chairs, plows, and automobiles are elements of technology, but so are such things as knowing how to domesticate wild plants and animals.
- *Economy.* A society's **economy** is the organized system whereby goods and services are produced, distributed, and exchanged among individuals and groups.

Production refers to such things as what goods are produced, who produces them, what tools or techniques are used in their production, and who owns the basic materials that enter into the process of production. *Distribution* involves the manner in which the items produced are allocated to various individuals and groups within the society. *Exchange* is carried out when individuals and groups transfer valuables to one another in return for other valuables. A society's means of distributing goods and services is generally dependent upon the means by which they are produced.

- *Ecology.* **Ecology** includes the totality of the physical environment to which humans must adapt. It involves such things as types of soils, the nature of climates, patterns of rainfall, the nature of plant and animal life, and the availability of natural resources. In a strict sense, ecology is not a part of a sociocultural system; it is the external environment to which sociocultural systems must adjust. However, since ecological factors are frequently crucial determinants of various aspects of social life, ecology is here treated as a fundamental component of sociocultural systems.
- *Demography.* **Demographic** factors are those involving the nature and dynamics of human populations. The size and density of the population; its growth, decline, or stability; and its age and sex composition are important things to know in studying any society. Demographic factors also include techniques of population regulation or birth control and the intensity with which these are applied.

Social Structure

This component of a sociocultural system consists of the organized patterns of social life carried out among the members of a society, excluding those social patterns that belong to the infrastructure. It is imperative to note that the **social structure** always

Table 3.1   THE BASIC COMPONENTS OF SOCIOCULTURAL SYSTEMS

Ideological superstructure	• General ideology • Religion • Science • Art • Literature
Social structure	• Social stratification (or its absence) • Racial and ethnic stratification (or their absence) • Polity • Gender division of labor and gender inequality • Family and kinship • Education
Material infrastructure	• Technology • Economy • Ecology • Demography

refers to actual behavioral patterns, as opposed to images or mental conceptions that people have about those patterns. In other words, the social structure consists of what people actually do, not what they say they do, think they do, or think they ought to do. For present purposes, the social structure consists of six subunits:

• *Social stratification (or its absence).* Social stratification refers to the existence within a society of groups of unequal wealth and power. Not all societies have social stratification. In the study of any society, it is crucial to note whether or not it is stratified; if so, the particular nature and degree of stratification must be ascertained.

• *Racial and ethnic stratification (or their absence).* This refers to whether or not there exist within a society groups that may be distinguished by racial or ethnic characteristics, and, if so, whether or not such groups occupy unequal positions with respect to each other. (Racial groups are those that are distinguishable on the basis of observable physical characteristics; ethnic groups are those that exhibit a cultural distinctiveness.) Many societies

in human history have not had racial or ethnic stratification. In the past several hundred years, however, racial/ethnic stratification has been a prominent feature of numerous complex societies.

• *Polity.* This refers to a society's organized means of maintaining internal law and order, as well as to its means of regulating or conducting intersocietal relationships. All societies have political systems, although the nature of such systems varies greatly from one society to another.

• *Gender division of labor and gender inequality.* This involves the way in which men and women are allocated to specific tasks or roles within the social division of labor. It also includes the way in which and the degree to which men and women occupy positions of unequal rank, power, and privilege within a society. Although the gender division of labor and gender inequality are universal, there is great variation among societies in terms of the specific forms these phenomena take.

• *Family and kinship.* All societies have family and kinship systems, or organized sociocultural patterns devoted to mating and reproduction. Once again, however, the specific nature of these systems varies greatly from one society to another. Furthermore, different subcultures within a society often reveal different family and kinship patterns.

- *Education.* Education is any formalized or semiformalized system of cultural or intellectual instruction. Most societies have lacked highly formalized educational systems, but no society has failed to develop some sort of procedure for transmitting knowledge, skills, or values to the next generation.

Ideological Superstructure

The **ideological superstructure** involves the patterned ways in which the members of a society think, conceptualize, evaluate, and feel, as opposed to what they actually do. Whereas the structure refers to behavior, the superstructure refers to thought. The superstructure includes the following subcomponents:

- *General ideology.* This refers to the predominant beliefs, values, and norms characteristic of a society or some segment of a society. **Beliefs** are shared cognitive assumptions about what is true and what is false. They concern such things as the nature of the universe, what child-training techniques produce children with healthy personalities, what differences exist between men and women, and literally thousands of other things. **Values** are socially defined conceptions of worth. They order our experience of what is good and bad, right and wrong, beautiful and ugly, desirable and undesirable, and so on. **Norms** represent shared standards or rules regarding proper and improper social conduct. They are the do's and don'ts that societies attempt to instill in their members. All societies create beliefs, values, and norms, but the diversity of these phenomena is extraordinary.
- *Religion.* Religion consists of shared beliefs and values pertaining to the postula-

tion of supernatural beings, powers, or forces. Such beings, powers, or forces are generally held to intervene directly in the operation of society, or at least to have some indirect connection with it. Like many of the other components of sociocultural systems, religion is a universal feature of human social life.

- *Science.* Science is a set of techniques for the acquisition of knowledge relying upon observation and experience (i.e., collection of factual evidence, demonstration, proof, etc.). It includes not only the techniques and procedures for producing knowledge, but also the accumulated body of knowledge itself. Conceived in this way, science is not a cultural universal, but has flourished only in certain places at certain times.
- *Art.* Art is a universal component of sociocultural systems. It consists of the symbolic images or representations having esthetic, emotional, or intellectual value for the members of a society or segment of a society. The symbolic images or representations in question are of a physical nature.
- *Literature.* Literature also consists of symbolic images or representations having esthetic, emotional, or intellectual value. However, in this case the images or representations are verbal (oral or written) rather than physical in nature. Conceived in this way, myth, legend, and the plays of Shakespeare all count as literature.

THE NATURE OF SOCIOCULTURAL EVOLUTION

What Is Sociocultural Evolution?

One problem with using the term *evolution* to identify changes that occur in sociocultural systems is that the literal meaning of the term is itself misleading. As Elman Service (1971a) has noted, the term derives from the Latin *evolutis*, meaning an "unrolling."

This clearly implies that evolution involves an "unfolding" or a "development," a process whereby a sociocultural system comes to realize the potentialities originally inherent within it. It implies that evolution is movement toward some "goal" or final end state, that societies evolve in much the same way that the embryo matures to become a healthy organism living outside its mother's body. It implies, in other words, that sociocultural evolution is a teleological process. The problem is that sociocultural evolution is not like that at all. As in the case of biological evolution, there is no ultimate "purpose" or "goal" to sociocultural evolution. There is no "unfolding" toward some end state.

In order to avoid misconstruing the nature of sociocultural evolution, it is necessary to stay clear of the literal meaning of the term and the dangers with which it is fraught. As a rough first approximation, we can define **sociocultural evolution** as *a process of change whereby one sociocultural form is transformed into another.* Conceptualized in this way, sociocultural evolution is a process involving *qualitative,* rather than quantitative, change. Quantitative changes are changes from less of something to more of something, or vice versa. Qualitative changes, by contrast, are those in which a new *type* or *form* replaces an old type or form. Of course, qualitative changes are themselves the results of a series of prior quantitative changes. When quantitative changes accumulate over time they eventually result in those kinds of transformations that we term qualitative. Nonetheless, we cannot really speak of evolutionary transformation until the level of qualitative change has been reached. Thus the shift of a society from dependence upon hunting and gathering to dependence upon agriculture for its food supply is an evolutionary change, as is the shift from agriculture to industry. Likewise, the emergence within a society of so-

cial class divisions where none existed before is an evolutionary change. The expansion of the number of villages found within a society, however, is not an evolutionary change so long as the new villages are essentially replicas of the old ones.

But there is somewhat more to the notion of evolution than is implied by the idea of qualitative change. Therefore, to complete our definition of sociocultural evolution we need to add that *it is change that exhibits a certain directionality.* What is meant is that sociocultural evolution is patterned change that manifests a trend of a linear nature. For example, changes in the level of technology that increase the sophistication and efficiency of tools and productive techniques signify a directional trend. Such a trend is also indicated by an increase in the level and intensity of class inequality.

Many evolutionists have thought that the chief directional trend in sociocultural evolution is that of increased societal complexity (cf. Parsons, 1966, 1971). Robert Carneiro (1972), for example, has claimed that in fact this is what evolution is—change in a direction of increasing complexity—and that any other use of the concept weakens and debases it. But while it must be acknowledged that growing social complexity is an important dimension of social evolution, there is no warrant for regarding it as the only, or as the most important, dimension. Sociocultural evolution has many dimensions, and thus many directional trends, and we should not restrict ourselves to analyzing a single one.

Sociocultural evolution involves both entire sociocultural systems and the individual components of such systems. What normally occurs is that change begins in one component (or subcomponent) and this change produces changes in the other components. An entire chain of cause and effect is set off that eventually results in the transformation of entire sociocultural systems.

Some scholars have insisted upon a distinction between the terms *history* and *evolution*. Most notable in this regard is Leslie White (1945). White's argument is that history is concerned with unique events or changes, while evolution involves *patterns* of change characteristic of human societies in general. According to this view, to be concerned with history is to limit one's attention to the specific details of historical change going on within any particular society; to be concerned with evolution, however, is to extend one's analysis to the regular and systematic changes characteristic of all or most societies. While there is some justification for White's distinction, it is rather artificial and overdrawn. All changes in sociocultural systems may be regarded as evolutionary to the extent that they involve qualitative and directional transformations of the whole or one or more of the parts. This is true, whether such changes occur in only one society or whether there are similar changes occurring within hundreds of societies (M. Harris, 1968). However, true to at least the spirit of White's claim, we shall seek an understanding of those major evolutionary transformations that have characterized a large number of the world's societies.

Special care must be taken to avoid identifying sociocultural evolution with progress. This was the great error of the major nineteenth-century evolutionists. These thinkers tended to read into evolution a general record of improvement in human rationality, morality, and happiness, and for this they were justifiably criticized by later scholars. The term *progress* is a moral notion and should not be applied to data gathered in the scientific attempt to understand basic patterns of evolutionary change. Since all societies represent, to one extent or another, adaptive solutions to fundamental human needs, it is an error of the utmost seriousness to assume that some so-cieties are superior to others simply because they occur later in history or because they are more evolutionarily complex.

Parallel, Convergent, and Divergent Evolution

Sociocultural evolution is not a singular, unitary process occurring in the same way in all societies. Like biological evolution, sociocultural evolution has a "dual" character (Sahlins, 1960). On the one hand, it is a process involving the overall transformation of human societies. It exhibits a general character and directional pattern in the case of all societies that undergo it. This process is usually known as *general evolution* (Sahlins, 1960). On the other hand, sociocultural evolution reveals an adaptive diversification along many different lines in many societies. The specific details of evolutionary change commonly differ from one society to another. This pattern of change is typically called *specific evolution* (Sahlins, 1960).

This distinction can be further clarified by introducing three additional concepts: parallel, convergent, and divergent evolution (M. Harris, 1968). **Parallel evolution** occurs when two or more societies evolve in basically similar ways and at similar rates. Beginning about 10,000 years ago, for example, human communities in various regions of the world independently began to domesticate plants and animals and subsist by agriculture rather than by hunting and gathering. The adoption of agriculture in these communities led to strikingly similar changes in their overall sociocultural patterns. **Convergent evolution** results when societies that have originally been dissimilar evolve in ways that make them increasingly alike. The United States and Japan, for example, have evolved along convergent lines in the past hundred years or so. **Divergent evolution** occurs when originally similar societies evolve along lines of increasing dissimilarity. An excellent example of this phenomenon results from the comparison of Japan and Indonesia (Geertz, 1963). These societies were very similar in the early seventeenth century, but today they are strikingly different: Japan is a modern industrial nation with a high standard of living, while Indonesia is a poor, underdeveloped country. (Some of the reasons for the divergence between Japan and Indonesia will be suggested in Chapter 9.)

These forms of evolution constitute the fundamental ways in which evolutionary transformations have occurred throughout human history, and social-scientific efforts are devoted to studying all of them. However, considerable evidence suggests that parallel and convergent evolution have been much more prominent features of human history than divergent evolution (M. Harris, 1968). This book therefore gives primary emphasis to parallelism and convergence, while at the same time not neglecting divergent outcomes.

Continuity, Devolution, and Extinction

Sociocultural evolution is a pervasive feature of human social life, and there is no such thing as a society that is completely static or unchanging. Nevertheless, there are numerous examples of societies that have presumably undergone no significant changes for thousands of years. This phenomenon is called **sociocultural continuity.** Many hunting and gathering societies, for instance, have survived into the present, and the majority of them have probably experienced no major change for hundreds or thousands of years.

Just as it is imperative to ask why some societies undergo major transformations, it is necessary to ask why others do not. Sociocultural evolution is an adaptive result of changing conditions. Societies evolve in order to meet new demands and needs. However, societies do not always confront new demands and needs. In such situations, existing sociocultural patterns are adequate for solving the basic problems of human existence, and no evolutionary changes need be undergone. Continuity, then, like evolution, is an adaptive process. Which of these will occur depends upon whether or not the basic underlying conditions necessary to human existence and well-being are changing or remaining the same.

Most human societies are characterized either by relative stability or by evolutionary transformation. In some instances, however, a society may undergo a **devolutionary** change: it may shift back to a form with characteristics of an earlier evolutionary stage. This might mean a decrease in societal complexity, or perhaps a loss of social cohesion. A striking illustration of such an occurrence comes from Colin Turnbull's (1972) description of the Ik of Uganda. The Ik were a hunting and gathering people who experienced economic disaster when their traditional hunting grounds were turned into a game preserve by the Ugandan government. This event precipitated the virtual collapse of the Ik sociocultural system. With the loss of their traditional means of subsistence, and with the shift to agriculture made difficult or impossible, the Ik experienced a substantial decline in population, lost their basis of political cohesion, and even experienced a general erosion of relationships among family members. What resulted was a way of life in which the social ties between all persons were largely broken.

Another example of a devolutionary transformation is the collapse of the Roman Empire in the fifth century A.D. Rome had created a huge empire, which extended all the way from Egypt in the south to the British Isles in the north. The diverse regions of the empire were linked by a marvelous system of roads, and the empire was centralized economically, politically, and militarily. When the empire finally collapsed after a long and slow period of decline, Europe devolved into a vast region filled with largely economically self-sufficient villages and principalities.

Some societies, of course, come to be extinguished altogether. This process is known as **sociocultural extinction.** Such a fate has happened to numerous hunting and gathering societies in recent times, as well as to various societies of greater evolutionary complexity. A sociocultural system can become extinct either through the complete physical extermination of its members, or through its absorption into another society by means of political conquest. Both of these processes have occurred frequently in human history, especially since the rise of modern capitalism in the sixteenth century. The North American continent, for example, was once filled with hundreds of Indian tribes. With the emergence and expansion of the new American civilization, most of the members of these tribes were killed in bloody wars. Those who remained were eventually herded onto reservations, their aboriginal way of life largely lost.

Sociocultural Evolution as an Adaptive Process

This book emphasizes the adaptive character of sociocultural evolution and therefore makes extensive use of the concept of **sociocultural adaptation.** Unfortunately, the concept of adaptation is a highly contentious one in modern sociology. Some sociologists reject the concept altogether, claiming that it is an inherently functionalist one that has markedly conservative connotations (Zeitlin, 1973; Giddens, 1981). These sociologists recommend that it therefore be discarded. However, such radical surgery is

by no means called for. The concept is a useful—indeed, necessary—one that we would be extremely foolish to abandon. What is called for is not abandonment of the concept, but judicious and careful use of it.

What is meant by calling sociocultural evolution an adaptive process is that *social patterns are created by humans as rational responses to the problems of existence that they confront, and that when the nature of these problems changes, as invariably happens, the responses must and will change as well.* We must now clarify and qualify the meaning of this statement.

First, to say that a sociocultural pattern is adaptive is not to imply that it is therefore "good" or "morally desirable." A claim about adaptation is a scientific assessment of how various types of sociocultural patterns originate, persist, and change. A claim about "goodness," by contrast, is completely different. It is a judgment about whether we like or approve of the things that people do. Thus, it is perfectly possible to identify a sociocultural pattern as adaptive and feel a moral repugnance for that pattern. For example, the Yanomama Indians of South America regularly slaughter one another in deadly wars and kill a given percentage of their female infants, yet such practices can be seen as highly adaptive responses to overpopulation and a scarcity of resources (M. Harris, 1974, 1977). To understand this fact is to make a scientific statement, not a judgment of moral desirability.

We also need to be clear about the kind of unit to which the concept of adaptation applies—about just what it is that does the adapting. Some sociologists have assumed that it is an entire sociocultural system. This is especially true of the functionalists and functionalist evolutionists (cf. Parsons, 1966, 1971). But such a notion is misplaced. As argued in Chapter 1, sociocultural systems are not comparable to organisms or individual persons; they do not have needs or

desires, and thus they cannot adapt to anything. Since only individual persons have
needs and desires, only they can be units of
adaptation. Of course, we sometimes speak
about whether or not a sociocultural pattern
is adaptive for a group or even a whole society, but when we do this it is clear that we
can only be referring to an aggregate of individuals, and that it is from the point of view
of each separate individual that the adaptation or adaptedness is judged.

This leads us to recognize another crucial point strongly emphasized by the conflict theorists: that an adaptive sociocultural pattern may not be equally beneficial
for all individuals or groups within a society. It is frequently the case that a pattern
that benefits some individuals or groups is
maladaptive for others. Indeed, the more
evolutionarily complex a society the more
this is likely to be the case. Early industrial
capitalism, for example, was adaptive for
wealthy factory owners, but it was highly
maladaptive for the thousands of factory
workers who died from exhaustion, malnutrition, and disease (Engels, 1973; orig.
1845). And modern world capitalism is
much more adaptive for the members of
some societies than the members of others.

It is extremely important to recognize
that it is entirely inappropriate to claim that
adaptation is somehow a quality that increases throughout sociocultural evolution.
Many evolutionists have equated sociocultural evolution with improved adaptation,
claiming that evolutionarily later societies
have increased their "adaptive capacity."
This idea has been promoted most strongly
by Talcott Parsons and other functionalist
evolutionists, but it has also been endorsed
by some evolutionary materialists (cf.
Childe, 1936; L. White, 1959). However, this
book strongly rejects such a view, which
tends toward ethnocentrism and which is
difficult to support by scientifically objective criteria (Granovetter, 1979). New socio-

cultural forms emerge as adaptations, but
these altered adaptations are simply *new*
rather than *better* ones.*

Finally, we must acknowledge that not
all sociocultural patterns are adaptations,
and thus the concept of adaptation does not
have universal applicability. But even
though we cannot use the concept everywhere and at all times, we are still far better
off with it than without it. Indeed, by having a notion of adaptation as a guiding element we will be in a position to identify
which sociocultural traits are not adaptations and why they are not.

Biological Versus Sociocultural Evolution

Social scientists have long been interested
in the relationship between biological and
sociocultural evolution. These processes
possess both important parallels and significant differences, and it may be instructive
to outline them.

Two basic similarities between these
types of evolution can be identified. In the
first place, both biological and sociocultural
evolution are adaptive processes. New biological forms, like new sociocultural patterns, arise largely as adaptations to changing circumstances. Second, both forms of
evolution have the "dual" character identified by Marshall Sahlins: both exhibit overall directional tendencies as well as a variety of radiations along many specific lines.

We could go further and say that the
processes of parallel, convergent, and divergent evolution apply to both biological and
sociocultural evolution. This would be
technically true, but it would also be misleading, because most biological evolution

---

*Actually, in a number of important respects the
level of adaptation clearly *decreases* throughout long-
term sociocultural evolution. Chapter 18 summarizes
the most important regressive dimensions of sociocultural evolution.

is in fact divergent evolution (the preferred biological term is *cladogenesis*). Most biological evolution involves the adaptive radiation of species at the same phylogenetic level, and evolutionary shifts to new phylogenetic levels are a relatively rare occurrence (Stebbins, 1969, 1974). By contrast, most sociocultural evolution is of the parallel and convergent types. This means that biological evolutionists spend most of their time studying the production of unique life forms, whereas social evolutionists concentrate their energies on the emergence of similar sociocultural patterns in various regions of the world (Sanderson, 1990).

A second difference concerns the extent to which sociocultural evolution can be said to be based on a process of natural selection. Since much of sociocultural evolution involves the selection of adaptive traits, it must also involve a kind of natural selection process (cf. Carneiro, 1985). However, this is true only in the most general way. Strictly speaking, the way in which natural selection works in the biological world is quite different from the way it works in social life. The difference involves the source of the variations on which selection operates. We have seen that in biological evolution the genetic variations that are selected for or against arise entirely at random. Although some social evolutionists claim that sociocultural variations arise in the same way (Campbell, 1965; Langton, 1979; Runciman, 1989), this is very unlikely. There is overwhelming evidence that most sociocultural innovations are deliberately introduced and are anything but random (Cavalli-Sforza and Feldman, 1981; Hallpike, 1986).

Two other differences between evolution in the two realms are also important. One of these has to do with the pace of change. Sociocultural evolution is extraordinarily faster, even taking into account the first 99 percent of human history (some four million years), during which things changed very slowly. In fact, sociocultural evolution has itself evolved, so that the pace of change is now exceptionally rapid. (The extraordinary rapidity of sociocultural evolution is obviously linked to the fact that sociocultural variations are deliberate and purposive rather than random.) Finally, there is a sociocultural evolutionary process known as **diffusion** that has no parallel in the biological world. Diffusion involves the spread of sociocultural traits from one sociocultural system to another. This may occur through deliberate borrowing or through the imposition of a set of traits by a more powerful society on a weaker one. Often diffusion makes up for invention in the sense that a society can take from another what it would otherwise be interested in developing on its own (Ingold, 1986). There is nothing like this process in the world of nature. Organisms cannot borrow genes from each other in order to cope with changing environmental conditions.

THE MATERIALIST APPROACH TO SOCIOCULTURAL STRUCTURE AND EVOLUTION

The most important question about sociocultural systems concerns the causes of their specific features and the changes these undergo. As mentioned in Chapter 1, this book takes a **materialist** approach to the nature of causation. The contemporary materialist approach to the study of social life finds its roots in the "materialist conception of history" of Marx and Engels. However, the modern version of the materialist strategy is a substantial elaboration of their ideas. Like Marx and Engels, contemporary materialists see such material factors as technology and economy as being among the leading causes of social life. But they also expand the notion of material factors to include ecological and demographic variables, and they see these as additional leading causes of sociocultural phenomena. Contemporary materialism is thus a more complex and sophisticated version of the original Marxian form. The most insistent contemporary spokesman for a materialist theoretical strategy is Marvin Harris (1974, 1977, 1979), whose ideas provide the foundation for much of the materialist theoretical argument developed here.

The materialist approach is a general theoretical strategy designed to explain the basic features of sociocultural systems and the parallel, convergent, and divergent evolutionary changes these features undergo. It is also designed to explain sociocultural continuity, devolution, and extinction. In fact, the totality of sociocultural similarities and differences represents its arena of application. Since the materialist approach is a theoretical strategy, there are many specific materialist *theories* that are included within it. Many of these theories will be discussed in the following chapters.

General Nature of the Materialist Approach*

The materialist theoretical approach used in this book specifies that a society's infrastructure is the primary cause of its structure, and the structure, in turn, is the primary cause of its superstructure. That is, infrastructural conditions are the primary causes of a society's basic patterns of interpersonal behavior, and these behavioral patterns in turn call forth specific patterns of thought that justify and interpret behavioral realities. Ideas therefore find their origin in the concrete patterns of behavior systematically engaged in by the members of a soci-

ety, and these patterns of behavior originate in conjunction with the infrastructural conditions whereby people solve the basic problems of human existence.

The materialist approach is, of course, a means of explaining both the structure and evolution of sociocultural systems. As an approach to evolution, it holds that change ordinarily begins in one or more infrastructural factors. Changes within the infrastructure subsequently lead to reverberating changes in both the structure and the superstructure. Hence, changes in modes of thinking ordinarily depend upon prior changes in patterns of behavior, and these latter changes are themselves largely products of prior infrastructural changes.

The materialist strategy holds that infrastructural factors are the primary, but not the only, causes of structural and superstructural phenomena. Indeed, the structure and the superstructure have a partial independence from the infrastructure, and they may occasionally act as causal forces in their own right. However, the impact of structure and superstructure on the infrastructure is much less than is the converse.

One great advantage of the materialist approach is that it provides a logical set of research priorities for the study of sociocultural life. As Marvin Harris (1979) notes, it directs any investigator to begin the search for the causes of sociocultural phenomena with an examination of infrastructural conditions. It is likely that these conditions provide the clue to explaining the phenomenon in question. If a diligent search fails to reveal the causal impact of infrastructural factors, an investigator is warranted to turn to the examination of structural conditions as possible causes of the phenomenon. Failure to find structural causes in turn licenses the investigator to explore the possibility of superstructural causation. Thus, superstructural causation may be searched for only after the investigator has failed to demonstrate the operation of infrastructural and

---

*A much more detailed presentation of the evolutionary materialist approach can be found in Sanderson (1994c, 1995a).

structural causes. This approach is immensely preferable to those frequently employed by other investigators: reversing the procedure by working from superstructure to structure to infrastructure, or assuming that all three components have a mutual causal influence upon each other.

This brief discussion of the materialist approach is necessarily a somewhat oversimplified account of the nature of causation in sociocultural systems. It does not specify, for instance, which particular infrastructural factor or factors may be most causally important in any given situation. However, it is impossible to make a statement to this effect in the abstract. Depending upon the phenomenon under investigation, any infrastructural factor (or any combination of factors) may be of prime causal importance. In some cases technological factors may be of greatest significance, while in other cases ecological, demographic, or economic factors may assume causal priority. Specification of the precise nature of infrastructural causation can only be done through the investigation of concrete sociocultural phenomena.

Related to the above problem is the fact that causal relationships exist *within*, and not simply among, the sociocultural components themselves. Ecological and demographic factors, for example, are among the primary determinants of the level of technology, and the latter in turn is an important cause of the nature of the economic system (see Chapter 4). Furthermore, the presence of social stratification, itself an element of the social structure, is an important cause of other elements of the structure. Although these problems are noted here, there will be no attempt to build into our abstract materialist formulation all of the causal relationships that exist within and among the basic sociocultural components. To do this would make it unwieldy and hence reduce its usefulness as a general analytic tool.

The Logical Priority of Infrastructure

There are essentially two ways in which a materialist approach to social life can be shown to be preferable to any of the theoretical alternatives that currently exist in the social sciences. One way is to submit the materialist strategy to detailed and rigorous empirical testing against a wide range of sociocultural differences and similarities. If a materialist strategy can successfully explain a large number of these differences and similarities, then the theoretical utility of the approach is at once confirmed. This book takes the position that such rigorous empirical testing has been carried out on a wide enough scale, and with sufficiently satisfactory results, that the usefulness of the approach can no longer be seriously doubted. A materialist approach is unable to explain all relevant sociocultural phenomena, but an approach that could do so does not exist. In any event, the materialist approach has had far greater explanatory success than any of its competitors, and that alone is sufficient justification for its employment as a general theoretical strategy.

The other way of justifying the choice of a materialist strategy rests on logical, rather than empirical, grounds. It is claimed that infrastructural factors have a logical causal priority over structural and superstructural factors. Materialists hold that infrastructural variables take priority because they constitute the fundamental means whereby human beings solve the most basic problems of human existence. Before humans can formulate marriage rules, organize political systems, and construct abstract religious concepts, they must organize the means whereby they will survive. Marx and Engels clearly understood this elementary fact. As Engels put it in his famous eulogy at Marx's graveside (Engels, 1963:188–189; orig. 1883):

> Just as Darwin discovered the law of evolution in organic nature, so Marx discovered

the law of evolution in human history; he discovered the simple fact, hitherto concealed by an overgrowth of ideology, that mankind must first of all eat and drink, have shelter and clothing, before it can pursue politics, science, religion, art, etc., and that therefore the production of the immediate material means of subsistence and consequently the degree of economic development attained by a given people or during a given epoch, form the foundation upon which the state institutions, the legal conceptions, the art and even the religious ideas of the people concerned have been evolved, and in the light of which these things must therefore be explained, instead of *vice versa* as had hitherto been the case.

Marvin Harris has argued for the logical priority of infrastructure along similar lines (1979:57):

> Infrastructure . . . is the principal interface between culture and nature, the boundary across which the ecological, chemical, and physical restraints to which human action is subject interact with the principal sociocultural practices aimed at overcoming or modifying those restraints. The order of cultural materialist priorities from infrastructure to the remaining behavioral components and finally to the mental superstructure reflects the increasing remoteness of these components from the culture/nature interface. . . . Priority for theory building logically settles upon those sectors under the greatest direct restraints from the givens of nature. To endow the mental superstructure with strategic priority, as the cultural idealists advocate, is a bad bet. Nature is indifferent to whether God is a loving father or a bloodthirsty cannibal. But nature is not indifferent to whether the fallow period in a swidden field is one year or ten. We know that powerful restraints exist on the infrastructural level; hence it is a good bet that these restraints are passed on to the structural and superstructural components.

THE MAJOR PRINCIPLES OF THE EVOLUTIONARY MATERIALIST THEORETICAL STRATEGY

The evolutionary materialist approach to sociocultural life has certain major principles that serve as the guiding themes throughout the remainder of this book.

The Principle of Sociocultural Adaptation

The **Principle of Sociocultural Adaptation** holds that sociocultural phenomena are adaptive consequences of the basic needs and desires of human beings. Social patterns are generally created by humans as rational responses to the fundamental problems that they must solve. When the nature of these problems changes, the responses to them change as well. All of the cautions we discussed earlier about use of the concept of adaptation apply fully to the application of this principle.

The Conflict Principle

The **Conflict Principle** is derived from a conflict theoretical strategy, and it typically plays an important role in the thinking of most materialists. It holds that conflict or struggle among individuals and groups over scarce resources is a pervasive occurrence in social life, and that such conflict is an important determinant of basic sociocultural patterns. Conflict most frequently occurs over the material resources that support human existence. Such conflict often leads to social stratification: to the formation of sociocultural patterns in which some groups gain economic and political dominance over others. Emerging patterns of social stratification play a significant role in shaping other aspects of sociocultural life.

The Conflict Principle asserts that people generally act so as to maximize their own interests. Under many conditions, the attempt to maximize self-interest results in overt conflict and structured patterns of economic and political dominance and subordination. These patterns are frequently productive of further conflict and struggle. However, under some circumstances (to be specified in later chapters), the attempt to maximize self-interest takes the form of cooperation and harmony rather than overt conflict. Individuals frequently cooperate with one another because they recognize that such cooperation is essential to their own survival and well-being. This phenomenon has been labeled **antagonistic cooperation** or **enlightened self-interest** (Lenski, 1966).

The Principle of Infrastructural Determinism

The **Principle of Infrastructural Determinism,** the most important of all the principles of the materialist evolutionary strategy, has already been discussed. It holds that infrastructural factors are the primary causes of structural and superstructural arrangements. It is designed to explain the entire range of sociocultural similarities and differences that result from sociocultural continuity, evolution, and devolution.

The Principle of Sociocultural Integration

The **Principle of Sociocultural Integration** refers to the tendency of the major components of sociocultural systems to fit together into a more or less consistent whole. Any particular kind of infrastructure is compatible with only a limited range of structures and superstructures. While it is not possible to make precise predictions about the nature of structure and superstructure from a knowledge of infrastructure, it is certainly possible to indicate the

kinds of structures or superstructures that would rarely or never be found with a particular infrastructure. For example, centralized governments are never found among hunting and gathering societies, but all modern industrialized societies have them. Likewise, societies dependent upon simple forms of agriculture for their food supply commonly have large-scale kinship groups known as clans, but such kin groups are never found in modern industrial societies.

SUMMARY

1. A useful way of compartmentalizing sociocultural systems is the tripartite distinction between infrastructure, structure, and superstructure. The infrastructure consists of the raw materials and organizational forms necessary for the production and reproduction of human social life; the structure, of the basic patterns of regularized social behavior characteristic of the members of a society; the superstructure, of the symbols, thoughts, ideas, and ideals shared by individuals as members of society.

2. Sociocultural evolution is a process of directional social change involving the transformation of old social forms into new ones. One important dimension of the directionality of social evolution is that of increasing societal complexity. However, this is only one of several important dimensions.

3. Many social scientists believe that sociocultural evolution is a teleological process of "unrolling," one in which societies pass through stages of development toward some end state or goal. It is also often assumed that this alleged developmental process involves progress or improvement in the human condition. But these connotations of the concept of sociocultural evolution are flatly rejected in the present book.

4. It is necessary to recognize three different types of evolutionary change: parallel, convergent, and divergent evolution. Parallel

evolution involves a similar type, rate, and direction of change in several societies; convergent evolution occurs when dissimilar societies become increasingly alike; and divergent evolution occurs when societies change in increasingly dissimilar ways. The first two appear to have been the most prominent types in human history.

5. Not all societies undergo evolutionary modifications. Some remain more or less the same, even for thousands of years, a process known as sociocultural continuity. Many societies have been obliterated altogether due to the encroachment of more powerful societies; this has been a frequent result of the expansion of Western capitalism. Occasionally societies change in a direction of increasing simplicity of organization; this process is known as social devolution.

6. Sociocultural evolution is an adaptive process, which means that it occurs as a result of the efforts made by individuals to satisfy their needs and wants. The basic unit of sociocultural adaptation is the individual person, not a sociocultural system. Sociocultural systems do not have needs, desires, or purposes; only individuals do. Hence, only individuals can adapt.

7. Use of the concept of adaptation often leads to the misunderstanding that adaptation is something that improves with sociocultural evolution. Some evolutionists maintain that this is so, but the present book vigorously rejects such a notion. New sociocultural adaptations are more accurately described as being simply different, rather than better, social forms.

8. Sociocultural and biological evolution are processes that share both similarities and differences. The main similarities concern their adaptive and their "dual" characters. The basic differences between them involve the pace of evolution; the origin of variations; the fact that most biological evolution is divergent, whereas most sociocultural evolution is parallel and convergent; and the fact that the sociocultural process of diffusion has no parallel in biological evolution.

9. The basic theoretical model of sociocultural structure and evolution used throughout this book is a materialist model. It holds that the material infrastructure constitutes the foundation on which the other components of society are built. Changes tend to occur in it first, and these changes produce reverberating changes in the other components. Those who adhere to the materialist model use it as a starting point for their analyses and are persistent in their search for material causes of social life. Structural and superstructural factors are entertained as possible causal variables only after a conscientious search for material causes has proven fruitless.

10. A materialist model may be justified on empirical or logical grounds. This book presents a large body of empirical evidence to support the model. But the model may also be justified logically by assuming that material conditions have a priority in the organization of social life because they involve the most fundamental areas of human concern.

11. The basic theoretical principles used in this book are the Principle of Sociocultural Adaptation, which holds that people create social patterns as responses to their needs and desires; the Conflict Principle, which suggests that people generally behave in accordance with their self-interests, and that the social conflict, domination, and subordination that result from this play a major role in shaping social patterns; the Principle of Infrastructural Determinism, which emphasizes the causal priority of the material conditions of social life; and the Principle of Sociocultural Integration, which suggests a consistency among the parts of sociocultural life.

SPECIAL TOPIC: SACRED COWS AND ABOMINABLE PIGS

One of the best-known applications of the evolutionary materialist perspective is Marvin Harris's examination of the origins of religiously based food taboos. Harris has devoted particular attention to explaining why in India the Hindu religion considers the cow sacred and regards beef as forbidden flesh. He has also made a rather thorough study of the ancient Israelites' taboo on the consumption of pork because they viewed the pig as a dirty animal. He believes that these food taboos can best be understood as adaptive responses to the specific constellation of material conditions faced by the populations that adopted them.

It is widely known that a central tenet of Hindu religious ideology is the sanctification of the cow. The cow is regarded as a holy animal, the slaughter and consumption of which is unthinkable. To most Westerners this taboo is a clear case of the irrational mismanagement of resources and is responsible for the perpetuation of widespread poverty and misery on the Indian subcontinent. The whole complex of cow worship is thought to be a classic example of the way in which mystical religious practices lead to undesirable and unnecessary economic results. But Harris (1974, 1977) thinks this is not the case, and in fact believes that the Hindu cow-love complex is a rational—indeed, necessary—response to the ecological and economic circumstances in which the great majority of Indian peasant farmers find themselves.

Harris claims that the cow performs vital functions in the context of the Indian ecology and economy, functions that it can perform only if kept alive. Cow dung is particularly valuable to the Indian farmer. It serves as a fertilizer for the fields, as a source of fuel for cooking, and, when mixed with water to form a paste, as an acceptable flooring material for houses. But by far the most useful role played by the cow is that of traction animal for the plowing of fields. Since Indian farmers cannot buy tractors, the cow is the only means by which they can plow. As Harris has argued emphatically, Indian farmers who yielded to temptation in times of particular stress to slaughter their cattle for food would in fact be bringing disaster upon themselves, for they would never be able to plow again. Hence, the cow is far more useful alive than dead to the average Indian farmer. However, since the temptation to slaughter one's cattle during periods of drought or famine was an ever-recurrent problem to most Indian farmers, it was necessary to find a means of removing this temptation. This means, Harris claims, was found in the establishment of a religious taboo deifying the cow and making it an unholy and unthinkable act to kill and consume it.

Just how the cow came to be sanctified in India can be better understood through a sense of historical perspective. As Harris notes, throughout much of Indian history cattle were regularly eaten and there was nothing considered particularly holy about them. He believes that it may not have been until sometime after A.D. 700 that the cow-love complex developed into its now familiar form. Regardless of exactly when the cow came to be worshiped in India, we do know that Brahman priests were "for centuries the sacrificers and consumers of animal flesh" (Harris, 1977:145). Under what kinds of conditions would these priests have been transformed from ritual sacrificers of cattle into their ritual protectors? Harris suggests that the answer to this question involves increasing population density and declining standards of living. As populations became denser, land became increasingly scarce and farms got smaller. It became more and more costly for farmers to raise animals for food, and they gradually had to be eliminated. All, that is, but one. The cow could not be eliminated because of its necessity in pulling the plow.

It is also commonly known that modern Judaism bans the eating of pork. Indeed, since the ancient Israelites, Judaism has officially regarded the pig as an abominable animal not suitable for human consumption. But the Jews have hardly been typical in their refusal to eat the flesh of the pig. Pork has been enjoyed for centuries throughout such regions as China and Europe, and the members of many tribal societies not only eat pork but think so highly of pigs that they practically treat them as members of the family (Harris, 1974). Since the members of so many other religions have shown no aversion whatsoever to the consumption of pork, why have the Jews treated it as such an abomination?

Perhaps the most common answer to this question is that the pig is an unclean animal: it wallows in its own excrement and is a carrier of disease. Yet as Harris (1974, 1977) has shown, this explanation is not satisfactory. Pigs are not particularly dirty animals when they live in habitats for which they are well suited. Since pigs cannot sweat, they are better adapted to environments where the temperature does not get too hot. But in dry, hot environments (such as that of the Middle East), pigs have considerable trouble keeping cool, and therefore they wallow in their excrement in order to cool their bodies. Concerning the fact that pigs transmit certain diseases, Harris admits that this is true, but he also notes that other animals that have been widely consumed (such as the cow) are also carriers of disease.

Harris believes that the ancient Israelites forbade pork for reasons that have specifically to do with the ecology of the Middle East. He holds that the consumption of the pig came to be tabooed because the raising of pigs constituted a threat to the entire subsistence system of the ancient Jews. After about 1200 B.C., when the Israelites arrived in Palestine, they settled on previously uncultivated land and began cutting down woodlands and building irrigated terraces. Land suitable for pig raising became increasingly scarce, and pigs increasingly had to be fed grains as dietary supplements, making them directly competitive with humans. Artificial shade and moisture had to be provided, making them even more costly. If pigs were ecologically costly, yet continued to be a source of temptation, the solution, Harris argues, would be to forbid the raising and consumption of pigs entirely; and the best way to make such a prohibition stick would be to establish it as a matter of divine interdiction: as a religious taboo. To remove this costly but tempting threat, the pig came to be redefined as an abomination.

Although Harris's theory has been subject to criticism, its plausibility is considerably enhanced by the fact that the ancient Jews shared the pig taboo with many of their neighbors. The taboo on pork was (and still is) found throughout the driest areas of North Africa, the Middle East, and Central Asia. Even the Egyptians, mortal enemies of the Israelites, tabooed the eating of pork. And with the rise of Islam in the seventh century A.D., the pork taboo became part of yet another major religious tradition. It thus appears to be specifically in those hot, dry regions of the world—regions to which the pig was poorly adapted and where special provisions had to be made for raising it—where the flesh of pigs came to be forbidden. By contrast, wetter, cooler areas of the world better suited to pig raising knew no pig taboo, and pigs were frequently dined upon with gusto in these areas.

Although the pig and the cow have both been the subject of strict religious taboos in which the consumption of their flesh was expressly forbidden, the pig and cow taboos were strikingly different; in India the cow was made holy, whereas the ancient Jews made the pig an abomination. Why this should be so should now be clear, at least if Harris's theories are valid interpretations. The cow was vitally necessary for Indian agriculture, and therefore it came to be sanctified. But the pig among the ancient Jews was of no use as a farm animal and only constituted a threat; hence it came to be defined as an unclean and undesirable creature.

FOR FURTHER READING

Carneiro, Robert L. "The four faces of evolution." In J. J. Honigmann (ed.), *Handbook of Social and Cultural Anthropology.* Chicago: Rand McNally, 1973. A useful discussion of the nature of sociocultural evolution and the various ways in which it has been conceptualized by social scientists.

Harris, Marvin. *Cannibals and Kings: The Origins of Cultures.* New York: Random House, 1977. An absorbing look at the role played by infrastructural factors in shaping the major outlines of sociocultural evolution over the past 10,000 years. A major contribution to evolutionary materialist theory written in an extremely accessible style.

Harris, Marvin. *Cultural Materialism: The Struggle for a Science of Culture.* New York: Random House, 1979. A passionate and highly persuasive argument for a materialist theoretical approach to the study of sociocultural life by one of the leading social scientists of our time.

Harris, Marvin. *Good to Eat: Riddles of Food and Culture.* New York: Simon & Schuster, 1985. A provocative discussion of food taboos and dietary preferences throughout the world from a materialist perspective. Contains highly informative and captivating discussions of food habits, with special attention to cattle, pigs, horses, insects, dogs, milk, and people. (The paperback version has been retitled *Sacred Cows and Abominable Pigs.*)

Mann, Michael. *The Sources of Social Power. Volume 1: A History of Power from the Beginning to A.D. 1760.* Cambridge: Cambridge University Press, 1986. An extraordinarily comprehensive treatment of the major milestones of world prehistory and history. Written from an eclectic theoretical perspective that leans strongly toward a type of Weberianism. A broad evolutionism stressed in the early chapters.

Marx, Karl, and Friedrich Engels. *The German Ideology.* Edited by C. J. Arthur. New York: International Publishers, 1970. (Originally written 1846.) The original statement of the "materialist conception of history" by its founders. Provides the classical intellectual foundations for the contemporary materialist approach.

Runciman, W. G. *A Treatise on Social Theory. Volume 2: Substantive Social Theory.* Cambridge: Cambridge University Press, 1989. A comprehensive attempt to develop a natural selectionist theory of social evolution. Although the author mistakenly claims that sociocultural variations are random in their origins, this book contains many excellent insights about the process of social evolution.

Sanderson, Stephen K. *Social Transformations: A General Theory of Historical Development.* Oxford: Blackwell, 1995. A detailed formal statement of evolutionary materialism and its application to understanding the three most important evolutionary transformations of the last 10,000 years of world history and prehistory.

Tainter, Joseph A. *The Collapse of Complex Societies.* New York: Cambridge University Press, 1988. A fascinating look at the process of social devolution in complex agrarian civilizations of the past. Sets forth a general theory of societal collapse based on the assumption that the increasing development of societal complexity is frequently counterproductive because it is unsustainable.

Wenke, Robert J. *Patterns in Prehistory: Mankind's First Three Million Years.* Third edition. New York: Oxford University Press, 1990. An excellent survey of world prehistory.

Chapter
4

Preindustrial Societies

In order to survive, all societies must establish technological and economic systems. Technology and economy are very closely related in every society, yet they are by no means the same thing. A society's technology consists of the tools, techniques, and knowledge that its members have created in order to meet their needs and wants. A society's economy, on the other hand, consists of the socially organized way in which goods and services are produced and distributed. This chapter begins the discussion of the evolution of technology, conceived here as *subsistence technology,* or the technology directly related to the getting of a living. Examination is limited to five types of subsistence technology arranged in a general evolutionary order: hunting and gathering, simple horticulture, intensive horticulture, agrarianism or intensive agriculture, and pastoralism.* Of concern are both the nature of these subsistence technologies and the reasons one has replaced another in the evolutionary history of the human species. Industrialism as a mode of subsistence technology is not discussed until Chapter 8.

---

*Hunting and gathering, horticultural, and sometimes pastoral societies are often known collectively as **primitive societies.** Although some social scientists object to the use of this term, feeling that it is derogatory, there is no reason not to use it from time to time for convenience. The term refers only to the level of technological development, and its usage does not imply any judgment about cultural inferiority.

HUNTER-GATHERER SOCIETIES

For about 99 percent of their history, humans subsisted entirely by hunting wild animals and gathering wild plant foods. The total monopoly of the hunting and gathering way of life was not broken until some 10,000 years ago, when some societies began to subsist by the practice of agriculture. During the past 10,000 years, **hunter-gatherer societies** have grown fewer and fewer in number, and only a handful remain today. Most of these are found in relatively isolated geographical locations, such as the arid and semiarid regions of Australia, the central rain forest and southwestern desert regions of Africa, and the Arctic. It is unlikely that even these will survive more than a few decades longer, and by the early part of the twenty-first century the hunting and gathering way of life is destined to be only a historical relic known to ethnography and archaeology.

Most of what is currently known about hunter-gatherers is based on fieldwork conducted among surviving hunting and gathering groups. It cannot be known with any certainty how similar these groups may be to hunting and gathering societies of prehistoric times. No doubt there are a number of differences, but it is also likely that there are many striking similarities. In any event, the description of the hunting and gathering way of life that follows is based primarily on the results of contemporary ethnographic research.

Hunters and gatherers live in small groups known as *local bands.* These are groups of about 25 to 50 men, women, and children who cooperate with each other in the quest for subsistence. Each local band is a more or less politically autonomous and economically self-sufficient unit. However, many local bands are usually connected by ties of intermarriage into a much larger cultural unit, sometimes known as a **tribe.** A tribe is a network of bands all of whose members share the same cultural patterns and speak the same language. Furthermore, the composition of each local band is constantly shifting. Persons frequently move from one band to another. Such movement may arise from marriage or from a need to create a more even balance between population size and the food supply.

How do hunter-gatherers divide their time between hunting and gathering? Some years ago Richard Lee (1968) estimated that contemporary hunting and gathering societies derive approximately two-thirds of their diet from gathered foods of all sorts, holding that this figure closely corresponds to the subsistence activities of prehistoric hunter-gatherers. This idea has come to be widely accepted by social scientists, even to the extent that the suggestion has been made that such societies might be more appropriately named "gatherer-hunter" societies.

However, a closer look suggests a rather different picture. Carol Ember (1978), using a sample of 181 contemporary hunting and gathering societies drawn from the *Ethnographic Atlas* (Murdock, 1967), a larger and more inclusive sample than the one used by Lee, has shown that hunter-gatherer societies are rather evenly divided in their emphasis on the activities of gathering, hunting, and fishing. Gathering is the most important activity in 30 percent of the societies, hunting most important in 25 percent, and fishing most important in 38 percent. However, if we treat fishing as a type of hunting, which is logical since fishing involves the procurement of wild animal protein, then 63 percent of hunter-gatherer societies emphasize hunting over gathering. Another way of looking at this problem is to calculate the percentage of societies in which a particular subsistence activity contributes half or more of the calories that people consume. Ember shows that in only 23 percent of societies does gathering contribute more than half of the calories. If

Ember's data are reliable, then, they show that in hunting and gathering societies hunting is clearly the dominant subsistence activity. This is consistent with what we have long known about hunter-gatherers: that they usually spend more time in hunting than in gathering activities, and that meat is more highly valued than plant food.

Since hunter-gatherers are food collectors rather than food producers, they must wander over wide geographical areas in search of food. They are thus generally nomadic, and the establishment of permanent settlements is highly unusual.

The technological inventory of hunting and gathering societies is quite limited. The tools and weapons used directly for subsistence typically include spears, bows and arrows, nets, and traps used in hunting, as well as digging sticks used for plant collecting. Tools are crude and simple, generally being made of stone, wood, bone, or other natural materials. There are usually few or no techniques for food storage or preservation, and food is thus generally consumed immediately or within a short span of time.

Hunting and gathering societies are the simplest in structure of all human societies. The division of labor is based almost exclusively on age and sex distinctions. Primary responsibility for subsistence ordinarily falls to persons who are in middle adulthood, with both young and old members contributing less to the subsistence needs of the group. Hunting is conducted by males, gathering by females. Although women may occasionally engage in the hunting or trapping of small game animals, they are seldom involved in big game hunting. Likewise, men sometimes share in gathering activities, but they are the principal gatherers in no hunting and gathering society. Hunter-gatherers are notoriously lacking in occupational specialization beyond subsistence tasks. There are no specialized "arrow mak-

ers" or "bow makers." Each man makes all of the tools that he needs in the subsistence quest. The women do the same.

The primary unit of subsistence among hunter-gatherers is the family, and hence economic life may be termed *familistic* (Service, 1966). Yet individual families within each local band are linked together into a total economic unit, the local band itself. While individual families produce their own subsistence, they also contribute in significant ways to the subsistence of other families within their band.

Hunter-gatherers, or at least most of them, are well known for their failure to produce an **economic surplus,** an excess of goods over and above what is needed for subsistence. Until recently it was widely believed that this was due simply to an inability to do so, an inability resulting from a marginal and precarious existence. Contemporary research contradicts this view. Social scientists now generally agree that the failure to produce a surplus is due to a lack of any real need. Since the resources of nature are always there for the taking, nature itself becomes a kind of great storehouse.

However, in recent years it has come to be increasingly recognized that some hunter-gatherers do produce an economic surplus, in some cases a considerable one. This has led to an important distinction between hunter-gatherer societies that store food and those that do not (Testart, 1982, 1988). Although nonstoring hunter-gatherers predominate, hunter-gatherers who store food are probably more common than we have realized, and in any event differ in important respects from those societies that do not. Storing hunter-gatherers are more likely to be sedentary rather than nomadic, to have bigger populations and higher population densities, and to be organized in a more complex way.

Contemporary hunter-gatherers who store can be found, but such groups seem to have been particularly prominent in the last few millennia before the development of agriculture (around 15,000 to 10,000 years ago) (M. Cohen, 1985), and probably represented hunting and gathering societies on the verge of developing an agricultural economy. It might be useful to call both prehistoric and contemporary hunter-gatherers who do not store food *simple* hunter-gatherers, while referring to those who do store food as *complex* hunter-gatherers (cf. Kelly, 1995).

The Original Affluent Society

Social scientists used to depict hunter-gatherers in largely negative terms. It was widely believed that they led a precarious and difficult life, one in which people had to work hard and long just to eke out a bare subsistence. As Marshall Sahlins noted a quarter-century ago (1972:1):

> Almost universally committed to the proposition that life was hard in the paleolithic, our textbooks compete to convey a sense of impending doom, leaving one to wonder not only how hunters managed to live, but whether, after all, this was living? The specter of starvation stalks the stalker through these pages. His technical incompetence is said to enjoin continuous work just to survive, affording him neither respite nor surplus, hence not even the "leisure" to "build culture."

Within the past three decades social scientists have radically altered this view of hunter-gatherers. In a famous argument, Sahlins (1972) dubbed them the "original affluent society." By this he did not mean that they are rich and enjoy a great abundance of material possessions, which would be an absurd claim. That is affluence in the modern sense. What Sahlins meant was that hunter-gatherers have very limited needs and wants and are able to satisfy them with a minimum of effort. To assess Sahlins's claim, we need to look carefully at the hunter-gatherer standard of living and at how hard and long hunter-gatherers typically work.

Despite the fact that virtually all contemporary hunter-gatherers exist in marginal environments, these environments often turn out to be surprisingly abundant in resources. For example, Richard Lee (1968) notes that the !Kung San (the "!" stands for a click sound in the language) of southwestern Africa are able to rely on a wide variety of resources of considerable quality. Their most important food source is mongongo nuts, and thousands of pounds of these rot on the ground each year for want of picking. Furthermore, the !Kung habitat contains 84 other species of edible plants, and !Kung gathering never exhausts all the available plant foods of an area. Similarly, James Woodburn (1968) has shown that the Hadza of Tanzania enjoy an exceptional abundance of game, and he thinks it is almost inconceivable that they would die of starvation. It would thus appear that both the !Kung and the Hadza obtain a standard of living that is perfectly adequate in meeting basic human subsistence requirements.

This impression is reinforced by Mark Cohen's (1989) survey of studies of diet and nutrition among many contemporary hunting and gathering groups. Cohen's review of numerous studies suggests to him that most hunter-gatherers generally enjoy diets that are fully adequate in nutrition. Some groups, such as the !Kung, may only barely obtain a sufficient number of calories, but their diets are otherwise abundant in animal proteins and various nutrients. It also seems to be the case that many hunter-gatherers experience seasonal bouts of hunger and food anxiety, and starvation may sometimes occur (Yesner, 1994). However, there is nothing unusual about hunter-gatherers in this respect. Settled agricultural populations also experience such difficulties, and quite likely to an even greater extent.

If hunter-gatherers generally enjoy adequate diets, how long and hard do they have to work to obtain them? A good deal of evidence suggests that many such groups work neither hard nor long. Reviewing data collected on the subsistence activities of the hunter-gatherers of Arnhem Land in northern Australia, Sahlins (1972) notes that these people do not work hard or continuously, that the subsistence quest is highly intermittent, and that plenty of spare time is available. Along the same lines, Lee (1979) has calculated that the typical !Kung adult spends an average of only 17 hours per week in direct food-getting activities. Woodburn (1968) has shown that the Hadza obtain sufficient food with relative ease, and that life for them is anything but a difficult struggle for existence. He believes that they spend less time and energy in obtaining subsistence than do their agricultural neighbors.

Some other studies of hunter-gatherer workloads are not as encouraging, at least on the surface. Since Lee's data on !Kung work patterns were collected during the dry season, John Yellen (1977) studied a group of !Kung during the wet season. He found that during this time of year they worked considerably longer. In addition, Kim Hill, Hilliard Kaplan, Kristen Hawkes, and Ana Magdelena Hurtado (1985) found that men among the Aché, a hunter-gatherer society in Paraguay, spent perhaps 40 to 50 hours a week hunting. But this figure is probably highly atypical. Robert Kelly (1995) has presented data on the workload in eleven hunter-gatherer societies in five different world regions. These data show that the average amount of time both men and women spend foraging is only about 3.8 hours a day, which comes to slightly less than 27 hours a week (assuming that foraging occurs on a daily basis). If we calculate the total subsistence effort in these same eleven societies by adding in the amount of time people spend at such tasks as manufacturing and repairing tools and processing food, then people are spending only 6.5 hours a day (45.5

hours a week). This is well below the figure for the members of modern industrial societies, who work a 40-hour week and spend many more hours in such subsistence related activities as getting to and from work, shopping for food, cooking, and maintaining the household. Most interestingly, Bruce Winterhalder (1993) has shown that most hunter-gatherers must limit their subsistence efforts because failure to do so will be counterproductive. In most hunter-gatherer environments, if people work too hard they will deplete their resources and lower their productivity in the long run. As he notes, low to intermediate levels of effort are associated with the largest sustainable populations and the highest rates of food acquisition.

It would seem, when all is said and done, that Sahlins's original affluent society thesis holds up reasonably well. This appears to be especially true when we realize that most of what we know about the standard of living and the work patterns of hunter-gatherers is based on contemporary groups. Since nearly all of these groups survive in marginal environments, prehistoric hunter-gatherers, most of whom would have existed in much more favorable environments, would have been even better off. It is crucial that we avoid romanticizing the hunting and gathering lifestyle as being some sort of primitive paradise. Clearly that would be a terrible oversimplification. Nonetheless, hunter-gatherers have fared much better than we used to imagine. As Elizabeth Cashdan (1989:26) has concluded, it is now possible to "demolish with confidence the old stereotype that hunter-gatherers had to work all the time simply to get enough food to eat." And it is also possible to demolish with confidence the old stereotype that hunter-gatherers did not eat well.

The !Kung San

Some 45,000 San are found scattered throughout the territories of Botswana, Angola, and Namibia in southern Africa. These people are divided into several different linguistic groups, one of which is !Kung, spoken by about 13,000 people. Many of these are now either under the direct control of local governments or heavily influenced in their way of life through contact with more technologically advanced peoples. The last of the hunting and gathering !Kung number some 1600 clustered around water holes in northwestern Botswana. The ethnographic account that follows is based on a population of 466 !Kung located in the Dobe area of Botswana studied by Richard Lee (1972; cf. Lee, 1979, 1984).

!Kung life is organized around eight permanent water holes and 14 independent camps. These camps are moved about five or six times a year. The population density is approximately 0.4 persons per square mile, a density typical for hunter-gatherers. The habitat is the Kalahari Desert, a region surprisingly abundant in resources. Nearly 500 species of plants and animals are known and named by the !Kung. The climate is characterized by hot summers with a four-month rainy season and by moderate winters with no rainfall.

The !Kung enjoy a secure existence. They depend primarily on vegetable foods (Lee estimates that about 37 percent of their diet consists of meat). Their most important food plant is the mongongo or mangetti nut, a highly nutritious and superabundant staple. Other major plant foods are also available, but the !Kung tend to eat only those that are more attractive in terms of taste or ease of collection. Game animals are less abundant and less predictable. A type of large antelope is regularly hunted, as are warthogs and smaller antelopes. Game birds are captured in ingenious snares, and a large tortoise is a great favorite.

The camp or local band is the basic residential unit and the primary focus of subsistence activities. Members of each local group move out each day individually or in small groups to exploit the surrounding area, returning each evening to pool collected resources. Women do the gathering in groups of three to five. The men do the hunting, which is primarily an individual activity. Bows and poisoned arrows serve as effective weapons. Food is extensively shared, although the sharing of meat is more formally organized than the sharing of vegetable foods. Large game is butchered and divided into three portions: about one-fifth remains with the family, one-fifth is cut into strips for drying, and the remaining three-fifths are distributed to closely related households. Meat division is carried out with considerable care. The hunter may call in other men to advise him, or he may even ask his father-in-law to conduct the division. Absolute sharing is the ideal in !Kung camps even though it is seldom attained in practice. It is noteworthy that the most common verbal disputes concern accusations of improper meat distribution and improper gift exchange.

SIMPLE HORTICULTURAL SOCIETIES

The Neolithic Revolution

Although hunters and gatherers have probably known for tens of thousands of years how plants and animals could be domesticated, it was not until about 10,000 years ago that some of them began to live in settled villages devoted to the practice of agriculture. The transition of humankind to an agricultural (technically, horticultural) mode of existence is known as the **Neolithic Revolution.** Actually the term *Neolithic Revolution* is somewhat misleading, since there was not a single revolutionary transition. The transition to agriculture occurred on an independent basis in several different regions of the world and at somewhat different times.

The adoption of agriculture occurred first in southwest Asia. The most important domesticated plants were wheat and barley, while the major domesticated animals were sheep, goats, and pigs. The actual process of domestication appears to have followed the emergence of sedentary villages organized around the harvesting of the wild ancestors of wheat and barley (Fagan, 1989; Wenke, 1990).

Agricultural communities emerged independently of the southwest Asian Neolithic in both China and Southeast Asia. In China agriculture can be dated to at least 7000 B.P., and possibly earlier (Chang, 1986). The principal domesticates were millet and pigs, with rice and soybeans being added later. Cattle, sheep, and goats were also domesticated, as were dogs and water buffalo. In south China taro and yams were grown in addition to the main crop, rice. The Southeast Asian Neolithic is dated to around 9000 B.P. (M. Cohen, 1977; Fagan, 1989). The main domesticates in this region were yams, taro, and rice.

Agricultural communities emerged independently in two other areas of the Old World: Europe and Africa. In Europe agriculture developed earliest in Greece and adjacent regions, probably around 8000 B.P. Wheat was the most important domesticated plant, although barley, millet, lentils, and legumes were also grown. Cattle, sheep, and pigs were the main domesticated animals (Milisauskas, 1978; Fagan, 1989). After about 7000 B.P. agriculture spread into temperate Europe, arriving in northern Europe (Scandinavia and the British Isles) sometime after 5500 B.P. The agricultural system focused on wheat, barley, cattle, sheep, and goats (Fagan, 1989). In Africa agriculture developed earliest in Egypt (around 7000 B.P.) where the principal domesticates were wheat, barley, cattle, sheep, goats, and pigs. Agriculture emerged slightly later in West and central Africa (around 6500 B.P.), the

Sudan (around 6000 B.P.), Ethiopia (around 6000 B.P.), and northern Kenya (around 4500 B.P.). In most of Africa below the equator, agriculture is much more recent, not beginning until after A.D. 1 (Phillipson, 1985).

Agriculture was also independently adopted in several regions of the New World: Mesoamerica (what is now Mexico and parts of Central America), South America, and North America. In Mesoamerica agriculture can be dated from about 7000 B.P. (MacNeish, 1978), although it is possible that it might have begun in some regions as early as 9000 B.P. (Fiedel, 1987). Settled village life, however, did not emerge until several thousand years later. This provides a striking contrast with the Old World, where agriculture and sedentary village life usually emerged together, although in some cases sedentism began prior to agriculture (M. Harris, 1977). In Mesoamerica the major plant domesticate was maize, the wild ancestor of which was a plant known as *teosinte*. Beans, gourds, squash, and chili peppers were also grown (Fiedel, 1987). Another contrast between Old World agriculture and that in Mesoamerica was the absence of any large animal domesticates in the latter, apparently because of a lack of species suitable for domestication (M. Harris, 1977). Indeed, the only large domesticated animal of any significance in all of the New World was the llama, which was domesticated in Peru around 5500 B.P.

In Peru, agriculture arose around 8000 B.P. or perhaps somewhat later. Here maize, potatoes, squash, gourds, beans, and quinoa were the major domesticated plants (B. Stark, 1986; Fagan, 1989). In Ecuador, it is possible that maize was being grown as early as 5000 B.P., and in the Amazon Basin it is thought that manioc was being cultivated perhaps as early as 4000 B.P. (Fiedel, 1987).

In North America maize was introduced around 5500 B.P., and beans were being grown by around 3000 B.P. (Fiedel,

1987). In the American southwest several major agricultural traditions dating from about 2350 B.P. have become well known. In eastern North America, agriculture centered around maize and beans developed after A.D. 400, although such plants as sunflowers, used for their edible seeds and oil, had been domesticated as early as 4000 B.P. (Fagan, 1989; B. Stark, 1986).

Contemporary Simple Horticulturalists

The first agricultural societies were not based on true agriculture but on simple **horticulture.** A number of **simple horticultural societies** have survived into the modern world. Most of these are found in Melanesia, a chain of islands in the southern Pacific (generally said to include New Guinea), and in various regions of South America. Extensive ethnographic research has been conducted among these societies, and the results of this research provide the basis for the discussion that follows.

Simple horticulturalists live in small villages ordinarily containing from 100 to 200 persons. Although villages substantially larger than this are known to exist, they are not common. Each village is in essence economically and politically self-sufficient. Nevertheless, important intervillage ties do exist. Marriage often takes place between individuals from different villages, and persons residing in separate villages often come together on ceremonial occasions. Members of culturally and linguistically related villages collectively constitute a tribe, a sociocultural unit that may contain tens of thousands or even hundreds of thousands of persons.

Most simple horticulturalists in recent times have lived in heavily forested environments and practice a form of cultivation known as *slash-and-burn* (also known as shifting cultivation). This cultivation technique involves cutting down a section of forest growth and then setting fire to the accumulated debris. The ashes that remain serve as a fertilizer, and usually no other fertilizer is added. The crops are then planted in these cleared plots (usually no more than an acre in size) with the aid of a digging stick, a long pole with a sharpened and fire-hardened end. A given plot may be devoted to a single crop, but a more common practice is to plant several minor crops along with one main staple (Sahlins, 1968). The task of clearing and preparing the plots generally falls to the men, while that of planting and harvesting is typically considered the responsibility of women.

Since wood ashes generally serve as the only fertilizer, slash-and-burn cultivation is associated with short-term soil fertility. Freshly produced ashes are washed away by rain after a year or two, and for this reason a plot of land can only be cultivated for that length of time. It must then be allowed to remain fallow long enough for the forest to regenerate so that new ashes can be produced. The fallow period ordinarily lasts approximately 20 to 30 years. When the forest growth has returned, the process of cutting, burning, and cultivating can begin again.

Because the slash-and-burn system requires lengthy fallow periods, any society practicing it must have much more land at its disposal than it will have under actual cultivation at any given time (Sahlins, 1968). The Tsembaga Maring of New Guinea, for example, had only 42 acres of land under actual cultivation in 1962–1963, but about 864 acres of their territory had been gardened at one time or another (M. Harris, 1975). Such land use requirements put limits on population density, and tropical forest cultivators often maintain population densities of less than ten persons per square mile (Sahlins, 1968).

Cultivated plants constitute the bulk of the dietary intake among simple horticulturalists. However, a number of simple horticultural societies also possess domesticated animals. Domesticated pigs, for instance, are found throughout Melanesia. But most simple horticulturalists lack domesticated animals, and such groups must rely upon hunting or fishing for their supply of animal protein.

Simple horticulturalists produce more food per unit of land than do hunters and gatherers. Some simple horticulturalists even produce small economic surpluses. Yet it cannot be concluded from these facts that they enjoy a superior standard of living. Indeed, it has been suggested that their standard of living is *inferior* to that of hunter-gatherers (M. Cohen, 1977, 1989) (see the Special Topic at the end of this chapter). They do not consume more calories, and their intake of protein appears to be lower. Furthermore, considerable evidence has accumulated in recent years to show that simple horticulturalists commonly work harder than hunters and gatherers (M. Cohen, 1977). It generally takes more time and energy to clear land and plant, tend, and harvest crops than to collect what nature automatically provides. Thus, simple horticulture is a more intensive system of technology than hunting and gathering, but it does not lead to greater material benefits.

The Yanomama

The Yanomama are a South American Indian tribe living in southern Venezuela and adjacent portions of northern Brazil. There are perhaps some 125 widely scattered villages having populations ranging from 40 to 250 inhabitants, with an average village size of about 75 to 80 persons. Several hundred years ago the Yanomama may have been devoted largely to a hunting and gathering subsistence pattern, and so they may only have recently made the transition to a horticultural existence (Colchester, 1984). Be that as it may, their current subsistence

practices nicely illustrate the simple horticultural mode of production. These practices have been described in some detail by Napoleon Chagnon (1983), one of their principal ethnographers.

The natural environment of the Yanomama is a relatively dense tropical forest. The land is entirely covered with jungle, even the tops of mountain ridges. The Yanomama survive in this environment with only a simple technology. All tools and techniques are uncomplicated, and none requires the use of specialized labor. Among the elements of technology the Yanomama have developed are crude clay pots, bows and arrows, agouti-tooth knives (made from the lower incisor of the agouti, a rodent), and canoes (which are so crude that they are generally used only once and then discarded).

The Yanomama are slash-and-burn cultivators. In earlier times, they had only stone axes for clearing the land, but they now have steel axes that have been supplied by local missionaries. Each man clears his own land. Each village has a local headman, and he typically has the largest garden. The headman must produce larger quantities of food as he is expected to give food away at feasts. By far the largest crop is plantains (similar to bananas), and each garden usually contains three or four varieties of both plantains and bananas. A root crop, sweet manioc, is also grown, and this is refined into a rough flour and then converted into a thick, baked bread. Other crops include taro, sweet potatoes, and a palm tree that produces a large crop of fruit. Maize is cultivated as an emergency crop, but it does not figure prominently in the daily diet. Tobacco is another cultivated crop, and the men, women, and children all chew it. Cotton is also grown and is used for making hammocks.

While perhaps 85 percent or more of the Yanomama diet consists of cultivated plants, the Yanomama spend almost as much time hunting as they do gardening. Since they have no domesticated animals, they rely exclusively upon hunting (as well as some fishing and the collecting of small animals) for their source of animal protein. Game animals are not abundant, a situation that is typical of tropical forest environments. The most commonly hunted game animals are several species of monkeys, two species of wild pig, armadillos, anteaters, deer, a small alligator, small rodents, and several species of smaller birds. All game animals are shot with arrows. Several varieties of insects, some species of caterpillar, and large spiders are collected and eaten. Wild honey, considered a real delicacy, is collected in large quantities.

The suggestion that the Yanomama were hunter-gatherers in the recent past seems confirmed by the fact that some villages have made the transition to horticulture only very incompletely. People in these villages regularly leave them to spend long periods of time trekking through the forest, surviving largely on whatever game they can kill and plant foods they collect (Good, 1987, 1993). These treks may last anywhere from three to six weeks, and as many as six treks might be made in a year's time. It is easily seen that these groups of Yanomama spend nearly as much time away from their villages as in them.

INTENSIVE HORTICULTURAL SOCIETIES

Many of the simple horticultural societies that were ushered into existence by the Neolithic Revolution in due time evolved into **intensive horticultural societies.** No doubt hundreds of intensive horticultural societies have existed during the past several thousand years of human history. Until the influx of the Europeans in the late eighteenth century, such societies were widespread throughout Polynesia, a vast island chain in the southern Pacific that includes the islands of Hawaii, Tahiti, and Tonga, among many others. Prior to the end of the nineteenth century, they flourished throughout large parts of sub-Saharan Africa. South America and Southeast Asia are also regions where numerous intensive horticulturalists were once located. Today, however, few remain. Most of these are found in parts of sub-Saharan Africa, and perhaps in some portions of South America and Southeast Asia.

Like simple horticulturalists, intensive horticulturalists are dependent upon cultivated garden products for the bulk of their food supply, and they cultivate by the slash-and-burn method. Some of them keep domesticated animals, and those that do not engage in hunting or fishing for their supply of meat. Yet intensive horticulturalists differ in several significant ways from simple horticulturalists. One principal difference involves the length of time that land is allowed to remain fallow. Simple horticulturists generally permit the land to lie fallow for twenty or thirty years before using it again. Intensive horticulturalists, by contrast, shorten the fallow period to perhaps as little as five to ten years, thus cropping a given plot of land more frequently. Some intensive horticulturalists have reduced the length of the follow period even further, occasionally to the point of cultivating land almost continuously. Ancient Hawaii, for example, fell into this category. To compensate for the decrease in soil fertility that accompanies more frequent cropping, intensive horticulturalists further fertilize the soil by adding such things as humus or animal manure.

The shortening of the fallow period has the effect of eventually converting thick forest growth to bush. Land that has been cleared of bush must be prepared for cultivation in a way that is not necessary for land cleared of forest. Thus, many intensive horticulturalists have invented or adopted hoes for the purpose of properly preparing land for cultivation. As Boserup explains (1965:24):

> After the burning of real forest the soil is loose and free of weeds and hoeing of the land is unnecessary. By contrast, when the period of fallow is shortened and, therefore, the natural vegetation before clearing is thin or grassy the land must be prepared with a hoe or similar instrument before the seeds or roots can be placed.

Some intensive horticulturalists employ elements of technology in addition to, or instead of, the ones mentioned above. Polynesian intensive horticulturalists, for example, although they never made use of hoes, did engage in the terracing and irrigation of land. It is clear, then, that intensive horticulturalists have achieved a level of technological development beyond what is typical for simple horticulturalists. It is also clear that people work harder and longer under intensive horticulture. Preparing the land by hoeing and the terracing and irrigation of land are demanding and time-consuming activities. Since people work harder and longer, and since any given area of land is cultivated more frequently, it is obvious why this mode of subsistence technology is referred to as *intensive* horticulture.

Compared to simple horticulture, intensive horticulture is considerably more productive per unit of land. Intensive horticulturalists, in fact, produce sizable economic surpluses, and these surpluses are used to support a class of persons who are freed from direct involvement in agricultural production. In many intensive horticultural societies, the members of this class are regarded, theoretically at least, as the owners of all the land, and in all such societies they direct many economic activities. Their standard of living is higher than that of everyone else. The standard of living of most of the members of intensive horticultural societies is difficult to determine, but

it seems likely that it differs little from that typically found among simple horticulturalists. Yet it should not be forgotten that intensive horticulturalists work significantly harder just to achieve the same material results.

Aboriginal Tahiti

Most of the population of aboriginal Polynesia lived on the so-called high islands. These islands are rugged, eroded remnants of great volcanic cones. The arable land is very rich, and it is covered with dense tropical growth. One of these high islands is Tahiti, a member of the Society Islands group. Tahiti is about 35 miles long and about half as wide. In the eighteenth century the island supported a population of approximately 100,000. The description of Tahitian society given here depicts their aboriginal way of life as it is presented by Elman Service (1963).

The Tahitians are sophisticated horticulturalists, considerably more so than groups like the Yanomama. They make very efficient use of the land for their gardens by terracing hillsides, diverting streams for irrigation, and enriching the soil in various ways. The prime horticultural tool is the simple digging stick. Since there are no metals, they have never developed the metal hoes characteristic of many other intensive horticulturalists.

Tahiti's main domesticated plants were brought from Indonesia, and these include coconut palms, breadfruit trees, taro, yams, sweet potatoes, bananas and plantains, and sugar cane. The most important food is breadfruit, a fruit that is plentiful and nutritious and stores well. The most versatile domesticated plant is the coconut palm. The coconut meat is a nourishing food and coconut milk is used for drinking. Palm leaves are used for thatch, and the fiber is used for the manufacture of mats and baskets.

Fishing is also an important part of the Tahitian subsistence pattern, and the technology available for it is diversified and elaborate. This technology includes basketry traps, many forms of nets, fish poisons, harpoons, and many kinds of hooks and lines. Tahitians of both sexes are excellent swimmers. Women dive for crabs and other shellfish and even capture octopi. Men and boys dive to great depths for pearl oysters, the flesh of which is used for food and the shell for various implements and ornaments. Aside from seafood, the main source of protein is pork, and pigs are carefully fed and tended. Chickens are also raised.

The Tahitian horticultural system is intensive enough to produce a sizable economic surplus, and this surplus is used to support a class of persons known as the *Ari'i:* chiefs and their families. The chiefs and their families live off this surplus and thus have no direct involvement in agricultural production. They also use it to support a set of administrative officials who carry out the daily business of political rule. A good deal of this surplus is also returned to the people through the holding of elaborate feasts.

AGRARIAN SOCIETIES

The first **agrarian societies** arose approximately 5000 years ago in Egypt and Mesopotamia and slightly later in China and India. It was not long before agrarian societies were to be found over much of the globe. From the time when agrarian societies first emerged until the present day, the majority of persons who have ever lived have done so according to the agrarian way of life. To the extent that this way of life remains today, it exists largely in substantially altered form in societies that are at least partially industrialized and are part of a worldwide capitalist economy. Hence

there are no true agrarian societies left in the world. But what were agrarian societies of the past like?

Agrarian societies rest upon true **agriculture.** Land is cleared of all vegetation and cultivated with the use of the plow and draft animals hitched to the plow. Fields are extensively fertilized, usually with animal manure. When land is cultivated in this fashion, it may be used more or less continually. Thus, fallow periods are either very short or do not exist. Farmers often crop a given plot of land annually, and in some cases several harvests may be reaped from the same plot of land in a single year.

A number of agrarian societies have existed in areas where rainfall was sufficient to nourish crops. Agrarian societies throughout Europe, for instance, were based on rainfall farming. But in many other agrarian societies, arid or semiarid climates have made rainfall farming impossible, and farmers have had to construct irrigation systems to water their crops. Farmers in ancient Egypt, Mesopotamia, China, and India, for example, practiced irrigation agriculture.

Agrarian farmers work much harder than do the members of earlier types of societies (cf. Minge-Klevana, 1980). The tasks of clearing land, plowing, sowing and harvesting crops, tending animals, and so on require extensive labor inputs. Where irrigation systems must be constructed, people work even harder. Because of their efforts, agrarian farmers produce much more per unit of land than do horticulturalists, and much of what they produce constitutes an economic surplus. But their greater efforts and larger surpluses do not yield for them a higher standard of living. Indeed, their standard of living is generally lower, and in some cases much lower, than that enjoyed by the members of horticultural societies. Part of the reason for this apparent paradox is explained at the end of this chapter, but this phenomenon cannot be fully understood until the rise of social stratification is discussed in Chapter 6.

Most members of agrarian societies are **peasants.** They are the primary producers, the persons who farm the land from day to day. Eric Wolf (1966) calls them *dependent cultivators* because they exist in a politically and economically dependent or subordinate relationship to the principal owners of the land. They themselves frequently do not own land, but are merely allowed the use of it. In this sense, they are tenants on the land. In those cases where peasants do own their land, they have far from full control over the dispensation of the produce from this land. But not all of the primary producers in agrarian societies are peasants. Some are slaves. Slaves differ from peasants in that they are legally owned and can be bought and sold. In some agrarian societies—ancient Rome and Greece, for example—slaves actually outnumbered peasants.

Medieval England

Medieval England serves as an excellent example of the agrarian mode of subsistence technology. H. S. Bennett's (1937) study of how English peasants from the twelfth to the fifteenth centuries farmed the land provides the basis for the following discussion.

English peasants lived in an overwhelmingly rural society, one in which there were few, comparatively small cities. The peasants lived in small villages that commonly numbered in the vicinity of a hundred persons. They spent most of their lives doing farm work, much of which was carried out by teams of peasants working cooperatively.

Some peasants farmed the land in a "two-field" fashion. They would work on one field in one year while allowing the other one to remain fallow; then the next year they would reverse the process. Other peasants farmed the land using a "three-field" system. One field would be planted in

the autumn with wheat or possibly rye; another would be planted with oats, vetches, or barley the following spring; in the meantime, the third field would lie fallow. The next year the fallow field would be sown with wheat, the first field with oats, vetches, or barley, and the second field would remain fallow, and so on. Naturally, by rotating crops and fields in this manner the peasants were trying to keep the fertility of the soil as high as possible.

Peasants also applied animal manure to the soil to aid in its fertility, but getting enough manure was a constant struggle. There were a number of reasons for this. In the first place, the peasant seldom had enough animals to produce all the manure he needed. Also, peasants did not have unrestricted use of their animals, for their landlords appropriated them on some occasions. Fodder to produce a sufficient quantity of manure was also in short supply. So the peasant did the best he could under difficult conditions, and this meant that he sometimes worked marl or lime into the ground as an additional fertilizer. Numerous animals were kept by peasants, both as means of working the farm and as sources of food. Oxen and cows were extremely important for farm work, and both were used for food and hides. Naturally, cows provided milk as a food product. Sheep were kept for their wool and for food. Pigs were also kept, and they were perhaps the most highly valued of all farm animals, at least as food sources. They had special significance as food sources because they could be economically fed, they put on weight quickly, and they could be efficiently prepared for slaughter.

Farm work for the average English peasant was extremely demanding, and peasants put in many long, hard hours in order to meet their subsistence needs and pay their taxes. The following description of peasant labor should convey just how demanding peasant life really was (Bennett, 1937:82–83):

Once all this was finished the peasant's labours were not so pressing, and he could turn to the many other secondary jobs waiting to be done. If the land was heavy, draining operations were constantly necessary and worth while; ditches wanted digging out after the winter floods, and the good earth put on to the land again; hedges and enclosures round the little home or any private bit of enclosure required attention, and so on. Then . . . it was time for the first ploughing of the fallow field, and the busy activities in the garden where such vegetables and fruits as were then available were grown.

So the days went by with plenty to occupy men till the end of May. The coming of June saw them making renewed efforts. The haymaking called for all their strength: first, there were the numerous compulsory days which they had to spend in getting in the lord's hay. . . .

With the coming of August the peasant's activities reached their climax. Once again the demands made upon him by his lord were often very heavy. He had to appear in person again and again to gather in the lord's crops—and, although he usually worked one or two days more a week from August to Michaelmas than at other times in the year, this was not enough, and he had to give several extra days of his time as a boon or gift to his lord. And further, he had to come with all his family: everyone able to work, save perhaps the housewife, was pressed into service for so many days. This made the getting-in of his own crops a more difficult and anxious matter, and work during these crucial weeks must have been wellnigh unending.

Thus it was that the medieval English peasant toiled in his fields in a manner that the average hunter-gatherer or horticulturalist would have considered unthinkable.

PASTORAL SOCIETIES

Pastoralism (or pastoral nomadism) is a highly specialized subsistence adaptation found in arid regions of the world poorly suited to agriculture. It is based on the tending of animal herds rather than the growing of crops. Exactly when and how pastoralism first emerged is still debated. It has been suggested that it arose as early as 8000 B.P. in parts of the Middle East (Hole, 1997; Cribb, 1991), but such an early date cannot be accepted with certainty. There is evidence that early in prehistory a number of groups seemed to depend heavily on domesticated animals. However, true pastoralism—exclusive or near-exclusive dependence on animal herds, with little or no agriculture—may be a more recent phenomenon, dating only from approximately 3500 B.P. (Sahlins, 1968; cf. Cribb, 1991:10). In any event, although classic pastoralism occurs later in history than cultivation, it is not evolutionarily "higher" or "more advanced" than agriculture. Rather, it is an alternative to agriculture in environments where aridity makes cultivation of the land difficult or impossible.

Pastoralists tend their animal herds year round and move seasonally with them in search of pasture (hence the name pastoral *nomadism*). Animals most frequently kept include sheep, goats, camels, cattle, and, in some cases, reindeer. Some pastoral groups depend on a single animal species, whereas others herd a number of different species. Some pastoralists practice no agriculture at all. These groups obtain agricultural products for their diet by trade relations with agricultural neighbors. It is not uncommon, however, for pastoral groups to engage in some agriculture in order to supplement the foods they obtain from their animal herds, but this is always distinctly secondary to their herding activities.

Pastoralists live and travel in relatively small groups that usually do not exceed 100 to 200 members. Population densities are quite low, usually fewer than five persons per square mile.

Most of what pastoralists eat, of course, comes from their animal herds.

They subsist principally on milk, meat, and blood. In eastern Africa, for instance, many pastoral groups have as their major dietary item a mixture of blood and milk obtained from their cattle. Although agricultural products generally supplement the diet, for some groups they do so only to a very small extent.

Most pastoralists have been located in the dry regions of Asia and Africa: in southwest Asia, northern Africa, and the grasslands of eastern Africa. Sheep, goats, and camels are the most commonly herded animals in Asia and northern Africa, while eastern Africa is famous for cattle herding. Pastoralism is also found in certain northern Eurasian forest regions, and here reindeer herders predominate (Sahlins, 1968). Marshall Sahlins (1968:33) has noted that the "classic locus of pastoral tribes is the transcontinental dry belt of Asia and Africa: Manchuria, Mongolia, Tibet, Turkestan, Iran, Arabia, the Sahara and its environs." Probably the most famous pastoralists have been those in northern China. For most of the time period since about 2500 B.P., mounted nomads from the steppes of northern China preyed upon Chinese agrarian civilization by regularly raiding it and wreaking all sorts of havoc (Barfield, 1989). The most notorious of these nomads were, of course, the Mongols. This is a common practice among pastoralists: they raid their agricultural neighbors and then escape with relative impunity.

The Basseri

The Basseri are pastoralists who live in the dry steppes and mountains of southern Iran. Numbering about 16,000 in the entire tribe, they are tent dwellers who move about with their animal herds. Their habitat is hot and dry. Annual rainfall is generally 10 inches or less, and most of this falls in the winter. The discussion of the subsistence pattern of this group is based on the detailed study by Fredrik Barth (1961).

The Basseri keep a number of domesticated animals, the most important of which are sheep and goats. The products of these animals provide the major part of subsistence. Donkeys are kept for transport and for riding, horses for riding only. Camels are maintained for use in heavy transport, and their wool is also of value. Dogs are used as camp watchdogs. Poultry is sometimes found as a source of meat, but the eggs are not eaten.

The milk obtained from sheep and goats is a most important product. Sour milk is a staple and is processed for storage. Cheese is made, although seldom during the periods of daily migrations. The best cheese is allegedly made during the summer, when the Basseri maintain a stationary residence.

Lambs are slaughtered for meat that is never smoked, salted, or dried, but always eaten fresh. The hides of slaughtered animals are sold in markets and also used as bags for storing water, sour milk, and buttermilk.

Wool is also an important animal product. Felt is made out of lamb's wool, and sheep's wool and camel hair are sold and used in weaving and rope making. Goat hair is also of value and is spun and woven.

Many agricultural products are included in the typical diet of the Basseri. Some of these are produced by the Basseri themselves, the rest being obtained in trade. Cereal crops like wheat are planted when the tribesmen first arrive in their summer camps, and these are harvested before the departure from the camps. The agriculture performed by the Basseri themselves is very rough, and, in general, disliked and disdained. Therefore, many of the Basseri are reluctant to engage in agricultural activity.

Many of the Basseri's necessities are obtained through trade. Flour, sugar, tea, dates, and fruits and vegetables are obtained exclusively or mainly by trade. Material for clothes, finished clothes and shoes, cooking utensils, and saddles are purchased in markets. For all these items the Basseri exchange clarified butter, wool, lambskins, and some livestock.

THE CAUSES OF THE EVOLUTION OF PREINDUSTRIAL TECHNOLOGIES

We must now consider the crucial question of what accounts for the evolution of preindustrial technologies from one stage to the next.

It was once widely believed by social scientists of all sorts that technology is a self-generating, independent force in its own right. It was thought that technological changes occur as the cumulative result of the inventive powers of the human species. In addition, it was felt that whenever new forms of technology become available, people automatically adopt them because they see the benefits they will bring.

Most social scientists have now abandoned this view of technological change. Many embrace instead the view proposed some three decades ago by Ester Boserup (1965, 1981; cf. R. Wilkinson, 1973). Boserup holds that people have no inherent desire to advance their level of technology. She postulates that people wish to make a living by the simplest and easiest means possible. Their natural inclinations are to meet their subsistent needs with the least amount of work. Since adopting new technologies actually results in people having to work harder, they will not switch to new methods unless special conditions compel them to do so. Boserup believes that the principal condition compelling people to advance their technology is **population pressure.** Population pressure exists when population growth causes people to press against food resources. As the number of mouths to be fed increases, a point is eventually reached at which people begin to deplete their resources and suffer a significant drop in their standard of living. Boserup argues that it is at this point that people will start to intensify production. They adopt new forms of technology and work harder and longer in order to produce more food to feed more people. Simple horticulturalists, for example, may begin to adopt more intensive horticultural techniques. Likewise, intensive horticulturalists may switch to plow agriculture.

It is imperative to realize that Boserup's argument does not assume that the switch to more intensive technologies will lead to the resumption of old standards of living, let alone to any long-term improvement in the standard of living. While this may occur in the short run (Conelly, 1992), the effect over the long haul is almost inevitably the continued deterioration of living standards. Her argument is simply that the adoption of more intensive modes of production is necessary in order to maintain as high a living standard as possible under the imposition of greater numbers.

Mark Cohen (1977, 1985) believes that Boserup's argument is relevant to understanding the origin of agriculture on a worldwide basis. Cohen notes that ancient hunter-gatherers had probably long understood how to domesticate plants and animals, but waited for perhaps tens of thousands of years before putting their knowledge to use. Apparently they saw no benefits to the practice of agriculture, and they probably saw it as a less desirable way of making a living than collecting food from nature's storehouse. Indeed, when contemporary hunter-gatherers are asked by ethnographers why they do not practice agriculture, they usually respond with something like, "Why should we work harder in order to live no better than we're living now?"

Table 4.1   PREINDUSTRIAL SUBSISTENCE STRATEGIES

Subsistence Strategy	Principal Technological Characteristics
Hunting and gathering	Hunting of wild animals with the use of spears, spear throwers, bows and arrows, nets, and traps. Gathering of wild plant food using a digging stick. Fishing may be undertaken, and in some environments may be a principal subsistence activity. Division of labor is based mainly on age and sex, with hunters generally males and gatherers generally females. Nomadic bands of 25 to 50 persons follow the supply of game and plants. Labor inputs are normally low.
Simple horticulture	Small-scale gardening, generally using the slash-and-burn method of cultivation. The men prepare garden sites, but the women are commonly the principal cultivators and harvesters. Gardens are moved frequently, and fallow periods are generally long (20 to 30 years). Labor inputs are typically low.
Intensive horticulture	Small-scale gardening, normally using slash-and-burn techniques but with more frequent and intensive usage of each plot of land and shorter fallow periods (5 to 10 years). May also involve extension of the technological inventory to include metal hoes and the construction of irrigation systems, as well as more extensive fertilization of garden plots. Labor inputs moderate.
Agrarianism	Large-scale intensive agriculture employing the plow and traction animals. Fields are entirely cleared of vegetation and are cultivated permanently or semipermanently. Extensive fertilization to maintain soil fertility. Requires high labor inputs, but is capable of generating large economic surpluses.
Pastoralism	Reliance on animal herds in arid environments not well suited for cultivation of the soil. Herds are moved on a seasonal basis, and thus a nomadic existence is maintained. Some cultivation may be practiced, or vegetable matter may be obtained through trade.

Richard Lee (1979), for example, asked a !Kung man named /Xashe why the !Kung did not adopt some of the practices of their agricultural neighbors, and /Xashe replied, "Why should we plant when there are so many mongongos in the world?" If, then, ancient hunter-gatherers knew how to plant crops but avoided doing so, what finally compelled some of them to cross the threshold to the agricultural way of life? Cohen believes that the reason was a "food crisis" due to growing population. He holds that hunting and gathering groups in several regions of the world finally outgrew the capacity of their environments to sustain them at an acceptable standard of living.

When this occurred, they were forced to start producing their own food in order to stave off the "food crisis." They became willing to work harder, because they now had something to gain from it.

Cohen's theory of the origin of agriculture is still widely debated by archaeologists, who are the social scientists best qualified to judge it. Yet it is extremely plausible in terms of what we know about the attitude of modern hunter-gatherers to the practice of agriculture, and a number of modern anthropologists and archaeologists have developed theories of agricultural origins that give population pressure a significant role (Binford, 1968; Harner, 1970; Flannery, 1973; M. Harris, 1977). The leading current competitors to Cohen's theory are either theories that emphasize the role of climate change (Henry, 1989; McCorriston and Hole, 1991), or theories that make resource stress the major causal factor (M. Harris, 1977; D. Harris, 1977; Hayden, 1981). These theories have serious problems, however, the most significant of which is that they are usually designed to explain the Neolithic in only one part (or at most a few parts) of the world. The theories of Henry and of McCorriston and Hole are intended to explain only the southwest Asian Neolithic—these authors deny the possibility of any general theory of the worldwide transition to agriculture—and Marvin Harris's theory is unsatisfactory in explaining the Neolithic in southwest Asia, Southeast Asia, or China (Fiedel, 1987). (Hayden's theory has other serious difficulties, but these are too complicated to discuss in a general textbook.) It is precisely where these theories fail that Cohen's succeeds. His theory is predicated on the enormously important fact of the *worldwide* transition to agriculture, as well as on the fact that many different regions of the world began the adoption of agriculture independently of one another. As Cohen has argued, the worldwide charac-

ter of the Neolithic at approximately the same time in world prehistory is of such striking significance that only a general theory that explains this whole process can hope to succeed.

But while there is still a good deal of disagreement concerning the causes of the early transition to agriculture, social scientists are more certain about the role of population pressure in leading to the **intensification of agricultural production.** Boserup herself presents considerable evidence that changes in the level of population density precede changes in the mode of economic production. For example, she points to the fact that the population increase in Japan from about 1600 to about 1850 was closely followed by a shift in the intensity of production. Boserup also notes that decreases in population density often seem to be followed by an actual *regression* in cultivation techniques. For example, in recent centuries some areas of South America have experienced population reductions as the result of new diseases introduced by encroaching Europeans, and the indigenous societies of these regions have regressed to less intensive cultivation techniques. Likewise, earlier in this century farmers in Tanganyika, Vietnam, Ceylon, and India adopted less intensive agricultural methods when they were resettled by their governments to less populated regions and given more land to use. And this was true even when the purpose of the resettlement was to spread more intensive methods to the areas of immigration.

Much additional research has supported the view that population pressure is the basic cause of preindustrial technological evolution. Increasingly intensive systems of agricultural production seem to have arisen as a response to growing numbers in such diverse regions of the world as South America, New Guinea, ancient Mesoamerica, and ancient Mesopotamia (Carneiro, 1968; Clarke, 1966; Sanders, 1972; Adams, 1972).

As noted earlier, although the demographic theory of agricultural intensification has won wide acceptance, some social scientists remain highly critical of it (cf. Bronson, 1972; Cowgill, 1975; B. White, 1982). George Cowgill (1975) and Benjamin White (1982), for example, argue that the theory incorrectly assumes some natural tendency of human populations to grow. For his part, White claims that population growth is not natural or automatic, but depends on a range of social, economic, and political circumstances. He contends that since there is no inherent tendency for population to grow, then population pressure cannot logically be invoked as a cause of advancements in the level of agricultural technology.

But while it is true that demographic change is influenced by a variety of social factors, it does not follow that there is no inherent tendency for population to grow under most preindustrial conditions. There is considerable evidence that preindustrial peoples devote an enormous amount of attention to attempting to regulate numbers, and this suggests that they are up against potent biological realities (cf. Harris and Ross, 1987). In particular, the widespread existence of female infanticide is powerful evidence of the need people have to control their numbers (Harris and Ross, 1987; R. Wilkinson, 1973; Cohen, Malpass, and Klein, 1980).

Demographic change interacts in complex ways with the various components of sociocultural systems, and it can hardly be considered some sort of universal cause of sociocultural evolution. More recent evolutionary events, such as the Industrial Revolution or the impoverishment of two-thirds of the population of the contemporary world, have resulted from very different causes. But at the preindustrial level population growth seems to be our best bet as the critical stimulus for the advance of subsistence technology (cf. Johnson and Earle, 1987). At least no

one has yet proposed a theory that is as convincing as the theory of population pressure.

SUMMARY

1. Hunting and gathering societies monopolized 99 percent of human history, and some still survive today. The members of these societies survive by hunting wild animals and collecting wild plant and vegetable matter. It was long thought that their members exist at a bare margin of survival, but more recent evidence suggests that most live adequately with a minimum of work effort. In fact, it has been suggested that they constitute a kind of "original affluent society."

2. Some human communities in various parts of the world began to adopt agricultural techniques of subsistence some 10,000 years ago. The transition to agriculture is generally known as the Neolithic Revolution. It is now known that the transition to agriculture occurred independently in several different world regions. The development of agriculture was a slow and gradual transition out of hunting and gathering, and it seems that people were actually beginning for the first time to use knowledge they had long possessed.

3. The earliest agriculturalists practiced a rudimentary form of agriculture known as simple horticulture. Many simple horticulturalists survive today in remote regions of the world, especially tropical forest areas. Simple horticulturalists commonly cultivate land by cutting down forest growth, burning the accumulated debris, and planting crops in the ashes that remain. Such groups generally rotate their gardens frequently and allow previously cultivated plots to remain fallow for long periods.

4. Many past and present societies have used a more intensive form of horticulture. They shorten the fallow period of previously used plots and often make use of additional fertilizers. They might also develop hoes for cultivation, and some have invented techniques such as terracing and irrigation of land. Just

as simple horticulture is more productive per unit of land than hunting and gathering, intensive horticulture is more productive than simple horticulture.

5. Agrarian societies began to emerge some 5000 years ago. The members of these societies practice what some regard as "true" agriculture. This involves cultivating large plots of land with the plow and draft animals and the continuous or semicontinuous usage of land. An agrarian mode of subsistence technology uses the land very intensively, requires enormous labor inputs, and achieves very high levels of economic productivity.

6. Pastoralism is an alternative to agriculture in dry regions not suitable for agriculture. Pastoralists live off their animal herds, especially from blood and dairy products. They are nomadic, driving their herds from pasture to pasture as the seasons change. Pastoralists

either practice agriculture on a very small scale or avoid it altogether.

7. Social scientists used to treat technological change more or less as a given. People were seen as advancing their level of technology when they knew how to because they obviously sought the benefits of more advanced techniques. This older view is now in serious disrepute. There is much evidence that technological inertia is built into most preindustrial societies. It seems that people resist technological advances because they require greater work efforts. Some have theorized that technological advances will only be made under severe population pressure that compels people to change in order to prevent further reductions in their standard of living. One of the great ironics of technological evolution is that it is associated with lower, rather than higher, standards of living.

SPECIAL TOPIC: AGRICULTURAL ORIGINS AND THE DECLINING STANDARD OF LIVING

The notion that cultural progress has accompanied technological advance is a strongly entrenched belief in Western civilization. One aspect of this notion is the belief that technological innovation over the millennia has brought about continuous improvement in the standard of living. Recent research by archaeologists and biological anthropologists into some of the consequences of the transition from hunting and gathering to agriculture, however, sharply challenges this assumption. These scientists have drawn upon the recent technique of paleopathology—the examination of the evidence of biological stress and disease in ancient skeletal remains—to assess the implications for health and nutrition of the adoption of agriculture.

One intriguing paleopathological study has been carried out by the biological anthropologist J. Lawrence Angel (1975). Angel examined some 2,200 human skeletal remains drawn from sites representing the past 30,000 years of human history. Through various painstaking analyses, he estimated the general dietary adequacy of the populations represented by the remains. He found that longevity increased little from 30,000 years ago through the time when complex agricultural systems predominated. For instance, he estimated that hunter-gatherers of 30,000 years ago had a life expectancy of approximately 31 years. By 5000 B.P. the life expectancy was virtually the same; by the early Roman Empire it was only about 37 years; and by late medieval times it was only about 34 years. In addition, Angel found a general decline in body stature over this period, as well as an increase in the incidence of dental disease. These findings clearly suggest an overall deterioration in nutritional and health status, especially a notable reduction in protein intake.

A great deal of evidence consistent with Angel's findings has been added in recent years. At a conference held in Plattsburgh, New York, Mark Cohen and George Armelagos (1984) summarized the paleopathological findings presented by over a dozen biological anthropologists. The participants at the conference "were asked to make comparative statements about the occurrence of as many as possible of a common set of indexes of health, diet, and pathology derived from recent summaries of paleopathological techniques" (M. N. Cohen, 1984:4). The participants addressed questions in regard to such phenomena as life expectancies, the occurrence of indicators of stress that would have disturbed childhood growth patterns, indicators of infection, changes in bone growth indicative of malnutrition, and the prevalence of dental cavities and other oral disease. The skeletal remains on which the paleopathological investigations were performed were drawn from throughout the world. There were eight analyses based on North America, one on Mesoamerica, three on South America, two on Europe, two on the Middle East, one on southern Asia, and one on North Africa.

With few exceptions, these studies strongly point to the conclusion that the standard of living declined with the adoption of agriculture. In regard to infection, most of the studies found that it was a more frequent and severe problem for farming populations than for hunter-gatherers. Evidence regarding chronic malnutrition yields the same result. The investigators looked for the incidence of porotic hyperostosis and cribia orbitalia (porosity of the skull and orbits), bone diseases generally considered good indicators of anemia. Most of the studies showed that these were primarily diseases of agricultural rather than hunting and gathering populations. Other indicators of malnutrition, such as the thinning of long-bone cortices and changes in the skull base and pelvic inlet, were also discovered to be more common in agricultural groups.

Indicators of biological stresses leading to the disruption of childhood growth tell basically the same story as the other indicators. Various defects in tooth enamel are considered good indicators of growth-disrupting stress. Cohen and Armelagos note that ten studies "all report that the frequency and/or severity of this indicator of growth disruption increases in farming and later populations in comparison to hunter-gatherers" (1984:589). Finally, the studies generally show that mean age at death actually declined after the adoption of agriculture, a conclusion even more provocative than Angel's finding in this regard.

The findings reported at the Plattsburgh conference are of major significance for theories of sociocultural evolution inasmuch as they strongly challenge the prevailing wisdom of Western civilization, a wisdom not only of the general members of society but of the majority of social scientists as well. As Cohen and Armelagos comment (1984:594):

> Taken as a whole, these indicators fairly clearly suggest an overall decline in the quality—and probably in the length—of human life associated with the adoption of agriculture. . . . The studies support recent ethnographic statements and theoretical arguments about the relatively good health and nutrition of hunter-gatherers. They also suggest that hunter-gatherers were relatively well buffered against episodic stress. These data call into question simplistic popular ideas about human progress.

FOR FURTHER READING

Bates, Daniel G., and Fred Plog. *Human Adaptive Strategies.* New York: McGraw-Hill, 1991. A good introduction to the basic subsistence adaptations discussed in this chapter.

Bettinger, Robert L. *Hunter-Gatherers: Archaeological and Evolutionary Theory.* New York: Plenum, 1991. A useful recent work on several dimensions of, as well as several perspectives on, hunter-gatherer societies.

Boserup, Ester. *The Conditions of Agricultural Growth.* Chicago: Aldine, 1965. The classic work on population pressure as the engine driving the intensification of economic production in preindustrial societies.

Burch, Ernest S. Jr., and Linda J. Ellanna (eds.), *Key Issues in Hunter-Gatherer Research.* Oxford:

Berg, 1994. A useful collection of recent essays on various aspects of hunter-gatherer societies, including gender, territoriality, hunter affluence, culture contact, and government intervention.

Chagnon, Napoleon A. *Yanomamö: The Last Days of Eden.* San Diego: Harcourt Brace Jovanovich, 1992. One of the most fascinating ethnographies ever written on a horticultural society. This latest edition contains an important discussion of the disrupting influence of modern society and speculations about the future of this famous tribal society.

Cohen, Mark N. *The Food Crisis in Prehistory.* New Haven: Yale University Press, 1977. The application of Boserup's hypothesis to explaining the worldwide origin of agriculture.

Harris, Marvin, and Eric B. Ross. *Death, Sex, and Fertility: Population Regulation in Preindustrial and Developing Societies.* New York: Columbia University Press, 1987. A major work on the demography of preindustrial societies.

Johnson, Allen W., and Timothy Earle. *The Evolution of Human Societies.* Stanford, Calif.: Stanford University Press, 1987. Excellent discussions of subsistence practices among the main types of preindustrial societies. Proposes population pressure as the basic cause of the advancement of subsistence technology.

Kelly, Robert L. *The Foraging Spectrum: Diversity in Hunter-Gatherer Lifeways.* Washington, D.C.: Smithsonian Institution Press, 1995. An excellent and highly comprehensive analysis of the most important dimensions of hunter-gatherer lifeways and the most important discussions and debates concerning these dimensions. The best book on hunter-gatherers in the last quarter-century.

Kirch, Patrick Vinton. *The Wet and the Dry: Irrigation and Agricultural Intensification in Polynesia.* Chicago: University of Chicago Press, 1994. Contains some very useful discussions of aspects of agricultural intensification in Polynesia by a leading expert on Polynesian societies.

Minge-Klevana, Wanda. "Does labor time decrease with industrialization? A survey of time-allocation studies." *Current Anthropology* 21:279–298, 1980. Contains extensive data on the workloads of preindustrial societies at different levels of technological development.

Price, T. Douglas, and James A. Brown (eds.). *Prehistoric Hunter-Gatherers.* Orlando: Academic Press, 1985. Some valuable archaeological investigations of hunting and gathering societies, especially of complex hunter-gatherers.

Winterhalder, Bruce, and Eric Alden Smith (eds.). *Hunter-Gatherer Foraging Strategies: Ethnographic and Archaeological Analyses.* Chicago: University of Chicago Press, 1981. A collection of essays applying the recent approach known as optimal foraging theory to the analysis of hunter-gatherer subsistence practices.

Chapter
5

Precapitalist Economic Systems

Every society has an economic system that is closely intertwined with its mode of subsistence technology. Yet there is a crucial difference between economy and technology. Technology involves the tools, techniques, and knowledge that the members of a society possess and use in the process of making a living. Economic activity is impossible without technology, but the economy is something more than the level of technology. The **economy** consists of the *social relationships that organize the production, distribution, and exchange of goods and services in any society*. **Production** is the socially organized process whereby goods and services are created. Questions about who owns the forces of production and how they decide to use these forces are questions about production. **Distribution** is the socially organized process of allocating the goods and services that the society produces—who gets what, how, and why. **Exchange** is the process of transferring valuables in return for other valuables, for example, exchanging gifts or purchasing items in a marketplace.

This chapter discusses those economic systems that existed prior to the development of a worldwide capitalist market economy or, if they exist today, display economic characteristics of a noncapitalist type.

A crucial concern of the chapter is to show the ways in which **precapitalist economies** are both similar to and different from modern capitalism.

PRODUCTION-FOR-USE VERSUS PRODUCTION-FOR-EXCHANGE

All goods have two distinct types of value, known generally as use-value and exchange-value. The **use-value** of a good is its direct utility, that is, the benefit it confers upon the user when it is used in the manner for which it is intended. For instance, the use-value of a shoe is its benefit to the wearer as a device that protects the foot, keeps the foot warm and dry, and so on. Likewise, the use-value of an automobile is its utility as a transporting vehicle.

But shoes, automobiles, and all other items also have the type of value called **exchange-value.** The exchange-value of these items is the value of some other item they will fetch when they are exchanged for that other item. For instance, if someone agrees to give to another person 300 pairs of shoes in return for that person's automobile, then the exchange value of the automobile in this situation is 300 pairs of shoes. Put another way, we may say that the exchange-value of the pair of shoes is 1/300 of an automobile. Exchange-value may be reckoned in terms of other useful goods, or in terms of some medium of exchange, that is, money. In capitalist, market-based societies, exchange-value is almost always calculated in money terms; in precapitalist societies, on the other hand, the exchange-value of goods is as often as not reckoned in terms of other goods rather than in some type of money.

While all goods in all economic systems have both use-value and exchange-value, economic systems themselves tend to be organized around one or the other of these types of value. Precapitalist societies are organized primarily around activities in which the production of goods for their use-value is the sole concern of the producers. In this case, the goods are produced so they can be consumed, not so they can be exchanged for other goods. When this type of activity dominates economic action, then a **production-for-use** economy exists.

Modern capitalism, by contrast, produces a vast quantity of goods primarily for their exchange-value, for the amount of money they will bring to the capitalist producers when they are sold in the market. Of course, these goods have use-value; otherwise no individuals would be interested in purchasing them. But that is beside the point. The *motivation* of modern capitalists to produce them relates to their exchange-value rather than to their use-value. Thus, modern capitalism is a **production-for-exchange** economy, or one in which production-for-exchange takes priority over production-for-use.

It should not be assumed that production-for-use economies do not have production-for-exchange. Indeed they do, at least to some small extent. It is simply that production-for-exchange plays a very secondary role in these types of economies. Nor should it be assumed that production-for-use economies are capable only of meeting the subsistence needs of their members. On the contrary, many precapitalist economic systems produce great wealth and marked economic inequalities among their members. However, the point to be stressed is that such wealth and inequality do not arise from production-for-exchange relationships, but from production-for-use relationships. Only in modern capitalism does the existence of vast wealth and economic inequality result primarily from production-for-exchange relationships. This important point will be developed more thoroughly as the chapter unfolds.

MODES OF OWNERSHIP IN PRECAPITALIST SOCIETIES

When considering how goods are produced in all societies, a vital question concerns who owns the forces of production—that is, who owns those resources that are of greatest significance in carrying out productive activities. In modern capitalism, the vital forces of production are principally owned by a tiny fraction of the population, and this small group of capitalists directs the overall process of economic production. In modern socialist societies, such as the former Soviet Union, ownership of the productive forces resided in the government, which claimed to direct production for the general good of society. Thus, in both modern capitalism and socialism the production process is strongly determined by those persons or groups who are the owners of crucial resources.

In precapitalist societies as well, economic production is shaped by the desires and choices of the owners of the productive forces. It is useful to distinguish four broad modes of ownership in precapitalist societies: primitive communism, lineage ownership, chiefly ownership, and seigneurial ownership. These types are not exhaustive of all modes of property ownership in precapitalist economies, and there are important variations within each type, but they are more or less representative of the ways in which property ownership is organized in the precapitalist world.

Primitive Communism

In the middle of the nineteenth century, Karl Marx speculated that the earliest mode of economic life in human history was what he termed **primitive communism.** By primitive communism, Marx meant a type of society in which people subsisted by hunting and gathering or by simple forms of agriculture, and in which all of the vital resources of nature were held in common. Private ownership of resources by individuals or small groups was not found, he thought, in this type of society.

Although many social scientists over the years have challenged Marx's view on this matter, contemporary social science provides considerable evidence that Marx was basically correct. The vast majority of hunter-gatherers studied by modern anthropologists display a mode of resource ownership that can be adequately characterized by Marx's notion of primitive communism. While much economic activity among hunter-gatherers is centered around the family, all individuals in such societies have equal access to those resources of nature that are necessary for their subsistence. No person in a hunting and gathering band may be deprived by any other person or group of an equal opportunity to hunt game, collect plants, use a water hole, or camp on the land. Everyone thus owns these resources collectively (it is sometimes said that since everyone has an equal right to their use, *no one* owns them). In fact, some hunter-gatherers do not even restrict the ownership of resources to their own local band; instead, they provide equal access to resources to all other individuals and groups who may have need for them (Woodburn, 1968). Even in those instances where resources may be "owned" privately by individual families, there are typically no restrictions placed against other families *using* these resources. Among the !Kung San, for instance, water holes are frequently said to be "owned" by individual families, but these families do not prevent other families from using them (Lee, 1968, 1972).

It is true that among hunter-gatherers items such as jewelry and art objects are owned privately, but this fact does not invalidate the claim that primitive communism is the principal ownership mode of hunting and gathering peoples. Jewelry and art objects are not a part of the forces of production, as Marx called the vital resources necessary to economic production. Rather, they are items of what is more appropriately referred to as *personal property*. Since they are not used in the productive process, the nature of their ownership is irrelevant to the Marxian thesis of primitive communism. Even then, we find that these items of personal property are seldom kept for long as private objects. Instead, they continually circulate among members of the group, and thus their use is community-wide.

Lineage Ownership

Among many small-scale horticultural peoples, primitive communism in the strict sense ordinarily does not prevail. Instead, most low-energy horticulturalists have a mode of property ownership that can best be designated **lineage ownership.** Lineage ownership occurs when large-scale kinship groups, known as lineages (or sometimes as clans), hold property in common. Of course, in such societies the most important form of property is land. When lineages own land in common, individual members of the group participate in the use of lineage land only because they are lineage members. Their right to the use of this land is only granted by the lineage itself as a corporate body; the leaders of the lineage, acting as representatives of the lineage as a whole, bestow these rights.

Lineage ownership is similar to primitive communism in that it is not a private form of property holding. Property is still held and used communally. But there is an important difference between lineage ownership and primitive communism. Lineage ownership is more exclusive or more restrictive inasmuch as it makes ownership and use of valuable resources dependent on kinship group membership. In societies resting on lineage ownership, not all members of the society have equal access to the forces of production, even though all members of the same lineage do. Lineage ownership is thus a small step away from primitive communism and toward private ownership. Still, it is closer to primitive communism than to private ownership, since in true lineage ownership the lineages themselves have relatively equal access to resources.

Chiefly Ownership

Chiefly ownership is an evolutionary variation on the theme of lineage ownership. It is ordinarily found among more intensive horticultural societies, although it has been known to exist in a few atypical hunting and gathering societies. Chiefly ownership prevails when a powerful individual—a chief—who is the head of a lineage, of an entire village, or of a vast network of integrated villages, claims personal ownership of the land within his realm and attempts to deprive those persons living on this land of full rights to its use. In order to use the land, these persons must observe certain restrictions on their production, such as turning over a part of their harvests to the chief.

Actually, the ownership of all the land within his realm by a chief is to a certain extent a fiction. The ownership rights of the chief are not as "real" as they are often made out to be. The Kpelle of Liberia in West Africa are intensive horticulturalists with a chiefly mode of ownership, yet the ownership rights of the chief are quite limited. As James Gibbs explains (1965:200–201):

Formally, land is said to be "owned" by the paramount chief, who divides it into portions for each town in the chiefdom, using for boundaries cottonwood and kola trees, creeks and hills. Each town chief divides the land for his town into segments for each quarter, using similar boundaries. These portions, in turn, are further split ... into parcels for each of the "families" or unnamed lineages....

Because each man in the lineage is entitled to the use of a portion of the land, the lineage head cannot refuse to allot a piece of it to each household head in the lineage. Once land is parceled out, it stays within the lineage and reverts to the quarter elder or other original "owner" only when a lineage dies out or some other unusual event occurs. Thus, although a town chief, a quarter elder, or a lineage head is, like a paramount chief, called "owner of the land," each is really a steward, holding the land for the group he represents.

Actually, in everyday situations, the head of the household to whom lineage land has been allocated is spoken of as the owner of the land. He decides which bit of "his" land he will work during a given year and which portions he will allow to lie fallow. Most farms are individually owned by the heads of the households and are worked with the help of the farmer's household group and cooperative work groups.

Thus, even though chiefs are the official owners of the land among the Kpelle, the powers of these chiefs appear to be significantly restricted. Since ordinary individuals make most of the daily decisions regarding the actual productive use of the land, these individuals are, in a sense, also its "owners."

Seigneurial Ownership

Although chiefly ownership represents a significant movement in the direction of private ownership, it has many of the characteristics of lineage ownership and is by no means a true mode of private ownership. True private ownership is reached with the evolution of **seigneurial ownership.** Seigneurial ownership prevails when a small class of persons,

generally known as landlords (*seigneurs* in French), claims private ownership of vast tracts of land on which there live and work peasants or slaves who pay rent, taxes, and labor services to these lords. There is nothing fictitious about this type of ownership, since landlords have the power to deprive others of the unrestricted use of land, and these other persons frequently do *not* make the day-to-day decisions about how the land is to be productively used.

Seigneurial ownership has been most characteristic of large-scale agrarian societies, although it has occasionally been found among some especially intensive horticulturalists. It is clear that it is associated with a very intensive mode of agricultural production. In medieval Europe, under the politico-economic system known as feudalism, seigneurial ownership prevailed for many centuries between the fall of the Roman Empire and the rise of modern capitalism. Following Max Weber (1978; orig. 1923), Eric Wolf (1966) has called the type of seigneurial ownership characteristic of medieval Europe **patrimonial ownership.** In this type of ownership, land is privately owned by a class of landlords who inherit it through family lines and who personally oversee its cultivation. Wolf has identified another type of seigneurial ownership that he calls **prebendal ownership.** Prebendal ownership exists when land is owned by a powerful government that designates officials to supervise its cultivation and draw an income from it. As Wolf notes, prebendal ownership was "characteristically associated with strongly centralized bureaucratic states—such as the Sassanid Empire of Persia, the Ottoman Empire, the Mogul Empire in India, and traditional China. The political organization of these empires attempted to curtail heritable claims to land and tribute, and asserted instead the eminent domain of a sovereign, a despot, whose claims overrode all inferior claims to domain" (1966:51).

Ownership Versus Control

The evolution of property rights has been a steady movement away from communal rights toward private rights, from the right of everyone to use vital resources to the right of only a few to the full use of these resources. But to be clear as to just what the important dimension of ownership is, it is important to avoid a narrow, legalistic conception of ownership, of ownership as "title." Rather, what is important is not "title" but *control.* For example, among the !Kung individual families "own" water holes, that is, have a "title" to them. But this ownership in the sense of "title" means little, since these families have no capacity or inclination to deprive other families of using the water holes. Thus, among the !Kung the control over water holes is communal, and that is what is important. In a similar vein, in medieval Europe there were numerous free peasants who owned their own land, that is, who had "title." Yet these peasants were effectively deprived of full control over their own land, since the landlord class held the administrative right to levy taxes against these peasants and to control them in other ways as well. Thus, the peasants owned their land, but the landlords heavily controlled it. Again, it is control that determines just what transpires within a system of production, and when ownership and control do not correspond, it is the latter to which social scientists must attend.

MODES OF DISTRIBUTION IN PRECAPITALIST SOCIETIES

The evolution of modes of property ownership in precapitalist societies is closely associated with the evolution of modes of resource distribution. The more privatized the system of ownership, the more unequal the system of distribution. It is useful to think of four major modes of distribution in precapitalist societies: reciprocity, pure redistribution, partial redistribution, and surplus expropriation.

Reciprocity

Reciprocity is the obligation to repay others for what they have given to or done for us, or the overt act of repaying others. Two distinct types of reciprocity, known as balanced and generalized reciprocity, exist. **Balanced reciprocity** occurs when individuals are obligated to provide equivalent and, frequently, immediate repayment to others. Balanced reciprocity can be identified by the fact that individuals deliberately and openly calculate what they are giving each other and openly declare the nature of the repayment to be made. Each party to the transaction expects to benefit in some way, but there is a clear expectation of mutual benefit and a lack of "exploitation."

Generalized reciprocity occurs when individuals are obligated to give to others without expecting any immediate or equivalent repayment. As opposed to balanced reciprocity, generalized reciprocity does not involve any direct or open agreement between the parties involved. There is a general expectation that equivalent repayment of a debt shall be made, but there is no particular time limit set for the repayment, nor is there any specification as to just how the repayment shall be made. The terms of repayment in generalized reciprocity are notoriously vague.

Marvin Harris (1974) has noted that one can tell whether generalized reciprocity is the prevailing mode of distribution by noticing whether people say "thank you." As Harris (1974:124) puts it, when generalized reciprocity is the distributive mode

it is rude to be openly grateful for the receipt of material goods or services. Among the Semai of central Malaya, for example, no one ever expresses gratitude for the meat that a hunter gives away in exactly equal portions to his companions. Robert Dentan, who has lived with the Semai, found that to say thank you was very rude because it suggested either that you were calculating the size of the piece of meat you had been given, or that you were surprised by the success and generosity of the hunter.

One might also say that it is rude to say "thank you" when generalized reciprocity is the distributive mode because under such circumstances giving things away to others is a social obligation, not an act of kindness.

While generalized reciprocity occurs to some extent in all societies (it occurs among friends and family members in our own society, for instance), it constitutes the very essence of economic life among hunter-gatherers, where it is most frequently found. Hunting and gathering peoples are famed for their extensive food-sharing. Individuals constantly give food to others and receive food in return. When a man returns to camp with an animal that he has killed, he will divide it into portions and then give these away, typically first to members of his family and then to other members of the band. Similarly, women constantly give away portions of food they have gathered. When a hunter gives meat to others he expects only that he will probably be repaid in some way at some time. The hunter may give to others time after time without any repayment taking place and without any mention being made of this fact. He understands that the chances are excellent that his acts will eventually be reciprocated. A failure to reciprocate only becomes a cause for concern and conflict when it appears that one person is "freeloading" off another.

Where generalized reciprocity is a pervasive feature of economic life, sharing and individual humility become compulsory social habits. As Richard Lee comments in regard to the !Kung (1978:888):

The most serious accusations that one !Kung can level against another are the charge of stinginess and the charge of arrogance. To be stingy or "far-hearted" is to hoard one's goods jealously and secretively, guarding them "like a hyena." The corrective for this in the !Kung view is to make the hoarder give "till it hurts," that is, to make him give generously and without stint until everyone can see that he is truly cleaned out. In order to ensure compliance with this cardinal rule, the !Kung browbeat each other constantly to be more generous and not to set themselves apart by hoarding a little nest-egg. . . .

But as seriously as they regard the fault of stinginess, the !Kung's most scathing criticisms are reserved for an even more serious shortcoming: the crime of arrogance. . . . A boasting hunter who comes into camp announcing "I have killed a big animal in the bush" is being arrogant. A woman who gives a gift and announces her great generosity to all is being arrogant. Even an anthropologist who claims to have chosen the biggest ox of the year to slaughter for Christmas is being arrogant. The !Kung perceive this behavior as a danger sign, and they have evolved elaborate devices for puncturing the bubble of conceit and enforcing humility. These leveling devices are in constant daily use, minimizing the size of others' kills, downplaying the value of others' gifts, and treating one's own efforts in a self-deprecating way. "Please" and "thank you" are hardly ever found in their vocabulary; in their stead we find a vocabulary of rough humor, backhanded compliments, putdowns, and damning with faint praise.

One possible reason generalized reciprocity is the dominant distributive mode among hunter-gatherers is that it is due to a "natural" tendency to share found among peoples who have yet to develop the corrupting influences of private property. Yet this explanation seems dubious because it paints an unduly romantic picture of hunter-gatherers. The explanation is more likely to be found in the necessity of close forms of cooperation among the members of such groups. Hunter-gatherers intimately depend on one another for survival. While resources are typically not highly scarce in a general sense, they are notoriously subject to marked fluctuations in availability. Thus a man may encounter a long run of bad luck in hunting. If others do not give meat to him during this time, he must go without. They give meat to him because they know that they too will eventually have their turn with bad hunting luck, during which time they will expect to receive meat from him. Therefore to give regularly to others is to help ensure one's own well-being in the long run (Weissner, 1982; Cashdan, 1985). Generalized reciprocity is thus a special instance of the phenomenon we earlier identified as *enlightened self-interest*. There can be nothing surprising in the fact that hunters and gatherers show great disdain for the occasional individual who is competitive, selfish, and boastful. Such a person is a direct threat to the economic well-being of others and must be subjected to severe pressure to change his or her ways.

Pure Redistribution*

Another process whereby goods are circulated in precapitalist societies is known as **redistribution.** When redistribution occurs, products are funneled from individual households to a central source and then returned to those households in some sort of systematic manner. Redistribution differs from reciprocity in that redistribution is a more formalized process involving the movement of goods into the hands of some person or group that serves as the focal point for their reallocation.

Two types of redistribution may be identified: *pure* and *partial* (Moseley and

*This section owes much to M. Harris (1974: 111–130).

Wallerstein, 1978), sometimes called *egalitarian* and *stratified* (M. Harris, 1975). In **pure redistribution,** the redistributive process is complete in the sense that the redistributive agent reallocates all goods and keeps no extra portion for himself. Thus pure redistribution is associated with economic equality. In **partial redistribution,** the redistributive process is incomplete inasmuch as the redistributive agent keeps a portion of goods for himself. Thus partial redistribution is associated with economic inequality.

Pure redistributive economies, which are most commonly associated with small-scale horticulturalists, work somewhat differently from one society to another. One version of a redistributive economy is widespread among simple horticultural groups in Melanesia. These societies contain extremely ambitious men known as **big men.** Big men are individuals who seek prestige and renown through their roles as organizers of economic production. The typical aspiring big man begins his career by cultivating larger gardens and raising bigger pig herds. He does this by drawing on the help of close relatives and neighbors, who themselves have a stake in his success. If he is successful at his attempts to increase the productivity of his own gardens and herds, he will eventually have accumulated enough foodstuffs to hold a large feast, at which time these foodstuffs will be redistributed to other village members. Prestige and some renown fall upon him through the holding of a successful feast. But there are usually other individuals in his village with the same aspirations holding feasts of their own. If he is consistently able to hold larger feasts than those held by his competitors, he is generally recognized as the village big man and given considerable prestige. But should he falter at this task, his status is quickly lost, and he will be replaced by one of the competitors who has outdone him. Also, he is expected to be generous in his distribution of products and must place considerable emphasis on the welfare of the entire village. Big men who are not sufficiently generous and keep too much for themselves are frequently killed.

The quest for high status on the part of aspiring Melanesian big men has definite economic consequences. Such a quest strongly enhances economic productivity, leading to a general increase in the quantity of garden products, domesticated animals, fish, and other economic products (Oliver, 1955). The circulation of goods is also substantially increased, as feast preparation involves numerous exchanges of goods and services. In addition, there is typically a notable increase in the consumption of many goods by the members of the entire village (Oliver, 1955). The process of competitive feasting is, then, a vital part of the economic systems of Melanesian horticulturalists.

The Kaoka-speakers, a simple horticultural group in Melanesia, are characterized by a classic big-man redistributive system (Hogbin, 1964). The native expression for a leader of prestige and renown is *mwanekama*, which literally means "man-big." The natives generally agree that there is at any given time only one real big man to a village. He is usually a man over 40 years old who carries himself with assurance and dignity, lives in the most solidly built house, extends extraordinary hospitality, and is shown deference by the villagers.

To win the support of relatives and neighbors in order to launch a career toward bigmanship, a man must be forceful, even-tempered, tactful, industrious, and a good organizer. A man's ambition to pursue such a career usually becomes apparent in his early thirties. When a man intends to strive toward bigmanship, he begins by cultivating larger gardens, a task for which he enlists the aid of close relatives. He also attempts to increase the size of his pig herd. When in time his gardens are flourishing and he has

perhaps ten fat pigs and several smaller ones, the man makes it known that he wishes to build a new dwelling, one that is larger and better built than usual. This move is usually taken as a public declaration that he is a candidate for the highest honors of the village. The celebration to mark the end of the job, what the Kaoka-speakers call "the feast-to-remove-the-splinters," is highly elaborate.

One such feast was that of Atana, a man who was already notable but not as yet a rival to the acknowledged village big man. Toward this feast, Atana and his immediate kinsmen contributed 250 pounds of dried fish, 3000 yam cakes, 11 bowls of yam pudding, and 8 pigs. Other villagers attending the feast also brought along additional foodstuffs. When these were added to what was provided by Atana and his kinsmen, the final count was 300 pounds of fish, almost 5000 yam cakes, 19 bowls of pudding, and 13 pigs. It was then Atana's task to redistribute this food to all those who were in some way connected with the feast. By the time he was finished, he had made 257 separate presentations, and only the remnants were left for him. The Kaoka-speakers considered this to be the proper result. As they said, "The giver of the feast takes the bones and the stale cakes; the meat and the fat go to others."

Further progress toward village big-manship requires that there be more and bigger feasts. If a man can continue to do this, he is eventually likely to become the village big man. If he does succeed, however, he can never rest on his laurels. As soon as the size of his gardens and pig herds begins to shrink, he subsides into insignificance. He is always faced with competitors who are waiting to take his place should he be unable to maintain a sufficiently intense level of economic productivity.

What accounts for the evolution of such redistributive systems? Marvin Harris

(1974, 1977) argues that the big man is an *economic intensifier:* his role is to increase the level of production beyond what it would otherwise be. Harris believes that this increase in the level of production has adaptive significance for small-scale horticultural groups. As he explains (1974:118): "Under conditions where everyone has equal access to the means of subsistence, competitive feasting serves the practical function of preventing the labor force from falling back to levels of productivity that offer no margin of safety in crises such as war and crop failures."

Michael Harner (1975) offers a similar, yet slightly different, explanation. He theorizes that big-man systems are products of labor scarcity. Where people cultivate the land by simple horticultural methods, vast tracts of land are usually available, and it is labor, rather than land, that is a scarce resource. Under conditions of labor scarcity, the role of big man arises as the principal mechanism for the attainment of power and prestige. Thus Harner focuses on the evolution of the big-man system from the point of view of benefits to the individual, whereas Harris's explanation stresses the society-wide benefits of the big-man system. Nonetheless, their explanations appear complementary rather than contradictory; that is, in this particular situation, the individual's selfish interests and everyone's economic needs are simultaneously satisfied through the same social activities.

Given Harris's explanation of the big-man system, it is easy to see why big men are not found among hunter-gatherers. Big men in hunting and gathering societies would be economically maladaptive, for they would exploit the resources of nature beyond their natural recovery points and thus destroy the ecological and economic foundation of hunter-gatherer society (Harris, 1974). Thus, the very personalities that may be highly beneficial for many horticul-tural societies would produce disastrous consequences for hunter-gatherers.

Partial Redistribution

Partial redistributive systems are most commonly found in societies in which intensive horticulture is the technological mode and chiefly ownership the prevailing mode of property rights. Chiefly ownership is a vital aspect of partial redistribution.

Marshall Sahlins (1963) highlights the important differences between pure and partial redistribution by comparing the distributional systems of Melanesian and Polynesian societies. As he notes, most Melanesian societies have had small-scale horticulture and big-man systems, whereas most Polynesian societies have been characterized by more intensive horticulture and partial redistribution.

Melanesian big men are persons who *seek prestige and renown* through the holding of elaborate feasts. They have little real power over their constituents, however, and their prestige and renown quickly disappear when their elaborate feast-giving declines. By contrast, Polynesian chiefs are *installed in office* through a system of hereditary succession. These chiefs exercise considerable power over their followers, and they hold substantial economic leverage over the large mass of ordinary folk. One of their primary aims is the production and maintenance of a constant economic surplus. They accomplish this by compelling the people to give up a portion of their harvests. This leads to the formation of a "public treasury," a great storehouse over which the chief exercises control. The uses to which this storehouse is put are many. Chiefs support themselves and their families from it. They also use it for providing lavish entertainment for visiting dignitaries, initiating major public projects such as irrigation works, building temples, sponsoring military campaigns, and supporting a vast range of political functionaries and administrative officials. In addition, portions of the storehouse are redistributed to the people as the need arises, and chiefs are expected to be generous with it. Those who are not sufficiently generous or who make excessive demands on the people's harvests are sometimes put to death.

Polynesian partial redistributive systems are redistributive in the sense that they involve a continual flow of goods between the chiefs and the people. In this case, however, the flow of goods is an unequal flow: the people clearly give more than they receive in return. While clearly similar in principle to the pure redistributive systems of small-scale horticulturalists, these intensified redistributive systems of more advanced horticulturalists are different in that they serve to promote a system of economic inequality. As such, they constitute a notable evolutionary development beyond the pure redistributive level.

Michael Harner (1975) has suggested that the key factor behind this significant evolutionary outcome is land scarcity. When population pressure forces small-scale horticultural groups to adopt more intensive methods of cultivation, it is clear that land is becoming a scarce resource. Indeed, that is precisely why each particular unit of land must be cultivated more intensively. Land scarcity, in Harner's view, results in increased competition over valuable land, and some persons end up with greater access to land than others. Former big men, with a relatively weak power base resting on their own efforts and the voluntary assistance of their followers, turn into chiefs, persons whose power base is made much stronger by their control over land.

Surplus Expropriation and Exploitation

Surplus expropriation is a distributive mode most generally found in agrarian societies organized in terms of a seigneurial system of property rights. It occurs when a class of landlords compels another class of dependent economic producers to produce a surplus from their fields and hand this surplus over to them. The surplus is handed over in the form of rent, taxation of various sorts, and various types of labor services.

Some students of precapitalist economies, notably the economic historian Karl Polanyi (1957), do not distinguish between expropriation and partial redistribution. Instead, they use the concept of redistribution to cover both types of economic activity. Yet this seems a serious mistake and at the very least highly misleading. There are several crucial differences between expropriation and partial redistribution, two worth noting here. First, landlords have considerably greater power than chiefs, and they use this power to place many more economic burdens upon peasant producers than chiefs are capable of placing on their followers. Second, the flow of goods and services between peasants and lords is substantially more unequal than is the flow of valuables between chiefs and commoners. The flow of valuables between peasants and lords can scarcely be described as redistribution, since there is little counterflow from lords to peasants; indeed, the flow of valuables is largely in one direction only: from peasants to lords. Although there may be in some situations a fine line between partial redistribution and expropriation, in most cases it is not difficult to tell whether redistribution or expropriation is operating within a society.

Under medieval European feudalism, surplus expropriation was the dominant distributive mode. Peasants owed landlords a specified rent for the use of the landlord's land that they paid either as a portion of their harvests (rent in kind), or by money (cash rent), or some combination of the two. In the earlier days of the feudal period, rent in kind was the standard form of rent payment; but as the feudal system evolved in the later Middle Ages, cash rent began to replace rent in kind. Since the peasant was thus producing both for himself and for his landlord, he had to increase his own toil as well as that of his family in order to meet these economic demands placed upon him. Peasants also had economic burdens in the form of taxes. For instance, peasants had to pay a tax to grind their grain in the lord's mill, another tax to bake their bread in the lord's oven, and yet another to fish in the lord's fishpond. (Since peasants did not own these resources, they fell into this sort of dependence on their lords.) A third type of economic burden placed on medieval European peasants was that of labor services. Peasants were required to spend so many days working on the lord's demesne (his home farm, or personal land on which he, and not his peasants, lived), tilling the soil and tending the animal herds. This burden often became very oppressive and left the peasant little time to provide for his own family's subsistence by working his own lands.

In ancient Rome a vast system of surplus expropriation also existed, but this system rested primarily on slave rather than peasant labor. The huge supply of slaves on which Rome relied was acquired by political conquest of foreign lands. Slave labor was much cheaper than peasant labor and therefore was the principal labor mode in Roman society (Cameron, 1973). There were many great Roman estates that had large slave gangs working on them; Pliny, for instance, mentions one estate that had 4117 slaves (Cameron, 1973). Where slavery rather than serfdom is the principal labor mode, the system of surplus expropriation is more direct and obvious. For example, to calculate their economic gain, the Roman landowners simply had to determine the amount of wealth their slaves produced for them and subtract from this the cost of acquiring and maintaining a slave labor force.

Many scholars have applied the term **exploitation** to the relationships between lords and peasants, masters and slaves, and, to some extent, chiefs and commoners. At the same time, others have objected to the use of this term. George Dalton (1974), for instance, has argued that the term is a highly prejudicial and emotion-ridden one that is used by those who do not like a particular economic system simply to condemn it. Since Dalton believes that the term is used merely to register disapproval rather than to engage in scientific analysis, he recommends that it be dropped from the vocabulary of social scientists. Dalton does suggest, however, that if the term is to be used, then it should be made to depend upon people's subjective judgments of whether or not exploitation is taking place—that is, of whether or not they themselves are being exploited. Dalton thus believes that objective definitions and calculations of exploitation are not possible and that exploitation can only be said to exist if people think it does. In other words, if a peasant does not *feel* exploited by his lord, then he isn't.

Dalton's wholly subjective approach to the problem of exploitation is unacceptable. Saying that exploitation does not exist when people do not feel exploited is very much like saying that people are not suffering from heart disease if they think they aren't. Like heart disease, exploitation is an objective phenomenon, and hence must be conceptualized and measured by objective criteria, not by people's subjective thoughts and feelings (Moore, 1966; Zeitlin, 1973).

The following objective definition of exploitation is offered here: *Exploitation exists when one party is compelled to give to another party more than it receives in return.* Two aspects of this definition must be emphasized. First, exploitation obviously occurs only when two parties to a relationship receive unequal benefits as the result of that relationship. Second, the unequal benefits must occur because one of the parties is being compelled to give or do something. That is, one party does not voluntarily enter the relationship, or, if there is voluntary entrance into the relationship, it is because alternative relationships would produce no improvement in that party's economic situation.

This definition of exploitation is somewhat easier to state, unfortunately, than to apply. Nonetheless, it can be applied with reasonable success. Dalton (1972) suggests that no objective assessment of the fairness of the flow and counterflow of goods and services between lord and peasant can be made. But this viewpoint seems unduly pessimistic. While it is perhaps difficult to do, it is by no means impossible. The products and services that peasants give to lords have already been noted. What do lords give in return to peasants? As Dalton (1972) himself mentions, they offer military protection against invaders, police protection against robbery, juridical services to settle disputes, feasts at special holidays, food on days when peasants work on the lord's demesne, and emergency food provisions. Dalton argues that there is no way to tell whether or not this set of exchanges is fair or unfair, exploitative or nonexploitative, except by appealing to the thoughts and feelings of the peasants.

But what is the one resource that lords never give to peasants? As Marvin Harris (1980) points out, it is the free and unrestricted use of land. Were they to do this, the relationship between lord and peasant would not be economically unbalanced, for peasants would then have no obligations to provide rent, taxes, and services to lords and undoubtedly would not do so. The economic situation of peasants would thus improve, while that of lords would deteriorate. In other words, even though lords provide valuable goods and services to peasants, they do not provide unrestricted access to the resource that is of greatest value in agrarian societies. Thus, it seems fair to conclude that peasants receive unequal benefits as the result of their relationship with lords, that they do so under a particular type of compulsion, and that they enter the relationship involuntarily or because alternatives are no more (and quite possibly less) attractive. It therefore seems reasonable to conclude that peasants are exploited by landlords.

Are, then, commoners exploited as well by chiefs? Probably they are, at least to some degree, although it appears that the level of exploitation is substantially less than in the landlord-peasant relationship. In fact, it seems fair to suggest that the very beginnings of exploitation, in an evolutionary sense, are to be found in intensive horticultural societies with chiefly modes of ownership and partial redistributive systems. Big-man and other pure redistributive systems, as well as systems of balanced and generalized reciprocity, are notable for their lack of any genuinely exploitative elements. In fact, these appear to be the only types of economic systems in which exploitation does not appear as a structured part of everyday social life.[*]

THE EMERGENCE OF ECONOMIC MARKETS

That economic institution known as the **market** exists when people offer goods and services for sale to others in some more or less systematic and organized way. It is important to distinguish between the terms *market* and *marketplace.* A **marketplace** is a physical site where goods and services are brought for sale and where buyers assemble to purchase these goods and services. In precapitalist societies, marketplaces are physical sites found at a small number of designated locations within the society. But in modern capitalism, the marketplace is "diffuse," that is, spread pervasively throughout society. The market, by contrast, is not a

---

[*]In later chapters we shall inquire as to whether modern capitalist and socialist economies operate according to exploitative principles.

physical place but a social institution, or a set of social relationships organized around the process of buying and selling valuables.

Societies in Relation to the Market

Paul Bohannan and George Dalton (1962) have distinguished three kinds of societies with respect to their relationship to the market: marketless societies, peripheral market societies, and market-dominated societies.

Marketless societies have neither markets nor marketplaces. Although there may be a few economic transactions based on buying and selling, these are casual and few and far between. Since marketless societies have no markets, subsistence is not provided by market principles, but by the mechanisms of reciprocity or redistribution. The !Kung, the Kaoka-speakers, and the Yanomama are marketless societies, as are indeed the vast majority of hunter-gatherer and horticultural groups.

Peripheral market societies have marketplaces but market principles clearly do not serve to organize economic life. In such societies, people may frequently be involved in marketplace activity, either as buyers or sellers, but this activity is a very secondary economic phenomenon. People do not receive their subsistence through marketplace activities, but through reciprocity, redistribution, and expropriation. In peripheral market societies, "most people are not engaged in producing for the market or selling in the market, or those who are so engaged are only part-time marketers" (Bohannan and Dalton, 1962:7).

Peripheral markets are found quite frequently among intensive horticulturalists, and almost universally in agrarian societies. The Aztecs, highly intensive horticulturalists who dominated Mexico during the fifteenth and sixteenth centuries, had peripheral markets of considerable scope and significance (Beals and Hoijer, 1971). In each

city throughout the Aztec empire there existed large markets, and these markets were connected to each other and to the Aztec capital city of Tenochtitlán by a system of traveling merchants known as *pochtecah* (Hassig, 1985). A huge market located in a suburb of Tenochtitlán took place every fifth day. Potential buyers came to this market from miles around to buy the many and varied goods that were offered in it: gold, silver, jewels, clothing, chocolate, tobacco, hides, footwear, slaves, fruits and vegetables, salt, honey, tools, pottery, household furnishings, and many other items.

Peripheral markets were also significant in medieval Europe (Heilbroner, 1985). Markets in the small cities of medieval Europe were places where peasants would bring some of their harvests for sale. Merchants and artisans who lived in these cities, however, were more important to the life of the marketplace. These merchants and artisans manufactured goods to be sold in the markets and made their livings from such sale. Medieval Europe also had a special kind of marketplace activity known as a *fair*, which flourished in the thirteenth and fourteenth centuries (Abu-Lughod, 1989). This was a type of traveling market, held usually once a year, to which merchants from all over Europe came to sell their products. The fair combined social holiday, religious festival, and intense economic activity. At some of these fairs, merchants brought a considerable variety of products for sale, such as silks, horses, drugs, spices, books and parchments, and many other items (Heilbroner, 1985).

Market-dominated societies have both markets and marketplaces (i.e., "diffuse" marketplaces), and the market principle— the principle of buying and selling goods according to the forces of supply and demand—governs all important decisions concerning production, distribution, and exchange. In these societies, various types of reciprocity and redistribution may be found, but they are of very minor significance indeed. The only genuine market-dominated societies are those characterized by modern capitalism. Since we shall examine market-dominated societies in detail later in this book, the rest of the discussion in this section of the chapter concerns peripheral market societies. Our focus is on the kind of highly developed peripheral market activity characteristic of most agrarian societies and typically located in cities.

Aspects of the Market in Precapitalist Societies

Manufacturing and the Guilds In precapitalist societies in which manufacturing occurs as a substantial economic activity, it is usually a small-scale undertaking, generally confined to the homes of artisans or to a few small shops located in the marketplaces (Sjoberg, 1960). Even the largest workshops in precapitalist societies would be quite small by modern standards of manufacturing. With no mass market for goods, and thus strict limits upon the formation of capital, productive units must necessarily remain small.

Precapitalist forms of specialization occur relative to the product rather than the production process. Each craftsman fashions an entire product himself, from beginning to end. As Gideon Sjoberg notes: "Specialization in product is often carried to the point that the craftsman devotes his full time to producing items made from a particular raw material; thus we have goldsmiths, coppersmiths, silversmiths, silk weavers, wool weavers, and so on, each with their own guild" (1960:197). In addition, the precapitalist craftsman typically functions as his own merchant in selling the final product.

In virtually all large-scale precapitalist societies with significant manufacturing sectors, craftsmen and merchants are organized into work organizations known as *guilds.* Guilds are specialized by occupa-

tion; they include as their members all persons who perform the same occupation or highly specialized branch of an occupation. Sjoberg (1960), for instance, lists the following guilds in just one precapitalist city, Beijing in the 1920s: carpenters (Sacred Lu Pan Society), shoe fasteners (Sewers of Boots and Shoes Guild, or Double Thread Guild), tinkers (Clever Stove Guild), clock stores (The Clock Watch Commercial Guild Association), leather stores (Five Sages Hide and Skins Guild), vegetable merchants (Green or Fresh Vegetable Guild), barbers (Beautify the Face Guild), and waiters (Tea Guild).

The most important function of guilds is creating and maintaining a monopoly over a specific type of economic activity: "The right to pursue almost any occupation concerned with manufacturing or trade, or even services, is possible only through membership in the guild that controls it" (Sjoberg, 1960:190). In exercising their monopolistic control over occupations, guilds engage in a variety of activities. As Sjoberg points out, they determine the selection of personnel for an occupation; train members for their work, usually through a master-apprentice relationship; set standards of workmanship for their members; control the output generated by their members; protect their members from excessive restrictions that might be placed upon them by governmental or religious bodies; and assist their members in establishing shops or purchasing the raw materials they need to complete their work.

Clearly guilds play a crucial role in the lives of precapitalist craftsmen and merchants. Indeed, they are roughly comparable in their basic aims to our modern-day labor unions and business and professional organizations.

Price Determination in Precapitalist Markets In modern capitalism, prices for goods and services are determined by abstract supply and demand forces. Individuals may expect to go into stores and find fixed prices already attached to items. Prices in precapitalist settings, however, are usually not established in this way, but are set by what is called *haggling*. Haggling occurs when a potential purchaser asks a merchant how much he wants for an item, the merchant replies, and then the purchaser offers a counterprice, which is usually much lower than that mentioned by the merchant. The seller and buyer then negotiate (haggle over) the price until eventually an agreement is reached or the buyer leaves in disgust. Sjoberg adds the following about the haggling process (1960:205):

> In the process the verbal duel may wax violent. Usually the customer belittles the item in question and tries to evince little interest in purchasing it, while the seller uses counterarguments to persuade the customer to buy it at the asking price. Occasionally friends, even strangers, will join in, interposing remarks as to the probable worth of the article. Not only does the skill of the participants enter into the final figure, but the relationship of the buyer to the seller is a decisive factor. Friends are likely to obtain goods at favored prices.

Haggling is the typical mode of price determination in societies where mass markets do not exist and thus where sellers and buyers have little "knowledge of the market" for any given item. In addition, since haggling can take up large amounts of time, time must not be a valuable and scarce resource, as it is in modern capitalism. Therefore, haggling can only occur in settings in which people are seldom in a hurry to accomplish their everyday tasks (Sjoberg, 1960).

Nonrationality of Economic Activity

Modern capitalism is a supremely rational type of economic system in the sense that there are a variety of sophisticated techniques used in the conduct of business— techniques designed to maximize economic productivity and growth. Thus, modern capitalists use advanced forms of accounting, finance, workplace organization, and marketing in the conduct of their business activity, and these procedures are crucial to their success.

In precapitalist markets, however, such a rational organization of economic activity is typically absent (Sjoberg, 1960). This nonrationality (not to be confused with "irrationality") of economic activity is expressed in numerous ways. For one thing, artisans and merchants commonly do not adhere to fixed work schedules closely regulated by the clock. On the contrary, they often start work at different hours in the morning and stop work at different times later in the day, according to the nature of other noneconomic activities in which they are engaged. In addition, precapitalist manufacturing is normally characterized by little synchronization of effort. Workers in one sector of manufacturing have little knowledge of what is happening in other sectors, and they make little if any effort to coordinate their activities with the activities being undertaken in these other sectors. Finally, the marketing of goods in precapitalist societies is generally subject to little standardization. For example, merchants seldom grade or sort their products, and there is little standardization of weights and measures. As Sjoberg notes, this lack of standardization is linked to the absence of a mass market and thus to the highly personalized nature of market activity.

Some Qualifications: Precapitalist Commercialism and Its Growth

Although these views about the role of the market in human societies have been widely accepted by comparative social scientists, in recent years some social scientists have strongly challenged them. Kajsa Ekholm and Jonathan Friedman (1982), for example, have suggested that market activities and production-for-exchange have played a much greater role in earlier societies than has generally been recognized. They oppose the traditional division of "the world's history into distinctive market/nonmarket or capitalist/pre-capitalist systems," and maintain the "point of view that there exists a form of 'capitalism' in the ancient world" (1982:87–88). In other words, Ekholm and Friedman object to the very conceptualization of peripheral market societies, or at least claim that this conceptual category does not apply as broadly as ordinarily thought.

Ekholm and Friedman do not claim that there are no differences between ancient societies and modern capitalism; they argue simply that the differences are less great than we have been taught to believe. Other scholars go even further. Barry Gills and Andre Gunder Frank (1992), for example, suggest that there has been extensive commercial activity in many agrarian societies over the last 5000 years, and that the shift to modern capitalism in the sixteenth century was less radical than is usually thought. They believe that the extent of markets and commercialism over the last few millennia has been greatly underestimated. Gills and Frank rely on studies of precapitalist markets by such social scientists as Morris Silver (1985), Philip Kohl (1978, 1989), and Joan Oates (1978). These scholars show that in ancient agrarian societies there frequently existed large-scale markets, including price-setting markets regulated by supply and demand; private warehouses stocked with goods; merchant middlemen; extensive investment in capital goods; large-scale trade networks; strong profit motives; and the accumulation of capital. Indeed, some societies—the Phoenicians of the late second and early first millennium B.C., for example, or the Italian city-states of the thirteenth and fourteenth centuries A.D.—were highly specialized for trade and overwhelmingly dependent on it.

Gills and Frank make an extremely important point, and it has become increasingly clear in recent years that the traditional view of the limited significance of markets in the precapitalist world must be strongly qualified. Production-for-use clearly dominated in precapitalist societies, but in many of them, especially the more advanced agrarian ones, production-for-exchange played an important role. Indeed, I would argue that since about 5000 B.P. there has been an important process of *expanding world commercialization* (Sanderson, 1994b). The existence of such a process is indicated by growth in the size and density of trade networks, as well as by increases in the number of large cities and the size of these cities. In the first few centuries after 5000 B.P. most trade networks were relatively small and a limited quantity of goods passed through them. Trade networks were either local or, at best, regional in scope. By about 2200 B.P.—in the early beginnings of the ancient Roman world— there had emerged a large-scale trade network stretching all the way from China through the Middle East to Mediterranean Europe (Curtin, 1984). This was a trade network obviously spread over a large portion of the world, and a much greater quantity of goods passed through this network than anything seen in the local or regional trade networks of earlier times. By about A.D. 1000 trade networks had become even more extensive and with a still greater volume of trade (McNeill, 1982; Wilkinson, 1992). The growth of cities tells the same story. In 4250 B.P. there were only 8 cities in the world with populations greater than 30,000, but by 2430 B.P. there were 51 cities of this size, together totalling 2,877,000 in population. After a decline in cities following the fall of Rome, the process of urbanization accelerated once again. By A.D. 1000 there were 70 cities having populations between 40,000 and 450,000 (totalling 5,629,000), and by A.D. 1500 there were over 75 cities with populations between 45,000 and 672,000 (totalling 7,454,000) (Wilkinson 1992, 1993).

It is clear, then, that the traditional view of precapitalist market and commercial behavior cannot stand unchallenged. Commercialism was frequently of considerable importance in the precapitalist world, and it grew steadily in importance over a period of some 4500 years. Moreover, as we shall see in Chapter 7, the growth of world commercialization had major implications, for it contributed decisively to the massive takeoff into modern capitalism that began in sixteenth-century Europe. Indeed, without acknowledging this long-term process of world commercial expansion, it is not possible to explain the emergence of the modern capitalist world.

SUMMARY

1. All societies have economies, or means of organizing the production, distribution, and exchange of goods and services. Two fundamentally different types of economic activity are production-for-use and production-for-exchange. Although both forms of economic activity are found in precapitalist societies, production-for-use is clearly dominant. In modern capitalism, though, production-for-exchange overwhelmingly displaces production-for-use.

2. Several modes of resource ownership can be distinguished in precapitalist societies and viewed from an evolutionary perspective. In hunting and gathering societies, primitive communism predominates. In most simple horticultural societies, a communal pattern of ownership prevails, but ownership is restricted to the members of particular kinship groups (lineage ownership). The beginnings of private property are found with the emergence of chiefly ownership in more advanced horticultural societies. In agrarian societies a highly restrictive form of ownership known as seigneurial ownership prevails. Here a tiny class of landlords claims ownership of land and imposes various penalties on the huge class of peasants who must have access to this land. There is a clear trend toward the evolution of increasingly private and restrictive modes of ownership.

3. Generalized reciprocity is a mode of resource distribution in which individuals give to others without any expectation of equivalent or immediate repayment. This form of behavior is characterized by strong demands for generosity, cooperation, and hospitality. Generalized reciprocity is at the center of the economic behavior of most hunter-gatherers.

4. Horticultural societies commonly emphasize redistributive modes of resource allocation. Pure redistribution prevails when individuals such as "big men" return to everyone the goods they have accumulated. Partial redistribution exists in more advanced horticultural societies and generally involves the activities of more powerful political leaders who redistribute only a portion of what they accumulate.

5. Surplus expropriation exists in agrarian societies. Here the powerful owners of the land compel those who cultivate it to produce large economic surpluses and turn them over to the owners.

6. Economic exploitation exists when one party compels another party to give up more than it receives in return. Exploitation should be seen as an objective phenomenon, not as something subjectively dependent on people's feelings about their situation. Where reciprocity and pure redistribution prevail, exploitation does not exist. Exploitation exists to some extent where partial redistributive systems are found, and it is a fundamental feature of economic life in agrarian societies with their seigneurial ownership and surplus expropriation.

7. Markets exist in many precapitalist societies, but they do not dominate economic

Table 5.1   OWNERSHIP, DISTRIBUTION, AND EXCHANGE IN PRECAPITALIST SOCIETIES

Mode of Subsistence Technology	Mode of Ownership	Mode of Distribution	Mode of Exchange
Hunting and gathering	Normally, primitive communism. The vital resources that sustain life are owned by the entire community, and no person may deprive others of the full right to use these resources.	Generalized reciprocity. Sharing and generosity are pervasive and are compulsory social habits.	Although some exchange does occur, markets and marketplaces are generally absent.
Simple horticulture	Typically, lineage ownership. This is a variation on primitive communism in which resources are communally owned, but the owning group is a kinship group rather than the entire community.	Pure or egalitarian redistribution. Goods are funeled into the hands of a leader, who is responsible for reallocating them to the entire community in an essentially egalitarian fashion.	Again, marketless societies, as above.
Intensive horticulture	Usually chiefly ownership. Powerful chiefs claim ownership of vast tracts of land and exert considerable control over how this land is used. However, the primary producers who live on the land retain substantial decision-making power over the day-to-day cultivation activities.	Partial or stratified redistribution. Goods are funeled into the hands of a centralized social group, but this group retains a large portion of these goods for its own subsistence and for building and maintaining a governmental administrative apparatus. Some reallocation, though, does occur.	Peripheral market societies. Markets exist and may have considerable importance, but are distinctly secondary to production-for-use activities.
Agrarianism	Typically, some type of seigneurial ownership. Land is owned and controlled by a private class of landlords, or by a powerful governmental apparatus functioning in the role of landlord. Landlords exert enomous power over the primary producers (peasants) who cultivate the land, and impose severe penalties on them for the use of this land.	Surplus expropriation. A highly imbalanced and exploitative relationship exists between landlords and the primary producers. Landlords extract surplus through rent, taxation, demands for labor services, and other mechanisms.	Peripheral market societies, but with greater importance of market activities. In some cases—for example, in ancient Rome—market exchange becomes very important. Exchange activities are often strongly promoted by elaborate intersocietal networks of trade. Throughout the agrarian era commercial and market activity becomes increasingly important over time; trade networks grow in size and density and cities grow and proliferate.

activity, most of which is still based on production-for-use. Precapitalist market activity is normally organized in ways different from the elaborate market economy of modern capitalism. The extraordinary "rationality" of modern capitalism is usually absent from precapitalist economic systems. Nonetheless, in some precapitalist societies and at certain historical periods substantial market behavior did exist and was inserted into networks of intersocietal and interregional trade. Commercialism was more important in precapitalist societies than normally thought, and the level of commercialism increased steadily throughout the several millennia of the agrarian epoch.

SPECIAL TOPIC: THE POTLATCH

The Northwest Coast of North America, an area that stretches from northern California to northern British Columbia, has in recent centuries been populated by Indian tribes who practiced a fascinating and seemingly bizarre custom known as the **potlatch**. The potlatch, which reached its highest level of development among the tribe known as the Kwakiutl, was an elaborate give-away feast held by village chiefs as a means of validating and reinforcing their high social and political status. The highest status went to those chiefs who could give away the most property and by doing so compel other chiefs to give away their property too.

A potlatch worked more or less in the following manner. The chief of one group would announce that he was holding a potlatch and publicly invite another chief and his followers weeks in advance of the big occasion. Elaborate preparations would then be made for the potlatch. The host chief would assemble a vast array of valuables, including fish, fish oil, berries, animal skins, blankets, and many other valuables (M. Harris, 1974). At the appointed time the visiting group would arrive, and serious feasting would begin. When the feasting itself had concluded, the host chief would begin the process of presenting gifts to the visitors. The more gifts he was able to bestow upon them, in the viewpoint of the Northwest Coast tribes, the greater he was and the more honor and respect he deserved. As the host chief gave away his valuables, he would sing and chant about his greatness. Ruth Benedict records the following speech made by a Kwakiutl chief (1934:191):

> I am the first of the tribes,
> I am the only one of the tribes.
> The chiefs of the tribes are only local chiefs.
> I am the only one among the tribes.
> I search among all the invited chiefs for greatness like mine.
> I cannot find one chief among the guests.
> They never return feasts,
> The orphans, poor people, chiefs of the tribes!
> They disgrace themselves,
> I am he who gives these sea otters to the chiefs, the guests, the chiefs of the tribes.
> I am he who gives canoes to the chiefs, the guests, the chiefs of the tribes.

The most successful potlatches were those in which a chief would give away all his property and, to demonstrate his true greatness, pour oil on his house and burn it to the ground. Thus the potlatch sometimes reached extreme and bizarre proportions. The successful potlatch not only brought greatness to the host chief, but it heaped shame upon the visiting chiefs unless they were able to reply with even greater potlatches of their own. Thus chiefs to whom much property had been given were highly motivated to organize future potlatches, at which time they could banish their shame and reassert their own greatness.

The potlatch has been the subject of considerable theoretical work attempting to make sense of it. A popular early theory was the ecological functionalist interpretation of Stuart Piddocke (1965). The Northwest Coast tribes lived amidst great material abundance due to the extraordinarily productive nature of their environments. Although possessing only a hunting and gathering technology, these tribes were able to support large populations because of their bounteous environments. However, as Piddocke points out, this picture of material abundance on the Northwest Coast can be somewhat misleading. Despite resource abundance, there was sharp regional variation and seasonal fluctuation in both plants and animals. Because of sharp seasonal fluctuations, at times some areas would have more than they needed, whereas others would suffer from considerable resource scarcity. Piddocke (1965:247) reports that the abundance "was great enough to support a population larger than the usual size reported for hunting and gathering societies; but this population lived sufficiently close to the margins of subsistence so that variations in productivity which fell below normal could threaten parts of the population with famine and death from starvation."

On the basis of these considerations, Piddocke's theory is that the potlatch system arose as a specialized type of redistributional mechanism designed to even out sharp variations in resources, and thus contribute to the survival and well-being of entire groups. Piddocke holds that without considerable distribution of food from better-off groups to poorer ones, the poorer groups might often have died from starvation. The potlatch was, to Piddocke's mind, a unique type of pure redistribution designed to level out resource variation over wide areas.

However, in recent years it has been shown that the potlatch's role in the movement of resources from place to place was limited (Kelly, 1995). As a result, a number of investigators have turned away from this sort of functionalist interpretation in favor of more conflict-oriented analyses. The potlatch may have been simply a matter of individuals striving for power and prestige in an environment with bountiful resources. Robert Kelly has given this type of argument a sociobiological twist. As he puts it (1995:327–328), "An evolutionary model would suggest that high-ranking individuals stood to enhance their fitness by participating in prestige competition, acquiring greater utility from the social relationships and prestige they gained than from the resources they gave away to get prestige, whereas commoners stood to gain more by assisting than by not assisting high-ranking individuals."

It might still be wondered, though, why the potlatch reached the kind of bizarre proportions seldom found in other systems of status competition, such as chiefs burning down their own houses. This may have been due to the intrusions of Western civilization, in particular its pouring of great wealth into the Northwest Coast economy. Peter Farb explains further (1978:158):

> It must be remembered . . . that the potlatches observed in the nineteenth century were outlandish exaggerations of the indigenous tradition, the result of contacts with Whites. The Whites, in their scramble to obtain sea-otter and fur-seal pelts, pumped vast amounts of fresh wealth into the Northwest Coast societies. The potlatch simply could not handle the sudden flood of mass-produced fabrics, guns, kitchen utensils, metal tools, cheap jewelry, and other products of industrialized Europe and the United States. So one cause for the explosion of the potlatch was a deluge of White wealth.

Another cause of the explosive growth of the aboriginal potlatch could have been the severe depopulation of the Northwest Coast tribes resulting from European-induced diseases and warfare. As Farb notes, the numerous deaths opened up far more noble titles than there were high-ranking individuals to hold them. This created widespread competition among the tribesmen to rise to these positions of high rank, and the potlatches were highly exaggerated as a result.

It thus appears that the Northwest Coast potlatch was a very unusual form of partial redistribution occurring under an unusual combination of circumstances. Rather than appearing as some sort of inexplicable phenomenon, as it has to many, it seems to have been an exaggerated version of a mundane phenomenon rooted in individuals' drives for status competition.

FOR FURTHER READING

Chaudhuri, K. N. *Trade and Civilisation in the Indian Ocean.* Cambridge: Cambridge University Press, 1985. An excellent discussion of commercialism and trade in the Indian Ocean between the seventh and eighteenth centuries.

Curtin, Philip D. *Cross-Cultural Trade in World History.* New York: Cambridge University Press, 1984. Perhaps the definitive work on large-scale intersocietal trade throughout history.

Dalton, George. *Tribal and Peasant Economies.* Austin: University of Texas Press, 1967. A well-known collection of previously published articles and essays on numerous aspects of precapitalist economic life. Discussions of, among other things, primitive money, chiefly forms of landownership, trade, the manorial economy of medieval Europe, and varieties of peasantry.

Harris, Marvin. *Cows, Pigs, Wars, and Witches: The Riddles of Culture.* New York: Random House, 1974. The chapter entitled "Potlatch" contains not only an analysis of that phenomenon but also a general analysis of reciprocity and redistribution in primitive societies.

Harris, Marvin. *Cannibals and Kings: The Origins of Cultures.* New York: Random House, 1977. Additional discussions of redistribution, plus discussions of the evolution of economic systems from pure redistribution to expropriation.

Hodges, Richard. *Primitive and Peasant Markets.* Oxford: Blackwell, 1988. A recent work on market exchange in precapitalist societies.

Lee, Richard B. *The !Kung San: Men, Women, and Work in a Foraging Society.* New York: Cambridge University Press, 1979. A detailed analysis of the best-known of all contemporary hunter-gatherer societies, with a major focus on economic life. Considerable attention is given to technology, the work roles of men and women, ownership patterns, and recent economic changes resulting from increasing contact with more advanced societies.

Plattner, Stuart (ed.). *Economic Anthropology.* Stanford, Calif.: Stanford University Press, 1989. A recent textbook that explores economic behavior throughout the whole range of precapitalist societies.

Popkin, Samuel L. *The Rational Peasant.* Berkeley: University of California Press, 1979. A well-known study of the rational basis of peasant economic life.

Sahlins, Marshall. *Stone Age Economics.* Chicago: Aldine, 1972. A well-known work on precapitalist economic systems written from a perspective different in important respects from that of the present book.

Chapter
6

The Origin and Evolution of Social Stratification

This chapter begins the discussion of social stratification, a phenomenon of central concern to sociologists, comparative macrosociologists especially. It explores the way in which social stratification originates and is intensified in human societies, and examines the nature of stratification (or its absence) in hunter-gatherer, horticultural, and agrarian societies. The principal theories offered to account for the origin and evolution of stratification are compared and contrasted and their general explanatory power is assessed. The extremely important issue of the nature of stratification in industrialized societies is postponed until Chapter 10.

THE NATURE OF SOCIAL STRATIFICATION

An important distinction must be drawn between the concepts of **social inequality** and **social stratification.** Failure to make this crucial distinction has led to much confusion among sociologists as to whether social stratification is actually a universal feature of social life.

Social inequality refers to *the existence of differential degrees of social influence or prestige among individual members of the same society.* There are two important facets of this definition. First, social inequality refers only to distinctions between individuals in terms of **social influence**—the degree to which the actions of an individual will be followed or copied by others; or **prestige**—the degree to which an individual is accorded honor or respect. Thus, inequality *does not refer to differential degrees of power and wealth.* Inequality can and does exist in human societies without any differential access of individuals or groups to wealth or to the resources of nature that sustain life. Second, social inequality implies *an inequality between individuals, not between discrete groups.* Where only inequality prevails, individual persons attain differential social standing, but they do so only as individuals, not as members of groups. Indeed, the fact of mere inequality implies the absence of distinct groups that are differentially ranked. Thus conceived, social inequality is a universal feature of human societies, for there is no record of a society that fails to make at least some evaluative distinctions between some individuals.

In contrast to social inequality, social stratification involves *the existence within a single society of two or more differentially ranked groups, the members of which control unequal amounts of power, privilege, and prestige.* This definition of stratification closely follows the conception of stratified society developed by the anthropologist Morton Fried. As Fried notes, "A stratified society is one in which members of the same sex and equivalent age status do not have equal access to the basic resources that sustain life" (1967:186). The key notion contained in Fried's definition is **differential access to resources.** This clearly goes beyond the fact of simple inequalities in influence or respect and into the realm of fundamental inequities in **power** and **privilege.** Power involves the capacity of some persons to command the actions of others, even against their will and despite their resistance. Privilege refers to wealth and other material benefits and opportunities. Differences in prestige also are a part of stratification systems, and it is usually the case that in stratified societies inequalities of prestige derive from inequalities of power and privilege.

Another crucial characteristic of stratification is that *it involves not individuals, but groups.* The degree of power, privilege, and prestige that individuals have in stratified society depends on their membership in actual social groups, not on their personal characteristics. These differentially ranked groups constitute **social strata** (singular = **stratum**), or layers of the overall sociocultural system, and they have a strongly hereditary character. Hence in stratified societies individuals are born into a particular social stratum that gives them a social position and identity regardless of their own personal characteristics. This hereditary quality of stratification clearly sets it apart from inequality. In unstratified societies, the inequalities that emerge (beyond those based on age and sex) are due mainly to individual effort and ability, rather than to hereditary social placement.

Stratification is by no means a universal characteristic of human societies. While there is no such thing as a society in which all persons are perfectly equal, there have been many societies lacking stratification. Stratification tends to be found for the first time among those societies that have evolved to an intensive horticultural level of technological development (although it is occasionally found below this evolutionary stage). Yet despite the fact that stratification has not been universal, it has been a common feature of many societies, and it is indeed universal among all complex societies.

SOCIAL STRATIFICATION IN EVOLUTIONARY PERSPECTIVE

A brief synopsis of the evolution of stratification in preindustrial societies is presented in Table 6.1. This synopsis may be useful in approaching the discussions that follow.

Inequality without Stratification: Hunting and Gathering Societies

Generally speaking, hunting and gathering societies are unstratified. Their economies are characterized by generalized reciprocity, by an intense sharing and cooperativeness among all members. Hunter-gatherers generally exhibit "primitive communism": ownership (or at least right of use) of basic resources is communal, and no individual is deprived of access to the resources of nature that sustain life and well being. Hunting and gathering societies are not characterized, therefore, by any fundamental inequalities of privilege, and no social strata can be said to exist.

Yet the absence of social strata does not mean that perfect equality prevails among the members of hunter-gatherer societies. Inequalities do exist. These are mainly inequalities of prestige or social influence and are typically based on such factors as age, sex, and certain personal characteristics. As is common throughout the world, men tend to have higher status than women among hunter-gatherers, and, likewise, the older members of society are often given more honor and respect than the younger ones. In addition, the possession of certain personal traits is generally a basis for the acquisition of prestige. Men who are particularly skilled hunters, who show spe-

Table 6.1   THE EVOLUTION OF SOCIAL STRATIFICATION IN PREINDUSTRIAL SOCIETIES

Type of Society	Nature of Social Stratification
Hunting and gathering	Typically, no stratification. Inequalities of privilege generally absent. Mild inequalities exist based on age, sex, and personal characteristics, such as courage and hunting skill, but these are inequalities of prestige and influence only. General equality permeates entire society.
Simple horticultural	Typically, no stratification. Inequalities of privilege generally absent. Inequalities based on age and sex exist. Outside of gender inequality, main form of inequality is personal prestige and renown accumulated by redistributor big men. These are frequently "rank" societies in Fried's sense of the term.
Intensive horticultural	Typically, first emergence of genuine stratification. Common pattern is division of society into three social strata (chiefs, subchiefs, commoners). Power and privilege of chiefs limited by people's demands for their generosity. Redistributive ethic still prevails, preventing extreme stratification.
Agrarian	Typically, extreme stratification. Bulk of population is a subjugated and exploited peasantry. Rulers and governing classes possess great wealth and power. Serfdom and slavery are most common forms of subordination of bulk of the population. Caste system of unique nature in southern Asia. Poverty and suffering are widespread. Placement of individuals in class structure is largely by birth, but some mobility does occur.

cial courage, or who are thought of as having great wisdom are often accorded high prestige. Such individuals typically assume leadership functions because they are deemed to be worthy of the trust and confidence of others.

However, men of prestige and influence among hunter-gatherers are no more than "firsts among equals," and they typically have no special privileges not available to others. It must also be noted that the acquisition of prestige and influence comes from an individual's own abilities and efforts, not from any mechanism of social heredity. Prestige is both personally gained and personally lost. Individuals must continually justify such honor, and should their abilities or efforts fail them, their status will fall and others will replace them. Thus, hunting and gathering societies permit virtually complete equality of opportunity for individuals to gain high status. In such societies, talent, effort, and social reward are closely aligned, a fact that sets them sharply apart from highly stratified societies.

It must be stressed that the degree of prestige that can be gained among hunter-gatherers is very mild when compared to the nature of prestige in other societies. Hunter-gatherers loathe boasting and self-glorification, and they use strong sanctions against those persons who come to think too highly of themselves. Their emphasis is clearly on communal well-being and general social equality. In this sense they are quite aptly described as *egalitarian* societies (Woodburn, 1982).

Yet not all hunter-gatherers have been egalitarian, and some have been characterized by considerable inequalities in privilege. The distinction made by Alain Testart (1982) between storing and nonstoring hunter-gatherers is relevant here. Using a representative sample of 40 hunter-gatherer societies, Testart has shown that 8 of the 10 that can be considered food-storing societies are stratified, whereas only 2 of the 30 nonstoring societies have stratification. There is obviously a pronounced relationship between food storing and the presence of stratification.

By far the best examples of stratified hunting and gathering societies are those Indian tribes that have inhabited the Northwest Coast of the United States. Although there has been some disagreement as to the actual nature and extent of the inequalities present, a number of anthropologists believe that the Northwest Coast was characterized by an exploitative class system. Anthropologist Eugene Ruyle (1973), for instance, makes a strong claim for the existence of a ruling class, rent or taxation, and slavery. These societies have been famous among social scientists for their elaborate competitive feasts known as potlatches, a phenomenon encountered in the last chapter. During their potlatches Northwest Coast chiefs would attempt to shame rival chiefs by giving away large quantities of wealth and by ranting and raving about their own greatness. Among the Kwakiutl, for example, chiefs seemed obsessed with maintaining and enhancing their high status.

There is also strong evidence that a number of hunter-gatherer societies in late pre-Neolithic times (about 12,000–10,000 years ago) had crossed the threshold into stratification, or at least had developed extensive inequalities of social status or rank (Mellars, 1985). Like the Northwest Coast tribes, these societies very likely consisted of dense populations in regions of abundant resources that had adopted the practice of food storing. And, also like the Northwest Coast tribes, these prehistoric societies were highly uncharacteristic of hunter-gatherer societies the world over. Their uniqueness should not be allowed to detract from what is most commonly found at the hunting and gathering stage of social life— pervasive social and economic equality.

It might be suspected that the striking egalitarianism of hunter-gatherers is a "natural" phenomenon, or one that results from the absence of motivations toward status seeking and wealth acquisition at this stage of social life. Such motivations, it might be presumed, develop only at later evolutionary stages. But this would be a seriously incorrect inference. As Elizabeth Cashdan (1980) and James Woodburn (1982) have pointed out, social and economic equality is always threatened by individuals who seek to attain more than others, and it takes constant vigilance to maintain it. The equality that results from pervasive reciprocity and sharing seems to be an essential condition for human survival and well-being among most hunter-gatherers because it is a necessary means of overcoming temporal and spatial variations in the food supply. But since there is nothing "natural" about strict equality, powerful techniques of socialization must be used to bring it about and maintain it (Cashdan, 1980; Lee, 1978). The emergence of significant inequalities, then, results from the lifting of restrictions once placed on human motivations (Cashdan, 1980). It is among food-storing hunter-gatherers and, more significantly, horticultural and agrarian societies that these restrictions come to be lifted.

Inequality without Stratification: Simple Horticultural Societies

Simple horticultural societies have greater opportunities than hunter-gatherers for the creation of various social inequalities. Greater inequalities are indeed characteristic of simple horticulturalists, but these are not inequalities of privilege or wealth. Rather, they are inequalities of prestige. For this reason, simple horticultural societies are not stratified but are frequently examples of what Morton Fried (1967) has termed

rank societies. As Fried defines it, "A rank society is one in which positions of valued status are somehow limited so that not all those of sufficient talent to occupy such statuses actually achieve them" (1967:109). Put another way, rank societies establish a prestige-ranking system characterized by a limited number of high status positions that confer no special material advantage.

As discussed in Chapter 5, simple horticultural societies generally display economies resting upon egalitarian (or pure) redistribution. The prestige-ranking system of such societies is intimately connected with this redistributive pattern. In many simple horticultural societies, individuals who work hard, make sacrifices, and solicit the help of their kinsmen are ultimately able to accumulate a considerable number of products from their gardens and animal herds. This fund of valuables may be used for the holding of large feasts, at which time a general redistribution of the products is made. Individuals who repeatedly demonstrate their prowess in holding successful feasts come to be persons of high rank: They come to be held in considerable respect, envy, and sometimes even awe. As noted in the last chapter, these individuals acquire the status of "big men."

Big men typically have many rivals who wish to oust them from their high rank. Although a society may have only one genuine big man, there are likely to be other persons who are also held in high regard. High rank must be earned through talent and effort; it cannot be acquired hereditarily. To become a big man, a number of personal qualities are necessary. Perhaps paramount among these is generosity. Big men accumulate wealth, but they do not gain their status through hoarding it; rather, prestige comes to them through their generous distribution of this wealth to others. Individuals who hoard their wealth rather than give it away are looked upon with great disfavor. Rank societies are therefore strongly antagonistic in principle to the existence of differential material advantage, and they contain strong built-in pressures working to prevent such a development. In this way, a system of ranking works to serve the common good (through the redistributive actions of persons of high status) while at the same time preventing the formation of differentially advantaged social strata.

The Siuai of Bougainville in the Solomon Islands are simple horticulturalists with a ranking system of the type envisioned by Fried (Oliver, 1955). Among the Siuai, individuals must possess a number of qualities in order to attain high rank. One of these, of course, is the possession of a considerable supply of valuables available for redistributive feasting. But mere possession of wealth does not by itself guarantee high rank. Men are also expected to be generous with this wealth, to be willing to distribute it to others. The Siuai actively dislike individuals who are miserly with their wealth, and they take a generally negative attitude toward selfishness. Selfishness in a spouse is a basis for divorce, and miserly men who do not aid their kinsmen in times of need are referred to as "stone-hearts." Misers are often feared and suspected of sorcery, are rarely liked, and cannot advance to positions of high rank and leadership. By contrast, generous men are universally liked and respected and, contingent upon their successful feast giving, have good opportunities for attaining high rank. Men who give frequent feasts that are well attended generally gain renown for themselves.

In recognition of the accomplishments of successful feast givers, the Siuai heap considerable praise upon these men of high rank. They also show much respect for a high-ranking individual's name and person. He is generally not addressed by name, but usually called instead by a kinship term or simply *mumi* ("big man"). Even in reference his personal name may not be used, and on these occasions he may be referred to by the name of his clubhouse or by the name of one of his assistants. The respect given his name typically continues even after his death. High-ranking persons are also usually given considerable deference. As the Siuai's principal ethnographer, Douglas Oliver, comments (1955:401):

> Leaders are usually spared menial jobs; others fetch water for them, and climb palms to get coconuts and areca nuts for their refreshment. Boisterous talk usually becomes quieter when a leader approaches, and boys leave off rough-housing. In fact, one of the sternest lessons impressed upon a child is to stay away from a leader, or else remain quiet in his presence. ("Never play when a mumi is nearby; you might disturb him or hit him with your toys.") Females, especially, appear awed near the great men, often looking shyly to the ground. Men usually wait for a leader to open conversations, and take their cues from him concerning when to laugh, to commend, or to decry.
>
> No supernaturally sanctioned taboos surround a leader's person in order to insulate him from plain physical contact with other natives, but few people would assume enough familiarity with him to place a friendly hand on his shoulder—a common gesture among equals.

Oliver's comments make clear the social meaning of rank in Siuai society. As a fairly typical example of the structure of inequality in most simple horticultural societies, the Siuai effectively demonstrate the nature of a system of ranking in the absence of stratification. Such a ranking system represents a definite evolutionary movement beyond the typical pattern of inequality prevalent among hunter-gatherers, where no man could be shown the kind of deference given to a Siuai mumi. On the other hand,

Siuai mumis would themselves be in awe of the attainments of their chiefly counterparts in truly stratified societies.

Intensive Horticultural Societies and the Emergence of Stratification

Social stratification generally emerges with the transition to intensive horticultural societies. These societies frequently exhibit hereditary social strata or classes, the true mark of stratified society. Three main social strata (consisting roughly of chiefs, subchiefs, and commoners) are a common pattern. Thus what appear only as differences of rank or status among simple horticulturalists are transformed among intensive horticulturalists into genuine inequalities involving differential access to the basic resources of nature. Appearing on the scene are separate groups of persons distinguished by their differences in social rank, power, dress and ornamentation, patterns of consumption of luxury and other goods, direct involvement in economic production, availability of leisure time, and general styles of life. Membership in such groups is hereditary, and the placement of individuals in the stratified order is largely unrelated to individual talents or efforts. Social status is determined by a person's genealogical relationship to the chief or king.

Yet because chiefs and commoners are related through kinship ties, the stratification system has definite restraints placed upon it. Kinship ties function to soften the nature and consequences of inequality, and chiefs are still expected to be generous with their wealth and to have a concern for the common good. As Lenski (1966) notes, the "redistributive ethic" still prevails in such societies, preventing too great a use of the surplus for the chief's own ends. Although members of the chiefly class enjoy substantial (and often great) privilege, chiefs are still regarded as "great providers" who must constantly consider the needs and wishes of their distant kinsmen in the commoner class.

Stratification systems of this type have been found among many of the intensive horticultural societies of sub-Saharan Africa as they existed in the eighteenth and nineteenth centuries. Here the familiar three-class system of stratified life was frequently found (Lenski, 1966). The dominant class consisted of a small minority of powerful and privileged persons who lived off the economic surplus generated from below. An intermediate class of officials and specialists served the fancies of the dominant class and carried out some of the lesser functions of political rule. The lowest class consisted of the large majority of ordinary people who were charged with producing enough economic goods to support the other two classes.

Chiefs or kings in some of these societies were treated with great respect and were often exalted and deified. In Dahomey, for instance, extreme acts of deference were shown the king. Even his ministers of state were expected to grovel in the dust in his presence, all the while throwing dirt over their heads and bodies (Lenski, 1966). Also, "No one could appear in his presence with his shoulders covered, or wearing sandals, shoes, or hat. No one could sit on a stool in his presence; if they sat, they were obliged to sit on the ground" (Lenski, 1966:154). Dahomean kings also possessed great wealth, both in the form of property and wives. They were nominally regarded as the owners of all property within the kingdom, were permitted to engage in incestuous marriages, controlled all appointments to public office, and approved the inheritance of property. Such exalted figures also possessed life-and-death power over their subjects, for persons who displeased the king could be (and often were) put to death.

Even though considerable stratification among African horticulturalists did exist, such societies were still permeated by a basic redistributive ethic. Among the Southern Bantu, for example, a chief was expected to be generous, and a failure to display such behavior was cause for a sharp decline in his popularity. As Lenski notes (1966:165):

> Though he is the wealthiest man in his tribe, he cannot use his wealth solely for the satisfaction of personal needs and desires. He is obliged to provide for the support of his ministers and courtiers. He must entertain all those who come to visit him. On great public occasions he is expected to slaughter many of his cattle and provide beer and porridge for all who gather at his village. He lends cattle, supports destitute widows and orphans, sends food to sick people and newly confined mothers, and in time of famine distributes corn from his own granaries or, if this is insufficient, purchases supplies from neighboring groups.

Similar systems of stratified life have also existed among many of the aboriginal societies of Polynesia. Aboriginal Hawaii affords an excellent example from this region of the world. According to the description given by Marshall Sahlins (1958), Hawaii was divided into three main social strata: the "high chiefs" and their families, local stewards who administered the various domains of a chiefdom, and commoners. A paramount chief managed the use of lands throughout an entire island. This chief had the right to redistribute all lands upon his accession to office. In addition, he could alienate the land of any lower-ranking manager and transfer it to someone else. Commoners could be dispossessed from land for such reasons as hoarding surplus production, failing to contribute labor for the construction of irrigation works, and failing to make one's household plot adequately productive. High chiefs and local stewards also controlled and supervised access to water used in irrigation. Local stewards directly supervised household economic production,

making sure that the land was being cultivated. In general, persons of high status could call upon those of lower rank for the performance of various labor services; commoners, of course, were the major source of labor for communal projects. Refusal by a commoner to comply with a demand for labor could result in his being put to death. It is clear that the major responsibilities of labor and economic production were carried out by the commoner class, and high chiefs and their families were freed from direct involvement in subsistence production. In this sense, chiefs constituted a kind of primitive "leisure class," putting others beneath them to work.

The stratified nature of Hawaiian society is also indicated by the existence of class differences in consumption patterns. Though differences in food consumption between classes were not prominent, certain choice foods were reserved for high chiefs. The chiefly redistributive ethic guaranteed an adequate food supply for all, and commoners have been described as "prosperous." Concerning the consumption of luxury goods, however, the matter is different. Luxury goods were often confined to high-status persons and served as insignia of rank. The use of certain luxury items for dress and ornamentation was restricted to high chiefs, and the quality of housing was highly associated with rank.

The Hawaiian paramount chief was considered divine. Because of the aura of sanctity that surrounded him, a series of elaborate taboos existed concerning contact with him, violation of which could result in death. For example, it was prohibited to let one's shadow fall on the paramount's house or possessions, to pass through his door ahead of him, or to put on his robe. Commoners were generally prohibited from touching anything used by the chief. In his presence, others were expected to prostrate themselves on the ground in a demonstration of extreme humility. When he traveled, people were warned of his coming so they could properly prepare themselves.

Stratification in Agrarian Societies

With the transition from intensive horticultural to agrarian societies, the limitations formerly placed on the stratification system were removed. The disappearance of the chiefly redistributive ethic and the removal of kinship ties between the members of different social classes were connected with the emergence of extreme forms of social stratification in which the majority of persons were frequently thrown into conditions of extreme poverty and degradation. One of the most striking characteristics of agrarian societies was the immense gap in power, privilege, and prestige that existed between the dominant and subordinate classes. Indeed, agrarian societies are by far the most highly stratified of all preindustrial societies. Unless otherwise noted, the following discussion is based on the description of agrarian stratification provided by Lenski (1966).

Agrarian stratification systems generally contained the following social strata:

• A political-economic elite consisting of the ruler and his royal family and a landowning governing class.
• The retainer class.
• The merchant class.
• The priestly class.
• The peasantry.
• Artisans.
• Expendables.

While the first four of these strata may be considered privileged groups, the privileged segment of greatest significance in all agrarian societies was, of course, the political-economic elite: the ruler and the governing class. Likewise, while peasants, artisans, and expendables were all highly subordinate classes, the peasantry, since it constituted a

majority of the population, was far and away the primary subjugated class.

The ruler in agrarian societies—monarch, king, emperor, or of whatever title—was that person who officially stood at the political head of society. The governing class consisted of those persons who were ordinarily the primary owners of land and who received the benefits that accompanied such ownership. But in fact both the ruler and the governing class tended to be both major landowners and major wielders of political power, and there were vital connections between these two segments of the elite. Taken together, they typically comprised no more than one or two percent of the population while receiving approximately half to two-thirds of the total wealth. The specific relationship between ruler and governing class varied from one agrarian society to another. In some societies, the power and wealth of the ruler was considerably diminished at the hands of the governing class, and the governing class itself was the primary holder of political power. This situation was found, for instance, in medieval Europe. In other agrarian societies, such as Ottoman Turkey or Mughal India, political power was highly concentrated in the hands of the ruler, and the ruler himself was the largest landowner. Under this situation, the prerogatives of the governing class (in terms of power, ownership and control of land, and wealth) were substantially reduced.

Regardless of the specific relationship between ruler and governing class, each typically enjoyed a considerable (and often enormous) amount of power, privilege, and prestige in comparison to other classes. A majority of the huge economic surplus generated within agrarian societies almost always found its way into the hands of the entire politico-economic elite. The rulers of agrarian societies have generally controlled great wealth. By the end of the fourteenth century, for example, English kings had an average income of approximately £135,000 a year, an amount that was equal to 85 percent of the combined incomes of the 2,200 members of the nobility and squirearchy. Rulers of some of the great agrarian bureaucratic empires have fared much better than this. Xerxes, emperor of Persia in pre-Christian times, is said to have had an annual income that would have totaled $35 million by modern standards. Similarly, the annual income of Suleiman the Magnificent of Turkey was judged to have equaled $421 million; the figures for Akbar the Great of India and his successor, Aurangzeb, are estimated at $120 million and $270 million, respectively. As for the wealth of the governing class, Lenski estimates that this class probably received on the average at least one-quarter of the total income of most agrarian societies. In late nineteenth-century China, for instance, the Chinese portion of the governing class (that is, excluding the Manchu segment of this class) received approximately 645 million taels per year in total income, a figure that amounted to 24 percent of the gross national product. Averaging out to about 450 taels per family head, the Chinese segment of the governing class had an annual income roughly twenty times that of the remainder of Chinese society.

Standing directly below the ruler and governing class in agrarian societies was that social stratum that has been termed the retainer class. This class consisted of such functionaries as government officials, professional soldiers, household servants, and other persons who are directly employed to serve the ruler and governing class. Lenski estimates that the retainer class probably constituted around five percent of the population of most agrarian societies. A crucial role of this class was to mediate the relations between the elite and the common people. As Lenski notes, it was various officials of the retainer class who actually carried out the day-to-day work necessary for transferring the economic surplus into the hands of the ruler and governing class. The actual privilege and social status of members of the retainer class varied considerably. While certain members of this class enjoyed greater privilege than some lower-ranking members of the governing class, others of the class often enjoyed no special measure of privilege, their overall standing in society has been perhaps only slightly better than that of the average peasant. On the average, however, members of the retainer class tended to share to a significant degree in the benefits of the wealth controlled by their employers. While the retainer class was in effect a service class, its general position in society was clearly nearer that of the privileged than of the disprivileged.

Also standing among the privileged segments of agrarian societies was the merchant class. Merchants, of course, engaged in commercial activity and were a vital part of the agrarian urban economy. The merchant class was often of great value to the ruler and governing class, since merchants dealt in many of the luxury goods that were purchased by the elite. Although many merchants remained poor, some amassed substantial wealth, and a few were wealthier than some members of the governing class. Yet, despite these material benefits, merchants were usually accorded very low prestige. In the traditional status-ranking system of China, for example, merchants were placed near the very bottom of the social scale, ranking even below peasants and artisans. In medieval Europe merchants fared somewhat better, but they were still regarded as highly inferior to the governing class. Merchants appear to have been well aware of their low status, and many strove to raise their status to the level of the governing class by imitating its lifestyle.

Although the priestly class in agrarian societies was often internally stratified, in general it is appropriate to consider it a privileged stratum. Indeed, priests have frequently commanded substantial wealth in many agrarian societies, and it has been a common pattern for them to be close allies of rulers and governing classes. In Egypt in the twelfth century B.C., for example, as well as in eighteenth-century France, priests owned 15 percent of the land. In pre-Reformation Sweden the Church owned 21 percent of the land, while in Ceylon, Buddhist monasteries are said to have been in control of about one-third of the land. This privileged status of the priestly class as a whole no doubt resulted from the political alliances typically forged between priests and rulers and governing classes. The latter two groups have commonly sought priestly support for their oppressive and exploitative activities. Priests have therefore been properly rewarded for their aid to these dominant groups. However, it must not be overlooked that the privilege of the priestly class was typically insecure. The holdings of this class were often stripped away by acts of confiscation by the political elite, indicating that the economic alliance between the priesthood and the elite was often a shaky one. In addition, it is imperative to recognize that not all priests were wealthy and of high rank. In medieval Europe, for instance, priests were divided into an upper and lower clergy. While the upper clergy lived in a privileged style consistent with their noble background, members of the lower clergy—parish priests directly serving the common people—lived in a style resembling that of the common people themselves.

In most agrarian societies the bulk of the population has consisted of peasants. As a class, peasants have occupied a distinctly inferior social, economic, and political status. Economically, their lot has generally been a miserable one, although the specific degree of their exploitation has varied from one society and one time to another. A major burden placed upon all peasants has

been taxation, the principal means of separating the peasant from his surplus product. The oppressiveness of taxation has varied considerably. During the Tokugawa era in Japan, the rate of taxation of the peasantry varied from as little as 30 percent to as much as 70 percent of the crop. In China, approximately 40 to 50 percent of total peasant agricultural production was commonly claimed by landowners. In pre-British India, peasants apparently handed over from one-third to one-half of their crops to both Muslim and Hindu rulers. In Babylon during the time of Hammurabi, taxes ranged from one-third to one-half of the crop. In Ottoman Turkey, the tax rate varied from 10 to 50 percent. In sixteenth- and seventeenth-century Russia, the rate was 20 to 50 percent. In a number of agrarian societies, multiple forms of taxation have existed. One of the most striking illustrations of a system of multiple taxation comes from the period of Ottoman rule in Bulgaria. Here the Turks imposed nearly 80 different kinds of taxes and obligations upon the peasantry. One such tax was known as the "tooth tax," a levy placed on a village by the Turks after they had eaten and drunk there. In official terms, the tax was said to compensate the Turks "for the wear and tear sustained by their teeth during the meal" (Lenski, 1966:269). Incredible as such a tax seems, it does indicate the lengths to which many agrarian elites have gone to benefit themselves at the expense of the bulk of the population.

In addition to the burdens of taxation, peasants were also subjected to other hardships. One of these was the **corvée,** or system of forced labor. Under this system, peasants were obligated to provide so many days of labor either for their lord or for the state. In medieval Europe, for example, peasants were obligated to work on their lord's land a specified number of days per week throughout the year. During the building of the Great Wall in China, some peasants were kept on forced labor projects nearly their entire adult lives. Peasant hardships did not end with the burdens of taxation and forced labor. If the peasant's lord operated a mill, oven, or wine press (and he frequently did), the peasant was under obligation to use them and to compensate the lord handsomely for such use. In some agrarian societies, the lord could take anything he desired from a peasant's personal property, and he could do so without payment. In medieval Europe, when a man died, his lord could claim his best beast. Furthermore, if a man's daughter married off the manor or without the lord's permission, the girl's father could be fined.

It should be obvious that the life of the average peasant was an extremely difficult one. By and large, life was lived with but the barest necessities for existence. The peasant diet was generally a poor one in terms of the quantity, variety, and nutritional adequacy of the food. Household furniture was extremely meager, and most peasants slept on straw-covered earthen floors. Sometimes conditions became so bad that a living was no longer possible and peasants had to abandon the land and attempt to sustain themselves by other means.

In addition to the severe economic deprivation typically suffered by peasants, the peasantry occupied a very low social status in all agrarian societies. A great gulf separated the lifestyles of peasants and the elite. The elite (and, to varying degrees, other classes as well) regarded peasants as extreme social inferiors, frequently conceiving of them as something less than fully human. In some agrarian societies, peasants were formally classified in various documents as belonging to roughly the same category as the livestock. Lacking all but the barest necessities of life, and deprived of any opportunity to pursue even such unremarkable amenities as an education or the cultivation of good manners, the peasantry stood in stark contrast to the privileged elite, where the social trappings of high status were a fundamental part of everyday life.

Standing below the peasantry in the agrarian stratified order were two other classes. One of these consisted of artisans, or trained craftsmen, a class that Lenski estimates probably represented about three to seven percent of the population in most agrarian societies. Artisans were mainly recruited from among the ranks of the dispossessed peasantry. Although the incomes of peasants and artisans overlapped, artisans were generally worse off economically than most peasants. Many apparently lived in destitute circumstances on the verge of starvation. At the very bottom of virtually every agrarian society could be found a class of "expendables." Constituting approximately five to ten percent of most agrarian populations, these persons were found in urban areas. Their ranks were filled by beggars, petty thieves, outlaws, underemployed itinerant workers, and other persons who, as Lenski has noted, were "forced to live solely by their wits or by charity" (1966:281). Members of this class suffered from extreme economic deprivation, malnutrition, and disease, and had a very high death rate. The sons and daughters of poor peasants who inherited nothing often fell into this extraordinarily hapless class.

One's class position in all agrarian societies was overwhelmingly determined by social heredity. Most persons died as members of the class into which they were born. This does not mean, however, that social mobility was impossible or nonexistent in such societies, and a small amount of it did occur. Occasionally a person rose in rank to one of the privileged classes. Nevertheless, such upward movement seldom occurred; far more common was downward mobility. As noted above, children who inherited nothing from their poor peasant parents were often forced into either the artisan or expendable class in order to maintain any sort of existence at all. Thus, the possibility of improving one's disadvantaged position in an agrarian society was greatly limited.

Because of the complexity of agrarian stratification systems, a diagrammatic representation may be useful in getting a clearer picture of how these systems were structured. Such a representation is available in Figure 6.1.

THEORIES OF THE ORIGIN OF STRATIFICATION

The Functionalist Evolutionary Theory

A number of theories have been proposed by social scientists to account for the developments recounted in the preceding pages. One very well-known theory of the origin of stratification is the functionalist evolution-

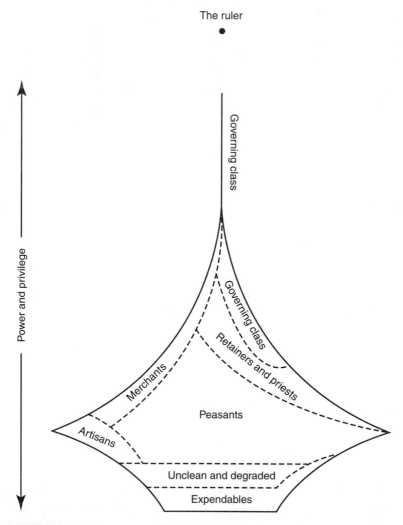

FIGURE 6.1
Simplified diagram of agrarian stratification systems. (*Source: Gerhard E. Lenski, Power and Privilege: A Theory of Social Stratification.* New York: McGraw-Hill, 1966, p. 284.)

ary theory of sociologist Talcott Parsons (1966, 1977) Parsons sees the emergence of stratification as a crucial aspect of the evolution of "increased adaptive capacity" in social life. It is for him an "evolutionary breakthrough," a great accomplishment allowing societies to function more efficiently and handle a larger number of functional problems. Stratification has such significance for Parsons because he believes that it allows societies to overcome the limitations placed upon them by social equality. When everyone is treated equally, no individual will have the motivation to assume important leadership roles necessary for a society to deal with many of the important problems and challenges it must face. With the emergence of stratification, though, some individuals will be inclined toward assuming these leadership roles because they know they will be rewarded for doing so with a superior measure of privilege and prestige. Stratification is thus a necessary device whereby societies begin to centralize many of their activities in order to solve problems and meet challenges with which they would otherwise be unable to deal.

There are numerous difficulties with this interpretation of the origin of stratified social life. In the first place, Parsons's concept of "increased adaptive capacity" is highly questionable. Parsons is suggesting that more recent and more complex societies are really superior in their organizational effectiveness to earlier societies. While it is certainly the case that more recent societies have *different* adaptive mechanisms from those found in earlier societies, most sociologists find little empirical support for the claim that these mechanisms are superior. A second difficulty with Parsons's theory is that, in stressing the alleged benefits to society of the emergence of stratification, it seems to overlook entirely the negative consequences of stratification. These include, among other things, the oppression, exploitation, and misery suffered by the lower strata. Indeed, one of the most significant consequences of the rise of stratification is an increase in the degree of conflict in social life. It is very difficult to see how these phenomena can be regarded as examples of "increased adaptive capacity."

Lenski's Surplus Theory

The sociologist Gerhard Lenski (1966) has presented another well-known theory of stratification, but one that has a strong materialistic and conflict-theoretical orientation. It therefore stands in sharp contrast to Parsons's theory. Although this theory has been known by a variety of names, we shall refer to it here as the *surplus theory*. The theory is represented diagrammatically in Figure 6.2.

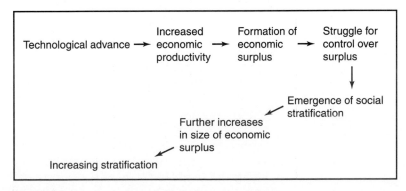

FIGURE 6.2
Lenski's surplus theory of the origin of social stratification.

Lenski's theory assumes that humans are essentially self-interested creatures who strive to maximize their own well-being. Individuals behave largely according to a principle of enlightened self-interest, cooperating with each other when it can further their interests, and struggling with each other when that seems the avenue to the satisfaction of their interests. The theory also assumes that the objects individuals seek are always scarce relative to the desire for them, and that individuals are unequally endowed by nature to compete for the attainment of scarce objects.

Lenski believes that basic equality will prevail in those societies in which cooperation is essential to the satisfaction of individual interests. People will share with each other when such sharing is to the long-run benefit of the sharers. When this condition is not met, conflict and stratification are expected to arise. This condition is not met when a society produces an economic surplus. When a surplus becomes available, a struggle for control of it seems inevitably to arise, and the surplus ends up largely in the hands of the most powerful individuals and groups.

Surplus economic production, then, is the key to the development of stratification, and the larger the surplus, the greater the extent of stratification. What determines the size of the surplus? According to Lenski, it is a society's technological capacity. There should thus be a very close association between a society's degree of technological development and its degree of stratification. The simplest societies, such as those of hunter-gatherers and simple horticulturalists, should be characterized by little or no stratification. With technological advance, substantial economic surpluses arise and the struggles over these should produce increasing stratification. Thus, intensive horticultural and agrarian societies should display proportionately increasing levels of stratification.

The empirical data discussed earlier on the evolution of stratification are highly consistent with Lenski's theory. Yet there are some significant problems with the theory, and the close association between technological development and stratification pointed to by Lenski seems to mislead us theoretically. Although highly correlated with stratification, technological development may not be the actual causal factor.

The major difficulty with Lenski's theory involves his assumption about the origin of an economic surplus. Lenski appears to assume that economic surpluses are more or less automatic results of technological advance. Yet this cannot really be the case. Technological advance makes surpluses possible; however, as Ester Boserup (1965) points out, people will not automatically desire to produce them because to do so involves more work for questionable results. (The discussion in Chapter 4 suggested that people are highly motivated to resist technological change in order to prevent increases in the workload.) If people are not naturally inclined to produce surpluses, then the question arises as to how surpluses can originate at all. The answer would seem to involve political compulsion: People produce surpluses because other people compel them to do so. And if this is the case, then stratification, at least in the sense of differential power, already exists. Surpluses, then, actually follow closely upon the heels of the development of stratification (cf. Elster, 1985:169). To see how this can happen, and to see what is ultimately behind such a process, the so-called *scarcity theory of stratification* must be examined.

The Scarcity Theory

The presentation here of the scarcity theory of stratification is derived from suggestions made in the work of Michael Harner (1970), Morton Fried (1967), Richard Wilkinson (1973), and Rae Lesser Blumberg (1978).

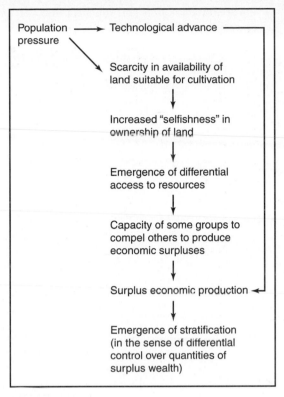

FIGURE 6.3
Scarcity theory of the origin of social stratification.

This theory is represented diagrammatically in Figure 6.3.

The scarcity theory holds that the basic cause of the emergence and intensification of stratification is population pressure. The following scenario may be imagined for purposes of illustrating the theory. Population pressure against resources has eventually led hunter-gatherers to begin adopting agricultural modes of subsistence. Agriculture eventually entirely displaces hunting and gathering. The "primitive communism" of hunter-gatherers gives way to the ownership of land by large kinship groups, but nonetheless ownership is still largely communal rather than private. However, further increases in population pressure cause horticulturalists to become more concerned about landownership. Increasing **scarcity** in the availability of land suitable for cultivation leads some families to increased "selfishness" in landownership, and some families begin to own more land than others. Additional population pressure leads to still greater "selfishness" in landownership, and eventually private relations of production (in the Marxian sense) emerge out of what was originally communal ownership. Differential access to resources now exists, and one group may compel others to work harder in order to produce economic surpluses off which the owning group may live, a group that is now emerging as a primitive "leisure class." Since technological advance has accompanied population pressure and declining standards of living, surpluses are now technologically feasible. With additional advances in population pressure and technology, differential access to resources becomes even more severe, and stratification intensifies under greater political compulsion by owning groups.

The scarcity theory holds that something probably very much like this process has happened in human history, no doubt not just once, but many times. It is important to see that the scarcity theory and the surplus theory are similar in some ways. Both are materialistic, conflict-oriented theories that are strikingly different from the functionalist evolutionary interpretation. But whereas the surplus theory regards technological advance as the basic cause of the development of stratification, the scarcity theory claims that the causal relationship between technology and stratification is illusory. It holds that both are results of population pressure and the scarcity of resources that this produces. The scarcity theory is favored in this book because the surplus theory is contradicted by Boserup's interpretation of the causes of technological change and the data that support her interpretation, yet the scarcity theory fits Boserup's claim very nicely.

It is important to realize that, once initiated, stratification has, so to speak, a "life of its own." Lenski himself recognizes this and stresses it. That is to say, once there emerge in society groups with differential access to the means of production, advantaged groups are highly motivated to maintain their advantage, and enhance it if possible. Thus stratification systems tend to be inherently self-perpetuating and self-enhancing.

SUMMARY

1. All societies are characterized by social inequality, or differentials between individuals in their levels of prestige and social influence. Many societies, though, go considerably beyond social inequality and establish social stratification, or hierarchies of hereditary social groups having unequal levels of social power and privilege.

2. In hunting and gathering societies inequality generally prevails in the absence of stratification. Individuals in such societies generally possess equal access to the resources of nature that sustain life. Equality is reinforced by strong norms compelling people to share and punishing them for failure to do so. The inequalities in hunter-gatherer societies are generally those of prestige and influence only, with the most skilled and courageous hunters and the wisest leaders commanding the most respect.

3. Simple horticultural societies commonly lack stratification as well. Many of them are examples of rank societies, or those in which a few individuals are accorded very high levels of respect. These individuals, though, do not inherit their positions but attain them competitively through their efforts as economic organizers. The superior prestige of village leaders does not translate into superior power and privilege.

4. Genuine stratification tends to emerge for the first time in more intensive horticultural societies. Many of these societies have stratification systems in which unequal groups composed of chiefs, subchiefs, and common-

ers are found. Chiefs and subchiefs have considerable control over economic production, and the large commoner class has a number of restrictions placed on its ownership and use of land.

5. Stratification reaches extreme proportions in agrarian societies. The two main social classes are landlords and peasants, but a number of other classes exist as well. These include merchants, priests, artisans, and "expendables." The extreme differences in power and privilege between different social classes is accompanied by major differences in styles of life and in levels of prestige.

6. One well-known interpretation of the origin of stratification is the functionalist evolutionary theory of Talcott Parsons. Parsons has theorized that stratification arose in human history in order to meet crucial societal needs. Societies with stratification could function more effectively than those without it. By rewarding some individuals more highly than others, societies could motivate those persons to assume important positions of societal leadership and thus direct the affairs of society in a more effective way.

7. The evolutionary materialist view suggests a sharply opposing interpretation. One version of this view is the surplus theory of Gerhard Lenski and others. Lenski sees stratification arising through the creation of economic surpluses, themselves produced by technological advance. When surpluses exist, individuals and groups struggle over their allocation, and some groups will win out over others. The bigger the surplus, the more severe the struggles and the more elaborate the stratification system.

8. An alternative materialist interpretation is the scarcity theory. This theory holds that population growth is the main engine of the rise of stratification. Population growth produces scarcity in resources, and with increasing resource scarcity individuals turn from more communal to more private modes of ownership. As some individuals gain control over resources, they gain the capacity to compel others to engage in surplus production. Owning groups take away (expropriate) this surplus and use it as the source of their own livelihoods.

SPECIAL TOPIC: A MATERIALIST PERSPECTIVE ON THE CASTE SYSTEM

The term **caste** generally refers to an especially rigid form of stratification characterized by the existence of endogamous (in-marrying) social strata that practice ritual avoidance of one another and out of which mobility is said to be impossible. While a number of societies have been said to have caste or castelike systems, by far the best-known (and perhaps the only true) caste system is the one that has prevailed among the Hindus of India for some 2000 years or more. In Hindu ideology, the caste system is said to operate such "that each person is assigned a place in society at birth, that contact between different ranks is 'impure,' that intermarriage between castes is forbidden, and that every social act is governed by caste rules" (McCord and McCord, 1977:30).

Five main castes have constituted the structure of Indian society: (1) *Brahmans,* or priests and landowners; (2) *Kshatriyas,* or warriors and political leaders; (3) *Vaisyas,* or workers performing agricultural and mercantile functions; (4) *Sudras,* or servants, menial laborers, and peasants; and (5) *Harijans,* or "untouchables," persons regarded as impure and degraded. The five major castes, or *varnas,* though, are not the basic functional units of the caste system. These units are the *jatis,* or subcastes. Each major *varna* is subdivided into hundreds of *jatis,* and there are several thousand *jatis* throughout India. An individual's *jati* is the social group that regulates all aspects of his or her everyday social life: It places the individual within the economic division of labor; it regulates marriage and family life; it coordinates religious ritual; it enforces caste taboos and imposes sanctions for their violation; and so on.

The Hindu caste system is undoubtedly the most elaborate and rigid form of stratification the world has ever known. It is also probably one of the least understood social phenomena in all of social science. Many attempts have been made over the decades to explain the origins of this unique system, but consensus among theoreticians is yet to be achieved. Because so much of Indian history is shrouded in mystery, it is unlikely that a really satisfactory solution can be given to so large and complex a problem.

A more limited and manageable question is the extent to which the caste system is, like other complex stratified orders, closely associated with economic exploitation. The traditional view has been to conceptualize the caste system as an elaborate status system that rests basically upon a widespread social consensus. The members of all castes, it has been asserted, view the caste system positively because they see it as promoting the interests of all groups within Indian society and thus as contributing to a fundamental social harmony. Yet in recent years this traditional view has been seriously challenged. As Joan Mencher (1974, 1980) has remarked, it is difficult to see the caste system as being any more harmonious than any other type of stratification system. When it is viewed from the perspective of those near the bottom of the system, it appears to be anything but harmonious.

On the basis of several years of field study in India, Mencher has tried to show how the caste system works to the disadvantage of lower-caste groups, especially Harijans (who make up about 15 percent of Indian society). Harijans, she believes, suffer from two main disadvantages: economic exploitation and a stigmatized identity. Harijans in the villages where Mencher lived were poorer than the members of all other castes, and possessed the least land for cultivation. As she points out (1980:265–266):

> While not all of the landless laborers are by any means untouchables, it is certainly clear that being an untouchable carries additional burdens along with it. In a sample of five villages in Chingleput District studied in 1967, 85% of the Paraiyans [untouchables] had less than

1 acre of land, and derived their main income from agricultural labor; whereas this was the case with only 56% of the Naickers (the other large agricultural community in this region). . . . In a larger sample of eight villages surveyed in 1971, 94% of the Paraiyans owned 1 acre or less; 54% of Naickers owned 1 acre or less. . . .

In the village in Kerala where I was working in 1971, none of the Cherumakkal [untouchable] families owned over 1 acre of land, whereas among other castes that furnish agricultural laborers, there are a sizable number of people having modest though adequate landholdings. In general many villages in Kerala have a few Harijans who own a little over 1 acre of land. . . . Nonetheless, the vast majority of Harijans in Kerala are landless, apart from a few cents of land (1 cent = .01 acre) around their house site. . . .

Thus it should be clear from the outset that a very high percentage of rural Harijans belong to the lowest social class in the economic system.

Mencher devotes particular attention to the problem of stigmatized identity among Harijans. Harijans are generally perceived by members of higher castes as impure and degraded, indeed, as "polluting." They are made aware of this social identity in numerous ways: Members of higher castes frequently object to their wearing clean clothes, sandals, or pressed shirts in public; they are often made to walk alongside a bullock cart rather than allowed to ride on it; they may be compelled to eat their meals in the road outside their employer's compound; when out of necessity Harijans in one particular village began to take water from a nearby pump, the pump's high-caste owner put cow dung in the water; in central Kerala, Harijans commonly use demeaning terms of self-reference (e.g., *adiyan*, or "slave") when conversing with members of certain higher castes; Harijans are generally forbidden to enter local temples, and in some cases are not allowed to use private temples and bathing pools. Mencher points out that although there are laws against many of these practices, high-caste landowners may use economic sanctions against those who violate these traditional caste rules. They simply do not hire the offending parties.

Mencher firmly believes that Harijans do not accept their stigmatized identity as legitimate and deserved. On the contrary, there is considerable evidence that they deeply resent it. Moreover, Mencher has collected ample evidence that Harijans view their poor economic situation as resulting from economic exploitation by wealthy landowners. When she questioned Harijans about why they thought their economic situation was the way it was, they often referred to the concentration of landownership among members of higher castes, or specifically mentioned the ability of higher-caste persons to use force against them. On the basis of Harijans' remarks and her own observations, Mencher concludes that power relations dominate life in Indian villages and that fear of oppression and violence is commonplace among Harijans. "Even where the landlord may appear cordial and sympathetic," she says, "village Harijans know how easily friendliness has turned to hate and oppression elsewhere, and carefully control their behavior" (1980:291).

FOR FURTHER READING

Berreman, Gerald D. (ed.). *Social Inequality: Comparative and Developmental Approaches.* New York: Academic Press, 1981. A good collection of articles on numerous aspects of stratification in a diverse range of societies.

de Ste. Croix, G. E. M. *The Class Struggle in the Ancient Greek World.* Ithaca, N.Y.: Cornell University Press, 1981. An extraordinary and much praised analysis of the class structure of ancient Greece and Rome, with a proper focus on the role of slavery in the economic life of antiquity. The first, and perhaps still the only, Marxian study of the ancient world.

Fried, Morton H. *The Evolution of Political Society*. New York: Random House, 1967. An interesting treatment by a leading anthropologist of the evolution from "egalitarian" through "rank" to "stratified" societies. Suggests that population pressure and attendant scarcity are the causal forces in the emergence of stratified society.

Harner, Michael. "Population pressure and the social evolution of agriculturalists." *Southwestern Journal of Anthropology* 26:67–86, 1970. An intriguing study that tries to show that population pressure is the basic cause of the origin and evolution of stratification. Uses a large sample of the world's societies.

Lenski, Gerhard E. *Power and Privilege: A Theory of Social Stratification*. New York: McGraw-Hill, 1966. An important work in which the author presents his surplus theory of the origin of stratification. Also presents a vast array of valuable data on the nature of inequality and stratification throughout the entire evolutionary range of human societies.

Patterson, Orlando. *Slavery and Social Death: A Comparative Study*. Cambridge, Mass.: Harvard University Press, 1982. An unusually comprehensive study of slavery in the world's societies. Discusses all manner and type of slavery, and emphasizes the status and honor-conferring aspects of slavery over its economic dimensions. Quite valuable and insightful despite being marred by a kind of idealist approach.

Sahlins, Marshall. *Social Stratification in Polynesia*. Seattle: University of Washington Press, 1958. A dated but still interesting study of the variations in stratified social life found among the major aboriginal Polynesian societies. Puts forth an essentially surplus interpretation of the evolution of stratification.

Scott, James C. *Domination and the Arts of Resistance*. New Haven: Yale University Press, 1990. An important study of the variety of ways in which subordinated groups resist being dominated by superordinate groups.

Woodburn, James. "Egalitarian societies." *Man* 17:431–451, 1982. A valuable treatment of the most essential features of egalitarian societies, especially those of hunter-gatherers.

7

The Origins of Modern Capitalism

This chapter begins the discussion of perhaps the greatest social transformation in world history: the transition from the medieval feudal economy in western Europe to the capitalist mode of production. Attention is focused on the early development of capitalism prior to the Industrial Revolution, that is, the period from the early sixteenth century to the middle of the eighteenth century. It will be shown that during this period there was also a relatively independent process of capitalist development in Japan. Particular attention is also given to explaining the transition from feudalism to capitalism in both Europe and Japan. The development of capitalism from the Industrial Revolution to the present day is the subject of the next chapter.

THE FEUDAL MODE OF PRODUCTION

The system of economic life that prevailed in western Europe from approximately the collapse of the Roman Empire until the advent of modern capitalism was known as **feudalism.** Feudalism was especially characteristic of France, Germany, and the British Isles, although it existed in other parts of western Europe as well. The basic unit of economic production under feudalism was the **manor.** The manor was overseen by a powerful feudal landlord and cultivated by numerous peasants. The average peasant held perhaps as much as 30 acres of land on which he lived and that he cultivated for his own living. The land held directly by the lord for his own use was known as the **demesne.** As seen in the two preceding chapters, the relationship between lord and peasant was a highly unbalanced and exploitative one. The peasant owed the lord so many days of work on the demesne, and he also had to pay dues of various sorts. For instance, he often rendered certain food products and paid certain fees, such as those exacted by the lord when the peasant used his winepress, his oven, or his grinding mill.

Just how different the feudal system was from modern industrial society can be seen in the following remarks about feudalism by Douglass North and Robert Thomas (1973:11):

> Thus the customs of the manor became the unwritten "constitution," or the fundamental institutional arrangement of an essentially anarchic world, most properly viewed as small isolated settlements, frequently in the lee of a fortified place and surrounded by wilderness. The wooden or earth castle, the knight, and the relatively self-sufficient manor had emerged as the most viable response to the collapse of order and the recurrent invasions of Norsemen, Moslems, and Magyars. While the terror of foreign marauders had declined by the middle of the tenth century, the land seethed with continual warfare and brigandage as the power of local lords waxed and waned. Feudalism provided a measure of stability and order in this fragmented world. . . .
>
> Commerce between different parts of Europe had always been potentially of mutual benefit, since the variety of resources and climatic conditions induced differentiation of crops and livestock. But trade had been sporadic because so many dangers within the wilderness beset the traveling merchant. As peace and security now revived, so did the profitability of exchanging varied products. In response, towns were taking form in the more densely settled areas either under the protection of a lord or as independent entities with their own walls, government, and military defense. Here skills and crafts flourished, providing "manufactured" goods to trade for the needed food and raw materials from the countryside.

It is clear that the feudal economy was overwhelmingly one of production-for-use. The basic economic relationship was that between landlord and peasant, the latter producing for them both. Life was tied securely to the soil and was very plain and simple—especially for the peasant, but for the lord as well. Production-for-exchange played a small role in economic life. Markets existed, but they were of limited significance. Towns existed and became more prominent as feudalism advanced, but the individuals and groups who lived and worked there—merchants and artisans primarily—had little impact on the functioning of the feudal economy. Trade also existed, but until the eleventh and twelfth centuries it was primarily local and very limited in extent of items traded.

This relatively simple economy persisted for hundreds of years in medieval Europe, but by the beginning of the fourteenth century it entered a period of crisis from which it was not to recover. The crisis led to two major attempts by the feudal nobility to improve its declining economic fortunes: leasing out the demesne to tenants who paid a money rent and who began to farm the land in the manner of a capitalist enterprise, and enclosing land for the pasturing of sheep. These new forms of landholding and land use spelled the end of the old feudal system and were among the earliest signals of the beginnings of the transition to a capitalist mode of economic production.

THE RISE OF THE CAPITALIST MODE OF PRODUCTION

The Nature of Capitalism

With the breakdown of feudalism, production-for-exchange slowly began to replace production-for-use as the principal type of economic activity throughout western Europe. At some point in this transition, the system we call **capitalism** began. But exactly when capitalism began is a question that can only be answered when we know what capitalism *is*. Contemporary scholars disagree in their answers to this fundamental question.

One of history's most prominent students of the capitalist system was Karl Marx. Marx was relatively clear as to just what capitalism was and when it began in European history. Although he conceived it as a type of economy in which people ran companies in an effort to earn **profits,** he knew that this kind of enterprise had existed for thousands of years, and he did not refer to these earlier modes of economic behavior as capitalist. Capitalism involved something more than merely the search for profits.

For Marx, capitalism was a type of economic system in which some individuals owned vital productive resources that they used in an effort to make the maximum profit. These individuals, whom Marx referred to as the **bourgeoisie,** employed another group of persons, whom Marx called the **proletariat,** who through their labor produced goods that the capitalists could exchange in the market for a profit. The capitalist was able to earn a profit because he paid the worker less than the full value of the goods that the worker produced. Marx was quite clear in his belief that the profits of the capitalist did not arise through the simple process of the exchange of goods— through mere buying and selling. Rather, profits were generated through the process of production itself, and the act of selling goods only served to realize the profits that were already there in the creation of the product by the worker.

In Marx's view, then, capitalism required the existence of a class of workers who sold their labor power to capitalists for wages. Only through the exploitation of workers by capitalists in the wage relationship could profits be generated. Marx thus identified the beginnings of the capitalist mode of production with the Industrial Revolution in England in the middle of the eighteenth century, because it was not until this time that wage labor and the factory system became prominent economic phenomena.

Of course, Marx was well aware that the vigorous search for profits began in western Europe long before the Industrial Revolution. Beginning as early as the late fifteenth century, some European nations embarked on colonial expeditions in which the search for profits was of paramount significance. And during the seventeenth century the search for profits was an obsession of governments throughout Europe. Yet Marx argued that the mode in which profits were realized in these centuries was fundamentally different from the mode in which they were obtained after the Industrial Revolution. Before the Industrial Revolution, profits were obtained through exchange rather than production relationships: through buying and selling rather than through the exploitation of a class of wage workers. A company could make profits by buying a product in one region of the world and selling it in another region in which a greater price could be asked. Marx identified this type of economic activity as a sort of capitalism, but he called it **merchant capitalism** in order to distinguish it from the **industrial capitalism** of a later era. Only industrial capitalism was a "true" system of capitalism for Marx.

Some contemporary social scientists believe that Marx's distinction should be strictly maintained. Eric Wolf (1982), for example, identifies the emergence of capitalism only with the Industrial Revolution, referring to the preindustrial period between the fifteenth and eighteenth centuries as a transitional period in which there was a "search for wealth," not a "search for profits." In fact, Wolf goes a step beyond Marx when he asserts (1982:79): "There is no such thing as mercantile or merchant capitalism. . . . There is only mercantile wealth. Capitalism, to be capitalism, must be capitalism-in-production."

Other social scientists, including many Marxists, hold a different view. Most notable among these is Immanuel Wallerstein (1974a, b). Wallerstein rejects Marx's distinction between merchant and industrial capitalism and claims that capitalism is simply production in a market in which the aim of the producers is to realize the maximum profit. For Wallerstein, it does not matter whether there are wage workers or not. Indeed, for him several types of coercive, non-wage labor have existed within the capitalist mode of production. What is crucial about capitalism for Wallerstein is that the maximum accumulation of profits over time be the guiding aim of economic activity. Wallerstein believes that this requires the exploitation of workers, but that this exploitation may take a variety of forms, not just the exploitation of wage laborers. Given his conception of capitalism, Wallerstein sees it originating in the late fifteenth century with the rise of European colonialism.

This book is more sympathetic to Wallerstein's point of view but frankly recognizes that the Industrial Revolution of the eighteenth century dramatically changed the nature of capitalism. Indeed, it inaugurated a phase of capitalist development that was in certain crucial respects qualitatively different from anything that had previously existed. In siding with Wallerstein, we can scarcely overlook this important fact.

Early Capitalism between the Thirteenth and Sixteenth Centuries

Sometime after A.D. 1000, and especially after 1100, parts of the continent of Europe began to undergo significant commercial expansion. This was a major part of the long-term world-historical trend toward expanding world commercialization that was discussed in Chapter 5. The most important commercial centers of Europe were in the northwest, primarily in what is now Belgium, and in southern Europe, especially in the Italian city-states. The commercial expansion of this period contributed in a very significant way to the capitalist "great leap forward" that began in the sixteenth century.

In the northwest the city of Bruges was an integral part of a growing center of merchant capitalism. It was part of a large trading area that covered the Mediterranean, Portugal, France, England, the Rhineland, and the Hanseatic League (Braudel, 1984). The Hanseatic League was a trading association of merchant capitalists who carried out their activities all the way from England to the Baltic Sea. In the south a vigorous form of merchant capitalism developed in such Italian city-states as Florence, Pisa, Rome, Genoa, Venice, Siena, Prato, and Lucca (Cohen, 1980). The most important of these city-states were overwhelmingly specialized for trade. Banking became significantly developed, and merchants were highly admired and respected. The famous Medici, who were the richest Florentine bankers, merchants, and industrialists, were ensconced at the very top of the social and economic ladder (Cohen, 1980). Jere Cohen (1980) argues that many of the capitalist methods and practices developed in Italy during this time provided the basis for the spread of capitalism to other parts of Europe. As he notes, double-entry bookkeeping, marine insurance, and commercial law were invented by the Italians, who were the only ones to use them until the sixteenth century. The greatest of all the Italian city-states was Venice. This city-state was overwhelmingly devoted to foreign trade, the return on which has been estimated at an extraordinary 40 percent (Braudel, 1984). According to the great French historian Fernand Braudel (1984:123), Venice's "merchants firmly controlled all the major commodity trades in the Mediterranean—pepper, spices, Syrian cotton, grain, wine and salt." Venice's wealth and significance were also evident in the number of her galleys and cargo vessels.

While the capitalism of these centuries was for the most part merchant capitalism, a surprising amount of industry and manufacturing had developed. Some textile industries were highly mechanized, and manufacturing played an important part in the economies of several city-states, Venice included (Cohen, 1980). For example, "in Florence in 1338 there were said to be as many as 200 workshops engaged in cloth manufacture, employing a total of 30,000 workmen or about a quarter of the whole occupied population of the city" (Dobb, 1963:157).

The Seventeenth Century and Mercantilism*

By the sixteenth century, the center of capitalist activity in Europe had begun to shift from Italy to northwest Europe, first to Antwerp and then later to the Netherlands, England, and France. And, as Braudel (1984) has noted, capitalism came to be associated with large territorial states rather than small city-states. In the seventeenth century these large territorial states vigorously promoted capitalism in the form of **mercantilism.** Mercantilism involved governments' granting of monopolies to trading companies so that the companies could benefit from trade between the European nation and its colonies elsewhere. Monopolies for trading companies were not new to the mercantilist era, but the specific economic context in which these monopolies were granted—that of colonial trade—was.

Mercantilist practices created an economic situation in which manufacturers in the European country could receive extremely favorable terms of exchange for their products. Efforts were undertaken to prevent the colonies from manufacturing items that would compete with those being produced in the home country. Moreover, every effort was made to encourage the import of raw materials from the colonies to the home country, the raw materials to be brought in at low prices, turned into manufactured goods, and then sold at very high profits.

The great mercantilist trading companies of the seventeenth century were established in the Netherlands, England, and France. In 1602 the Dutch East India Company was formed. This company acquired a monopoly on trade with India, forbidding the English, the Portuguese, and the French to engage in such trade. The company had an army of nearly 12,000 men and a navy of between 40 and 60 ships. It brought into Europe each year between 10 and 12 million florins worth of goods. Between 1619 and 1663 the Dutch came to dominate the routes of the Far East. From 1648 to 1650 they imported from this area pepper and spices in quantities constituting 66 percent of all purchases and, in the same period, textiles totaling 14 percent of all purchases. They also began sugarcane production in Java. On the home front, the Netherlands established important processing industries,

---

*Unless otherwise noted, much of this section is attributable to Michel Beaud (1983).

such as wool and linen processing; diamond cutting, and the dyeing, weaving, and spinning of silk. Other industries included sugar refining, brewing, distilling, tobacco and cocoa refining, and lead working.

England became a major rival of the Netherlands during the seventeenth century. In 1600 the English East India Company was formed under a charter from Queen Elizabeth, and within 15 years the company had established more than 20 trading posts. These were located in India, certain islands in the Indian Ocean, Indonesia, and in Hiratsuka, Japan. Between 1610 and 1640 England's foreign trade increased by ten times. English kings "distributed privileges and monopolies, regulated and organized the control of manufacturers, prohibited the export of wool, and raised taxes on imported French and Dutch fabrics; Acts of Parliament went so far as to make obligatory the use of woolen cloth for mourning clothes" (Beaud, 1983:28–29). Moreover, especially vigorous mercantilist practices were carried out under the guidance of the statesman Oliver Cromwell. He issued a navigation act specifying that "European goods could be transported only on English ships or on ships belonging to their country of origin; products from Africa, Asia, or America could be imported only on ships of England or the colonies" (Beaud, 1983:29).

Mercantilist policies were also prominent in France. Cardinal Richelieu, Louis XIV, and Jean-Baptiste Colbert were the principal governmental personages associated with French mercantilism. Under Cardinal Richelieu, who was called upon to handle royal finances in 1624, various protectionist measures were established. These involved such things as a protective tariff on textiles in 1644 and a 50 cent per ton tax on foreign ships in 1659. But mercantilism in France reached its apex between 1663 and 1685 under Louis XIV and his chief economic minister, Colbert. For these men, the trading companies were regarded as the armies of the king, the manufacturers of France as his reserves (Beaud, 1983:39):

> [Colbert] watched over the establishment of more than 400 manufactures. There were "collective" works which brought together several artisan centers which benefited as a group from conferred privileges.... There were "private" works, individual enterprises (Van Robais in Abbeville), or large companies with branches in several provinces, especially in mining and metallurgy ... and woolen goods. Finally there were royal manufactures, which were the property of the sovereign.... The counterpart to the privileges (monopolies, of production or of sale, exemptions and financing) was strict controls (norms, quantity, quality). These policies developed luxury and export production (tapestries, porcelain, glassware, luxury fabrics) as well as basic production (iron working, paper making, armaments) and products for common consumption (woolen and linen fabrics, etc.)....
>
> State policy extended to commerce as well as production. The French East Indies Company (1664) received a fifty-year monopoly on trade and navigation in the Indian Ocean and the Pacific Ocean.

Capitalism as a World-System

An extremely influential perspective on the development of capitalism has been presented by Immanuel Wallerstein in his multivolumed *The Modern World-System* (1974a, 1980, 1989). Wallerstein regards capitalism as constituting, from the sixteenth century on, what he calls a **world-system.** Wallerstein defines a world-system as any relatively large social system having three principal characteristics:

- a high degree of autonomy; that is, the system is self-contained in the sense that it does not depend for its existence on something outside it, although it will interact to some degree with other world regions;

- an extensive division of labor or specialization of roles within the system; this specialization is both geographical and economic, there being different kinds of economic activities devoted to different kinds of products in various geographical zones of the system;
- a multiplicity of cultures, or the existence of different groups adhering to different traditions and speaking different languages.

Wallerstein identifies two basic types of world-system: world-empires and world-economies. A **world-empire** is a world-system that is politically centralized and unified, every group within the empire being subordinate to one political center. Ancient Rome and classical China and India, for example, were organized according to this type of world-system. A **world-economy** is a world-system that lacks political centralization and unification. It therefore contains not only a multiplicity of cultures, but a multiplicity of sovereign political units as well. In the past there may have been numerous world-economies, but all of these either collapsed or quickly became converted into world-empires. In the modern world, however, there is only one world-economy: the capitalist world-economy, which has existed from the sixteenth century to the present day. Although Wallerstein notes that there have been attempts to turn this world-economy into a world-empire (most notably by Spain in the sixteenth century), these attempts have failed, and capitalism to this day has remained a politically decentralized system. Wallerstein holds that this political decentralization has greatly contributed to the long-term persistence of capitalism, inasmuch as empires tend to stifle innovation and individual creativity, factors that are basic to the capitalist organization of production.

But what exactly is a world-economy? What integrates it, or holds it together?

Rather than being integrated by an overarching political structure, the capitalist world-economy is held together by a set of economic relationships, relationships of production and exchange of valued goods and services. In this sense the world-economy does not have the "tightness" of integration of a world-empire, but is a rather loosely structured network of economic relationships. These relationships involve extensive geographical and labor specialization. On the basis of such specialization, Wallerstein identifies three basic types of economic units that compose the world-economy.

The **core** consists of those regions and nation-states that dominate the capitalist world-economy and expropriate the bulk of the surplus produced within it. In the core are found those societies that are the most economically advanced or developed, that have the greatest degree of technological advancement, and that have the strongest governments and military structures. In the core, **wage labor**—work performed by employees bargained for by employers in a labor market—predominates. Wallerstein suggests that this is the case because work in the core is more highly skilled than work elsewhere, and more highly skilled work can be done more efficiently (i.e., more profitably) when wage labor is employed. The wealthiest capitalists within the entire world-economy are to be found residing in the core, establishing economic enterprises there and in other parts of the world-system.

The **periphery** is that segment of the world-economy that is most extensively subjected to surplus expropriation by the core. There is an intimate economic relationship between the core and the periphery, one in which the core dominates and exploits the periphery, which in turn becomes economically dependent on the core. The periphery has in most respects those characteristics that are the reverse of what we find in the core. The societies and regions of the periphery are those that are least economically developed, have the lowest level of technological advancement, and have the weakest governments and military units (or no sovereign governments or military units at all). Forced labor, rather than wage labor, predominates here (or at least has done so historically). **Forced labor** is any system of labor in which workers are not legally free to sell their labor in a market and are therefore politically compelled by members of some other group to work for them. The main historical types of forced labor have been slavery and serfdom. Under slavery, workers are owned outright and are under the complete political control of their owners. Under serfdom workers are tied to specific parcels of land from which they have no freedom to move away. Wallerstein believes that since most work in the periphery is unskilled compared to work in the core, forced labor systems are more suitable because they are less costly.

The **semiperiphery** is that segment of the world-economy that operates between the core and the periphery. Wallerstein conceives of it as both an exploiter and as itself being exploited: it is an exploiter of the periphery, but it is exploited by the core. The societies of the semiperiphery are more technologically and economically advanced than those of the periphery, but less so than those of the core. They have stronger governments and military units than those found in the periphery, but weaker governments and military units than those possessed by core societies. Another way of characterizing the semiperiphery is to say that it contains features of both core and peripheral societies. For example, semiperipheral societies, at least historically, have combined wage labor with certain types of forced labor. They thus carry out certain economic activities that are typical of core societies in conjunction with other economic activities characteristic of the periphery.

It is crucial to see that for Wallerstein capitalism is a vast system of surplus expropriation that goes on not only within regions, but *between* them as well. Marx focused his attention on the surplus expropriation that went on within core societies, using England as a model. Wallerstein, though, has broadened the Marxian model of capitalism to a worldwide level. He recognizes with Marx that capitalists exploit workers within the developed European nations, but he goes a step further in asserting that there are crucial relations of economic exploitation that go on between nations, that is, primarily between core and periphery. Wallerstein views the periphery as having a vital role to play in the capitalist world-economy. Peripheral societies are primarily organized by capitalists in the core to serve as raw material-producing units whose products can be exported to the core and turned into finished goods. Regions selected for peripheral development will be those that are most geographically suited for the production of certain raw materials at a certain time. (The relationship between core and periphery will become clearer in due course, especially in Chapter 9 where the problem of economic development and underdevelopment is discussed.)

It is also important to see that Wallerstein's notion that capitalism has constituted a world-system from its very inception is a rather revolutionary idea. Before Wallerstein, all analysts of capitalism, including Marx himself, limited their analyses to individual nation-states. But Wallerstein believes that the proper unit to deal with in analyzing capitalism is the world-system as a whole. He argues that one cannot understand what goes on in any single part of the world-system without understanding what is simultaneously going on in other parts of that system, indeed in the world-system as a whole. He believes that in order to understand the modern world from about 1500 on, societies can no longer be viewed as separate, independent units. Instead, they must be viewed in terms of their participation in or connection with a world-economy. This is a very bold idea, and the extent to which Wallerstein is correct is still hotly debated (cf. Skocpol, 1977; Brenner, 1977; Zolberg, 1981). Certainly one must be careful about pushing Wallerstein's world-system concept too far. However, whatever its limitations, the concept does appear to be a vital one for understanding the modern world and its evolution over the past five centuries.

The Capitalist World-Economy from the Sixteenth to the Eighteenth Centuries

Since its inception in the fifteenth century, the capitalist world-economy has been undergoing continual *expansion* and *evolution*. By saying that it has been expanding,

we mean that it has been increasing its geographical range to cover ever wider areas of the globe (see Figures 7.1 and 7.2). By saying that it has been an evolving system, we mean that its various components—core, periphery, and semiperiphery—have been changing their structure as parts of the whole. As we will see in the next two chapters, capitalism is now a vastly complex and technologically sophisticated system that covers most of the globe. But, as a world-system, what was it like during its early stages?

The first European nations to make a bid for core status in the sixteenth century were Spain and Portugal. These were the first European societies to engage in colonial expeditions in other regions of the world. Spain, in fact, attempted to turn the capitalist world-economy into its own world-empire—an attempt that failed. By the late sixteenth century it was clear that

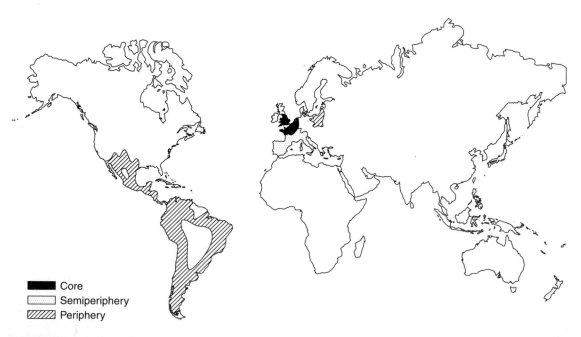

■ Core
▢ Semiperiphery
▨ Periphery

FIGURE 7.1
The capitalist world-economy, c. 1600.

FIGURE 7.2
The capitalist world-economy, c. 1750.

these societies would no longer be at the head of the world-economy. Their places were taken by the Netherlands, England, and France, the main core societies from the late sixteenth century on. Of these, the Netherlands was initially dominant. In these societies the principal economic activity was capitalist farming. Nobles increasingly leased their land out to tenants for a money rent and the land came to be farmed for profit. Many former nobles and peasants were converted into capitalist farmers. Much land was also turned over to the grazing of sheep, giving rise to an important woolen industry in England. Cottage industries were also of growing significance in these core societies.

The periphery in the sixteenth century consisted of two major world regions: Iberian (Hispanic and Portuguese) America and eastern Europe. In Hispanic America,

the Spaniards had established important colonies given over to large-scale agriculture and, more importantly, to gold and silver mining. Forced labor systems established by the Spaniards produced large quantities of gold and silver ore, which were exported back to Europe to be turned into coinage. The influx of these precious metals contributed in a major way to the expansion of the money supply in Europe and thus had a great impact on the world-economy. In Portuguese America (Brazil), sugar plantations were established and came to depend on extensive slave labor imported from Africa. Sugar became a commodity greatly valued in Europe for sweetening coffee and making chocolate. In the other major peripheral region, eastern Europe, large-scale grain farming was the primary economic activity. This was carried out under a forced labor system that was essentially like the serfdom of earlier days. The peasant-landlord relation still prevailed, but peasants were producing for a world economic market, not simply for their lords. During the sixteenth century, eastern Europe, Poland especially, was a major exporter of grain to western Europe.

The semiperiphery in the sixteenth century was located in Mediterranean Europe, primarily in Italy and ultimately in Spain and Portugal. Sharecropping was the principal form of agricultural labor, and industry mainly involved the production of high-cost products, such as silks.

After the middle of the seventeenth century, England began to replace the Netherlands as the major core society, due in large part to the military defeats the English imposed on the Dutch. France also began to supersede the Netherlands, but the French did not attain the degree of success that the English did. During this time, several new societies entered the periphery. The most important of these were the U.S. South, a slave colony of England devoted to the production of numerous agricultural goods; and the slave societies of the West Indies, established primarily under the influence of the British and the French. The Caribbean slave-plantation societies were devoted heavily to sugar production. The semiperiphery at this time also expanded to include Sweden, Prussia, and the U.S. North.

The Development of Capitalism in Japan

Traditionally the rise of modern capitalism has been understood as a distinctly European phenomenon, and thus Europe has been viewed as containing a developmental dynamic that was largely absent in the rest of the world. This argument, though, can no longer be sustained, for at least one other so-ciety, Tokugawa Japan (1600–1868), also revealed a marked tendency toward capitalist economic development. Moreover, this capitalist development was a largely indigenous phenomenon and had little to do with any European influence. This must be so, for between 1639 and 1853 Japan adopted a policy of almost complete isolation from economic and political contact with Europe (Pearson, 1991).

Japan was the one society outside Europe to develop a genuinely feudal politico-economic system (P. Anderson, 1974b). Feudalism emerged perhaps as early as 1185, but it is generally argued that the full development of the feudal system did not occur until 1338. The period from 1338 to 1600 has been called the classical age of Japanese feudalism, and the period from 1600 to 1868 (the Tokugawa era) the period of late feudalism (Reischauer, 1956; J. W. Hall, 1970).

It used to be thought that the Tokugawa period was one of economic stagnation, but in the last several decades it has come to be recognized that this period was actually one of great economic vitality. Daniel Spencer (1958) has claimed that during this period Japan experienced the widespread commercialization of agriculture, an increasing flight of peasants into the towns and cities, large-scale urbanization, a worsening economic condition of the feudal nobility, increased monetization of the economy, and the beginnings of the factory system. Urbanization was so extensive that John Whitney Hall (1970) calls it "astounding." The growth of Edo (modern Tokyo) was truly remarkable; at the end of the sixteenth century it was only a small village, but by the early eighteenth century it had reached 500,000 inhabitants, and by the end of the eighteenth century it was well past one million in population. By the early nineteenth century Japan was even more urbanized than Europe, and Edo had become the world's largest city.

Another striking feature of Japanese economic development during the Tokugawa epoch was the gradual *proletarianization* of the labor force (T. C. Smith, 1959; Leupp, 1992). Proletarianization is the process whereby workers are gradually converted from forced labor, such as serfdom, to wage labor, and it is an unmistakable sign of capitalist development. Proletarianization was most marked in urban areas, but it occurred in rural areas as well. By the end of the Tokugawa period, wage labor had become the dominant mode of compensating labor in the urban economy.

Recognition that modern Japan's capitalist roots extend back several centuries is a tremendously important accomplishment and a badly needed corrective to the old view of Tokugawa economic stagnation. Yet focusing on the Tokugawa period may itself be starting too late, for the true roots of Japanese capitalism may be found several centuries earlier. It seems that important economic developments were occurring in Japan as early as the thirteenth century. At this time Japan was deeply enmeshed in a network of foreign trade with other parts of Asia, especially China. During the fifteenth and sixteenth centuries foreign trade grew rapidly, and trade ventures were extended to more distant parts of the Far East. Japan was clearly a maritime economic power in these times (Sansom, 1961; Reischauer, 1956; J. W. Hall, 1970).

It is my view that by the end of the Tokugawa period Japan had become an essentially capitalist society in economic terms, even though it still retained old-fashioned feudal political and social institutions. By this time the economy was clearly in the hands of the urban merchants rather than the feudal landlords (Spencer, 1958). As we shall see, this relatively independent trajectory of capitalist development in Japan holds major implications for understanding the rise of modern capitalism.

EXPLAINING THE TRANSITION FROM FEUDALISM TO CAPITALISM

Explaining the transition from feudalism to capitalism has turned out to be one of the knottiest theoretical problems in contemporary social science. Numerous theories have been offered, but there has been little consensus about them. Most of these theories fall into four main categories:

- *Marxian theories*, which emphasize economic factors, the revival of world trade, or class struggle and exploitation (Dobb, 1963; Sweezy, 1976 [orig. 1950]; Wallerstein, 1974a; Brenner, 1976, 1977).
- *Weberian theories*, which emphasize the Protestant work ethic, Christianity, the role of the nation-state, or a "spirit of rationality" (Weber, 1958 [orig. 1905]; Collins, 1980; Mann, 1986; Chirot, 1985, 1986).
- *World-system theories*, which focus on geopolitical shifts within world trade networks (Abu-Lughod, 1989).
- *Demographic theories*, which stress population growth, population decline, or some combination of the two (Postan, 1972; Wilkinson, 1973; Le Roy Ladurie, 1974; M. Harris, 1977; P. Anderson, 1974a).

All of these theories contain weaknesses critical enough to preclude any of them offering a satisfactory explanation of the transition to capitalism. (An extended explication and critique of these theories may be found in Sanderson, 1994a.) A serious weakness in nearly all of these theories is that they have been developed exclusively with respect to the European transition, ignoring the Japanese transition to capitalism altogether. My own interpretation of the transition to modern capitalism, by contrast, has been explicitly developed to explain both the European and Japanese transitions, and thus is designed as a general theory. My assumption is that any adequate social-scientific theory must apply to as many instances of a phenomenon as possible. Concerning the rise of capitalism, as there are only two cases, an adequate theory of this phenomenon should apply equally to both, and not to one alone.

My interpretation of the rise of capitalism contains two parts. First, there were several common characteristics of Europe and Japan that I think operated as important preconditions facilitating their transition from feudal to capitalist economies. Second, there was a great historical trend—expanding world commercialization—that provided the necessary context within which the preconditions operated to facilitate a capitalist transition. It was the interaction of these two kinds of factors—common preconditions on the one hand and a major historical trend on the other—that led to the transition to modern capitalism when and where it occurred. (A much more detailed presentation of my theory is found in Sanderson, 1994a.)

I would suggest that medieval Europe and medieval Japan shared a minimum of four basic characteristics, each of which contributed in its own way to the emergence of modern capitalism. First, there is the factor of *size.* Japan and two of the three leading capitalist countries of early modern Europe, England and the Netherlands, were very small. Small geographical size minimizes the costs necessary to create systems of transportation and communication that help bring about economic development. Europe and Japan contrasted markedly with most of Asia, because most Asian societies, such as those found in China and India, were bureaucratic empires spread out over large landmasses. The costs of maintaining large empires constitute a serious obstacle to capitalist development.

Second, there is *geography.* Japan and the leading capitalist countries of northwest Europe were located on large bodies of water that allowed them to give predominance to maritime rather than overland trade. Historically, in the long agrarian era those societies containing the greatest amount of production-for-exchange—a kind of early capitalism or "protocapitalism"—have generally been ones in which maritime trade predominated (Amin, 1991). Maritime trade allows for a much more extensive and efficient development of networks of economic exchange than does overland trade.

A third factor is *climate.* Europe and Japan both had temperate climates, which is important when we recognize that the greater part of the world colonized by Europe had tropical or subtropical climates. Japan's temperate climate, or perhaps its far northerly location, allowed it to escape European colonization, which meant that its economy never became subordinated to or dominated by some foreign economic power. In the modern world the least economically developed nation-states have generally been those exposed to many years of colonial domination by Europe. One of the reasons why Europe and Japan were the colonizers rather than the colonized was probably their temperate climate and northern latitudes.

Finally, the *political structures* of Europe and Japan were similar in that they were the only true feudal regimes in world history (P. Anderson, 1974b). The key to feudalism is political decentralization or fragmentation (see Chapter 11), and it is widely agreed that feudalism contributes to capitalist development because of the economic freedom it gives to merchant classes. Large centrally organized empires tend to stifle mercantile activity because it is a threat to the mode of surplus extraction used by rulers and governing classes. The freedom given to merchants under the feudal regimes of medieval Europe and Japan was probably the most important precondition that helped push these parts of the world forward as the first states to undergo a capitalist revolution.

These four preconditions did not operate in a vacuum, however, but occurred in the context of a great historical trend, that of expanding world commercialization, which we discussed in Chapter 5. My argument is that the rise of capitalism could only be a slow and gradual process because of the generalized hostility of landholding classes to merchants, the carriers of capitalism throughout history. As discussed in Chapter 5, merchants generally occupied a very low position in the status-ranking systems of agrarian societies, despite the great wealth they sometimes accumulated. Therefore, mercantile activity could not expand rapidly because landlords would not allow it. Nevertheless, landlords were still dependent on merchants because they desired many of the goods merchants offered. Mercantile activity thus had to be preserved, and this gave merchants the opportunity to expand their activities slowly but surely. And in due time mercantile activity had expanded to the point at which it could act as a kind of "critical mass" stimulating the huge leap in capitalist development after the sixteenth century.

Explaining the emergence of modern capitalism means explaining why capitalism arose when it did (why in the sixteenth century rather than in earlier or later periods), and also why it occurred first in particular regions (northwest Europe and Japan rather than other parts of Europe, Asia, or elsewhere). The theory offered here explains this "when" and "where" of capitalist development. Capitalism could not have occurred earlier (or at least much earlier) in world history because of the slow expansion of world commercialization and the need for a "critical mass" of mercantile activity to trigger a capitalist takeoff. That critical mass

was not reached until sometime around A.D. 1000–1500. Numerous economic historians have thought that China during the time of the Sung Dynasty (A.D. 960–1275) was ready to take off into capitalism, but the tremendous economic advances it made during this time were eventually short-circuited (Elvin, 1973; E. L. Jones, 1988). The reason why this Chinese economic development petered out can be found in its unfavorable preconditions, especially the fact that China had a large landmass and a highly centralized and very powerful bureaucratic state. Northwest Europe and Japan had the most favorable preconditions for capitalist development at that time in world history during which a critical mass of commercialization had been achieved, and thus they were the world's first regions to experience the transition to the system that we now know as modern capitalism.

SUMMARY

1. The feudal economy of western Europe was a production-for-use economy organized around the manor. Landlords subjugated a peasantry who cultivated for their own subsistence and rendered taxes, rent, and labor services to their lords. Production-for-exchange played little role in economic life. Although towns and trade existed, they had little impact on the functioning of the feudal economy.

2. This system was eventually replaced by the capitalist mode of production. The capitalist system is one in which the selling of commodities for maximum profit is the essence of economic life. Marx and many other Marxists view capitalism as based on the wage-labor relationship and as developing with the Industrial Revolution in the late eighteenth century. They distinguish between industrial capitalism (or "true" capitalism) and a type of capitalism known as merchant capitalism that existed between the sixteenth and eighteenth centuries.

Others reject the distinction between merchant and industrial capitalism and date capitalist origins from the sixteenth century.

3. Although most scholars do not consider capitalism to have developed in Europe until at least the sixteenth century, in fact a vigorous form of merchant capitalism could be found as early as the thirteenth century in northwest Europe and in the Italian city-states. The Italian city-states were highly specialized for trade and merchant capitalists dominated social and economic life. The Italians developed banking, double-entry bookkeeping, marine insurance, and commercial law.

4. After the beginning of the sixteenth century a major capitalist takeoff began, and by the seventeenth century capitalism had come to be the dominant economic form in northwest Europe. The seventeenth century has been known as the age of mercantilism. In this era governments granted monopolies to companies to engage in international trade. Huge profits were earned by European trading companies through trade with their colonies elsewhere in the world.

5. A major effort to interpret the historical development of capitalism has been made by Wallerstein. Wallerstein sees capitalism as a world-system that has always had a complex division of labor along both occupational and geographical lines. This world-system has been geographically expanding for several hundred years and is now nearly worldwide in scope.

6. Wallerstein divides the capitalist world-system into core, peripheral, and semiperipheral nations and regions. Core areas are politically and economically dominant and engage in extensive surplus extraction from peripheral regions they create in order to exploit. Core regions are the most technologically and economically advanced. Peripheral regions have historically functioned in the world-economy as raw-material-producing areas whose products are desired by the core. Semiperipheral nations and regions are economically intermediate between core and peripheral nations and regions and have many of the characteristics of both.

7. For Wallerstein capitalism began in the sixteenth century with the emergence of Spain and Portugal as colonially expanding European powers. When they declined, their place was taken by the Netherlands, England, and France, core nations that dominated the world-system by the middle of the seventeenth century. The major peripheral regions during this period were Iberian America and eastern Europe. The semiperiphery consisted of Mediterranean Europe.

8. The development of capitalism was not unique to Europe, for during the same centuries Japan underwent a largely independent process of capitalist development. During its Tokugawa epoch Japan was witness to increased commercialization and monetization of the economy, rapidly expanding urbanization, and the growing importance of the urban merchants. By the middle of the nineteenth century Japan had become a substantially capitalist society in economic terms even if feudal social and political relations were still dominant.

9. Many theories of the development of modern capitalism have been presented without any real consensus being reached regarding them. My own interpretation focuses on four commonalities between medieval Europe and Japan—small geographical size, location on a large body of water, temperate climate, and feudal politico-economic relations—and on the gradual buildup of the forces of world trade and commercialization. The commonalities between Europe and Japan constituted preconditions that helped facilitate capitalist development in these regions, and the absence of most or all of these preconditions elsewhere was a hindrance to the development of capitalism. However, these preconditions by themselves could not have led to the emergence of modern capitalism. They occurred in the context of a long-term historical trend—expanding world commercialization—whose slow and gradual development had built up by about A.D. 1000–1500 to a "critical mass," or a level sufficient to trigger a dramatic capitalist takeoff. It was the interaction of the four preconditions with the level of world commercialization that led to the emergence of capitalism after the sixteenth century in northwest Europe and Japan.

SPECIAL TOPIC: INDUSTRY BEFORE THE INDUSTRIAL REVOLUTION

The Industrial Revolution of the late eighteenth century unleashed industrial activity on a massive scale and converted European capitalism into a highly urbanized, manufacturing-oriented economic activity. Yet in the principally agrarian life of Europe before the Industrial Revolution, industry was not lacking. Indeed, a good deal of it existed. But it was organized very differently from the later industry that developed under industrial capitalism.

The French social historian Fernand Braudel (1982) has distinguished four forms of industrial activity in early capitalist Europe. At the simplest level were *family workshops*. There were countless numbers of these tiny industrial units throughout Europe. Each workshop was normally headed by a master tradesman and contained two or three journeymen and an apprentice or two. The division of labor was very simple or there was none at all. Braudel includes in this category the cutler, the nail maker, the village blacksmith, the cobbler, the goldsmith, the locksmith, and the lace maker, as well as the baker, the miller, the cheese maker, and the butcher.

A second type of industrial activity might be termed the *dispersed factory*. In this type of arrangement, workshops were scattered over possibly wide areas yet connected to one another. A merchant entrepreneur served as a kind of director or coordinator. This entrepreneur provided raw materials to the individual workshops, ensured that the work got done, made payments of wages to the workers, and marketed the finished product. This category of industry was perhaps most commonly found in textile manufacturing, but it was also associated with cutlery, nail making, and iron working.

A third category of industry involved *concentrated manufacture*, or the *manufactory*, a form that represented a significant break with the first two types. Rather than remaining in their own homes, workers came together under one roof to complete a series of tasks. A division of labor ensued, leading to an increase in the level of productivity. This type of work organization had penetrated textile manufacturing to some extent, and was also found in connection with brewing, tanning, glassworking, and a number of other industries.

The fourth type of industrial activity was very similar to the third, but was distinguished by the level of technology employed. In manufactories, work was done primarily by hand, but in the fourth category—*factories*—work was accomplished through considerable reliance upon machinery. Of course, factories did not become a significant feature of capitalism until the late eighteenth and early nineteenth centuries, but they existed to some extent nonetheless. As Braudel comments (1982:301–302):

> I would regard the typical modern mine of the sixteenth century for instance, such as existed in central Europe . . . as an example, and an important one, of mechanization, even if steam was only introduced two hundred years later and then only very slowly and grudgingly. . . . Other examples are the naval yards of Saardam near Amsterdam in the seventeenth century, with their mechanical saws, their cranes, their masterecting machines; and so many little "factories" using hydraulic wheels: paper-mills, saw-mills or the sword-works in Vienne in the Dauphine, where the grindstones and bellows were mechanically operated.

The most famous form of industrial activity throughout preindustrial Europe was what in Germany came to be known as the *Verlagssystem*, more commonly known as the **putting-out system,** or sometimes simply as **cottage industry.** This is a version of the second category of industry discussed above. In the *Verlagssystem*, a merchant served as "the middleman between the producer of raw materials and the artisan, between the artisan and the purchaser of the finished product, and between his local town and foreign markets" (Braudel, 1982:318). As Braudel notes, this merchant "had one foot in the town and the other in the country" (1982:318). The merchant organized industrial activity by providing workers with raw materials and an initial wage and then placing an order for a certain quantity of finished products. Workers remained in their homes to manufacture the products. The merchant paid the remaining wages when the products were turned over to him, and he saw to the selling of the products in the available markets.

The putting-out system developed very early in preindustrial Europe, even before the sixteenth century. Although it was originally named by the Germans and first analyzed by German historians, it was not invented in Germany. Braudel suggests that it probably originated in the Netherlands and in Italy, perhaps as early as the thirteenth century. It soon spread throughout Europe.

Although many forms of industry were organized by the *Verlagssystem*, the principal industry with which it was associated was textile manufacturing. Braudel gives us a vivid picture of the *Verlagssystem* as applied to lace manufacture in eighteenth-century Germany (1982:318):

> In the month of June 1775, an observant traveller crossing the Erzgebirge from Freyberg to Augustusberg, journeyed through the string of mountain villages where cotton was spun and lace made. . . . Since it was summertime, all the women were sitting outside on their doorsteps; under a lime tree, a circle of girls sat round an old grenadier. And everyone, including the old soldier, was hard at work. It was a matter of life and death: the lacemaker's fingers only stopped for a moment to pick up a piece of bread or a boiled potato sprinkled with salt. At the end of the week, she would take her work either to the local market (but that was the exception) or more probably to the Spitzenherr, the "lord of the lace," who had provided her with thread and patterns from Holland and France, and who had placed an advance order for her work.

This system is an excellent example of a type of productive activity that was different in its very essence from the one that came to dominate after the Industrial Revolution. The organization of work associated with industrial capitalism was completely absent, and the workers retained their traditional craft skills. The merchants' concerns were limited to the marketing of the final product and did not involve attempts to alter the production process. Thus, the putting-out system was a classic form of merchant capitalism.

FOR FURTHER READING

Abu-Lughod, Janet L. *Before European Hegemony: The World-System* A.D. *1250–1350.* New York: Oxford University Press, 1989. Argues that there was a major world-system, within which Europe was peripheral, in operation several centuries before Wallerstein's postulated European-based world system. Shows that the level of world commercialization by the thirteenth century was very great and was of more significance than Wallerstein is willing to grant.

Beaud, Michel. *A History of Capitalism, 1500–1980.* New York: Monthly Review Press, 1983. A valuable general sketch by a French Marxian economist of the historical development of capitalism.

Braudel, Fernand. *Civilization and Capitalism, 15th–18th Century.* New York: Harper & Row, 1981–1984. An extraordinary economic history of capitalism before the Industrial Revolution by an eminent French historian who has had a great influence on Wallerstein. Volume 1, *The Structures of Everyday Life,* explores such basic aspects of human material existence as population, housing, food and drink, and technology. Volume 2, *The Wheels of Commerce,* examines many intricate details of economic exchange and commerce. Volume 3, *The Perspective of the World*, is the most theoretical of all the volumes and examines the early history of capitalism from a perspective similar to Wallerstein's world-system approach.

Chirot, Daniel. *Social Change in the Modern Era*. San Diego: Harcourt Brace Jovanovich, 1986. A critique and reformulation of Wallerstein's conception of the world capitalist system. Presents a neo-Weberian interpretation of the rise of modern capitalism.

Duby, Georges. *Rural Economy and Country Life in the Medieval West*. Translated by Cynthia Postan. Columbia: University of South Carolina Press, 1968. A classic treatment of the feudal economy of medieval Europe. Truly unsurpassed.

Hilton, Rodney (ed.). *The Transition from Feudalism to Capitalism*. London: Verso, 1976. A collection of articles written by Marxian historians and social scientists on the transition to modern capitalism. The articles by Dobb and Sweezy are the most famous Marxian analyses of this issue.

Kriedte, Peter. *Peasants, Landlords and Merchant Capitalists: Europe and the World Economy, 1500–1800*. Cambridge: Cambridge University Press, 1983. A good brief treatment of the development of capitalism during its early centuries.

Mann, Michael. *The Sources of Social Power. Volume 1: A History of Power from the Beginning to A.D. 1760*. Cambridge: Cambridge University Press, 1986. Several chapters near the end treat in considerable detail the rise of modern capitalism. Adopts basically a Weberian perspective and locates the roots of capitalism several centuries earlier than most treatments.

Sanderson, Stephen K. "The transition from feudalism to capitalism: The theoretical significance of the Japanese case." Review 17: 15–55, 1994. An explication and critique of the major theories of the transition from feudalism to capitalism, along with a more detailed version of my theory of this great social transformation.

Smith, Alan K. *Creating a World Economy: Merchant Capital, Colonialism, and World Trade 1400–1825*. Boulder, Colo.: Westview Press, 1991. A useful overview of some of the leading aspects of the emergence and evolution of the capitalist world-economy through the early nineteenth century.

Wallerstein, Immanuel. *The Modern World-System: Capitalist Agriculture and the Origins of the European World-Economy in the Sixteenth Century*. New York: Academic Press, 1974. An outstanding, but highly controversial, work on the emergence of capitalism by a noted sociologist. The first of four planned volumes on the development of capitalism from Wallerstein's world-system perspective. Already a modern classic, it is absolutely essential reading for anyone interested in the general history of capitalism.

Wallerstein, Immanuel. *The Modern World-System II: Mercantilism and the Consolidation of the European World-Economy, 1600–1750*. New York: Academic Press, 1980. The second volume of Wallerstein's planned four-volume opus.

Weber, Max. *The Protestant Ethic and the Spirit of Capitalism*. Translated by Talcott Parsons. New York: Charles Scribner's Sons, 1958. (Originally published 1905.) The most famous explanation ever advanced for the rise of modern capitalism. Argues that the Protestant Reformation of the sixteenth century provided a critical stimulus to capitalist development.

Wolf, Eric. *Europe and the People Without History*. Berkeley: University of California Press, 1982. An absorbing historical analysis of capitalism in which the author gives special emphasis to the impact of capitalism on the precapitalist societies that fell under capitalist influence.

Chapter

8

Capitalism and Socialism Since the Industrial Revolution

Immanuel Wallerstein (1984d) has claimed that there have been three great trends in the evolution of the capitalist world-economy: increasing mechanization of production, increasing commodification of the factors of production, and increasing proletarianization of the labor force. Increasing **mechanization** involves the increasing application of advanced technology, especially machinery, to production tasks. The level of **commodification** of the factors of production advances when land, labor, technology, and other productive forces increasingly come to be regulated by the market and by considerations of their exchange-value. Increasing **proletarianization** results when a larger percentage of the workforce is compensated in the form of wages. Taken together, these three trends mark what is known as a "deepening" of capitalist development (Shannon, 1996). This chapter and the next explore the deepening of capitalism over the past two centuries. Of particular concern in the present chapter is what has been called the Industrial Revolution: what it was, when and why it occurred, and what its consequences were for the capitalist system. The chapter also explores the evolution and expansion of capitalism from the late nineteenth century to the present. After 1917, and particularly after 1945, some capitalist societies began efforts to withdraw from the capitalist system and to establish socialist economies. The nature and significance of these efforts is also a major topic of the chapter.

THE INDUSTRIAL REVOLUTION AND THE EMERGENCE OF INDUSTRIAL CAPITALISM

The Industrial Revolution and Its Causes

The Industrial Revolution involved the transformation of a technology resting heavily on human and animal labor into a technology characterized by *machines* (Landes, 1969). Along with this came the transition from a heavy reliance on agricultural production to a reliance on the manufacture of goods for sale in the context of a factory system. The Industrial Revolution was, at bottom, a revolution in technology; it created, nevertheless, new and profound changes in the very economic structure of society, bringing new methods of production and exchange of goods, and profound changes in the organization of labor.

The Industrial Revolution began in England during the second half of the eighteenth century, its first phase typically being dated from about 1760 to 1830 (Landes, 1969). This initial phase of **industrialization** was characterized by the great expansion of the textile industry and by major developments in the manufacture of iron and the mining of coal. The textile industry, especially the manufacture of cotton cloth, was advanced through the invention of the spinning jenny, the water frame, the power loom, and the cotton gin. The growth of textile manufacture spurred the development of the factory system. The invention of the steam engine was also an important part of this process, as it was used to power the heavy machinery housed in the textile factories. Textiles formed a vital part of the English economy and were a major export in the international capitalist system.

The iron industry also underwent significant expansion in the first phase of industrial development. Iron was increasingly in demand for the manufacture of steam engines and machine tools; machine tool production itself became a significant feature of the English economy. The increasing manufacture of these products, in turn, caused an increase in the demand for coal and the expansion of the coal-mining industry.

Industrial technology was soon to be found in several other parts of Europe during the nineteenth century, especially in France, Belgium, and Germany. The United States also began to emerge as a major industrial society during this time. By the late nineteenth century, both Russia and Japan had begun to industrialize.

The Industrial Revolution created a new mode of economic production, *industrial capitalism*. As indicated in the last chapter, industrial capitalism differs from other forms of capitalism in that it involves the earning of profit through the exploitation of wage workers. The establishment of industrial capitalism on a major scale thus required the reorganization of the workforce into the factory system, and the factory became the basic social unit of capitalist production. Michel Beaud has said the following in regard to the emergence of industrial capitalism (1983:83):

> During the nineteenth century it was chiefly through the establishment of mechanized industry that the capitalist mode of production was extended. The "mills" which had begun to be built in England at the end of the eighteenth century became more widespread, not only in England itself, but in Belgium, France, Switzerland, Germany, and the United States. The development of these mills was particularly striking in the "driving" sectors of the time: textiles and metallurgy. Men who had previously been traders or merchants, as well as foremen and the sons of artisans, became manufacturers and availed themselves of a

labor force that had become available through the transformation of the country-side or through immigration. These laborers were employed with the intention of extracting the maximum, and it was in conditions of misery and unbearable oppression that the original core of the modern working class was formed.

Obviously, industrialization did not end with these technological and economic developments. Rather than as an event or a series of events, industrialization is better thought of as a continual process that has existed down to the present time. In the middle of the nineteenth century, further technological innovations emerged and existing technologies were elaborated and applied to capitalist production on a wider scale. For example, the steam engine came to be applied to transportation. It was used to create the first steam railway and was applied as well to navigation with the invention of the steamboat. It was during this time that railroads began to emerge as an extremely significant aspect of capitalist investment (Dobb, 1963).

By the turn of the twentieth century, the automobile, electrical, and petroleum industries were becoming important features of life in industrial societies (Lenski, 1970). By World War II, the aviation, aluminum, and electronics industries were achieving major economic significance (Lenski, 1970). Recent years have witnessed such notable technological developments as the harnessing of nuclear energy and the manufacture of highly sophisticated computers on a major scale. And it takes no particularly acute vision of the future to see that such developments are probably only the beginning of a series of enormous technological accomplishments.

This picture of the Industrial Revolution is highly schematic, but it should nonetheless serve to make clear just how significant were the technological changes that were taking place. These changes were to produce major changes in the structure of social life throughout virtually the entire world. But why did the Industrial Revolution occur when and where it did? Indeed, why did it occur at all?

Some scholars have seen the Industrial Revolution as rooted in population pressure (R. Wilkinson, 1973; Boserup, 1981). They thus see industrialization as simply another technological advance that, like earlier technological advances such as the Neolithic Revolution or the emergence of the plow, is rooted in the desire to stave off declining standards of living created by increasing numbers. It is unlikely, though, that industrialization can be explained by demographic growth. We are dealing here with a technological change far different from the technological changes of earlier eras.

A much better explanation is that the Industrial Revolution was the logical and predictable outcome of the evolving European world-economy (Wallerstein, 1989). By the middle of the eighteenth century, England had clearly emerged as the dominant power within this economy. England had expanded its import and export markets throughout the capitalist system and had concentrated within itself enormous quantities of wealth. This wealth became essential as capital to be used in financing factories and machinery, and thus England was in a uniquely favorable financial position to engage in industrial development. But as Eric Hobsbawm (1968) has pointed out, capitalism has no inherent bias toward technological innovation for its own sake. It only has a bias toward increased profitability and will innovate only when it is profitable to do so. With this insight, it is easy to see why England was strongly oriented toward major industrial development. Industrialization permitted increasing productivity and lowered costs, which in turn allowed for the expansion of England's existing domestic and foreign markets and for the creation of new ones. The result was the increasing accumulation of capital on a grand scale.

The Industrial Revolution was thus the historical product of the European capitalist world-economy, and it was initiated by the nation that was best suited economically to bring it about. This fact also helps explain why the Industrial Revolution occurred when it did rather than much earlier or later. It could not have occurred much earlier since its emergence closely depended upon the creation and substantial expansion of a capitalist world-economy. Its occurrence at some much later time was also unlikely, since industrial technology was an important—indeed, an essential—component of an expanding economic system fundamentally committed to unlimited growth.

It is also important to see why the Industrial Revolution did not occur outside Europe. Of all the non-European societies, China was in one sense the most likely to have had an industrial revolution. As Wallerstein (1974a) has pointed out, in A.D. 1500 China was technologically at least as advanced as, if not more advanced than, western Europe (cf. McNeill, 1982). But by 1800 western Europe had far surpassed China. This demonstrates that technological change is surely not an autonomous process, occurring for its own sake. Rather, it depends upon particular conditions. Western Europe, and England especially, had precisely those conditions logically leading to major technological innovation. But what did China have (or not have) that impeded major technological advance? For one thing, it was not organized around a capitalist mode of production in the eighteenth century. In addition, it had an imperial bureaucratic state that did not depend upon technological advance for its enrichment and that actively squashed many technological innovations because of their potential economic threat (Wallerstein, 1974a). Imperial China was thus very poorly situated to experience the world's first industrial revolution.

The Industrial Revolution in World-System Perspective

In the third volume of his *The Modern World-System* (1989), Wallerstein has suggested that the notion of the Industrial Revolution is something of a myth, or at least that the way in which most scholars have spoken of these changes is highly misleading. Wallerstein is essentially making three closely related points: first, that the changes were not as dramatic or as revolutionary as commonly thought; second, that the so-called Industrial Revolution is not some sort of great dividing point between the past and the modern world; and finally, that what we call the Industrial Revolution was part and parcel of the evolution of the world-economy as a whole, not of individual societies within it.

As noted earlier, Wallerstein has argued that one of the great evolutionary trends of the capitalist world-economy is increasing mechanization. This occurs throughout the entire system, but is carried out faster and far more extensively in core societies. Increasing mechanization has gone on continually, even if not smoothly, throughout the history of capitalism. From this perspective, the Industrial Revolution of the eighteenth century was simply one phase in this evolutionary process, and therefore not really revolutionary at all. Considerable mechanization had occurred in earlier centuries, especially during the period between 1540 and 1640 (Nef, 1964). All of this means that the "great divide" in world history is not the Industrial Revolution, as many social scientists argue, but the transition to capitalism that began some three centuries earlier.

In addition, if the Industrial Revolution was simply part of the evolution of the capitalist world-economy as a whole, then we have to use the entire system as a reference point in understanding why it occurred. In this regard Wallerstein insists that what we call the Industrial Revolution occurred in certain core societies during what he terms "the second era of great expansion of the capitalist world-economy" (Wallerstein, 1989). Capitalism was born in the fifteenth and sixteenth centuries and expanded throughout a significant portion of the globe during that time. Then, in the seventeenth century, it continued to expand, but at a much slower rate (Wallerstein, 1980). After about 1730, it entered a third phase, which was its second phase of rapid expansion. By the end of this phase—sometime during the middle of the nineteenth century—it had come to cover a large portion of the globe (most of it by the end of that century; see Figure 8.1). And it was during this third phase that extensive industrialization occurred within the major core societies, and for reasons that have already been explained.

To my mind, Wallerstein's overall position is basically correct, but with the important qualification that he underestimates the extensiveness of the technological and economic changes after the middle of the eighteenth century. To be sure, increasing mechanization has been a continual process in the history of capitalism, but it has also been very sporadic and uneven. It is an exaggeration to imply that the technological changes before 1760 were on the same scale as those that occurred after that time. Therefore, while many scholars may overrate the significance of the Industrial Revo-

lution, Wallerstein is underrating its significance.

Some Social Consequences of Industrialization

In fact, industrial development has had enormous consequences for the organization of social life, and virtually every aspect of social life has been touched by it. One of the most fundamental consequences of industrialization has been an enormous increase in economic productivity, an increase on a scale totally unprecedented in human history. To take a simple case, in 1750 the import of raw cotton for spinning amounted to £3 million, but by 1784 the figure had climbed to £11 million, by 1799 to £43 million, and by 1802 to £60 million (Heilbroner, 1972). Likewise, the production of pig iron increased dramatically from 68,000 tons in 1788 to 1,347,000 tons in 1839 (Heilbroner, 1972). Moreover, the productivity of labor has increased continually from these early days of industrial capitalism to the present and is far greater today than it was in the early nineteenth century.

A second consequence of industrialization, already touched upon, was the creation of an industrial proletariat within the core capitalist societies. This was the first great wave of proletarianization in the history of capitalism. This proletariat consisted of the mass of workers—men, women, and children—who worked in the factories. In the early days of industrial capitalism, these workers labored under conditions of severe hardship. They were brutally overworked in the factories and paid extremely low wages, in many cases barely enough to keep them alive. They lived in overcrowded slums and suffered frequently from malnutrition and disease. Many of them were children, who could be paid even lower wages than adult men and women. The situation in industrial

England in the first half of the nineteenth century was thus one characterized by the exploitation and degradation of a large mass of the population. It was precisely this situation that led to Marx's (1967; orig. 1867) scathing critique of capitalism. Commenting on life in the English factory towns, Eric Hobsbawm writes (1968:67–68):

> And what cities! It was not merely that smoke hung over them and filth impregnated them, that the elementary public services—water-supply, sanitation, street cleaning, open spaces, etc.—could not keep pace with the mass migration of men into the cities, thus producing, especially after 1830, epidemics of cholera, typhoid and an appalling constant toll of the two great groups of nineteenth-century urban killers— air pollution and water pollution, or respiratory and intestinal disease. It was not merely that the new city populations, sometimes entirely unused to nonagrarian life, like the Irish, pressed into overcrowded and bleak slums, whose very sight froze the heart of the observer. "Civilization works its miracles," wrote the great French liberal de Tocqueville of Manchester, "and civilized man is turned back almost into a savage."

A third consequence of industrialization has also occurred within the realm of work: the increasing specialization of labor. This phenomenon, whereby the worker has increasingly become a small cog in a large machine, has developed especially rapidly and extensively since the late nineteenth century. In the view of Karl Marx, this growing specialization of labor made work more and more meaningless and stifling for the worker. This was another feature of industrial capitalism that led him to be extremely critical of it. In a very real sense, the increasing specialization of labor signifies all three major trends of capitalist evolution. It results from a combination of proletarianization and mechanization, and it leads to the increasing commodification of work and the worker. We shall have more to say about this process shortly.

A fourth consequence of the emergence of industrial capitalism has been the extensive urbanization of society. Social life has shifted from the rural countryside to cities, many of them of vast scale. As Heilbroner (1972) notes in regard to the urban development of the United States, in 1790 only 24 towns and cities exceeded 2500 citizens, and collectively these towns constituted only 6 percent of the total population. But by 1860, 20 percent of the population was located in the 392 largest cities, and by 1970, much of the eastern seaboard had evolved into practically one gigantic city containing more than 60 percent of the total population of the country.

A fifth and final consequence of industrialization to be noted is demographic in nature. Industrialization has generally produced what is called the **demographic transition** (Harris and Ross, 1987; cf. Handwerker, 1986). This involves, initially, a lowering of the mortality rate because of improvements in sanitation, health care, and so on. People begin to live longer, healthier lives. The fall in the death rate is eventually followed by a dramatic decrease in the birth rate. Children are a strong economic asset in societies dominated by agricultural production, as they can be put to good use as farm workers. People in agrarian societies are thus generally motivated to have large families. But in industrial societies children become economic liabilities. As this occurs, people are motivated to reduce their family size. Instead of having six or eight children, they have two or three and invest more in each child. This sharp reduction in the birth rate has led to much lower rates of population increase in industrial societies than in societies still having a large agricultural population (Harris and Ross, 1987). (For some comparative statistical data on population growth rates in the world's societies, see Table 9.1 in Chapter 9.)

INDUSTRIAL CAPITALISM SINCE THE LATE NINETEENTH CENTURY

By the last quarter of the nineteenth century, the capitalist world-economy was dominated by four core societies (see Figure 8.1): the United Kingdom, the United States, Germany, and France (Chirot, 1986). These four societies were the most highly industrialized and urbanized societies in the world. In 1900 they collectively produced approximately three-quarters of all the world's manufactured goods, despite having only about one-eighth of the world's population (Chirot, 1977).

According to Daniel Chirot (1986), membership in the capitalist core was also held by five other societies: the Netherlands, Belgium, Switzerland, Sweden, and Denmark. These five societies were substantially overshadowed economically by the four main core powers. The semiperiphery at this time consisted mainly of Spain, Austria-Hungary, Italy, Russia, and Japan (Chirot, 1986). The periphery consisted of Portugal, China, the Ottoman Empire, the eastern European countries, and all or nearly all of Latin America, Asia, and Africa (see Figure 8.1).

World capitalism around the turn of the twentieth century had a number of crucial features that cannot be overlooked. One of these was the relative decline of Britain in the world economy and the relative rise of several other nations, especially the United States. As Beaud (1983) notes, Britain's share of world industrial production fell from 32 percent in 1870 to 14 per-

Core
Semiperiphery
Periphery

FIGURE 8.1
The capitalist world-economy, c. 1900.

cent just before World War I, and then to only 9 percent by 1930. At the same time the U.S. share of world production was increasing. In 1870 the United States produced 23 percent of the world's goods; by the eve of World War I it was producing 38 percent; and its share of world production had climbed to a full 42 percent by 1930. By the early twentieth century the United States had clearly replaced Britain as the world's major core power.

Another crucial feature of world capitalism at this time was its entry into a new phase of capitalist development, what has often been termed **monopoly capitalism.** Under monopoly capitalism, the competitive character of capitalism is increasingly reduced as capitalist companies grow in size and in their concentration of capital. Large corporations begin to dominate the market and drive out smaller producers by ruining them economically and then swallowing them up. Eventually a few giant corporations dominate the market for many industries. Beaud sums up the extent to which capital was being centralized in the hands of fewer and fewer companies during this time (1983:136–137):

> Everywhere, the average size of business establishments and industrial companies increased. . . . In times of crisis mergers took place which benefited the most powerful companies; thus during the period 1880–1918 in Britain, 655 companies "disappeared" into 74 merger companies.
>
> Above all, unprecedented concentrations of capital occurred, under the direction of a capitalist or of a family; trusts or groups very quickly came to dominate an entire industrial sector within a nation, especially in the United States and in Germany. In the United States in 1908, the seven largest trusts owned or controlled 1,638 companies. By 1900, the percentage represented by the trusts included 50 percent of textile production, 54 percent of the glassmaking industry,

60 percent of the book and paper industry, 62 percent of the food industry, 72 percent of the liquor industry, 77 percent of nonferrous metals, 81 percent of the chemical industries, and 84 percent of iron and steel. These included companies such as the United States Steel Corporation, founded by J. P. Morgan and E. H. Gary, which incorporated the Carnegie steel mills, and Standard Oil, founded in 1870 by J. D. Rockefeller, which in 1870 refined only 4 percent of American petroleum but by 1879 controlled 90 percent of the American refineries, and by 1904 controlled 85 percent of the domestic business and 90 percent of the export business as well.

In Germany the Krupp industrial empire employed 7,000 workers in 1873, and 78,000 in 1913; the AEG electrical industry, through an astonishing process of concentration, by 1911 controlled 175 to 200 companies, and employed more than 60,000 workers.

The emergence of monopoly capitalism was also characterized by a substantial increase in foreign investment by the core capitalist nations. Foreign investments quadrupled in Britain from the early 1890s to the early 1910s. In Germany, such investments doubled between 1883 and 1893, and then doubled again between 1893 and 1914. In France, they tripled between 1880 and 1914 (Beaud, 1983). About half of the foreign investments of the core powers were made outside Europe and North America. Latin America accounted for 19 percent, Asia for 16 percent, Africa for 9 percent, and Oceania for 5 percent (Beaud, 1983).

By the middle of the twentieth century, a new economic unit had become prominent in the capitalist world-economy: the **transnational corporation** (Barnet and Müller, 1974). The transnational corporation is today the central economic entity within world capitalism (Bornschier and Chase-Dunn, 1985). A transnational corporation is a company that has branches of production in more than one country. Long before the rise of such a corporation, capitalists *sold* their products in a world market, but the rise of the transnational corporation marked the emergence of international *production.*

The huge importance of the transnational corporations can be gleaned from a comparison of their sales with the gross national products (GNPs) of some smaller European nations (Heilbroner, 1972). For example, in the late 1960s General Motors had a sales level exceeding each of the GNPs of Belgium, Switzerland, Denmark, Austria, Norway, Greece, and Portugal. Similarly, the sales of Standard Oil of New Jersey exceeded the GNPs of all these countries except for those of Belgium and Switzerland.

The transnational corporation is only the latest in a series of strategies used by capitalists in the historic process of capital accumulation. By internationalizing production, capitalists are able to overcome certain barriers imposed on their accumulationist activities. One of these barriers is the existence of tariffs on imports. By locating a branch of their company in a foreign country, capitalists are able to produce and sell their products directly in that country and avoid costly tariffs.

In the capitalist world-system today the great core powers are the United States, Germany, France, and Japan. Although the United States is still the leading core power, its dominance is not as great as it once was. Most of the other nations of Western Europe, as well as Canada and Australia, are also members of the core. The semiperiphery principally consists of European nations such as Spain, Italy, and Greece; some of the better-off less-developed countries, such as Argentina, Venezuela, South Africa, and Taiwan; and the resource-rich OPEC countries of the Middle East. The periphery consists of the rest of the less-developed world in Africa, Asia, and Latin America (see Figure 8.2). (The next chapter will provide a close look at these nations of the contemporary capitalist periphery and semiperiphery, with an eye to explaining their low levels of economic development.)

THE JAPANESE TRANSITION TO INDUSTRIAL CAPITALISM

The discussion of industrial capitalism thus far has concentrated on Europe and North America, but of course it is well known that Japan has in recent decades emerged as a major industrial capitalist society and a world economic power. Many people, social scientists and laypersons alike, expect Japan to be the leading world economic power by the beginning of the twenty-first century.

Japan was incorporated into the world-economy after 1853, when Western ships landed in its harbors and demanded that it put an end to its two centuries of economic isolation from the West. Japan somewhat reluctantly accepted its inability to prevent Western contact and influence, but it took important steps to guarantee that Western contact would not do serious harm to its economy and society. In 1868 Japan underwent a major social and political transformation known as the Meiji restoration, which not only changed the form of government, but more importantly initiated a major program of economic development and industrialization. It is important to recognize that Japan was incorporated into the capitalist world-economy as a semiperipheral rather than a peripheral country. It was economically strong at the time of incorporation, and thus it was able to resist becoming a peripheral country devoted to producing raw materials for the benefit of core societies.

One of the first tasks of the modern national state that was created in Japan in 1868 was to make vigorous efforts to encourage large-scale industrialization, and

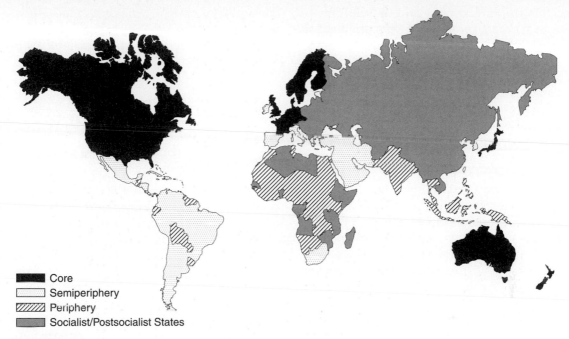

FIGURE 8.2
The capitalist world-economy, c. 1999.

the state came to play an extremely important role in the organization and development of the economy. Japanese industrialization involved direct government action to a degree far greater than was the case among the earlier European industrializing nations. Frances Moulder (1977) has identified three major ways in which the Japanese state involved itself in moving the economy forward:

- It established pilot projects with its own funds and administered them.
- It subsidized industries, especially heavy industry, railway construction, shipping, and mining; railways were a major government activity, as was mining; by the 1880s six mines (devoted to the mining of iron, lead, gold, silver, copper, and coal) were being operated by the government, and these were virtually the only ones that were worked on a large scale with modern machinery; the government also

became heavily involved in manufacturing during the 1870s, especially in the textile industry.
- It encouraged the formation of a system of national banks that would provide long-term loans at low interest rates to investors in modern industry.

The state continued to play a crucial role in Japanese economic development throughout the twentieth century, and plays such a role even today. The involvement of the Japanese government in the economy is so great that the country is sometimes jokingly referred to as "Japan, Inc." (Chirot, 1986).

It is mainly in the last four or five decades that Japan has risen to the position of a leading world economic power. From the mid-1950s through the 1980s the Japanese economy grew at a phenomenal rate. In 1989 Japan produced one-quarter of all the passenger cars manufactured throughout the world. By 1991 it produced about 30 percent of the passenger cars sold in the United States (this figure includes cars produced in Japanese factories in the United States). Japan has also outproduced other major industrial capitalist nations, or at least strongly challenged them, in the manufacture of such products as radios, quartz watches, televisions, calculators, video cassette recorders, stereophonics, computers, silicon memory chips, and robotics (Hane, 1992).

There are certain important differences between the capitalist economies of Japan and the West (Hane, 1992; Yoshihara, 1986). Japanese companies generally provide lifetime employment for their employees, with workers seldom moving from one company to another. Japanese workers at all levels of the workplace show a striking loyalty to their companies that is almost unimaginable in Western capitalism. Labor-management relations are also different in Japan. Japanese workers are asked for far more input into the decision-making process than are Western workers, and this has seemingly created a much greater harmony between management and labor. Mikiso Hane (1992) reports that the number of days lost to labor disputes in Japan in the 1980s was only about four percent of the days lost in the United States. Additionally, Japanese capitalists place emphasis on long-term rather than short-term profits, just the opposite of the situation in the West, where the mentality of the "quick buck" tends to predominate. Finally, it has become increasingly apparent in recent years that Japanese companies collaborate very closely with one another, forming conglomerates known as *zaibatsu* or *keiretsu*. This is a system in which a giant producer, such as Toyota or Sony, forms linkages with satellite firms that supply it with the materials needed to make its product. Members of these conglomerates confer with one another and coordinate their efforts, often in great detail.

These conglomerates behave like closed clubs—outsiders are kept out—and they tremendously facilitate the profitability of Japanese companies.

THE EMERGENCE OF STATE SOCIALIST SOCIETIES

The Origin and Nature of State Socialism

The world's first socialist society was born in 1917 when Russia underwent the Bolshevik revolution and became the Soviet Union. Elsewhere in Europe other socialist societies began to emerge in the mid- to late 1940s, and in the less developed part of the world a number of socialist societies arose somewhat later, mostly in the 1970s. Table 8.1 lists the major socialist societies of the world as of 1987. All of these societies are ones in which Marxism-Leninism is the dominant political ideology and the Communist party is in control of the state. (There are or have been a few other societies claiming to be socialist in a sense other than Marxist-Leninist. These are not included here.) These societies are perhaps best termed **state socialist** because of the strong role the state plays in the direction of the economy. To complicate matters, many of these societies have, since 1989 throughout Eastern Europe and 1991 in the Soviet Union, abandoned state socialism (at least in its classical version) and shifted markedly toward a more capitalist, market-oriented economy. In these same societies the Communist party has lost its monopoly of power, and substantial political liberalization has been achieved. For the sake of terminological clarity, I propose to use the term *state socialism* (or *state socialist*) to refer to these societies as they were before 1989 (Eastern Europe) or 1991 (Soviet Union), and to use the term **postsocialism** (or **postsocialist**) to refer to them from these

Table 8.1 STATE SOCIALIST SOCIETIES IN 1987

Country	Year of Transition to State Socialism
Soviet Union	1917
Mongolia	1921
Albania	1944
Yugoslavia	1945
Bulgaria	1947
Czechoslovakia	1948
Hungary	1948
Poland	1948
Romania	1948
North Korea	1948
China	1949
East Germany	1949
Vietnam[a]	1954
Cuba	1959
Congo	1963
Somalia	1969
South Yemen	1969
Benin	1972
Ethiopia	1974
Angola	1975
Kampuchea	1975
Laos	1975
Mozambique	1975
Afghanistan	1978
Nicaragua	1979
Zimbabwe	1980

[a]The date 1954 refers only to the northern part of the country. The southern part became socialist in 1975, when Vietnam again became a unified state.

Source: János Kornai, *The Socialist System: The Political Economy of Communism.* Princeton: Princeton University Press, 1990, pp. 6–7.

dates forward (the term *postsocialist* was coined by the Hungarian economist János Kornai, an astute analyst of the state socialist economy and its postsocialist transition; see Kornai, 1992).

In analyzing these societies, I first want to discuss their economic structure during their classical state socialist phase. At a later point we will look at the economic reforms they experienced in the 1970s and 1980s that led to the dramatic economic and political upheavals of 1989 and 1991. This will allow us to consider them as they are now—that is, as postsocialist societies. In this chapter I am concerned only with those state socialist societies that have undergone substantial industrialization: the Soviet Union and the socialist societies of Eastern Europe. I shall discuss both state socialism and postsocialism in the present tense, mainly because much of state socialism remains today within postsocialism. We cannot speak of state socialism as if it were a historical phenomenon that has been completely eliminated and transcended, for nothing of the sort has occurred.

In the classical exemplar of state socialism, the Soviet Union, private property has been almost completely eliminated, with the exception of consumer goods. Thus, one can own one's own house, car, or wardrobe privately (as items of personal property), but one cannot privately own the means of economic production. Most of the industrial sector and part of the agricultural sector have been nationalized. Indeed, all sectors of the economy, except for small plots of land cultivated by collective farmers, have been brought under the control of national economic planning. The very core of the Soviet economy is its state sector; all major industries are state owned and state operated in the areas of mining, heavy construction, railroads, communications, power production, urban retailing, large cooperative farms, and others. The major means of production are thus publicly owned, and all employees work for the state. The private enterprise that does exist, such as small-scale artisans operating small farms in remote areas, is very limited (Lane, 1985; Kornai, 1992). The Eastern European state socialist societies are based more or less on the Soviet model, but they have had a tendency to be somewhat more open to capitalist or market-oriented economic activity, a phenomenon that became rather prominent in the 1970s (Abonyi, 1982). This is especially true in Hungary and Yugoslavia. Yugoslavia was experimenting with market economics as early as the 1950s. It attempted to create a form of "market socialism," which involved retaining a basic state socialist economy but allowing considerable development of capitalist businesses alongside socialist operations.

However, the classical state socialist system, as represented best by the Soviet Union, has kept market activity to an absolute minimum and given overwhelming emphasis to state management and state economic planning. As Janos Kornai (1992:115) has written, in classical state socialism "the 'life or death' of a firm as a collective organization or organism is determined not by the 'natural selection' of market competition but by the bureaucracy.

There is a complete absence of . . . entrepreneurs who introduce new products or new technologies, establish new organizations, and conquer new markets, while obsolete production and ossified organizations are squeezed out."

This absence of a market principle is perhaps nowhere more salient to the functioning of the economy than with respect to money and prices. Classical socialism is, according to Kornai (1992), not a fully monetized, but rather a *semimonetized* economy. Money exists, but it does not act as a universal means of exchange in the way that it does within capitalism, nor is it convertible into foreign currencies. Kornai also notes that prices are not set by market principles, but rather by bureaucratic decree. This means that they are not sensitive to the basic laws of supply and demand, and thus cannot be used as indicators of how much of what products to produce. As we shall see, these economic characteristics have had dramatic consequences for the functioning and evolution of the state socialist system.

Industrialization in the state socialist societies has taken place under the close control of the state (Gershenkron, 1962). In the Soviet Union, the major drive toward industrialization occurred from the late 1920s through World War II under the leadership of the Stalinist regime. In a very short time the Soviet Union was transformed from a largely agrarian society into one of the world's major industrial societies. The speed of industrialization in the Soviet Union, and the fervor with which the Soviet leaders carried it out, took a terrible human toll. Millions of peasants were either killed or sent to labor camps in order to make the transition from agriculture to industry. This was one of the sorriest sagas in human history.

By the second half of the twentieth century the state socialist societies came to closely resemble the industrial capitalist societies in several important respects. To a large extent, industrialization has created notable similarities in the basic social patterns of both types of society. However, the state socialist world, although it has made considerable progress in this regard, has not been able to achieve the truly high levels of economic prosperity characteristic of modern capitalism. By the late 1980s the levels of per capita income of the state socialist societies were still only about one-third to one-half of those of the industrial capitalist nations. Indeed, despite considerable economic progress, by the 1970s state socialism seemed to run up against severe constraints on further economic development. State socialist economies began to stagnate and suffer from a variety of ills. These ills led to various programs of economic reform that culminated in the postsocialist transition of the late 1980s and early 1990s. Shortly we shall look in detail at these reforms and what motivated them.

State Socialism and the Capitalist World-Economy

The relationship between the socialist states and the capitalist world-economy has been the subject of recent and intense debate, especially among Western Marxian social scientists. Christopher Chase-Dunn (1982), for instance, argues a position that has become popular among Wallersteinian world-system theorists in recent years. He holds not only that the state socialist nations have close economic ties with world capitalism, but, indeed, that the socialist states are integral parts of the capitalist world-economy. The position they occupy in the world-system is in the semiperiphery. The socialist states have this role, Chase-Dunn claims, because they engage in commodity production for a world market and have important dealings with the capitalist

transnational corporations. It is thus Chase-Dunn's view that the socialist societies are not really socialist at all. Rather, they are essentially capitalist societies whose governments are led by socialist political parties.

At the opposite extreme from Chase-Dunn is Albert Szymanski (1982). Szymanski argues that the state socialist nations are thoroughly socialist. They have economies that are geared only to production-for-use and not to production-for-profit. Moreover, the state socialist economies are basically autonomous from Western capitalism, the economic exchanges between the capitalist and socialist nations being mainly of a nonessential or luxury nature.

Szymanski offers several lines of evidence to support his position (his analysis is based almost entirely on the case of the Soviet Union). First, the agreements with Western capitalists that the Soviet Union has entered into—agreements that involve various exchanges of goods or technology— have been made on the Soviet Union's own terms. These agreements cannot significantly have affected economic processes within the Soviet Union because they have not involved any direct investment or management rights for capitalists in Soviet enterprises. Second, although the state socialist societies invest in both core and peripheral capitalist societies, these investments are extremely small in comparison to those of the advanced capitalist nations. For example, in 1978 U.S. investments in the peripheral capitalist countries exceeded Soviet investments in those countries by a factor of 2200. Third, the state socialist societies trade far more among themselves than with the advanced capitalist societies. For example, in 1978 about 60 percent of Soviet trade occurred with the other state socialist nations, but only 28 percent of its trade was with the core capitalist nations. Moreover, in the same year only about 4 percent of the trade of the core capitalist societies was with the socialist states. Finally, if there were a close economic tie between the socialist and capitalist countries, the economic fluctuations so characteristic of capitalism should be reflected in similar fluctuations in the socialist nations. However, the correlation between the capitalist and socialist societies in this regard is not strong. Indeed, "the period of the most rapid industrial growth in the USSR, 1928–1941, coincided with the period of the most protracted and deep depression in the modern history of capitalism" (Szymanski, 1982:75).

The disagreement between Chase-Dunn and Szymanski is a complex one that involves a wide range of issues, and it is therefore difficult to resolve in a definitive way. Indeed, this disagreement is only part of a much larger discussion about the nature of the economic systems in the Soviet Union and Eastern Europe (cf. Sweezy, 1980; Lane, 1985: Chapter 3). On Szymanski's side, it must be recognized that the state socialist societies do have economies that are different in important ways from Western capitalism. The state socialist societies have no private capitalist class engaged in profit maximization as an end in itself; they make use of centralized economic planning to a degree that is unheard of in Western capitalism; and they, the Soviet Union in particular, have made relatively minimal use of market mechanisms to guide economic decisions. Thus, the state socialist societies obviously do have some important characteristics that we normally associate with a socialist mode of economic organization (Gorin, 1985; H. Davis and Scase, 1985).

On the other hand, Szymanski clearly errs in viewing the state socialist societies as having essentially fulfilled the expectations of Marx and Engels regarding the content of socialist society. The plain and simple truth is that the Soviet Union and Eastern Europe depart markedly from the classical Marxian conception of socialism.

Although Marx did not spell out in any detail what he thought the future socialist society would look like, we know some of the basic things he had in mind. For one, he was thinking of a society with a level of economic equality much greater than that which has prevailed in the Soviet Union and Eastern Europe (see Chapter 10). For another, he thought of socialism as being relatively democratic in nature, as giving everyone a strong voice in the whole process of social and economic planning. The politically repressive character of state socialism throughout most of its history shows that this expectation has not been even remotely realized. Finally, and in some ways most significantly, there is the fact that Marx conceived of genuine socialism as being built around production-for-use rather than production-for-exchange. State socialist societies likewise do not live up to this expectation as their economies are devoted greatly to the production of commodities—goods that are designed to augment the value that they originally had when created. In sum, it is a serious error to refer to contemporary socialist states as "Marxist states." Although these states have historically characterized themselves as Marxist, this is at best only a very partial truth.

This brings us back to Chase-Dunn's position. It is important to understand that he is not claiming that the state socialist societies are capitalist in the same way that Western capitalist societies are. He recognizes that the socialist societies have had unique forms of internal economic organization. His position springs from his world-system outlook. The state socialist societies have been, he claims, important experiments in socialism that have failed largely because these societies have been greatly constrained by the existence of the capitalist world-economy (Chase-Dunn, 1989a). Socialist societies have great difficulty surviving within a capitalist world-system;

they are compelled to interact to some extent with that system, and as this happens they tend to be drawn back increasingly toward a capitalist mode of operation. Thus, the Soviet Union and Eastern Europe had become gradually reincorporated into the capitalist world-economy and had lost most of whatever socialist content they once possessed. There is a good deal of evidence to show that this is precisely what has been happening over the past two or three decades, more rapidly and substantially in Eastern Europe than in the Soviet Union itself (Frank, 1980; Abonyi, 1982; Rossides, 1990). Andre Gunder Frank (1980), for example, has shown in considerable detail the extent to which the state socialist societies have reinserted themselves into global capitalism. Since the early 1970s they have begun to trade with Western capitalism much more vigorously, and many important financial and industrial agreements have been established. Frank's analysis ends in 1979, but it looks as though the process of reintegration he described for the decade of the 1970s has accelerated throughout the 1980s and 1990s. Indeed, it appears that this process is currently growing by leaps and bounds (cf. Aganbegyan, 1989).

In the end, then, Chase-Dunn's position turns out to be the more valid and enlightening one. The state socialist societies had only a limited Marxian socialist content to begin with and by now have lost most of what they had. This conclusion has implications for a final important question: Have the socialist countries ever had relations among themselves comparable to the relations among more- and less-developed capitalist countries? To the extent that there ever was a separate socialist world-system, it seems clear that this system never structurally resembled the capitalist world-system (Chase-Dunn, 1982; Chirot, 1986). In other words, the Soviet Union never acted like a socialist "core" that exploited

its Eastern European neighbors or less developed socialist countries such as Cuba. The Soviet Union has not been dependent upon other socialist countries for its essential raw materials. In fact, it has played an important role in *exporting* raw materials to other socialist countries (Chirot, 1986). Moreover, the Soviet Union has historically acted in ways that have apparently been designed to help less-developed socialist countries enhance their economic development. For example, it has paid Cuba well above the world market price for Cuban sugar (Eckstein, 1986). While it is true that the Soviet Union has engaged in political and military domination over the Eastern European states, as well as over many less-developed socialist countries, this domination is not comparable to the economic domination that some nations exert over others within the world capitalist system.

The Democratic Socialism of Scandinavia

Mention must also be made of the variety of "socialism" that has arisen in the Scandinavian nations, primarily in Sweden, Denmark, and Norway. (This variety has also arisen, although to a lesser extent, in such Western European nations as England and the Netherlands.) Actually, the Scandinavian nations are not socialist at all, at least not in any economic sense. Their economies are still overwhelmingly capitalist. The great bulk of the means of production is privately owned and production takes place for profit. There has, however, been some nationalization. Some heavy industries and utilities are owned and operated by the government.

The Scandinavian societies are only really "socialist" in a political sense. Beginning in the 1930s, socialist political parties came to occupy a dominant place in the government, and they still do today. These parties have had the express aim of reforming the economy so as to make it more just and egalitarian. Although production can take place for profit in most spheres of economic life, the government considers that private companies should have a strong concern for the national interest. It has entered into close collaboration with private business in order to manage the economy for the public good. The state closely watches over and helps to regulate prices, wages, interest rates, and so on.

The Scandinavian version of "socialism" is even more removed from the classical Marxian conception of socialism than is state socialism. Marx held that capitalism was incapable of being reformed, and that socialism necessarily involved the complete abolition of private property and the collective ownership of the means of production. He would have taken a very dim view of any social experiment designed merely to reform the capitalist system. (In Chapter 10 we will examine the degree to which this experiment has been successful.)

REFORM WITHIN STATE SOCIALISM AND THE TRANSITION TO POSTSOCIALISM

As early as the 1970s the socialist economies of Eastern Europe began to combine state economic planning with considerable private ownership and market-oriented economic behavior. They were well ahead of the Soviet Union in making this move. Nevertheless, by the mid-1980s the Soviet Union itself was spurred into the same basic kind of action. Economic reform in the Soviet Union began in earnest with the rise in 1985 of Mikhail Gorbachev to the position of General Secretary of the Communist party, the most powerful political office in all of Soviet society. Gorbachev pursued a strategy known as *perestroika,* or economic restructuring. The most fundamental aspects of this plan of economic reform were the following (Lapidus, 1988; Kushnirsky, 1988; Leggett, 1988; Zemtsov and Farrar, 1989):

- Whereas centralized economic planning was to be maintained as a guiding policy, individual firms were given increased responsibility to make decisions about their production activities. These firms were required to compete with each other, with the level of profitability being the main criterion for success. Firms that were not sufficiently profitable would be eliminated. Moreover, managers of firms were increasingly to be elected, rather than simply rising to power through the political patronage system traditionally in effect.
- The wage structure was to be overhauled in the direction of greater wage differentials. This was designed to serve as an incentive for workers to work harder and better. As a further incentive, workers could be fired for poor work and for excessive absenteeism. With this reform, unemployment would become a reality for the first time since the early years of Soviet society.
- New joint ventures with Western firms were to be undertaken. These ventures were designed primarily to attract Western capital and enhance the production of consumer goods.

What all of these changes had in common was obviously a recognition of the limitations of centralized economic planning, and thus an increased reliance on the market (Lapidus, 1988; Aganbegyan, 1988, 1989). The changes were designed to shift the Soviet economy in a more "capitalistic" direction, a move that would not surprise Wallerstein and the world-system theorists, since they see the Soviet Union as already substantially capitalist.

What lay behind these reforms? Why were they undertaken at this particular historical juncture? A large part of the answer obviously has to do with the deteriorating economic conditions that the Soviet Union began to face in the 1970s, conditions that had reached crisis proportions by 1985 (Leggett, 1988; Lapidus, 1988; Zemtsov and Farrar, 1989; Kaneda, 1988; Mandel, 1989). This was, and still remains, a crisis that has been accompanied by a serious demoralization of many segments of Soviet society. Robert Leggett (1988) and Tatsuo Kaneda (1988) summarize the dimensions of the problem:

> Growth has been trending downward for several decades as the economy experienced repeated harvest failures, bottlenecks in industry, shortages of energy and labor, and chronically low productivity. GNP growth during the 11th Five-Year Plan (1981–85) had its worst showing of any five-year period since World War II.
>
> Meanwhile, improvements in living standards have tapered off as a result of the worsening performance of the economy, and popular discontent has grown. The latter has manifested itself in declining worker morale, more materialistic attitudes, an increase in "deviant" and "delinquent" behavior by Soviet youth, rising crime rates, alcohol and drug abuse, and a rising anti-Russian nationalism among ethnic groups (Leggett, 1988:23, 25).

Soviet leaders face the wastefulness of their entire economy; a decrease in the Soviet capacity for technological development; dependency on the technological progress of the West; a drop in international competitiveness; chronic shortages of basic necessities; the existence of black markets; widespread bribery and corruption; growing debt; feelings of alienation and habitual drinking among the people, who avoid work and whose rates of illness and mortality are increasing (Kaneda, 1988:81).

But then if a severely deteriorating economic situation was the motivation for Gorbachev's economic reforms, what were the underlying causes of the economic problems? János Kornai (1992), one of the world's leading experts on the political economy of state socialism, has argued that these difficulties were inherent in the classical socialist system from the beginning, even if they took decades to fully manifest themselves. According to Kornai, bureaucratic economic planning in the absence of a market principle has had especially severe consequences primarily because it fails to provide a rational pricing system that is sensitive to the basic laws of supply and demand. Because prices are not determined by consumer demand there is no way for economic planners to know how to adjust supply so that it is in harmony with demand. Indeed, the system works so that whatever is produced will always be consumed, and therefore producers have no incentives to increase supply. This leads inexorably to a situation of chronic shortage. Moreover, Kornai argues, in contrast to capitalism, the state socialist system has always given priority to the production of means of production—those things, such as machinery, that are used for the production of goods—rather than to the production of consumer goods, which indicates that the standard of living increases slowly. Two other features that Kornai sees as inherent in state socialism are, first, the existence of little incentive to create an indigenous technology and thus the need to borrow most of it from the West, a situation that severely reduces economic innovation; and, second, a strong emphasis on the quantity rather than the quality of goods produced, which leads, of course, to severe problems with product quality.

A special point needs to be made with respect to the difficulty state socialism has had in producing high levels of high-quality consumer goods. In its first several decades the Soviet economy worked reasonably well, and in fact was capable of producing industrialization on a scale sufficient to nar-row the gap appreciably between itself and Western capitalism (Szelenyi, 1992; Chirot, 1991). However, the Soviet economy and state socialism in general seemed to run up against inherent limitations after a certain period. As Daniel Chirot (1991) has said, by the middle of the twentieth century the So-viet system was successful in creating an in-dustrial economy based on steel, electrical machinery, and organic chemistry—a stage of industrialization that such economic powers as Germany and the United States had attained in the period between 1870 and World War I—but it became stagnant at that stage. It was never capable of moving into the next stage of industrial development, which in Western capitalism involved the production of such things as automobiles, consumer electrical goods, and services.

However, the problems inherent in state socialism as a mode of economic pro-duction may not be the entire basis for the economic reforms. Certainly state socialism has some tremendous built-in limitations, but the crisis it began to suffer in the 1970s may have other causes as well. In particular, we also need to consider the role of the capi-talist world-system in imposing constraints on the functioning of state socialism. As noted earlier, in recent decades the Soviet Union has begun to reinsert its economy into the capitalist world-economy and to act more and more like a traditional capitalist state in the international economic arena. And why should this be? Christopher Chase-Dunn (1982, 1989a) points out that the capitalist world-economy exists as a hostile economic ocean within which state socialism must try to swim. Because of the external economic pressures the world-system creates, state socialist economies have serious obstacles put in the path of their economic functioning. These obstacles include the costs associated with needed military buildup and embargoes against trade. As a result of these obstacles, Chase-

Dunn says, socialist states within the world-system tend either to be crushed by that system or pulled back into line as capi-talist states. The impairment of their func-tioning by the capitalist world-system may give them little choice but to play the game according to capitalist rules.

That the Soviet Union has been in the process of being pulled back into line as a member of the capitalist system is strongly confirmed by Abel Aganbegyan's *Inside Per-estroika: The Future of the Soviet Economy* (1989). Aganbegyan, who was at one time Gorbachev's principal economic advisor, makes clear the extraordinary extent to which the Soviet Union has desired for some time to compete in the capitalist world-economy using capitalist ground rules. According to Aganbegyan, a key fea-ture of *perestroika* involves an economic shift toward export promotion. The Soviet Union has been reorganizing itself so as to be able to manufacture and sell commodi-ties competitively in the world market. For the world's most prominent socialist state, this is an extraordinary departure from tra-ditional economic practices, and it surely indicates a pronounced shift in the eco-nomic outlook and interests of a sizable seg-ment of the Soviet elite. It also suggests, as Aganbegyan is at pains to point out, that *perestroika* is no mere economic tinkering. Gorbachev and his supporters have seemed to be doing much more than just repairing the flaws in the Soviet economy. They have seemed to be attempting to complete the shift, begun some time before them (and, be it noted, *before* the full-scale economic cri-sis), of the Soviet Union toward full-fledged participation in the world capitalist system.

But what is the current situation, and where are the postsocialist societies headed? In many ways the economic situation has continued to deteriorate (Ericson, 1995). As of the early 1990s Russia was in the midst of financial and monetary chaos and ram-pant corruption. Indeed, it has been charged that perhaps as much of half of the Russian economy has fallen under the control of the Russian mafia (Remnick, 1997). Moreover, between 1992 and 1993 the Russian economy contracted alarmingly. For example, real national income fell by 32 percent, and industrial production declined by 31 percent (Ericson, 1995).

Calling Russia and the other Eastern European societies postsocialist tells us, unfortunately, more about what they are not than about what they are. They are "after socialism," and they have taken serious steps toward capitalism on the Western model. As Richard Ericson (1995) has noted, by the end of 1992 there were over 60,000 small businesses, over 135,000 family farms, and more than 2,000 independent joint stock companies. Some 24,000 state enterprises had been privatized, and approximately one-third of all trade and service enterprises had become private. Nearly one million businesses had come to be organized under nonstate forms, and a vigorous drive toward mass privatization of large-scale industry began in 1993. Yet despite all of this privatization, the postsocialist societies, Russia in particular, are rather unwieldy mixtures of the old state socialism and the new "capitalism." It has been suggested that these societies are evolving a kind of "market socialism," or a capitalism that still retains substantial state-directed economic planning. Perhaps this is so, but it has also been suggested by János Kornai (1992) and others that such a polyglot economy is unworkable and thus can provide no real solution. Kornai vigorously asserts that the socialist system is unreformable in principle. It must be eradicated in whole, he says, and replaced with a market-dominated system for a viable economy to emerge.

So where exactly are the former socialist states heading at this point in history? The answer is that no one knows for sure. My prediction is that they will eventually be fully reincorporated into the capitalist system, but how long that will take, and whether that will improve or worsen their economic situation, are questions to which I will not at this point risk answers.

SUMMARY

1. The Industrial Revolution began in England in the second half of the eighteenth century. By the nineteenth century it had spread to other western European countries and to the United States. It was a massive economic and technological transformation in which machines and the factory system came to dominate production. Industrial capitalist society was the child of this massive change.

2. The Industrial Revolution occurred as a major phase in the development of the capitalist system. It was inaugurated by capitalists as a means of greatly expanding their productivity and lowering their operating costs. In effect it established a fundamentally new means whereby capitalists could earn profits: by extracting surplus value at the point of production. Industrialization developed earliest in the most economically advanced capitalist societies.

3. Some major consequences of industrialization have been an enormous increase in the productivity of labor, the creation of a large and socially significant urban proletariat, an increase in the specialization of labor, the extensive urbanization of society, and a marked decline in the rate of population growth because of a decline in the birth rate.

4. In the late nineteenth century capitalism entered a monopoly phase. This involved the emergence of the large corporation as the basic economic unit and a corresponding reduction of the competitive character of economic life. Monopoly capitalism also involved extensive investment of advanced capitalist nations in poorer regions of the world.

5. The capitalist world-system today is constituted approximately as follows: The major core nations are the United States, Germany, France, and Japan; the periphery consists of the poorest nations of Asia, Latin America, and Africa; and the semiperiphery includes

some of the less-developed European nations, as well as some of the better-off nations in Latin America, Asia, and Africa.

6. Japan has been the only non-Western society to experience a full transition to industrial capitalism. Japan entered the European-based world-economy in the 1850s, doing so as a semiperipheral rather than a peripheral country. Japanese industrialization was spurred by the modern nation-state created by the Meiji restoration in 1868. Japanese capitalism took a strongly state-directed form, with the state playing a much greater role in the economy than it did in Western capitalism. In the late nineteenth century the state helped advance capitalist development by such means as establishing pilot projects, subsidizing industries, and encouraging the formation of national banks. Today Japanese capitalism differs from Western capitalism in such ways as the loyalty of employees to their companies, labor-management relations, and emphasis on short-term versus long-term profits.

7. State socialist societies arose in Russia in 1917, in Eastern Europe after World War II, and in parts of the less-developed world in the 1970s. In these societies the state directs most economic activity in the relative absence of private enterprise and markets. Industrialization in these societies was driven by the state in a forced way and did not result from the profit-seeking activities of capitalist entrepreneurs. Much debate continues to rage about the specific economic character of these societies. Some sociologists, world-system theorists in particular, see them as basically an alternative version of capitalist commodity production ("state capitalism"), whereas others believe they have uniquely socialist features. In recent years it appears that they have increasingly lost whatever socialist content

they originally had and have moved toward closer integration into the capitalist world-economy.

8. The economic systems of the state socialist societies should not be confused with the allegedly socialist economies of Scandinavia. The Scandinavian economies are fundamentally capitalist in the sense that private production for profit is the basis of economic life. The Scandinavian version of "socialism" is an attempt to reform capitalism through political measures while leaving the economy basically intact.

9. By the 1970s most of the Eastern European socialist countries had initiated economic reforms directed toward increasing the amount of private ownership and production for profit, or in other words mixing market economic principles with centralized state planning. In the mid-1980s the Soviet Union embarked on its program of economic reform known as *perestroika*. This was designed to bring it into fuller participation in the capitalist world-economy and to allow it to function as a competitive capitalist state following capitalist ground rules. These economic reforms have undoubtedly been a response to the economic stagnation of the 1970s and the mounting crises of the 1980s. These stagnations and crises were undoubtedly precipitated, at least in part, by various internal deficiencies of state socialism rooted in the absence of market principles. However, the external pressures of the capitalist world-system have probably played an important role as well in inducing economic malfunctioning within state socialism. It is difficult for socialist states to function effectively within a surrounding capitalist world-economy because of the hostility of that economy toward socialism.

SPECIAL TOPIC: THE RISE OF A POSTINDUSTRIAL SOCIETY?

One of the most influential sociological works of the last quarter century is Daniel Bell's *The Coming of Post-Industrial Society* (1973). Since Bell's work was published, the phrase *postindustrial society* has appeared frequently and approvingly in numerous sociological textbooks and other works. Bell argues that a new type of society, the postindustrial society, has in recent decades begun to emerge in the most economically advanced nations of the West, the United States in particular. The most fundamental feature of this type of society is its emphasis on the production of services rather than goods, and especially certain types of services. Whereas the industrial society delivers services in such areas as transportation, utilities, and telecommunications, the postindustrial society emphasizes services involving health, science, and education.

The emergence of a postindustrial society thus involves a major transformation in the very basis of society. An industrial society, Bell argues, is based on property; a postindustrial society, on the other hand, rests on knowledge, particularly theoretical knowledge. As Bell puts it rather provocatively, the rise of a postindustrial society marks the transition from a labor theory of value to a "knowledge theory of value." This change in the very basis of social life is also marked by a change in the class structure. The new dominant social class is no longer a property-owning bourgeoisie, but a "social intelligentsia": a class of highly educated individuals whose social dominance rests upon their possession of advanced forms of theoretical knowledge. The most important members of this class are teachers, physicians, lawyers, scientists, and engineers, people for whom work has become a "game between people" rather than a game between people and things.

For Bell, then, the postindustrial society is one whose overall character is vastly different from industrial or "capitalist" society. The desire for profit is no longer the driving force of economic and social life. Life becomes oriented around the accumulation of knowledge and its use for human betterment. Corporations come to be subordinated to what Bell calls the "sociologizing mode." This means that their emphasis shifts toward providing extensive benefits for their employees as well as toward their "social responsibility." In addition to and in conjunction with these changes, the postindustrial society gives a new emphasis to leisure. People acquire advanced forms of education not only for their important social uses, but for enjoyment and intellectual uplift. In general, a postindustrial society is far better educated than an industrial one.

Although Bell's ideas have gained widespread acceptance among many contemporary sociologists, there is cause to be highly skeptical of most of them. The basic difficulties with Bell's analysis have been insightfully delineated by Stephen Berger (1974). Berger suggests that many of the developments discussed by Bell do not represent the emergence of a new type of society that is opposed to capitalism, but rather of a new phase in the very development of capitalism. The expansion of government services, for example, may be understood as a necessary step in the political management of an advanced capitalist society. Moreover, Berger argues, the original motivation behind technological forecasting was military in nature, and most of the recent expansion of science has been due to government involvement in defense and space exploration. Berger's central argument against Bell is best expressed as follows (1974:102):

> I would argue that these changes, if they are real, represent only the continued operation of the logic of industry. That logic, as analyzed by . . . Karl Marx, included the continuous enlargement of the areas of human work which were dominated by commodity production and the continuous use of scientists and engineers to create machines, techniques, and modes of organization to replace and control workers. . . .
>
> . . . The shifts from goods to services and from manual to professional and technical workers make sense within an analysis of the dynamics of capitalism.

To Berger's remarks several critical comments may be added. One concerns Bell's notion that a propertyless intelligentsia has emerged as the dominant class within postindustrial society. A better interpretation, I believe, would hold that such a group, to the extent that it exists, lacks any real social power and is by and large in a service capacity to the capitalist system. After all, most teachers, scientists, and engineers are employed in large public bureaucracies. As Berger has noted, these public bureaucracies may be viewed from the perspective of the capitalist-induced expansion of government. A second comment involves Bell's treatment of the expansion of education. In this regard, Bell seems to confuse education with "schooling" (Berger, 1974). While it is certainly true that schooling has been expanding on a vast scale in the contemporary United States, this should not be construed, as Bell seems to do, as resulting from the greater need and desire for knowledge. A more realistic interpretation, in my view, is that schooling has been expanding as a result of the process of the inflation of educational credentials so characteristic of advanced industrial societies in this century, the United States in particular. It is not the thirst for knowledge that leads people to stay in school for ever longer periods, but the desire for educational certificates that translate into better-paying and higher-prestige jobs (see Chapter 16).

In sum, then, modern industrial economies have increasingly become "service and information economies," but this is not a process of the overturning of capitalism. Capitalism is alive and well, and the increased focus on service and information is simply another aspect of the commodification of social life. Industrialism and capitalism have been extended rather than negated.

FOR FURTHER READING

Beaud, Michel. *A History of Capitalism, 1500–1980.* New York: Monthly Review Press, 1983. Contains some very informative material on the emergence and development of industrial capitalism.

Braverman, Harry. *Labor and Monopoly Capital: The Degradation of Work in the Twentieth Century.* New York: Monthly Review Press, 1974. An excellent work in which the author analyzes in depth the transformation of the workplace in capitalist society since the late nineteenth century. A major extension of the Marxian conception of alienation.

Chase-Dunn, Christopher (ed.). *Socialist States in the World-System.* Beverly Hills, Calif.: Sage, 1982. A provocative set of essays in which a number of contemporary Marxian scholars debate the nature of state socialism and its relationship to the capitalist world.

Chase-Dunn, Christopher. *Global Formation: Structures of the World-Economy.* Oxford: Blackwell, 1989. An extremely comprehensive extension and reformulation of Wallersteinian world-system theory. An outstanding work that applies world-system concepts and principles in considering a vast range of issues in the contemporary world-system, and in its past and its future.

Chirot, Daniel. *Social Change in the Modern Era.* Orlando: Harcourt Brace Jovanovich, 1986. Despite having an unconvincing Weberian approach to the origins of the modern world, a very good treatment of many of the most basic social, economic, and political changes in the capitalist world-economy since the early nineteenth century, and especially since 1900. Also contains a good analysis of state socialism. (An earlier version of this book was published in 1977 under the title *Social Change in the Twentieth Century.* It is substantially different in parts, owing more to Wallerstein, and can still be valuably consulted.)

Davis, Howard, and Richard Scase. *Western Capitalism and State Socialism: An Introduction.* Oxford: Blackwell, 1985. A very good and easily understood treatment of the basic socioeconomic character of contemporary Western capitalist and state socialist societies.

Hobsbawm, E. J. *Industry and Empire.* New York: Pantheon Books, 1968. A valuable study by an eminent British historian of the Industrial Revolution in England and the development of the English economy since that time.

Kornai, János. *The Socialist System: The Political Economy of Communism.* Princeton:

Princeton University Press, 1992. The definitive work outlining the basic principles undergirding the functioning and evolution of state socialism.

Kumar, Krishan. *From Post-Industrial to Post-Modern Society: New Theories of the Contemporary World.* Oxford: Blackwell, 1995. A critical analysis of the theory of postindustrial society and related theories.

Lane, David. *Soviet Economy and Society.* New York: Blackwell, 1985. Some important discussions of various dimensions of Soviet economic life.

Shannon, Thomas Richard. *An Introduction to the World-System Perspective.* Second edition. Boulder, Colo.: Westview, 1996. The first textbook on world-system theory. An excellent and very succinct summary of the leading features of world-system theory and the critical reaction to it.

Wallerstein, Immanuel. *The Modern World-System III: The Second Era of Great Expansion of the Capitalist World-Economy, 1730–1840s.* San Diego: Academic Press, 1989. The long-awaited third volume of Wallerstein's multivolume work on the history of the capitalist world-economy.

Yoshihara, Kunio. *Japanese Economic Development.* Second edition. Tokyo: Oxford University Press, 1986. A good brief introduction to the development of industrial capitalism in Japan.

Chapter
9

Capitalism and Economic Underdevelopment

Sometime after the end of World War II social scientists began to speak of three "worlds." These worlds represented social, economic, and political categories into which contemporary societies could be placed. The First World consisted of the industrially advanced capitalist nations, which had parliamentary democratic forms of government: the United States, Canada, England, France, the Netherlands, Sweden, most of the rest of western and northern Europe, and also Australia and Japan. The Second World was industrially advanced, or at least on the path toward industrial development, but the societies of this category had socialist economies and totalitarian forms of government. Included in this category were the Soviet Union and the Eastern European socialist states. The rest of the world, not counting primitive or preliterate cultures, was the Third World. This world consisted of the poor, technologically backward, economically underdeveloped societies constituting most of Latin America, Africa, and Asia.

Having conceptualized something called a Third World, social scientists proceeded vigorously to study it. Many kinds of social scientists became involved in investigations focusing on different aspects of life in the Third World. Yet the overriding question for most investigators was why the societies of the Third World had failed to achieve the levels of technological and economic development, as well as the social patterns, so characteristic of the First World, and to some degree of the Second.

This question is the focus of the current chapter. After discussing the nature of underdevelopment, this chapter proceeds to examine the major theories that social scientists have proposed to explain underdevelopment. These theories are critically assessed in light of the most recent evidence that social-scientific research has been able to produce. The chapter concludes with a brief look at the increasing involvement of the Third World in the rapidly accelerating process of the globalization of economic production.

THE NATURE OF UNDERDEVELOPMENT

Social scientists first called the societies of the Third World "backward nations," but later abandoned this expression as derogatory, adopting instead the expressions "underdeveloped nations," or "underdevelopment." Although these terms have also been criticized and others proposed, they have stuck and continue to be used by most social scientists. To understand exactly what is meant by underdevelopment, or by an underdeveloped nation, a useful first step is to distinguish between *under*development and *un*development (Frank, 1966). **Undeveloped societies** may be regarded as those outside the framework of a capitalist world-economy that have not yet gotten beyond a preindustrial stage of technological development and a precapitalist stage of economic development. Societies surviving by hunting and gathering, horticultural, pastoral, or agrarian methods of production and having some sort of production-for-use, premarket economy are referred to as *undeveloped*. The term *underdevelopment* is reserved for societies incorporated into a capitalist world-economy and functioning within it in some way. **Underdeveloped societies** may thus be regarded as the least technologically and economically advanced members of the modern world-system.

The most commonly used measure of economic development is a nation's per capita Gross National Product (GNP), which is the total value of goods and services it produces per person in a given year. This and other measures of underdevelopment are represented in Table 9.1. It can be seen that most of the underdeveloped nations have per capita GNPs that are strikingly low when compared to those of the developed nations. All of the African nations shown in Table 9.1, for example, have per capita GNPs of less than $1,000. These levels of economic productivity are low indeed when compared with those of the developed capitalist nations, where the per capita GNP averages over $25,000 per year. Many Asian nations are at about the same level of economic productivity as contemporary African societies, although Asia displays considerable variation. South Korea and Hong Kong have very high levels of economic development for countries traditionally thought of as belonging to the Third World, and have had some of the fastest growing economies in the world over the past three or four decades. (The Special Topic at the end of the chapter offers an explanation for the dramatic development of South Korea and Hong Kong and why they have become exceptions to the developmental potential of most Third World countries.) The Latin American nations, especially those in South America, are on the whole notably higher in economic productivity than the nations of Africa and Asia, but even the most developed Latin American countries compare very unfavorably with the developed world.

The general measure of technological advancement used in Table 9.1 is the number of scientists, engineers, and technicians

Table 9.1   SOCIAL, DEMOGRAPHIC, AND ECONOMIC CHARACTERISTICS OF SELECTED CONTEMPORARY NATIONS AT DIFFERENT LEVELS OF ECONOMIC DEVELOPMENT

Nation	POP	RNI	IMR	LFA	GNP	SCE
Developed capitalist nations						
Denmark	5.2	0.3	6	6	29,890	429
Sweden	8.8	0.6	4	—	23,750	618
United Kingdom	58.5	0.3	6	2	18,700	292
France	58.1	0.5	6	5	24,990	500
Germany[a]	81.9	0.6	6	4	27,510	626[b]
Netherlands	15.5	0.7	6	5	24,000	434
Canada	29.6	1.3	6	3	19,380	326
United States	263.1	1.0	8	3	26,980	293[c]
Australia	18.1	1.1	6	6	18,720	321
Japan	125.2	0.3	4	7	39,640	586
State socialist nations						
Soviet Union	289.0	1.0	25	20	8,375	532[c]
Czechoslovakia	15.6	0.2	13	13	7,876*	715
East Germany	16.6	0.1	9	—	9,669*	1,187
Poland	38.2	0.6	18	28	4,625*	239
Hungary	10.6	−0.2	17	21	6,119*	348
Postsocialist nations						
Croatia	4.8	0.0	16	16	3,250	—
Czech Republic	10.3	−0.1	8	11	3,870	300**
Hungary	10.2	−0.3	11	15	4,120	200**
Poland	38.6	0.3	14	27	2,790	200**
Slovak Republic	5.4	0.3	11	12	2,950	—
Russia	148.2	0.0	18	14	2,240	700**
Underdeveloped nations						
Latin America						
Mexico	91.8	1.9	33	28	3,320	50**
Brazil	159.2	1.5	44	23	3,640	37[c]
Venezuela	21.7	2.3	23	12	3,020	44
Peru	23.8	2.0	47	36	2,310	29[c]
Bolivia	7.4	2.4	69	47	800	40**
El Salvador	5.6	2.2	36	36	1,610	34
Guatemala	10.6	2.9	44	52	1,340	20**
Africa						
Egypt	57.8	2.0	56	40	790	56
Nigeria	111.3	2.9	80	43	260	7
Senegal	8.5	2.7	62	77	600	8
Kenya	26.7	2.7	58	80	280	3
Tanzania	29.6	3.0	82	84	120	—
Ghana	17.1	2.8	73	59	390	—
Asia						
Saudi Arabia	19.0	3.7	21	19	7,040	—
India	929.4	1.8	68	64	340	20
China	1,200.2	1.1	34	72	620	160**

continued

Table 9.1   (Continued)

Nation	POP	RNI	IMR	LFA	GNP	SCE
Indonesia	193.3	1.6	51	55	980	17c
Jordan	4.2	5.7	31	15	1,520	10**
South Korea	44.9	0.9	10	18	9,700	216
Hong Kong	6.2	1.6	5	1	22,990	—

Legend: POP = total population in millions (1995); RNI = annual percentage of population increase (1990–1995); IMR = infant mortality rate, calculated as annual number of deaths to infants under one year of age per 1000 live births (1995); LFA = percentage of the labor force engaged in agriculture (1990); GNP = Gross National Product per capita calculated in U.S. dollars (1995); SCE = number of scientists, engineers, and technicians engaged in research and experimental development per 100,000 population (years vary from 1975 to 1988, but are mostly for the mid- to late 1980s).

aThese data refer to unified Germany.

bThis figure is the average for former West Germany and former East Germany. The figure for West Germany is 472, that for East Germany 1,187.

cThis figure excludes technicians and therefore may be underrepresentative.

Sources: With the exceptions noted below, data in columns 1–5 are from the World Bank's World Development Report, New York: Oxford University Press, 1997, Tables 1, 4, and 6. Also with the exceptions noted below, data in column 6 are from the United Nations's Statistical Yearbook, New York: United Nations, 1992, Table 121.

The sources for the data on state socialist societies are as follows: Data in columns 1, 2, 3, and 5 come from the World Population Data Sheet, Washington, D.C.: Population Reference Bureau, 1989 (with the exception of those data marked with an asterisk—see below). Data for column 4 come from the United Nations's Human Development Report, New York: Oxford University Press, 1992, Tables 16 and 36. Data in column 6 are from the United Nations's Statistical Yearbook, New York: United Nations, 1992, Table 121.

Data marked with an asterisk come from U.S. Bureau of the Census, Statistical Abstract of the United States, Washington, D.C.: U.S. Government Printing Office, 1992, Table 1371, and are for the year 1989. Data marked with a double asterisk come from the United Nations's Human Development Report, New York: Oxford University Press, 1995, Tables 10 and 21 and are for the period 1988–92.

employed in research and experimentation. The developed countries (both capitalist and state socialist) average 486 scientists, engineers, and technicians engaged in research per 100,000 population. But the underdeveloped nations average only about 47 research and experimental personnel per 100,000 population. (This figure is inflated because of the large contribution made by South Korea; if South Korea is removed, the average is only 36.)

In most of the underdeveloped world today, agriculture is still the dominant economic activity, and peasants commonly outnumber workers of any other type. Most of these peasants farm small plots of land using techniques inherited from their ancestors thousands of years ago. Although industrialization has proceeded to some extent in all underdeveloped nations, in most it has not gone very far. In many of the underdeveloped nations shown in Table 9.1, one-third or more of the population is engaged in agricultural pursuits, and in some of these nations the proportion ranges from one-half to three-quarters. (The average for the underdeveloped countries is 43 percent.) In contrast, the figures for the developed countries indicate that 7 percent or fewer of the population is agriculturally employed in all capitalist nations. (The average for the developed capitalist countries is 5 percent, whereas for the state socialist countries it is 21 percent.)

Yet underdevelopment involves considerably more than low levels of technological and economic development. It also involves important social dimensions. Social and economic inequality is an especially important characteristic of underdeveloped societies. In most underdeveloped societies, wealth is enormously concentrated in the hands of a few, and tiny elites generally dominate the manufacturing and agricultural sectors of the economy. Throughout the Third World the bulk of the land is normally owned by a tiny fraction of the population. What is true of the inequality of wealth also holds for income inequality. As Table 9.2 reveals, income inequality in un-

Table 9.2   INCOME INEQUALITY IN DEVELOPED AND UNDERDEVELOPED NATIONS

Nation	Income Share of Bottom 20%[a]	Income Share of Top 10%[b]	Ratio of Top 10% to Bottom 20%	Year[c]
Developed nations				
Australia	4.4	25.8	5.9:1	1985
United Kingdom	4.6	27.8	6.0:1	1988
Canada	5.7	24.1	4.2:1	1987
Netherlands	8.2	21.9	2.7:1	1988
France	5.6	26.1	4.7:1	1989
Sweden	8.0	20.8	2.6:1	1981
Germany	7.0	24.4	3.5:1	1988
United States	4.7	25.0	5.3:1	1985
Denmark	5.4	22.3	4.1:1	1981
Japan	8.7	22.4	2.6:1	1979
Averages	6.2	24.0	3.9:1	
Underdeveloped nations				
Tanzania	6.9	30.2	4.4:1	1993
Uganda	6.8	33.4	4.9:1	1992
Nepal	9.1	25.0	2.7:1	1985
Kenya	3.4	47.7	14.0:1	1992
Nigeria	4.0	31.3	7.8:1	1993
India	8.5	28.4	3.3:1	1992
China	6.2	26.8	4.3:1	1992
Philippines	6.5	32.1	4.9:1	1988
Thailand	5.6	37.1	6.6:1	1992
Malaysia	4.6	37.9	8.2:1	1989
Bolivia	5.6	31.7	5.7:1	1990
Guatemala	2.1	46.6	22.2:1	1989
Dominican Republic	4.2	39.6	9.4:1	1989
Brazil	2.1	51.3	24.4:1	1989
Mexico	4.1	39.2	9.6:1	1992
Averages	5.3	35.9	6.8:1	

[a]Proportion of the total national income received by the bottom 20% of the population.

[b]Proportion of the total national income received by the top 10% of the population.

[c]Year in which the data for these computations were collected.

Source: World Bank, *World Development Report,* New York: Oxford University Press, 1996, Table 5. Data range from 1980–1993 but are mostly for the late 1980s or early 1990s.

derdeveloped nations is notably higher than in the industrialized countries.

Yet these data on income inequality, useful as they may be, do not tell us what we really want to know about underdeveloped nations: what the standard of living is for the majority of the population. Using a sample of 24 underdeveloped countries, Table 9.3 shows the percentage of the population of each country living in poverty. As can clearly be seen, the standard of living in most underdeveloped nations is very low. For this sample of countries, some 41 per-

cent is living below the poverty line. The situation is worst in Africa, where 52 percent of the population is living in poverty. Latin America is the best-off region, but still 31 percent of the population is living in poverty. It also needs to be borne in mind that the poverty line is set much lower in the less-developed countries than in the advanced industrial countries. Were poverty in the less-developed world to be measured in the same way as it is in the industrialized world, then the extent of poverty in the Third World would turn out to be much

Table 9.3 POVERTY LEVELS IN UNDERDEVELOPED NATIONS

Nation	Poverty Line	Percentage in Poverty	Year
Botswana	$372/cap/yr	37	1985
Ivory Coast	$372/cap/yr	27	1985
Ghana	$372/cap/yr	60	1985
Kenya	$365/cap/yr	63	1983
Lesotho	$365/cap/yr	52	1987
Rwanda	$365/cap/yr	58	1985
Tanzania	$365/cap/yr	43	1991
Uganda	$365/cap/yr	72	1990
Afghanistan	$372/cap/yr	57	1985
China	$365/cap/yr	14	1990
India	$365/cap/yr	71	1990
Indonesia	$365/cap/yr	22	1990
Nepal	$365/cap/yr	44	1985
Pakistan	$372/cap/yr	26	1985
Philippines	$372/cap/yr	34	1985
Sri Lanka	$365/cap/yr	47	1985
Brazil	$365/cap/yr	31	1989
Chile	$365/cap/yr	16	1989
Guatemala	$372/cap/yr	57	1985
Honduras	$365/cap/yr	61	1989
Mexico	$365/cap/yr	23	1984
Panama	$365/cap/yr	27	1989
Peru	$365/cap/yr	24	1986
Venezuela	$365/cap/yr	7	1987

Source: Hamid Tabatabai, *Statistics on Poverty and Income Distribution.* Geneva: International Labour Office, 1996.

greater. This means that, by the standards familiar to members of the advanced industrial countries, Table 9.3 grossly underestimates Third World poverty.*

Underdeveloped societies also stand out because of their demographic features. They are growing at a rate some three to four times as fast as the developed nations (see Table 9.1). This greater rate of growth is primarily attributable to the fact that birth rates remain high in the underdeveloped world, especially among peasant farmers who desire large numbers of children as farm workers (Harris and Ross, 1987). The underdeveloped nations currently constitute about three-fourths of the world's population, but because of their rapid growth rates an ever greater percentage of the world's population will live in these nations in the years ahead. Rapid population growth is creating increasingly severe problems in the underdeveloped world, and for some Asian and African nations population growth has created problems of crisis proportions.

A final characteristic of the underdeveloped world that is important to note involves general standards of nutrition and health. One of the most useful measures of a nation's overall nutritional and health status is its infant mortality rate. As can be seen from Table 9.1, infant mortality rates are dramatically higher in underdeveloped countries. Whereas the developed capitalist nations have infant mortality rates of approximately 6 per 1,000 births, and the developed state socialist nations have rates of around 15 to 20

per 1,000 births, many underdeveloped nations have rates between 50 and 100 per 1,000 births. (The average infant mortality rate for the underdeveloped countries shown in Table 9.1 is 46.) Infant mortality rates are especially high in Asia and Africa but are also high throughout Latin America.

Much of what has been surveyed from a statistical point of view can be summarized and seen more vividly by imagining what daily life is like for a more or less typical member of a more or less typical underdeveloped nation. Robert Heilbroner's attempt to evoke such a daily life imaginatively is worth quoting in its full detail (1963:23–27):

> We must conjure up in our mind's eye what underdevelopment means for the two billion human beings for whom it is not a statistic but a living experience of daily life. . . .
>
> It is not easy to make this mental jump. But let us attempt it by imagining how a typical American family . . . could be transformed into an equally typical family of the underdeveloped world.
>
> We begin by invading the house of our imaginary American family to strip it of its furniture. Everything goes: beds, chairs, tables, television set, lamps. We will leave the family with a few old blankets, a kitchen table, a wooden chair. Along with the bureaus go the clothes. Each member of the family may keep in his "wardrobe" his oldest suit or dress, a shirt or blouse. We will permit a pair of shoes to the head of the family, but none for the wife or children.
>
> We move into the kitchen. The appliances have already been taken out, so we turn to the cupboards and larder. The box of matches may stay, a small bag of flour, some sugar and salt. A few moldy potatoes, already in the garbage can, must be hastily rescued, for they will provide much of tonight's meal. We will leave a handful of onions, and a dish of dried beans. All the rest we take away: the meat, the fresh vegetables, the canned goods, the crackers, the candy.

---

*On the other hand, the data in Table 9.3 are based on income received from economic activities that take place within the context of an economic market, such as wage work or the selling of products in local markets. These figures therefore underestimate the real income available to peasant farmers, most of which is provided by subsistence farming. Nonetheless, the figures in Table 9.3 still demonstrate markedly low living standards in the underdeveloped world.

Now we have stripped the house: the bathroom has been dismantled, the running water shut off, the electric wires taken out. Next we take away the house. The family can move to the toolshed. It is crowded, but much better than the situation in Hong Kong, where (a United Nations report tells us) "it is not uncommon for a family of four or more to live in a bedspace, that is, on a bunk bed and the space it occupies—sometimes in two or three tiers—their only privacy provided by curtains."

But we have only begun. All the other houses in the neighborhood have also been removed; our suburb has become a shantytown. Still, our family is fortunate to have a shelter; 250,000 people in Calcutta have none at all and simply live in the streets. Our family is now about on a par with the city of Cali in Colombia, where, an official of the World Bank writes, "on a hillside alone, the slum population is estimated at 40,000—without water, sanitation, or electric light. And not all the poor of Cali are as fortunate as that. Others have built their shacks near the city on land which lies beneath the flood mark. To these people the immediate environment is the open sewer of the city, a sewer which flows through their huts when the river rises."

And still we have not reduced our American family to the level at which life is lived in the greatest part of the globe. Communication must go next. No more newspapers, magazines, books—not that they are missed, since we must take away our family's literacy as well. Instead, in our shantytown we will allow one radio. In India the national average of radio ownership is one per 250 people, but since the majority of radios is owned by city dwellers, our allowance is fairly generous.

Now government services must go. No more postman, no more fireman. There is a school, but it is three miles away and consists of two classrooms. They are not too overcrowded since only half the children in the neighborhood go to school. There are, of course, no hospitals or doctors nearby. The nearest clinic is ten miles away and is tended by a midwife. It can be reached by bicycle, provided that the family has a bicycle, which is unlikely. Or one can go by bus—not always inside, but there is usually room on top.

Finally, money. We will allow our family a cash hoard of five dollars. This will prevent our breadwinner from experiencing the tragedy of an Iranian peasant who went blind because he could not raise the $3.94 which he mistakenly thought he needed to secure admission to a hospital where he could have been cured.

Meanwhile the head of our family must earn his keep. As a peasant cultivator with three acres to tend, he may raise the equivalent of $100 to $300 worth of crops a year. If he is a tenant farmer, which is more than likely, a third or so of his crop will go to his landlord, and probably another 10 percent to the local moneylender. But there will be enough to eat. Or almost enough. The human body requires an input of at least 2,000 calories to replenish the energy consumed by its living cells. If our displaced American fares no better than an Indian peasant, he will average a replenishment of no more than 1,700–1,900 calories. His body, like any insufficiently fueled machine, will run down. That is one reason why life expectancy at birth in India today averages less than forty years.

But children may help. If they are fortunate, they may find work and thus earn some cash to supplement the family's income. For example, they may be employed as are children in Hyderabad, Pakistan, sealing the ends of bangles over a small kerosene flame, a simple task which can be done at home. To be sure, the pay is small: eight annas—about ten cents—for sealing bangles. That is, eight annas per *gross* of bangles. And if they cannot find work? Well, they can scavenge, as do the children in Iran who in times of hunger search for the undigested oats in the droppings of horses.

And so we have brought our typical American family down to the very bottom of the human scale. It is, however, a bottom in which we can find, give or take a hundred million souls, at least a billion people. Of the remaining billion in the backward areas, most are slightly better off, but not much so; a few are comfortable; a handful rich.

Of course, this is only an impression of life in the underdeveloped lands. It is not life itself. There is still lacking the things that underdevelopment gives as well as those it takes away: the urinous smell of poverty, the display of disease, the flies, the open sewers. And there is lacking, too, a softening sense of familiarity. Even in a charnel house life has its passions and pleasures. A tableau, shocking to American eyes, is less shocking to eyes that have never known any other. But it gives one a general idea. It begins to add pictures of reality to the statistics by which underdevelopment is ordinarily measured. When we are told that half the world's population enjoys a standard of living "less than $100 a year," this is what the figures mean.

Heilbroner wrote these words well over three decades ago, and to some extent they have to be updated for the late 1990s. Yet much of what Heilbroner is saying still applies to the state of the underdeveloped world today. There is still much poverty and misery throughout the Third World, as Table 9.3 clearly reveals. And to some extent it may be even more difficult for the members of highly developed, affluent societies to imagine life in the Third World, for the gap between the richest and the poorest nations has actually widened rather than closed. Only a handful of Third World countries have taken major strides toward economic development on the Western model. How can we explain not only the historical problem of underdevelopment, but the marked failure of most of the underdeveloped world to move toward the status of the developed nations?

THE MODERNIZATION APPROACH TO UNDERDEVELOPMENT

Social scientists have developed three principal theoretical approaches to the problem of underdevelopment: **modernization theory, dependency theory,** and **world-system theory.** In many ways world-system theory is a more flexible version of dependency theory, and so these two approaches are very similar. They stand sharply opposed, however, to modernization theory, and in fact originally emerged as alternatives to that approach.

The General Nature of Modernization Theory

Modernization theory is a very broad theoretical strategy that includes a variety of complementary, but also competing, theories. By and large, it is a specialized version of an even broader theoretical strategy, the functionalist evolutionary approach to sociocultural evolution (A. D. Smith, 1973; Sanderson, 1990). The diverse theories that coexist within the modernization approach are united by two fundamental assumptions. First, underdevelopment tends to be seen as an "original state," as a condition of society that has always existed in some form or another. Modernization theorists tend to conceive underdevelopment as a social and economic process that long predates the emergence of modern capitalism. Indeed, they suggest that it was only with the rise of modern capitalist societies that underdevelopment was first overcome, despite the fact that many contemporary nations have not yet been able to reach this developmental stage. For the modernization theorists, then, such societies as the Yanomama, the Aztecs, and medieval England were or are underdeveloped in much the same way that contemporary Brazil, Thailand, and Nigeria are. This view is in sharp contrast to the point made earlier about development and underdevelopment being meaningful concepts only when they are applied to nations incorporated into a capitalist world-economy.

A second major assumption of modernization theory is that underdevelopment results from the internal deficiencies of a society. This notion is the counterpart to the claim that development results from certain special qualities of those societies having achieved it, qualities that set them apart from the rest. Three broad kinds of internal deficiencies are proposed by modernization theorists as causes of underdevelopment. One of these is insufficient capital formation. Many economists argue that underdeveloped societies have been unable to generate an amount of capital sufficient to get them to a "takeoff point": a point at which they could begin rapid economic growth.

Other modernization theorists have mentioned outdated business techniques and practices as factors preventing economic development. They suggest that underdeveloped societies commonly do not have the modern rational techniques of marketing, accounting, finance, sales, and so on, that are so common in the developed nations. The failure of such societies to adopt these modern rational business practices keeps their productivity and profit rates low and prevents significant development within them.

Finally, more sociologically oriented modernization theorists stress that underdeveloped societies generally lack the kind of consciousness or mentality—the kind of outlook on the world—that promotes development. Development is said to occur when people adopt rational, future-oriented value and ethical systems, and religions or philosophies that embody these kinds of values and ethics. It is alleged that most people in underdeveloped countries are governed by attitudes and values stressing the past and the importance of custom and tradition. Moreover, they are often caught up in religions that emphasize that human suffering can only be changed in the afterlife and that attempting to change the secular world is futile. Thus people are rendered fatalistic and generally accept their situation

in life rather than make rational efforts to change it. When people remain passive in regard to changing their situation, their underdeveloped state is perpetuated.

Rostow's Evolutionary Interpretation

Perhaps the best-known modernization theory is that of the economist W. W. Rostow (1960). According to Rostow, economic development involves the passage of a society through five evolutionary stages: the stage of traditional society, the stage of the preconditions for takeoff, the takeoff stage, the drive to maturity, and the age of high mass consumption. All underdeveloped societies are in the stage that Rostow calls traditional society. This is a type of society, past or present, that in Rostow's view has been little touched by modern capitalism and by modern science and technology. In this kind of society people are attached to the land, their families, and the forces of custom and tradition. Societies begin the transition out of this stage of social and economic life when they acquire the preconditions for takeoff. The idea spreads that economic progress is both possible and desirable. Education broadens, banks and other capital-mobilizing institutions appear, as do modern manufacturing enterprises using the latest technology. The takeoff is achieved when a society has reached the point at which it can carry on sustained economic growth. The drive to maturity involves a long period of sustained economic progress during which a society attempts to apply its new technological capacity to a wider and more diverse range of economic activities. Finally, a society becomes ready to enter the stage of high mass consumption. At this point the economy is capable of producing a wide range of consumer goods, and individuals are capable of consuming at a level that is beyond their basic needs for food, shelter, and clothing.

Although Rostow's analysis focuses more on development than on underdevelopment, there is clearly implied in his work a theoretical conception of underdevelopment. Underdeveloped societies are those that have not passed beyond the stage of traditional society. They have yet to experience those crucial stimuli that prompt people to want to reorganize their society so that self-sustaining economic growth can be realized. Underdeveloped societies lack the social patterns, political structures, and values that promote economic progress. Instead, the traditional features of these societies lead to a perpetuation of historically low levels of economic productivity.

Despite its considerable fame, Rostow's analysis of development and underdevelopment is not particularly impressive. The vast majority of his discussion is taken up with detailed descriptions of his stages, especially the last four. This sort of detailed description is of limited use. As Baran and Hobsbawm (1973) have pointed out, once a takeoff stage has been posited, the stages that precede and follow it are logically implied by it. Thus, the identification of these stages tells us little that we do not already know. Moreover, simply "pigeonholing [an underdeveloped society] in one of Rostow's 'stages' does not bring us any closer to an understanding of the country's economic and social condition or give us a clue to the country's developmental possibilities and prospects" (Baran and Hobsbawm, 1973:51) In other words, it gives us no insight into what the causes of development and underdevelopment are.

The Failures of Modernization Theory

The critical stance toward Rostow's particular interpretation may be extended to modernization theory in general. By and large, it has failed to produce an acceptable interpretation of the conditions that stimulate development and of those that establish obstacles to it. One major failing of the modernization theorists lies in the concept of "traditional society." A major difficulty with this concept is its highly global character. Traditional societies include not only ancient Rome, medieval Europe, and classical China, but also contemporary Kenya, Chile, and India. These societies differ dramatically in terms of a whole range of social, technological, economic, and political patterns, yet the concept of traditional society is used to cover them all. Can a concept that is applied so globally, and that ignores crucial differences among societies, really be a useful one?

There is another crucial difference among the societies mentioned above: their relationship to world capitalism. Ancient Rome, medieval Europe, and classical China were all historic civilizations that existed before the development of European capitalism; but contemporary Kenya, Chile, and India are all nations that have been subjected, at one time or another and in one form or another, to European colonialism. This suggests another major weakness of modernization theory: its virtual neglect of the economic and political relations that have historically existed between contemporary underdeveloped nations and the nations of the developed world (Frank, 1967). It is difficult to see how social scientists can justify paying little or no attention to these relations when formulating theories of underdevelopment.

As important as these weakness are, the real failing of modernization theory has been its inability to predict successfully the way development can be produced. Various modernization theorists have served as advisors to governments in developed nations and have made numerous recommendations regarding methods by which development in the Third World can be stimulated. In general, they recommend closer contact between the developed and the underdeveloped countries. Greater capital investment in the Third World, or large amounts of foreign aid to poor countries, are among the most frequent recommendations that have been made. Also, sociologically sensitive modernization theorists commonly recommend that underdeveloped countries should seek to imitate the social patterns of the advanced industrial nations. Yet despite the implementation of these recommendations, in some cases on a grand scale, most of the underdeveloped nations have not been developing as the modernization theorists have predicted. The economic gap between the developed and the underdeveloped countries is actually larger today than it was several decades ago, and the absolute amount of poverty and misery in the Third World has conceivably been growing rather than lessening. Such facts scarcely speak well for modernization theory.

Despite the severe criticism that it has received, modernization theory has never died out. Not only does it survive, but it probably is still the most widely embraced of the theoretical approaches to underdevelopment, at least outside of sociology (cf. Apter, 1987). Nevertheless, it must share theoretical attention with the approaches that came to challenge it in the 1960s, the first of which was dependency theory.

THE DEPENDENCY APPROACH TO UNDERDEVELOPMENT

Dependency theory was first developed in Latin America and came to the attention of North American and European social scientists largely through the writings of the American-educated economist Andre Gunder Frank (1966, 1967, 1969). By the mid-1970s this approach had become very popular, especially among sociologists. In many ways dependency theory is a specialized offshoot of the Marxian theory of capitalism.

The General Nature of the Dependency Approach

The basic underlying assumptions of the dependency approach stand in stark contrast to those of modernization theory. Rather than conceiving underdevelopment as an "original state," as something characteristic of a "traditional society," underdevelopment is viewed as something created within a precapitalist society that begins to experience certain forms of economic and political relations with one or more capitalist societies. Underdevelopment is not a product of certain internal deficiencies, as modernization theory holds. It results not from the absence of something, but from the *presence* of something. Thus, dependency theory would not regard India in 1700 as an underdeveloped society. At that time it was an agrarian, precapitalist empire. But by 1850 it was well on the road to becoming underdeveloped due to its relationship to British capitalism.

The root cause of underdevelopment in the dependency perspective is **economic dependency.** Economic dependency exists when one society falls under the sway of some foreign society's economic system, and when the first society's economy is organized by persons in the foreign society so as to benefit primarily the foreign economy. Economic dependency implies that there are relations of economic domination and subordination between two or more societies.

The concept of dependency as an explanation for economic underdevelopment has been developed most prominently by Andre Gunder Frank (1966, 1979) and Samir Amin (1974). For Frank the concepts of development and underdevelopment have meaning only when applied to nations within the capitalist world-economy. Frank envisions this world-economy as being divided into two major components, *metropolis* and *satellite*. (These concepts are basically equivalent to Wallerstein's concepts of core and periphery.) The flow of economic surplus in the world-economy is from the satellite (or periphery) to the metropolis (or core), and the world-economy is organized to make this happen. The underdeveloped nations therefore have become and remain underdeveloped because they are economically dominated by developed capitalist nations that have continually been extracting wealth from them. Frank has called this process the *development of underdevelopment* (1966). In this view, the development of the rich nations and the underdevelopment of the poor ones are but two sides of the same coin; underdevelopment of some nations has made development for others possible. The primary victims of this process are the vast majority of peasants and urban workers of the underdeveloped world itself. And who benefits from such a system? The members of developed nations certainly do, since their standard of living is raised substantially. But the greatest benefits go to capitalists in the metropolitan countries, as well as to the agricultural and industrial elites of the satellite countries. The latter have close economic and political ties to the metropolitan elite and play a crucial role in maintaining the situation of economic dependency.

Samir Amin's (1974) contributions to dependency theory center on his concepts of **articulated** and **disarticulated economies.** According to Amin, the developed nations have highly articulated economies, or ones whose multiple sectors closely interrelate such that development in any one sector stimulates development in the other sectors. Underdeveloped societies, by contrast, have disarticulated economies. These are economies whose various sectors do not closely interrelate. As a result, development in any one sector is commonly unable to stimulate development in the other sectors. Those sectors that are most developed in disarticulated economies involve the production of raw materials for export to the developed countries. What is the cause of economic disarticulation? According to

Amin, it is foreign control of the economy. Capitalists in the developed world have important connections with those peripheral capitalists who control raw-materials production.

What disarticulation really means, Amin argues, is that the kind of development characteristic of the advanced industrial societies cannot occur. When a society's economy becomes disarticulated due to foreign economic control, attention is directed to the development of those economic activities that benefit core capitalists. Those activities that would involve production for the overall benefit of the domestic economy are consequently neglected.

Types and Varieties of Economic Dependency

The concept of dependency can be understood more thoroughly by examining its various forms. Theotonio Dos Santos (1970) has suggested three historical forms of dependency through which the now-underdeveloped nations have passed. The first of these he calls *colonial dependence.* Under this form of dependency, which began as early as the sixteenth century in some parts of the world, European capitalist powers colonized precapitalist regions and established a monopoly over land, mines, and labor. Surplus wealth was extracted from these regions by means of European control over trade relations. The economic character of these colonized regions was powerfully shaped by their subordination to European nations.

A second historical form of dependency identified by Dos Santos is *financial-industrial dependence.* This form of dependence began in the late nineteenth century. It was characterized by the expansion of European industrial capital (as opposed to the earlier merchant capital) into the backward regions of the world. This form of dependence was part and parcel of the monopoly phase of capitalist development. Financial-industrial dependence involved heavy investment of big capitalists in the world's backward regions mainly for the purpose of producing raw materials to be exported back to the core nations.

The most recent form of dependency is termed by Dos Santos *the new dependence.* This kind of dependence is a post–World War II phenomenon and involves the emergence of multinational corporations that engage in extensive economic investment in Third World countries.

In addition to this concern about the forms of dependency, there is the question of how economic dependency creates and perpetuates underdevelopment. Dependency theorists often disagree with respect to the particular mechanisms whereby this occurs. Several different mechanisms through which dependency induces underdevelopment have been proposed by various theoreticians, and more than one is sometimes proposed even by the same theorist. Four possible dependency mechanisms are most frequently suggested in the current dependency literature (Chase-Dunn, 1975; Delacroix and Ragin, 1981; Barrett and Whyte, 1982):

- *Exploitation through repatriation.* It is often suggested in dependency writings that foreign firms reinvest only a portion of their profits derived from Third World investments in the Third World itself. The bulk of these profits is shipped home (repatriated) for the benefit of the investing nation.
- *Elite complicity.* A common theme in dependency writings is the claim that the rich capitalists of Third World countries enter into various types of agreements with rich core capitalists to maintain the status quo of the underdeveloped country. This occurs because the elites of both countries benefit from the prevailing economic situation.
- *Structural distortion.* Some dependency theorists argue that economic dependency leads to a distortion of the economy in the underdeveloped nation. This distortion then creates severe barriers to economic development. This argument, for example, is the kind made by Amin when he speaks of the disarticulation of the economy that results from the dependence of Third World countries on the capitalist core.
- *Market vulnerability.* It is sometimes argued that the peripheral nations are especially harmed by world market conditions. World demand for the primary products of peripheral countries tends to decline over time, and this decline is aggravated by price fluctuations for primary products.

These four ways in which dependency can induce underdevelopment should not be thought of as mutually exclusive. It is entirely possible that underdevelopment could result from more than one mechanism operating at the same time, or even from the simultaneous operation of all of them.

Recent Empirical Tests of Dependency Theory

In recent years numerous sociologists and other social scientists have conducted empirical investigations designed to test the basic claims of dependency theory. These studies generally examine a large number of the world's nations and employ the most advanced and sophisticated statistical procedures. A work by Volker Bornschier, Christopher Chase-Dunn, and Richard

Rubinson (1978) attempts to synthesize the results of 16 such studies (cf. Rubinson and Holtzman, 1981).

Most of the studies reviewed by Bornschier et al. examine economic growth from about 1960 until the early 1970s. Initial examination of the studies indicated that some found that dependency promoted economic growth, whereas others found that dependency retarded economic growth. Bornschier et al. have gone on to scrutinize these studies to determine what would have produced such apparently contradictory findings. They have shown that the findings of each study are closely linked to the way dependency is conceptualized and measured. By and large, the studies that show that foreign investment promotes economic growth conceptualize and measure investment in terms of *recent flows of investment capital.* By contrast, those studies demonstrating that foreign investment retards growth conceptualize and measure investment in terms of *long-term stocks of foreign investment.* The authors believe this finding to be of great substantive significance. On the basis of it, they conclude that "the immediate effect of inflows of foreign capital and aid is to increase the rate of economic growth, while the long-run cumulative effects operate to reduce the rate of economic growth" (1978:667). Moreover, they go on to say (1978:667–668):

> These results tend to confirm the hypothesis that current inflows of investment capital and aid cause short-term increases in growth due to the contribution to capital formation and demand as foreign corporations purchase land, labor, and materials and start production, while the long-run structural distortions of the national economy produced by foreign investment and the exporting of profits tend to produce negative effects over time. We conclude, then, that the effect of short-term flows of investment and aid has positive effects on growth, but

that their cumulative effect over time is negative. Many of the seemingly contradictory findings of these studies can be reconciled under this proposition.

In more recent work, Bornschier and Chase-Dunn (1985) have expanded this line of inquiry to include a greater number of studies (36 rather than 16), and have reached the same basic conclusions. Moreover, using a sample of 103 nations, they have gone on to conduct new original research on the developmental effects of short-term capital flows versus long-term stocks of capital. They regard this original research as eliminating some of the flaws of the earlier studies. Once again, the same basic conclusions are forthcoming, the most important of which is that long-term penetration by foreign capital hinders a country's chances of economic development.

Unfortunately, despite Bornschier et al.'s seemingly elegant solution to confusion, things cannot be resolved quite so easily. Bornschier et al.'s conclusions have recently been challenged by Glenn Firebaugh (1992). Firebaugh's challenge is methodologically complex and subtle, but his point is basically that Bornschier et al. interpreted their statistical analyses backwards. The long-term effect of foreign investment in the Third World, Firebaugh claims, is to *promote* rather than inhibit development. Firebaugh admits that domestic investment produces a higher rate of growth in the Third World than foreign investment, but he claims that the effects of foreign investment are nonetheless positive: Foreign investment is better than no investment at all. Firebaugh's attack has prompted a counterattack from the dependency perspective by William Dixon and Terry Boswell (1996a), which in turn has prompted a renewed attack by Firebaugh (1996) and a renewed counterattack by Dixon and Boswell (1996b). The disagreement is at this point unresolved and may stay unresolved for some time. About the most that can be said now is that the issue is still an open one: We still cannot be sure of the effects of foreign investment on economic development in the Third World.

The Effects of Economic Dependency: Some Historical Case Studies

Recent studies are thus inconclusive concerning the contemporary effects of economic dependency. However, even if these studies were highly conclusive they would still have to be viewed as having definite limitations, the most important of which is the restricted time span they explore. Most of the studies examine economic growth within a time span of only 10 to 15 years. Moreover, all the studies concentrate on economic growth since the late 1950s. Yet the Third World countries being explored in these studies were already underdeveloped by that time, and dependency theorists would argue that this underdevelopment was the result of a long-term historical process of economic dependency of one sort or another. To carry out a genuinely meaningful test of dependency theory, then, a long-term historical perspective on underdevelopment is needed. This can be accomplished through the use of two carefully selected historical comparisons: the economic divergence of China and Japan since the nineteenth century, and the differential economic outcomes that have occurred in the Americas over the past few centuries.

China and Japan A historical comparison of China and Japan seems especially appropriate inasmuch as Japan is today by far the most economically developed country in Asia. In her book *Japan, China and the Modern World Economy* (1977), Frances Moulder suggests that a major reason Japan became developed and China did not was the incorporation of China into the capitalist world-economy as a peripheral society.

According to Moulder, China first came to be incorporated into the world-economy as a trading partner of Great Britain. For centuries China had engaged in a luxury trade with Europe, but in the late eighteenth and early nineteenth centuries the trade relations between China and Europe underwent a major change. Trade between China and Britain became a trade in staples rather than in luxury items. As tea became a staple item in Britain, nearly all of the tea that the British imported came from China in the first half of the nineteenth century. This import was a very important source of revenue for the British government. "In 1855, for instance, about 10 percent of the gross revenue of the British government was derived from duties on imported tea" (Moulder, 1977:99). In addition, an interesting trade network developed among Britain, China, and India. The British found a market in China for the raw cotton they were producing in India and thus exported much of this cotton to China. Moreover, after the middle of the eighteenth century the British gained control of opium production in India and substantially increased its output. They eventually succeeded in addicting a portion of the Chinese population to opium and thus developed a vast opium market in China, a market supplied, of course, by Indian opium.

Another aspect of Britain's trade with China involved the development of Britain's textile industry. As British cotton textile production increased, there was increasing concern to find foreign markets for the sale of these products, and China was seen as an important market. In their development of China as an export market for British cotton goods, it was necessary for Britain to deprive the Chinese of a home market for their own textile industry. British rather than Chinese manufactures increasingly came to be sold in China. By the late nineteenth century, other industrializing nations, such as France, the United States, and Germany, began to follow Britain's lead and sell a portion of their manufactures in China. By the end of the nineteenth century China's consumption of Western goods was substantial.

The incorporation of China into the world-economy involved foreign investment as well as trade. Shipbuilding became an important form of foreign investment, "and by the 1930s over half the tonnage built in China was the work of foreign-controlled firms" (Moulder, 1977:113). This industry was primarily controlled by the British. But the most important form of foreign investment in China involved railroads and mining. As Moulder notes (1977:114):

> Since the 1860s, Western merchants and statesmen continually sought out Chinese officials and urged railroad and mine construction. They offered to construct railways and to open mines or to lend the money to the government to do so. . . .
>
> The Sino-Japanese War marked the end of the government's ability to resist foreign investment in railroads and mines, as it had in manufacturing. After 1895 the Chinese government was forced to grant railway and mining concessions to various Western nations and Japan (a concession granted the sole right to construct railroads or open modern mines within a specified territory). France received railway concessions in various places on the borders between Indochina and China, Russia obtained concessions in Manchuria and Liaotung (whose railways ultimately came under control of Japan), the Germans in Shantung (which also came under control of Japan after World War I), and the English in the Canton area.
>
> By 1911, 41 percent of the railway mileage in China was owned by foreigners and the remainder had largely been built by the Chinese government with foreign loans. . . .

Numerous mining concessions were granted from 1896 to 1913 to the British, Germans, Russians, French, Americans, Belgians, and Japanese.

Japan's experience with European capitalism has been very different. By 1639 Japan had completed the establishment of its famous policy of economic and political isolation from the West. For more than two centuries thereafter, Japan had very little contact with western Europe. For a number of reasons Japan, unlike its Asian neighbors, never fell victim to colonization (or foreign economic penetration). During this time the economic relations between Japan and the West were limited to some minor and closely regulated forms of trade. After the middle of the nineteenth century, Japan was compelled to reverse its isolationist policy and begin opening up to Western contact and influence. However, the nature of its economic relationship to the West even after this time was very different from China's. Although trade with the West did increase and some foreign investment did develop, these never approached the levels reached in China. Moulder concludes that throughout the nineteenth century China was a tightly integrated peripheral zone of Western capitalism and Japan was not. And it was these different relations to Western capitalism, Moulder argues, that led to the divergent economic outcomes observable today. In other words, it was the emergence of economic dependency in China and the failure of dependency to develop in Japan that lay, respectively, behind modern China's underdevelopment and modern Japan's development. (Of course, it took more than just the absence of peripheralization for Japan to achieve the economic status that it has today. There were of necessity positive factors that helped promote development as well as an absence of inhibiting factors. In Chapter 7, I have delineated what I believe to have been the major positive factors.)

The Americas   Andre Gunder Frank (1979) has given particular attention to explaining the historical underdevelopment of Latin America and the development of North America (exclusive of Mexico and Central America). Within this latter category he has tried to explain why the northeastern region of the United States led the way into economic development in the nineteenth century, whereas the U.S. South experienced its own form of underdevelopment and did not begin to develop until much later.

According to Frank, Latin America's current underdevelopment is the historical legacy of centuries of dependent development—of the development of underdevelopment. Much of Latin America fell under European colonial domination from the sixteenth century on. Contemporary Mexico and Peru, for example, were colonized in the sixteenth century by Spain. Although the Spaniards first imposed slavery on the indigenous population, this was quickly abandoned. It was replaced by a form of labor control known as the *encomienda*. Under this system (Frank, 1979:45)

> Indians of designated communities were assigned to particular Spaniards, who did not receive ownership of their persons, lands or other property, but were authorised to exact tribute in personal services, goods and money from them. This tribute was the principal source of the Spaniards' capital, and the *encomenderos* invested it in a variety of mining, agricultural, commercial and other enterprises, such as further conquests, that permitted the realisation of this tribute for shipment abroad and for further capital accumulation in Mexico itself.

The *encomienda* was soon replaced by a labor system known as the *repartimiento*. This was similar to the *encomienda* but more flexible. Under the *repartimiento* a state official would assign a certain number of man-days of labor to particular Spaniards. Beginning in the late sixteenth century, this system was itself replaced by the *hacienda* system. In this system, Indians were tied to particular Spaniards through a form of debt, and these Indians had to work for their overlords until such debts were repaid. The *hacienda* system was generally organized so that it was virtually impossible for debts to be repaid, and thus the Spaniards were more or less assured of a continual supply of cheap labor.

In Brazil, under the direction of the Portuguese, a slave plantation system was established using imported Africans as slaves. This system prevailed from the sixteenth until the late nineteenth century. Slave plantation systems prevailed as well in the Caribbean, where they were established by the British, the French, the Dutch, and the Spaniards.

In North America, suitable geographical conditions favored the establishment of a slave society in the Southern colonies of the United States. Slavery using imported Africans as workers prevailed there from the late seventeenth century until the middle of the nineteenth century. Frank believes that this slave society, as well as those in Latin America, functioned as a vital part of the capitalist world-economy. It served in the first half of the nineteenth century, for example, as a major producer of raw cotton, a product that fed the flourishing textile industries of Britain and the U.S. North. It was therefore an important part of the capitalist periphery.

But what of the U.S. North itself? What prompted it to take off into enormous industrial development beginning around 1830? Frank notes that the original Northern colonies were not highly regarded by the British. Unlike the Southern colonies, they did not have a long growing season and were not deemed to be particularly suitable for large-scale agricultural production. This low assessment of the economic value of the Northern colonies led to what Frank calls their "benign neglect." They were never peripheralized or made an economic dependency of some European country, as were the Southern colonies and much of Latin America. Instead, the U.S. North became a *settler colony*, a region settled by individuals from a foreign country but then left more or less alone economically. The U.S. North was in the seventeenth and eighteenth centuries largely a society of small independent farmers and craftsmen, very different indeed from its neighbors in the U.S. South and Latin America.

Frank is suggesting, then, that the U.S. North was not constrained by a foreign power, and thus was free to develop its own resources for itself rather than for the benefit of others. But what could have stimulated the enormous development it did experience? Frank argues that it was the North's unique role in world capitalist trade networks, a role no doubt conditioned by its geographical location, that was responsible (Frank, 1979:61):

> The North-eastern colonies came to occupy a position in the expanding world mercantile capitalist system and in the process of capital accumulation which permitted them to share in the latter as a sub-metropolis of Western Europe in the exploitation of the South, the West Indies, and indeed of Africa and indirectly of the mining regions and the Orient. This privileged position—not shared by others in the New World—must be considered as contributing crucially to the economic development of the North-east during colonial times and to its successful political policy of Independence and further development thereafter. This privileged position and role impinged on northern transport, mercantile and financial participation in southern and western export (and import) trade; the North-east's advantageous participation in the West

India trade, the slave trade and indeed world trade; north-eastern manufacturing development, largely for export; and in the associated capital accumulation and concentration in northern cities.

In sum, Frank is persuasively suggesting for the Americas what Moulder argued in the case of China and Japan: that underdevelopment is the historical outcome of a situation of economic dependency, whereas development requires (at the very least) economic autonomy.

FROM DEPENDENCY THEORY TO THE WORLD-SYSTEM

Despite its superiority to modernization theory in explaining historical and contemporary patterns of underdevelopment, dependency theory has certain weaknesses that cannot be overlooked. By the late 1970s these weaknesses had begun to be noticed even by many of this approach's most enthusiastic supporters, and today dependency theory is regarded as a flawed, if still highly useful, perspective. Of the objections that have been raised against it, the most important are essentially as follows (Roxborough, 1979; Hoogvelt, 1982; Leys, 1982; Blomstrom and Hettne, 1984):

• In spite of its severe criticism of modernization theory's failure to place contemporary underdeveloped societies in their historical context, in its own peculiar way dependency theory is also ahistorical. While it gives great attention to the historical relationship of underdeveloped societies to the capitalist core, it tends to ignore the precapitalist history of these societies. This history is very important, however, in conditioning the way in which a particular precapitalist society will be incorporated into the capitalist system and the results of that incorporation (Chase-Dunn, 1989a; Lenski and Nolan, 1984).

- Dependency theory tends to overgeneralize about contemporary underdeveloped nations. It assumes that their dependent status renders them all essentially alike. Yet there are important differences between these nations with respect to such things as class structure, political system, and geographical and demographic size, and these differences play a role in shaping a nation's current development level and future developmental prospects. Another way of putting this is to say that dependency theory concentrates too much attention on the external relations between an underdeveloped society and the capitalist core, and not enough attention on its internal characteristics.
- The poverty and misery of contemporary Third World countries cannot simply be blamed on the economic intrusion of the more advanced capitalist countries (Chirot, 1977, 1986). Most of the countries and regions that fell under the economic control of the more advanced countries already had extensive poverty before they came to be dominated by these countries. While in some instances this poverty and misery may have become worse as a result of foreign influence, by and large that poverty and misery were already there from the beginning.
- Dependency theory is too pessimistic in asserting that economic dependency makes economic development impossible. This is contradicted by the experience of a number of countries in recent decades. For example, Brazil underwent substantial economic growth between the mid-1960s and the mid-1970s, and east Asian countries like Taiwan and South Korea have experienced very rapid growth since the 1950s.
- Dependency theory's main policy recommendation for the underdeveloped countries—breaking out of the capitalist system by socialist revolution—has produced little. The vast majority of the Third World countries that have opted for socialism in recent decades have failed to generate any real developmental impetus; in fact, their record is inferior to that of several countries that have remained capitalist.

These criticisms have considerable force, but it needs to be understood that they are directed more to some dependency theorists than to others. It is essential to distinguish two rather different strands of dependency theory (Bornschier and Chase-Dunn, 1985), what might be called "hard" and "soft" dependency theories.

The hard version of dependency theory is associated primarily with the works of Frank and Amin discussed earlier. It sees economic dependency as always generating the development of underdevelopment, and thus as rendering development impossible (or at least extremely difficult) so long as it continues. The soft version is associated mainly with Fernando Henrique Cardoso (1982; Cardoso and Faletto, 1979) and Peter Evans (1979; cf. Bornschier and Chase-Dunn, 1985). It does not assume that dependency must always lead to the development of underdevelopment. Under some circumstances there can occur what Cardoso has called "associated dependent development," or simply "dependent development." This is a type of economic growth that occurs primarily as the result of extensive investment in manufacturing industries by transnational corporations. Soft dependency theorists insist that in recent decades a new form of dependency has grown up alongside the old form. In the older, or "classical," dependency, core countries use peripheral countries as sources of investment in raw agricultural and mineral products. But in the new dependency, investment occurs within the industrial sector. And this form of dependency, it is argued, is not incompatible with certain amounts of economic development.

It is obvious that the soft version of dependency theory is much more flexible than the hard version, and thus largely free from the criticisms cited earlier, especially the third. Dependency and development can coexist. However, it is vital that this point not be overinterpreted. It seems clear that the kind of development that occurs under the new dependency is quite different from the kind that has occurred within the core capitalist countries. For one thing, it has not gone nearly as far, and for another it has some peculiarities not associated with development in the core. Contemporary Brazil, which both Cardoso and Evans take as the leading exemplar of dependent development, illustrates both of these points. After about the mid-1960s Brazil experienced a spurt in economic growth that occurred simultaneously with extensive transnational industrial investment. This growth was so rapid that many observers began to speak of a "Brazilian miracle" (Skidmore and Smith, 1989). However, by about the middle of the 1970s this growth had slowed greatly, eventually virtually stopping altogether. Brazil's current per capita GNP is still meager when compared with the per capita GNPs found in the core (see Table 9.1). Moreover, the economic growth that did occur in this period seemed to benefit primarily a small segment of the population, perhaps less than 20 percent. Income inequality has increased sharply, and there is now a great gap between persons working in the modern industrial and service sector and those still living and working in traditional occupations (Skidmore and Smith, 1989) (Brazil now has one of the most unequal income distributions in the world). To make matters worse, to finance its dependent development Brazil borrowed huge sums of money from core financial institutions, and now it has accumulated a huge foreign debt that is a severe obstacle to further economic growth (cf. World Bank, 1988).

It is but a short step from the theory of dependent development to a full-blown world-system theory of underdevelopment. Wallerstein has claimed that it is the capitalist world-system as a whole that develops, not particular societies. He acknowledges that internal characteristics of societies matter, but they exert their effects only in the context of a society's position within the world-system at a particular time in history. As the world-system evolves, there is increasing polarization between core and periphery, and it is difficult for less-developed nations to improve their status, or at least improve it very much. However, at particular historical junctures opportunities are created for some countries to move up. Wallerstein (1979b) proposes three basic strategies that nations can adopt to accomplish this: "seizing the chance," "development by invitation," and "self-reliance."

During periods of contraction of the world-economy, core countries may be in a weakened economic position. If so, peripheral or semiperipheral countries may be able to use aggressive state action to improve their position. This is the strategy of seizing the chance. Wallerstein suggests that Russia adopted this strategy in the late nineteenth century, and that it was employed by Brazil and Mexico during the 1930s.

Development by invitation, by contrast, occurs during periods of expansion of the world-economy. During these periods, "space" or "room" is created for some countries to move up because there is an increased level of demand for commodities on a world scale. Underdeveloped countries with just the right internal characteristics (especially geopolitical circumstances) may be treated unusually favorably by core countries. As a result they may be able to use the resulting economic advantages to inaugurate a developmental surge. Wallerstein suggests that Scotland followed this developmental strategy in the late eighteenth century. Perhaps the best recent exemplars of the strategy are the east Asian countries of Taiwan and South Korea (see the Special Topic at the end of the chapter).

Some countries, though, may see their best chance for economic development resting on withdrawal from the world-system and adoption of some version of socialism. No doubt the most successful employment of this strategy—self-reliance—has been by Russia (the Soviet Union), beginning in 1917.

Despite the differences between world-system theory and classical dependency theory, it is clear that the former is only a version of the latter. Wallerstein stresses what he calls "limited possibilities" for transformation of underdeveloped countries within the world-economy. Most countries don't move up, and those that do don't move very far. They move from the periphery into the semiperiphery, or from a lower to a higher semiperipheral position. There is no example of a country ever having been truly peripheral and moving from that position all the way into the core. Since most nations continue to stagnate rather than move up, and since there is increasing polarization within the system, Wallerstein is not optimistic about the fate of the underdeveloped countries within a capitalist context. For him, the only real solution to the problems of the underdeveloped world is a long-term one: the ultimate worldwide collapse of capitalism and its replacement by a socialist world-government.

THE PROCESS OF GLOBALIZATION

A word that seems to be on almost everyone's lips these days in discussions of current economic issues is *globalization*, by which is generally meant a process of the increasing internationalization of economic production, a process usually thought to include associated social and political changes. Globalization is occurring most extensively and rapidly among the advanced industrial countries themselves. In the last 20 years or so there has been a tremendous acceleration of capital investment by the industrial capitalist countries in each other (Alderson, 1997). However, from the perspective of this chapter the most important aspect of globalization involves the increasing relocation of manufacturing industries from the core to the periphery and semiperiphery.

Among the first to discuss the relocation of manufacturing from core economies to the Third World were the German scholars Folker Fröbel, Jürgen Heinrichs, and Otto Kreye (1980). They saw emerging in the 1970s what they called a "new international division of labor." Primarily as the result of innovations in communication and transportation, it became economically feasible for core capitalists to move many of their production operations into the periphery and semiperiphery, where a huge supply of cheap labor could be found. The increasing migration of capital abroad had not only important consequences for the countries into which capital increasingly moved; there were also consequences for the core countries themselves, especially in the form of deindustrialization. In the United States, for example, deindustrialization became most prominent in the highly industrialized and urbanized northeastern part of the country (Bluestone and Harrison, 1982; Ross and Trachte, 1990).

In their book *Global Capitalism: The New Leviathan*, Robert Ross and Kent Trachte (1990) see the process of globalization as creating a new form of capitalism, what they call *global capitalism*, that is highly distinctive from earlier forms of capitalism (competitive and monopoly capitalism). Global capitalism is primarily distinguished by the existence of a world market in sites for manufacturing production, the spatial division of production tasks throughout the world, and the extensive migration of capital from region to region in the search for profits. Although the periphery has traditionally been associated with raw materials production, under global capitalism a significant segment of it has been increasingly reoriented to the production of manufactured goods. Much manufacturing in the Third World takes place in what have been called *free production zones* (Fröbel et al., 1980; Ross and Trachte, 1990). These are geographical zones within a country, in many cases physically demarcated by fences or other barriers, within which foreign investors organize production that is little restricted by labor regulations. Workers engage in high-intensity work, work long hours, and receive very low wages. Usually labor unions are prohibited and workers have few or no rights. Sometimes workers, who are most commonly young, unmarried women, are bussed in from hinterlands and live in prison-style barracks. Often employment is of short duration, and capitalists may pick up their operations and take them elsewhere if it is more profitable for them to do so. The reason Third World countries agree to such labor conditions is that they must make concessions to attract foreign capital investment, which they believe will enhance their economic development.

But the process of globalization is not simply about the relocation of manufacturing from core to periphery or semiperiphery, although this is, of course, a major part of the process. Globalization involves all of the basic types of economy activity carried on in economies throughout the world. Manuel Castells (1996) argues that we are now making the transition from a world-economy to a truly global economy. A world-economy is one in which capital accumulation goes on throughout the world,

but a global economy is *one that has the capacity to work as a single unit on a planetary scale.* In a global economy (Castells, 1996:93–95),

> Capital is managed around the clock in globally integrated financial markets working in real time for the first time in history: billion dollars-worth of transactions take place in seconds in the electronic circuits throughout the globe. . . . [There has been an extraordinary growth in the scale] of transborder flows for major market economies: their share of GDP increased by a factor of about 10 in 1980–92. New technologies allow capital to be shuttled back and forth between economies in very short time, so that capital, and therefore savings and investment, are interconnected worldwide, from banks to pension funds, stock exchange markets, and currency exchange. Since currencies are interdependent, so are economies everywhere. . . .
>
> Labor markets are not truly global, except for a small but growing segment of professionals and scientists . . . , but labor is a global resource in at least three ways: firms may choose to locate in a variety of places worldwide to find the labor supply they need, be it in terms of skills, costs, or social control; firms everywhere may also solicit highly skilled labor from everywhere, and they will obtain it provided they offer the right remuneration and working conditions; and labor will enter any market on its own initiative, coming from anywhere, when human beings are pushed from their homes by poverty and war or pulled towards a new life by hope for their children. . . .
>
> Science, technology, and information are also organized in global flows . . .
>
> In spite of the persistence of protectionism and restrictions to free trade, markets for goods and services are becoming increasingly global. This does not mean that all firms sell worldwide. But it does mean that the strategic aim of firms, large and small, is to sell wherever they can throughout the world, either directly or via their linkage with networks that operate in the world

market. . . . the *dominant segments and firms, the strategic cores* of all economies are deeply connected to the world market, and their fate is a function of their performance in such a market.

From the perspective of the semiperiphery and periphery, perhaps the most relevant question at this point is the extent to which the industrialization of the Third World can lead it forward into a process of major economic development. Both Fröbel et al. (1980) and Ross and Trachte (1990) are highly pessimistic, adopting a stance much like that of dependency theory. Castells's (1996) answer is more complicated. He notes that the new global economy is highly dynamic, strongly exclusionary, and very unstable in its boundaries. It is an exacting taskmaster that suffers no fools gladly. To succeed in this extremely competitive world, four basic traits are necessary: technological capacity; access to a large, well integrated, and affluent market (e.g., the European Union, the North American trade zone); a significant differential between cost of production at the production site and prices in the destination market; and the capacity of governments to steer the growth strategies of the economies that they regulate. Societies that have these traits must use them to integrate themselves centrally into the global economy (or, as the case may be, to keep themselves centrally integrated). Those that can compete will do so, and those that cannot will be brutally excluded and marginalized. And to refuse to play the new global game is no option, for that will bring certain disaster. To a large extent, old patterns of domination and dependency will be perpetuated. Most of Africa and large parts of Latin America and Asia will continue to be marginalized, and their suffering may increase. (Few are inviting Africa to play the game, because they are seen as having little or nothing to offer.) At the same time, some peripheral and semiperipheral countries—or, more exactly, some segments of these countries—will be in a position to improve their situation. The Pearl River Delta area of China, for example, is already benefitting from its connection to the dynamic Asian Pacific economy centered on Japan. It has succeeded in attracting an enormous amount of foreign investment since the early 1980s, and between 1980 and 1990 had one of the fastest growing economies in the world. Foreign investment since 1990 has grown to much greater proportions.

In conclusion, we need to ask just how new this "new global economy" is. World-system theorists generally, and Chase-Dunn in particular, take the position that this is just old wine in new bottles. Capitalist production has always been global, they insist. Social scientists such as Ross and Trachte and Castells, on the other hand, see a qualitatively new economic structure emerging. But can we really answer definitively at this point? Probably not. It will take another decade or two before we can have clear sight of what we are looking at. Understanding any dramatic historical phenomenon, if that is what we are witnessing, has always taken many years of serious reflection.

SUMMARY

1. Worldwide differences in levels of economic and social development have long been a crucial concern of many social scientists. Underdeveloped nations are those that have the lowest levels of technological and economic development within the capitalist world-economy. They should not be confused with undeveloped societies, which are truly preindustrial and precapitalist. Developed nations are those advanced industrial countries that have attained the highest levels of technological development and economic prosperity within the world-economy.

2. Underdevelopment is perhaps best assessed in terms of a society's level of per capita GNP, but there are numerous other indicators of underdevelopment. These include marked levels of economic inequality, high rates of population growth, poor standards of nutrition and health, and a high percentage of the population still employed in agriculture.

3. The modernization approach to underdevelopment is an older approach still favored by most social scientists, at least those in the developed world. It postulates that underdevelopment occurs because a society has certain internal deficiencies preventing it from transcending economic and social traditionalism. These deficiencies include insufficient capital formation, outdated techniques of business practice, and a value system oriented to the past.

4. Rostow's theory is perhaps the leading example of modernization theory. Rostow postulates that societies pass through a definite series of stages on their way to becoming developed—traditionalism, preconditions for takeoff, economic takeoff, sustained growth, and drive to maturity. Underdeveloped nations have remained stuck in the stage of traditionalism.

5. In general, the modernization theorists believe that intellectuals and leaders of business and government in the developed world can help promote development in the Third World by helping Third World nations overcome their fundamental deficiencies.

6. In the late 1960s and early 1970s dependency theory began to emerge as an alternative to modernization theory. This theory is a version of the Marxian theory of capitalism applied to a world level. It holds that underdevelopment results from the economic dependency on foreign economies into which many nations have fallen. Frank has suggested that the advanced capitalist countries have dominated and exploited the poorer regions in order to attain high levels of prosperity. Amin suggests that the domination of one nation by another produces an economic disarticulation that inhibits economic development.

7. Two different versions of dependency theory can be identified. A hard version, associated with Frank and Amin, sees economic dependency as always leading to the development of underdevelopment. In this version, development cannot occur as long as dependency continues, and the only real hope for underdeveloped countries is therefore to withdraw from the capitalist system through socialist revolution. A softer version of dependency theory holds that economic dependency is the basic root cause of historical patterns of underdevelopment, but that development is possible under certain recent forms of dependency. This version of dependency theory is preferable to the harder version, but the versions are more similar than different and both are highly preferable to modernization theory.

8. Wallerstein's world-system theory is very similar to the softer version of dependency theory. Wallerstein claims that contemporary underdeveloped nations have become what they are as the result of centuries of domination by the capitalist core. Most of these countries are continuing to fall ever farther and farther behind the core. However, a few of these countries may be able to improve their position in the world-economy by seizing upon opportunities available at certain historical junctures in the development of capitalism.

9. Beginning as early as the 1970s, a process of globalization has linked the economies of the world more tightly together. Core societies have begun to relocate many of their manufacturing operations in the Third World because labor costs there are much lower. The production process has become spatially differentiated at a world level, which has been made possible by major innovations in transportation and communication. Economies have become increasingly interdependent and competitive. Firms not only increasingly produce in a world market, but increasingly sell there too. The new global economy is a fast-changing, highly dynamic system that societies must plug into in order to be economically successful. Within it many of the old relations of domination and dependency will be preserved, but there will also be possibilities for the most fortunate peripheral and semiperipheral countries to take advantage of their circumstances to undergo significant economic development.

SPECIAL TOPIC: EAST ASIA AND THEORIES OF UNDERDEVELOPMENT

Since about the mid-1950s a startling degree of economic development has occurred in the east Asian societies of Taiwan, South Korea, Hong Kong, and Singapore. Before 1950 these societies were very poor members of the capitalist periphery, but they are now among the most prosperous societies outside the capitalist core. South Korea has a per capita GNP of $9,700 a year, and Hong Kong's and Singapore's levels of per capita economic productivity are more than double that figure (see Table 9.1). All of these societies have extremely low infant mortality rates for non-core nations, as well as rates of population growth more similar to core than to non-core societies (see Table 9.1). Moreover, at least in Taiwan and South Korea, this development has occurred without producing the extremely sharp income inequalities so characteristic of other rapidly growing less-developed countries. These countries today have income distributions that resemble those of core nations, or that are even more egalitarian.

Collectively, these four east Asian countries are frequently known as the "Newly Industrializing Countries," or NICs. It has frequently been asserted that the economic development of the NICs is a fatal blow to dependency theory (Barrett and Whyte, 1982; Berger, 1986). Certainly if we are talking about the strong version of dependency theory, it is impossible to deny that assertion (Bienefeld, 1981). However, this east Asian development is not inconsistent with the soft dependency theory or with world-system theory. Indeed, it would seem that world-system theory is extremely well suited to explain what has been happening in recent decades in the NICs. In order to show that this is so, I shall confine myself to Taiwan and South Korea. Hong Kong and Singapore are really city-states rather than countries, and they have only a tiny agricultural sector. Because of their unique nature, they are not particularly good test cases for any theory of underdevelopment.

Taiwan and South Korea seem to be exceptionally good examples of what Wallerstein has called "development by invitation" (Bienefeld, 1981; Cumings, 1984), and their accomplishments result from a unique combination of five circumstances. Some of these circumstances involve internal characteristics of the societies themselves, while others involve the larger world-economy and their relationship to it (Cumings, 1984; Crane, 1982; Koo, 1987; Evans, 1987; Aseniero, 1994).

First, it is true that both Taiwan and South Korea have a history of economic dependency, but the dependency they experienced has been unique. Around the turn of the twentieth century Taiwan (then known as Formosa) and Korea (which, of course, had not yet been divided into South Korea and North Korea) became colonies of Japan. But Japan was no ordinary colonizer, for it engaged in practices not found among European colonizers. The Japanese built up in these colonies a large infrastructure of transportation and communication, and even established heavy industries, especially in steel, chemicals, and hydroelectric power. Thus, although Taiwan and Korea became dependent, they nonetheless acquired certain technological and economic resources generally absent in other dependent countries. These resources helped establish a foundation for developmental efforts once Japanese colonialism ended.

Second, both Taiwan and South Korea undertook major land reforms after World War II. These reforms produced a much more egalitarian distribution of land. It is well known that land-reform efforts have failed, or not even been attempted, in most other less-developed countries. In most of these countries land is enormously concentrated in the hands of a few rich landowners, and this uneven distribution is a major obstacle to development. But land reform in Taiwan and South Korea led to major increases in agricultural output, and industrialization efforts could therefore begin to succeed.

However, as important as these conditions were, they could never have led to significant economic development if Taiwan and South Korea had not been favored by two features of the external environment. First, there was the unique geopolitical situation these countries were in. During the 1950s the United States became the world's leading economic power, and it began to perceive a severe threat to its economic position from the Soviet Union and China, the latter having just had a revolution (in 1949) and become part of the socialist world. There was great fear that both Taiwan and South Korea would become part of this world, and so the United States began to pump huge amounts of money, in the form of both aid and loans, into both countries. Although the United States had given aid and loans to many other countries, the amounts going into Taiwan and South Korea were unparalleled. There is no doubt that this economic assistance played a crucial role in helping launch these countries' developmental efforts.

All of this was happening during a period in which the world-economy was undergoing major expansion. Thus, the increase in world economic demand made "room" or "space" available for some countries to improve their position. Moreover, the United States directly encouraged the upward mobility of Taiwan and South Korea by opening its own domestic markets to the products of these countries. This occurred primarily after 1960. In the 1950s the industrialization of Taiwan and South Korea was oriented mainly to producing for their domestic markets, but after 1960 it shifted toward an emphasis on selling competitively in the world market. This kind of industrialization, known generally as *export-led industrialization,* is a common developmental strategy of less-developed countries. Whether it works or not is another question. That it has worked so well for these two countries depended significantly on the protected markets that the United States carved out for them in its own territory.

Finally, it cannot be overlooked that the largest single investor and the largest director of economic growth in both countries was the state. This, too, was the legacy of Japanese colonialism. Both Taiwan and South Korea had structured their state apparatuses on the Japanese model and had developed the kind of highly efficient state that could, in the context of the other four conditions, lead them into significant economic development. Specifically, the state in these two countries played a major role in keeping the wages of workers down, which is essential for export-led industrialization because it makes products cheaper and thus more competitive on the world market. It also built up military-style discipline in the factories, thus contributing to high productivity.

Because of the success of Taiwan and South Korea, the question has naturally arisen as to whether they constitute models for economic development that other countries could imitate. Some social scientists who are especially enthusiastic about east Asian development believe that they do (cf. Berger, 1986). Yet this is a very dubious notion. As Bruce Cumings has said, "The developmental 'successes' of Taiwan and Korea are historically and regionally specific, and therefore provide no readily adaptable models for other developing countries interested in emulation" (1984:38). Indeed, it is not even clear the extent to which Taiwan and South Korea can sustain their development in the decades ahead. South Korea has, in fact, encountered a number of economic problems. Its economic growth has slowed somewhat since 1980, and it has now accumulated a huge foreign debt. It has moved from the periphery into the semiperiphery, but how much further it may be able to move is unclear. Taiwan continues on a smoother course, but historical precedent suggests great caution in expecting too much of it (Cumings, 1984).

In summary, some important things have been happening in east Asia since the end of the Second World War, but these events do not suggest a fundamental flaw in dependency or world-system theories of underdevelopment, especially world-system theory. East Asian development is not only compatible with world-system theory, but can only be properly understood in terms of it.

FOR FURTHER READING

Amin, Samir. *Accumulation on a World Scale.* New York: Monthly Review Press, 1974. A detailed statement of Amin's version of dependency theory.

Bradshaw, York W., and Michael Wallace. *Global Inequalities.* Thousand Oaks, Calif.: Pine Forge Press, 1996. A useful introduction to many of the issues discussed in this chapter.

Castells, Manuel. *The Information Age: Economy, Society, and Culture. Volume I: The Rise of the Network Society.* Oxford: Blackwell, 1996. An excellent analysis of the so-called information technology revolution and its relationship to the globalization of economic production. The first of three volumes.

Chirot, Daniel. *Social Change in the Modern Era.* Orlando: Harcourt Brace Jovanovich, 1986. An exploration of the development and contemporary character of the capitalist world-economy that takes up many aspects of the social, economic, and political situation of Third World nations. Focuses closely on the relationship between the Third World countries and the capitalist core. (The reader is reminded that the 1977 version of this book is still worth consulting.)

Evans, Peter B. *Dependent Development: The Alliance of Multinational, State, and Local Capital in Brazil.* Princeton, N.J.: Princeton University Press, 1979. An excellent case study of dependent development in Brazil. Focuses on the shaping of Brazilian economic development by three groups: foreign capitalists, local capitalists, and the Brazilian state.

Frank, Andre Gunder. *Dependent Accumulation and Underdevelopment.* New York: Monthly Review Press, 1979. A major statement of dependency theory by one of its chief formulators.

Fröbel, Folker, Jürgen Heinrichs, and Otto Kreye. *The New International Division of Labour.* Cambridge: Cambridge University Press, 1980. Postulates that a "new international division of labor" is being created through the relocation by core capitalists of many segments of their operations in the capitalist periphery. Contains detailed case studies of this phenomenon.

Gereffi, Gary, and Donald L. Wyman (eds.). *Manufacturing Miracles: Paths of Industrialization in Latin America and East Asia.* Princeton, N.J.: Princeton University Press, 1990. A collection of very useful essays on the "dependent development" of the most rapidly growing countries in Latin America and east Asia.

Hoogvelt, Ankie M. M. *The Third World in Global Development.* London: Macmillan, 1982. One of the better introductions to current issues and theoretical debates in the study of underdevelopment.

Moulder, Frances V. *Japan, China and the Modern World Economy.* New York: Cambridge University Press, 1977. An impressive attempt to explain the historical divergence of China and Japan as the result of their relationship to the capitalist world-economy.

Ross, Robert J. S., and Kent C. Trachte. *Global Capitalism: The New Leviathan.* Albany: State University of New York Press, 1990. Sets forth the argument, similar to that of Fröbel, Heinrichs, and Kreye, that around 1970 the world-economy entered a new phase characterized by an extensive and intensive global organization of production on a scale never before witnessed. An important extension of the basic argument of world-system theory.

So, Alvin Y. *Social Change and Development: Modernization, Dependency, and World-System Theories.* Newbury Park, Calif.: Sage, 1990. A very good overview and critical analysis of the three major theories of underdevelopment.

Wolf, Eric. *Europe and the People Without History.* Berkeley: University of California Press, 1982. Written from a type of world-system perspective, this book contains much useful information regarding the historical impact of expanding European capitalism upon many precapitalist societies.

Chapter
10

Social Stratification in Industrial Societies

This chapter continues the discussion of social stratification begun in Chapter 6. As that chapter showed, there is a striking trend in the evolution of forms of stratified life throughout human history. The movement of societies from the hunter-gatherer to the agrarian stage is closely associated with the development of increasingly complex and extreme forms of stratification. However, as Gerhard Lenski (1966) has shown, with the passage from agrarian to industrial societies a reversal of this trend seems to have taken place. In industrial societies the dominant economic class claims a smaller share of national income and wealth, and there has been a diffusion of income throughout the population to an extent unimaginable to the average members of agrarian societies.

Nonetheless, the inequalities of contemporary industrial societies are sharp enough and significant enough to permit analysis on their own terms, not just in terms of a broad comparison with the past (Rossides, 1976). That is the aim of this chapter. Its focus is a close comparative analysis of the stratification systems of the two major types of industrial societies, capitalist and state socialist. An effort is made to ascertain to what extent the state socialist societies have fulfilled Marx's prediction about a "classless society" resulting from the collectivization of the means of production. In addition, the major sociological theories of stratification within contemporary capitalist societies particularly those of Karl Marx and Max Weber—are explored and assessed.

STRATIFICATION IN INDUSTRIAL CAPITALIST SOCIETIES

The Distribution of Income and Wealth: The United States and Britain

Data collected under the auspices of the U.S. government (U.S. Bureau of the Census, 1984) show that, for 1982, the highest-paid 5 percent of Americans received 16.0 percent of the total national income (Table 10.1). When the data are divided into income quintiles (fifths) of the population, they show the following: The top income quintile received 42.7 percent of the total national income; the next quintile received 24.3 percent; the middle quintile received 17.1 percent; the next-to-lowest quintile received 11.2 percent; and the bottom quintile received a mere 4.7 percent of the total.

These data demonstrate a highly unequal distribution of income in American society. They show that the most prosperous 5 percent of the population received nearly four times the income of the least prosperous 20 percent. Looked at another way, they show that the top 20 percent received a greater total income than the bottom 60 percent combined. In addition, the figures reveal virtually no change at all in the income distribution over a period of 35 years.

Such data, however, do not fully reveal the actual extent of income disparities. A more adequate picture of overall income distribution is obtained when income deciles (tenths), rather than quintiles, are used in the analysis. Gabriel Kolko (1962) has calculated the distribution of income in the United States from 1910 to 1959 using income deciles. The data he presents reveal a highly unequal distribution of income that has not changed in any major way during this entire period. For example, in 1910 the top income decile received 33.9 percent of the total income, while the bottom decile received only 3.4 percent of the total. By 1959 the income share going to the top tenth had declined slightly, to 28.9 percent, but so had the share going to the bottom tenth, to 1.1 percent. The bottom 50 percent of the population received only 27 percent of the national personal income in 1910, and by 1959 the share of this poorer half had even declined slightly, to 23 percent. Thus, for both 1910 and 1959 the top 10 percent of the population received a greater total income than the bottom 50 percent. Throughout the entire period the only income groups to experience significant increases in income shares were the second- and third-richest income deciles, which experienced modest increases. As hardly needs saying, these groups were not among those in serious need of a greater share of the national income (Kolko, 1962).

These data support two major conclusions: There are vast inequalities in the distribution of income in the United States, and this pattern of unequal distribution has shown no significant trend toward greater equalization over a 50-year period. While there have been major increases in the standard of living for a large part of the American population during the twentieth century, such increases should not be confused, as they often are, with any trend toward income equalization.

It is likely, however, that even these figures understate the real extent of income inequality in American society, for there are forms of income that go unreflected in the figures. Many persons receive considerable amounts of "income in kind" rather than in direct cash payments, and such income is quite disproportionately concentrated among

Table 10.1 INCOME DISTRIBUTION IN THE UNITED STATES, 1947–1982

Year	Income at Selected Positions (dollars)ᵃ					Percentage Distribution of Aggregate Income					
	Lowest	Second	Middle	Fourth	Top 5%	Lowest Fifth	Second Fifth	Middle Fifth	Fourth Fifth	Highest 5%	Top
1982	11,200	19,354	27,750	39,992	64,000	4.7	11.2	17.1	24.3	42.7	16.0
1977	7,903	13,273	18,800	26,000	40,493	5.2	11.6	17.5	24.2	41.5	15.7
1972	5,612	9,300	12,855	17,760	27,836	5.4	11.9	17.5	23.9	41.4	15.9
1967	4,097	6,700	9,000	12,270	19,025	5.5	12.4	17.9	23.9	40.4	15.2
1962	3,000	5,000	6,800	9,500	14,900	5.0	12.1	17.6	24.0	41.3	15.7
1957	2,488	4,234	5,594	7,505	11,494	5.1	12.7	18.1	23.8	40.4	15.6
1952	2,053	3,321	4,493	6,077	9,455	4.9	12.3	17.4	23.4	41.9	17.4
1947	1,584	2,556	3,466	4,918	8,072	5.0	11.9	17.0	23.1	43.0	17.5

ᵃUpper limit of each fifth.

Source: U.S. Bureau of the Census, *Current Population Reports, Series P-60, No. 142. Money Income of Households, Families and Persons in the United States 1982.* Washington, D.C.: U.S. Government Printing Office, 1984, Table 17. The figures are based on all families and unrelated individuals. Dollar figures are given in current dollars.

the already wealthy. Income in kind is especially prominent among the top income tenth, and especially among the top 5 percent (Kolko, 1962). It takes the form of expense accounts and many other types of executive benefits, and such benefits have long been an acknowledged form of the remuneration of many corporate executives (Kolko, 1962). Large-scale and often unlimited expense accounts are now commonly extended to persons employed in or near the upper reaches of the corporate world. The top corporate elite also commonly receive such material benefits as a company car, a gas credit card, country club memberships, and even such luxuries as the use of yachts and private planes and company-paid jaunts to private retreats and exotic watering places (Kolko, 1962). While all these benefits do not count as forms of reportable personal income, they constitute just as real forms of material privilege nonetheless.

The existing income distribution figures also fail to reflect income that goes unreported and dividend income from stock ownership that remains undisbursed to stock owners. Kolko believes that this unreported income, mainly in the form of dividends, interest, and so on, is largely confined to persons in the upper-income brackets. Not reporting such income is, of course, illegal, but it is apparently a widespread practice nevertheless. Were such income to be included in the income distribution figures, the pattern of income inequality would be even more extreme than it already is. In addition to such practices, there are legal ways in which actual income can go unreported. As Kolko notes, corporations often vote to retain dividend earnings on stock so that their wealthy, stock-owning directors will not be personally liable to pay taxes on the dividend income. The upshot of this practice is that "the corporations represent vast income reserves for the economic elite" (Kolko, 1962:23).

It is widely believed that taxation, through the allegedly "progressive" income tax, has served to reduce income inequalities and bring about a redistribution of income from wealthier to poorer individuals. This belief, however, is largely unjustified. Available studies show that taxation produces no notable equalization of income (Rossides, 1976). Actual rates of taxation of the American public indicate a huge gap between theory and practice in the tax structure. While the federal income tax is, in principle, progressive, the rich have built so many loopholes and safeguards into the tax laws that they are able to avoid any major redistribution of their huge incomes. Indeed, the rich have become so skilled at tax avoidance that they have placed the actual burden of taxation onto the shoulders of low and middle-income groups (Kolko, 1962).

The distribution of total wealth (i.e., total assets minus liabilities) in the United States reveals much greater extremes than the distribution of income. Indeed, wealth is enormously concentrated at the top. Data collected by the federal government (Office of Management and the Budget, 1973) show the following pattern of distribution for 1962: The wealthiest quintile of the population owned 76 percent of the total wealth; the next quintile owned 15.5 percent; the middle quintile owned 6.2 percent; the next-to-poorest quintile possessed but 2.1 percent; and the poorest fifth could claim only 0.2 percent. Such figures reveal an enormous concentration of property, demonstrating that the wealthiest 20 percent of the population possesses more than three times the total wealth available to the remaining 80 percent.

Additional data on the concentration of wealth show essentially the same pattern. In 1972 the top 1 percent of the population held 56.5 percent of the total corporate stock, 60 percent of all bonds, and 89.9 percent of all trusts (U.S. Bureau of the

Census, 1982). Closer scrutiny reveals that most of these assets are actually concentrated within the top 0.5 percent of the population. For the same year the top 0.5 percent owned 49.3 percent of the corporate stock, 52.2 percent of the bonds, and 80.8 percent of the trusts (U.S. Bureau of the Census, 1982).

Britain displays similar inequalities in the distribution of income and wealth. Estimates show that in 1979 the top income tenth in the United Kingdom commanded 26.1 percent of the total income, while the bottom 30 percent received only 10.4 percent (Atkinson, 1983:63). This pattern has changed little since 1954, when the top income tenth received 30.1 percent of the income and the bottom 30 percent received 10.3 percent (Atkinson, 1983:63). These are pretax figures, but calculations show that, for the United Kingdom just as for the United States, taxation has affected the income distribution only in the very slightest way (Atkinson, 1983:63).

Regarding the distribution of wealth, Westergaard and Resler (1975) show that, in 1954, the richest 5 percent of the population owned 48 percent of all cash and bank deposits, 71 percent of all government and municipal securities, and 96 percent of corporate stock. More recent data for all wealth categories show that the richest 5 percent possessed 45 percent of the wealth in 1979 (Atkinson, 1983:161). Although the distribution of wealth is somewhat less unequal now than it was 40 years ago (Atkinson, 1983:168), the concentration of wealth is still enormous. Britain remains, like the United States and all modern capitalist societies, a society permeated by deep economic inequalities (Westergaard and Resler, 1975).

Some Comparisons and Recent Trends

Although the industrial capitalist societies are broadly similar in their distributions of income and wealth, and although they have similar class structures, it should not be as-

sumed that they are exactly alike in these respects. Recent evidence shows, in fact, some surprising differences. It would appear that the United States has the most unequal distribution of income, whereas Japan is the most egalitarian. Kevin Phillips, in his recent book *The Politics of Rich and Poor* (1990), has assembled some comparative data on income distribution. These data, all of which are for the time period around the late 1970s and early 1980s, show that in the United States at that time the ratio of the top income quintile to the bottom quintile was 12:1;* the ratio of the top quintile to the bottom quintile in Japan was, by contrast, only 4:1. The corresponding ratios for several other industrial capitalist nations were as follows: France and Canada, 9:1; Britain, 8:1; and West Germany, Sweden, and the Netherlands, 5:1. That the United States has the most unequal income distribution will not surprise many sociologists and other social scientists. The United States is also a leader among industrial capitalist countries in the extent of poverty. It has a very large class of poor—rural and urban, black and white—and many members of this class are concentrated in inner-city ghettoes whose economic condition has been deteriorating for decades and continues to deteriorate (M. Harris, 1981; W. Wilson, 1987).

It has also been shown that income inequality has been increasing in most industrial capitalist countries in recent years. This is particularly true in the United States. The conservative social and economic policies of the Reagan administration during the period 1981–1989 are often blamed for this. However, this can only be

---

*This figure seems a bit inflated and is inconsistent with Table 10.1, where it is shown that the ratio of the top income quintile to the bottom quintile in 1982 was approximately 9:1 rather than 12:1. However, this would still mean that the United States is one of the most inegalitarian industrial capitalist societies.

part of the story, for income inequality has been widening since at least the mid-1970s, and possibly as early as the beginning of that decade (Phillips, 1990). Table 10.2 displays the changing income distribution in the United States for the period 1977–1988. These data show that 80 percent of the population experienced real income losses, with only the top two income deciles experiencing income gains. Moreover, it was at the very top of the income hierarchy that the greatest income gains were realized, with the top 1 percent of the population enjoying an income increase of nearly 50 percent; and it can clearly be seen that it was at the bottom of the income hierarchy that the worst losses were suffered. This is one of the most recent versions of "the rich getting richer and the poor getting poorer."

The Class Structure of Industrial Capitalist Societies

There is currently no broad consensus among sociologists about how to characterize the class structure of contemporary capitalism or, for that matter, about how to define the concept of **class** itself. Instead, two distinct approaches to the definition of class and the identification of the major classes within contemporary capitalism exist: the conventional approach and the Marxian approach. The *conventional approach* designates occupation as the principal criterion for distinguishing classes from one another. This approach conceives of classes as broad groupings of persons who share similar levels of privilege and prestige on the basis of their roles within the occupational structure. The *Marxian approach* identifies ownership or nonownership of the crucial forces of production (in this case, capital) as the distinguishing feature of a social class. It thus conceives of classes as social groups organized around forms of property ownership. However, the Marxian approach is not a singular one, for Marxists disagree with one another in important ways about the class structure of contemporary capitalism.

The Conventional Approach A good illustration of the conventional approach is found in Daniel Rossides's (1990) analysis of the class structure of contemporary American

Table 10.2   INCOME LOSSES AND GAINS IN THE UNITED STATES, 1977–1988

Income Decile	Average Family Income		% Change	Change in Average Family Income
	1977	1988	1977–1988	1977–1988
Bottom	$ 4,113	3,504	−14.8%	$ −609
Second	8,334	7,669	−8.0	−665
Third	13,140	12,327	−6.2	−813
Fourth	18,436	17,220	−6.6	−1,216
Fifth	23,896	22,389	−6.3	−1,507
Sixth	29,824	28,205	−5.4	−1,619
Seventh	36,405	34,828	−4.3	−1,577
Eighth	44,305	43,507	−1.8	−798
Ninth	55,487	56,064	+1.0	+577
Tenth	102,722	119,635	+16.5	+16,913
Top 5%	134,543	166,016	+23.4	+31,473
Top 1%	270,053	404,566	+49.8	+134,513

All incomes are calculated in 1987 dollars.

Source: Kevin Phillips, *The Politics of Rich and Poor.* New York: Random House, 1990, Table 10.1

society. Rossides identifies five major social classes in the contemporary United States: the upper class, the upper-middle class, the lower-middle class, the working class, and the lower class.

The upper class, no more than 1 or 2 percent of the population, consists of those families possessing great wealth and power, much of which is derived from inheritance. The members of this class occupy the key positions in corporations, banks, insurance companies, and so on. They enjoy very high prestige and are often strongly oriented toward the consumption of elite symbolic culture (e.g., fine art and music). In short, this class is an extraordinarily privileged, powerful, and prestigious segment of the American social structure.

The upper-middle class is composed primarily of successful business managers, members of the learned professions (e.g., law, medicine, architecture), and well-placed civil and military officials. It includes approximately 10 percent of the population. Its members generally earn high incomes and accumulate substantial wealth through savings and investment, and they typically enjoy high social prestige.

The lower-middle class, consisting of approximately 30 percent of the population, mainly includes small businessmen, lower-level professionals (e.g., public school teachers, social workers, nurses), and sales and clerical workers. Most persons in this class receive moderate incomes and have but small amounts of savings and other personal wealth. Only fairly modest levels of prestige are accorded the members of this class.

The working class in American society comprises roughly 40 percent of the population. The members of this class are employed as skilled, semiskilled, or unskilled manual and service workers. The class as a whole is subject to fairly high rates of unemployment, and its members frequently suffer under the burdens of no savings or in-

vestments and low social prestige. The incomes received by persons in this class are relatively low, on average, when compared to the incomes received by members of higher classes.

The lower class, roughly 20 percent of the American population, consists of those persons who may be regarded as living under conditions of poverty. Included in this class are "the chronically unemployed, underemployed, and underpaid, abandoned mothers, and the poor who are sick, disabled, or old" (Rossides, 1976:28). The members of this class suffer from greater or lesser degrees of acute economic distress, and have extremely low social prestige. Indeed, they are often regarded as lazy and worthless persons who constitute drains on society's resources.

Marxian sociologists have generally been quite critical of this approach to the problem of class (Wright, Hachen, Costello, and Sprague, 1982; Wright, 1979, 1985). They point out that it generally conceives of social classes as large-scale occupational groupings. The difficulty with equating class and occupation, as the Marxists see it, is that it focuses attention exclusively on the content of jobs and fails to consider the social relations that people enter into doing these jobs. From the Marxian point of view, class relations are largely about the domination and exploitation that occur as individuals carry out the content of their work. As several Marxian sociologists have put it, "A carpenter, for example, could easily be a worker, a semiautonomous employee, a manager or a petty bourgeois artisan. In each of these cases the technical content of the job remains largely the same (transforming lumber into buildings or whatever), but the social relational content changes" (Wright et al., 1982:719).

How, then, do contemporary Marxists conceptualize class and arrange the class structure of modern capitalism?

A Marxian Approach Karl Marx defined social classes as groups organized around property relations. He identified two major classes in the early industrial capitalist society of his time: the bourgeoisie, or capitalists, the owners of capital; and the proletariat, or workers, those who were propertyless and thus had to sell their labor power to the capitalists in order to make a living. Marx recognized the existence of other minor social classes, but he saw the nature of capitalist society as revolving mainly around the relationship between capitalists and workers.

Capitalism has changed a great deal since Marx's day. The major change most relevant to our discussion here is the rapid growth of numerous classes located somewhere between the traditional bourgeoisie and the traditional proletariat, classes that are hard to identify and categorize unambiguously. It has been extremely difficult for modern Marxists to identify these classes within an orthodox Marxian framework that claims that classes are organized purely around modes of property ownership. Therefore, most modern Marxists have modified and updated the Marxian conception of class. They have generally done so by arguing that contemporary classes rest not only on forms of property ownership, but also on *modes of domination and control*— that is, on ways in which some persons direct the activities of others within the work process (Parkin, 1979).

One of the most impressive efforts to develop a Marxian conception of classes under contemporary capitalism is that of Erik Wright (1979; Wright et al., 1982). Wright stresses that classes in modern capitalism cannot be thought of simply as being different levels or gradations of privilege and prestige, as the conventional approach tends to assume; rather, they must be conceptualized as groups whose members occupy positions within the social relations of eco-nomic production. These relations involve differential property ownership and differential levels of domination and control. Wright thus stresses that social classes are *relational*, rather than *gradational*, categories.

In order to capture the complexity of the contemporary capitalist class structure, Wright distinguishes between what he calls basic class locations and contradictory class locations. **Basic class locations** are positions in the social organization of production that are relatively unambiguous concerning the nature of property ownership and domination and control. **Contradictory class locations** are positions within the productive process that are characterized by some of the elements of two different basic class locations. Contradictory class locations are therefore not consistent where property and domination are concerned. For this reason it is more difficult to categorize social positions not belonging to basic class locations.

A diagrammatic representation of Wright's image of the contemporary capitalist class structure is given in Figure 10.1. Within his category of basic class locations, Wright identifies three basic social classes: the bourgeoisie, the proletariat, and the petty bourgeoisie. The *bourgeoisie* consists of the major owners of capital, that is, the leading members of corporations, banks, insurance companies, and so on. The economic basis of this class is property ownership pure and simple. The members of this class derive their income and wealth, in the classical Marxian formulation, from the exploitation of the working class: from the extraction of surplus labor and surplus value from workers. This class probably constitutes less than 2 percent of the population. Its members have ultimate power over all other positions within the productive apparatus of modern capitalism. The *proletariat* consists of workers in the classical Marxian sense. In Wright's formulation, it consists of

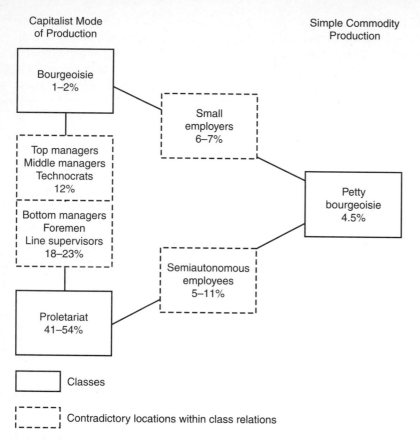

Capitalist Mode
of Production

Simple Commodity
Production

Bourgeoisie
1–2%

Small
employers
6–7%

Top managers
Middle managers
Technocrats
12%

Bottom managers
Foremen
Line supervisors
18–23%

Petty
bourgeoisie
4.5%

Semiautonomous
employees
5–11%

Proletariat
41–54%

☐ Classes

⌐⌐⌐⌐ Contradictory locations within class relations

FIGURE 10.1
Wright's model of the contemporary capitalist class structure. (*Source:* Erik Olin Wright, *Class, Crisis and the State.* London: New Left Books, 1978, p. 63.)

those propertyless persons who sell their labor power to capitalists. Moreover, workers are at the bottom of the ladder in terms of domination and control within the workplace. They give orders to no one, but their own work is closely directed and supervised by others. Wright estimates that the proletariat consists of approximately 41 to 54 percent of the population of capitalist societies.

Capitalists and workers occupy the basic class locations within the capitalist

mode of production. This mode is characterized by the extraction of surplus value from the labor of workers and the continual accumulation of capital over time. As Wright notes, however, not all economic positions within modern capitalist society are within the pure capitalist mode of production. Some are in the *simple commodity mode of production,* a minor mode that exists alongside the pure capitalist mode. In the simple commodity mode of production, profits do not result from extracting surplus value—

from exploitation of labor—but from the individual producer's own efforts. Furthermore, these profits are usually so small that little if any accumulation can result. There is one basic social class within this simple commodity mode, the *petty bourgeoisie*. It constitutes less than 5 percent of the population in Wright's estimate. Members of this class are small businesspersons and craftspersons who employ no workers, exploit no labor power, and dominate no one within an authority hierarchy. The income of this class's members comes from small-scale property ownership. This class is, in a sense, a holdover from an earlier phase of capitalism, and it is destined to disappear with the further evolution of the capitalist system.

Within the category of contradictory class locations Wright also identifies three classes: managers and supervisors, small employers, and semiautonomous employees. *Managers and supervisors* occupy a contradictory class location between the bourgeoisie and the proletariat. Persons in these positions own no property and must therefore sell their labor power and earn their livings through salaries or wages. This is a characteristic they share in common with the proletariat. Yet, although they must sell their labor power, they occupy a position within the hierarchy of production in which they dominate or control others, particularly the proletariat. Top and middle managers are closer to the bourgeoisie. They have considerable authority to organize production and the very top managers earn at least a portion of their incomes by sharing in the profits of the company. Lower-level managers, foremen, and other supervisors are, on the other hand, closer to the proletariat. In fact, Wright believes that some are so close that they might just as well be placed within it. These persons directly supervise the routine work of others but are

themselves extensively controlled by top and middle managers. Wright estimates that managers and supervisors taken together make up about 30 percent of the population.

Small employers, about 6 or 7 percent of the population, occupy a contradictory position between the bourgeoisie and the petty bourgeoisie and thus share characteristics of both. Unlike the petty bourgeoisie, they employ at least one worker, and therefore at least part of their income is derived from the exploitation of labor power. Unlike the bourgeoisie proper, however, they exist on a relatively small scale and have much less opportunity to accumulate capital.

Semiautonomous employees are professional workers within bureaucratic organizations. They occupy a contradictory class location between the petty bourgeoisie and the proletariat. Probably no more than 10 percent of the population, these workers must sell their labor power to others and earn their incomes through salaries. But unlike other workers, they have considerable freedom in the direction of their work. Although subject to the authority of managers, their high level of specialized knowledge dictates that they be allowed much personal decision making in carrying out assignments. Lawyers in corporations, physicians in research organizations, professors in universities, and engineers in organizational settings are prime examples of semiautonomous employees.

Although Wright's scheme is not always easy to apply to concrete persons and positions within modern capitalism, in some respects it is an improvement on the conventional approach, which essentially equates class with occupation. In fact, Wright has compared his scheme with the conventional class-as-occupation approach in terms of their respective abilities to predict income inequality, and empirically his scheme has proved the better predictor

(Wright, 1979). This is one reason for preferring it to the conventional approach.*

Social Mobility within Modern Capitalism

A belief widespread among the members of modern capitalist societies is that one's class position need not be fixed at birth. It is thought that all individuals have good opportunities for moving up to a higher class—that is, for upward **social mobility.** This idea has taken a particularly strong hold in the United States, where it tends to dominate thinking about the nature of stratification. Most Americans appear to believe that the American class system is highly "open," permitting a high degree of upward movement for persons who have the necessary motivation to get ahead. To what extent is this belief in the opportunity structure of modern capitalism justified?

The best-known study of social mobility in American society is that of sociologists Peter Blau and Otis Dudley Duncan (1967). Drawing upon a sample of more than 20,000 American men between the ages of 20 and 64 collected in 1962, Blau and Dun-

can came to the following general conclusions about mobility in the United States (summarized in Vanfossen, 1979):

- Mobility has been a fairly widespread characteristic of American society.
- Mobility is far more common over short rather than long distances.
- Upward mobility is more common than downward mobility.
- The expansion and contraction of certain occupational groupings accounts for some of the observed mobility.
- Proprietorship represents a significant source of rigidity in the occupation structure; that is, independent professionals, proprietors, and farmers display the greatest occupational inheritance and self-recruitment.
- The education received by a son is of considerable importance in determining his adult occupational position.
- Rates of social mobility have increased very little, if at all, during the past 50 years.

While one of Blau and Duncan's major conclusions is that mobility is widespread

---

*In a more recent work, Wright (1985) has made some substantial modifications in his conceptualization of class and in his class scheme. He has eliminated the category of semiautonomous employees and subdivided the managerial/supervisory class into numerous subclasses, largely according to the extent of possession of educational credentials. These changes stem from a questioning of the use of domination or authority relations as a dimension of class relations. Wright has attempted to move toward a reconceptualization of class that makes the concept of exploitation central. Since exploitation is a central Marxian notion in a way that domination is not, as a Marxist he undoubtedly feels that this is preferable. However, the results leave much to be desired. Wright ends up using the concept of exploitation in non-Marxian ways and stretches it beyond the breaking point. Moreover, his new class scheme contains 12 classes, making it rather unwieldy, and many of these classes are ill-defined. Thus one can raise serious questions about whether Wright's latest ideas are an intellectual advance. Indeed, Wright himself recognizes that his new formulations present a number of new problems.

Obviously the difficulties Wright is having suggest that there are serious obstacles in the path of any effort to produce a coherent Marxian analysis of class relevant to the late twentieth century. To make a Marxian scheme applicable at all, ideas from different intellectual traditions—especially the Weberian tradition—have to be imported into it (Parkin, 1979). There is nothing wrong with that, except when these ideas are twisted out of shape in order to call them Marxian. Perhaps the most sensible thing to do is simply to confront them on their own terms, which is what I try to do later in the chapter.

For these reasons, and because Wright's new analysis is much too technical and abstract to be presented in an introductory textbook, I have retained his original position as probably the best illustration of a Marxian approach to class.

in American society, this judgment must be carefully assessed in the context of their other findings and the nature of their data. As Vanfossen (1979) points out, the larger the number of occupational categories that are used in a study, the larger will be the measured rate of social mobility. Blau and Duncan used 17 occupational categories, far more than usually employed. It is not surprising, then, that they found considerable movement within the occupational structure. In light of this, one of their other major conclusions must be taken very seriously: that most upward mobility is of short distance. In other words, while many men are upwardly mobile during their lifetimes, most do not move very far. In fact, a great deal of observed mobility consists of movement from lower to upper blue-collar (manual) positions, from upper blue-collar to lower white-collar (nonmanual) positions, or from lower white-collar to upper white-collar jobs. There is very little movement of persons from near the bottom to near the top of the class structure, and movement from the lower class into the upper-class elite is a rare phenomenon indeed. It therefore seems just as important to emphasize the rigidity, as opposed to the flexibility, inherent in the American class structure, for the direct familial inheritance of class position is a fundamental feature of life in all major capitalist societies.

A considerable amount of mobility is due to factors having nothing at all to do with an ideology of equal opportunity. As Blau and Duncan themselves note, the expansion and contraction of occupational groupings due to technological change is a significant factor promoting mobility. Throughout the twentieth century all major industrial societies have undergone major technological changes that have greatly expanded the number of white-collar jobs available. Many of these jobs could be filled only by recruiting persons from lower-

status backgrounds. In addition, differential class fertility rates force a certain amount of upward mobility. Persons in higher-class positions tend to have fewer children than those in lower-class positions. This means that not all higher-class positions can be filled by children of persons from the same class. Therefore, some recruitment from subordinate classes is always necessary.

What conclusions are warranted regarding social mobility in the United States? There is a substantial amount of upward movement of individuals within the class structure; however, this fact by itself means very little, for most movement is over short distances. Most persons, therefore, end up in adulthood at or near the level attained by their parents, and movement from the very bottom stratum to the very top is practically nonexistent. Furthermore, it is incorrect to ascribe all the mobility that does occur to America's alleged ideological commitment to equality of opportunity. While some persons do indeed improve their positions by exceptional intelligence, motivation, hard work, or even luck, much mobility is an inherent feature of the structure of modern capitalism: of the constant technological and occupational change produced by that system. Above all, it is important not to exaggerate the extent of mobility in American society and thereby underemphasize the heavy inheritance of class position that does take place.

What has been said above regarding the United States also holds for the most part for industrial capitalist societies in general. Most current studies show that, while they do display some differences, industrial capitalist societies are strikingly alike in their mobility patterns and overall levels of fluidity. This is true even when the societies in question have differed appreciably in the extent to which they have tried to promote high levels of mobility, and it is also a pattern that has held over a considerable period of time (Kerckhoff, Campbell, and Winfield-Laird, 1985; Erikson, Goldthorpe, and Porto-carero, 1982; Goldthorpe, 1980; Halsey, Heath, and Ridge, 1980).

PATTERNS OF STRATIFIED SOCIAL LIFE IN STATE SOCIALIST SOCIETIES

We now turn our attention to the question of the extent to which class distinctions are to be found in the state socialist societies.

Basic Class Structure and Inequalities of Privilege

Frank Parkin (1971) has provided a useful historical overview of the changing nature of social stratification in the Soviet Union. As he notes, in the period immediately following the rise of the Communist party to power, there was a marked tendency toward the establishment of economic equality. Fundamental reforms were put into effect in order to equalize the distribution of incomes, and a drastic reduction of the wage differential between blue-collar and white-collar workers was achieved. (Similar income equalization policies were pursued as well after World War II in the other major Eastern European Communist nations.) In addition to these measures, established privilege was attacked via major educational reforms. These reforms were designed to bring large numbers of youth from subordinate classes into higher education.

Beginning in the early 1930s, however, this major egalitarian push was halted and even partially reversed through new policies established by Stalin. Stalin launched a major attack on all equalization programs, declaring himself steadfastly against *uravnilovka* ("equality-mongering"). It was argued that, in order to achieve full industrialization and the building of a modern society, greater material incentives had to be offered to persons engaged in more highly skilled forms of work. This policy was responsible for the reestablishment of sharp income differences between major occupational groups. Such new economic inequalities continued until approximately the mid-1950s. Around this time, a new attack on income inequality began and income differentials were reduced once again. Since the late 1980s, the program of economic reforms known as *perestroika* has included an attempt to increase income differentials. This is consistent with the Soviet Union's shift toward a more market-oriented, capitalist economy.

In recent times, it is clear that there are a number of social groupings that can be distinguished by different income levels and other forms of privilege. Whether or not these groups should be called "classes" is to some extent a matter of definition. Official Soviet ideology (at least prior to 1985 and the beginnings of *perestroika* and *glasnost*) referred to them as "nonantagonistic strata," noting that the groups were not distinguished by the ownership of private property, which had been formally abolished in the Soviet Union. Thus so-called *nonegalitarian classlessness* has been said to prevail under state socialism. That is, there are different social groups possessing unequal amounts of material privilege, but these groups cannot be thought of as classes since their level of privilege does not depend on their possession or lack of property. Since private ownership of property is absent, one group does not gain by holding other groups down, and the social relations between such groups are therefore not antagonistic ones.

From a classical Marxian viewpoint, which equates class with property ownership, the official Soviet view is not unreasonable. But the Western Marxian conception of class has been substantially modified in recent years, and as we have seen Western Marxists include the notion of domination or control as an essential component of their concept of class. Following this line of reasoning, it seems perfectly sensible to regard the major socioeconomic groups within state socialist society as classes, since they are in fact based on different levels of control over economic resources.

Parkin (1971) has characterized the class structure of state socialist society in the following manner (listing the classes from highest to lowest):

- The white-collar intelligentsia, consisting mainly of individuals in professional, managerial, and administrative positions.
- Skilled manual workers.
- Lower-level white-collar workers.
- Unskilled workers.
- Peasant farmers.

From this perspective the dominant and most privileged class within state socialism is the white-collar intelligentsia. Parkin suggests that the major class cleavage within state socialism is between this group and all the rest. Members of the intelligentsia not only receive higher incomes than the rest, but also receive bonuses and special wage supplements, as well as other less measurable rewards: high-quality accommodations, opportunities to travel abroad, the use of official cars and state property, and others. Furthermore, the social distinction between the intelligentsia and other classes is magnified by the fact that its members are more likely to be party members. Party membership in itself confers additional benefits. These include the pulling of strings or the winning of favors, an opportunity to acquire the best theater tickets, or the ensuring of a place for one's children at good schools and universities.

Whereas Parkin sees the major class division within state socialism as between the intelligentsia and the rest of society, others would emphasize a line of demarcation between a tiny portion of the intelligentsia and everyone else. This group is what is most commonly called the *nomenklatura*. The intelligentsia makes up perhaps as much as 20 percent of state socialist society, but the *nomenklatura* at most would include 1 percent. It consists of individuals at the very highest levels of the Communist party bureaucracy. Milovan Djilas (1957) has regarded the *nomenklatura* as a ruling elite broadly similar to the ruling classes of capitalist societies. He sees this elite, which he has referred to as a "new class," as a property-owning, highly privileged, and self-perpetuating class that dominates the rest of state socialist society. This argument has considerable merit, but it must be qualified. Anthony Giddens (1980), for example, while not disputing the existence of such an elite group, argues that it cannot be strictly compared to a capitalist ruling class. He observes that in state socialist society the dominant class enjoys rights only over the dispensation of collective property, and that this gives it a different character from capitalist classes, which have control over large supplies of private capital.

Victor Zaslavsky (1995) provides additional insight into the stratification system in the Soviet Union. He points out that this system consists of "several interrelated subsystems of political, economic, territorial, and ethnic stratification, controlled by the state" (1995: 118). He gives special attention to the most favored members of the intelligentsia, who are those working in the military sector of the economy. In their behalf, a whole system of "closed enterprises" and "closed cities" has been created. Zaslavsky tells us more (1995:120–121):

Having introduced the top-priority category of "closed cities," the redistributive state had taken a decisive step in the organization and administration of this territorial-based system of social stratification. Closed cities were considered the most important settlements in the country, with rights to permanent residence conferred only by birth or by special permission of the city administration. The hierarchy of population settlements in the redistributive state led to the establishment of a stable hierarchy of status and to the emergence of new social groups and categories whose members had different life chances and enjoyed very different levels of consumption. The closed cities also played an increasingly important role in structuring access to higher education and promoting the growth of the group of Soviet specialists traditionally known as the intelligentsia. Indeed, the major universities of the country were all located within these closed cities, as were the majority of specialists with a higher education. The proliferation of elite schools and specialized services such as private tutoring in closed cities gave their residents a decisive advantage in access to prestigious universities and other institutions of higher education. Membership in the Soviet elite and educated middle classes, thus, took on an increasingly hereditary character. . . .

These and analogous policies of creating special "top priority" enterprises and entire industrial sectors, privileged geographic regions and settlements, and an accompanying system of most- and least-favored social and ethnic groups exemplify the enormous role the Soviet redistributive state played in creating and maintaining a hierarchical social structure. Using its position both as the sole employer for the entire labor force and as the primary agency of redistribution, the state established a political-administrative ascription for membership in major social groups and categories.

Class Structuration under State Socialism

The degree to which a class hierarchy has inherent rigidities such that the classes become relatively isolated from one another and hence impermeable to the exchange of members is known as **class structuration** (Giddens, 1980). The main indicators of the degree of class structuration in any society are its rate of social mobility and the extent to which its classes have become culturally distinctive groupings. A society with high class structuration will consist of classes

that are sharply distinguishable culturally and are largely impermeable, self-recruiting groups. By contrast, low class structuration prevails when the rate of social mobility is high and when the cultural differences among classes are minimal. What is the overall level of class structuration in state socialist society?

There is widespread agreement that rates of social mobility in the major state socialist societies are relatively high, or at least that they were in the past (Parkin, 1971; Giddens, 1980; Yanowitch, 1977). For example, a 1963 study of Hungary showed that nearly 77 percent of white-collar intelligentsia positions were filled by persons from worker and peasant backgrounds (Parkin, 1971). In addition, the Yugoslavian census of 1960 indicates that 62 percent of persons in managerial and administrative positions came from manual backgrounds (Parkin, 1971). Furthermore, in the Soviet Union in the late 1960s the proportion of the intelligentsia recruited from manual and peasant families amounted to approximately 40 to 50 percent (Yanowitch, 1977). When recruitment to the intelligentsia from lower-level white-collar families is added to that supplied by manual and peasant families, it becomes clear that a majority of the intelligentsia was recruited from classes outside their own (Yanowitch, 1977).

These data support the conclusion that there is a marked "openness" to state socialist class structures. Not only are rates of social mobility notably high, but a good deal of this mobility is of the "long-distance" sort. As Parkin has remarked in this connection (1971:157): "What, perhaps, gives mobility rates in socialist society their special significance is the fact that they indicate large-scale movements across the entire range of the reward hierarchy, not merely the interchange of personnel at the class margins."

The data on mobility indicate a relatively low degree of class structuration in state socialist society. What is known about the cultural distinctions among classes tends to support the same conclusion. Although Yanowitch stresses the fact that Soviet classes are distinguished by lifestyle and consumption habits, it does not appear that the differences are of major significance. Indeed, Parkin argues for a low degree of cultural distinctiveness of classes under state socialism. In support of his claim, he points out that negative or defensive value-orientations do not seem to have developed among the members of subordinate classes; that there appears to be no distinctive "working-class subculture" such as that found in capitalist societies; and that members of the intelligentsia have failed to develop a highly distinctive culture, accent, and mode of dress similar to that typical of capitalist elites. These considerations compel Parkin to conclude (1971:158): "Those theorists who claim that socialist society is 'classless' because it lacks sharp [cultural distinctions among classes] have thus touched upon an important feature of this type of society."

The exceptionally high mobility rates of state socialist societies are undoubtedly a thing of the past. With the onset of major economic difficulties in the 1970s, there ensued declining educational opportunities and thus greater restrictions on upward mobility for many individuals (Lapidus, 1983). The high mobility rates of the period prior to the mid-1970s were due largely to major changes in the occupational structure as the result of massive technological change, and so it is not surprising that these rates would be markedly reduced as the result of economic stagnation.

Stratification and the Postsocialist Transition

Because of the instability and uncertainties of postsocialist economies, it is difficult to tell just what forms new postsocialist stratification systems will take. However, as these societies become more capitalistic it is almost a certainty that inequalities of income and wealth will become increasingly prominent. There is clear evidence of this already. In Russia the disintegration of the old Soviet Union has caused the *nomenklatura* to lose its monopoly on political power, and as a result the careers of many members of that group have been destroyed (Zaslavsky, 1995). At the same time many members of this group have been in an excellent position to benefit from the new privatization. They have been able to strike deals with new private firms, often becoming co-owners, and are in the process of forming a fast-growing class of property owners. Many members of this class have already become extremely rich and flaunt their wealth in the most garish ways (Zaslavsky, 1995). They provide a striking contrast with the highly impoverished individuals whose numbers are also rapidly growing, especially in Russia, where near economic chaos prevails.

THEORIES OF INDUSTRIAL STRATIFICATION SYSTEMS

Sociologists have proposed three main theories to explain the character of modern industrial stratification systems: the functionalist theory, the Marxian approach, and the major alternative to Marxism, the Weberian approach.

The Functionalist Theory

The functionalist theory of stratification is set forth by sociologists Kingsley Davis and Wilbert Moore (1945). Davis and Moore's leading argument is that stratification arises from the basic functional requirements of organized social life and is therefore a fundamentally necessary and inevitable feature of human societies.

Davis and Moore reason that, in order to survive or function effectively, all societies face the fundamental problem of motivating a sufficient number of their members to fill the most "functionally important" social positions. They believe that a system of stratification—a system of unequal rewards—is the mechanism that societies settle upon to solve this crucial problem. Stratification therefore arises as an incentive system, as a means of motivating people to carry out vital social responsibilities. For those talented persons who are willing to work hard and make sacrifices in order to gain entry into certain crucial occupational positions, top rewards will be forthcoming. Likewise, untalented or unmotivated individuals will have to settle for less demanding roles accompanied by lower rewards.

Davis and Moore point out that the rank of a social position (i.e., the level of rewards accompanying it) in any society is determined by two principal factors. One of these is the position's alleged "functional importance," a concept that is crucial to Davis and Moore's argument. They note that not all social positions are "equally important" to societal functioning. Some are more important in that they make a greater contribution to the survival and well-being of society. The second factor said to determine positional rank is the scarcity of personnel available to fill the position. Other things being equal, a position for which available personnel are relatively scarce should have a high rank. Scarcity of personnel can result either from a lack of sufficient talent in the population or from the strong demands of training associated with some positions. Concerning the latter point, Davis and Moore observe that modern medicine is within the abilities of most persons, but that the training for medical careers is so demanding that many persons will ordinarily be reluctant to undertake it. Attaching high rewards to the role of physician is, therefore, a socially created device designed to eliminate scarcity of personnel qualified for the position.

The Davis-Moore theory has been extensively criticized and widely debated over the years (Tumin, 1953; Huaco, 1963; Anderson and Gibson, 1978; Chambliss and Ryther, 1975). Perhaps the most telling argument against it is that its concept of "functional importance" will not stand up to careful inspection. In what sense, for example, can the engineers of a factory be considered more important to that factory than the less rewarded manual workers (Tumin, 1953)? It is clear that both play necessary roles in such an organization. This line of reasoning can be extended indefinitely. By Davis and Moore's logic, garbage collectors should be extremely low in functional importance, since such positions receive very low rewards and are widely regarded as undesirable. Yet without garbage collection, severe sanitation and health problems would soon develop in our major cities, problems such as New York and Paris witnessed in the 1960s. Many other social positions that are poorly rewarded in many societies can be shown to have considerable functional importance for those societies. There appear, then, to be serious difficulties with the functional importance concept, a concept that is vital to the entire functionalist explanation.

Other important objections can also be raised against the theory (Tumin, 1953). For example, Davis and Moore's assumption that the stratification system promotes efficient use of a society's supply of talent is highly questionable. The more rigid a stratification system is, the less a society can discover just how much talent it has, since social rewards will be largely determined by inheritance rather than by effort. Moreover, stratification not only impedes a society's discovery of its range of talent, but also blocks its full use of available talent.

Additionally, it is conceivable that rewards other than economic privilege and prestige may be effective motivators of people. For instance, such rewards as "joy in work" and "social duty" might serve as important inducements for people to perform important social roles (Tumin, 1953). Finally, stratification systems clearly seem to have many negative social consequences. For example, they unequally distribute favorable and unfavorable self-images; they encourage hostility, suspicion, and distrust between individuals and groups; and they unequally distribute the sense of membership and identification that people feel with society (Tumin, 1953).

The functionalist theory thus seems inadequate as an explanation of stratification in industrial societies. In fact, some sociologists regard it as little more than a rationalization and ideological justification for prevailing social and economic inequalities (Anderson and Gibson, 1978; Rossides, 1976). What, then, would a more acceptable theory of industrial stratification systems look like?

The Marxian Approach

Classical Marxism regards stratification as arising from the continual struggle between and among individuals and groups for access to scarce resources, the most important of which is economic property. Groups that gain control of property—the crucial forces of production—are able to use this control to exploit others and reap rewards for themselves. Their superior position with regard to property gives them power over others, and this superior privilege and power are translated into superior prestige. Dominant groups, in addition, commonly develop ideologies designed to justify their superior power and privilege, to make them seem right and honorable. For example, modern capitalists justify their superior wealth by asserting that it is their just reward for risk taking in investment. Moreover, they claim that their entrepreneurial activities lead to a general improvement in the total social wealth and therefore benefit everyone. They

utter statements like "What is good for General Motors is good for the country." Contemporary Marxists would argue that this statement is an aspect of a self-serving ideology, and that, moreover, it is basically false. They would claim instead that what is good for General Motors (i.e., the top owners and managers of that company) may very well be bad in several respects for much of the rest of the country.

Erik Wright (1979) has carried out a valuable study that attempts to test the overall merits of the Marxian approach to stratification. He uses his class scheme as a predictor of income inequality in the contemporary United States. (Wright's scheme, of course, departs notably from the classical Marxian formulation of class as based on property.) Wright begins by specifying the basis for income in each of his classes. The bourgeoisie receives its income from the exploitation of workers, which it carries out by paying them less than the full value of the goods and services they produce. The proletariat receives its income in the form of wages paid by capitalists. The level of these wages is determined by the market for labor. Capitalists generally attempt to hold these wages down as low as possible, for in the classical Marxian formulation their profits are determined by the level of wages they pay. The wages paid to workers derive from the respective bargaining strengths of capitalists and workers, and these strengths are determined by numerous historical, social, and economic factors (e.g., level of unionization, relative demand for labor power, and so on).

Members of the petty bourgeoisie employ no workers and therefore cannot rely on the exploitation of labor for their income. Instead, they must rely on their own efforts. The harder they are willing to work, the more income they stand to receive.

Managers and supervisors derive their income from salaries (or wages) paid them by the capitalist class. Their income levels will vary closely in accordance with their position in the hierarchy of authority within their organization. Top managers perform activities crucial to the making of profit by the company, and therefore they must be paid high salaries as inducements for them to carry out their functions well.* As Wright notes (1979:89), "Large income differentials between hierarchical levels are essential for underwriting the legitimacy of authority."

Small employers derive their income both from their own efforts and from their exploitation of labor. The closer they are to the bourgeoisie, the more their income is derived from such exploitation. Some small employers, such as lawyers and physicians engaged in self-employed private practices, derive their income not from exploiting labor power but from their control over prices (fees). Their income comes from their capacity to manipulate market forces to their advantage. Semiautonomous employees derive their incomes from paid salaries. These incomes are usually fairly high because income level must serve as an inducement for them to perform well in tasks demanding creativity and responsibility.

Most of Wright's predictions about the income levels of different classes were well supported by his empirical results. He found a significant income gap between managers/supervisors and workers. Moreover, the income of managers and supervisors was, as expected, closely tied to position within the managerial hierarchy. The data also showed that small employers had a higher income level than all other classes except the bourgeoisie. An important limitation of Wright's study is that it did not in-

clude members of the true bourgeoisie, who are extremely difficult to capture in the kind of survey research employed by Wright. But, as Wright (1979:224) points out, "in spite of the partial nature of the analysis of property relations, the results clearly demonstrate that even small property ownership is consequential. The mean income of small employers is over twice that of workers. . . . Furthermore, the income gap between employers and workers is much greater than between workers and managers."

In more recent research based on a modified and expanded version of his class categories, Wright (1985) has obtained slightly different results. His data for the United States show that "expert managers"—managers with advanced educational credentials—earn somewhat more than small employers. The data for Sweden are even more striking. They show that four categories of managers and supervisors, including even those with moderate educational credentials, earn more than small employers. Overall, the American and the Swedish data show that educational credentials and organizational authority are major determinants of income level. Although Wright tries to interpret these findings in Marxian terms, he ties himself in theoretical knots in doing so. After all, educational credentials and organizational authority are phenomena that are alien to a Marxian approach to stratification. What his findings really suggest are the limitations of Marxism and the relevance of certain Weberian ideas to understanding contemporary stratification patterns.

The Weberian Alternative to Marxism

Max Weber (1978; orig. 1923) agreed with Marx that the concept of class was a central one for the analysis of stratification in capitalist societies. But Weber saw Marx's analysis of stratification as limited to the

*Is this, perhaps, an instance of the small kernel of truth that most of us recognize within the functionalist theory?

discussion of class and therefore as too narrow. Weber believed that there were two other types of stratified groups that played important roles in any society's stratification system: status groups and parties. **Status groups** were identified by Weber as groups whose members share common lifestyles and levels of social honor or prestige. A **party** is a political association whose members share in the exercise of a certain amount of social power.

Weber identified three aspects of stratification—property, honor and lifestyle, and power—and three types of stratified groups corresponding to these criteria. He also went on to point out that property, honor, and power may operate somewhat independently of one another. That is, a group that possesses property may not rank high in terms of status and power; likewise, a group that has a high status might not be a property-owning group. But Weber also stressed that although the three criteria are logically independent, they tend to be closely associated. Thus, property ownership generally does confer considerable status and power.

Weber's concepts of class, status group, and party are abstract analytical categories and can be difficult to apply in clear and distinct ways to concrete social groups. A given social group might be characterized as both a class and a status group, for instance. Using Weber's criteria, we would have to identify the nobility of the European Middle Ages as both a class and a status group: its economic position was rooted in the ownership of land, but it lived a lifestyle emphasizing the pursuit of warfare as an occupation, chivalrous conduct, and disdain for commercial activity.

A Weberian analysis of contemporary capitalism recognizes the existence of a powerful, property-owning bourgeoisie that has great impact on the functioning of modern society. But it also acknowledges the existence of other groups whose social posi-

tion is not tied to property ownership. Members of the learned professions, for example, possess considerable privilege and high social status, but not as property owners. These groups are better thought of, therefore, as status groups than as classes. What accounts for their superior privilege and status?

Weber used another concept in his analysis of stratification that is at least as important as, if not more important than, the concepts of class, status group, and party: the concept of **social closure** (Weber, 1978; orig. 1923; cf. Parkin, 1979; Murphy, 1988). Weber used this concept to indicate the strong tendency for social groups to seize upon certain social criteria as marks of distinction, as means by which to set themselves apart from outsiders. These criteria include such things as sex, race, cultural background (nationality), educational level, and common occupation. By using some criterion to close themselves off from others, the members of a social group attempt to monopolize resources that will bring them economic success and social esteem.

Weber's concept of social closure is an important supplement to the Marxian analysis of modern stratification systems. It may in fact be the case that the Marxian stress on property ownership can be subsumed under the concept of social closure (Parkin, 1979). That is, property ownership may be viewed as simply one form (although an especially important form) of social closure. Members of the capitalist class, for example, use their ownership of huge supplies of capital as a means for creating and maintaining their extremely high privilege and prestige.

But other criteria may be used by other groups. Parkin notes that in modern society educational credentials seem to have emerged as one of the most important means of social closure. By achieving a certain level of education (which means the possession of a certain type of diploma), the members of a group hope to establish a minimum credential for entry into certain occupations with high payoffs in terms of privilege and prestige. As Ivar Berg has noted in this connection (1971:185; cited in Parkin, 1979:59):

> Educational credentials have become the new property in America. That nation, which has attempted to make the transmission of real and personal property difficult, has contrived to replace it with an inheritable set of values concerning degrees and diplomas which will most certainly reinforce the formidable class barriers that remain, even without the right within families to pass benefices from parents to their children.

Recall also that in recent research on the United States and Sweden Erik Wright (1985) has shown that educational credentials are a major determinant of income level. In both countries, managerial personnel with advanced educational credentials earn approximately twice the income of managers without such credentials.

If educational credentials are a major means of social closure in modern industrial societies, they are not the only ones. The learned professions rely to some extent on these credentials as criteria for setting themselves apart, but they also use two other means that have been crucial to their economic success: the manipulation of symbolic culture, and the development of powerful forms of political organization (Weber's "party"). Law and medicine, for example, are in most industrial societies, and especially in the United States, highly lucrative professions that bring great social prestige to their members. Lawyers and physicians have long understood how to achieve high levels of economic and social success. They monopolize specialized forms of knowledge that are crucial to their clients' and patients' well-being. In order to display

their monopolization of an esoteric body of knowledge, they have developed elaborate terminological systems that are derived from Latin and that only they adequately understand. These systems are designed, at least in part, to impress those they serve. This makes it easier for the members of such professions to claim that they are uniquely deserving of the high economic rewards they receive.

The monopolization of a body of specialized knowledge is necessary to the success of the learned professions, but by itself it is not sufficient. There must be a form of political organization designed to protect and promote privilege and prestige. Physicians have such an organization in the American Medical Association, lawyers in the American Bar Association. The AMA has been called the second most powerful political lobby in the United States (the first is the oil corporation lobby). For decades it has restricted admissions to medical schools, thereby keeping the supply of doctors low relative to the demand (Freeman, 1976). This artificial manipulation of the market helps to insure much higher incomes than would otherwise be possible (Freeman, 1976). In addition, for many years the AMA has vigorously opposed even the hint of socialized medicine in the United States. It has lobbied in the federal government to preserve the "free enterprise" system of health care, and has successfully prevented the development of any major form of nationalized health care. It seems worthy of note that in those modern industrial societies that have health care systems closely regulated by the government, the income level and social status of physicians relative to the rest of the population is notably lower than in the United States (cf. Starr, 1982:6).

To accept much of what the Weberian approach to stratification has to offer does not mean that the Marxian approach must be abandoned. On the contrary, the Weberian and Marxian approaches may usefully be regarded as complementary rather than contradictory. Yet there is at least one sense in which the Weberian approach is clearly superior, and that is in the analysis of state socialist societies. Since these societies have not had private forms of property ownership, classical Marxian theory is really helpless to explain why they have been highly stratified. But the stratification systems of these societies can be accounted for by employing a Weberian perspective. The Soviet bureaucratic elite and other members of the intelligentsia have used educational credentials and party membership as means of social closure.

SUMMARY

1. Income is very unequally distributed in industrial capitalist societies, and there has been no major change in this distribution in the twentieth century. Wealth is much more unevenly distributed than income. In the

Table 10.3 THEORIES OF STRATIFICATION IN INDUSTRIAL SOCIETIES

Theory	Characteristics	Evaluation
Functionalist theory	Argues that stratification is a universal and inevitable feature of human societies because it makes a crucial contribution to any society's survival and well-being. In particular, unequal rewards function as an incentive to motivate people to take on a society's most functionally important roles and thus get the important work of society effectively done. An individual's level of economic and social reward is commensurate with his or her contribution to societal functioning.	Has numerous serious weaknesses, and is more an ideological justification for stratification than an explanation of it. Rejected in this book.
Marxian theories	Emphasize private ownership of property as the key determinant of the structure of stratification. The main axis of stratification in capitalist societies is the struggle between the bourgeoisie and the proletariat. Individuals command privilege and prestige in proportion to their level of property ownership.	Identify a critical dimension of stratification in capitalist societies, but have difficulty explaining the high rewards of persons who are not property owners, such as learned professionals and many business managers. Also have difficulty explaining the stratification patterns of state socialist societies.
Weberian theories	Emphasize the importance of dimensions of stratification not rooted in property relations. Focus on the various ways in which groups attempt to monopolize resources in order to acquire high levels of privilege and prestige. Thus, individuals' levels of social and economic reward are proportional to their control over important resources.	Are extremely useful supplements to Marxism in that they seem able to explain aspects of stratification inadequately dealt with by Marxian theories. Also seem to have a higher level of realism about the likelihood of abolishing stratification in future societies.

United States, for example, more than half of the corporate stocks, bonds, and trusts is owned by only 0.5 percent of the population.

2. Industrial capitalist societies differ among themselves in terms of their levels of economic inequality. The United States and France have the greatest income inequality, while Japan has the most egalitarian distribution of income. Since the mid-1970s, in most industrial capitalist societies income inequality has been rising significantly. In the United States the top 5 percent of the population has experienced a large increase in real income during this period, whereas the bottom 20 percent has experienced a significant income loss.

3. Sociologists have not been able to agree completely on just what a social class is or what the class structure of modern capitalism looks like. Traditional sociologists define class in terms of occupation and generally identify an upper class, an upper-middle class, a lower-middle class, a working class, and a lower class. Marxian sociologists conceptualize class in terms of relations of property ownership and workplace authority. The Marxian sociologist Erik Wright identifies six basic classes within contemporary capitalism: the bourgeoisie, the proletariat, the petty bourgeoisie, managers and supervisors, small employers, and semiautonomous employees. Both traditional and Marxian approaches have strengths and weaknesses.

4. Considerable mobility occurs within modern capitalist societies, although its extent is usually exaggerated. Most changes of class position are over short distances, and movement from near the bottom to near the top of the class structure is rare. Much mobility in industrial capitalism is due to technological and occupational change.

5. State socialist societies are stratified into groups with different levels of control over economic resources. Party membership and educational credentials are the keys to economic and social success. The basic classes are the *nomenklatura*, the white-collar intelligentsia, skilled manual workers, lower white-collar workers, unskilled workers, and peasants. The *nomenklatura*, the highest echelon within the white-collar intelligentsia, constitutes a ruling class; this ruling class, though, is not strictly comparable to a capitalist bourgeoisie.

6. Capitalist and state socialist societies are similar in their divisions of labor, the kinds of work people do, and their emphasis on individual achievement. The main differences between these societies' stratification systems are: (a) the range of income inequality is much less under state socialism; (b) lower white-collar workers are less highly regarded under state socialism; (c) the dominant class under state socialism is less wealthy and less hereditary in character; (d) state socialist societies have class groupings that are less culturally distinctive, and the rate of mobility from one class to another is notably greater; (e) state socialist stratification derives from political decisions rather than property ownership and market forces.

7. As a result of the postsocialist transition currently underway in the European state socialist societies, the stratification patterns of state socialism are starting to change in important respects. The most important of these changes are increasing income inequality, increasing class structuration, and the emergence of a bourgeoisie out of the old *nomenklatura*.

8. There is still much disagreement among sociologists about how to explain stratification systems in industrial societies. The three major theories that have been developed are the functionalist, Marxian, and Weberian theories. These theories are summarized and assessed in Table 10.3.

SPECIAL TOPIC: STRATIFICATION AND THE WELFARE STATE

In the twentieth century all modern industrial capitalist societies have created large-scale welfare states that, to one extent or another, have been designed to improve the situation of various groups in society, in particular the working class. But there is no single type of welfare state, there being considerable variation in its nature. Gøsta Esping-Andersen (1990) has identified three different welfare state clusters. First there is what he calls the *liberal* welfare state. This type of welfare state is a "minimalist" system in that the government provides citizens with meager to modest income support and a limited amount of assistance in other ways. The clientele consists largely of the lowest-income segments of the working class. Strong work-ethic norms prevail, and entitlement rules are very strict. The United Kingdom, the United States, Canada, and Australia are the best examples of this type of welfare system.

Conservative welfare states are found in such European countries as Austria, France, Germany, and Italy. Here social benefits are provided to the large mass of the population, but these are highly status-differentiated. There are numerous social insurance schemes, each with its own particular rules, finances, and benefit structure. For example, in Germany "Bismarck's pension for workers was not to be blended with that for miners and certainly not with the social policy for civil servants or for white-collar employees" (Esping-Andersen, 1990:60). Social insurance normally excludes nonworking wives, and family benefits are designed so as to encourage motherhood. Day care services are poorly developed.

The final type of welfare state, the *social democratic* state, provides the greatest number and degree of benefits. This "maximalist" welfare state stands at the opposite extreme from the minimalist or liberal welfare state. The social democratic welfare state aims to provide a high level of social and economic equality for all citizens, with the working class enjoying the same benefits as the members of higher social classes. As Esping-Andersen notes, everyone benefits and everyone feels obligated to pay for the benefits that all receive. This type of welfare state is most characteristic of Sweden, Denmark, Norway, and to some extent the Netherlands.

Esping-Andersen argues that the most critical feature of a welfare state is the degree to which it has decommodified work. Capitalism is the essence of commodified work. Work is commodified when its function is to provide the labor that will produce profits for capitalists, and when little or no provision has been made for the well-being of the worker. Work is decommodified to the extent that the debilitating effects of its profit-inducing capacities are counterbalanced by concerns for the quality of life of the worker. This means that workers enjoy extensive benefits in regard to such things as medical insurance and sick days, maternity or parental leave, educational leave, unemployment insurance, and retirement (early or otherwise). As Esping-Andersen (1990:23) puts it, work is decommodified when "citizens can freely, and without potential loss of job, income, or general welfare, opt out of work when they themselves consider it necessary." These are benefits that are normally enjoyed by civil servants and other white-collar workers, but in the most advanced welfare states they are extended as well to the working class. Thus the social democratic welfare states are the most decommodified, and the liberal welfare states are the least decommodified. As Esping-Andersen (1990:141) explains, the most decommodified type of welfare state

> has deliberately abandoned the minimalist philosophy, and espouses entirely new principles with regard to its proper role in the life-cycle, now often committing itself to optimize people's capacities to work, to find work, and even to count on a good job with good pay and working environment. The goal is to allow individuals to harmonize working life with familyhood, to square the dilemmas of having children and working, and to combine productive activity with meaningful and rewarding leisure. In some countries, at least, this philosophy has buttressed recent decades of social-policy development; indeed, it often underpins the legitimacy and common understanding of many contemporary welfare states.

Upon their emergence early in this century, one of the aims of the social democratic welfare states in Scandinavia was to create a more equal income distribution throughout the population. Various studies have suggested that the Scandinavian countries have been relatively unsuccessful in this endeavor, for their income distributions, even after taxation, do not differ all that much from the distributions found in other industrial capitalist societies (Parkin, 1971; Stevenson, 1974, 1982). However, as Esping-Andersen points out, looking at income distributions alone provides too narrow a framework for evaluating the achievements of the most advanced type of welfare state. For one thing, it has done a great deal to eliminate poverty. The percentage of the aged living in poverty in the United Kingdom and the United States is, respectively, 29 percent and 24 percent, whereas in Sweden it is a mere 1 percent.

In addition, criteria for measuring the quality of life involve more than just the level of paid income. One has to look at such additional resources as health, housing, education, and social and political effectiveness, not to mention the extent of workplace decommodification. Esping-Andersen notes that periodic national surveys have been conducted in Sweden and Denmark since 1968 concerning the welfare state's equalizing effects. These studies show that, despite worsening economic conditions throughout the Western world during this time, living conditions have improved and there is a trend toward greater equality in the possession of economic resources. Thus, "for Scandinavia at least, the welfare state is a mighty opponent to the economy's inegalitarian thrust" (Esping-Andersen, 1990:57). The accomplishments of the social democratic welfare state are therefore much greater than a simple inspection of income distributions would suggest.

FOR FURTHER READING

Davis, Howard, and Richard Scase. *Western Capitalism and State Socialism: An Introduction*. Oxford: Blackwell, 1985. Useful material on stratification patterns in industrial capitalist and state socialist societies.

Erikson, Robert, and John H. Goldthorpe. *The Constant Flux: A Study of Class Mobility in Industrial Societies*. Oxford: Oxford University Press (Clarendon Press), 1993. An extremely comprehensive analysis of social mobility in a dozen industrial societies. Perhaps the best study of social mobility in several decades.

Esping-Andersen, Gøsta. *The Three Worlds of Welfare Capitalism*. Princeton, N.J.: Princeton University Press, 1990. One of the best sociological analyses of the modern welfare state available. Provides many useful insights into the different types of welfare states, their origins, and their accomplishments.

Giddens, Anthony. *The Class Structure of the Advanced Societies*. Second edition. London: Hutchinson, 1980. A valuable theoretically informed analysis of many of the issues involved in studying classes in modern industrial societies. Useful discussions of Marx and Weber on capitalist society and of the nature of classes under contemporary state socialism.

Giddens, Anthony, and David Held (eds.). *Classes, Power, and Conflict: Classical and Contemporary Debates*. Berkeley: University of California Press, 1982. An excellent collection of essays on numerous aspects of stratification in industrial societies.

Lane, David. *The End of Social Inequality? Class, Status, and Power Under State Socialism*. London: Allen and Unwin, 1982. A worthwhile examination of many features of stratification within state socialist societies by a well-known student of the subject.

Matthews, Mervyn. *Privilege in the Soviet Union*. London: Allen and Unwin, 1978. One of the best and most detailed studies of the social and economic privileges of the Soviet elite.

Murphy, Raymond. *Social Closure: The Theory of Monopolization and Exclusion*. Oxford: Clarendon Press, 1988. A valuable assess-

ment and extension of the neo-Weberian closure theories of Frank Parkin and Randall
Collins.

Parkin, Frank. *Marxism and Class Theory: A
Bourgeois Critique.* New York: Columbia
University Press, 1979. A very provocative
critique of the Marxian approach to class in
industrial societies. Parkin suggests that a
Weberian approach provides the best alternative to Marxism.

Phillips, Kevin. *The Politics of Rich and Poor:
Wealth and the American Electorate in the
Reagan Aftermath.* New York: Random
House, 1990. A valuable and much-needed
examination of recent trends toward greater
inequality in the distribution of income and
wealth in the United States and other industrial capitalist societies.

Szymanski, Albert. *Class Structure: A Critical
Perspective.* New York: Praeger, 1983. Despite Szymanski's predictable Marxian ex-
cesses, as well as a tendency to view state
socialism unrealistically, contains useful
discussions of many features of stratification
within industrial capitalism.

Wright, Erik Olin. *Class Structure and Income
Determination.* New York: Academic Press,
1979. One of the most impressive attempts
by a Marxist to conceptualize the contemporary capitalist class structure and to show
how such a conceptualization is a good predictor of economic inequality. (Readers interested in this book should consult the
same author's *Classes* [London: Verso, 1985],
a work in which Wright significantly modi-
fies some of his thinking.)

Chapter

11

Political Evolution and the Origin of the State

In this chapter and the next we explore the evolution of political organization. As we shall see, forms of polity are closely tied to the nature of economic organization and social stratification. The chapter examines four major stages in political evolution widely recognized by social scientists: bands, tribes, chiefdoms, and states. Particular emphasis is given to the key differences between societies organized into states and prestate societies. Some well-known theories of the origin of the state in human history are also examined. In the following chapter, the crucial problem of the evolution of the state since the emergence of modern capitalism is considered.

THE NATURE OF POLITICAL ORGANIZATION

Broadly conceived, the **polity** is the aspect of society that serves to maintain law and order within a society and to regulate the external relations between or among societies. The political system establishes a means of social control or regulation designed to keep the behavior of individuals and groups within certain bounds and to make and implement decisions in behalf of the entire society or certain segments of it. The polity is universally found in human societies since all societies have some established means of social control and decision making. The specific nature of political control and decision making, however, varies greatly from one society to another. Different kinds of societies will have different mechanisms for keeping things under control and insuring that decisions and plans can be successfully implemented. It is useful to think of three such political mechanisms: influence, power, and authority.

Influence is *the likelihood that the behavior, decisions, or advice of one or more persons will be followed or copied by others.* Influence is a strictly informal process of social control occurring as a regular result of constant and close social interaction. This form of control predominates in societies that are small, relatively simple in structure, and characterized by the regular face-to-face interaction of most of their members. While influence is not necessarily the only mechanism of political control in such societies, it is overwhelmingly the predominant mechanism. What is most characteristic of influence is that it lacks "teeth." It cannot guarantee that decisions or advice will be followed, but can only make it more or less likely that they will be. A political leader possessing only influence, then, has no capacity to force others to do his bidding; he may only suggest or implore and hope to be effective.

A distinctively different mechanism for bringing about social control is **power,** a central feature of most political systems. Paraphrasing the classic definition given by Max Weber (1978; orig. 1923), power may be defined as *the capacity to control the behavior of others even against their resistance.* Power contains precisely the element that is lacking in the case of influence, namely, the capacity to overcome resistance and insure that the will of the powerholder prevails. Behind power, then, lurks the constant threat of *coercion* or *force* should orders or decisions not be willingly complied with. Given these considerations, power re-

quires a certain level of organizational development. Therefore it usually begins to appear as a prominent feature of social life only with the transition to intensive horticultural societies possessing social stratification. It is at this stage of sociocultural evolution that the administrative machinery that power requires can be created.

The strength of power is that it is backed by the capacity to use force. Paradoxically, this is also its weakness, for that force may not always be sufficient to prevail against the will of those persons and groups subjected to it. The weakness of force is that it is an *external* means of getting people to comply; it does not require their psychological commitment to rules and orders, but demands only that such rules and orders be obeyed. Yet because power requires no psychological allegiance to commands, those commands may go unheeded when the threat of force is inadequate. The holders of power throughout human history have clearly understood this fact; and for this reason they have generally been eager to gain not only compliance with commands, but psychological commitment to them as well. Such psychological identification with the ruling powers naturally increases the likelihood of compliance. When such psychological identification has been created, the use of power has been *legitimized*—that is, justified or rationalized as morally right and proper—by the people themselves. When this occurs, power gives way to **authority,** the political form that Weber identified as *rule by the consent of the governed.*

Sociologists have generally made much of the notions of authority and **legitimacy,** arguing that most political regimes have rested on authority rather than on raw force—that the people have committed their hearts and minds to their own subordination. Some sociologists, though, have suggested that this picture of political systems is not a realistic one. Immanuel Wallerstein

(1974a) and Pierre van den Berghe (1978), for example, insist that the consent of the governed has been largely absent from most political regimes. They believe that most complex political systems have been to one extent or another outright tyrannies resting on a solid foundation of physical force.

Wallerstein and van den Berghe have a significant point to make. Social scientists have undoubtedly exaggerated the extent to which genuine legitimacy has prevailed within political systems. Numerous peasant and slave rebellions throughout human history, for example, bear witness to the frequent withholding of legitimacy. Yet it seems that the view of Wallerstein and van den Berghe goes too far in the other direction. Indeed, a number of political systems have been vigorously supported by the masses. The contemporary U.S. government, for instance, undoubtedly enjoys an enormous level of legitimacy, as do the governments of all industrial capitalist societies. In any event, the question of the extent to which polities receive legitimation

is an empirical one that will have to be settled by the concrete examination of particular cases.

THE GENERAL PATTERN OF POLITICAL EVOLUTION

Like the study of sociocultural evolution in general, the investigation of political evolution initially requires a typology of stages. The best-known and most widely adopted typology of political stages is that developed by Elman Service (1971b), who distinguishes four major stages in political evolution: band, tribe, chiefdom, and state. His typology is the basis for the discussion of the major evolutionary transformations within political society. The typology is outlined in Table 11.1.

Bands

The most rudimentary form of political society is the **band,** a form of polity typically associated with hunting and gathering soci-

Table 11.1 STAGES IN THE EVOLUTION OF POLITICAL ORGANIZATION

Stage	Characteristics	Mode of Subsistence Technology
Band	Primary political role is that of headman, with informal leadership capacity and no power over others.	Hunting and gathering
Tribe	Political leaders generally acquire leadership through their roles as economic redistributors. Leaders have high prestige but little or no power. Leadership typically limited to local village level. Villages are largely autonomous political segments; that is, there is no unification of villages into a common political framework.	Simple horticulturalists and some pastoralists
Chiefdom	A centralized polity organized into a hierarchy of powerful chiefs and subchiefs. Individual villages lose their political autonomy and are subordinated to centralized authority.	Intensive horticulturalists, a few hunter-gatherers, and many pastoralists
State	A political system having great concentration of power in a few hands, monopolization of the means of violence, expropriation of surplus production, and a legitimizing ideology.	Agrarian, some intensive horticultural, and all modern industrial societies

eties. As Service (1971b) points out, all band-level political structures are found within hunting and gathering societies, even though not all hunter-gatherers are politically organized at the band level; and such societies as have developed beyond the band level have had some infrastructural features unusual for hunter-gatherers.

Morton Fried (1967) has provided a valuable description of the nature of political leadership in band-level society. As he points out, it rests on influence and typically lacks any sort of real power. In addition, leadership tends to be displayed in transient fashion, frequently shifting from one person to another. These shifts in leadership appear to be associated more with the nature of social situations than with the nature of persons. Fried also notes that the nature of leadership bears a close relation to variations in ecology and demography. More extensive leadership (and greater power underlying leadership) is associated with denser populations and more productive subsistence patterns.

The political structure of band-level societies is thus a rather loosely organized pattern of frequently shifting, informal leadership. This leadership is typically invested in a person known as a *headman*, although he is often not the only person who exercises influence or leadership. Some band-level societies are so loosely organized that they appear to lack any sort of leadership structure altogether. The Eskimos are an excellent example of this most rudimentary of all known political structures. Perhaps more typical of band-level society are the !Kung San, who have a somewhat more regular structure of leadership (Fried, 1967). Even here, however, leadership is quite loosely and informally organized. !Kung San leaders direct migration and subsistence activities and perform certain ceremonies, but the position they hold contains no power, honors, or rewards. Fried appears to catch

the essence of political organization at the band level when he says (1967:83):

> It is difficult, in ethnographies of simple egalitarian societies [i.e., band-level societies], to find cases in which one individual tells one or more others, "Do this!" or some command equivalent. The literature is replete with examples of individuals saying the equivalent of "If this is done, it will be good," possibly or possibly not followed by somebody else doing it. More usually the person who initiates the idea also performs the activity. . . . The leader is unable to compel any of the others to carry out his wish.

Tribes

Perhaps the clearest and most consistent usage of the term **tribe** has been provided by Elman Service (1971b) and Marshall Sahlins (1963, 1968; cf. Fried, 1967). Both Service and Sahlins conceive of a tribal society as one in which a larger unit, typically identified in cultural and linguistic terms, is divided into a number of smaller, relatively unintegrated villages. These smaller village units, while culturally identified with the tribe as a whole, are characteristically economically self-sufficient and politically autonomous. The tribe therefore has a *segmentary* character. The individual village units of the tribe maintain a high degree of autonomy and there is no unification of the villages into a single political unit. To seek the nature of the political organization of tribal society, then, one must look within the villages themselves rather than at the tribal units as as whole.

The tribe is typically associated with simple horticultural and some pastoral societies. Marshall Sahlins (1963) has described the basic features of one type of tribal politics through reference to the famous Melanesian big-man systems of leadership. As the primary political leaders of tribal society big men are individuals whose public actions are designed to make invidious comparisons with others. Big men, however, do not come to office in the sense that they acquire a hereditary position by birthright. Rather they must achieve the position by their own actions and the status of big man is therefore personally acquired. Qualities necessary to the attainment of big man status generally include ability as an organizer of economic production and a redistributor of wealth, skill in oratory, magical powers and perhaps bravery in war. Success in competitive feasting is, as noted earlier, an especially important quality necessary to the attainment of top leadership. Tribal politics is therefore personal politics; the status of big man is not a title to be conferred, but a position to be earned through skill and hard work. Although the status is not easily won, it can be easily lost should laziness creep in and important skills deteriorate.

The status of big man confers great prestige and renown on the person who achieves in. However this status confers no real power or authority to command the actions of others. Big men advise, suggest, and cajole, and more often than not their wishes will be followed. But they lack any real power since they lack the capacity to force others to do their bidding. The political structure of big-man leadership, therefore, rests on influence. Lacking the capacity to command others, big men are successful leaders only to the extent that they serve the public good. In a real sense they are *servants* of the people, servants who depend on the good graces of their followers to retain high status. The status of big man is symbiotic with society at large; in exchange for prestige and renown, big men must serve long-range societal interests, or else they will not continue to be big men. Failure to serve the public good ends in demotion from big-man status.

The Nuer are also a society in which a tribal form of politics prevails. The Nuer are pastoralists who inhabit a part of the Sudan in eastern Africa. Among them a number of positions of informal leadership exists, but none confers any real power or authority. One of the most important positions of leadership among the Nuer is that of "leopard-skin chief." The leopard-skin chief is charged with special responsibilities in regard to the ending of feuds, but this should "not imply that he has any right to command obedience. The right to wear a leopard-skin cloak is the privilege and the symbol of his position" (Mair, 1964:41). Lucy Mair summarizes the tribal character of politics among the Nuer (1964:63):

> Among them certain persons are leaders in the sense that they are respected, and people will wait to see what they do and then follow suit; others have ritual powers that are not shared by all members of the community, and certain ceremonies can be performed only by these men. But none of these persons can claim to give orders, nor do they even announce decisions which have been taken collectively.

Law and Order in Band and Tribal Societies

Band and tribal societies lack any specialized kind of legal or political machinery. They have no political officials with the power or authority to make decisions and implement them. The question therefore arises as to how such societies maintain law and order, or an acceptable level of internal peace and harmony. They obviously do, since social breakdown or anarchy are no more characteristic of band and tribal societies than of any other type of society.

Numerous mechanisms exist to maintain internal peace in societies lacking formalized political and legal authorities. Mention may be made here of only two. Among the Eskimos, a well-known mechanism for settling conflict and restoring order is the "song duel." The song duel is a social ritual in which individuals who are engaged in a difficult dispute attempt to settle it by "out-singing" each other. One person begins by singing aloud his grievances against the other, and the other person is given his chance to sing a reply. In their songs, the disputants attempt to shame each other. The winner of this contest is decided by community agreement. Once the community has decided upon the winner, the loser usually accepts the decision and the dispute is put to an end.

A more widespread mechanism for keeping the peace is found in the beliefs and fears that many band and tribal societies have about the practice of witchcraft. Many anthropologists have suggested that the fear of witchcraft, or of being accused of practicing witchcraft, serves as an important mechanism of social control when formalized political controls are absent. Beatrice Whiting (1950) and Guy Swanson (1960) have attempted to test this idea empirically. In a study of 26 small-scale societies, Whiting found that of 16 societies in which beliefs and fears about witchcraft were important, 15 (94 percent) lacked political officials with the legitimate right to levy punishments for offenses. By contrast, in the 10 societies that had no significant concerns about the practice of witchcraft, only 2 (20 percent) lacked such political officials. Similar results were obtained in Guy Swanson's research. In his study of 28 societies, he found (Wallace, 1966:182) that "witchcraft is highly prevalent—indeed, occurs almost exclusively—in those societies where social roles are not subject to effective control by secular authority."

Anthony Wallace (1966) suggests that when people fear having witchcraft used against them, or fear being accused of practicing witchcraft, they will be especially careful to "toe the line" so as to avoid offending others. Under such circumstances, people become convinced of how important it is not to be taken as a perpetrator of evil,

and this generally makes them more cooperative (M. Harris, 1971).

Since band and tribal societies typically lack social class divisions, conflict does not arise between and among social groups with differential access to the most valued economic resources, but rather tends to be highly personal and individualized. In societies where disputes are primarily of this personal sort, maintaining an effective social peace is not especially difficult, and elaborate political institutions are not required. However, specialized and elaborate forms of political machinery *are* required in more complex societies where structured class conflict becomes a significant feature of social life.

Chiefdoms

The next major evolutionary stage beyond the tribal level of political society is the **chiefdom,** a form of political organization strikingly different in several basic respects from the tribal polity. Chiefdoms are most characteristically found among intensive horticultural and pastoral societies. What distinctively separates chiefdoms from tribes is that the former achieve a political unification and centralization conspicuously lacking in the latter. The chiefdom is marked by the integration of many separate villages into a centrally coordinated complex whole governed from the top down. Marshall Sahlins (1963) again offers a classic description.

Sahlins's analysis of this form of political society is based upon the classical chiefdoms of Polynesia as they existed prior to European contact in the late eighteenth century (cf. Kirch, 1984). The most advanced of the Polynesian chiefdoms were found on the islands of Tonga, Tahiti, and Hawaii. Here were sovereignties that included as many as tens of thousands of persons spread over areas as extensive as hundreds of square miles. The classical Polynesian chiefdom was a pyramidal arrangement of higher and lower chiefs. These chiefs were regular and official holders of offices and titles, and they claimed authority over permanently established groups of followers. Authority resided in the office itself, and not merely in the person holding the position. Chiefs gained access to their positions through a line of hereditary succession.

Polynesian chiefs had rights of call on the labor and agricultural produce within their domain, which gave them considerable economic leverage over a large number of people. Through extraction of economic surplus, they established and controlled large storehouses that were used for such things as the lavish entertainment of the people and visiting chiefs, the subsidizing of craft production and technical construction works such as irrigation systems, and the organization and conduct of military campaigns. While a portion of the storehouses was redistributed to the people, a substantial part of it was used to support a permanent administrative apparatus created to carry out a variety of political functions. Such administrative officials as supervisors of the stores, talking chiefs, ceremonial attendants, and high priests, as well as specialized warrior corps, were supported from this chiefly surplus.

The pastoral Basseri are also politically organized as a chiefdom. The central leader is a chief who is granted considerable authority to command the actions of others. As Fredrik Barth (1961) notes, power is conceived as emanating from him, not delegated to him by his followers. The chief plays a major political role in settling disputes that the contending parties have been unable to settle informally. In this regard, Barth comments that the chief (1961:77)

> constitutes the only "court" in the tribal system. The chief is not bound by custom or precedent in his decision—the cases that are brought before him are precisely such as can-

not be mediated within the framework of tradition, for reasons of their subject, or the personalities involved. . . . Quite explicitly, he is expected to make the decision which he feels is "best for the tribe"—he is expected to exercise his privileged arbitrary authority within a very wide area of free grace, unhampered by considerations of individual justice as derived from rules. Only in disputes over the division of inheritance does he restrict his autocratic power—such cases he frequently refers for decision to a religious judge in a sedentary community.

It is clear that a significant evolutionary gulf separates tribal leaders of all sorts from genuine chiefs. Indeed, the chiefdom marks the beginning of the institutionalization of political power and authority in social life. Polynesian chiefs (and other genuine chiefs as well) developed the powers of government to the point where they no longer had to depend upon the voluntary compliance of their followers in order to make and implement decisions. As Sahlins has pointed out, their followers were now dependent *on them*, a complete reversal of the political arrangements of tribal society. The real beginnings of power and authority emerge with the chiefdom because it is there that the necessary administrative machinery needed to compel compliance is created. Polynesian chiefs could not only issue commands, but could back them up as well. When that is possible, genuine power has become a significant social force. Richard Lee has nicely caught the nature of the evolutionary shift from tribal leaders to true chiefs (1990:238):

> At some point in the development of these redistributive societies [chiefdoms] there was an ideological shift of great magnitude, a changeover in the demeanor of leaders from modesty to self-aggrandizement, and from self-denial to self-praise. This shift removed a constraint on the behavior of leaders, lifting a ban that opened the way for

the accumulation of power, prestige, and wealth.

Yet we must be careful not to overstate the case, for there are definite limitations placed upon the power of chiefs. Chiefs are still related to the common people through kinship ties, and they are expected to be generous and benevolent and to serve the common good. The Basseri, for example, clearly anticipate that a chief will show his followers the utmost consideration. There is much concern that he be hospitable by providing such gifts as weapons and horses to his most prominent followers (Barth, 1961).

Chiefs who fail to meet these expectations frequently find themselves in the midst of a popular, and more than likely successful, revolt. In ancient Polynesia, for instance, many a chief who "ate the powers of government too much" was dethroned and put to death (Sahlins, 1963). Thus, while chiefdoms have been able to institutionalize genuine power and authority, there are clear restraints on their coercive capacities. Lacking a genuine monopoly of force, and tied to the people through kinship and expectations of generosity, primitive chiefs have not been allowed to become true tyrants.

States

The chiefdom, containing only a limited capacity for compulsion, is inadequately backed by the administrative machinery necessary to overcome the most severe forms of resistance. When this administrative machinery is finally created, that form of political society known as the **state** has evolved.

The state not only continues the general evolutionary process of the increasing concentration of power; it also establishes a *monopoly of force* necessary to back that power up and ensure that the will of the power holders shall prevail. Indeed, this capture of a monopoly of force is essential to the very definition of a state.* As Morton Fried notes (1967:230):

> Of great importance is the claim of the state to paramountcy in the application of naked force to social problems. Frequently this means that warfare and killing become monopolies of the state and may only be carried out at times, in places, and under the specific conditions set by the state.
>
> In the final analysis the power of a state can be manifested in a real physical force, an army, a militia, a police force, a constabulary, with specialized weaponry, drill, conscription, a hierarchy of command, and the other paraphernalia of structured control.

While holding a monopoly of force is crucial to the nature of the state, other characteristics of state-level polity are also significant. One is that the state emerges under conditions in which the significance of kinship ties is reduced. Kinship ties, such as those of chiefdoms, serve to mitigate the development of coercive power. With the transition to the state, these ties between ruler and ruled are generally eliminated. Therefore, state-level rulers no longer subjugate their kinsmen, but dominate a great mass of unrelated individuals.

States have two additional characteristics worth noting (van den Berghe, 1978).

---

*Some social scientists have challenged this notion. Anthony Giddens (1985) and Robert Carneiro (1981), for example, point out that many societies that are almost universally considered to be states have lacked a true (i.e., complete) monopoly over the means of violence. Some individuals and groups outside the state, they claim, sometimes possess a certain capacity to use various means of violence. While this is undoubtedly true, the fact remains that in these societies the state's capacity for overcoming organized resistance to its rule is still enormous, and this is the key idea implied by usage of the word *monopoly*.

One is the extent to which they promote elaborate legitimizing ideologies. The naked use of force alone may be insufficient to guarantee compliance with the state's wishes, and rulers therefore commonly attempt to convince the people of their moral right to rule. The greater the psychological commitment of the people to the state, the less the likelihood of rebellion against it. Legitimizing ideologies have taken a variety of forms, but a very common tactic has been for state rulers to justify their rule in religious terms: to claim supernatural sanction of their role in society. The second characteristic is that states, unlike chiefdoms, have generally not been redistributive centers. The flow of the surplus to the state has been a one-way flow, and such surplus expropriation has resulted in substantial—indeed, often enormous—enrichment of the ruling powers.

As a stage in political evolution, the state typically emerges within agrarian societies, and most states throughout history have therefore been *agrarian states*. While these states have shared certain basic characteristics, there have been several different forms of the agrarian state (see the Special Topic at the end of this chapter). Not all states, however, have been confined to the agrarian level. There have been a few instances of *primitive states*, those formed within essentially primitive, intensive horticultural societies. Most notable are those that flourished in the nineteenth century in western and southern Africa, such as the west African Ashanti state and the south African Zulu state. George Peter Murdock (1959) has called such states *African despotisms*. He lists among their prominent features such attributes as monarchical absolutism, conceptions of divine kingship, ritual isolation of kings, insignia of office, royal courts, territorial bureaucracy, and ministers of state. The intensive horticultural chiefdoms of Polynesia also appear to have evolved into short-lived primitive states immediately after European contact (Service, 1975).

Of course, with the rise of capitalism and industrialism, states were by no means eliminated from the scene, and all industrial societies are organized into powerful and extensive state systems; we may thus speak of *modern states*. There have been two major forms of the state in modern industrial societies. In the West, the principal form of the state is a parliamentary democracy. Here the all-powerful and despotic nature of the state has been significantly tempered with the introduction of certain basic freedoms and at least some semblance of control by the people of the basic apparatus of government. Even though the parliamentary democracies have not actually created a genuine democratic order, they have at least eliminated some of the worst and most despotic forms of state power. The other major kind of modern industrial state, the totalitarian state, has arisen in the non-Western state socialist societies. Here, despite some pretense of democracy, the state operates in a more typical despotic fashion, except in this case with an awesome monopoly of force made possible by an industrial level of technology. (Western parliamentary democracies and non-Western totalitarian states are discussed in detail in the next chapter.)

Thus the state in one form or another represents the outcome of a long process of political evolution in which democracy and equality were increasingly undermined and replaced with the domination of the many by the few. Although the evolution of the state was achieved in gradual rather than sudden fashion, its actual emergence represents a great watershed in human history. For it was here that powerful leaders no longer needed to promise to be generous to their followers. They could and did promise their followers little or nothing, save continual subjugation and constant toil, and they had a sufficient monopoly of force to back up their rule. What was the nature of the earliest states, and how and why did they come into existence?

THE ORIGIN OF THE STATE

Pristine Versus Secondary States

In order to analyze the rise of the state in human society, it is useful to follow Morton Fried's (1967) distinction between **pristine** and **secondary states.** According to Fried, secondary states are those that have arisen as the result of the presence of one or more preexisting states. Contact between a non-state society and one or more state-level societies may create conditions in which the former is rapidly turned into a state. Many, if not most, of the primitive states in Polynesia and Africa arose in this manner. Secondary states, however, need not form through intersocietal contact. When new forms of the state gradually or suddenly replace old states within the same sociocultural system, then we can also speak of the new state as a secondary state. According to this conception of a secondary state, the overwhelming majority of states in human history have been secondary in nature.

On the other hand, the very first states arose under conditions in which there was no preexisting state. These are the states that Fried has termed *pristine.* As he says, "When a pristine state emerges it does so in a political vacuum. That is, there is no other more highly developed state present that might help it toward stateship" (Fried, 1967:231–232).

Obviously there have been only a handful of pristine states in human history. Pristine states arose in at least six regions of the Old World and at least two regions of the New World. The earliest of the Old World states evolved in Mesopotamia (what is now mainly Iraq) and Egypt in approximately 5000 B.P. (Fagan, 1989; Wenke, 1990). Pristine states arose in other parts of

Africa somewhat later—for example, in 3600 B.P. in Kerma on the middle Nile, in 2500 B.P. in Axum in Ethiopia, and in Jenne in west Africa in approximately A.D. 200 (Connah, 1987). In China an indigenous state began to emerge with the creation of the Shang Dynasty around 3800 B.P. (Chang, 1986). In the Indus River valley in north India (in what is now Pakistan), the famous state known as the Harappan was evolving around 4600 B.P. (Possehl, 1990). There were also pristine states in Europe. In Mediterranean Europe (mainly Greece) the first true states arose no later than 2700 B.P. (Champion, Gamble, Shennan, and Whittle, 1984) and possibly as early as 4000 B.P. (Milisauskas, 1978; Fagan, 1989). In temperate Europe the first states, those of the Celts, were emerging around 2200 B.P. (Champion et al., 1984). Many of these Old World states emerged in geographical regions dominated by major rivers, or, in the case of Mediterranean Europe, in the vicinity of a large sea. Thus the earliest Mesopotamian states arose in the fertile area between the Tigris and Euphrates Rivers, the state in China evolved along the Yellow River in northern China, and the earliest Indian state emerged along the Indus River.

In the New World, pristine states evolved somewhat later. The two regions of New World state formation were Mesoamerica (mostly what is now Mexico and parts of Central America) and Peru. In the Mesoamerican lowlands, the first states to emerge were those created by the Olmec and Maya civilizations. The Olmec state flourished between 3200 and 2800 B.P. The Mayan state achieved its peak between approximately A.D. 300 and 900 (Fiedel, 1987). In the Mesoamerican highlands, just north of what is now Mexico City, the first state was formed around the city of Teotihuacán in approximately 2000 B.P. (Fiedel, 1987). The most powerful of the Mesoamerican highland states, though, was established by the Aztecs, whose capital city was known as Tenochtitlán. The Aztecs reached the apex of their development in the early sixteenth century. Sometime around 2000 B.P. in Peru, a series of wars and conquests led to the formation of more complex and extensive political units. These eventually reached imperial scope and culminated in the establishment of the Inca empire, which reached its zenith in the fifteenth and sixteenth centuries (Fiedel, 1987).

The Emergence of Pristine States

A study that presents a clear picture of the main features of pristine state formation has been carried out by Robert Adams (1966). Adams's study is devoted to a comparative analysis of pristine state formation in one Old World case—Mesopotamia—and one New World case—central Mexico. A major conclusion concerns the striking similarities in state formation in each instance. His analysis therefore offers considerable insight into state formation as a classic process of parallel evolution. It is highly probable that the processes involved in state formation in Mesopotamia and Mexico were broadly similar to those involved in the emergence of the other pristine states.

Basic to the emergence of the state in these two cases was the development of social stratification. Adams characterizes Early Dynastic Mesopotamia as being highly stratified. At the pinnacle of Mesopotamian society stood princely families who, during late Early Dynastic and Akkadian times, were increasingly extending their control of land. These ruling families apparently headed manorial estates. A significant proportion of the labor force employed on these estates consisted of slaves.

At the top of the Aztec social hierarchy were royal households that in due time evolved into an endogamous (in-marrying) nobility sharply distinguished from the rest of the population by wealth, education, diet, and dress. Great estates were at the king's

disposal; large amounts of surplus production were generated by these estates, the surplus flowing as tribute from commoners to the ruling class. At an intermediate level in the social hierarchy were groups of warriors and merchants. Below them were localized kin groups that were internally stratified and held corporate (collective) title to land. Below these, in turn, were persons who cultivated the private lands of the nobility and who have been likened to medieval serfs. At the very bottom of the social order stood slaves.

In both Mesopotamia and Mexico we find a general pattern of political evolution characterized by the emergence of theocratic polities and their eventual transformation into militaristic and, ultimately, conquest states. The early formation of the state in both cases was marked by a decidedly religious focus, with much emphasis on temple building and governance by priesthoods. The dominance of religious groups, however, soon gave way to the rise to power of militaristic groups. Political power came to be increasingly concentrated in dynastic institutions at the expense of earlier communal and religious bodies. Archaeological evidence demonstrates the existence of palaces containing private apartments for the ruling family and the families of top-ranking administrative officials and personal servants. In Mesopotamia there is good evidence for the existence of an array of political functionaries such as gatekeepers, cooks, servants, messengers, and slaves. Clearly the palace structure associated with both states indicates the development of highly stratified societies in which the power and complexity of governing bodies had been erected on a major scale. Both societies had parallel conceptions of kingship, and both ultimately evolved into major conquest states that extended their territorial control over wide regions. This increasing conquest of neighboring lands and peoples brought greater demands for tribute, increasing stratification, and yet further intensification of the autocratic features of the state.

Theories of the Origin of the State

A variety of theories attempting to explain the general process of pristine state formation have been proposed by social scientists. The most important of these are:

- *Functionalist* theories, which stress the role of the state as a societal integrator and see it arising as a necessary organizational structure to coordinate complex sociocultural systems.
- *Marxian* theories, which give priority to the importance of class struggle in explaining the rise of the state.
- *Ecological* theories, which place emphasis on the role of population pressure and the natural environment in the formation of the state.

A Functionalist Theory A well-known functionalist theory of the state is found in the work of Elman Service (1975, 1978). Rather than conceiving of the state as an oppressive and exploitative institution, Service thinks of it as a form of centralized leadership that organizes and coordinates society for the mutual benefit of its various individuals and groups. When the state arises, therefore, the principal distinction within society is not between wealthy and poor or oppressors and oppressed, but between governing and governed groups. The state originates in order to serve more effectively the needs of the governed.

Service sees three principal types of benefits arising from the creation of the state. The first concerns economic redistribution. The state is an organ that mobilizes natural resources and persons for important production and consumption functions. More diversified ecological zones are said to be exploited through state-level organization. The products of skilled workers and diverse ecological zones are seen as being brought together for the benefit of the court, the bureaucracy, the priesthood, the army, and also for the citizenry at large. A second major benefit conceived by Service is that provided by new forms of war organization. Intensified warfare is said to be an integrative feature of society in that it brings in increasing wealth in the form of booty, captives, and tribute and thus enhances the "national pride." A third major benefit allegedly produced by the state is that of public works. The state oversees the construction of temples, tombs, pyramids, walls, roads, irrigation systems, and many other public projects.

I would suggest that great skepticism is warranted with respect to this theory. It seems unduly optimistic in the extreme to argue that the rise of the state produced positive benefits for the members of society collectively. Of course, the rise of the state did produce certain crucial benefits, yet not for society as a whole. On the contrary, these benefits largely accrued to the ruling class. Service suggests that the waging of war was a benefit, again for society as a whole. Yet the spoils of war were primarily claimed by the most privileged members of society, especially the ruling class. Service also claims that the building of temples, tombs, pyramids, and other public works was a great social benefit. Yet the vast majority of the citizenry did not have their lives improved by such public works. In fact, many persons suffered much additional hardship because of these construction projects, since they were the ones who contributed the labor necessary to their realization.

The Marxian Theory The alternative to a functionalist interpretation of the origin of the state is some type of conflict theory, one version of which is the Marxian theory. The classical Marxian view of the state holds that the state, in Marx's own words, is "the executive committee of the ruling class." That is, the state is a political body that exists primarily as a means of protecting the economic interests of the dominant social class within a stratified society. With the division of society into classes, the state becomes a virtual necessity from the standpoint of the dominant class. Morton Fried (1967, 1978) is a vigorous contemporary defender of this view of the origin of the state. For Fried, once a society has developed a system of social stratification, the emergence of the state is all but assured. The appearance of differential access to resources means the emergence of privileged and disprivileged groups, and those holding a privileged position must secure and protect it against the threats of the disprivileged to take it away. Indeed, Fried's conception of "state" and of "stratified society" are fundamentally the same.

One difficulty with Fried's version of the Marxian argument concerns his claim that there are no known societies that are stratified and that also lack a state. Actually, there have been a number of stratified societies that lacked true state-level polities. Classical chiefdoms, such as those of Polynesia, were certainly stratified, since there was a division of those societies into social groups having unequal control over productive resources. But the classical Polynesian chiefdoms were by definition not states, since they lacked a sufficient monopoly of force to override the will of their members consistently.

Nevertheless, with appropriate modification Fried's general point holds up well: Societies with especially elaborate and intense stratification systems do have states, and in these societies there is a very close connection between the dominant economic class and the state. And, although the question is still an open one, considerable evidence suggests that elaborate strati-

fication systems with their ruling classes historically came first and then were followed by the emergence of the state (Fried, 1978:46; Haas, 1982). All of this points to considerable merit on the part of the Marxian theory, or at least suggests that it is moving us in a more fruitful direction than Service's functionalist theory.

However, the issue cannot be settled so easily, for there is a different conflict theory that we have yet to consider—Carneiro's famous circumscription theory—that seems at least as compelling as the Marxian interpretation.

The Circumscription Theory   Many scholars have called attention to the role of demographic and ecological factors in the rise of the state (cf. Kirch, 1984; Johnson and Earle, 1987), but the best-known theory of this type is Robert Carneiro's (1970, 1981, 1987) *circumscription theory*. This theory is in fact more than just a theory of the origin of the state; it is a theory of the entire course of political evolution.

Carneiro notes that a factor common to all major areas of the world where pristine states arose was what he has called *environmental circumscription*. This exists when areas of rich agricultural land are surrounded either by areas of very poor or unusable land or by natural barriers, such as major mountain ranges or large bodies of water. The potential operation of this factor can be seen in such areas of pristine state formation as the Middle East, where fertile river valleys were surrounded by vast expanses of arid land deficient in rainfall, and in Peru, where fertile valleys were blockaded by major mountain ranges.

In order to show the likely consequences of circumscribed environments, Carneiro begins with an illustration of a completely different kind of ecological situation, the Amazon Basin of South America. Here was a vast area of tropical forest in which nothing even approaching indigenous state formation occurred. This region of the world has probably long been occupied by numerous horticultural villages. An abundance of land was available for horticulture, population density was typically quite low, and hence there was little if any problem of population pressure. Warfare, while common in many horticultural societies of the region, was not fought directly over land itself. With an abundance of land suitable for horticulture, defeat in warfare meant that the defeated group could simply move away and reestablish itself on new land. Under such circumstances, we would expect that individual societies would be able to maintain their autonomy and preserve their existing sociopolitical adaptation to the environment.

The situation is different where environmental circumscription is present. As Carneiro notes, where there are sharp limits on the availability of productive land, population growth soon leads to growth in the number of villages occupying the land, with the result that all arable land is eventually under cultivation. This puts pressure on individual villages for the intensification of production in order to feed the expanding population. With continuing population growth, population pressure becomes a severe problem, leading, most likely, to the intensification of warfare in order to capture additional land. Under such circumstances, the consequences of warfare for the defeated group cannot be dispersal to a new region, since there is no suitable place to go. The conquered group will therefore likely be politically subordinated to the victorious group, leading to the establishment of complex political systems at the chiefdom level. With further population growth and increased militarism over the struggle for land, chiefdoms will ultimately evolve into yet more complex, state-level polities. The ultimate outcome of such an evolutionary process might well be the formation of vast political empires, such as those that prevailed in such circumscribed areas as Peru and the Middle East.

Two wrinkles that Carneiro has added to this basic theory involve the concepts of *social circumscription* and *resource concentration.* Social circumscription occurs when the barriers to human movements are other societies rather than features of the geographical environment. This can operate as a factor in political evolution apart from, or in addition to, physical circumscription. Resource concentration exists when an environment is especially abundant in plant and animal resources. This abundance tends to attract people to the area and stimulate population growth. Population pressure is a likely result, but movement out of the area may be impeded by the presence of other groups—by social circumscription. Warfare and political conquest, and thus political evolution, are expected outcomes. Carneiro (1987) suggests that it is this kind of process that has produced substantial political evolution in uncircumscribed environments, such as some regions of Amazonia.

The circumscription theory is perhaps the most impressive theory of political evolution we have, and it has stood the test of time remarkably well (Graber and Roscoe, 1988). It has been extensively tested through archaeological and anthropological research, and the results have been much more on the positive than on the negative side (Kirch, 1984, 1988; Schacht, 1988; Carneiro, 1988). It is likely that Carneiro has come very close to identifying some of the key elements in long-term political evolution. However, one nagging difficulty concerns Carneiro's strong emphasis on warfare and his relative neglect of economic processes in political evolution. As Patrick Kirch (1988) and Robert Schacht (1988) have pointed out, there is a very close correlation between agricultural intensification and political evolution, and both of these are closely related to population pressure and environmental circumscription. Could it be that chiefdoms and states are political responses to the growth of the stratification systems that are associated with agricultural intensification, as the Marxian theory is basically suggesting? Could such economic changes be more important than, or at least as important as, warfare (cf. Lee, 1990; Earle, 1991)? More research is clearly needed to establish solid answers to these crucial questions, and so in the meantime it is difficult to make a clear choice between the circumscription theory and the Marxian theory—assuming, of course, that such a choice needs to be made.

SUMMARY

1. Political systems are the means whereby societies maintain internal law and order and manage intersocietal relations. In many societies political leaders have acquired power and authority over others. Power involves the capacity to compel the actions of others, whereas authority gives moral legitimacy to political rule. In the simplest societies only social influence prevails. This is an informal means of political control lacking any features of compulsion.

2. The band is the simplest level of political organization. Bands are characteristic of hunter-gatherers. Power and authority are absent, and leadership tends to be highly informal. Tribes are also political structures in

Table 11.2 THEORIES OF POLITICAL EVOLUTION

Theory	Characteristics	Evaluation
Functionalist theory	Long-term political evolution produces increasingly well-adapted political structures, the best-adapted of which is the state. The earliest states more adequately served societal needs than did previous political structures. Early states functioned as important economic redistributors, as superior war machines, and as administrative units devoted to the construction of important public monuments.	A very dubious theory that greatly overrates the beneficial consequences of chiefdoms and states for society as a whole, and greatly undervalues the narrow self-interest of elites in generating and sustaining chiefdoms and states
Marxian theory	More powerful and advanced political systems accompany the rise and evolution of social stratification. The state comes into play in order to protect and enhance the interests of the economically dominant class in a situation in which it is threatened by subordinate classes.	Far superior to the functionalist argument, but by itself not a fully adequate or complete explanation
Circumscription theory	Political evolution occurs most rapidly and extensively in environments posing physical or social barriers to territorial expansion. When population pressure reaches high levels in such regions, people can no longer avoid its negative consequences by migrating to new regions. The result is increasing social conflict culminating in higher and higher levels of political conquest. The state ultimately emerges from this process.	An extremely impressive theory that undoubtedly captures many of the most important dimensions of political evolution. May be complementary to the Marxian theory.

which power and authority are not present. Tribes have often been described as segmentary forms of political organization. Different villages within a larger cultural unit are highly autonomous and there is no overarching structure of the whole.

3. Band and tribal forms of political organization have no formalized means of political control, but they are anything but anarchic. Numerous informal mechanisms, such as witchcraft accusations and song duels, exist in order to maintain law and order.

4. A third stage of political evolution is the chiefdom, which marks the beginnings of power and authority in social life. Chiefs have considerable control over their followers, including the capacity to use force. Chiefdoms are unified, integrated political systems in which villages lose their autonomy and are subordinated to the whole. They have been found among many intensive horticulturalists and pastoralists.

5. A crucial watershed in political evolution was the origin of the state. The key characteristic of the state is its monopolization of the means of violence within a territory. This means that the state has a highly developed capacity to overcome numerous forms of resistance to it.

6. The first states arose some 5000 years ago in Mesopotamia and Egypt, and somewhat later in other parts of Africa, Europe, China, and India. States first arose in the New World around 3000 B.P. in Mesoamerica and some time after 2000 B.P. in Peru. These first states are generally known as pristine states. Once pristine states formed in these regions of the world, they created the conditions for the establishment of many other states, which are known as secondary states. The process of pristine state formation is a classic instance of parallel evolution. Explaining this process is one of the crucial problems of modern macrosociology.

7. The most important theories of political evolution in general, and the evolution of the state in particular, are the functionalist, Marxian, and circumscription theories. The basic features of these theories, and an evaluation of them, are found in Table 11.2.

SPECIAL TOPIC: FEUDALISM AND ORIENTAL DESPOTISM

All agrarian societies are highly stratified, state-organized societies. However, just as agrarian societies have differed in their modes of economic and social organization, so have they differed in their state structures. Two types of agrarian states have been of persistent interest to social scientists: **feudal states** and what might be termed **agrobureaucratic states.**

In feudal societies landownership is private, and the landowning nobility subjects a class of peasants beneath them; over this class they exercise political rule and legal jurisdiction. However, such landownership is not unconditional or absolute, acquired once and for all and without strings. Rather, land is acquired in the form of a **fief.** A fief is a grant of land given by a superior lord to a lesser lord (vassal) in return for the performance of certain obligations, especially military service and personal protection. The vassal granted a fief acquires with it the legal jurisdiction over the peasantry who are associated with it. Ownership and control of land are thus intimately connected with the political institution known as **vassalage.** Vassalage is the personal tie between unequally ranked landlords. It takes the form of a contract binding the parties into mutual obligations, and it is symbolized by personal oaths of loyalty. Through this institution, a complex hierarchy of lords is established, extending from the lowest-ranking vassal at the bottom all the way to the king or monarch at the top. In principle, the monarch may be the owner of all land, but in actuality this land is granted out as fiefs to a whole series of lords of different rank. Each lord exercises jurisdiction only over those lands that have been granted him.

Vassalage and the fief therefore establish a particular kind of political system characterized by its *decentralization,* by what Perry Anderson (1974a) calls the "parcellization of sovereignty" among a hierarchy of lords. Rather than investing power in a centrally coordinated state, the feudal polity spreads it out among a host of lords, each of whom has strictly circumscribed jurisdiction over a limited geographical region and a limited number of persons. Because of the decentralized nature of the feudal polity, the residence of lords is in the countryside (i.e., in their castles), and an ideology exalting the virtues of rural life typically accompanies this practice.

True feudal systems fitting the above description have by no means typified agrarian societies. Indeed, only two major examples of feudal societies are generally agreed on by historians. The prototype of feudalism prevailed in western Europe from about the ninth to the fifteenth century. In addition, historians are generally agreed that a type of feudalism existed in Japan from about the twelfth to the nineteenth century. Despite their local differences, the European and the Japanese feudal systems were strikingly similar. In both cases we find the essential features of feudalism (P. Anderson, 1974b:413):

> The links between military service, conditional landownership and seigneurial jurisdiction. . . . The graded hierarchy between lord, vassal, and rear-vassal, to form a chain of suzerainty and dependence. . . . An aristocracy of mounted knights formed a hereditary ruling class.

What accounts for feudal regimes? Most students of this problem have suggested that feudal forms of government arise as responses to the new military needs encountered after the breakdown of large centralized empires. European feudalism, for example, was created in the aftermath of the fall of Rome. The collapse of Roman political authority left communities vulnerable to attack by marauding Germanic tribes that preyed upon much of what was formerly the Roman Empire. It was therefore necessary to fuse political rule with military specialization as a means of protection against these attacks.

While many agrarian societies have been called feudal, most have developed political systems that contrast sharply with the decentralized character of feudal regimes. Indeed, the general tendency in agrarian societies has been for the *centralization,* rather than the fragmentation, of power. Many agrarian civilizations have been marked by highly centralized, bureaucratic, and intensely powerful states in which the masses were highly subordinated to a tiny elite.

The kind of state that we have called an agrobureaucratic state is one having essentially the following characteristics: Massive amounts of power are concentrated in the hands of a tiny group of persons or, indeed, in the hands of a single ruler standing at the apex of society; private ownership of land may exist to some extent, but land is primarily owned by the state itself; the state involves itself intensively in directing various forms of public works affecting the entire society; and the state rules the mass of people in despotic fashion, severely punishing any activity perceived as a threat to its existence. Such states have been found in many of the great agrarian civilizations, such as China, India, and ancient Mesopotamia and Egypt. No doubt other agrarian societies have had similar state systems. These states stand quite far removed from the vassalage and fief systems of feudal regimes. They are all-powerful, despotic states severely repressing their subjects (M. Harris, 1977:157):

Despite the development of philosophies and religions advocating justice and mercy, the rulers of these vast realms frequently had to rely on intimidation, force, and naked terror to maintain law and order. Total submissiveness was demanded of underlings, the supreme symbol of which was the obligation to prostrate oneself and grovel in the presence of the mighty. . . . In all of these ancient empires there were ruthless systems for routing out and punishing disobedient persons. Spies kept the rulers informed about potential troublemakers. Punishments ranged from beatings to death by torture. . . . In ancient India the magistrates condemned disobedient subjects to eighteen different kinds of torture, including beatings on the soles of the feet, suspension upside down, and burning of finger joints. . . . In China the emperor punished those who expressed incautious opinions by having them castrated in a darkened cell.

The modern notion of despotic agrobureaucratic states is based upon Marx's famous idea that many non-European societies were typified by a peculiar **Asiatic mode of production.** Marx argued that such great Asian societies as India and China were strikingly different from European feudalism. He held that the Asiatic mode of production was especially characterized by an absence of private ownership of land and by the presence of a centralized state that regulated complex irrigation systems throughout vast territories. He thought that large-scale hydraulic agriculture, necessitated by arid climates, was the technological basis for the lack of private landownership and for the centralizing and despotic character of the state.

The most prominent modern scholar to elaborate upon the notion of an Asiatic mode of production is Karl Wittfogel. Wittfogel (1957) has argued the case for a particular type of society—what he has most frequently called **Oriental despotism**—typified by state ownership of land; the presence of large-scale irrigation works necessary for hydraulic agriculture; and the existence of a cruel, despotic state claiming total power over its subjects. Like Marx, Wittfogel claims that the basis for such a despotic state is the need for hydraulic agriculture in arid climates. Wittfogel believes that the centralized powers of government were required to create and maintain a vast network of irrigation works. The larger these works became, the greater became the centralized and despotic character of the state. Wittfogel, however, has gone at least one major step beyond Marx. He has extended the idea of Oriental despotism to include non-Asian societies with small-scale waterworks (such as Hawaii) as well as non-Asian societies having no irrigation systems at all (such as Russia). In the latter case, Wittfogel has argued that once an Oriental despotism developed, it could be carried by diffusion to other societies. Ultimately Wittfogel has come to view many quite diverse societies in many parts of the world as examples of Oriental despotism.

Wittfogel ultimately carries the notion of despotic hydraulic civilizations too far. He has been sharply criticized for mixing into a common type many highly diverse societies (P. Anderson, 1974b). This criticism seems justified when Wittfogel offers as examples of hydraulic civilizations such primitive and stateless societies as aboriginal Hawaii and the horticultural Hopi Indians of the southwestern United States. He has also been criticized on the grounds that a number of societies had developed the centralizing features of government before complex irrigation systems were found within them. Yet Wittfogel's theory is not one of the origin of the state, but of the emergence of a *particular kind* of unusually despotic state (M. Harris, 1977). And in this respect Wittfogel has vigorous defenders. Marvin Harris (1977), for example, argues that the record of archaeological discoveries generally reveals step-by-step increases in the despotic power of the state that parallel respective increases in the size and complexity of irrigation works.

Although there can be no doubt that in certain respects Wittfogel has carried his theory beyond its feasible limits, the real point is whether there is a basic core of truth in Wittfogel's principal claims. Such civilizations as China and India most certainly were despotic, centralized, agrobureaucratic states. But whether or not hydraulic agriculture was the technological basis for such despotisms is still an unsettled question.

FOR FURTHER READING

Earle, Timothy (ed.). *Chiefdoms: Power, Economy, and Ideology.* New York: Cambridge University Press, 1991. An excellent collection of recent essays on various aspects of chiefdoms.

Fried, Morton H. *The Evolution of Political Society.* New York: Random House, 1967. An important work developing Fried's conception of the major stages in the evolution of political organization. Of particular significance is Fried's analysis of the emergence of social stratification and the state.

Haas, Jonathan. *The Evolution of the Prehistoric State.* New York: Columbia University Press, 1982. A discussion of archaeological evidence regarding the origin of the state with a particular focus on the opposition between functionalist and conflict theories of state origins. Comes down basically on the conflict side.

Harris, Marvin. *Cannibals and Kings: The Origins of Cultures.* New York: Random House, 1977. Several chapters of this engaging work deal with the emergence of various forms of state-organized society. Material, especially ecological, factors are given primary emphasis in Harris's theoretical analyses.

Johnson, Allen W., and Timothy Earle. *The Evolution of Human Societies.* Stanford, Calif.: Stanford University Press, 1987. A valuable treatment of general social evolution with a particular emphasis on political evolution. The theoretical perspective is materialist, with a strong role being given to population pressure.

Kirch, Patrick Vinton. *The Evolution of the Polynesian Chiefdoms.* New York: Cambridge University Press, 1984. An extremely thorough archaeological analysis of social and political evolution in Polynesia by a recognized expert. The most comprehensive evolutionary analysis of this important region of the world to date.

Mair, Lucy. *Primitive Government.* Baltimore: Penguin Books, 1964. A well-known discussion of various types of political systems among primitive societies, from bands to states. The ethnographic examples are drawn from Africa, the region in which Mair specializes.

Sahlins, Marshall. "Poor Man, Rich Man, Big Man, Chief: Political Types in Melanesia and Polynesia." *Comparative Studies in Society and History* 5:285–303, 1963. A fascinating discussion of the contrast between tribes and chiefdoms using Melanesian and Polynesian societies as case studies.

Service, Elman R. *Primitive Social Organization: An Evolutionary Perspective.* Second edition. New York: Random House, 1971. The development of Service's conception of the major stages in political evolution: band, tribe, chiefdom, and state.

Service, Elman R. *Origins of the State and Civilization.* New York: Norton, 1975. A valuable discussion of some well-known primitive states and of the rise of pristine states in both the Old and New Worlds. Contains much useful descriptive material as well as Service's functionalist explanation of the origin of pristine states.

Upham, Steadman (ed.). *The Evolution of Political Systems.* New York: Cambridge University Press, 1990. Some valuable recent essays by specialists on political evolution in its early stages. The essay by Richard Lee is especially recommended.

Wenke, Robert J. *Patterns in Prehistory: Mankind's First Three Million Years.* Third edition. New York: Oxford University Press, 1990. Extensive discussion of the origin of the state in all the major centers of pristine state formation.

Chapter
12

Capitalism, Socialism, and the Evolution of the State

This chapter continues the discussion of political evolution begun in Chapter 11. Its focus is on the development of the state since the rise of modern capitalism. The chapter begins by looking at the formation of powerful national states out of the relatively weak feudal states that prevailed in Europe before the sixteenth century. Attention then shifts to the capitalist origins of parliamentary democracy in the West. The state in modern state socialist societies is also examined, particularly in terms of why a totalitarian mode of government has accompanied the socialist organization of the economy. The last section of the chapter takes up a discussion of the collapse of Communism in the Soviet Union and Eastern Europe after 1989.

THE FORMATION OF NATIONAL STATES IN EARLY MODERN EUROPE

In his pathbreaking work *Coercion, Capital, and European States* (1990), Charles Tilly has identified three major types of state that existed in Europe during the millennium from A.D. 990 to 1990: large territorial states; small states with extremely fragmented sovereignty, such as city-states and urban federations; and national states. Tilly has shown that these states were not randomly situated in space and time; on the contrary, each type of state was found in a particular time and was associated with a particular form of economic organization.

The large territorial states were associated with regions where the landlord class was overwhelmingly dominant in the economy and where capital was weak and capitalists few. Russia, Poland, Hungary, and Brandenburg Prussia (now part of modern Germany) were states of this type. Here there was an extremely strong alliance between the landlord class and the state. City-states and urban federations, by contrast, were found where there were many powerful capitalists who had concentrated large amounts of capital. As a result, there was a strong alliance between capitalists and the state, and the state was largely devoted to serving the economic interests of capitalists. City-states and urban federations were most characteristic of what Tilly has called the inner geographical core of Europe, especially the Italian city-states and the Dutch Republic.

These two different forms of the state were found in the first half of the millennium we are considering—from A.D. 990 to 1490. After the latter date, **national states** began to form. During the first half of this millennium there was nothing resembling a national state, that is, a large centrally coordinated state highly identified with a particular nationality, what today we call, for example, England, France, or Germany. In fact, during these earlier times England, France, and Germany did not yet exist. These regions and many others were divided into hundreds of smaller states. As Tilly (1990:39) has said, there was an "enormous fragmentation of sovereignty then prevailing throughout the territory that would become Europe." There were perhaps as many as 500 states within the boundaries of Eu-

rope. In the Italian peninsula there were roughly 200 to 300 independent city-states, and in what is now southern Germany there were 69 free cities and numerous bishropics, duchies, and principalities. What a contrast with the present, where there are, or at least were before the Eastern European nationalist movements of the early 1990s, only 25 to 28 sovereign European states (Tilly, 1990).

According to Tilly, the national states of Europe formed as a result of the strong concentration of both capital and military might. The new national states beginning to evolve in the sixteenth century were massive structures compared to most of their predecessors. Huge state bureaucracies were built, and these bureaucracies were devoted to both economic and military activities. They played a large role in managing and guiding the economy and making war against other national states. Large standing armies were created to replace the relatively small private armies characteristic of feudalism. Historians have commonly referred to these new national states in their early years as forms of **absolutism** or **absolutist monarchy.** Perhaps the most important of the new monarchies were Spain, England, and France. In Spain, beginning in the late fifteenth century, the Hapsburg Dynasty came to power with the marriage of Ferdinand and Isabella. The Hapsburgs concentrated their attention on plundering the wealth of the New World through the establishment of colonies in the Americas. The treasure controlled by the Hapsburgs was greatly swelled by the precious metals shipped back to Spain from its overseas colonies. Absolutism in France was the result of a gradual development dating as far back as the fourteenth century (P. Anderson, 1974b). But it was in the late seventeenth century, under the reign of Louis XIV, that French absolutism achieved the zenith of its power. Louis XIV was the supreme symbol of absolute rule throughout all of Europe. He is reputed to have said *"l'État, c'est moi"* (I am the state). While he may never have uttered those precise words, such language clearly expresses his view of his own power (Burns, 1973). The weakest and most short-lived of all the western European absolutisms was formed in England. Absolutism began there in the late fifteenth century with the rise to power of the Tudors, who were eventually replaced by the Stuarts at the beginning of the seventeenth century. English absolutism was not to survive past the end of the seventeenth century.

Thus it was that, after the sixteenth century, a system of interlocking yet highly competitive states was created, what we today call the interstate system. This system was initially confined to Europe, but by the late twentieth century it had spread to encompass the entire world. The world is today divided into some 180 sovereign states that engage in numerous economic, political, and military interactions with one another.

THE EMERGENCE OF MODERN STATES

In the contemporary industrialized world we find two major forms of the state. In the West the state takes the form of a **parliamentary democracy.** Such a state is characteristic of the major industrial capitalist societies of Western Europe and North America, although it prevails elsewhere as well. In general, where we find highly developed capitalist societies, we find parliamentary democracy as the dominant form of polity.

It is necessary to indicate briefly what is meant here by the term *democratic,* since this concept is subject to important variations in meaning. In its literal sense, democracy means "government by and for the people." This meaning implies the absence of a ruling elite that makes governmental decisions independently of the wishes of the populace as a whole. It would be a grave distortion to restrict the concept to this literal meaning, since it is doubtful that any such form of government exists anywhere in the world above the tribal level of society. Rather, borrowing from Rueschemeyer, Stephens, and Stephens (1992), this book shall conceive of democracy as a system of government having the following four features:

- The existence of a parliamentary or congressional body having a power base separate from that of presidents or prime ministers.
- The regular, free, and fair election of government officials to office by means of universal suffrage (i.e., the entire adult population maintains the right to vote).
- Responsibility of the remaining segments of government to the parliament or congress.
- The granting of individual rights and freedoms to the mass of the population and the general honoring of these liberties.

A distinction should be drawn between *formal* and *substantive* democracy, and also of benefit will be the use of the term *restricted* democracy (Rueschemeyer, Stephens, and Stephens, 1992). A formal democracy is a government that has officially declared itself to be a democracy, but whose actions are in fact inconsistent with its declarations. Formal democracies are governments that lack genuine democratic behavior and that are democratic in name only. Throughout the Third World today, and especially in Latin America, we find many countries that fall into this category. Substantive democracies, on the other hand, are genuine democracies, those that are democratic in both name and deed. Finally, a restricted democracy is one in which the four principles mentioned above prevail, but in which there is some restriction or limitation placed on them. For example, individual rights and freedoms may be limited in various ways, or the right to vote may be restricted to certain sections of the population by such factors as gender, race, or property ownership. All of today's societies with full substantive democracies began as restricted democracies, and several of these societies have had full democracy for only a surprisingly short length of time.

The other major form of the state in modern society is a **totalitarian dictatorship.** This form of the state has prevailed in the Soviet Union and its satellites in Eastern Europe; that is, it has prevailed where state socialism is the economic form. A totalitarian dictatorship is typified by the marked absence of those principal features characteristic of parliamentary democracy. Power is massively concentrated in a central agency that directs the affairs of society, individual liberties do not exist, free elections are not held, and no opposition to the government is permitted, either ideologically or in actual practice. In short, a general state of political repression prevails.

Why have such divergent political outcomes been associated with today's major industrial societies? Why did parliamentary democracy arise in such places as England, France, and the United States, whereas totalitarianism arose in Russia and Eastern Europe?

THE ORIGIN OF WESTERN PARLIAMENTARY DEMOCRACIES

In a famous study Barrington Moore (1966) has traced the roots of the very first parliamentary democracies. The earliest originated in England during the English Civil War of the 1640s. The outcome of the war was one that increased the political significance of parliament at the expense of the king. The outcome was also, Moore points

out, a victory for the forces of capitalism—for the interests of the commercially minded members of the landed upper classes, or former landlords that had turned toward capitalist agriculture. The next two parliamentary democracies were born in the United States and France. In the United States, as hardly needs explaining to readers of this book, parliamentary democracy emerged with the American Revolution of 1776 and was further solidified with the writing of the Constitution in 1787. Another major step toward genuine democracy was made with the outcome of the Civil War in 1865. Slavery was abolished, destroying the economic and political power of the old Southern slavocracy, the closest thing in America to a feudal nobility. In France it was the French Revolution of the 1790s that led to the turn toward democracy. As Moore notes, the Revolution destroyed the entire complex of aristocratic class privilege—monarchy and landed nobility—and did so in the name of private property and the legal equality of the citizenry. The famous slogan of the French Revolution was *"Liberté! Egalité! Fraternité!":* freedom, equality, and brotherhood.

It should be noted that in none of these societies did anything like full substantive democracy exist until after the middle of the nineteenth century. The governments Moore is discussing were basically parliamentary systems that had very little real democracy. In the United States, for example, voting rights were originally extended only to free, white, adult men who owned property, and it would be many years before blacks and women gained voting privileges. Likewise, what occurred in France in the decades after the French Revolution has little resemblance to what prevails there now.

In the formation of modern parliamentary democracies the parliamentary aspect came first; it would be many years before full democracy was achieved. It was not until the middle of the nineteenth century that universal suffrage began to be installed in governments that were already parliamentary in nature. The first four governments to grant full voting rights to at least the male segment of the population were Switzerland (1848), France (1877), Norway (1898), and Denmark (1915). These four were followed fairly rapidly by four more: Sweden, Belgium, the Netherlands, and Great Britain. The earliest democracies to develop outside western Europe emerged in the United States, Canada, Australia, and New Zealand. All of these societies were settler colonies that originally hived off from Great Britain. There were several other European countries that made the transition to full democracy but that were able to maintain democratic institutions only for a brief period. These societies were Austria-Hungary, Spain, Italy, and Germany. All four have since regained democratic institutions, but it is clear that their paths to democracy were strewn with severe obstacles (Rueschemeyer, Stephens, and Stephens, 1992).

How do we explain the evolution of parliamentary democratic modes of government? It will not escape attention that democracy has evolved in the West, and especially in connection with the development of modern capitalism. Indeed, every core capitalist society in the world today is, without exception, characterized by a genuinely democratic political system. Such a striking correlation cannot possibly have occurred by accident, and a causal connection is undoubtedly present. But what kind of connection? There is a Marxian line of argument, and it goes something like this: The form of government is a result of the form of economy and the social class that dominates the economy. Capitalist societies are dominated by a bourgeoisie, and parliamentary democracy is the form of government best suited to advancing the economic interests of the bourgeoisie. This is because parliamentary democracy gives capitalists the maximum economic freedom to maneuver, both locally and globally, in their search for profits. It interferes minimally with what capitalists want to do. Monarchy suited feudalism and early capitalism, but with the advance of capitalism the restrictions of monarchy were too great, and so it had to be destroyed and replaced by the form of government that we see in capitalist societies today.

This line of argument has been advanced by Barrington Moore in his classic *Social Origins of Dictatorship and Democracy* (1966), as well as by Albert Szymanski (1978). Moore has argued that the English Civil War of the 1640s marked parliament's gaining the upper hand in government (over the king) because of the rise to dominance of capitalist farmers in England. Parliamentary democracy became dominant because parliament represented the economic interests of capitalists. Szymanski has said the following about the connection between the rise of capitalism and the emergence of parliamentary government (1978:147, 150):

> As the commercial class became the dominant class in society, it established republican and parliamentary forms as the instruments of its rule. These forms are best suited to articulate the diverse interests within this class and work out a common class will. . . .
>
> . . . Because of this immense diversity of economic and hence political interests, the commercial classes have encouraged the development of parliamentary and republican forms of government to work out compromises and a common will that benefits the maximum number of divergent interests within the class.
>
> . . . businesses must have assurances from the state that it will not arbitrarily interfere with the system of contracts and expectations. The best guarantee of moderation and lack of arbitrariness on the part of the state is the parliamentary form.

. . .

Parliamentary forms developed further and consolidated themselves earlier in England because England was always a major and eventually *the* leading commercial power in the world. The development and triumph of parliamentarianism in the British Isles must be understood as the natural result of the early development of commercial, and later industrial capitalist forms in that country.

The Marxian argument does seem to be correct for the parliamentary dimension of democracy, but it does not hold up for that dimension of democracy that many will regard as the most important—universal suffrage. This has been shown in a superb study by Dietrich Rueschemeyer, Evelyne Huber Stephens, and John D. Stephens, *Capitalist Development and Democracy* (1992). In an extraordinarily detailed comparative and historical analysis, these authors have shown that in most cases capitalists have been hostile to the political inclusion of the masses, largely because they fear the power that workers might be given through the vote. There are almost no instances, they claim, in which the bourgeoisie has favored the development of genuine democracy in Western capitalist societies. Then why is there such a striking association between capitalism and democracy? Rueschemeyer, Stephens, and Stephens's answer is that capitalism has promoted the development of a large working class, which has organized itself and pressed hard for citizenship rights, especially the right to vote. The authors show that democracy developed earliest and most fully in those capitalist societies that were in the forefront of capitalist development and thus had the largest and best-organized working classes.

Democracy was most greatly resisted, on the other hand, in those societies where capitalist development was retarded. In these societies, industrialization was slower and as a result the working class remained small and politically anemic. Moreover, such societies were ones in which the landlord class still exerted considerable economic and political power, and this class is virtually always extremely hostile to democracy. Landlords are engaged in the exploitation of peasants through their direct submission and political subordination—what Rueschemeyer, Stephens, and Stephens call *labor-repressive agriculture*—and as long as landlords remain important in the economy democracy can advance but little. The authors point to Austria-Hungary, Spain, Italy, and Germany as the four western European societies in which democracy emerged late and with great difficulty, and indeed all four societies are those in which landlords maintained considerable economic power well into the twentieth century. Of these four, Spain has been the last to develop democratic institutions, doing so only in recent years, and it has been a society whose landed upper class has been slow to disappear.

Rueschemeyer, Stephens, and Stephens argue that the route to democracy in the British settler colonies was somewhat different. These were all countries that inherited the political achievements of Great Britain, and this gave them a favorable and early start. In addition, the enormous availability of cheap land allowed for the development of a large class of independent farmers. Except for the slavery in the U.S. South, there was no system of labor-repressive agriculture. They also note that, and again with the exception of the U.S. South, the landed upper class did not control the state. Finally, they point out that eventually the working class in these societies did become strong and press for political inclusion. All of these conditions were highly favorable to the development of full substantive democracy.

Rueschemeyer, Stephens, and Stephens also look at the failure of much substantive democracy to develop in Latin America, arguing that the great economic power of landed upper classes in this region has been a severe barrier to democracy. We shall have more to say about this in a later section.

The theory of Rueschemeyer, Stephens, and Stephens is a non-Marxian materialist interpretation that seeks the explanation for the emergence and growth of democracy in the development of capitalism, but it is not because of the economic interests of capitalists that democracy advances. It advances *in spite of* the economic interests of capitalists, and because of one of the fundamental *contradictions* of capitalism: the creation of a large working class that is able to use its strength in numbers and organization to advance its own interests against the interests of capitalists. Rueschemeyer, Stephens, and Stephens's work is an enormous intellectual advance, a tremendous achievement in our understanding of the evolution of modern democracy.

THE STATE IN THE CONTEXT OF THE CAPITALIST WORLD-SYSTEM

So far our discussion has not explicitly considered the world-system context in which modern capitalist states exist. Just as problems of economic organization in the modern world cannot be understood apart from the existence of a capitalist world-economy, the nature of states throughout the world cannot be properly understood without recognition of their role in a worldwide system of political order. The world-system perspective, then, adds an important dimension to an understanding of modern capitalist states (cf. Chirot, 1977; Bollen, 1983).

The Interstate System

A fundamental characteristic of the capitalist world-system since the beginning of its existence is its politically decentralized character. The capitalist system has always consisted of a multitude of competing and conflicting states, a form of political organization known as the **interstate system** (Wallerstein, 1974a,b; Chase-Dunn, 1989a). No single state has ever succeeded in achieving such a level of political control over all of the others that a world-empire would have resulted. There have been several efforts at such world-empire creation—most notably by the Hapsburgs in the sixteenth and seventeenth centuries, by Napoleonic France in the early nineteenth century, and by Germany in the twentieth century (Chase-Dunn, 1989a)—but each of these efforts failed. It would seem that the very logic of capitalism as an economic system makes it extremely difficult for a world-empire to emerge. As soon as any state begins to follow a path that it hopes will lead to world political domination, the other states start to gang up on it so as to prevent such an occurrence. Thus capitalist economics and the interstate system go hand in hand. Indeed, had the capitalist world-system ever succumbed to world-imperial domination, it is doubtless the case that its essentially capitalist nature would have disintegrated (Wallerstein, 1974a,b; Chase-Dunn, 1989a).

Much controversy has arisen over whether the capitalist world-economy and the interstate system are fused together as part of a single reality, or whether the interstate system is a substantially autonomous reality in its own right. Contemporary Weberians see the interstate system as largely autonomous (Skocpol, 1977; Zolberg, 1981; R. Collins, 1986b). They believe that capitalism and the interstate system are intertwined, but that the world political system must be studied as a reality in its own right. States are actors in a world political order in which political and military objectives cannot be understood simply in terms of capitalist economic interests. There is no doubt a good deal of truth in this assertion, but the position adopted in this book is that the political and military objectives of capitalist states cannot seriously depart from the capitalist economic interests that form the context in which these states operate. In Christopher Chase-Dunn's (1989a) words, there is only "one logic" within the capitalist world-system, a single logic in which economics and politics are essentially inseparable. The driving force behind this logic is, of course, that of ceaseless capital accumulation.

World-System Status and the Form of the State

We must now consider the crucial question of how a nation-state's position within the capitalist world-system shapes the particular type of state structure that it evolves. Looking first at the capitalist core, we see that in this zone highly stable democratic governments are found. It was in the core, of course, that parliamentary democracy first arose, and today every core state is democratic. We have already seen why this should be the case. Parliamentary government was favored in core societies because this type of government was best suited to serve the needs of capitalists (Moore, 1966; Szymanski, 1978; Therborn, 1977). More significantly, core societies are those with the largest working classes, and the struggles of the working classes in the nineteenth and twentieth centuries for political inclusion were vital to the development of full substantive democracy (Rueschemeyer, Stephens, and Stephens, 1992). It might be added that in the late twentieth century core societies have large and highly educated middle classes that strongly expect— indeed, demand—that general rights and liberties be upheld (Chirot, 1977). By and large, the tradition of democratic government has become so strongly entrenched in the advanced capitalist societies that it has come to constitute an independent force in its own right. Democratic philosophies pervade the whole fabric of life in these societies.

In the capitalist periphery, democracy is very much the exception. Peripheral capitalist societies typically have one or another form of nondemocratic regime. Regimes based on military dictatorship, for example, are widespread throughout the peripheral capitalist world. In peripheral capitalist societies the industrial working class is small and politically weak, and the predominant ruling class consists of landlords incorporating a large peasantry into the process of labor-repressive agriculture. As Rueschemeyer, Stephens, and Stephens (1992) have pointed out, democracy is not possible in societies with such a balance of class forces. In addition, extreme forms of authoritarianism may be necessary to maintain sheer order under conditions of severe exploitation and abject human misery and suffering. Under such conditions democracy is, in a way, a "luxury" that peripheral capitalist societies (or, more accurately, their ruling classes) cannot "afford."

In the modern capitalist semiperiphery democracy is also seldom found. There have been a number of societies that have developed formal democracies, but these have had little real democratic content. Moreover, these societies have generally been vulnerable to political crises in which formal democracy has collapsed back into authoritarianism. Latin America is a region of the world that can be strongly characterized in these ways. The relative absence of substantive democracy in the semiperiphery can be explained in the same way that we explained democracy's relative absence in the periphery: landlords continue to dominate the economy, the working class remains small and politically anemic, and there is much discontent stemming from very high levels of exploitation and human misery. Because of the political weakness of the industrial working class, the limited democratic inroads that have been made have generally required a political coalition between the working class and the middle class (Rueschemeyer, Stephens, and Stephens, 1992).

But world-system theorists have also pointed to another possible reason why semiperipheral societies may have highly authoritarian states: these states can be a real advantage to semiperipheral societies seeking to improve their status in the world-economy. (South Korea since the early 1950s and Brazil from the mid-1960s to the mid-1970s are especially good illustrations of this point.) As Daniel Chirot (1977) has suggested, these types of state help to promote the economic aims of semiperipheral societies by holding down consumption in order to free more funds for investment, as well as by a variety of other economic measures. Such states may become important forces to contend with politically and militarily in the international arena, especially if they are strategically placed so as to be important to the interests of the major core powers.

In recent years there has been much talk about a "redemocratization" process occurring in parts of the periphery and semiperiphery, especially in Latin America. What has been happening is that some Latin American countries—Brazil, for example—have replaced military governments with civilian ones that have come to power through an electoral process. Some observers view this as perhaps the beginning of a movement away from authoritarian and repressive states and toward genuine democracy (Cammack, 1986)—or they at least think that the possibilities are there for the creation of a much more democratic order. Others are more pessimistic, or at least more cautious. Fernando Henrique Cardoso (1986) suggests that we should take the new democratizing trends with a grain of salt. As he says, "At the level of society, they exist and are universal; however, at the level of the state, they encounter resistance, and in some societies this resistance is successful" (1986:30). Herman and Petras

(1985) take an even stronger view, noting that military power has not been eroded despite the adoption of a formal democratic apparatus. Indeed, to the extent that it is not actually continuing, the use of state terror through "death squads" continually lurks in the background (Petras, 1987). Moreover, a sense of historical perspective also gives us reason to be more than just a little cautious about strong claims for the significance of the redemocratization trends. Throughout this century, politics in many Latin American countries has shown something of a cyclical alternation between more and less repressive regimes (Skidmore and Smith, 1989; E. Stephens, 1989). Given this pattern, the prediction of a directional trend toward democracy seems highly premature.

But even if the kind of democracy that is occurring in Latin America is more outer shell than real substance, what accounts for it? Bruce Cumings (1989) suggests both economic and political reasons. On the economic side, "Democratization was a political corollary to very strong demands for markets in developing countries to be opened up to American goods, especially service industries like banks and insurance, but also tobacco, grain and meat" (1989:30). Thus core, especially American, economic interests can create external pressures on Third World governments to adopt democratic arrangements. On the political side, the move toward democracy (or at least its outer shell) is a way of managing and defusing system-threatening discontent.

THE MODERN COMMUNIST STATE: LENINIST REGIMES

Modern totalitarian dictatorships are best represented by the Communist states in Eastern Europe: the Soviet Union and its satellites. The Communist state emerged in Russia in 1917, and shortly after the end of the Second World War East Germany, Poland, Czechoslovakia, Yugoslavia,

Hungary, Romania, and Bulgaria joined the Communist world mainly as a result of Soviet military intervention (Yugoslavia was the only one of these societies to adopt Communism by virtue of an internal revolution). Communist states arose in parts of the less-developed world at later points (see Table 8.1 in Chapter 8), but our concern here is only with the totalitarian states in industrialized or semi-industrialized countries. Of course, Communism collapsed throughout Eastern Europe in 1989 and in the Soviet Union in 1991. We shall discuss this collapse in some detail in the next section, but first we need to look at the structure of the Communist totalitarian state and consider the reasons for its existence.

A classic description of the contemporary Communist state has been provided by Milovan Djilas in his book *The New Class* (1957). Djilas is a former vice president of Yugoslavia who was expelled from the Communist party in 1954 after appealing for democratic reforms. In 1956 he was sentenced to a 10-year prison term for expressing the ideas contained in *The New Class.* Although released in 1961, he was reimprisoned in 1962 after the publication of his *Conversations with Stalin.*

As Djilas notes, "Everything happened differently in the U.S.S.R. and other Communist countries from what the leaders— even such prominent ones as Lenin, Stalin, Trotsky, and Bukharin—anticipated. They expected that the state would rapidly wither away, that democracy would be strengthened. The reverse happened" (1957:37). Djilas explains that the post-revolutionary Communist party had an extraordinarily high degree of ideological and organizational centralization. Remaining on the political scene long after victory, the party began strengthening and consolidating its power over the rest of society. It maintained an atmosphere of constant political vigilance; ideological unity within the party

was demanded and great attention was paid to rooting out both real and potential opposition. Terrorist and oppressive methods were needed to achieve these goals. The result was the creation, in Djilas's words, of "a class whose power over men is the most complete known to history"—the Communist bureaucratic elite or *nomenklatura.*

Until very recently, this bureaucratic elite had maintained an administrative monopoly over the entire social order, including complete control over virtually all economic activity; had tolerated no ideological deviation from the party line and swiftly used force to punish those who did deviate; and had tyrannized the mind by suppressing all intellectual and artistic discoveries and creations that contradicted official party dogma. It is little wonder that Djilas has called the power of this class the "most complete known to history."

The Communist states of Eastern Europe have often been referred to as "Marxist" or "Marxist-Leninist" states. While there is some justification for this, the terminology is highly misleading and should be either avoided or used with great care. The Soviet Union and its Eastern European satellites adopted some of the ideas spelled out by Marx in the middle of the nineteenth century as essential elements of socialism. They socialized the means of production, eliminated the bourgeoisie, and reorganized the economy around centralized state planning. However, in many ways they have been very un-Marxian. They produced an alternative version of capitalist commodity production, introduced the detailed division of labor into the workplace, failed utterly in abolishing alienated labor, failed to create a classless society, and failed miserably in producing a political system that Marx would have found acceptable. Marx argued that in their early stages the first socialist societies would be forced to adopt what he called the "dictatorship of the proletariat" as a form of government. This would be a highly authoritarian government that would be necessary to restore social order and facilitate the transition to full communism. However, it would be only temporary and in due time would give way to an entirely new form of political order based on the "withering away of the state." The state would cease to have any ruling or dictatorial powers and would be reduced to the role of manager and coordinator of the economy. It would be a highly democratic state, with the working class having direct input into political decision making.

Obviously nothing like this developed in the first socialist societies, but it is important to set the record straight about what Marx really said and wanted. And in setting that record straight I would urge the abandonment of the terms *Marxist* or *Marxist-Leninist* to characterize Communist states. Although these states use those terms themselves, that is no justification for keeping them. They use these terms not out of a desire for social-scientific accuracy but as part of an overarching legitimizing ideology. As Kenneth Jowitt (1978) and Daniel Chirot (1986) have suggested, it is more accurate to call them "Leninist societies" or "Leninist regimes." These regimes have the following basic features (Chirot, 1986:265):

- The Communist party claims an absolute monopoly of political power.
- All key sectors of the economy are controlled and operated by the state.
- There is a formal commitment to creating an industrially advanced and highly egalitarian society.
- The regime legitimizes itself by appeal to Marxism-Leninism as an overarching political ideology.
- The Communist party regards itself as the ultimate interpreter of scientific and political truth, and its decisions and actions are not subject to doubt.

- There is close regulation of the daily lives of individuals and sharp limitations placed on their freedom of movement, of speech, of association, and of philosophical or ideological commitment.

What accounts for the fact that the state socialist societies have deviated sharply from Marx's hope for a socialist state that was highly democratic? Why have these states been so politically repressive? In the case of Eastern Europe, of course, totalitarian regimes were originally imposed, and to a large extent maintained, from the outside by the Soviet Union (Yugoslavia being an exception). But what then is the reason for the totalitarian character of the Soviet Union itself? One type of explanation has been offered by Immanuel Wallerstein. He argues that Soviet totalitarianism resulted from the severe threat the Soviet Union experienced, both economically and militarily, from the Western capitalist world (cf. Chase-Dunn, 1982). In a genuine socialist society—the socialist world-government that will ultimately replace the capitalist world-economy—this threat will disappear, and the repressive state will then wither away (Wallerstein, 1984b).

Although this argument initially appears to contain a strong air of special pleading, it actually has much to recommend it. From about the late 1920s until sometime during the 1950s, the Soviet Union largely withdrew from the world capitalist system and followed an economic policy devoted to catching up with Western capitalism. It was precisely during this time that totalitarianism —indeed, Stalinist terrorism—was at its height (Nove, 1989). This terrorism substantially ceased after the death of Stalin in 1953, and with the shift to the new regime of Nikita Khrushchev a bit of openness first started to appear (Nove, 1989). And, indeed, it was during the Khrushchev period that the Soviet Union starting showing signs of moving back toward greater participation in the world-economy. The fact that the recent Soviet regime, with its strong orientation toward the world market, made such a dent in the totalitarian state strongly suggests that totalitarianism is a political strategy closely associated with closure to a hostile world-economy.

However, this may not be the whole story. A well-known competing explanation is at hand in the Weberian view of the state. Weber thought that socialism would necessarily lead to extensive bureaucratic centralization of power in the hands of a ruling minority. Such centralization would be necessary as a means of managing the affairs of a socialist economy. Thus, socialism would inevitably become much less democratic than capitalism. Bureaucracy encourages the concentration of power, and once such power has developed, it becomes self-perpetuating and its stranglehold is extremely difficult to break.

At this moment it is difficult to tell which of these two explanations, the world-system or the Weberian explanation, is the better one. The coming decade may provide a natural experiment that will help us make a choice. If Russia and Eastern Europe move significantly along the road to democracy, then the world-system explanation will appear to be vindicated. However, if they appear unable to go as far as it now appears they might, then Weber's argument about the self-perpetuating character of bureaucratic power will seem a potent one.

THE COLLAPSE OF COMMUNISM

As any reasonably alert citizen knows, dramatic political changes occurred in the Soviet Union and Eastern Europe in the late 1980s and early 1990s. After Mikhail Gorbachev rose to power in the Soviet Union in 1985 he inaugurated not only the economic reforms known as *perestroika*, but the polit-

ical reforms that have gone under the heading of *glasnost*. *Glasnost* was essentially devoted to greater "openness" in political and social life. The mass media were given more freedom to report events accurately and thoroughly; there was more toleration of intellectual and artistic freedom of expression; some elections of public officials were held; and some political prisoners were released. *Glasnost* cannot be understood, as some might think, as simply being some sort of philosophical or intellectual sea change based on a sudden awareness of the humanistic implications of democracy. It seems much more appropriate to think of *glasnost* as the political counterpart of *perestroika*: it is the political expression of the Soviet Union's shift toward full reintegration into the capitalist world-economy. Gorbachev and other Soviet leaders have seemed to think that the return to free-market capitalism requires a much greater degree of political openness than has previously been the case—that a more liberal economy requires a more liberal state (Kumar, 1992).

However, *glasnost* was only the beginning of the political changes. In the autumn of 1989 Poland, East Germany, Czechoslovakia, and Romania experienced major transformations in their totalitarian regimes. The political monopoly of the Communist party was broken and significant steps were taken in the direction of much greater democracy and openness. Then, in 1991, after a right-wing attempt to overthrow Gorbachev failed miserably, the Soviet Union was publicly delegitimated, the Communist party lost its monopoly of power, and Gorbachev was removed from office and replaced by his chief ultraliberal opponent, Boris Yeltsin. What happened in Eastern Europe in 1989 and the Soviet Union in 1991 was, quite literally, the collapse of Communism as a political and social movement and a state ideology. This collapse has been complicated and exacerbated by intense waves of nationalism all over the former Communist world. The Soviet Union disintegrated as a single state as a result of many of the old Soviet republics claiming political sovereignty (the largest and most politically significant of these new sovereign states is, of course, Russia). Czechoslovakia has separated into two states, Slovakia and the Czech Republic. And, in the most horrendous fashion, the state once known as Yugoslavia has been entirely broken apart, succumbing to some of the most virulent nationalist movements the modern world has ever seen.

The collapse of Communism beginning in the fall of 1989 took almost everyone—social scientists, journalists, political commentators, and ordinary citizens—by great surprise. No one expected that a political party with the level of political and military control that the Communist party has achieved could be so swiftly and decisively thrown out of power. How do we account for such a profound and surprising political transformation?

Daniel Chirot (1991) points to the economic failures of state socialism and, in particular, to what he thinks of as the moral decadence and moral rot of the whole system. In the last 20 years or so, he argues, the system simply became morally unbearable for the citizenry. People were constantly exposed to petty tyranny and endless lies and corruption, which led them in due time to turn away from the Communist state and to morally delegitimize it. The groups that were in the forefront of delegitimizing the system were the educated middle class and, especially, the intellectuals. Chirot comments that (1991:21) "the artistic and literary intellectuals who addressed their work to these middle classes helped them understand and interpret the immorality of the system, and so played a major role. They needed receptive audiences, but it was their work that undid East European communism." Chirot also goes on to note that over the past two or three decades it became increasingly obvious to the citizenry of the state socialist countries that the utopian model of Communism was not going to succeed; once that became clear, the immorality of the system, previously tolerable, became unbearable.

While Communism obviously came to be delegitimated in the 1980s, and while one can easily agree with Chirot that the whole system was full to the brim with corruption and moral rot, it is difficult to regard such phenomena as sufficient to bring about such a dramatic transformation. Chirot talks as if one of the most powerful types of political regime in human history could be brought to its knees simply by willing it. Things are not quite that simple.

An entirely different kind of explanation has been advanced by Randall Collins and David Waller (1992; R. Collins, 1986b). They view the collapse of the Soviet Union as the latest historical instance of the phenomenon that has been called *state breakdown*. This is a severe crisis within a state that leads to widespread political conflict and the collapse of a state's capacity to rule (Goldstone, 1991). Collins and Waller's theory is a kind of Weberian geopolitical argument. They root the breakdown of the Soviet state in the overextension of its "empire"—the incorporation of many different nationalities into the USSR after 1917 and again during World War II, and the military domination of its Eastern European satellites. This overextension created severe economic costs, especially in military buildup, which simply became unbearable over time. The system was ultimately unsustainable. Collins and Waller are saying, in essence, that the immediate causes of Soviet state breakdown have been economic, but that these economic problems have resulted from the geopolitics of the Soviet empire rather than from any inherent feature of state socialism as an economic system.*

Collins and Waller's argument has a good deal to recommend it, but I do not think it can be the whole story. One of the things the theory clearly does help to explain is the wave of nationalist movements that have erupted all over Eastern Europe. It also gives us one of the pieces to the puzzle of the Soviet Union's severe economic problems. However, the economic difficulties of state socialism cannot simply be laid at the door of the Soviet Union's geopolitical arrangements. For one thing, since Collins and Waller's argument applies only to the Soviet Union, it cannot explain the deep economic troubles of its Eastern European satellites. As we noted in Chapter 8, there do seem to be serious problems inherent in state socialism as an economic system. As János Kornai (1992) has shown, the intrinsic nature of state socialism turns it into a permanent shortage economy and produces economic difficulties that feed on themselves and worsen over time. State socialism was reasonably successful for a time in generating a great deal of industrialization and improvement in living standards in Eastern Europe, and especially in the Soviet Union. It has not been the abject failure that it has often been portrayed to be in recent years (Szelenyi and Szelenyi, 1992). Nevertheless, by the mid-1970s it began to stagnate, and the economic problems have only worsened since that time. As noted in Chapter 8, state socialism has not been an economy well suited to making the move into the production of mass consumer goods

and services, and thus it began to fall ever farther behind Western capitalism after about 1975. And, as also pointed out in Chapter 8, we cannot ignore the role of the surrounding capitalist world-economy in creating all kinds of pressures designed either to destroy socialism or cause it to want to relink itself with the world-capitalist system. This has been a source of economic difficulties quite apart from geopolitics.

Three additional points need to be made about state socialism's economic difficulties. First, it must be borne in mind that Russia and Eastern Europe have lagged behind the rest of Europe economically for many centuries, even long before the emergence of the capitalist world-economy in the sixteenth century (Zeman, 1991; Chirot, ed., 1989). This part of Europe has long suffered from historical economic backwardness, and thus it has had a long way to go in trying to catch up with the West. Second, it cannot be overlooked that the era during which state socialism's economic difficulties surfaced has been one of global economic downturn. This downturn has only served to exacerbate these economic problems (Frank, 1992a,b). Finally, during the 1970s and 1980s the differences in living standards between capitalist and state socialist societies became increasingly obvious to the residents of the latter as a result of portrayals of Western capitalism by the mass media (Hobsbawm, 1991a). This contributed significantly to popular discontent.

My conclusion is that the causes of the recent state breakdowns in the Soviet Union and Eastern Europe have been primarily economic. (This is not surprising, because economic difficulties have contributed in a major way to state breakdowns in earlier historical periods; see the Special Topic at the end of this chapter.) It was the economic problems created within state socialism, and from a variety of sources, that led to the economic reforms known as *perestroika* and the political reforms known as *glasnost*. But, in

---

*It might be noted in passing that the basic idea behind the Collins and Waller article was first articulated by Collins in 1980. Although Collins did not publish the article in which the idea appeared until 1986 (see R. Collins, 1986b:Chapter 8), it was written in 1980 as a specific prediction of the future breakdown of the Soviet empire. This is one of the few sociological predictions that has been right on target.

THE COLLAPSE OF COMMUNISM

essence, Gorbachev and the reformers created a monster they couldn't control. Once reforms began, they acquired a life of their own, especially as economic conditions worsened. By 1989 it had become obvious to many members of Eastern European societies that the Soviet Union was no longer willing to intervene militarily to quell popular discontent. And, with the Soviet Union's military control over Eastern Europe removed, people no longer had to fear that popular protest would be extremely dangerous, as it had been in the past. They took to the streets and demanded an end to the long-hated regimes, regimes that even many members of the Communist elites in Eastern European countries wanted to see ended. Things had been brewing under the surface for many years, and when they all came together in one explosive push it seemed as if it all simply happened overnight. But, as we have seen, these events had been developing for a long time.

Before concluding, I would like to tackle three more highly pertinent questions: Were these state breakdowns "people's revolutions," as they have often been made out to be, or something else? What are the future prospects for genuine democracy in Eastern Europe? After the collapse of Communism, what is the future of socialism?

That the collapse of Communism has been due in large part to popular rebellions by the masses has been a widespread interpretation among both intellectuals and journalists (Chirot, 1991). However, despite all the popular discontent throughout Eastern Europe, it is doubtful that this played more than a small role in bringing Communist regimes down. The movements against the Communist regimes, to the degree that they can be called revolutions at all, have not been people's revolutions but rather what some social scientists have called "revolutions from above"—revolutions initiated by one segment of the political elite against another. These revolutions have occurred both because of the shifting economic (and hence political) interests and outlook of an elite segment, and because the Soviet Union has greatly relaxed its military and political domination of Eastern Europe. A look at the recent past makes the point. In 1956 there was a people's uprising against the Hungarian Communist regime, and in 1968 an attempt at liberalization of the Communist regime in Czechoslovakia was made. Both movements were crushed powerfully and quickly by Soviet military force. What had changed between 1968 and 1989? The answer is, the Soviet elite, or at least a significant segment of it, had come to view things in an entirely new way. Indeed, it has been shown in some detail that Gorbachev and his supporters either desired or easily tolerated the regime transformations that occurred in Eastern Europe in 1989 (Kumar, 1992:345–349). Popular discontent figured in the downfall of these regimes only at the very end, when everything had basically been decided, and then more as show than as real substance. Krishan Kumar has captured the situation almost perfectly (1992:320–321):

> Is it not the case rather that it is only when the upper classes cannot maintain the old order that we find the clear evidence of the determination of the lower classes to end it? Does this not suggest that causal priority has to be assigned to the problems of the existing power structure and the existing power holders in society—that is, to the distemper at the top rather than at the bottom of society? Discontent, latent or manifest, among the lower classes can be taken as the more or less given of most stratified social orders. Regimes can be peppered with popular rebellions without succumbing to them, despite these expressions of manifest disaffection on the part of the people. This has been the case with the majority of the agrarian empires of the pre-industrial world.
>
> It is only when the ruling structures of society are in a clear state of decay or dissolution that popular discontent can express

itself in a confident way. Then we usually find spokesmen from the upper classes urging on popular feeling against the regime. Revolutionaries, often released from prison or returned from exile abroad, busy themselves with organizing the mass discontent. After the success of the revolution, the idea of a popular uprising against a hated tyranny becomes the official myth of the new regime. This conceals the fact that the old regime has died, often by its own hand, rather than been overthrown in a popular outburst of indignation.

Given the political changes thus far, what are the prospects for genuine democracy in Eastern Europe and the former Soviet Union? On the surface it might appear that the prospects are good, but a closer look reveals many problems, and indeed a number of social scientists are pessimistic, at least about the near future (Hobsbawm, 1991a; Jowitt, 1992; Steel, 1992). Ken Jowitt (1992), a leading specialist on Soviet and Eastern European politics, believes that the Leninist legacy of corrupt authoritarian regimes is likely to remain for some time and is a very inadequate foundation for constructing a genuinely democratic polity. He suggests that the postsocialist (and "post-Communist") countries in the future are more likely to resemble the Latin America of the past than the Western Europe of the present, that is, that they will experience the constant breakdown of attempts to establish democracy. The most one might hope for in the near future, he believes, is a kind of "liberal authoritarianism," or the type of highly restricted democracy that characterized the Western European states before the middle of the nineteenth century. Jowitt's pessimism is echoed by Ronald Steel (1992:170–171), and for largely the same reasons:

For all the justifiable euphoria that has greeted the downfall of Stalinist dictatorships in most of the region, the fact remains that the states of this region are, for the

most part, without a democratic tradition or modern economy. Some are quite likely to revert to previous forms of militarism and authoritarianism. All will probably be plagued by unemployment, inequality, and the consequent social unrest. The states of this traditionally unstable region have been frozen in an authoritarian mold for at least four decades, and some for many more. They have been cut off from the forces of democratization and modernization that have transformed Western Europe. They have a long history of anarchy, ethnic violence, endemic hatreds, regional warfare, and authoritarianism. The fact that they have been liberated from communist dictators does not mean that they will be pacific or democratic.

It is clear that genuine democracy will be a long time coming to Russia and the remaining postsocialist states of Eastern Europe. It took several hundred years to build substantive democracy in the West, and it is only in the twentieth century that it has become established on a wide scale. It will not take the postsocialist societies that long, for they exist in a different era and can benefit from the experiences of the West. Nevertheless, it will still take a good while to hammer out the political arrangements that are necessary to make genuine and stable democracy a reality (Rueschemeyer, Stephens, and Stephens, 1992). It certainly cannot be done overnight.

And then our final question: With the collapse of Communism in its twentieth-century form, what is the future of socialism as a political philosophy and worldwide sociopolitical movement? Is it dead once and for all, as many observers have been claiming? My answer would be a quite definite no. This *particular version* of socialism is dead, and deservedly so. However, the basic social problems that first called capitalism to task in the nineteenth century remain, and some have been added (Hobsbawm, 1991b). Despite the enormous affluence that capitalism has produced in the

West, social and economic inequalities remain, and on a world scale the inequalities among nation-states have grown to alarming proportions. And a new problem has surfaced, that of the environmental impact of capitalism. It is clear that this impact is so great that brakes have to be placed on the capitalist expansion of production, and this means establishing a form of economic planning that reins in the free market. Because of these problems, socialism is still higly relevant in the world, and it is inconceivable that it would disappear entirely. What will happen, I think, is that socialism will be rethought—indeed, that has been going on for some time on the part of Western Marxists and other intellectuals—and socialists will try to learn from the serious mistakes of the past. Too much central planning is obviously bad, and complete abandonment of the market principle produces major economic difficulties. Nonetheless, as Eric Hobsbawm (1991b:324) has remarked, "Socialists are there to remind the world that people and not production come first. That people must not be sacrified." And he continues (1991b:324–325): "The future of socialism rests on the fact that the need for it remains as great as ever, though the case for it is not the same as it was in some respects. It rests on the fact that capitalism still generates contradictions and problems it cannot solve." The challenge for socialists, as I see it, is not to turn against socialism, but to create a better form of socialism that can be combined with the best features of capitalism to produce a form of economic life truly superior to what the world has witnessed thus far.*

SUMMARY

1. In the period A.D. 990–1490 Europe contained many more sovereign states than it does now, perhaps as many as 500. After A.D. 1490 large, highly bureaucratic national states began to form, and the number of European states was reduced to about 25 to 28 by the late twentieth century. These new national states combined highly concentrated amounts of capital and military power. Once the national state formed, it was so militarily successful that other states were compelled to imitate it or suffer extinction.

2. The new national states of early modern Europe originally took the form of absolute monarchy, but monarchy gave way in due time to parliamentary government. Parliamentary governments are those in which power resides in legislative bodies as much as or more than in monarchs. Parliamentary government emergcd because it was the form of government best suited to preserve and promote the economic interests of capitalists.

3. Early parliamentary governments eventually became democratic, beginning to make the transition to full democracy after the middle of the nineteenth century. Democratic governments contain four essential features: a congressional or parliamentary body as a significant power base, election of government officials to office by the entire adult population, responsibility of other segments of government to the legislative body, and the granting of individual rights and freedoms to the population at large.

4. The rise of democracy is often interpreted in idealist terms as the intellectual working out of a political philosophy, but it is more accurately seen as part and parcel of the expansion of capitalism. Although capitalists have favored parliamentary government, they have generally been hostile to mass suffrage because of their fear of the power this would give the working class. Full substantive democracy has emerged in those societies with the greatest degree of industrial capitalism and the largest and best-organized working classes. It was the political struggles of these classes in the advanced capitalist countries that brought about democracy. The social class most hostile to democracy has been landlords, and democracy has been most successfully resisted in those societies where industrialization has been limited and landlords still dominate the economy.

*An excellent example of current socialist rethinking is Roemer (1994).

5. The world-system perspective on modern states has many insights to offer. There is an interstate system of competing and conflicting nation-states that is deeply intertwined with the capitalist world-economy. Within this interstate system, core states generally have parliamentary democracies. Peripheral states seldom enjoy democracy. The absence of democracy in peripheral societies is understandable given their small and politically weak working classes and their high levels of social and economic inequality. Semiperipheral societies, also seldom democratic, often develop authoritarian states in order to improve their status in the world-system.

6. The Soviet Union and its Eastern European state socialist satellites have been characterized by totalitarian governments, or what are best called Leninist regimes. In these regimes, until recently at least, the Communist party monopolized political power and regarded itself as the sole arbiter of truth, the regime legitimized itself by reference to Marxism-Leninism as a political ideology, and individuals enjoyed few freedoms and had their lives closely regulated by the state.

7. World-system theory suggests that totalitarianism has been associated with an economic policy of closure to the world-economy. It has been produced by a need for socialist states to protect themselves economically and militarily from the hostile world-capitalist system. An alternative interpretation, based on Weber, holds that state socialism leads naturally to a massive enlargement of the functions of the state, and thus to an enormous concentration of power in the hands of a state bureaucracy. Once in existence, this bureaucracy may be difficult to dislodge. Both of these explanations may contain significant insights.

8. After the mid-1980s the Soviet Union established a policy devoted to political liberalization that, in conjunction with severe and increasing economic stagnation throughout the state socialist world since 1975, ultimately led to the collapse of Communist regimes. This occurred in 1989 in Eastern Europe and 1991 in the Soviet Union. Various explanations of this dramatic political transformation have been given: unbearable moral corruption leading to massive popular discontent, the economic costs associated with the political overextension of the Soviet empire throughout Eastern Europe and Asia, and massive economic difficulties. It is likely that economic difficulties have been paramount in the collapse of Communist regimes. The state breakdowns in the Soviet Union and Eastern Europe were primarily "revolutions from above" rather than "people's revolutions."

9. The prospects for the establishment of genuine democracy in the postsocialist societies are not particularly good. The authoritarian legacy of Leninist regimes does not provide a solid base on which to build, and it will take some time to create a political apparatus that will sustain stable democracy. Reversions to militarism and authoritarianism on the part of some postsocialist states are likely in the near future.

10. Many Western social scientists and other intellectuals claim that socialism as a political ideology is dead once and for all. However, this judgment is likely very premature. The collapse of one particular version of socialism is not the same as the loss of faith in some sort of highly modified socialist philosophy. Socialist thinking is likely to be here for some time to come, because many of the serious problems of capitalism have not been solved and new ones are emerging.

SPECIAL TOPIC: REVOLUTIONS AND STATE BREAKDOWNS IN HISTORICAL EUROPE AND THE THIRD WORLD

An extremely important political phenomenon in recent centuries is that of **revolution.** Theda Skocpol (1979:4), one of the foremost sociological students of revolutions, distinguishes between social and political revolutions and defines social revolutions as "rapid, basic transformations of a society's state and class structures [that are] accompanied and in part carried through by class-based revolts from below." Political revolutions differ from social revolutions in that they involve only the transformation of state structures, there being no corresponding transformation of class or social structures.

Jack Goldstone, another major student of revolutions, has used the alternative term **state breakdown.** For him, a state breakdown occurs when a society's government undergoes a crisis so severe that there is a serious crippling of its capacity to govern. Only some state breakdowns become actual revolutions. Many state breakdowns lead to only limited political changes, ones that are not dramatic enough to warrant the label revolution.

What then are some of history's more prominent and interesting examples of revolutions and other sociopolitically conflictive phenomena? Heading the list are the so-called great revolutions: the French Revolution of 1789; the Bolshevik Revolution of 1917, which transformed Russia into the Soviet Union; and the Chinese Revolution that began in 1911 and culminated in 1949. To these may be added other social revolutions in the Third World, such as the Cuban Revolution in 1959, the Islamic Revolution in Iran in 1979, and the Nicaraguan Revolution of the same year.

How do we explain social revolutions? Several major theories of revolution have been developed, the most famous of which is undoubtedly the Marxian theory. Marx worked out a famous conception of revolution that emphasized the socioeconomic order and the struggle between classes. As everyone knows, Marx predicted the ultimate collapse of capitalism and its replacement by socialism, and he thought that this great transformation would most likely take place by revolutionary means. It all had to do with the logic of capitalism and the capitalist class struggle. As capitalism advanced, Marx said, the working class would expand in size. The capitalist class, through the gradual concentration of capital, would actually grow smaller, and ultimately a huge working class would confront a tiny bourgeoisie. There would also occur an economic polarization between the two classes, which would intensify the conflict between them. Moreover, with the advance of capitalism the working class would come to be better organized and at some point would rise up and overthrow the capitalist class by violence. Marx thought that the first revolution against capitalism would most likely occur in England, because it was at the time the world's most industrially advanced society; but this revolution also had a chance of occurring in other advanced capitalist societies.

Unfortunately for Marxists, this theory has been almost completely falsified by the history of the last century. No advanced capitalist society has ever even remotely experienced a socialist revolution of any sort; on the contrary, such revolutions have occurred in overwhelmingly agrarian societies, first in Russia in 1917, and then later in China and Cuba and other parts of the Third World. And it has been the peasantry, far more than the working class, that has been the social class most central to revolutionary change. Why has the Marxian theory failed so badly? Basically, because it systematically omits one major type of social factor, the political factor, in its overwhelming focus on the economy and class relations.

In her *States and Social Revolutions* (1979), Theda Skocpol has formulated one of the most impressive theories of revolution ever developed, and one that gives strong emphasis to the role of politics. Skocpol argues that a good theory of revolutions must focus heavily on the *international context* in which societies and governments are situated. For the past several hundred years there has existed a capitalist world-economy and an international system of states, and both of these, Skocpol insists, have contributed greatly to revolutionary situations and outcomes. Skocpol (1979:23) comments that "developments within the international states system as such—especially defeats in wars or threats of invasion and struggles over colonial controls—have directly contributed to virtually all outbreaks of revolutionary crisis."

Skocpol's theory is essentially this: The great revolutions resulted from a coming together of two overpowering circumstances, *a massive crisis within the state machineries* of France, Russia, and China, and *widespread rebellion and revolt on the part of the lower classes,* especially the peasantry. State crises resulted both from severe international political and military pressures and economic difficulties that produced widespread dissatisfaction for various social groups. In all three societies governments were unable to implement needed reforms or to promote sufficiently rapid economic development to be able to deal with the military threats that they encountered. Skocpol pays particular attention to the impact of war on the functioning of states. World War I, she holds, was critical to the revolutionary outcome that we know as the Bolshevik Revolution. The involvement of Russia in World War I, when combined with widespread economic dissatisfactions, produced a situation of economic and political chaos.

The other key ingredient in the great revolutions was *peasant revolt.* As Skocpol says, neither political crises nor peasant revolt alone could have brought about social revolution; it was the combination of the two that was necessary. Although various socioeconomic groups were a part of the total insurrectionary picture, Skocpol sees peasant revolt as absolutely critical. The peasantry was the largest social class, and other classes had insufficient potential to bring about a revolutionary outcome.

Skocpol's theory is most assuredly a very important advance. At the time it was published it was undoubtedly the most important theory of revolutions ever developed. But theoretical work on the part of others has added to the picture developed by Skocpol, and in some respects has contradicted her argument. One of the most important recent works on revolution has been produced by one of Skocpol's own students, Jack Goldstone, whose theory is really a more general theory of state breakdowns.

Goldstone argues that state breakdowns have been cyclical phenomena that have occurred over the past several hundred years in two major waves, one peaking in the mid-seventeenth century and the other peaking in the mid-nineteenth century. These waves occurred in both Europe and Asia, and between them there was approximately a century of relative political stability. Most of Goldstone's *Revolution and Rebellion in the Early Modern World* (1991) is devoted to the analysis of four cases of state breakdown: the English Revolution of the mid-seventeenth century, the French Revolution of the last decade of the eighteenth century, the Anatolian rebellions in the Ottoman Empire (which peaked in the mid-seventeenth century), and the fall of the Ming Dynasty in China in approximately 1644.

Goldstone's model of state breakdown is what he calls a *demographic/structural* model. It specifically considers the impact of population growth on various social groups so as to lead to widespread social and economic dissatisfaction and a state crisis. Goldstone notes that the large agrarian states of early modern Europe and Asia had considerable difficulty dealing with the effects of population growth. When population grew a whole series of negative consequences ensued. For one thing, prices increased because of increased demand. This had a negative impact on the tax system. As a result, with price inflation tax revenues lagged behind prices, and this gave states no option but to increase taxes. Since it was difficult to increase taxes to the extent of being able to maintain a stable fiscal situation, state fiscal crisis normally ensued, and it was intensified if military demands on the state purse increased, as they frequently did. In addition to all this, the growth of population had a negative impact on social and economic elites; because it increased the number of competitors for elite positions, an increasing number of aspirants for these positions would have their aims frustrated. Finally, the growth of population drove down wages. With higher prices and lower wages, both rural and urban misery increased, precipitating food riots and wage protests. The result of this combination of unfortunate circumstances was a widespread state crisis and, ultimately, a state breakdown.

Goldstone argues that the cyclical nature of state breakdowns in early modern Europe and Asia corresponded closely to the swings of population, and that these swings were largely determined by changes in mortality. Population grew when mortality fell, and stabilized or declined when mortality increased. What then caused the changes in mortality? Goldstone's answer is changes in the incidence of virulent disease.

Goldstone's theory is an impressive and fascinating one, and its demographic emphasis fits well with the emphasis we have given to population pressure in explaining important evolutionary developments. But is it right? Quite frankly, it is too early to tell. More research over a period of years will be needed before we can answer more definitively. But there is no doubt that this theory is as impressive and compelling as any theory of revolution we have.

But what about contemporary revolutions in the Third World? One of the most important works in this area is Timothy Wickham-Crowley's *Guerrillas and Revolution in Latin America*, published in 1992. Wickham-Crowley's analysis focuses on guerrilla movements in Latin America in the second half of the twentieth century. As Wickham-Crowley notes, peasant support of guerrilla movements is essential, but guerrillas need more than just peasant support to be successful. They also need *military strength*. But even when guerrillas are strongly supported by peasants, and even when they are also militarily strong, another factor is crucial: the nature of the state, especially *the extent of its vulnerability to revolutionary movements*. It is with respect to this last factor that Wickham-Crowley makes his most distinctive contribution to a theory of Third World revolutions.

As Wickham-Crowley shows, in the second half of the twentieth century successful revolutions have occurred in only two Latin American countries: Cuba in 1959 and Nicaragua in 1979. What is it that made these societies and their states distinctive? Let us look at Cuba first. Wickham-Crowley identifies several distinctive features of Cuban society and the Cuban state that made Cuba especially vulnerable to the actions of a revolutionary movement, and of these features three stand out:

- The Cuban middle and upper classes were relatively weak politically; this means that they had little capacity to influence the functioning of the state, from which they could thus be easily disaffected.
- The revolutionary movement that overthrew Batista in 1959 was a large-scale coalition. This coalition drew heavily on the peasantry, but it also included the middle class, the working class, and even portions of the upper class. In effect, virtually all of Cuban society was opposed to the Batista regime and wanted it overthrown; the third factor tells why.
- Most important of all, Cuba had a very distinctive type of state that has been called a *patrimonial praetorian regime*, a *neopatrimonial regime*, or, in Wickham-Crowley's words, a *mafiacracy*. This is a type of regime in which a highly corrupt ruler turns the state into his own personal property; he personally controls the military, suppresses political parties, and dispenses rewards and favors (and punishments) in a highly personalized manner. In short, the ruler dictatorially controls all of the state and society and bends them to his own personal whims. It is precisely this type of regime, Wickham-Crowley argues, that is most vulnerable to overthrow because the personal dictator eventually ends up alienating virtually all major social groups. This is what makes a broad revolutionary coalition—a coalition that includes groups that normally have strongly opposing interests—possible.

It turns out that a description of Nicaraguan state and society is strikingly similar to the one for Cuba. It had a state that was dominated by a dictator (Somoza) who engaged in massive corruption, personal control of the military, and violent attacks on his political opponents. In short, Nicaragua also had a neopatrimonial state or mafiacracy, and this state, as in Cuba, was overthrown by a large-scale revolutionary coalition.

Successful revolution in the Third World is obviously not easy, given its rarity. Nevertheless, movements in Latin American countries that lacked neopatrimonial regimes created a lot of worry, and sometimes came close to revolution, at least if they were militarily strong and had peasant support. Guerilla movements that failed to attract peasants, and that were not militarily strong, got nowhere. But the overall message is quite clear: so long as the state has enough support in the larger society, and so long as it does not become highly vulnerable to a large-scale revolutionary coalition, it will not become the victim of social revolution.

FOR FURTHER READING

Anderson, Perry. *Lineages of the Absolutist State.* London: New Left Books, 1974. A well-known attempt at a Marxian explanation of the rise of the absolute monarchies in Europe from the late fifteenth century on.

Blackburn, Robin (ed.). *After the Fall: The Failure of Communism and the Future of Socialism.* London: Verso, 1991. A good collection of recent essays, mostly by Marxists, on the collapse of Communism.

Carnoy, Martin. *The State and Political Theory.* Princeton, N.J.: Princeton University Press, 1984. An unsurpassed overview of theories of the modern state, with a particular stress on classical and contemporary Marxian theories.

Domhoff, G. William. *The Power Elite and the State: How Policy Is Made in America.* Hawthorne, N.Y.: Aldine de Gruyter, 1990. A valuable assessment of the main bones of contention among several theories of the locus of power in modern American society. Written by one of the leading figures in the debates about the American power structure.

Evans, Peter B., Dietrich Rueschemeyer, and Theda Skocpol (eds.). *Bringing the State Back In.* New York: Cambridge University Press, 1985. A fine collection of articles calling for more attention to the state as an autonomous social force rather than simply an agent of the capitalist class.

Giddens, Anthony. *The Nation-State and Violence.* Berkeley: University of California Press, 1985. A major work on the state and its long-term historical development.

Goldstone, Jack A. *Revolution and Rebellion in the Early Modern World.* Berkeley: University of California Press, 1991. A superb book, winner of a coveted prize, presenting a general theory of state breakdowns in agrarian empires and early modern societies over the past few centuries.

Lapidus, Gail W. (ed.). *The New Russia: Troubled Transformation.* Boulder, Colo.: Westview Press, 1995. A collection of insightful essays on the transition from the Soviet Union to Russia.

Mann, Michael. *The Sources of Social Power. Volume 1: A History of Power from the Beginning to A.D. 1760.* Cambridge: Cambridge University Press, 1986. Several chapters of this well-known and widely read book treat the development of the modern state from a basically Weberian perspective.

Rueschemeyer, Dietrich, Evelyne Huber Stephens, and John D. Stephens. *Capitalist Development and Democracy.* Chicago: University of Chicago Press, 1992. Easily the definitive treatment of the origin and evolution of democracy in Western Europe, North America, the Caribbean, and Latin America. Far outdistances previous contributions. Mandatory reading for the student of the rise of modern democratic governments.

Skocpol, Theda. *States and Social Revolutions: A Comparative Analysis of France, Russia, and China.* New York: Cambridge University Press, 1979. One of the best sociological analyses of the great historical revolutions ever written.

Szymanski, Albert. *The Capitalist State and the Politics of Class.* Cambridge, Mass.: Winthrop, 1978. An excellent general treatment from a Marxian perspective of the role of the state in modern capitalism.

Tilly, Charles. *Coercion, Capital, and European States, A.D. 990–1990.* Oxford: Basil Blackwell, 1990. An outstanding and superbly written analysis of the evolution of European states over the last millennium. No one is more qualified than Tilly to tackle this huge topic.

Wickham-Crowley, Timothy P. *Guerrillas and Revolution in Latin America.* Princton, N.J.: Princeton University Press, 1992. A superb treatment of the nature and causes of revolutions in Latin America in the second half of the twentieth century.

Comparative Patterns of Racial and Ethnic Stratification

The concepts of **race** and **ethnic group** have long been an important part of the terminological repertoire of sociologists and other social scientists. This is so because for at least the past several hundred years race and ethnicity have been factors extremely basic to the construction of numerous systems of stratification. This chapter discusses the various forms of stratified social life that have been erected along the lines of racial and ethnic distinctions. The discussion turns on how these systems originated and underwent various transformations, and special attention will be given to the underlying causes of such origins and transformations.

Until recently, the study of the relations between racial and ethnic groups suffered from a number of very serious impediments. Older approaches tended to be ahistorical and to lack any comparative foundation; most studies focused on contemporary American society. Great emphasis was given to the study of prejudice—an attitude of ill will of the members of one racial or ethnic group toward another—and this phenomenon was seen as being largely the result of certain personality configurations. Larger social forces, especially economic ones, were either excluded from consideration or treated as being of secondary significance. Racial and ethnic antagonism was frequently seen as the result of irrational or perverse psychological motives or needs on the part

of some individuals; the "cure" for this antagonism was seen to lie in the removal of
such unhealthy motives and needs. This
kind of approach was bound to run into an
intellectual dead end, and it did.

Sometime during the late 1960s, many
social scientists began to see the limitations
of these older approaches. Many stopped
talking about "prejudiced personalities" and
started talking about the larger social and
economic forces that generated racial and
ethnic divisions and inequalities and made
some people prejudiced in the first place. In
addition, interest in the study of slavery,
both in the U.S. South and elsewhere, was
greatly revived. Gradually the attention of
many social scientists has shifted toward a
more historical and comparative approach
in which racial and ethnic stratification is
simply seen as being a special case of the
more general phenomenon of stratified social life (van den Berghe, 1967). Much attention is now being given to how racial and
ethnic stratification results from large-scale
economic forces generating opposition between groups, and how these forces have
served to maintain or destroy certain patterns of racial and ethnic stratification. This
more recent kind of approach has already
yielded much greater insights than did the
older ones.

THE CONCEPTS OF RACE
AND ETHNICITY

The concept of race has for many years been
a rather difficult one for social scientists to
define. For a long time biological anthropologists approached this concept by conceiving it in strictly biological terms, races
being viewed as groups of persons separated
by constellations of distinctive genetic characteristics. Various classifications of racial
"stocks" and "substocks" were proposed.
But these anthropologists could not agree
among themselves on the number of stocks

and substocks that were to be identified, nor
could they agree on precisely how one stock
or substock was to be distinguished from
another (van den Berghe, 1967). In time it
came to be recognized that there was no
such thing as a distinct or "pure" race, and
that racial distinctions represented an almost infinite range of gradations and variations. Because of these problems, biological
anthropologists have recently restricted the
term *race* to refer to a "breeding population," a group of persons sharing a common
genetic heritage and within which the rate
of inbreeding is very high. Since breeding
populations frequently overlap in complex
ways, constellations of genetic traits form a
continuous series of small gradations rather
than a set of discrete, clear-cut groups.

Racial groups, however, represent
more than simply physically distinguishable categories of persons. They also represent important *social* categories, groups of
persons who identify themselves, and are
generally identified by others, as distinctive
and as occupying a particular social location
with regard to other groups. An excellent illustration of this point is afforded by the
contrasting systems of racial classification
of the United States and Brazil. Historically,
the United States has recognized only two
racial groups (whites and blacks) and has
classified persons into one group or the
other according to what Marvin Harris
(1964) has called the **rule of hypo-descent.**
According to this rule, any person known to
have any black ancestry, no matter how remote, is classified as black. The United
States has not recognized any intermediate
categories of racial identity. By contrast,
Brazil has never applied such a rigid descent
rule to the classification of racial identity.
In Brazil, as Harris points out (1964:57–58):

> Over a dozen racial categories may be recog-
> nized in conformity with the combinations
> of hair color, hair texture, eye color and skin
> color which actually occur. These types

grade into each other like the colors of the spectrum and no one category stands significantly isolated from all the rest. . . .

It was found, in addition, that a given Brazilian might be called by as many as thirteen different terms by other members of his community. These terms are spread out across practically the entire spectrum of theoretical racial types. A further consequence of the absence of a descent rule is that Brazilians apparently not only disagree about the racial identity of specific individuals, but they also seem to be in disagreement about the abstract meaning of the racial terms as defined by words and phrases.

Harris goes on to note that the Brazilian system makes it possible for people to change their racial identity in their lifetime. This change can be accomplished through the achievement of economic success or the attainment of advanced education. Brazilians have a saying that "money whitens the skin," which means that the greater the wealth a person acquires, the lighter will be the racial category to which he or she is assigned.

If we combine the sociologist's notion of race as involving social definitions with the biological anthropologist's conception of race as a biological category, we end up with essentially the following definition: a race is *a group or category of persons who identify themselves, and are identified by others, as having a socially meaningful distinctiveness that rests on physical or biological criteria.*

In contrast to the term *race*, the term *ethnic group* shall be used to refer to a *social group or category whose distinctiveness rests on cultural, rather than biological, criteria.* In reality, racial and ethnic groups often overlap: a group whose distinctiveness rests primarily on biological criteria may also have a cultural distinctiveness. Despite their frequent intermingling in reality, however, the concepts of race and ethnicity are analytically separate. Usage of the

terms in this chapter reflects this analytical distinction.

TWO TYPES OF RACE AND ETHNIC RELATIONS

A useful typology presenting two fundamentally different forms of racial and ethnic stratification has been developed by Pierre van den Berghe (1967) (Table 13.1). What is most useful about this typology is that it relates a society's particular form of racial/ethnic stratification to its material infrastructure and to the broader aspects of its social structure. In addition, as van den Berghe has stressed, the typology permits systematic comparative study of those societies that have been prominently stratified along racial and ethnic lines. It also allows an examination of the historical evolution of racial/ethnic stratification patterns and of the forces directing such evolutionary changes. The typology will therefore serve as the conceptual foundation for much of what follows in the rest of the chapter.

Van den Berghe distinguishes between **paternalistic** and **competitive race relations.** Paternalistic race relations are characteristic of complex preindustrial societies based on large-scale agricultural production, particularly plantation agriculture. The most prominent societies resting on paternalistic race relations are the preabolition regimes of Brazil, the southern United States, and South Africa. Under a paternalistic system, the society is rigidly stratified into racial groups having a "castelike" nature, and many social scientists have referred to these racially distinctive groups as "castes." There exists a tremendous gulf between these castes in status, wealth, occupation, education, health, and general lifestyle patterns. No mobility between racial castes is allowed. Race becomes the major criterion determining the division of labor. A highly developed ideology of racial superiority and inferiority exists.

Table 13.1 VAN DEN BERGHE'S PATERNALISTIC AND COMPETITIVE TYPES OF RACE RELATIONS

	Paternalistic	Competitive
Factors Determining the Prevailing Type of Race Relations		
1. Economy	Nonmanufacturing, agricultural, pastoral, handicraft. Mercantile capitalism. Plantation economy.	Typically manufacturing, but not necessarily so. Large-scale industrial capitalism.
2. Division of labor	Simple ("primitive") or intermediate (as in preindustrial large-scale societies). Division of labor along racial lines. Wide income gap between racial groups.	Complex (manufacturing) according to "rational" universalistic criteria. Narrow gap in wages, no longer strictly racial.
3. Mobility	Little mobility either vertically or horizontally (slaves, servants, or serfs "attached" in space).	Much mobility both vertical and horizontal (required by industrial economy).
4. Social stratification	Caste system with horizontal color bar. Aristocracy versus servile caste with wide gap in living standards (as indexed by income, education, death and birth rates). Homogeneous upper caste.	Caste system but with tendency for color bar to "tilt" to vertical position. Complex stratification into classes within castes. Narrower gaps between castes and greater range within castes.
5. Numerical ratio	Dominant group a small minority.	Dominant group a majority.
6. Value conflict	Integrated value system. No ideological conflict.	Conflict, at least in Western "Christian," "democratic," "liberal" type of society.
Aspects or Components of the Racial Situation		
1. Race relations	Accommodation. Everyone "in his place" and "knows it." Paternalism. Benevolent despotism.	Antagonism. Suspicion, hatred. Competitiveness (real or imaginary).
2. Roles and statuses	Sharply defined roles and statuses based on ascription (birth). Unequal status unthreatened.	Ill defined and based on achievement. Unequal status threatened.
3. Etiquette	Elaborate and definite.	Simple and indefinite.
4. Forms of aggression	Generally from lower caste: slave rebellions; nationalistic, revivalistic, or messianistic movements. Not directly racial.	Both from upper and lower caste. More frequent and directly racial: riots, lynchings, pogroms; passive resistance, sabotage, organized mass protests.
5. Miscegenation (interbreeding)	Condoned and frequent between upper-caste males and lower-caste females. Institutionalized concubinage.	Severely condemned and infrequent.
6. Segregation	Little of it. Status gap allows close but unequal contact.	Much of it. Narrowing of status gap makes for increase of spatial gap.

(continued)

Table 13.1   (Continued)

	Paternalistic	Competitive
7. Psychological syndrome	Internalized subservient status. No personality "need" for prejudice. "Pseudotolerance."	"Need" for prejudice. Linked with sexuality, sadism, frustration. Scapegoating.
8. Stereotypes of lower caste	Childish, immature, exuberant, uninhibited, lazy, impulsive, fun-loving, good humored. Inferior but lovable.	Aggressive, uppity, insolent, oversexed, dirty. Inferior, despicable and dangerous.
9. Intensity of prejudice	Fairly constant.	Variable and sensitive to provocative situations.

Source: Pierre L. van den Berghe, *Race and Racism: A Comparative Perspective.* New York: Wiley, 1967, pp. 31–32; slightly modified.

The dominant group views itself as inherently superior, either on biological or cultural grounds, or both, to the subordinate group. Members of the subordinate group are seen as childish, immature, irresponsible, fun-loving, and happy-go-lucky—as inherently inferior, but nevertheless as lovable when "in their place." The system is therefore construed along the lines of a strict master-servant model. The superordinate group dominates the economy (it owns the bulk of the land, labor, and other natural resources), and this economic dominance gives it firm control over the political system and the law. Thus, as van den Berghe is quick to point out, paternalistic race relations are extreme examples of the exploitation of, and the tyranny over, the many by the few. Corresponding to this master-servant system is a mode of social life marked by low physical distance (i.e., little physical segregation), but high social distance. An elaborate system of social etiquette governs the interaction between dominant and subordinate groups. Since subordinate group members are highly structured inferiors, they may be permitted close physical contact with members of the dominant group without this serving as a threat to the status of dominant group members.

The competitive type of race relations is in many ways the polar opposite of the paternalistic type. It is characteristic of industrial societies with a complex division of labor and with a system of production based on manufacturing. The dominant racial group may be either a numerical majority or a substantial minority. The contemporary United States, South Africa, and Britain are among the more prominent societies displaying competitive race relations. Under this type of racial stratification system, class differences become more important than differences based on racial caste distinctions, and race is no longer the primary criterion for the recruitment of persons to occupational positions. The political system is often what van den Berghe calls a **Herrenvolk democracy,** that is, one in which parliamentary democracy is limited in its application to the dominant racial group. The master-servant model collapses and is replaced by extreme competition between the subordinate racial group and the working class of the dominant group. Physical segregation becomes extensive in order to preserve the dominant group's privileged position. The dominant group's image of the subordinate group is transformed from one

of irresponsible and childish yet lovable inferiors to one of aggressive, "uppity," dis-
honest competitors for scarce resources and
challengers to the status quo. The conde-
scending benevolence characteristic of paternalistic race relations largely disappears
and is replaced by hostility and outright hatred by many members of the dominant
group for the subordinate group. Conflict
between the dominant and subordinate
groups becomes a frequent occurrence, taking the form of lynchings, race riots, and
mass movements of political opposition.
What is most characteristic of competitive
race relations is that many members of the
dominant racial group are thrown into open
competition with members of the subordinate group in the search for jobs (hence
the name "competitive"). This contrasts
markedly with the paternalistic situation
where the two groups are rigidly separated
in the occupational structure, where one
group is overwhelmingly the structured inferior of the other, and where the dominant
group holds the other down through a
benevolent despotism (hence the name "paternalistic").

   All of the systems of plantation slavery
that arose in the New World with the advent of modern capitalism have exhibited to
one extent or another versions of the paternalistic type of race relations. Furthermore,
several of these paternalistic systems
evolved into competitive systems with abolition and increasing industrialization.

SYSTEMS OF PLANTATION SLAVERY IN THE NEW WORLD

The Capitalist World-Economy and the Origins of New World Slavery

Slavery is *a mode of labor organization and
control in which some people are legally
owned for life as a form of human property,*
*are compelled to work by those who own
them, and are generally deprived of all or
most political liberties or rights.* Slavery of
one sort or another has existed in many different societies throughout history. It was,
for example, the principal form of labor organization in ancient Greece and Rome.
There, however, slavery was unconnected
with race. The kind of slavery we are concerned with here, on the other hand, was intimately connected with race, for nearly all
the slaves were black men and women
drawn from Africa. We may call this kind of
slavery *plantation slavery,* for the slaves
were put to work on large-scale plantations
producing cash crops for a world economic
market.

   It is no accident that systems of plantation slavery arose in conjunction with
the early development of the capitalist
world-economy. As Immanuel Wallerstein
(1974a:88) has pointed out, slavery "is pre-
eminently a capitalist institution, geared to
the early preindustrial stages of a capitalist
world-economy." New World plantation
slavery arose as a fundamental means of
labor organization oriented to the production of goods that could be sold in a world
economic market for profit. Slavery was
fundamentally an economic institution
from the very beginning. While it was also a
social and political institution—a whole
way of life for both masters and slaves—it
was originally and primarily brought into
existence for economic reasons. But why
was slavery basic to certain sectors of the
early capitalist economy? Why was it not
some other system of labor, such as serfdom
or wage labor? Wallerstein (1974a) argues
that slavery was a highly profitable system
of labor control under conditions of large-
scale plantation agriculture in which major
cash crops were being produced for an
extensive market. Hence slavery was a rational labor choice for early capitalist entrepreneurs who were pursuing large-scale

agricultural production for profit in faraway lands.

Major systems of plantation slavery developed in several areas of the New World. It is currently estimated that approximately 9.5 million Africans were imported as slaves into the New World via the Atlantic slave trade (Fogel and Engerman, 1974). The biggest consumer in the slave trade was Brazil, which took 38 percent of the total. The British Caribbean, the French Caribbean, and Spanish America took 17 percent each, and the United States and the Dutch, Danish, and Swedish Caribbean took another 6 percent each (Fogel and Engerman, 1974).

Many European nations were involved in the slave trade and the establishment of plantation societies in the New World. Portugal established Brazil as a major slave society. Spain established slavery in Mexico and various parts of South America and, after a lapse, established a substantial slave society in Cuba in the nineteenth century. England had the British West Indies (mainly Barbados and Jamaica) and, of course, the American colonies until their independence. France had the French West Indies, consisting mainly of St. Domingue (now Haiti) and Martinique. Even Holland and Denmark were involved, with the Dutch establishing a small slave society in Dutch Guiana (now Surinam) and the Danes another on the island of St. Croix.

By far the biggest cash crop produced by the New World slave systems was sugar, an item greatly in demand by Europeans for sweetening their coffee. Brazil, the British and French West Indies, and Cuba were the biggest producers of sugar. A number of other products were generated for the market by plantation slavery, among them coffee, cocoa, tobacco, indigo, hemp, and rice (Fogel and Engerman, 1974). Cotton, of course, was the major product of slavery in the United States, but its production did not become significant until after the beginning of the nineteenth century.

It should also be mentioned that not all slaves were put to work in plantation agriculture; in addition to those who worked as household servants, many were used in mining operations, particularly in Spanish America and Brazil.

Slavery in the U.S. South

Although slavery began in the U.S. South toward the end of the seventeenth century, the U.S. South did not emerge as a major slave society until the beginning of the nineteenth century. After this time, its principal commodity was, of course, cotton, the bulk of which was exported to England to feed its flourishing textile mills. By the middle of the nineteenth century slavery had expanded from its beginnings in Maryland and Virginia to encompass much of the Deep South, and it had spread as far west as Texas.

Blacks always constituted a numerical minority in the slave system of the United States. In the Southern colonies in 1650 they made up only 3 percent of the total population; by 1770 their percentage had risen to 40 percent (Fogel and Engerman, 1974). These figures are in striking contrast to what prevailed in many other plantation systems, where blacks were often a very large numerical majority. Furthermore, the average plantation size in the United States was considerably smaller than that in the prime sugar-producing societies. The average size of a slave holding in Virginia and Maryland at the end of the eighteenth century was less than 13 slaves (Fogel and Engerman, 1974). In the antebellum period (1800–1860), only the great planters had plantations with as many as 100 to 200 slaves, and the majority of plantations contained 30 or fewer slaves. These figures are quite small when we consider that many sugar plantations in the West Indies and Brazil had as many as 500 slaves.

The U.S. Southern slave system was dominated by a wealthy and powerful planter class, a slavocracy that consisted of only a small minority of all slaveholders. This planter class controlled the economy through its ownership of land and people, dominated the political system, and created the laws of the slave South to serve its own ends. Many historians have thought of the great planters as essentially an aristocratic class with an ideology that was antagonistic to the calculating outlook of capitalist entrepreneurs (Genovese, 1965, 1969). However, in their famous study of the economics of Southern slavery, *Time on the Cross* (1974), Robert Fogel and Stanley Engerman demonstrate convincingly that the planters were "shrewd capitalistic businessmen" with a highly rational and calculating outlook. Actually, given the larger economic system of which they were part, how could they have been otherwise? Since they were producing for a world economic market, it is inconceivable that they could have turned a deaf ear to questions of profit and loss and still have survived.

In the southern United States the relations between masters and slaves were governed by a pervasive social structure and ideology of paternalism. The plantation was a largely self-contained world where masters and slaves lived in close and continuous contact with one another. Social interaction between the races was regulated by a highly developed etiquette. Slaves were supposed to behave submissively toward their masters through the use of terms of respect as well as gestures and speech signifying their own inferiority, but masters addressed slaves by their first names. While sexual activity between black men and white women was severely condemned, white masters frequently had sexual relations with their black slave women. Young white boys often had their first sexual experience with slave girls, and it was a fairly common practice for masters to keep several slave women as concubines. In the ideological realm, whites held an elaborate set of stereotypes regarding the inferiority of blacks. Blacks were generally regarded as irresponsible grown-up children. Masters treated slaves much as a stern but loving father would treat his small children (van den Berghe, 1967).

Slavery in Brazil

One of the largest and most significant of all the New World plantation systems was developed by the Portuguese in Brazil. The first slaves were introduced into Brazil from Africa around the middle of the sixteenth century, and by the seventeenth century a well-developed slave system was in operation. The great majority of Brazilian slaves worked on sugar, coffee, cotton, and cacao plantations. Sugar dominated Brazilian slavery during the seventeenth century. A minimum of about 80 slaves seemed to be required for the operation of a successful sugar plantation, and some of the plantations employed several hundred slaves (van den Berghe, 1967). When the economic significance of sugar waned, Brazil shifted to the large-scale development of coffee plantations, and coffee was the dominant cash crop in the eighteenth and nineteenth centuries.

Brazil had an intense reliance on the Atlantic slave trade, taking, as previously noted, 38 percent of the total number of slaves imported into all of the New World. Brazilian slavery was based on large-scale operations, and black slaves came to outnumber whites throughout Brazil's slavery period. In 1789, out of a total population of 2.3 million, 1.5 million were African slaves. In 1872 whites still represented only 38 percent of the total population (van den Berghe, 1967). In contrast to the U.S. South, Brazil had a slave labor force that did not reproduce itself. Because of the continual influx of slaves, little attention was given to the reproductive powers of slave women, and they produced few offspring. Slaves were worked to the limit and replaced by new ones when they died.

The Brazilian slave system was highly paternalistic and bore many striking resemblances to the slave society of the southern United States. Van den Berghe provides an informative description of Brazilian plantation life (1967:65–66):

> It is clear that the *fazenda* [sugar-cane plantation] was a classic example of paternalistic race relations. It was a self-sufficient microcosm with its own food supply, repair shops, chapel, resident priest-tutor, cemetery, hospital, and school. . . .
>
> Residentially, the big house *(casa grande)*, inhabited by the owner's family and by domestic slaves, dominated the nearby slave quarters *(senzala)* that housed the field hands and skilled craftsmen. Relations between masters and house slaves were intimate, that is, both spatially and emotionally close, though socially very distant. White children were raised by Negro wet-nurses *(amas)* and given a slave of their age and sex as play companions. When a white boy reached sexual maturity, he was sexually initiated with one of his father's slaves and continued to engage in promiscuous concubinage with female slaves throughout his sexually active lifetime. Interracial concubinage with female slaves was completely accepted for white men, and, according to the dual standard of sexual morality, marriage was not considered an impediment to the maintenance of a slave harem. Even the Catholic clergy interbred extensively with women of color. . . .
>
> The division of labor along racial lines was quite clear-cut. The Portuguese aristocracy was a leisure class *par excellence*, engaged almost solely in war and love making. . . .
>
> Social distance between masters and slaves was maintained through a punctilious etiquette of subservience and dominance. Sumptuary regulations, forms of address, and symbolic gestures regulated social intercourse between people of vastly different status who were in constant and intimate contact with each other. For example, masters were carried about in litters and were accompanied by a retinue of slaves arranged in a well-regulated procession when going to public places. . . .
>
> Many stereotypes about the Negro developed during the slavery period and are still part of the Brazilian folklore. The Afro-Brazilian was regarded as a lascivious, physically unattractive, happy-go-lucky grown-up child.

With only a slight change in wording here and there, van den Berghe's description of Brazilian paternalism could equally well serve as a description of plantation life in the southern United States.

Slavery in the West Indies and Cuba

The British West Indies were composed of several small islands in the Caribbean, the most notable of which were Barbados and Jamaica. These islands were given over to extensive plantation slavery during the seventeenth and eighteenth centuries, and sugar was by far the largest cash crop. An increasing number of slaves were imported after the middle of the seventeenth century to work rapidly developing sugar plantations. By the eighteenth century the British West Indies had become totally dependent on sugar production (Foner, 1975). The economy and polity were dominated by a small planter class, the most important segment of which consisted of absentee owners. These owners lived in splendor off their great profits in England and left their plantations under the care of overseers (Foner, 1975). Philip Foner (1975) describes British West Indian slavery as especially harsh and cruel.

The French West Indies consisted of the islands of Guadeloupe, Martinique, and, most important, St. Domingue (Haiti). Great profits were made from the sugar plantations of St. Domingue in the eighteenth century. Like most sugar plantations elsewhere, those of the French West Indies were very large in scale. Black slaves, therefore, greatly outnumbered whites. In St. Domingue in 1790 there were 32,000 resident whites, 24,000 freedmen, and 48,000 slaves (Foner, 1975). The French planter class, like its British counterpart, consisted largely of absentee owners. French West Indian slavery was also characterized by great brutality (Foner, 1975).

The Danish West Indies consisted mainly of the small island of St. Croix. The Danes were mainly absentee owners on sugar plantations. The Dutch West Indies principally involved the country of Surinam (Dutch Guiana) on the northern coast of South America. Like most of the other West Indian planters, the Dutch were absentee owners. Surinam contained large sugar, coffee, cotton, and lumber plantations, on which the black slaves overwhelmingly outnumbered the whites. The Dutch were notorious for their atrocious treatment of slaves (Genovese, 1969).

Under the direction of Spain, Cuba became a major sugar-producing slave society in the nineteenth century when St. Domingue collapsed from a successful slave insurrection. Foner describes nineteenth-century Cuban slavery as extremely brutal and exploitative, and he further notes that the level of brutality increased proportionately with the intensification of sugar production.

The different slave systems of the West Indies shared many features in common. In all of them sugar production was the key to the economy. All were dominated by planter classes whose members consisted mainly of absentee owners. And all were exceptionally brutal. Under these kinds of conditions, the paternalism so characteristic of the U.S. South and Brazil undoubtedly could not develop fully (Genovese, 1969).

Slavery and the Capitalist World-Economy

In examining the plantation slave systems of the New World, one can look at them from two different, yet equally significant, points of view. One can look at their internal dynamics, at the nature of their master and slave classes and the relations between these classes. One can then get some insight into how the systems functioned and what consequences they had for those persons and groups who lived within them. One can also, however, look at these slave societies from a larger perspective, from the point of view of their involvement in a capitalist world-economy. From this perspective, it is possible to get a clearer idea of the fundamental forces that generated, sustained, and ultimately destroyed New World slave societies. So far, we have been looking at slavery from both points of view, but we have said less than we can about the relationship of individual slave societies to the capitalist world-economy.

An insightful study of the role played by slavery—particularly British West Indian slavery—in the development of British capitalism has been carried out by Eric Williams in his book *Capitalism and Slavery* (1966; orig. 1944). Williams's main argument is that slavery played a vital role in generating the profits that led to the great expansion of British capitalism and the financing of the Industrial Revolution.

Williams places great emphasis on the role of the *triangular trade* in the development of British capitalism. The triangular trade linked Africa, the British West Indies, and Britain together into a vast network of economic interdependence. Ships would sail from Britain with a supply of manufactured goods. These would be exchanged at a profit for Negroes in Africa. The African slaves were in turn traded on the plantations at another profit in exchange for plantation produce to be taken back to Britain.

The triangular trade stimulated a host of industries. Shipbuilding was one of the more prominent of these, for specific types of vessels were manufactured for the slave trade. The shipbuilding industry led to the development of the great British seaport towns of Bristol, Liverpool, and Glasgow. The manufacture of woolen and cotton goods also received a great boost, for these items were of considerable importance for the purchase of slaves. Another industry that grew in response to the triangular trade was sugar refining, and the prosperity of cities such as Bristol and Glasgow rested heavily on their sugar-refining industries. Since rum could be distilled as a by-product of sugar production, the rum-distillation industry also became important. The metallurgical industries expanded: chains and padlocks were manufactured for confining slaves; guns were shipped to Africa in exchange for slaves; and sugar stoves, rollers, wrought iron, and nails were manufactured for the plantations. Banking was directly stimulated, for shipbuilders and slave traders were instrumental in establishing the first banks. Insurance companies originated at this time, as slave traders felt a need to insure their human cargoes against loss.

The British West Indian plantations therefore played a crucial role in the economy of the British Empire in the eighteenth century. They were a key link in a vast economic network that led to the massive expansion of British capitalism. During this time the British North American colonies played a very secondary role in British economic life. But following the American Revolution the role of the British West Indies declined and that of the United States greatly accelerated. During the first half of

the nineteenth century, U.S. slavery played a major role in the advance of British capitalism. The great industry in Britain during this time was, of course, textile manufacturing, and Britain's demand for raw cotton increased enormously. By the middle of the nineteenth century the United States was providing the bulk of this cotton: "The United States supplied less than one-hundredth part of British cotton imports in the five years 1786–1790, three-quarters in the years 1826–1830, four-fifths in 1846–1850" (Williams, 1966:128). British capitalism was thus enormously responsible for the great expansion of the cotton kingdom of the U.S. slave South during the nineteenth century.

It is clear that plantation slavery was intimately involved in the whole process of Western capitalist development. The many slave regimes that flourished in the New World between the sixteenth and eighteenth centuries were inextricably intertwined with capitalist economic interests. Nonetheless, plantation slavery in the New World was to last only some three centuries. When and where did it come to an end, and, more important, why was it abolished?

The Abolition of Slavery and the Slave Trade

Britain and the United States abolished their roles in the slave trade in 1807, although much illegal slave trading continued after that time, the Atlantic slave trade not actually coming to a complete halt until 1867 (Blackburn, 1988; Fogel, 1989). The abolition of slavery did not occur until several decades after the official ending of the slave trade (see Table 13.2). Britain abolished slavery throughout her colonial empire in 1838, the United States ended its slave system in 1865, and Cuba abolished slavery in 1886. The last slave society to

Table 13.2   A CHRONOLOGY OF THE ABOLITION OF SLAVERY AND THE SLAVE TRADE

Date	Decision
1804	Slavery abolished in Haiti.
1807	England and the United States prohibit further engagement in the international slave trade.
1813	Gradual emancipation adopted in Argentina.
1814	Gradual emancipation begins in Colombia.
1823	Slavery abolished in Chile.
1824	Slavery abolished in Central America.
1829	Slavery abolished in Mexico.
1831	Slavery abolished in Bolivia.
1838	Slavery abolished in all British colonies.
1842	Slavery abolished in Uruguay.
1848	Slavery abolished in all French and Danish colonies.
1851	Slavery abolished in Ecuador.
1854	Slavery abolished in Peru and Venezuela.
1863	Slavery abolished in all Dutch colonies.
1865	Slavery abolished in the United States.
1873	Slavery abolished in Puerto Rico.
1886	Slavery abolished in Cuba.
1888	Slavery abolished in Brazil.

Source: Robert William Fogel, *Without Consent or Contract: The Rise and Fall of American Slavery.* New York: Norton, 1989, pp. 206–207, Table 6.

come to a halt was Brazil, which put an end to slavery in 1888.

What were the driving forces behind these events? As for Britain's abolition of the slave trade, Immanuel Wallerstein (1979a) suggests two reasons. First, by the beginning of the nineteenth century Britain was starting to make colonial intrusions into Africa in order to make use of it as a crop-producing area; as a result, Africans were becoming more valuable to Britain as colonized workers in their homelands than as slaves in distant lands. Second, Wallerstein claims that Britain wanted to deny its European competitors, especially the French, access to slaves. This second point has been reiterated by Dale Tomich (1990:54), who holds that French merchants and shippers "saw Britain's demand for the immediate abolition of the slave trade as a strategy that, by depriving the colonies of their indispensable labor supply, would at one stroke destroy the recovery of the colonies."

As for the abolition of slavery itself, generations of scholars have called attention to the role of humanitarian sentiments, arguing that these played a critical role in bringing slavery to a halt. As Robert William Fogel (1989) has shown, there were many groups—in Britain, the United States, and elsewhere—that, from the middle of the eighteenth century on, called for an end to slavery on the basis of moral considerations. For many of these groups the moral opposition to slavery was religious. However, it is unlikely that the moral and humanitarian crusade against slavery by itself made much difference. It is largely because the appeals of these groups coincided with larger political and economic interests that they could be taken seriously at all (Fogel, 1989). Moreover, in some cases humanitarian arguments against slavery were little more than a cover for underlying economic motives. Eric Williams (1966) has argued that this was very much the situation in British West Indian slavery. Williams notes, for example, that whereas many of the abolitionists were condemning West Indian slavery, they tolerated—indeed, encouraged—slavery in Brazil, Cuba, and the United States. This came about because, Williams argues, the West Indian plantations had become economically burdensome to Britain at the same time that Britain continued to have a vital economic interest in the perpetuation of slavery in Brazil, Cuba, and the United States. Williams explains further (1966:190–191):

> The abolitionists were boycotting the slave-grown produce of the British West Indies, dyed with the Negro's blood. But the very existence of British capitalism depended upon the slave-grown cotton of the United States, equally connected with slavery and polluted with blood. The West Indian could legitimately ask whether "slavery was only reprehensible in countries to which [sic] those members do not trade, and where their connections do not reside.". . . The boycotters of West Indian sugar sat upon chairs of Cuban mahogany, before desks of Brazilian rosewood, and used inkstands of slave-cut ebony. . . .
>
> Was Brazilian sugar necessary? The capitalists said yes; it was necessary to keep British capitalism going. The abolitionists took the side of the capitalists.

Williams obviously sees slavery and antislavery as rooted in economic considerations, and several other scholars have followed suit. Barrington Moore (1966) has emphasized economic factors in attempting to explain the Civil War and the abolition of slavery in the United States. Moore's argument is that the Southern slave system had eventually become incompatible with the economic interests of Northern industrial capitalists. Southern slaveholders and Northern industrialists, he claims, were locked in a bitter struggle over who was going to control the lands of the Western frontier, and it took a war to settle this struggle. The North won the war, of course, and this meant the defeat of the Southern slavocracy. Dale Tomich (1990) makes economics even more central. Speaking in particular of the slave colony in Martinique, he notes that slavery was finally abolished there in 1848 because it had become economically inefficient. Sugar production could only be made more profitable by abolishing slavery and replacing it with a new mode of labor organization. Immanuel Wallerstein (1979a) has also emphasized economic factors, but from the standpoint of the capitalist world-economy as a whole. Wallerstein argues that slavery had to be abolished because it was becoming too economically costly to a world-economy that had lost its major slave-producing region (Africa).

The most recent explanations of the abolition of slavery have focused on politics rather than economics (Fogel, 1989; Blackburn, 1988). In a book devoted to this subject, *The Overthrow of Colonial Slavery, 1776–1848*, Robin Blackburn (1988:520) comments that "slavery was not overthrown for economic reasons but where it became politically untenable." Blackburn has been able to show that there was a close relationship between the economic and political strength of slave regimes and the abolition of slavery. Slavery was strongest and survived longest in the United States, Brazil, and Cuba; conversely, slavery was ended earliest in those regions where the slave regimes were relatively weak: South America and the British and French West Indies. The strength of slavery was also correlated with the presence or absence of colonialism: slavery was strong where colonialism had been overthrown and political independence gained (in particular, in the

United States and Brazil), but it was much weaker where colonial ties remained (as in the West Indies). Blackburn concludes that antislavery made greatest progress in those areas where slaveholders became politically and economically marginal. This was especially true if such marginality coincided with the likelihood of successful slave rebellion, and if powerful groups other than slaveholders could benefit politically from the abolition of slavery.

Although he stresses politics over economics, Blackburn's argument is actually not that far from an economic explanation of antislavery. In taking up the argument of others that it was the advance of capitalism that produced the reaction against slavery, he says (1988:520), "To the extent that capitalist advance did promote anti-slavery it was indirectly, because of the class struggles to which it gave rise and because of the capacities of the new type of state created in the wake of industrial revolution." Also particularly worth noting is his comment that in the West Indies (1988:521) "the economic significance of slaveholding to the metropolitan ruling classes was small and trade with the colonial Caribbean in eclipse." So, for Blackburn, economics was certainly lurking in the background and formed the basis for the emergence of the political causes of antislavery.

In recent decades new life has been breathed into the study of the abolition of slavery and the slave trade. Much research is now being done, but no consensus has yet been reached, about the basic causes of antislavery. It may be some time before we will have a firm hold on this problem. My guess, though, is that it will be shown that economic forces loomed the largest in the antislavery movement throughout the New World. And I think it will additionally be shown that the specific kinds of economic factors that were involved varied from one slave regime and one time period to another. For example, slavery in the United States was probably ended, as Moore suggests, because it was incompatible with the further development of the economic interests of industrial capitalists. But this could not have been the case in the slave regimes in Cuba and Brazil, for these societies are not even today industrial capitalist societies. It is hard to imagine that there could be a single economic cause explaining the downfall of slave regimes in very diverse societies. I think it will be shown that political motives were important too, but only insofar as they were linked with deeper economic interests.

INDUSTRIAL CAPITALISM AND THE DEVELOPMENT OF COMPETITIVE RACE AND ETHNIC RELATIONS

With the eventual destruction of slavery by the late nineteenth century, people of African origin ceased to be slaves, but for the most part they did not cease to be highly oppressed members of racially divided societies. As the old paternalistic systems came apart, they were quickly replaced by racially stratified societies in which a new type of race relations—the competitive type—rose to prominence. In these societies, blacks were nominally free, but they still had to struggle against forces that sought to keep them at the bottom of the social order.

The Development of Competitive Race Relations in the United States

Pierre van den Berghe (1967) has provided a valuable discussion of the emergence and development of competitive race relations in the United States. As he notes, the end of slavery marked the beginning of a whole new phase in the relations between blacks and whites. The black man ceased to be seen as a "happy, singing slave" and increasingly came to be viewed as "uppity" and "pushy," as not knowing "his place," as an economic competitor with whites, and as a rapist of white women.

Economically, slavery gave way to a system of sharecropping and debt peonage. Many freedmen found that they had to stay on the land in order to eke out a living. The plantation owners divided their land into small plots that could be farmed by individual tenants. Freedmen were lent food, seeds, tools, and other necessary items in order to farm their share of the land. The plantation owners arranged things so that the black tenants could never repay these debts, and blacks therefore fell into a system of debt peonage in which they were as securely tied to the land and their landlords as they had been under slavery.

By the last quarter of the nineteenth century, lower-class whites found themselves in increasing contact and competition with millions of freed blacks. Whites and blacks were "forced by economic conditions to confront one another, bump shoulders, and compete on a wide scale for the same jobs" (W. Wilson, 1978:56). The increasing economic threat that blacks posed to whites gave rise to political disfranchisement and the development of an elaborate system of "Jim Crow" segregation. Especially in the South, segregation began to penetrate into virtually every sphere of social life: "It became a punishable offense against the laws or the mores for whites and Negroes to travel, eat, defecate, wait, be buried, make love, play, relax, and even speak together, except in the stereotyped context of master and servant interaction" (van den Berghe, 1967:89–90).

In addition to disfranchisement and segregation, there also arose another tactic designed to remove or neutralize the economic threat posed by blacks: terrorism. The Ku Klux Klan emerged and made extensive use of intimidation, brutality, and murder against blacks. Vigilante groups were also formed and these too engaged in acts of terrorism in order to keep the Negro "in his place." Lynching became a significant feature of social life as a device for maintaining white supremacy.

Around the time of World War I blacks began to migrate to the North in search of jobs in an expanding northern industrial economy. Here blacks competed intensely with whites for jobs. During this time blacks were frequently used by white businessmen as strikebreakers. The increasing influx of blacks created housing shortages in northern cities, and competition also arose between whites and blacks over access to facilities for recreation and relaxation, such as playgrounds and public beaches. These occurrences created great hostility between whites and blacks, and this hostility erupted into a number of race riots, among the more serious of which occurred in East St. Louis in 1917 and in Chicago in 1919. As William Wilson (1978:76) notes, "In the final analysis, the rioting served to underscore the effect of economic changes on the interracial arena, as all of the major interracial riots had either a direct or indirect connection with industrial strife."

By the 1930s the major cities of the North had sizable concentrations of blacks, and the black ghetto was well on its way to being consolidated. Most northern blacks were concentrated in these ghettoes. By the end of World War II, according to Wilson (1978), another era of American race relations was beginning, an era in which the social and economic fortunes of blacks were coming to be more determined by class than by racial factors.

Racial and Ethnic Stratification in South Africa

Van den Berghe (1967) has provided a perceptive analysis of the development of racial stratification in South Africa. What is now the Republic of South Africa was originally colonized by the Dutch, who began to settle there in 1652. By the end of the seventeenth century, a rigid system of racial stratification had come into play. In 1658 the Dutch began the importation of slaves. The form of slavery that came to be established was one based on medium-sized farms engaged in diversified agriculture rather than on large plantations. Nevertheless, South African slavery did develop a paternalistic character. The white farmer lived on an autonomous estate surrounded by his black slaves. The division of labor was clearly established along racial lines, with whites regarding manual work as degrading. An unequal status system was maintained through an elaborate racial etiquette.

Some of the Dutch were not slave owners, but seminomads who were constantly expanding into the frontier regions. These, known as the Boers, colonized native Hottentot pastoralists, whom they reduced to the status of serfs. Boer expansion was greatly slowed in the 1770s when the Boers encountered the Bantu tribes, but it began again in 1836 with the Great Trek, which lasted for a decade.

The era of competitive race relations in South Africa began toward the end of the nineteenth century. With the discovery of gold in 1886, South Africa began to industrialize, with the gold-mining industry leading the way. This industry was dominated by British colonists, who had begun to settle in South Africa around the turn of the nineteenth century. British mineowners had an enormous need for unskilled mine workers and set their sights on the many African tribesmen who lived throughout the region. Through a variety of coercive methods, many of these tribesmen were drawn into the gold-mining industry, where they eventually came to constitute a severe economic threat to white mine workers. The extreme economic competition between white and African mine workers led, particularly in the period 1910–1924, to the early formation of what is today the practice of *apartheid*, or a strict policy of racial segregation and exclusion directed against Africans. Apartheid did not become an official government policy until 1948 with the coming to power of the Afrikaner Nationalist party, but its essential foundations had been established by 1924 (Ndabezitha and Sanderson, 1988).

Today South Africa is undoubtedly the most conflict-ridden, racially divided society in the world. It is divided into four main racial groups:

- Europeans, or whites, totaling about 18 percent of the population.
- East Indians, who amount to about 3 percent of the population.
- Coloureds—persons of mixed European and native Hottentot ancestry—numbering about 10 percent of the total.
- Africans, who constitute the bulk of the population, with 70 percent of the total; this group consists of various African tribesmen who have been incorporated into the South African state at different intervals.

The last three groups are collectively known as "nonwhites," and a rigid caste line separates them from the Europeans.

The system of apartheid that has governed the relations between whites and nonwhites in South Africa is a vast social phenomenon that contains important social, economic, and political dimensions. More narrowly, it refers to a policy of strict separation between the races that applies to virtually every aspect of social life. Strict apartheid laws have been applied to housing, schools, transportation, hospitals, cemeteries, toilets, sports facilities, and churches as well as many other things. However, the economic and political dimensions of apartheid are more important in the sense that they have greater significance for the quality of life for the vast majority of the population.

The whites in South Africa hold a massive monopoly over power and wealth.

Whites own the bulk of the land, and the English own the bulk of the mining and manufacturing industries and control a great deal of South Africa's banking, finance, and commerce. Since 1948 the Afrikaners (descendants of the Dutch, who speak a modified form of Dutch known as Afrikaans) have monopolized political power. The army, navy, judiciary, and all the higher positions in the civil service are dominated by whites. Whites control nearly all the more attractive jobs, and nonwhites are overwhelmingly concentrated in the lower-paying, low-prestige jobs. In 1960 the average family income of whites was approximately 14 times that of Africans and 5 times that of Coloureds and Indians. (The ratio of white to African income had declined slightly by 1975, but was still very great: about 10:1 [Nattrass, 1981:288].)

A repressive political regime has characterized South Africa for many years. Although the nation is technically a parliamentary democracy, its democratic procedures have applied only to whites, and there has been no pretense of democracy for nonwhites. It is a classic example of a *Herrenvolk democracy*. Africans have no right to vote. At least until recently, they were required to carry identification cards with them everywhere and to present these to the police on demand. At one point more than a million Africans were being arrested each year, most on technical and minor violations of apartheid laws. Africans have spent their lives under the constant shadow of police surveillance, intimidation, and brutality.

In the past two decades there has been an enormous challenge to apartheid on the part of Africans through their various social and political movements. During this time have things gotten better or worse, or have they remained the same? Pierre van den Berghe (1990), a leading sociological specialist on South Africa, has reported on a recent stay some 30 years after he did intensive fieldwork there. He argues that many of the more trivial or petty aspects of apartheid have been eliminated; that, although South Africa still has a racial division of labor, it no longer has the rigid industrial color bar that was once the very heart of apartheid; and that the obsession with racial purity is largely gone. However, he says, much remains the same: the whole structure of political and economic inequality is largely unchanged and the huge black urban working class still lives in the same appalling shantytowns; education remains almost as segregated as ever; and, although there has been a massive withdrawal of the state from daily control over the lives of blacks, the police have simply substituted for this method of direct control "the covert methods of indirect rule, vigilantism, terrorism, and the encouragement of political factionalism, class and ethnic warfare, and predatory crime of blacks against blacks" (1990:27). Van den Berghe concludes that little has changed in terms of improving the living conditions and opportunities of the vast majority of Africans.

In 1994 a new coalition government involving both blacks and whites was elected to office and the legal aspects of apartheid were officially brought to an end. However, as the preceding discussion makes all too clear, because of the legacy of apartheid huge problems still remain, and these problems are now being complicated by major tribal divisions among blacks. As far as I am concerned, the short-term future in South Africa still looks extremely grim. Things are very likely to get worse before they get better.

Theories of Competitive Race Relations

A variety of theories have been proposed to explain the existence of racial antagonisms during the era of competitive race relations. The most valuable of these theories emphasize racial antagonism as an outcome of economic forces and class struggle. But even these economic theories present somewhat contrasting and conflicting interpretations of the basic causes of racial antagonism.

The *orthodox Marxian* interpretation argues that racial antagonism is a direct product of the conflict between capital and labor (Cox, 1948; Szymanski, 1976; Reich, 1977). Capitalists desire the cheapest labor possible and act in ways deliberately designed to keep the cost of labor down. Capitalists make use of racial distinctions to further their own economic interests. They consciously promote racial antagonism between white and black workers, thereby dividing the working class against itself. This prevents the working class from achieving a high degree of solidarity and making full use of its organizational potential, thus limiting its ability to push for higher wages.

Edna Bonacich (1972, 1979) has suggested that this interpretation is a considerable oversimplification of the dynamics of racial antagonism. She argues instead for a *split labor market theory*. The central assumption of this theory is that racial antagonism first develops in a labor market that is split along racial lines. For a labor market to be split, it "must contain at least two groups of workers whose price of labor differs for the same work, or would differ if they did the same work" (1972:549). The split labor market theory holds that, rather than being the result of a simple conflict between capitalists and workers, racial antagonism is the outcome of the relationships among three economic groups: capitalists, higher-paid labor, and cheaper labor. Capitalists have as their main aim the acquisition of as cheap and docile a labor force as possible. When labor costs are too high, capitalists will, if possible, turn to the use of cheaper labor. The main interest of higher-paid labor is to keep its wages up and prevent other groups of workers from undermining its economic security. It therefore fears competition from cheaper labor and will do what it can to remove it as a threat. Cheaper labor, naturally, wishes to maximize its economic interests and this frequently brings it into competition with higher-paid labor. Capitalists may attempt to use cheaper labor as strikebreakers and undercutters.

Racial or ethnic antagonism develops when higher-paid labor and cheaper labor are of different racial or ethnic groups. This antagonism may take one or the other of two principal forms, depending upon the underlying conditions: exclusion movements or caste systems.

Exclusion movements typically arise when the cheaper labor group lives outside a given territory but wishes to immigrate into it. With the movement of cheaper labor into a labor market previously controlled by higher-paid labor, higher-paid labor experiences a direct economic threat and begins making demands that the cheaper labor group be excluded from the labor market altogether. Bonacich argues that this is what happened when cheaper labor groups of Chinese and Japanese immigrated to the United States in the late nineteenth century. As Chinese and Japanese immigration increased, higher-paid labor perceived a direct threat to its economic well-being and began voicing demands that the Asian workers be prevented from immigrating; these demands were, in fact, acted upon by the U.S. government (cf. Boswell, 1986).

Caste systems rather than exclusion movements result when cheaper labor is already present in the labor market and cannot be excluded. Under this arrangement, higher-paid labor gains monopolistic control over the better, higher-paying jobs and consigns cheaper labor to poorer-paying jobs, thereby removing them as an undercutting threat. Bonacich argues that such caste systems have been most prominently represented by the racial stratification systems of the United States and South Africa (cf. Bonacich, 1972, 1981).

In contrast to orthodox Marxian theory, which sees racial antagonism as resulting simply from the conscious actions of capitalist entrepreneurs, Bonacich's split labor market theory sees racial antagonism as primarily the result of the conflict that arises between different segments of the working class. She therefore implicates higher-paid workers in the formation of racial antagonism in a way that is ignored by the orthodox Marxian interpretation. Although both theories emphasize economic conflict as the basis for racial/ethnic antagonism, they do so in distinctively different ways.

William Wilson (1978) believes that both the orthodox Marxian and split labor market interpretations have validity, but that they must be applied to different historical circumstances. Wilson divides the history of the United States into three different historical periods according to the pattern of race relations prevailing in each: the preindustrial, industrial, and modern industrial periods of race relations. The preindustrial period was characterized by the system of plantation slavery. Wilson argues that the orthodox Marxian theory satisfactorily explains the racial stratification system prevailing during this time. White slave owners constituted the dominant economic class and consciously turned blacks into slaves in order to advance their own economic interests.

With the end of slavery, the industrial period of American race relations began, lasting until about the end of World War II. This period was characterized by continual strife between white and black workers as freed blacks directly competed with whites for jobs. Wilson holds that the patterns of race relations prevailing during this period cannot be accounted for by the orthodox Marxian theory; rather, the split labor market theory is said to do a much better job of explaining the kinds of racial conflict that emerged. The evidence presented by Wilson seems to bear out this contention. Again and again we find capitalists interested in, and to a large extent succeeding in, employing cheaper black workers in large numbers. Yet white workers who were economically threatened by such actions were highly successful in trying to establish racial caste arrangements to protect their more privileged economic position.

Finally, the modern industrial period of race relations is said to characterize the United States from the end of World War II to the present. Wilson believes that neither theory can adequately explain the structure of racial stratification during this period (see the Special Topic at the end of this chapter).

Wilson's claim regarding the complementarity of the orthodox Marxian and split labor market theories also seems to apply to the history of racial antagonism in South Africa. The orthodox Marxian theory seems to apply to the preindustrial period in South Africa, but from the beginnings of South African industrialization the split labor market theory seems a much more adequate interpretation (Bonacich, 1981; Ndabezitha and Sanderson, 1988). As noted earlier, the era of competitive race relations in South Africa began with the development of large-scale gold mining in 1886. White mineowners used numerous coercive methods to attract Africans to the mines to work for wages. For a variety of reasons Africans could be employed at a markedly lower wage rate, and thus there was a split labor market present in South Africa right from the beginning of its competitive race relations era. Capitalist mine owners tried to employ Africans in ever larger numbers because of the cheapness of their labor, and this meant that they became an increasing economic threat to white mine workers. As a result, numerous forms of conflict broke out between white and African workers, and white workers vigorously attempted to prevent mineowners from gaining access to Africans. By 1924 white workers had succeeded in electing a government highly sensitive to their demands to exclude African workers from competition with them, and thus by that time the foundations of the modern system of apartheid had been established (Fredrickson, 1981). The exceptional repressiveness of the apartheid system in recent times no doubt reflects the desperate efforts of a privileged white numerical minority to protect itself against the tremendous economic threat posed by roughly two-thirds of the population.

THE ORIGIN AND EVOLUTION OF RACISM

The phenomenon known as **racism** has been of great concern to social scientists for some time. An excellent definition of racism has been provided by Pierre van den Berghe (1996). He holds that racism is *"the belief that certain physical attributes, such as skin pigmentation or facial features, are linked to attributes of intellect, morality or behavior, and thus establish a hierarchy of quality or worth between sub-groups of our species. The core of racism is thus the belief that inherited, visible phenotypes of physical appearance are causally linked to abilities or behaviors by biological inheritance"* (1996:1055; italics added). Racist doctrines assume that the social, economic, and political achievements of the members of one race are the result of their superior genetic endowment; likewise, the "failures" of the members of other races are said to be due to innate and largely unmodifiable deficiencies. As van den Berghe notes in his definition, these alleged deficiencies are usually thought to lie in the realm of intelligence and character, but racist doctrines fre-

quently extend themselves to include other traits as well.

Van den Berghe's definition of racism is what might be called a "classical" or "strict" definition. This is the conceptualization of racism that sociologists and other social scientists traditionally employed for many decades. Unfortunately, in the last quarter-century or so the term has come to be debased by dint of the extreme broadening of its meaning (see, for example, C. A. Wilson, 1996). As traditionally conceived, racism is an ideology or belief system and nothing more, but its current meaning has been stretched so as to include the notion of prejudice (which is an attitude) as well as numerous forms of behavior (van den Berghe, 1996). As van den Berghe notes, there is no longer any real distinction between scholarly and lay discourse on the matter. The concept of racism seems to refer to virtually any form of racial antagonism or any aspect of inequality whatsoever between racial groups (such as the lower scores of blacks on cognitive achievement tests, or the fact that few coaches of professional sports teams are black even though many of the players are).

A concept that has been so uncritically generalized and thus degraded in meaning can hardly be of much use. Therefore, in this book we retain the strict, traditional meaning of the term. In doing so, it is critical that racism be distinguished from three other concepts: ethnocentrism, prejudice, and discrimination. As discussed in Chapter 2, *ethnocentrism* refers to the beliefs held by the members of a culture that their way of life is superior to the lifeways of the members of other cultures. Ethnocentrism differs from racism in being a belief system based upon notions of cultural, rather than biological, superiority. Another difference is that ethnocentrism is a much more common feature of human social life, actually a true human universal.

Prejudice is an attitude of dislike or hostility held by a member of one racial or ethnic group toward the members of some other racial or ethnic group. Ordinarily, this attitude is applied categorically, that is, toward the members of a racial or ethnic group collectively. Whereas racism is a belief system, prejudice is an emotional response or feeling. Racism and prejudice are often found together in the same individuals or societies, but they do not have to correspond and sometimes do not. It is perfectly possible for the members of a society to be racists and yet at the same time relatively unprejudiced. This situation prevailed in the antebellum U.S. South, for example; white slaveowners held racist conceptions of blacks, yet in their racial paternalism they frequently found them to be "lovable creatures." And just as racists may be relatively unprejudiced, it is possible for persons to be prejudiced without harboring racist beliefs.

Finally, the concept of **discrimination** or **exclusion** refers to the unequal and unfair treatment of one racial or ethnic group at the hands of another. Discrimination is distinguished from ethnocentrism, racism, and prejudice in being a form of overt behavior. It involves what people do, not what they think or feel. It therefore follows that whereas discrimination is frequently associated with racist beliefs and prejudiced feelings, it does not have to be and sometimes is not.

Returning to the matter of racism, a crucial question concerns how cross-culturally and historically general it is. Is it found in many different kinds of societies, and was it characteristic of the ancient and medieval civilizations of the world, many of which had slavery? Ancient Greece and Rome had elaborate slave systems, for example, but were these systems intertwined with race in such a way as to produce an ideology of racism? Scholars are divided into two opposing camps on this question, those who claim that racism is old and widespread, perhaps even universal (Gossett, 1963; Kovel, 1984; Todorov, 1993), and those who claim that it is largely confined to the early modern and modern world (Cox, 1948; van den Berghe, 1967; Fredrickson, 1971; Smedley, 1993). Thomas Gossett (1963) claims to have located both racism and race prejudice in ancient India and Egypt, in early Chinese thought, and among the ancient Jews. On the other side of the issue, Audrey Smedley (1993) sees racism as a unique product of Western European and North American capitalist expansion between the sixteenth and nineteenth centuries. She is highly critical of scholars who, in her opinion, naively assume that humans have some sort of innate tendency toward racism and race prejudice. Oliver Cromwell Cox (1948) takes precisely the opposite view from Gossett, claiming that racial antagonism is a unique product of modern times and that none of the ancient civilizations exhibited it. The ancient Egyptians, Babylonians, and Persians were not racists, Cox says, nor were the Greeks and the Romans. The civilizations of classical antiquity used culture and language, and not race, as a basis for making invidious distinctions among groups—that is, distinctions of superiority and inferiority. Cox concludes that it was not until the beginning of capitalist exploitation of non-Western peoples that racism began. Van den Berghe concedes that racist ideologies of some type are occasionally found outside the modern Western world, but concludes nonetheless that racism is for the most part a product of Western capitalism and colonialism.

My student Joshua Dubrow and I (Dubrow and Sanderson, 1997) have studied the relevant literature on ancient civilizations in an attempt to adjudicate this issue (Sherwin-White, 1967; Lewis, 1971, 1990; Snowden, 1983; Thompson, 1989). This literature deals primarily with three civilizations: ancient Egypt, ancient Rome, and the Islamic world. From the evidence that we have been able to review, it seems as if some of the elements of racial antagonism—racial prejudice and racial exclusion or discrimination—did exist in the ancient civilizations of Rome and Islam. But ancient Egypt seems to have exhibited very little racialized thinking and gives even less evidence of any form of racial antagonism. And racism, in the strict sense in which we have defined it in this book, seems not to have existed in any of the three civilizations. Ancient Egypt exhibited almost no recognition of the concept of race, let alone an entire ideology of racial superiority and inferiority. Rome, while showing examples of mild forms of racial prejudice, was built on an ideology of status rather than one of race. As for Islam, while it was characterized by both racial prejudice and racial exclusion it seems not to have been a racist civilization.

It thus appears that racism, strictly defined, is a product of the early modern and modern world, and scholars who have claimed otherwise have fallen into error because they have failed to distinguish between racism and the other dimensions of racial antagonism. As noted earlier, these conceptual distinctions are vital. Racism arose in a general and somewhat rudimentary fashion in conjunction with European colonialism and the establishment of New World plantation slavery. It appeared to crystallize in the Western world in the eighteenth century and reached its peak in the nineteenth century (Noel, 1972a). Pierre van den Berghe (1967:15) has asserted that "it came of age in the third or fourth decade of the nineteenth century, achieved its golden age approximately between 1880 and 1920, and has since entered its period of decline." During this period it came to be greatly elaborated and intensified, penetrating into almost every nook and cranny of Western social life.

Some scholars believe that negative beliefs about and attitudes toward blacks preceded the existence of slavery and actually helped to give rise to it. Winthrop Jordan (1974), for example, makes much of the fact that Englishmen in the early sixteenth century held a number of negative conceptions of Africans, regarding them as "lustful," as "heathens," and even as "beasts." He believes that these early conceptions played at least some role in turning Africans into slaves in the North American colonies. But the conceptions that Jordan refers to were not components of a genuine racist ideology; rather, they no doubt represented the ethnocentric reaction of Europeans to people who differed radically from them in cultural terms. Englishmen of the early sixteenth century were highly ethnocentric, but they were not yet accustomed to racist thinking. And it scarcely seems plausible to argue that ethnocentrism gave rise to the necessity for slavery.

In a similar vein, Carl Degler (1972) has claimed that North American slavery was molded to a considerable extent by the prior existence of racial prejudice among the colonists. Degler is ultimately trying to show that slavery as a politico-economic and social system was heavily conditioned by the mental conceptions of those who established and maintained it. But, as Noel (1972b) remarks, Degler ends up blurring the distinction between racism, prejudice, ethnocentrism, and discrimination, and his argument only produces confusion. His preoccupation with the colonists' mental conceptions of blacks, furthermore, leads him to ignore the immense role of economic forces in the creation of slavery (Noel, 1972b).

It would seem that scholars such as Jordan and Degler have been looking at things from the wrong perspective: instead of examining how slavery may have been the result of certain mental conceptions, it would seem much more fruitful to examine how the establishment of slave systems led to the transformation of the slaveholders' ideological conceptions about the people they were enslaving. When we pose the question in this fashion, we may begin to understand how and why racism as an ideology came into being.

There is now a high degree of consensus among modern social scientists that racism emerged in order to justify and rationalize the brutal oppression and exploitation to which millions of people were subjected under the conditions of plantation slavery (Cox, 1948; Williams, 1966; Foner, 1975). Philip Foner indicates that racism was first applied by the Spanish to the enslavement of the Indians of the New World. But he goes on to comment that (1975:89) "racism's real development came with the importation of the more permanent slaves—the Africans—and it was the English who made the leading contribution toward this development." By indicating that racism arose as a rationalization and justification for slavery, it is not being suggested that those who harbored racist thoughts did not really believe in them—that they were merely trying to convince others of the moral propriety of what they were doing. On the contrary, those who harbored racist conceptions of blacks no doubt were deeply convinced of the basic correctness of their beliefs. And in being so convinced that what they were doing was justified by the inherent inferiority of blacks, they could continue to do it without feeling so guilty about it.

Noel (1972a) notes that the development of slavery coincided with the emergence of democratic political principles in the Western world. Since slavery was obviously so incompatible with those democratic ideals, it would have required special justification to avoid a massive contradiction. Racist ideologies, arguing that the natural inferiority of black Africans suited them only for a condition of servitude, provided such a justification.

It is still necessary to account for the tremendous intensification that racist thought underwent in the nineteenth century. This might be explained, paradoxically, in terms of the abolition of slavery itself. Abolition meant that millions of blacks were turned loose to compete in the labor market with whites, thus posing a severe economic threat. One way of meeting this threat would be to attempt to exclude blacks from many economic positions by virtue of their race alone. An elaborate racist ideology could be an extremely effective tool in this regard; it could be used as an ideological weapon to justify, under altered economic circumstances, the restriction of blacks to the lowest-paying jobs. This argument is strengthened by the fact that racism in the United States was at its peak when blacks posed the greatest economic threat to working-class whites, that is, from about 1890 to 1930 (W. Wilson, 1978). As William Julius Wilson observes (1973:42), "When the system of racial stratification is challenged both by subordinates seeking to share the dominant group's rights and privileges and by other individuals and groups opposed to race exploitation, the need for a more explicit and forceful justification of racial domination emerges. This is when dominant-group spokesmen with vested interests begin to denounce the subordinate racial group publicly." In other words, the point at which the system of racial stratification is under attack is the point at which an intensification of racism can be anticipated.

ETHNICITY IN EVOLUTIONARY PERSPECTIVE

Until recently, the dominant view of the future of ethnicity has been a functionalist one. The functionalist theory has argued that ethnic affiliations are primordial attachments characteristic of preindustrial societies, attachments destined to disappear with the full maturation of industrial society (cf. Hraba, 1979; A. D. Smith, 1981; Hechter, 1975, 1976). In the modern industrial world, ethnic ties are highly maladaptive and are thus increasingly dissolved. Modern industrial societies emphasize achievement and universalistic values incompatible with the particularism of ethnicity. Ethnic sentiments and ties are highly dysfunctional to the rational organization of labor systems basic to industrialism. Moreover, the expansion of international trade, transportation, and communication brings culturally diverse people into greater contact with one another and helps to erase ethnic differences.

The events of the twentieth century, and particularly of the past 30 or 40 years, have clearly shown that the functionalist theory of ethnic change is grossly inaccurate (A. D. Smith, 1981; Hechter, 1976). Rather than becoming less significant, ethnic ties have actually become considerably more significant as the twentieth century has progressed. As Anthony Smith points out (1981:12), "In every continent and practically every state, ethnicity has reappeared as a vital social and political force. The plural composition of most states; their policies of cultural integration; the increasing frequency and intensity of ethnic rivalries and conflicts; and the proliferation of ethnic movements: these are the main trends and phenomena which testify to the growing role of ethnicity in the modern world."

In the context of these remarks, Smith goes on to list several dozen examples of recent ethnic conflicts or ethnic movements, among them ethnic riots in Malaysia, Japanese hostility to Burakumin, the Muslim-Hindu conflict that divided Pakistan from India, civil war in Lebanon, the Palestinian conflict in the Middle East, racial conflict in South Africa, conflict between Hausa and Ibo in Nigeria, the Québecois movement in Canada, the black revolt in the United States, the conflict in Northern Ireland,

conflict between Flemings and Walloons in Belgium, and the Russian persecution of several ethnic minorities in the Soviet Union. Undoubtedly Smith's list, much longer than the one above, could be extended considerably.

Basically, there are two reasonable alternatives to the functionalist theory. One is an economic conflict theory. This theory suggests that the revival of ethnicity is the historical legacy of generations (or even centuries) of economic domination of some ethnic groups by others. Contemporary ethnic conflict is thus the ghost of historically subjugated minorities coming back to haunt dominant ethnic groups and force them to pay for their sins. This kind of theory has already been used in this chapter to explain several examples of ethnic and racial conflict, but it also seems to apply very well to many other instances. Two stand out in particular. The French Canadian Québecois movement for separation in Canada is a good example. Even in Quebec, where they substantially outnumber English speakers, French Canadians are a highly dominated ethnic minority. The economy is disproportionately controlled by English Canadians, and French Canadians are in general worse off economically than English Canadians.

The situation in Northern Ireland is even more clearly one in which economic conflict plays a major role. The conflict between Protestants and Catholics there is often interpreted as a battle over religion, but it is more appropriately viewed as a conflict in the socioeconomic sector. As Michael Hechter (1975) has shown, the roots of the present Irish conflict must be understood in terms of the history of British colonialism in Ireland. Ireland was for several centuries in a peripheral relationship to England. It was turned into a raw-material-producing-and-exporting region for England's benefit, and came to be an "internal colony." English colonization of Ireland was accompanied by extreme ethnic hostility.

English landlords in Ireland were Protestants who despised the traditional culture and religion of their Catholic peasant subordinates.

The ethnic antagonism in Northern Ireland today appears as the historical legacy of this economic situation. Catholics are disproportionately concentrated at the bottom of the socioeconomic ladder. They are subjected to economic discrimination and looked down upon by the Protestant majority. While undoubtedly the conflict between Protestants and Catholics is about more than socioeconomic differences, these are at the root of the conflict.

The other kind of theory that might help to explain the current persistence of ethnicity (if not its strong revival) is sometimes called **primordialism** (cf. van den Berghe, 1981; A. D. Smith, 1981, 1986). Primordialism holds that ethnic ties are fundamental, indeed irreducible, kinds of human attachments that can be softened but never entirely eliminated. Unlike the functionalist theory, this view holds that ethnic ties are fundamental to the basic character of human relations, including those in industrial societies.

The most substantial problem with many primordialist arguments is that they posit ethnic affiliation as a "natural" human tendency without actually telling us why this should be so. As van den Berghe has remarked (1981:17): "As a theoretical underpinning, the primordialists had nothing better to fall back on than the nebulous, romantic, indeed sometimes racist ideologies of nationalists to which the primordialists pointed as illustrations of their contention. What kind of mysterious and suspicious force was this 'voice of the blood' that moved people to tribalism, racism and ethnic intolerance?"

The sociobiological version of primordialism, however, overcomes this difficulty by suggesting that the tendency toward ethnic attachment is rooted in the human biogram (cf. van den Berghe, 1981; Reynolds, Falger, and Vine, 1986). Among ancient hominids strong group loyalties would have been highly adaptive as mechanisms for individual survival, and thus would have been favored by natural selection. This argument cannot be comfortably ignored, and it may be entirely complementary with explanations of ethnic attachment that emphasize economic conflict. Ethnic attachments are obviously greatly affected by a range of sociocultural conditions, especially economic ones. But, since they have a remarkable persistence throughout human space and time (cf. A. D. Smith, 1986), it is difficult to believe that they are simply at the mercy of sociocultural forces. Sociobiological arguments cannot contribute much toward explaining most of the dimensions of racial and ethnic stratification that we have explored in this chapter, but they may be relevant to explaining why at least some tendency toward ethnic affiliation and identity is a constant in human societies.

SUMMARY

1. Sociologists generally define racial groups as physically distinguishable populations accorded social significance. Ethnic groups are populations that are culturally, rather than physically, distinguishable. In reality, however, racial and ethnic groups often extensively overlap.

2. Two major types of race relations may be distinguished, paternalistic and competitive. Paternalistic race relations are characteristic of preindustrial societies based on plantation agriculture and slavery. Castelike divisions between a dominant racial group and a subordinate group emerge, and an elaborate racial etiquette regulates the relations between them. Competitive race relations are associated with industrial capitalist societies with a manufacturing economy and wage labor. The paternalism and racial etiquette of former times give way to extreme conflict

between racial groups over access to economic positions.

3. Slavery and the slave trade were a vital part of expanding capitalism in the New World. Slavery was found in peripheral capitalist societies and seemed to be the most profitable way of organizing a labor force under the particular economic arrangements of those societies. There was a close link between the slave economies and the development of capitalism in the core nations.

4. Slavery in the U.S. South was at its zenith in the period between 1800 and 1860, when it was largely given over to the production of cotton. A classical paternalistic system of race relations emerged from it. Slavery in Brazil differed from slavery in the U.S. South in a number of ways; nevertheless, Brazilian slavery generated a paternalistic pattern of race relations that was strikingly similar to U.S. Southern racial paternalism. Slavery also existed in the West Indies. Here it seemed to take an especially cruel and despotic form, and racial paternalism was largely absent, doubtless because most West Indian planters were absentee owners and because of the overwhelming demographic dominance of the slaves.

5. A popular argument suggests that the abolition of slavery and the slave trade resulted from moral and humanitarian opposition to slavery. However, it is unlikely that this opposition by itself could have brought slavery to an end. Other interpretations focus on economic and political factors. Britain's banning of the slave trade may have been motivated by a desire to deprive slaveholding competitors access to slaves. Slavery was abolished in the 1830s and 1840s in the West Indies, but by that time the slave system was economically in decline and the political power of slaveholders was becoming weaker. The abolition of slavery in the United States was likely due to the political and economic power of Northern industrial capitalists, whose economic interests were highly incompatible with slavery. Slavery lasted longest in societies that had become politically sovereign and in which slavery was economically sound and slaveholders politically strong.

6. The end of slavery ushered in the era of competitive race relations. In the United States extreme forms of economic and social conflict between whites and blacks began to arise in the late nineteenth century and have continued throughout much of the twentieth century. Whites have used segregation, terrorism, and a range of exclusionary practices as various means of counteracting the economic threat posed by blacks. The most extreme version of competitive race relations anywhere in the world has been found in South Africa for the past century. South Africa is dominated by a white numerical minority that holds an enormous monopoly over power and wealth. A rigid system of apartheid has governed the relations between whites and nonwhites. In recent years racial conflict has grown and has taken increasingly violent forms.

7. Two major theories of competitive race relations are the orthodox Marxian theory and the split labor market theory. The Marxian theory argues that capitalists attempt to stir up racial conflict so as to divide the working class and make it more exploitable. The split labor market theory views racial antagonism as emerging from a more complex situation in which higher-paid workers of the racial or ethnic majority attempt to prevent lower-paid workers of minority groups from economically competing with them on equal terms. This effort may result in exclusion movements or caste systems.

8. Racism is an ideology holding some racial groups to be biologically inferior to others. It must not be confused with prejudice, ethnocentrism, or discrimination. Racism seems to have been largely a unique product of Western capitalism, colonialism, and plantation slavery. Many sociologists argue that racism arose in the West as a means of giving moral justification to slavery, and its intensification after the end of slavery can be understood as the result of the enormous economic threat posed by blacks to whites at that time.

9. The functionalist evolutionary theory of ethnicity asserts that with the maturation of industrial societies ethnic distinctions will increasingly disappear. In the twentieth cen-

tury, though, ethnic distinctions have in many ways become more meaningful, and ethnic conflict has increased. Ethnic divisions are deeply intertwined with the economic organization of society and its conflicts, and are not simply symbolic expressions of traditional group attachments. It is also possible that a basic tendency toward ethnic affiliation has roots in the human biogram, as a number of sociobiologists have recently suggested.

SPECIAL TOPIC: THE QUESTION OF BLACK PROGRESS

In the past decade or so a crucial question for many social scientists has been the extent to which blacks in the United States have made progress in achieving equality with whites. As these social scientists note, the civil rights movement of the 1960s was specifically devoted to the accomplishment of this aim. So now, some 40 years after the beginning of that movement, what has been its degree of success?

Reynolds Farley (1984) has described three different views that have been taken on the question of black progress. The *optimistic view* holds that blacks have generally been making progress over the past decades; the *pessimistic view* claims that black progress has been illusory, or at least far more limited than generally believed; and the *polarization thesis* claims that, while some blacks have indeed been progressing significantly, a larger number have been experiencing a worsening of their opportunities and have been falling ever further behind whites.

Perhaps the best representative of the optimistic view is Farley himself. Farley acknowledges that in some areas blacks still lag as much behind whites as they did four decades ago. For example, black unemployment is still about twice as high as white unemployment, residential segregation between whites and blacks is still marked, and little progress has been made toward the integration of schools in the nation's largest cities. However, Farley claims that in other respects blacks have progressed significantly. Racial differences in educational attainment have declined, blacks are far more likely to hold prestigious and high-paying jobs, and the earnings of employed blacks have increased notably. Farley concludes that, on balance, black gains have been both substantial and widespread.

The pessimistic view has been embraced most vehemently by Alphonso Pinkney (1984). Pinkney does not claim that blacks have made no progress at all in recent years, but he does assert that the extent of this progress has been greatly exaggerated by both white and black social scientists. He focuses most heavily on what he believes is the strong persistence of racism, prejudice, and discrimination. He is convinced that the United States is still a thoroughly racist society, despite the decline of some of the more blatant forms of racism. This racism has allegedly become an autonomous and self-perpetuating ideology that is responsible for continuing racial discrimination and subordination. As a result, blacks have made only very limited gains in upgrading their occupations and income levels and in being treated as equal partners with whites.

Opposed to both of these views is the polarization thesis, which to my mind is the most sensible of the three. Undoubtedly the most important representative of this view is William Julius Wilson, a leading black sociologist. Wilson's view is a complex and subtle one that has been developed in two books written a decade apart. In *The Declining Significance of Race* (1978), Wilson argues that the United States has experienced three distinct historical periods of race relations: the preindustrial, industrial, and modern industrial periods. As noted in the main text, Wilson has argued that the orthodox Marxian theory seems to explain the pattern of race relations in the preindustrial period, while the split labor market theory does a much better job of explaining racial antagonism during the industrial period. But after the end of World War II the United States entered the modern industrial period of race relations, a period to which, Wilson believes, neither the orthodox Marxian nor the split labor market theory adequately applies. Indeed, he advances an entirely new thesis to account for the pattern of race relations during this period. He claims that the modern industrial period has witnessed the "declining significance of race" and, correspondingly, the increasing significance of class. That is, he argues that the economic fortunes of blacks are now determined more by the forces of *class* than by those of *race.*

Wilson rests the burden of his argument on an analysis of the changing shape of the black class structure over the past several decades. He notes that a black middle class began to form in the first quarter of the twentieth century. Until after World War II this class constituted only a very small proportion of the total black population. However, beginning around 1950 it began to expand considerably. It grew from 16 percent of the black population in 1950 to 24 percent in 1960 and approximately 35 percent in 1970. (Wilson's definition of "middle class" for the black population includes working-class blacks with stable incomes.) Wilson traces this increase primarily to a general expansion of the corporate and governmental sectors of the economy, arguing that such an expansion greatly increased the availability of white-collar job opportunities for the more talented and better-educated blacks.

This growth of a black middle class has been accompanied by the continued concentration of many blacks at the lowest rungs of the socioeconomic ladder, resulting in an income distribution among blacks now more unequal than among whites. Thus, despite the substantial upward mobility achieved by blacks in recent decades, a large black underclass of ghetto poor remains; furthermore, the economic situation of this underclass has been worsening significantly in recent years. These black poor, Wilson argues, represent the legacy of many decades of previous discrimination against blacks. But he also goes on to point out that, at the present time, their economic fortunes are determined more by the class position they share with lower-class whites than by their race. Wilson is saying that a large black underclass *came to be formed* through decades of systematic racial discrimination, but that its *persistence* owes more to its identity as a class than to continued racial discrimination.

In terms of the question of black progress, then, Wilson's argument is that over the past four or five decades the black community has become increasingly bifurcated into a small middle class and a large underclass. In *The Truly Disadvantaged* (1987), Wilson concentrates specifically on the situation of the black underclass. As he notes, just from the time he wrote his previous book this underclass has become increasingly impoverished, demoralized, and isolated. Its members have suffered from increasing joblessness, family breakdown, and welfare dependency, and have turned more and more to violent crime and other extralegal activities in order to cope with their deteriorating situation. Wilson invokes a number of factors to explain this continued deterioration. Although the black underclass was formed as a result of many decades of extreme racial discrimination, it is not discrimination that accounts for its worsening condition, but primarily a particular combination of economic, demographic, and social conditions. Many industries have left the central cities where the black underclass is concentrated, taking with them a large number of the jobs for which poorly educated blacks can most qualify. There has also been a major increase in the number of black youth, thus adding to the problem of joblessness. At the same time, the expansion of corporate and governmental sectors of the economy has, as already noted, permitted the more talented and better-educated blacks to move increasingly into stable white-collar jobs. As they have done so, these middle-class blacks have moved out of black neighborhoods, where they once lived with lower-class blacks, into formerly all-white working-class and middle-class neighborhoods. This has dealt an extremely serious blow to the social integration of black communities and contributed even further to the economic plight of lower-class blacks. As Wilson explains (1987:56–57):

The exodus of middle- and working-class families from many ghetto neighborhoods removes an important "social buffer" that could deflect the full impact of the kind of prolonged and increasing joblessness that plagued inner-city neighborhoods in the 1970s and early 1980s. . . . This argument is based on the assumption that even if the truly disadvantaged segments of an inner-city area experience a significant increase in long-term spells of joblessness, the basic institutions in that area (churches, schools, stores, recreational facilities, etc.) would remain viable if much of the base of their support comes from the more economically stable and secure families. Moreover, the very presence of these families during such periods provides mainstream role models that help keep alive the perception that education is meaningful, that steady employment is a viable alternative to welfare, and that family stability is the norm, not the exception.

. . .

Thus, in a neighborhood with a paucity of regularly employed families and with the overwhelming majority of families having spells of long-term joblessness, people experience a social isolation that excludes them from the job network system that permeates other neighborhoods and that is so important in learning about or being recommended for jobs that become available in various parts of the city. And as the prospects for employment diminish, other alternatives such as welfare and the underground economy are not only increasingly relied on, they come to be seen as a way of life.

How can this increasingly desperate situation be turned around? As Wilson argues convincingly, it cannot be done simply by so-called race-specific policies, such as affirmative action programs. Such programs are really only effective in opening up opportunities for the better-off blacks who need them the least. What is called for is nothing less than a fundamental government-led program of economic reform that would create many new jobs specifically obtainable by the black underclass. It remains to be seen whether such a program will be forthcoming in the near future.

FOR FURTHER READING

Blackburn, Robin. *The Overthrow of Colonial Slavery, 1776–1848.* London: Verso, 1988. An exceptionally comprehensive historical analysis of the abolition of slavery and the slave trade. Presents a political interpretation of antislavery.

Bonacich, Edna. "The Past, Present, and Future of Split Labor Market Theory." In Cora B. Marrett and Cheryl Leggon (eds.), *Research in Race and Ethnic Relations,* Volume 1. Greenwich, Conn.: JAI Press, 1979. An excellent survey by its originator of the split labor market theory of racial antagonism, of what it has accomplished, of currently ongoing research generated by it, and of some of its weaknesses that need to be addressed in the future.

Fogel, Robert William. *Without Consent or Contract: The Rise and Fall of American Slavery.* New York: Norton, 1989. A recapitulation and update of Fogel and Engerman's *Time on the Cross,* an outstanding recent study of the economics of slavery in the U.S. South. Also contains a detailed treatment of the abolitionist movement.

Fredrickson, George M. *White Supremacy: A Comparative Study in American and South African History.* New York: Oxford University Press, 1981. A well-known comparative treatment of the history of race relations in the United States and South Africa.

Harris, Marvin. *Patterns of Race in the Americas.* New York: Norton, 1964. An illuminating comparative study of paternalistic systems of labor organization and control in Latin America. Explains why the Spaniards developed a debt-peonage system in their New World colonies rather than the system of slavery that the Portuguese established in Brazil. Many useful insights regarding Brazil's slave system are provided.

Hechter, Michael. *Internal Colonialism: The Celtic Fringe in British National Development, 1536–1966.* Berkeley: University of California Press, 1975. A valuable study of the historical subjugation of the Celtic ethnic minorities in Britain from an essentially world-system perspective.

Layton-Henry, Zig. *The Politics of Race in Britain.* London: Allen and Unwin, 1984. An excellent depiction of the emergence of competitive race relations in Britain since the end of the Second World War.

Smith, Anthony D. *The Ethnic Revival.* Cambridge: Cambridge University Press, 1981. Although the author presents an unpersuasive theory of the revival of ethnic sentiments in the twentieth-century world, he does make some reasonable arguments concerning the limitations of materialist theories of ethnicity.

Tomich, Dale W. *Slavery in the Circuit of Sugar: Martinique and the World Economy, 1830–1848.* Baltimore: Johns Hopkins University Press, 1990. One of the latest in a series of studies on the relationship of New World plantation slavery to the rise and expansion of capitalism.

van den Berghe, Pierre L. *Race and Racism: A Comparative Perspective.* New York: Wiley, 1967. The presentation and illustration of van den Berghe's paternalistic-competitive typology of race relations through a historical and comparative analysis of four different societies. Must reading for the serious student of racial and ethnic stratification.

van den Berghe, Pierre L. *The Ethnic Phenomenon.* New York: Elsevier, 1981. The presentation of a wealth of comparative data on various types of racial and ethnic stratification. A typical van den Berghe book in being meaty, provocative, and well written.

van den Berghe, Pierre L. "South Africa after thirty years." *Social Dynamics* 16(2):16–37, 1990. An extremely penetrating assessment of what changed and what didn't in South Africa between 1960 and 1990.

Williams, Eric. *Capitalism and Slavery.* New York: Putnam, 1966. (Originally published 1944.) A classic study of the contribution of British West Indian slavery to the expansion of British capitalism and the Industrial Revolution.

Wilson, William Julius. *The Truly Disadvantaged: The Inner City, the Underclass, and Public Policy.* Chicago: University of Chicago Press, 1987. A seminal contribution to the worsening plight of the black underclass in the United States. Should be read in conjunction with the author's *The Declining Significance of Race* (University of Chicago Press, 1978).

Chapter

14

The Gender Division of Labor and Gender Inequality

Sociologists use the word **sex** to denote the biological differentiation between males and females. They use the word **gender,** on the other hand, to identify the entire corpus of socially acquired roles and relationships characterizing men and women in the world's societies. The gender relations of a society represent the social and cultural elaborations that society builds onto the biological differences between the sexes. Thus we may say that "sex = male/female," whereas "gender = man/woman." Sex and gender correspond, of course, but they do so only incompletely, and so the sex of a person by no means thoroughly determines his or her gender. One goal of this chapter shall be to determine the extent to which sex and gender correspond (or fail to correspond) in human societies, and why the degree of correspondence (or noncorrespondence) is as it is.

All human societies use sex as a major criterion for assigning individuals to tasks within the social division of labor. While all societies usually have a number of roles that can be suitably performed by either sex, they prescribe some roles as distinctly masculine and others as distinctly feminine. Indeed, no society anywhere in the world is either casual or random in the gender-typing of many of its tasks. Furthermore, not only do all societies have a gender division of labor, but all have as well corresponding ideological conceptions of the nature and significance of masculinity and femininity, including evaluative notions of the relative status of the sexes. Thus no society is either casual or random in evaluating the social standing of each sex or the differential contribution made by each sex to that society's overall functioning. In short, all societies have a gender division of labor, structured forms of **gender inequality,** and ideological conceptions of masculinity and femininity. This chapter attempts to describe and explain numerous aspects of these universal social phenomena.

THE GENDER DIVISION OF LABOR AND GENDER INEQUALITY: THE OVERALL PATTERN

There is considerable variation across societies in the assignment of people to gender-typed occupational roles. Some activities—such as pottery making, weaving, or horticulture—that are assigned to women in some societies are assigned to men in others. But despite these variations, there are a number of occupations that are consistently assigned to men and others that are consistently assigned to women in most of the world's societies.

Using a sample of 185 societies, Murdock and Provost (1973) have attempted to identify the most consistently "masculine" and "feminine" occupations found throughout the world. They identify as the most consistently masculine occupations the following: hunting large game animals; metalworking; smelting ores; lumbering; woodworking; making musical instruments; trapping; boatbuilding; stonework; working in bone, horn, and shell; mining; quarrying; and bonesetting. The most consistently feminine occupations are fuel gathering, preparing drinks, gathering and preparing wild plant foods, dairy production, laundering, water fetching, and cooking. Women are also extensively involved throughout the world in rearing children and performing general domestic activities.

In general, those activities that are consistently assigned to men tend to be ones requiring greater physical strength, higher levels of risk and danger, more frequent travel from home, higher levels of group cooperation, longer periods of technical training, and higher skill levels (Parker and Parker, 1979). By contrast, consistently feminine occupations involve relatively less danger, tend to be more repetitive, do not require intense concentration, are more easily interruptible, and require less training and fewer skills (Parker and Parker, 1979).

Of greater concern in this chapter is the relative status of the sexes: the degree to which they are unequally placed and valued, as well as the degree to which human societies are male- or female-centered. William Divale and Marvin Harris (1976) have identified the existence of a widespread material, social, and ideological complex of male supremacy in band and tribal societies. They note that male supremacist institutions in these societies are expressed in numerous ways. Marriage and kinship practices, for example, reveal marked gender asymmetry in their organization. Patrilocality and virilocality—forms of postmarital residence organized through males—are approximately eight times as frequently found as matrilocality and uxorilocality—forms of postmarital residence organized through females.* Furthermore, patriliny—the tracing of descent through males—is approximately five times as common as matriliny—the tracing of descent through females. Moreover, even matrilineal societies invest authority over the domestic group's affairs in the hands of males rather than females. Marked gender asymmetry is also revealed in marriage practices, inas-

---

*See Chapter 15 for fuller discussions of these and related terms.

much as polygyny—the marriage of one man to several wives—is found 141 times as often as polyandry—the marriage of one woman to several husbands.

Pervasive gender asymmetry is also highly characteristic of band and tribal political institutions. Headmanship is characteristic of hunting and gathering societies, but there is no such thing as "headwomanship." Likewise, bigmanship is widely found among horticulturalists, but its logical counterpart, "bigwomanship," has never been reported to exist. Male monopoly over political leadership is also expressed in the fact that men completely monopolize the weapons of war and the hunt, even to the extent that women are often forbidden to touch or handle these weapons.

Gender asymmetry is particularly characteristic of the ideological sector in band and tribal societies. Divale and Harris note here the existence of widespread beliefs emphasizing the inferiority of females. Women are widely believed in many societies to be sources of evil and pollution, and many taboos exist in order to restrict their activities, particularly during menstruation. Furthermore, male gods generally outnumber female gods, and legendary heroes outnumber legendary heroines. In many societies, men menace women with masks, bull roarers, and other sacred paraphernalia. Gender asymmetry in the ideological sector is also revealed by the widespread cultural preference for male children, a preference that is often embodied in the rule that the firstborn must be a male.

Many other examples of the male-centeredness of band and tribal social institutions can be added to the list provided by Divale and Harris. Male ritualistic activity is generally far more frequent and elaborate than the ritualistic activity associated with females; male secret societies have no strict female counterpart; men dominate the prestige spheres of economic activity; the labor performed by women is generally accorded lower status than that performed by men; and women are often subjected to forms of serious physical abuse (gang rape, for instance), whereas this is seldom if ever the case for men.

Gender-asymmetrical institutions are by no means confined to band and tribal societies, however. On the contrary, societies at more advanced evolutionary levels reveal new, and often more intensive, forms of female subordination. In agrarian societies, economic and political affairs are tightly organized under male control, and women are shunted off into the seclusion of a private, domestic world. In most such societies, the activities of women are very tightly controlled, and there is often special concern with women's sexuality. In short, the status of women in agrarian societies is generally so low that they are treated like dependent minors. The agrarian world is an almost completely male-centered and male-dominated world.

Industrial societies are also characterized by significant inequalities between the sexes, although not to the extreme found in the agrarian world. Men typically dominate positions of high status in all industrial societies, and industrial state systems are heavily under the control of men. Women are heavily confined either to lower-status, lower-paying jobs or to the domestic sector and its functions (or to both). Women are still widely regarded, both by men and by themselves, as holding a status that is secondary to men's. Gender equality is characteristic of no industrial society found in the world today.

The picture that strikingly emerges from the foregoing is one of widespread, indeed universal, female subordination. Of course, in some societies the overall status of women is fairly high, but there is no known society in which women achieve complete equality with men in all of the relevant sectors of social life. In each and every society about which we have reliable information, the social standing of men is higher than that of women. This is true even in the most gender egalitarian of all societies, hunters and gatherers. Here men monopolize positions of leadership; and hunting, a male monopoly, is defined as more prestigious than gathering, a female monopoly.

Despite an occasional dissenting voice (e.g., Leacock, 1978), a widespread consensus exists among social scientists concerning the universality of male dominance and female subordination. Certainly few take seriously the speculative claims of some nineteenth-century anthropologists about the original existence of primitive matriarchies, societies in which women dominated men. No matriarchy has ever been discovered, and it seems exceedingly unlikely that one ever will be. By the same token, few contemporary social scientists claim that there is any society in which complete gender equality can be found. The view of Michelle Rosaldo and Louise Lamphere (1974:3; cited in Giele, 1977) may be taken as representative of modern social-scientific opinion:

> Everywhere we find that women are excluded from certain crucial economic or political activities, that their roles as wives and mothers are associated with fewer powers and prerogatives than are the roles of men. It seems fair to say, then, that all contemporary societies are to some extent male-dominated, and although the degree and expression of female subordination vary greatly, sexual asymmetry is presently a universal fact of human social life.

THE GENDER DIVISION OF LABOR AND GENDER INEQUALITY IN EVOLUTIONARY PERSPECTIVE

As Rosaldo and Lamphere have noted in the quotation above, despite certain universal features of the relations between the sexes these relations vary markedly from one society to another. These variations are just as worthy of social-scientific study as are the universals. The best way to examine such variations is to explore the association between gender-role patterns and a society's technological adaptation.

Hunting and Gathering Societies

The principal economic roles in hunting and gathering societies are strongly gender-typed. Hunting is overwhelmingly the province of men, while gathering is basically the task of women. While women may occasionally hunt small game and do some fishing, big game hunting and deep-sea fishing are universally monopolized by men. Likewise, while men may sometimes participate in gathering activities, gathering is mostly a female concern. Hunting and gathering societies vary in the proportion of subsistence provided by either meat or plant food. Among some hunters and gatherers, such as the Eskimo, hunting accounts for nearly all of the total subsistence needs. Among most hunting and gathering societies, however, the foods provided by gathering account for a substantial portion of the total subsistence. This fact underlines the tremendous importance of gathering for most foragers, and indicates that women generally play a prominent productive role in such societies.

In assessing the relative status of the sexes among hunter-gatherers, Ernestine Friedl (1975) has noted that men generally have greater opportunities than women for the achievement of recognition and prestige, and that these greater opportunities stem primarily from their roles as hunters. Hunting gives men the opportunity for the extradomestic exchange of meat, the most prestigious food among foragers. Where men provide most of the food supply through meat, as among the Eskimo, their status is much higher than that of women. In the same way, where men do little hunting and where the contribution of women to subsistence is high, the status of men and women is more nearly equivalent.

The male contribution to subsistence through hunting also appears to give men an opportunity for control over women. Where men engage in little hunting or where the male monopoly over meat is low, men exercise little control over women. Polygyny, for example, is rare in societies of this type. But where male hunting provides the great bulk of the food supply, male aggression toward women is prominent and a pattern of strong male dominance exists. Among the Eskimo, for example, a generalized pattern of male dominance and female subordination is found. Women are treated as sex objects and have little control over their own destiny. Friedl thus concludes that male dominance is greatest where men monopolize economic production, and that gender equality is most nearly approached in foraging societies in which men and women work together to provide subsistence.

Generalizing about sex roles in hunting and gathering societies is no easy task, given the variable patterns that have been found. Among some foragers, such as the Eskimo or various Australian groups, male dominance is distinctly present and a virtual male-supremacy complex exists. Among other groups, such as the !Kung San, gender equality is closely approximated. Beyond these variable patterns, it appears that the following generalizations can be established: males tend to monopolize political decision making and to have at least somewhat higher status in all hunting and gathering groups; in most, but by no means all, groups, women enjoy a high degree of autonomy and relatively high status; gender equality is more nearly attained among foragers than among all other societal types.

Horticultural Societies

In their major study of the relations between the sexes, Kay Martin and Barbara Voorhies (1975) analyze women's position in horticultural societies. They do not make a distinction between simple and intensive horticulturalists.

Women generally continue their important role in economic production among horticulturalists. In analyzing a sample of 515 horticultural societies drawn from the *Ethnographic Atlas* (Murdock, 1967), Martin and Voorhies note that women dominate cultivation in 41 percent of these societies, men dominate cultivation in 22 percent, and in 37 percent men and women share in the performance of cultivative tasks. Furthermore, the greater the importance of crops in the total diet, the more likely males are to be involved in cultivation.

The status of women among horticulturalists cannot be analyzed independently of kinship patterns, since these bear a strong relationship to the nature of women's activities. Using a sample of 104 horticultural societies, Martin and Voorhies found that 56 percent had patrilineal descent and another 24 percent had matrilineal descent. In general, the status of women is higher among those horticulturalists practicing matrilineal descent. Among matrilineal horticulturalists, women are the focus of the entire social structure, and this elevates their overall social standing. Kinship links are traced through women, and men trace their genealogical connections through their mothers and sisters rather than through their fathers. In such societies, females are central to the conduct of economic activity. Land is owned matrilineally and women cultivate it on behalf of their own matrilineages, which means that women often wield considerable influence over political affairs. However, politics in matrilineal horticultural societies is still controlled by men, except that in these cases men exercise authority in their roles as brothers of women rather than as husbands. Thus, although matrilineal societies generally hold women in fairly high regard, women are still politically subordinated to men, and their general status ranks below that of men. Matriliny reduces, but does not eliminate, male dominance.

Since patrilineal societies trace descent through males, men become the focus of the social structure among patrilineal horticulturalists. Land is owned and inherited through men, and women hold a more peripheral relationship to economic resources than is the case in matrilineal horticultural societies. Women among patrilineal horticulturalists are economic producers for kin groups organized through and dominated by their husbands. It therefore follows that the status of women in these societies is generally quite low, and certainly lower than among horticulturalists organized matrilineally. In patrilineal societies a husband acquires rights in a woman as a childbearer, and any offspring belong to the father and his kin group. Women represent investments for the patrilineages of their husbands or fathers. In her father's patrilineage, a young girl performs valuable labor services, and upon her marriage she becomes valuable for both her labor and her reproductive services in the patrilineage of her husband. Women frequently transfer their kin group membership at marriage from their father's to their husband's patrilineage, and when this occurs marriage means that women enter a world of strangers. Women ordinarily hold very low status in this new world. They typically do not achieve respect and influence until they reach old age, and even then they do so only through their connections with sons or other male relatives.

A great range of variation in the status of women is found among horticulturalists. At one extreme we find groups like the Iroquois, a North American Indian society in which women had unusually high status and influence (Brown, 1975). At the other extreme we find societies like the Yanomama, where female subordination is intense and where social life is overwhelmingly male-centered (Chagnon, 1983). Among horticulturalists, the Iroquois are much more the exception than are the Yanomama, for women on balance tend to have a very low status. Certainly it seems reasonable to say that horticultural women generally hold lower status than their counterparts among hunter-gatherers. But it is in agrarian societies that the status of women reaches its depths.

Agrarian Societies

In the transition from horticultural to agrarian societies, profound changes took place in technology and economic life. These changes had major consequences for the nature of the relations between the sexes (Martin and Voorhies, 1975). With the shift to intensive forms of agrarian cultivation, women were largely cast out of an economically productive role, and economic production came to be strongly dominated by men. As men took control of production, women were assigned to the household and the domestic activity connected with it. There thus developed what Martin and Voorhies have called the "inside-outside dichotomy," or what others have termed the "public-domestic" distinction. This involves the partitioning of social life into two largely separate and distinct realms. On the one hand, there is the "public" sphere of activities that take place outside the domicile. This sphere includes economics, politics, religious life, education, and so on. It is a sphere monopolized by and for men. On the other hand, there is the "inside" or domestic sphere of household activity, a realm principally concerned with cooking, cleaning, laundering, and nursing and rearing children. This sphere came to be considered distinctly feminine in nature.

It appears that the inside-outside dichotomy did not emerge in fully identifiable form until the rise of agrarian societies, for most societies below the agrarian level either do not recognize such a distinction or have developed it only minimally. With the emergence of this distinction, men and women came to live in markedly different social worlds, and there developed an elaborate ideology celebrating the "natural" superiority of males and emphasizing the "natural" inferiority of females. The rise of the inside-outside dichotomy was associated with the descent of woman to the lowest point of her structured inferiority.

A widespread feature of life in most agrarian societies has been the seclusion of women and the restriction of many of their activities (Martin and Voorhies, 1975; Mandelbaum, 1988). Women have been forbidden to own property, to engage in politics, to pursue education, or to engage in virtually any activity outside the walls of their domiciles. In many agrarian societies, women have been legal minors and dependent wards of men. Their seclusion from men has been symbolized, especially in the Islamic world, by the wearing of clothing to conceal all body parts but the eyes. Agrarian societies have typically exercised very tight controls over female sexuality. Many agrarian societies demand premarital virginity on the part of girls, and both premarital and extramarital sexual activity can lead to severe punishment, even including the killing of the offending woman by her husband or other kinsmen. By contrast, agrarian societies have permitted and even encouraged nonmarital sexual activity for males. Women are also usually forbidden to initiate divorce, normally an exclusive male prerogative.

Agrarian societies generally think of males as ideally suited for those tasks that demand intelligence, strength, and emotional fitness. Women, by contrast, are deemed most suitable for roles that are menial, repetitive, and uncreative. By and large, women are social appendages of fathers and husbands and are in general completely economically dependent upon them. Women are viewed as dependent, immature, and in need of male protection and supervision; and these conceptions have been deeply imbedded in agrarian religion, morality, and law (Martin and Voorhies, 1975).

Whereas intensive male dominance is a widespread occurrence in many horticultural and some hunting and gathering societies, agrarian societies have been the most consistently, thoroughly, and intensively male supremacist. In the material, social, and ideological sectors of agrarian life, women have typically been assigned a highly inferior status. This fact is in all probability closely related to the character of agrarian economic production.

Industrial Societies

Industrial Capitalist Societies Capitalism and industrialism have been responsible for bringing women back into the sphere of economic production. Nevertheless, many aspects of the old agrarian gender-role pattern remain. Women still do the bulk of the domestic labor and men still dominate politics, the most prestigious and highly paid jobs, and other extradomestic spheres of social life. Women are still mainly confined to poorly paid, low-prestige jobs, those, for example, in clerical, secretarial, and service work. Women also dominate jobs that have a strong nurturant component, such as elementary school teaching and nursing. Only small inroads have been made by women into the top managerial and executive positions in corporate life, and men still monopolize the high-status professions, such as architecture, law, medicine, engineering, and university teaching. In situations in which men and women hold the same or similar jobs, women are usually paid significantly less. Currently, the median income of American women in full-time jobs is only about 72 percent of that of men (U.S. Bureau of the Census, 1992).

Many social scientists, Marxists in particular, have portrayed capitalism as actually having negative consequences for the social position of women (J. Thomas, 1988). Yet despite their generally subordinate status in many spheres of social life, women have in many respects been emancipated since the advent of capitalism. They have, for example, achieved virtual political and legal equality with men, and they are no longer regarded merely as legal minors and dependent wards of men. Compared to women in nearly all agrarian and Third World societies, as well as to women in many horticultural and pastoral societies, women under capitalism have achieved a dramatic improvement in their status and in their capacity to control their own lives free from male tyranny.

Edward Shorter (1976) has suggested that this improvement may have begun at least as early as the eighteenth century. Many women became integrated into the capitalist market economy through employment in cottage industries and early forms of factory work, and this newfound economic role improved women's overall power, autonomy, and status with regard to men. As Shorter notes (1976:520), "in the capitalist market economy, unlike the traditional moral economy, women's work brought in resources from outside.... Therewith the woman's contribution to the household economy became obvious and quantifiable. The weekly wage packet turned into a weapon in the struggle for domestic power." Shorter stresses that these changes in women's status were confined to peasants and workers, and that for the middle and upper classes the situation was perhaps different. In these more prosperous groups the status of women may actually have declined in the early phases of capitalism as women's economic dependence on their husbands grew. But as Shorter points out, peasant and working-class women constituted the great bulk of the population in these times.

The substantial improvement in the status of women in much more recent times can be linked to their rapid movement into the labor force in the twentieth century. Women are now a substantial portion of the labor force in all industrial capitalist societies (Table 14.1). In the late nineteenth century women were greatly in demand as secretaries and clerical workers. However, the vast majority of working women before World War II were single, widowed, or divorced. Most married women, especially those with dependent children, stayed in the home. For example, in the United States in 1930 only 11.7 percent of married women worked outside the home, compared to 50.5 percent of single women and 34.4 percent of women who were widowed or divorced (U.S. Department of Commerce, 1975). Since World War II, though, the increase in the labor force participation of married women, even those with young children, has been remarkable. In the United States in 1948, for example, only 10.8 percent of married women with children under six years of age were in the labor force (U.S. Department of Commerce, 1975); however, by 1980 45.1 percent of women in the same category were in the labor force, and by 1995 the proportion had climbed to 63.5 percent (U.S. Bureau of the Census, 1996).

Over the past few decades women have also made significant inroads into the learned professions. In the United States in 1960 women made up only 5.5 percent of physicians, 0.8 percent of dentists, 2.5 percent of lawyers, and 0.4 percent of engineers (U.S. Bureau of the Census, 1985). But by 1995 they constituted 24.4 percent of physicians, 13.4 percent of dentists, 26.4 percent of lawyers, and 8.4 percent of engineers (U.S. Bureau of the Census, 1996). Although women have hardly achieved equality with men in their access to these

Table 14.1 WOMEN'S LABOR FORCE PARTICIPATION IN SELECTED INDUSTRIAL COUNTRIES, 1960–1994

Country	% of Women in Labor Force[a]				Women as % of Labor Force		
	1960	1970	1980	1994	1970	1980	1994
United States	42.6	50.4	61.3	63.7	36.7	41.9	45.0
Canada	33.7	41.1	57.8	67.8	32.2	40.0	44.0
France	45.4	47.5	52.5	59.5	36.6	40.1	44.0
Germany[b]	49.2	48.1	50.0	61.8	35.9	37.8	41.0
Japan	60.1	55.4	54.9	62.1	39.3	38.7	40.0
Sweden	50.1	60.6	75.7	74.4	39.5	45.2	47.0
United Kingdom	46.1	53.5	61.7	65.4	36.2	40.3	43.0

[a]Labor force of all ages as a percentage of the population 15 to 64 years old.

[b]The figures for 1960–1980 pertain to former West Germany, those for 1994 to unified Germany.

Sources: U.S. Bureau of the Census, *Statistical Abstract of the United States.* Washington, D.C.: U.S. Government Printing Office, 1985, Table 1492, 1988, Table 1402; and 1996, Table 1349; World Bank, *World Development Report,* New York: Oxford University Press, 1996, Table 4.

professions, the situation has improved significantly nonetheless.

State Socialist Societies In the old Soviet Union women became half the labor force, and they were found at all levels of the Soviet work force. The high representation of women in the Soviet labor force has been due in large part to the great manpower shortage that resulted from the Soviet Union's participation in World War II. Following the war, women began to enter a great many occupations in very large numbers. In recent years Soviet women have been highly represented at all levels of the occupational structure, including the professions. It is particularly interesting to note the participation of women in the professional fields. As Bernice Rosenthal (1975) notes, women constituted 72 percent of the doctors; 35 percent of the lawyers; 47 percent of the judges and associate judges; 90 percent of the dentists, medics, and nurses; 58 percent of agricultural specialists with advanced degrees; 76 percent of the accountants, statisticians, and planners; 38 percent of all scientists; and 33 percent of engineers.

These figures seem to suggest an enormous stride by Soviet women toward equality in the economic sector. However, the figures are seriously misleading, as Rosenthal explains (1975:444–446):

> The position of a Soviet doctor cannot be compared to an American one. Medicine is notoriously ill-paid. . . . Within the medical profession, men head the hospitals and departments; they are the surgeons, the highest-paid specialty, and women are the general practitioners, midwives, nurses, and ward attendants. . . . Law is not a particularly lucrative profession either and within it the "advocats" (the best paid specialty) are usually men. Women judges and associate judges (the official figures lump the two together) are concentrated in the lower courts.

> . . .

> Within the research hierarchy, only 2 percent of the Full Members of the prestigious Soviet Academy of Science are women and only 2.5 percent of the Corresponding Members. No woman has ever been President, Vice-President, Chief Scientific Secretary, or member of the Presidium of the Soviet Academy of Science.

> . . .

In Soviet society, power, money, and prestige go to top executives in factories and collective farms. Women are extremely rare in positions of authority where they have to give orders to men. In factories, women are 6 percent of the directors, 16 percent of the chief engineers, and 12 percent of the department heads. . . . Women executives are most prominent in routine jobs; they do not set policy. Secondary-level positions such as bookkeepers, "rate-setters," and technicians are predominantly female.

. . .

Not only are the top levels of Soviet society less accessible to women than to men, but women are overly represented at the lowest levels of the Soviet economic spectrum. Though women constitute half the labor force, their total wages are only one quarter of all wages earned. . . . Well over half of Soviet women earn less than the average Soviet wage of 103 rubles/month. Furthermore, many women are paid at piece rates; their wages often fall below the official Soviet minimum wage of 60 rubles/month.

From Rosenthal's comments, it is clear that Soviet women have held a very secondary status in the Soviet economic structure, a status that, in fact, has closely resembled that of women in the occupational structures of the capitalist societies. Women have also been severely underrepresented in Soviet politics. The political participation of women in Soviet society has been heavily confined to positions in the lower reaches of government; they have seldom been found in top political positions (Rosenthal, 1975).

While women have played a major role in the Soviet economy, this has not excused them from domestic work. Household labor in the old Soviet Union is still viewed as work that is distinctly "feminine," and men contribute little or nothing to domestic work. This has given Soviet women a double burden: the responsibility for employment in the workplace as well as virtually full responsibility for domestic tasks. As Rosenthal comments (1975:429), "The 'dual burden' of home and work poses a formidable barrier to equality which is yet to be surmounted."

It thus seems clear that the Soviet Union has scarcely made any greater progress toward gender equality than have the major industrial capitalist societies. In both capitalism and state socialism, basic gender inequalities remain a very significant part of social life. To this point in human history, neither industrialization nor political ideology has been successful in putting an end to male dominance and the subordination of women. This fact can hardly be ignored in any explanation of the fundamental causes of gender inequality.

The Third World

In many ways the status of women in the contemporary underdeveloped world closely resembles that found in agrarian societies of the past (Ward, 1985). In the peasant agricultural sector men tend to dominate agricultural work, and this economic control gives them control over the other major institutional sectors of social life. Thus, strongly patriarchal relations between the sexes are a pervasive feature of peasant life in the Third World, with the old agrarian inside-outside dichotomy remaining firmly in place.

Outside the agricultural sector, work roles are of course very different, but the status of women still appears to be very low. Women tend to be heavily concentrated in the lowest-paying jobs with the lowest social prestige. They are notably underrepresented in professional and managerial positions and overrepresented in service work, especially in such domestic service jobs as housekeepers, cooks, wet nurses, governesses, and servants. Women are also heavily overrepresented in such traditional craft jobs as those involving pottery making, dressmaking, basket and mat making, and weaving (cf. Chinchilla, 1977; Arizpe, 1977).

Recent changes in the organization of the world capitalist system have had significant implications for women's work and status in the Third World (cf. Ward, 1985, 1990; Fuentes and Ehrenreich, 1983). As noted in Chapter 9, in the past two or three decades there has emerged a tendency toward a "new international division of labor" (Fröbel et al., 1980). Developed capitalist countries have been relocating many of their industries in the underdeveloped world as a means of using cheaper labor and cutting production costs. The industry most frequently the subject of this industrial relocation has been the textile industry, with countries such as Singapore, Hong Kong, South Korea, Taiwan, Jamaica, the Dominican Republic, El Salvador, and Mexico being some of the leading countries in which this relocation has been occurring (Safa, 1981; Fernandez-Kelly, 1983; Tiano, 1990). The Third World workers involved have been overwhelmingly women, especially young, single women.

What are the implications of these major economic changes for Third World women? One basically positive result is that their new employment gives many women a new economic autonomy and loosens the control of their families, especially their fathers, over them. Yet as Helen Safa (1981) has pointed out, this new economic autonomy seems to be accompanied by a severe form of economic exploitation. The jobs that women perform in these new industries require very little skill and pay poorly. For the most part the work is very tedious and often requires long periods of intense concentration. In electronics industries, where workers have to spend most of their time looking through microscopes, they often suffer from impaired vision after only a few years on the job (Safa, 1981). Moreover, not only is the pay extremely low, but fringe benefits are generally nonexistent, as are opportunities for worker unionization or other forms of worker organization that might improve conditions. In many Third World countries with these new industries, the governments have taken extreme measures to prevent workers from organizing, including the violent suppression of worker protest (Safa, 1981).

Firm generalizations about the status of women in the Third World are difficult to make, for there are some notable variations from country to country. By and large, though, women occupy a highly inferior status in the Third World, and it is doubtful that their position has improved with some of the most recent economic changes. The plight of the Third World today is a very serious one, and women clearly bear the burden of this plight more than men.

THEORIES OF GENDER INEQUALITY

A variety of theories have been proposed to account for the nature of the gender division of labor and gender inequality. Some of these theories focus primarily on explaining the universal pattern, while others are more concerned with accounting for variations in gender roles. *Sociobiological* theories attempt to explain the universality of male domination by reference to fundamental biological differences between the sexes. These theories assume that, regardless of the degree of social elaboration of gender inequality, gender-role differences are erected in accordance with certain basic features of human biology. *Materialist* theories, which come in both Marxian and non-Marxian versions, attempt to explain gender-role patterns as products of the infrastructural arrangements of a society. They concentrate more on the variations in gender-role systems, and generally assume that it is the nature of technology, economic production, and ecology, rather than biological necessity, that principally determines how the sexes relate to each other. *Political* theories also attempt to explain variations in gender-role patterns. The most prominent of these theories emphasize variations in the prevalence of warfare as the key determinant of variations in gender roles. Since these major types of theories endeavor to explain different aspects of gender inequality (universality versus variation), they may be complementary rather than contradictory.

Sociobiological Theories

Sociobiological interpretations of gender roles have been presented by Pierre van den Berghe (1973) and Steven Goldberg (1993). Van den Berghe presents a bioevolutionary theory based upon evidence from primate studies and a speculative reconstruction of hominid evolution. His main argument is that all contemporary gender-role arrangements reflect the basic "biogram" that modern humans inherited from their primate and hominid ancestors. This biogram is one that predisposes men to hunt, to make war, and to protect the group, and women to nurture children. Van den Berghe sees it as underlying the universal pattern of male political domination over females.

It is important to realize that van den Berghe offers this sociobiological theory only to account for the universality of male domination. Variations in the form or intensity of male domination, he says, are not due to biology, but to the various cultural elaborations on the human biogram. Thus there is nothing in this particular theory that is designed to explain the basic differences in gender arrangements from one society to another. Van den Berghe's theory is "biosocial" in that it proposes that both biological and sociocultural factors are necessary to account for all of the aspects of gender-role behavior.

In a recent book carrying the very politically incorrect title *Why Men Rule: A Theory of Male Dominance* (1993), Steven Goldberg attempts to explain why men everywhere monopolize a society's leadership roles and high-status positions. The reason for these patterns, he says, is neuroendocrinological: men have much larger concentrations of the male sex hormone testosterone than do women (in point of fact more than 10 times as much). Testosterone levels appear to relate closely to levels of aggression, dominance, and competitiveness. Therefore men's greater dominance and status attainment tendencies will mean that they will, on the whole, much more frequently aim for and achieve positions of leadership and high status. Women are simply at a natural disadvantage in the competition for these positions. Goldberg believes it is extremely noteworthy that there is not a single society known from sociological, anthropological, or historical research that constitutes an exception to the pattern he is discussing. All it would take to overthrow his theory, he says, is just one exception—yet none is forthcoming. Various exceptions have been proposed, but when these are scrutinized more closely they all collapse.

Most sociologists disagree with the kind of interpretation presented by van den Berghe and Goldberg, claiming that these features of gender roles are learned through the socialization process. Little boys are taught to be aggressive and dominant and little girls are taught to be nurturant. These are cultural patterns transmitted socially from generation to generation. However, as van den Berghe and Goldberg point out, the problem with this argument is that it fails to consider *why* little boys and little girls are taught in these ways throughout the world. Cultural patterns and socialization practices are simply reflections, they claim, of the fact that little boys *really are* more aggressive and little girls *really are* more nurturant. Or, as Goldberg puts it, these socialization patterns are simply social conformation to a basic psychophysiological reality that people in all societies readily recognize.

A good deal of evidence has now accumulated to suggest that the claims of van den Berghe and Goldberg are basically correct. Evidence from studies of infrahuman primate behavior, cross-cultural studies of sex differences, and studies of sex differences in human development all point toward the conclusion that human biology is a significant component in differential behavior of the sexes (Parker and Parker, 1979).

Seymour and Hilda Parker (1979) note that aggression is a behavioral difference between the sexes that is extremely widespread in the animal world. Among mammals males generally exhibit higher levels of aggression, and among the nonhuman primates males are generally reported to be substantially more prone to rough-and-tumble play and threat and dominance behaviors. Moreover, these differences seem to begin in early childhood and last throughout the organisms' lifetimes, just as they tend to do in humans. Parker and Parker also review a good deal of research evidence showing that testosterone is significantly linked to aggressive and dominance behavior among a variety of mammalian species. Studies using rhesus monkeys, for example, have shown that monkeys with higher levels of blood plasma testosterone are more inclined toward aggressive and dominance behavior and less inclined toward "maternal" forms of behavior. And when female monkeys are injected with testosterone, they behave more aggressively and engage in more dominance behavior.

Finally, the Parkers examine data on human development highly suggestive of differential biological propensities of the sexes (cf. Money and Ehrhardt, 1972). Longitudinal studies of females who prenatally had higher than normal levels of the male sex hormone androgen show that they develop differently from other females. They exhibit higher levels of aggression and energy expenditure, are more likely to select males rather than females as their companions, show less interest in doll play or other forms of feminine play associated with maternal behavior, show greater interest in nondomestic careers, and are more frequently described as tomboys.

On the basis of their detailed review of the above and other findings, Parker and Parker conclude that "there is a neat and logical fit between biopsychological sex differences and uniformities in the sexual division of labor" (1979:299).

In addition to the foregoing, we cannot overlook other obvious biological differences between the sexes: that men are physically larger and stronger and that women bear and nurse children. These biological facts no doubt play a crucial role in shaping certain aspects of the gender division of labor. It is clearly advantageous for hunter-gatherer societies to make men the hunters, for pregnant and lactating women would undoubtedly be less adept at hunting than men. Men are not burdened with these responsibilities, and they are as well swifter and stronger, facts that make males the logical choice as the sex to hunt wild game (especially big game).

Moreover, men's greater strength is certainly one reason they monopolize the more strenuous and demanding tasks in all societies. Women, for example, usually take a major part in cultivation in horticultural societies, this type of cultivation not requiring great physical strength or endurance. Men, however, monopolize economic production under intensive agriculture, and labor under such conditions requires high levels of strength and energy expenditure. In addition, it is not difficult to see why all societies make women the primary providers of child care, since it is the women who must bear and nurse children and who, therefore, have undoubtedly been built by biological evolution to have temperamental qualities essential to child-care tasks. There is also a sound reason why the world's societies tend to assign women jobs that are lower in skill level and more easily interruptible. Since child-care responsibilities require unpredictable and frequent interruptions of any other simultaneous task, less-skilled jobs requiring lower levels of concentration are more suited to the sex with primary child-care duties (cf. Blumberg, 1978).

Women's childbearing and childrearing responsibilities also seem to be pertinent to the overall participation of women in economic production, especially to the reasons why they lost so much of their productive role in the transition to agrarian societies. As just noted, men's greater physical strength and stamina have undoubtedly played an important role in their dominance of agrarian economic production. Yet women's responsibilities for producing and rearing children may have been just as important if not more important. Women tend to have more children in agrarian societies than in any other type, thus increasing their child-care obligations. It becomes very difficult for women with such duties to participate heavily in economic activities that would take them away from their children for long periods of time. It also becomes difficult for mothers to take their children into the fields with them, because agrarian activities like plowing often spell serious danger for young children (cf. Ember, 1983; Blumberg, 1978).

Human biology may also be implicated in the major transformation in gender roles that has occurred within the Israeli kibbutzim (Tiger and Shepher, 1975; Spiro, 1979). The kibbutzim (singular: kibbutz) are communal settlements established in Israel by immigrant eastern European Jews in the early part of the twentieth century. Many of these settlements remain in operation today and continue to thrive. The kibbutzim were established according to strong ideological principles of economic and gender egalitarianism. In the beginning men and women worked alongside one another in agricultural tasks; women were actively involved in political administration; children were reared in communal nurseries; and both men and women took responsibility for such service work as cooking, laundering, and childrearing.

From this initial position of near gender equality, the kibbutzim have changed within one or two generations into societies marked by sharp gender-role differences. Men now monopolize agricultural work, and women have taken primary responsibility for cooking, laundering, and attending to children in the nurseries. In addition, men have come to be highly overrepresented in political administration. Tiger and Shepher (1975) report that women have voluntarily removed themselves from agricultural production and from politics. They have also made increasingly vocal demands over the years for the opportunity to spend more time individually with their own children. Tiger and Shepher interpret these changes as arising from the natural biological propensities of the sexes: the natural inclination of men to perform strenuous labor and dominate politics, and the inclination of women toward service-related and child-rearing roles.

Marxian Theories

A Marxian interpretation of the subordination of women has been given by Friedrich Engels in his famous book *The Origin of the Family, Private Property, and the State* (1970; orig. 1884). Engels drew his inspiration for this book both from Marx's own ideas and from the work of the nineteenth-century evolutionary anthropologist Lewis Henry Morgan. According to Engels, early forms of human society were characterized by production-for-use economies. The household was communal in nature, and all work was done for the household as a whole. Women were equal participants in the affairs of the group and made important contributions to economic production.

With the development of private property, all this was swept away. Men came to be the owners of property and production-for-exchange replaced production-for-use. As the owners of private property, men rose to political dominance. Women began to produce for their husbands rather than for the group as a whole. Thus, according to Engels, it was the development of private property and its subsequent control by men that was the basic cause of the subordination of women.

This interpretation is at best only partially correct. Engels thought that societies lacking private property and social classes gave equal standing to women. But as we have clearly seen, this is not the case. Not only is some degree of male domination universal, but many prestate and preclass societies are characterized by intensive forms of female subordination. It certainly cannot be the case, then, that private property and social classes were *the* fundamental causes of woman's subordination. Nonetheless, these factors have in fact been associated with a precipitous overall *decline* in the status of women. Engels has therefore generated a significant insight even though his theory is not acceptable as a general theory of the subordination of women.

Karen Sacks (1975, 1979) has presented a Marxian elaboration of Engels's argument. She argues that in sociocultural evolution the general decline in women's status has been significantly correlated with the development of production-for-exchange and private property. This has occurred because of its advantages for ruling classes. Men are selected for the production of goods of value

for the ruling class because, not having to nurse and rear children, they can be more intensively exploited than women. Women therefore come to be shunted off into domestic work. Once the division is made between women's domestic work and men's work in the larger productive arena, the conditions are created that allow women to be defined as less than full adults and as dependent wards of men.

Sacks's overall effort to link women's status to the nature of a society's mode of production has much to commend it (cf. Hendrix and Hossain, 1988), but there is one aspect of her theory that is highly dubious: her proposal that males control economic production in class-divided societies because of the desires of ruling classes. It is unlikely that ruling classes have much to do with it. Even without the actions of a ruling class, males would still take charge of economic production in societies where production requires intensive labor inputs and where women's reproductive responsibilities interfere with a heavy participation in production.

Marxian theories focusing specifically on the subordination of women in modern capitalist societies have also been prominent in recent years (cf. Morton, 1971; Vogel, 1983). These theories link gender divisions to the need of capitalists for an exploitable labor force. They suggest that the dominance of men over women is an outcome of the dominance of capitalists over workers. Women play a crucial role in the reproduction of labor power that men cannot play. That is, since women are the childbearers they must produce and continue to produce more offspring as future workers for capitalists. This requires their concentration in domestic work, which helps to ensure the dominance of their husbands over them.

The notion that it is woman's special role as a childbearer that contributes to her subordinate position is an important idea. The concentration of women in domestic labor and their corresponding removal from the workforce deprives them of valuable resources that can be used in their struggle for equality with men. However, the problem with the Marxian analysis on this score is that it insists on seeing this as a class phenomenon. How then can we explain the inferior position of women who do not belong to the subordinate class? The difficulty Marxists have in answering this question with any theoretical consistency suggests that there is more to the subordination of women than they propose.

Non-Marxian Materialist Theories

An important non-Marxian materialist theory of gender relations has been developed by Martin and Voorhies (1975). They claim that gender relations should be viewed largely as adaptive consequences of particular ecological, technological, and economic arrangements.

That men hunt and women gather in hunter-gatherer societies is viewed as highly adaptive within the framework of that mode of production. Since women's gathering activities mean that they contribute heavily to subsistence, men are unable to monopolize economic resources and to use such monopolization to create strong forms of female subordination. Since women contribute in a major way to subsistence, they command resources of their own and are able to turn this resource control into relatively high status.

The status of women in horticultural societies is linked to the material conditions that determine their control over resources. In horticultural societies lacking severe pressure against natural resources, matrilineal descent is common. This generally gives women fairly high status because women become the focus of the entire social structure; land is owned and inherited by matrilineal

kin groups, and women's productive labor is undertaken for the benefit of their own matrilineages. In horticultural societies where there is severe pressure against resources, patrilineal descent typically develops. Women's labor is performed for the benefit of their husbands' or fathers' patrilineages, and women come to be viewed as resources to be used for the benefit of males. Under such conditions, the status of women is relatively low.

Male control of production in agrarian societies is viewed by Martin and Voorhies as highly adaptive. Men are much better suited than women to perform activities requiring intensive labor, since women must assume responsibility for bearing and nursing children. Male control over economic resources allows them to gain control over the entire extradomestic sphere of social life, and as they do so women's status drops to an extremely low point.

Industrial societies have historically perpetuated much of the old inside-outside dichotomy of agrarian societies largely because men have continued to dominate production. However, the advance of industrial technology has done much to alter many aspects of traditional gender relations. Increasingly sophisticated technology has now made it possible for women to perform quite ably a great many extradomestic roles. As they have begun to do this, their overall status has markedly improved.

A similar theory has been developed by Rae Lesser Blumberg (1984). Blumberg argues that the key factor determining the status of women in the world's societies is their *level of economic power*. Where women's economic power is high, women are able to translate this power into relatively high status; conversely, where the economic power of women is low, their overall social status is almost invariably low.

Blumberg proposes three factors that determine women's level of economic power.

One of these is the strategic indispensability of women's labor. This factor includes such things as the extent to which women contribute to total household subsistence needs, the control women workers may have over technical expertise, the degree to which women workers have freedom from male supervision, and the size and cohesiveness of female work groups. A second factor is the organization of the kinship system. Where matrilocality and matriliny prevail, women's economic power is higher because of their greater involvement in property ownership and management. A final factor is the overall character of the stratification system. Blumberg argues that women fare less well in societies with well-developed stratification systems because intensive stratification tends to reduce the overall level of economic power that women possess.

Blumberg stresses that the possession of economic power by women means more than simply the capacity to translate this power into high status—into a positive regard and respect for them on the part of men. It means as well an overall capacity to manage their own lives in ways relatively free from male control. As Blumberg puts it, economic power gives women substantial "life options." These options include the ability to control such things as reproduction, sexuality, marriage, divorce, household affairs, freedom of movement, and access to education.

The interpretations offered by Martin and Voorhies and by Blumberg appear to overcome the main limitations of a Marxian approach. These theorists convincingly demonstrate that gender roles are closely related to underlying infrastructural arrangements. They therefore make sense out of the entire range of variation presented by gender-role systems. Where women take a major part in production, they control resources, which they then convert into rela-

tively high status and control over their own lives. By contrast, where women are largely excluded from production they command few resources; male control over economic resources translates into the opportunity to control and subordinate women in all of the major spheres of social life, and men are quick to take advantage of this opportunity to advance their own interests.

Political Theories

Divale and Harris (1976) have proposed an ingenious theory to explain the predominance of male supremacist social institutions in band and tribal societies. According to this theory, male supremacist institutions in band and tribal societies arise as a by-product of warfare. Warfare, in turn, emerges as a means of regulating population pressure against scarce resources. Warfare reduces population pressure by dispersing populations and creating a more favorable ratio between population and the food supply, especially the supply of animal protein. The practice of female infanticide is also implicated as a factor that serves to regulate population pressure. By selectively killing off a certain proportion of female infants, band and village societies are able to stabilize their populations and prevent severe deterioration in their standards of living.

There thus arises what Divale and Harris call the "warfare–female infanticide–male supremacy complex," a functionally related pattern of traits. Both warfare and female infanticide contribute to the maintenance of male supremacist institutions. The superiority of men in using hand-held weapons means that they will become the warriors, and warfare makes it necessary to train males to become aggressive and militant. Likewise, females are trained to become passive because they become rewards for male success in battle (through the practice of polygyny). Female infanticide also has consequences for the creation of male supremacist institutions, because an ideology of male supremacy can be used as a justification for killing female babies.

Divale and Harris have tested their theory using data from 112 band and village societies, and they claim that the theory is supported by the data. Furthermore, Harris (1977) points to the intensive pattern of warfare, female infanticide, and male supremacy among the Yanomama as an ethnographic case that illustrates and supports the theory. The Yanomama are one of the world's most militant societies (Chagnon, 1983). Yanomama men are well known for their extreme levels of aggression, both against other men and against women. Intravillage male violence is commonplace, and intervillage warfare and preparation for warfare are chronic features of Yanomama life. And it would be difficult to find a society more thoroughly imbued with male supremacist institutions. Men thoroughly control the economic and political sectors of life, and kinship is strongly male-centered. Men dominate religious life, and only they are permitted to use the hallucinogenic drug *ebene*, an important part of Yanomama religious activity. Men regularly engage in various sorts of violent acts against women: striking them with axes, shooting them with arrows, holding glowing sticks against their flesh, pulling at their earrings until their earlobes are loosened from the head. Ideologically, Yanomama men consider women to be thoroughly inferior second-class citizens who deserve the position they have in life. Yanomama women seem more or less resigned to their fate, and young girls learn from an early age that their world will be an almost completely male-centered one.

Another social scientist to stress warfare as the key to understanding male domination is Randall Collins (1975, 1985b).

However, Collins's theory, more general than Divale and Harris's, applies across the full range of (at least preindustrial) societies. Collins suggests that in situations in which there is little military threat and weapons are not well developed, there is not much reason for males to organize into military groups. Under such circumstances, relatively egalitarian relations between men and women prevail. On the other hand, the need for well-developed military organization favors an emphasis on male physical and aggressive characteristics, and this tends to produce high levels of male domination.

These political theories are carefully reasoned and there is considerable evidence that militarism and male domination are linked. However, it seems implausible to regard such theories as constituting an acceptable general interpretation of male supremacist institutions, for it is unlikely that warfare is among the principal causes of male domination. There are too many examples of societies without warfare but with strong male domination, or with warfare but with considerable importance given to the role of women. Nonetheless, it may well be that warfare is an important factor leading to the *intensification* of a preexisting state of male domination. Among societies like the Yanomama, for example, male supremacist institutions are carried to an exaggerated extreme and are found in close connection with chronic warfare (cf. Chagnon, 1983). But this fact does not elevate warfare to the status of the primary determinant of male domination.

Theories of Gender Inequality: Some Conclusions

What may be concluded about the causes of the gender division of labor and gender inequality in human societies? In view of the considerable evidence reviewed, the following conclusions seem appropriate: marked and cross-culturally consistent asymmetries in the gender division of labor, as well as the universal pattern of at least some degree of male domination, are to be explained as results of the basic biological differences between the sexes; major cross-cultural variations in the gender division of labor and in the intensity of male domination are to be explained primarily by reference to ecological, technological, and economic arrangements; in some societies, militarism and warfare may strongly intensify patterns of male domination.

As the preceding suggests, there is no single factor or set of factors capable of completely explaining gender relations. Different factors have to be introduced to explain different aspects of gender arrangements. It also seems inappropriate to conceptualize gender hierarchies in exactly the same fashion as we conceive of hierarchies based on class and race. Class and racial hierarchies have little or nothing to do with biological differences among individuals or groups, but are largely consequences of particular systems of economic production. Hierarchies based on gender are also strongly conditioned by productive arrangements, but the matter does not appear to stop there. The evidence suggests that gender hierarchies, at least in terms of their universal features, are also erected upon the basic human biogram.*

---

*It needs to be stressed that the argument that human biology plays a role in the relations between the sexes is not being used here, and should not be used elsewhere, as a justification for any prevailing pattern of gender inequality. There is a huge difference between a scientific analysis of the conditions giving rise to a human situation and a moral endorsement of that situation. Furthermore, even to the extent that biology is significantly implicated in some aspects of gender-role patterns, as many social scientists have pointed out, it should be remembered that "anatomy is not destiny."

SUMMARY

1. All human societies have a gender division of labor and gender inequality. Men tend to be assigned work that involves greater physical strength and danger, more technical training, and more frequent absences from home. Women tend to be assigned roles that are more repetitive and require less concentration. Gender inequality universally favors the male sex. This is evident in societies' political and familial institutions, in their ideological superstructures, and in numerous other aspects of the daily interaction of men and women.

2. The variations in gender-role patterns among societies are also of crucial significance. Hunter-gatherer societies, more than any other type of society, approximate a condition of gender equality. Women often have considerable authority and autonomy in these societies, and strong beliefs in female inferiority are generally absent.

3. Horticulturalists vary markedly in the status given to women. In some horticultural groups, such as the Iroquois, women have very high status and great authority. In others, such as the Yanomama, women are intensively subordinated and subjected to a wide range of physical abuses. Variations in horticultural gender-role patterns have much to do with kinship structures.

4. It is in agrarian societies that the status of women is lowest. These societies are notable for their strong inside-outside dichotomies. Men tend to dominate all activities outside the household, while women are largely confined to life oriented around the household. In most agrarian societies women are regarded as dependent wards of men. Powerful beliefs in the inherent inferiority of the female sex are found in these societies.

5. Capitalism and industrialism have in many ways liberated women from the extreme subordination they suffered in the agrarian era. Women now have much greater autonomy and are held in much higher regard. In recent decades women have come to occupy increasingly prominent positions in the work

Table 14.2   THEORIES OF GENDER INEQUALITY

Theory	Characteristics	Evaluation
Sociobiological theories	Focus on the universal features of gender inequality. Suggest that male monopolization of politics, warfare, and a society's high-status positions is rooted in genes developed millions of years ago by our ancestors. Women's inclinations toward nurturant roles are also considered to be biologically rooted.	Much evidence has now accumulated to suggest some basic validity to many sociobiological claims. However, these theories are only relevant to explaining universal (or at least very widespread) features of gender inequality. They cannot explain important variations in patterns of gender inequality.
Marxian theories	Emphasize class divisions and patterns of economic exploitation as basic to understanding the subordination of women. Long-term evolutionary versions stress the evolutionary decline in the status of women and see it as resulting from the growth of private property, production-for-exchange, and class stratification. Versions focusing only on modern capitalism see women's subordination as stemming from capitalism's need for an exploitable labor force.	Are on the right track in seeing a general connection between the mode of economic production and the status of women, but go awry in tying the specific explanation of female subordination to stratification and class struggle.
Non-Marxian materialist theories	Link the relations between the sexes to specific technological, economic, demographic, and ecological conditions. Where these conditions favor the heavy participation of women in economic production and a high level of economic power for women, women will tend to have a relatively high status. Otherwise, they tend to be strongly subordinated to men.	Achieve the best explanations of historical and cross-cultural variations in patterns of gender inequality. Superior to Marxian theories in showing how class stratification and gender inequality are largely independent phenomena.
Political theories	View male domination as a by-product of warfare and militarism. Where warfare and military organization are prominent features of social life, a premium is placed on training men to be highly aggressive, and this leads to an exaggerated emphasis on masculinity and a corresponding demeaning of women.	Are not adequate as a general explanation of patterns of gender inequality, but may usefully supplement materialist theories in that they may help explain some features of extreme forms of male domination.

world, and they are even gaining greater access to the learned professions. Important dimensions of gender inequality remain, however. The high position of women in state socialist societies has been exaggerated. In some ways the position of women in these societies is actually less favorable than their position within industrial capitalism.

6. It is difficult to generalize about the status of women in Third World countries, but in general women seem to have a very low status. Moreover, they are more severely affected than men by the economic burdens of life in such societies.

7. Social scientists have proposed many theories of gender inequality. The most important of these are sociobiological, materialist, and political theories. They are described and evaluated in Table 14.2.

SPECIAL TOPIC: THE RISE OF MODERN FEMINISM

A striking feature of life in industrial capitalist societies in the past century has been the rise of feminism. There have actually been two waves of feminist activity. The first began around the middle of the nineteenth century and occurred off and on until around 1920. Women became very active in the antislavery movement, and they also led numerous crusades against vice, particularly alcohol consumption and prostitution. Probably the best known of these movements was the Women's Christian Temperance Union (R. Collins, 1985b). Around the turn of the twentieth century, women in many industrial societies were pushing vigorously for the right to vote. The first country to give women voting rights was New Zealand in 1893; Australia, Sweden, Norway, and Finland soon followed New Zealand's example. England extended suffrage to women in 1918, the United States in 1920, and France not until the late 1940s (R. Collins, 1985b).

Feminism was dormant in the major industrial capitalist societies from about 1920 until the early 1960s. Since that time a second major wave of feminism has occurred. Women have demanded equality with men in the major spheres of social life, and have made enormous inroads into the labor force. A new feminist consciousness has emerged: Women see themselves as the equals of men and as deserving of the same basic social rewards that men have traditionally received. In addition, many women have sought an autonomy and a separate identity heretofore denied them. They have come to view themselves as having an existence apart from their roles as wives and mothers, and have insisted that men acknowledge this separate identity. These phenomena are well illustrated by the increasing frequency with which women retain their maiden names upon marriage (or hyphenate their maiden names with their husbands'), by a rise in the number of marriage postponements, and by declining rates of marriage and childbearing.

The second wave of feminism has also witnessed a vigorous development of organizations designed to promote women's interests. Undoubtedly the most important of these has been the National Organization of Women (NOW), which was founded in the United States in 1966. The most important driving force behind this organization was Betty Friedan, who became its first president. Friedan had authored just three years earlier the book that some have seen as the intellectual catalyst of the modern feminist movement, *The Feminine Mystique* (1963), a book strongly condemning the subordination of women in contemporary society. NOW is today a major organization that lobbies for women's rights at a national level and opposes conditions that hinder women's efforts to achieve equality with men in all areas of social life. For instance, it vigorously pushes for women's rights to control their own childbearing and for strict legal equality between men and women. But it was an effective organization even in its early years, as Joan Mandle points out (1979:171):

The year 1970 was a major watershed for NOW as an organization and for the women's movement as a whole. In August, NOW sponsored a highly successful Women's Strike for Equality, the largest demonstration concerning women ever held in the United States. The strike was particularly important for the women's movement because it involved close cooperation between NOW and many other women's groups, all of which supported the action, and also because NOW's local chapters expanded rapidly in the aftermath of the massive publicity given to the strike.

The two waves of feminist activity have been closely associated with significant changes in the character of Western capitalism, particularly as these changes have affected the position of women in the labor force. The first wave of feminism coincided with the movement of women in large numbers into various types of white-collar secretarial and clerical jobs in the expanding corporate sector of the economy (R. Collins, 1985b). The most recent wave of feminism has closely corresponded to the rapid entry of married women with small children into many sectors of the workforce. According to Marvin Harris (1981), the labor of these women has been increasingly sought by capitalists to fill the rapidly growing number of service and information jobs in the economy. Harris believes that this increased participation of women in the labor force eventually encouraged in them a feminist consciousness. As they worked alongside men more closely, and as they came to see how much less they were being paid for essentially the same work men were doing, women came to be more acutely aware of the powerful forces of economic discrimination that were working against them. This understanding helped to promote a broader consciousness regarding the overall social position of women.

Thus Harris believes that modern feminism—both as an ideology and as an organized social movement—is ultimately traceable to major economic changes in which women have been increasingly incorporated into the work world outside the home. Given that further changes along these lines are likely in the decades ahead, the social power and feminist consciousness of an increasing number of women will continue to grow. As they do, women will advance still further along the road toward genuine equality with men.

FOR FURTHER READING

Blumberg, Rae Lesser. "A general theory of gender stratification." In Randall Collins (ed.), *Sociological Theory 1984*. San Francisco: Jossey-Bass, 1984. An important theory of gender inequality by a sociologist sensitive to the necessity of a historical and comparative perspective for intelligent theorizing.

Chafetz, Janet Saltzman. *Sex and Advantage: A Comparative, Macro-Structural Theory of Sex Stratification*. Totowa, N.J.: Rowman and Allanheld, 1984. A perspective on gender inequality much like that of Martin and Voorhies and of Blumberg.

Friedl, Ernestine. *Women and Men: An Anthropologist's View*. New York: Holt, Rinehart and Winston, 1975. A short but informative book that examines the relations between the sexes in hunter-gatherer and horticultural societies.

Goldberg, Steven. *Why Men Rule: A Theory of Male Dominance*. Chicago: Open Court, 1993. An extremely carefully reasoned discussion of the reasons for the male monopolization of leadership and high-status positions in every known society.

Leacock, Eleanor B., and Helen I. Safa (eds.). *Women's Work: Development and the Division of Labor by Gender.* South Hadley, Mass.: Bergin and Garvey, 1986. Essays and case studies focusing on the impact upon women of expanding capitalism in the Third World.

Martin, M. Kay, and Barbara Voorhies. *Female of the Species.* New York: Columbia University Press, 1975. A detailed evolutionary analysis of gender roles throughout the entire spectrum of human societies. Argues that gender roles are mainly adaptive consequences of ecological, technological, and economic forces.

Rossi, Alice S. "Gender and parenthood." *American Sociological Review* 49:1–19, 1984. A persuasive argument for the social importance of biological differences between the sexes, especially in regard to parenting. Originally delivered as the Presidential Address at the 1983 annual meetings of the American Sociological Association.

Thomas, Janet. "Women and capitalism: Oppression or emancipation?" *Comparative Studies in Society and History* 30:534–549, 1988. An overview of contrasting theoretical viewpoints regarding the impact of early capitalism and industrialism on the status of women.

Tiger, Lionel, and Joseph Shepher. *Women in the Kibbutz.* New York: Harcourt Brace Jovanovich, 1975. Tells an extremely important story of the reversion to traditional gender roles in a communal society dedicated to eradicating them.

van den Berghe, Pierre L. *Age and Sex in Human Societies: A Biosocial Perspective.* Belmont, Calif.: Wadsworth, 1973. Discusses sexual differentiation among primates, the human biology of sex, and the nature of gender-role differentiation across a wide range of human societies. Suggests that gender arrangements are rooted in biology but are elaborated in diverse ways by culture.

Vogel, Lise. *Marxism and the Oppression of Women: Toward a Unitary Theory.* New Brunswick, N.J.: Rutgers University Press, 1983. An interesting historical treatment of the various strands of thinking by Marxists on "the woman question," from Marx and Engels to contemporary Marxists. Also presents a Marxian theory of women's subordination under contemporary capitalism.

Ward, Kathryn (ed.). *Women Workers and Global Restructuring.* Ithaca, N.Y.: Cornell University Press (ILR Press), 1990. An important recent work containing essays on the impact of the rapidly changing global economy on the status of women.

Chapter
15

Marriage, Family, and Kinship in Comparative and Evolutionary Perspective

Systems of marriage, family, and kinship are the institutionalized means whereby human societies organize and carry out important activities involving mating and reproduction. Among other things, familial institutions provide for legitimate rights to sexual access, the procreation and training of children, the organization of domestic work groups in accord with a gender division of labor, and the transmission of property and other forms of inheritance. Familial institutions establish networks of social bonds between individuals based on **affinity** (i.e., marriage) and **consanguinity** (i.e., "blood" or genetic relatedness); these networks are devoted to the performance of crucial social functions.

Marriage, family, and kinship institutions are universal features of human societies. Nevertheless, the nature of these institutions differs markedly from one society to another. In modern industrial societies, family systems assume a role secondary to that of the economy and polity in organizing and integrating the society, and a great many social relationships in industrial societies lie outside the framework of family life. In preindustrial—and especially in primitive—societies, however, family assumes a predominant significance as a mode of organization of many spheres of social activity. In the primitive world, activities that are themselves principally economic, political, religious, and so on are carried out in the context of kinship groups. In primitive society, kinship is dominant, and so much so that many social scientists have referred to primitive societies as *kinship-based societies.*

The present chapter takes a very broad comparative and evolutionary look at family and kinship. The first half of the chapter focuses on family and kinship in preindustrial societies. Here we ignore many of the subtle details of family life, concentrating instead on the general types of family and kinship systems and their adaptive significance for individuals in various types of human societies. The second half of the chapter takes a somewhat closer look at family life in one particular civilization: Western capitalism. It is principally concerned with understanding the past 300 years of family evolution in the West and the reasons why Western family patterns have changed so substantially in this period of time.

THE NATURE OF KIN GROUPS

When all the many details are taken into consideration, there is a dazzling array of kinship groups found throughout the world. Yet when minor variations are ignored, there are only a few basic types of kinship groupings among the world's societies. It is convenient to think of three such types: nuclear families, extended families, and corporate descent groups. While not exhaustive, these three types include most of the fundamental kinship groupings found throughout the world.

The **nuclear family** is a kinship unit consisting of the married spouses and their immediate offspring who maintain a common household and act together as a social unit. It is widespread in human societies; indeed, it is found almost universally. Despite its widespread occurrence, however, the nuclear family is the principal kinship unit only in some societies. A great many hunting and gathering societies emphasize

the nuclear family as the predominant kin group. Furthermore, the nuclear family is the principal familial unit in all industrial societies (the only possible exception is Japan, which places considerable emphasis on larger groups of kin). As the smallest and simplest unit of kinship, the nuclear family is therefore limited in its significance to the extremes of the evolutionary spectrum. Among societies closer to the middle of the evolutionary spectrum—that is, among horticultural and agrarian societies—the nuclear family generally pales in significance and is subsumed within larger kinship groups. These larger kinship units may be either extended families or corporate descent groups.

The **extended family** is a kinship group consisting of a number of related nuclear families bound together and acting as a unit. Such a group, which may or may not share a common household, gets its name from the fact that it *extends* the range of kinship beyond the narrow boundaries of the nuclear family. Extended families are generally of much greater significance in preindustrial societies of all types than they are in industrial societies. Logically, however, some kind of extended family unit exists in all societies because the tracing of relatives obviously does not stop at the boundaries of the nuclear family. Even in industrial societies, the extended family is a unit of at least some social significance: Extended kins people often give financial and other forms of aid to one another, and holidays and other special occasions are frequently times at which the extended family convenes and acts as a unit.

Extended families usually consist of reasonably small networks of kin. In many societies, however, kinship ties can be extended even further to include a great many individuals within one's sphere of kinship. When this happens, **corporate descent groups** are frequently formed. These groups are networks of individuals who trace descent, or genealogical connection, from a common ancestor. Corporate descent groups, which may include hundreds or even thousands of persons, function as single, discrete units of kinship. They are the largest and most complex type of kin group found in human societies. Corporate descent groups are entirely nonexistent in industrial societies, and they are infrequently found among hunters and gatherers. Among horticulturalists and agriculturalists, however, they are extensively found; indeed, they are the predominant type of kinship unit in most horticultural societies.

SYSTEMS OF RESIDENCE AND DESCENT

Local Groups and Descent Groups

Two of the most important characteristics of kinship systems are **rules of residence** and **rules of descent.** All societies use these criteria for organizing individuals into various types of kinship groups. Rules of residence determine who goes to live with whom upon marriage. They establish *local groups,* or groups of kinspeople who cooperate in the performance of domestic and extradomestic activities. The primary rules of residence in use by the world's societies are depicted in Table 15.1.

As Table 15.3 clearly reveals, **patrilocality** is overwhelmingly the preferred residence rule in the world's cultures, accounting for slightly more than two-thirds of the residential practices in a sample of 857 societies. Under this residential system, husbands bring wives home to live with them in their father's households. Far less common is **matrilocality,** which accounts for only 13 percent of the residential practices of the sample of 857 cultures. With matrilocality, wives bring their husbands home to live with them in their extended family households. Rarer yet is the interesting practice of **avunculocality.** In this system, residence occurs with the husband's mother's brother. While this practice may seem rather bizarre at first glance, it actually can be shown to make perfectly good sense when the conditions under which it is found are revealed.

Some societies do not restrict marital residence exclusively to either the wife's or husband's kin groups. Thus arises the practice of **bilocality,** a system under which the married couple alternates its residence between the husband's and wife's kin groups. **Ambilocality** occurs when the married couple has a choice of living with either the husband's or wife's group. A rare, but quite fascinating, residence practice is **natolocality.** In this arrangement, husband and wife do not live together, but rather remain in their natal households (i.e., the households

Table 15.1   RULES OF POSTMARITAL RESIDENCE IN THE WORLD'S SOCIETIES

Patrilocality:	The married couple resides in the household of the husband's father.
Matrilocality:	The married couple resides in the household of the wife's mother.
Avunculocality:	The married couple resides in the household of the husband's mother's brother.
Bilocality:	The married couple alternates its residence between the husband's and wife's kinship groups.
Ambilocality:	The married couple may choose to take up residence either with the husband's or with the wife's kinship group.
Natolocality:	Husband and wife do not live together; each stays in the household into which he or she was born.
Neolocality:	The married couple establishes an independent residence of its own.

of their birth) Finally, there is the residence system that is most familiar to the members of Western industrial societies: **neolocality.** Under this system, the married couple establishes a new, independent household of its own. While neolocal residence is sometimes found in preindustrial societies, it is most frequently found in societies of the industrial type. Indeed, neolocality is the standard residence practice in virtually all industrial societies. Neolocal residence is highly adaptive in societies emphasizing the small nuclear family, such as our own.

By contrast with rules of residence, rules of descent establish broad networks of genealogically related individuals, many of whom frequently do not live together. Whereas local groups consist of individuals who reside together, descent groups include all individuals who maintain common genealogical ties, regardless of whether they live together. The distinction between local groups and descent groups is therefore one between *common residence* and a *sense of common identity.*

While all societies have descent rules, the nature of the kinship groups or categories formed by these rules differs significantly from one society to another. In the majority of the world's societies, the descent rule is combined with a kinship system resting on **ancestor-focus** (Fox, 1967). This situation creates what we have already termed corporate descent groups. These are groups of individuals who trace descent from a common ancestor (real or mythical) who is believed to have been the founder of the group. Membership in a corporate descent group defines for individuals the rights and obligations they have in regard to the other members of their group. Corporate descent groups generally have the following characteristics (W. Stephens, 1963):

- *Corporateness.* The group possesses a unity in the sense that the entire group may act as a single legal individual in behalf of any of its members.
- *A name.* Since the group has corporateness, it is natural for it to have a name to signify its identity. The names of corporate descent groups are frequently taken from plants, animals, or other natural phenomena.
- *Exogamy.* Most corporate descent groups forbid the marriage of their members to any other member of the group, thus forcing them to select marriage partners from among other descent groups.
- *Common religious observances.* The members of a corporate descent group frequently symbolize their identity through the enactment of common ritual and ceremony.
- *Corporate property ownership.* The members of a corporate descent group commonly hold collective title to land and other property. Individuals may therefore own land only as members of the group. This is perhaps the most crucial characteristic of a corporate descent group.
- *Obligations of mutual aid and hospitality.* Members of a corporate descent group are frequently called upon to render assistance to one another in times of need.

Corporate descent groups vary greatly in terms of size and complexity. They range from as small as a dozen or so members in some cases to as large as a million members in others (the latter, for example, in the case of the traditional Chinese clan). On average, they probably contain from a few dozen to a few hundred members. Such groups also vary in terms of the degree of certainty that members have of their relatedness. A corporate descent group whose members can precisely identify their genealogical connections to one another is commonly known as a **lineage.** When the members of a corporate descent group can only assume, rather than precisely identify, their genealogical connections, the group is generally known as a **clan.** Clans are therefore typically larger than lineages, and several lineages may be grouped together to form a clan.

Societies having corporate descent groups, as indicated earlier, base their kinship systems on ancestor-focus. A number of societies, however, use **ego-focus** as a basis for forming kin groups. When this occurs, kinship is traced from the point of view of *any given living individual,* rather than from some putative common ancestor (Fox, 1967). Ego-focus gives rise to small-scale personal kin groups known as **kindreds.** These groups are not corporate and maintain few of the functions of corporate descent groups. Kindreds are typically inactive much of the time, and are activated only on special occasions, for example, during times of festival or ritual or when the need arises for the group to aid one of its members. Kindreds are of greatest significance in societies that emphasize the nuclear family as the primary kinship group, that is, in industrial and in many hunting and gathering societies.

The primary rules of descent found in human societies are shown in Table 15.2.

Patrilineal Descent

Patrilineal descent is the most common of all the major types of descent groupings, accounting for nearly half of the world's descent systems (Table 15.3). Patrilineal descent systems are those in which descent is traced through males. This means that a young man, for example, would trace his primary kin ties through his father, his father's father, his father's father's father, and so on. This same young man would therefore belong to a descent group consisting of his father (and father's father, etc.), his father's brothers, his own brothers, and his own sons. His mother may or may not be a member of his patrilineal group (this varies from one patrilineal society to another), but certainly his mother's primary relatives (e.g., his mother's father, mother's mother, and mother's brothers and sisters) will not be members of his group.

Patrilineal societies vary in terms of the placement of wives in descent groups. A girl, of course, is born into the patrilineal group of her father. But what happens to her upon marriage cannot be predicted in the abstract. In many patrilineal societies, a woman remains a member for life of her

Table 15.2   DESCENT SYSTEMS IN THE WORLD'S SOCIETIES

I. Unilineal descent:	Descent traced through a single line only, either through males or through females.
A. Patrilineal descent:	Descent traced only through males (i.e., through one's father, father's father, father's father's father, etc.).
B. Matrilineal descent:	Descent traced only through females (i.e., through one's mother, mother's mother, mother's mother's mother, etc.).
C. Double descent:	A descent system in which both patrilineal and matrilineal descent exist side by side in the same society.
II. Cognatic descent:	A system in which both males and females are used in the establishment of descent groupings.
A. Ambilineal descent:	Descent in which corporate descent groups are formed by tracing relationships through either males or females.
B. Bilateral descent:	Descent in which personal kindreds are formed by tracing relationships through both males and females simultaneously.

Table 15.3 FREQUENCY OF OCCURRENCE OF RESIDENCE AND DESCENT SYSTEMS

	Rule of Descent									
	Patrilineal		Matrilineal		Double		Bilateral		Total	
Rule of Residence	N	%	N	%	N	%	N	%	N	%
Patrilocal	384	96.2	18	14.8	25	92.6	161	52.0	588	68.6
Matrilocal	0	0.0	44	36.0	0	0.0	67	21.7	111	13.0
Avunculocal	0	0.0	36	29.5	1	3.7	0	0.0	37	4.3
Bilocal	5	1.3	14	11.5	1	3.7	53	17.2	73	8.5
Neolocal	6	1.5	6	4.9	0	0.0	28	9.1	40	4.7
Duolocal	4	1.0	4	3.3	0	0.0	0	0.0	8	0.9
Total	399	100.0	122	100.0	27	100.0	309	100.0	857	100.0
Percent of grand total		46.5		14.2		3.2		36.1		100.0

Source: Slightly modified from Pierre L. van den Berghe, *Human Family Systems: An Evolutionary View.* New York: Elsevier, 1979, p. 111, Table 11.

father's patrilineage, and therefore upon marriage she is still something of an outsider in the patrilineal group of her husband. In other patrilineal societies, a woman is absorbed upon marriage into the patrilineal group of her husband. In this latter case, she may still retain some ties with her father's group despite the fact that her ties are now primarily to her husband's group.

The primary kinship tie in patrilineal societies is between father and son. The inheritance of land and other forms of property, for example, passes from father to son. Women are usually deemed important mainly as procreators; the continuity of the group, however, is established through males, since children are generally regarded as belonging primarily to their father rather than to their mother.

Of course, any individual has many more relatives in a patrilineal group than those listed here, since we have concentrated only on identifying primary kinspeople. The important point is that **patriliny** links people on the basis of their descent through the male line. A person's patrilineal relatives are therefore those who are related in the father's line, rather than in the

mother's. By using the principle of descent in the male line only, patrilineal societies are able to organize their members into neat, mutually exclusive, nonoverlapping kin groups of a corporate nature.

Matrilineal Descent

Although **matrilineal descent** is not nearly as common as the patrilineal variety, it does occur in approximately 14 percent of the world's societies and is therefore by no means rare (Table 15.3). This type of descent system has some very interesting features, and it is not simply the mirror opposite of patriliny (Fox, 1967).

Matrilineal descent traces kinship ties through females. A young man recognizes descent through his mother, mother's mother, mother's mother's mother, and so on. Any person is a member of a group constituted by his mother (and mother's mother, etc.), his sisters, his brothers, and his mother's sisters and brothers. A person's father, however, is never a member of his own matrilineal group. Thus, a woman's children belong to her matrilineal group, but a man's children do not belong to his. It is clear that husbands and wives do not share the same matrilineal group. Unlike some patrilineal societies, individuals in matrilineal societies never transfer their descent group membership upon marriage. One is born and remains for life in the same matrilineal descent group. Again, it is not advisable here to attempt to trace all potential relatives in a matrilineal system. The principle that matrilineal descent rests upon is that basic kinship ties run through females; thus women, and not men, are the perpetuators of matrilineal groups.

Matrilineal societies are different in several crucial respects from those based on patriliny. Indeed, matrilineal groups encounter one very special problem: While **matriliny** traces descent through females, it nevertheless leaves males in control of the affairs of descent groups. However, while men in patrilineal societies control their groups as fathers and husbands, men in matrilineal societies exercise control as *brothers and uncles*. A man in a matrilineal society actually has two primary social roles to play. On the one hand, he will be the husband of a woman in another matrilineage; on the other hand, he will be performing as a brother in his own matrilineage (i.e., that of his sister and mother). It is a man's role as a brother in his own matrilineage that is of greater social significance, for he has a special tie to his sister's children, especially her sons. He has a heavy responsibility for the training of these sons, and inheritance will pass from him (as a maternal uncle) to these nephews.

This fact gives rise to two basic kinds of "fatherhood" in matrilineal societies: "biological fatherhood" and "sociological fatherhood." A man will be a biological father to his own sons (who belong to the matrilineage of their mother) and a sociological father (as a maternal uncle) to his sister's sons (his maternal nephews) in his own matrilineage. This produces a strain in matrilineal societies that is not found under patriliny. In patrilineal societies, a man is only

a biological father to his own sons in his own patrilineage, but a man under matriliny is both a "father" and a "maternal uncle." Maternal uncles have primary responsibility for the rearing of young boys, but biological fathers often intrude upon the rights of these maternal uncles in attempting to assume responsibility for their own sons.

Because matrilineal societies trace descent through females but keep males in charge of the domestic group's affairs, they encounter some special problems that are absent with patrilineal descent. Since patriliny and matriliny are not simply mirror opposites of each other, it is desirable to summarize their principal differences (Zelditch, 1964; D. Schneider, 1961):

- Under patriliny, females can be severed from membership in their natal descent group and fully absorbed into the descent group of their husband. But under matriliny, no such severance can take place, and both men and women remain members of their natal descent group for life.
- With patriliny the roles of husband and father are of crucial importance. But with matriliny such roles are not even necessary to the maintenance of the group.
- The establishment of strong husband-wife bonds is not compatible with matrilineal descent. With patrilineal descent, however, such bonds are both compatible and desirable.
- In patrilineal systems, no special mechanisms are needed to deal with in-marrying affines. But in matrilineal systems, in-marrying affines are a threat to the descent group and special mechanisms are needed to deal with such threats.
- In matrilineal societies, the bonds that may develop between child and biological father tend to be in direct competition with the bond between that child and his mother's brother (his maternal uncle). In patrilineal societies, no such problem arises.

Bilateral Descent

Bilateral descent involves the tracing of genealogical relatedness through both males and females simultaneously. This does not result in the formation of corporate descent groups (it logically cannot result in such groups being formed); rather, small-scale, personalized, ego-focused groups known as *kindreds* are produced. Kindreds are in actuality only special-purpose extended kin groups that may long remain dormant and may only be activated on special occasions. Kindreds extensively overlap (father and son, for example, have overlapping, yet different, kindreds), and because of this they can never be corporate groups. Such groups are most common in many hunting and gathering and virtually all industrial societies. In our own society, for example, when a person makes reference to all the members of his extended family unit, he is referring to a bilateral kindred.

Forms of Residence Under Patriliny

As Table 15.3 reveals, patrilineal societies are overwhelmingly patrilocal. The great majority of patrilineal societies therefore neatly combine both residence and descent in the hands of males. The following examples will serve to illustrate the actual operation of patriliny and patrilocality (Fox, 1967).

In traditional China, descent was organized in terms of exogamous patrilineages. A lineage was divided into sublineages, and these were often dispersed throughout several villages. Residence was patrilocal. Upon marriage, a woman transferred her descent group membership from that of her father to that of her husband; she became completely severed from her natal patrilineage and was absorbed completely into her husband's group.

A patrilineal system of a somewhat different nature exists among the Tallensi of northern Ghana. Residence among the Tal-

lensi, who raise cattle as well as cultivate fields, is patrilocal. Descent groups exist in the form of patriclans, which are further divided into patrilineages. The rule of exogamy applies to the clan as well as the lineage. While women move in with their husbands, they never move far away, and therefore it is easy for them to retain close ties with their natal patrilineage. In this regard, the Tallensi contrast strikingly with traditional China. Whereas in China women were completely lost to their natal patrilineages, among the Tallensi women continue to play an important role in the descent group of their fathers and brothers.

Forms of Residence Under Matriliny

Since most patrilineal societies are patrilocal, descent and residence are neatly tied together. Things are not nearly so neat among matrilineal peoples. Matrilineal societies display a wide range of residence rules (Table 15.3). The most common residence rule associated with matriliny is matrilocality, but still only slightly more than one-third of matrilineal societies have adopted it. One such matrilocal-matrilineal society is that of the Hopi Indians of the American Southwest (Keesing, 1975). The major descent groups among the Hopi are exogamous matriclans, and these are landowning corporate groups. Hopi matriclans are further subdivided into unnamed matrilineages. An adult man takes up residence with his wife's household, where he is, of course, an outsider. Despite the fact that the men disperse upon marriage, they never move far away from their natal households, and thus it is relatively easy for them to continue to carry out important activities in their own matrilineal groups.

Matrilineal societies are almost as likely to adopt avunculocality as matrilocality (Table 15.3). A well-known matrilineal society practicing avunculocal residence is the Trobriand Islanders (Keesing, 1975).

Among these people, women go with their husbands to live in the household of the husband's mother's brother. During adolescence, a boy will move away from his parents' household and return to the village of his own matrilineal group. The boy's sisters will remain in their father's household until the time of their marriage; at this time, of course, they will move to the households of their husbands' mothers' brothers.

Forms of Residence Under Bilateral Descent

When bilateral descent is found among hunters and gatherers, it is very frequently associated with patrilocal residence. Matrilocality and bilocality, however, are also found to some extent in these societies. Among bilaterally organized industrial societies, residence is normally neolocal.

THE CAUSES OF RESIDENCE AND DESCENT SYSTEMS

As Robin Fox (1967) has pointed out, many scholars have talked about residence and descent systems as if they had simply dropped from the sky upon the peoples practicing them. Such a view is scarcely likely to provide much illumination about the causal dynamics of these systems. A better approach would be to examine residence and descent systems as adaptive consequences of the practical conditions of social life (Keesing, 1975; M. Harris, 1979; Goody, 1976).

An essential first premise holds that *residence systems are logically prior to descent systems.* This means that the members of a society must first organize themselves in workable household arrangements before they organize their descent patterns. From this point of view, descent systems largely reflect and serve to validate the kinds of household arrangements already established. To complete the causal chain, the problem is then one of determining the conditions likely to produce one residential pattern versus another. This approach yields some solid results. However, it must be borne in mind that, once in existence, descent patterns may have causal significance in their own right. It may sometimes be the case that some residential patterns actually result from the prior establishment of a particular kind of descent system. Such logic seems necessary in order to understand the otherwise puzzling phenomenon of avunculocality.

The Causes of Patrilocality and Patriliny

A number of factors have been proposed to explain the overwhelming popularity of patrilocality and patriliny. These include population pressure, limited land and resources, frequent warfare with neighboring groups, and the presence of concentrated forms of wealth (M. Harris, 1975; Martin and Voorhies, 1975). Under these kinds of conditions, keeping fathers, sons, and brothers physically together so they can pursue their common interests in land and people is a highly adaptive social arrangement (M. Harris, 1975). However, the most basic factor determining the male bias in residence and descent practices is very likely the more generalized male bias that occurs in all human societies. Based on what we learned in Chapter 14, there is no reason to be surprised that patrilocal and patrilineal societies greatly outnumber matrilocal and matrilineal societies.

Male-centered kinship practices are commonly found among widely differing societies. This suggests that patrilocality and patriliny are adaptive under a wide range of material conditions, and thus appear to have considerable adaptive flexibility. Hunting and gathering societies, for example, are frequently patrilocal. This probably reflects the need to keep male kinsmen together for crucial hunting purposes. The kinship systems of horticultural societies also tend strongly toward patrilocality and patriliny, and the factors proposed by Marvin Harris and by Martin and Voorhies may well be important determinants of the great prevalence of male-centered kinship among such peoples. Agrarian societies likewise frequently opt for patrilocality and patriliny. Since men overwhelmingly dominate economic production in such societies, there is a strong need to keep male kinsmen together to form cooperative work teams, and patriliny can easily result from such household arrangements.

The Causes of Matrilocality and Matriliny

Since patrilocality and patriliny are so common, and since they are found under such variable conditions, there is an especially critical need to identify the factors that cause some societies to adopt matrilocal and matrilineal institutions. It seems that the origin of matriliny is almost always to be found in a prior condition of matrilocal residence. The problem, then, is to determine the factors that make matrilocality highly adaptive.

The most widely accepted explanation of matrilocality at present is that offered by Melvin and Carol Ember (1971; C. Ember, 1974). They argue that when societies engage in at least some degree of internal warfare (i.e., warfare with neighboring societies close to home), patrilocal residence is the typical result. However, when societies engage in purely external warfare (i.e., warfare at long distances from home), and when this warfare requires women to be heavily involved in economic production, then matrilocality is the typical outcome. Thus, when men are gone from their home territories for long periods of time, and when this results in a heavy female contribution to subsistence, there is a strong need to keep the women of kin groups together. The available evidence tends to support Ember and Ember's conclusions. A classic instance of a society with matrilocal and matrilineal institutions is the Iroquois of western New York state. These people engaged in extensive warfare with societies hundreds of miles away. Men were frequently gone from home for extended periods on warfare and hunting expeditions. In addition, women took a predominant role in subsistence activities. The Iroquois thus demonstrate the validity of Ember and Ember's conclusions, as do many other societies.

The argument developed by the Embers can be generalized to suggest that *any activity* that produces long-term absence of males from home base puts pressure on a society to become matrilocal (M. Harris, 1975, 1979). For example, among the Navaho of the American Southwest (a matrilocal and matrilineal people) the women tended sheep close to their own households, but the men raised horses and worked for wages, activities that required long-term absences from home. Likewise, among the matrilineal (but avunculocal) Trobriand Islanders men were frequently absent from home on long-distance trading expeditions.

Even if the preceding arguments about the origins of matrilocality and matriliny are correct, we must still explain why almost as many matrilineal societies are avunculocal as are matrilocal. In this regard, it is necessary to abandon the assumption that residence is prior to descent, for avunculocality distinctly appears to be a result of the prior existence of matrilineal descent. As Fox (1967) has pointed out, matrilocal residence works best in those matrilineal societies where households are not highly dispersed and where concentrations of wealth are not large. If households were to become highly dispersed, or if large concentrations of wealth were to begin to form, then matrilocality would begin to present a problem. If the men were highly dispersed from their own matrilineal groups, it would be difficult for them to participate in the regular functions of such groups. Furthermore, with growing concentrations of wealth, men would have difficulty managing and controlling that wealth. Therefore, when a matrilineal society begins to grow in scale, complexity, and wealth concentration, there is considerable pressure placed upon it to shift away from matrilocality. The residence solution to which such a society is apt to shift is avunculocality, for this residence system once again physically unites the male directors of matrilineal corporate groups, allowing them to participate efficiently in the management of their groups' affairs. Avunculocality therefore appears to be an adaptive solution to problems encountered in the evolutionary growth of matrilineal systems.

The Causes of Bilateral Descent

The causes of bilateral systems are well known. These systems occur principally in hunter-gatherer and industrial societies. Both types of societies, despite their overwhelming differences in most respects, share one crucial characteristic: a technoeconomic system requiring a great deal of geographical mobility. Hunters and gatherers must be mobile because of their constant need to search for food. The members of industrial societies are frequently mobile because they are searching for jobs, getting transferred in their jobs, and so on. Under such conditions, a small-scale, loosely structured, and highly flexible family system is most adaptive. Bilateral kin groups provide just such a system.

MARRIAGE IN COMPARATIVE PERSPECTIVE

Three basic forms of marriage are found in the world's societies: monogamy, polygyny, and polyandry. (Some scholars have pro-

posed a form of "group marriage," but there is no good evidence that this has ever existed.) **Monogamy** refers to the marriage of one man to one woman. While this is the marriage form familiar to the members of Western industrial societies, it is clearly in the minority as a preferred marriage practice throughout the world. Only about 15 percent of all societies actually prefer this form and institutionalize it as the required practice. It is the legally required form of marriage in all contemporary industrial societies, and it is fairly common among hunter-gatherers. It is only occasionally found among horticulturalists. In agrarian societies throughout history monogamy has been virtually the only form of marriage among nonelite classes. The elites of agrarian societies, on the other hand, have generally preferred polygyny and practiced it whenever possible. In the ancient world the only notable agrarian societies to have institutionalized monogamy for all members of society were the ancient Greeks and Romans. With the rise of Christianity, and its extreme idealization of monogamy (or even chastity), medieval Christian Europe became monogamous (despite a few exceptions). Before we explore the possible reasons for monogamy, we first need to deal with the world's most strongly preferred form of marriage.

This form is **polygyny,** which involves the marriage of one man to two or more women. Approximately 85 percent of the world's societies prefer this type of marriage. Despite the overwhelming preference for polygyny, however, the practice is greatly limited in those societies in which it does occur. In fact, the majority of persons in most polygynous societies marry monogamously. It is not hard to see why this is so. With the number of males and females being approximately equal, it would be very difficult for all men to engage in polygynous marriage. Thus, normally only a minority of men actually have multiple wives in polygynous societies, and these are usually men of highest social rank.

Two main kinds of polygynous systems must be distinguished: *harem polygyny* and *hut polygyny* (van den Berghe, 1973). Harem polygyny occurs in agrarian societies and in some intensive horticultural societies. It involves a political ruler's having a very large number of wives (a harem) at his command. Far more common, however, is hut polygyny. Under this form of polygyny, a man typically has no more than three or four wives. The wives often have independent households, and the husband takes turns sleeping with all of them. Wives are often graded into senior and junior wives, and there are usually mechanisms available to deal with the jealousy that frequently arises among co-wives.

Polygyny is most common in horticultural societies and among the elites of agrarian societies. It is also found in a substantial number of hunter-gatherer societies. It is considerably more common in patrilineal than in matrilineal societies. Polygyny is still found today in many African societies and throughout the Middle East and other parts of the Islamic world, although many restrictions have been placed on it. In the contemporary world it is most likely to be found in the more traditional sectors of society and is much less common in the more urbanized and modernized sectors.

What accounts for this widespread preference for polygynous marriage? The most frequently invoked explanation is economic (White and Burton, 1988). As noted above, polygyny is most widely found in horticultural societies, and here women are economic assets because of their role as tillers and cultivators in "female farming" systems. Men can thus improve their economic situation by having more than one wife. It is true that in most polygynous societies women are economic assets, and in these societies men may be at least partially inclined toward polygyny because it can increase their wealth. However, the economic value of women is not likely the most basic cause of polygynous marriage.

A more convincing explanation is the sociobiological interpretation, which holds that polygyny is a natural result of the male's reproductive strategy (van den Berghe, 1979; Symons, 1979; Hartung, 1982). Men's desire to mate with many women stems from their desire for sexual quantity and variety, and this desire is a biological adaptation that evolved because it promotes a man's inclusive fitness—the representation of his genes in the society's total gene pool, both in the present and in subsequent generations. This argument is made extremely plausible by the fact that the male desire for sexual variety seems to be a true cultural universal (Symons, 1979). Even in societies in which monogamy is socially imposed, men still commonly acquire multiple mates by such means as extramarital affairs and the taking of concubines (legitimized sexual companions who do not enjoy the legal status of wife). But to some extent the sociobiological and economic explanations may be complementary (van den Berghe, 1979). After all, the enhancement of wealth certainly contributes to the promotion of the male's inclusive fitness, and thus a man's desire to increase his wealth may be rooted in the same portion of the human biogram that guides his desire for sexual variety.

Polyandry is a marriage form involving the marriage of one woman to two or more men. When polyandry occurs, it is often fraternal, which means that a woman marries a group of brothers. It is rare, occurring in less than one percent of all societies. Its rarity, especially when combined with the extreme prevalence of polygyny, is undoubtedly related to biological inclinations, especially those of men. From a sociobiological perspective, the type of marriage a man should least prefer would be polyandry, because it would be the marriage form least likely to promote his inclusive fitness and most likely to promote the inclusive fitness of other men (van den Berghe, 1979). Given the opposition between polyandry and the male's natural biological inclinations, the circumstances under which it occurs should be very unusual. How, therefore, can it be explained?

Societies having polyandry usually also have polygyny and monogamy. One interpretation holds that polyandry is usually associated with a situation of **hypergyny,** or one in which women marry men of higher social rank. This leads to the development of polygyny at the top of the society and a serious shortage of women at the bottom. In such a situation, unless lower-status men wish to remain celibate, polyandry is their only real option.

A different interpretation has been given by William Durham (1991) in his study of various peasant groups in Tibet. One group of Tibetans Durham studied had the full range of marriage practices. Fraternal polyandry was the most common, but monogamy and polygyny were also practiced, and there even existed an extremely unusual practice that has been dubbed **polygynandry,** which is the marriage of two or more men to two or more women—the closest thing possible to group marriage. The Tibetan peasants lived at a very high altitude and the land was so dry that its productivity was very limited. The most common way of establishing a household was for a group of brothers to inherit the same plot of land and to bring in a woman to serve as their wife. Durham argues that if the land had been split up among a group of brothers, each of whom married monogamously, then no one would have had enough land to produce a decent living, and everyone would have suffered. In addition, having several brothers making a living from the same plot of land increased available labor. Fraternal polyandry was thus a

rational response to a uniquely difficult economic situation. Why, then, were some marriages monogamous and others polygynous? A monogamous marriage could occur because a man had no brothers, so he inherited the land by himself and took on a wife. Polygyny could result from a monogamous marriage in which the first wife was deemed infertile and so a second one was added. It could also occur when a family had several daughters and no sons. In such a situation, the parents could arrange a marriage of their daughters to a man with no brothers. And polygynandry could result from a polyandrous household whose husbands took on a second wife because they believed the first wife to be infertile.

Although the above explanation of Tibetan polyandry is an economic one, Durham insists that there is really more going on than that. Durham has carried out computer simulations which show that in the long run (i.e., three or more generations) fraternal polyandry leads to higher levels of reproductive success than monogamy and the splitting up of family plots. Thus his explanation is at once economic and sociobiological. Fraternal polyandry is both economically and reproductively adaptive.

The reason monogamy is the exclusive form of marriage in some societies is still not clear, although several theories have been set forth. Monogamy among the nonelite sectors of agrarian societies is probably an adaptation to economic conditions. By and large, peasant men do not have the economic circumstances that allow them to support more than one wife. Indeed, many do not have the circumstances to take even a single wife, and thus are forced into bachelorhood. However, the economic cost of wives cannot really explain monogamy in modern industrial societies. In these societies, the standard of living is high enough so that many men, perhaps as much as 20 percent of the society, could afford more than one wife. What we really have to explain in regard to modern monogamy is its legally established, socially imposed nature.

Richard Alexander (1987) has offered a sociobiological explanation, claiming that socially-imposed monogamy is a strategy of *reproductive opportunity-leveling.* Since men compete for wives, giving men equal access to potential wives reduces conflict between males. Alexander claims that the result is greater cooperation among males, an essential ingredient in modern societies that wage wars with large pools of young men. Alexander also believes it noteworthy that legally-imposed monogamy is found in modern societies that publicly affirm justice to be equality of opportunity, and that hold to a concept of a single god who acts impartially in behalf of all people.

Another explanation has been offered by Richard Posner (1992). Posner claims that socially-imposed monogamy in industrial societies results from the fact that these societies have *companionate marriage.* As we shall see in some detail shortly, this form of marriage began to evolve in the Western world in the seventeenth and eighteenth centuries. It is based on an intimate relationship of lifelong companionship between a man and a woman, one key ingredient of which is sexual fidelity. Such a marriage system, Posner argues, would be radically undermined by polygyny, and thus as companionate marriage evolved polygyny had to go.

It is difficult to test this theory rigorously because Western societies were already monogamous when they began to evolve companionate marriage. Monogamy was a basic part of their Christian religious tradition. We therefore will never be able to know what would have happened had they been polygynous before companionate marriage emerged (although we would predict, of course, that they would have abandoned polygyny for monogamy). However, we do

know that Japan, a non-Christian society with a long history of polygyny and concubinage, outlawed these practices in a new civil code that was introduced in 1898, just at the time it was beginning its industrialization and modernization (Murstein, 1974).

In addition, we are in a position to learn what happens when Third World countries permitting polygyny industrialize and modernize. Polygyny is still widely practiced throughout much of Africa and the Islamic world today, although in some countries it has been outlawed and in most others various restrictions have been placed on it (Welch and Glick, 1981; Nasir, 1994; Pitshandenge, 1994). These restrictions usually involve such things as requiring a man to declare at the outset of his first marriage whether he has any intent of taking on additional wives (and disallowing future wives if he initially declares he will not take any). Since these parts of the Third World today contain a mixture of polygyny and monogamy, it is interesting to see who still practices polygyny and who has repudiated it. In a study of marriage practices in Nigeria in the early 1970s (Ware, 1979), it was shown that poorly-educated women from lower socioeconomic backgrounds were far more likely to be part of a polygynous marriage than well-educated women of higher socioeconomic backgrounds. For example, 58 percent of wives who had no formal education were in polygynous marriages, compared to only 4 percent of women who had university educations. And 57 percent of women from unskilled rural backgrounds were in polygynous marriages, compared to only 17 percent from professional backgrounds. The fact that it is especially the best-educated women who turn away from polygyny would seem to support Posner's interpretation. As Helen Ware (1979:191) has said in regard to marriage in Nigeria, "companionship may be the goal especially for those who are already cut off from their families of origin by migration or their formal education." And Alice Armstrong et al. (1993:337–338) make the same point with respect to Africa more generally: "Now many women perceive marriage in terms of companionship and love. Polygyny is unlikely to fulfil their expectations."

Unfortunately, it is difficult to see how Posner's theory can be applied to ancient Rome and Greece, since these societies certainly did not have companionate marriage. Moreover, what explains monogamy in medieval Europe, centuries before the rise of companionate marriage? And what of hunter-gatherer societies, which are frequently monogamous? Perhaps Alexander's sociobiological theory can explain the existence of socially-imposed monogamy in the ancient world, or perhaps medieval Europe was monogamous because of the influence of Christianity. All these are still open questions, and at this point it is very difficult to see how a single parsimonious theory can explain the various instances of monogamy that we observe in the world.

THE DEVELOPMENT OF THE MODERN WESTERN FAMILY

Most readers of this book live in a society whose family system is based on the strong affection and close companionship of the spouses, and in which the basis of marriage is romantic love rather than economics or family lineage. Young people expect to choose a spouse free from family dictates and to have a close companionate and sexual relationship with that person. Yet this mode of family and marital life is a unique creation of the modern world. Nowhere before about the seventeenth or eighteenth century in the West was family and marital life organized in this fashion. The remainder of this chapter tells the story of the evolution of the modern Western family system. It begins by examining family life in prein-

dustrial Europe and North America and describing the profound changes it began to undergo several centuries ago. It then moves on to discuss the dramatic changes that have been occurring in family life in the last third of the twentieth century.

Household Composition in the Preindustrial West

In all modern industrial societies the nuclear family is overwhelmingly dominant. The close relationship between the industrial mode of social life and the nuclear family once led sociologists to argue that industrialization caused the emergence of the nuclear family. It was thought that prior to industrialization people throughout western Europe and North America lived basically in large extended families. In the last 30 years or so, however, new research by sociologists and social historians interested in the history of the Western family has shown that this older view is incorrect, or at least that it must be strictly qualified.

Two of the earliest sociologists to challenge the traditional wisdom were Sidney Greenfield (1961) and Frank Furstenburg (1966). Both Greenfield and Furstenburg claimed that the nuclear family was commonly found in Colonial America and western Europe long before industrialization, and that the effects of industrialization on family structure had been exaggerated. But perhaps the most important research on this issue has been carried out by the British historical sociologist Peter Laslett and his colleagues (Laslett, 1977; Laslett and Wall, 1972). Detailed empirical studies have convinced Laslett that most people in Colonial America and in England, France, and Germany during the seventeenth and eighteenth centuries lived in nuclear family households whose average size was about five or six members. Moreover, Laslett argues that the predominance of the nuclear family was unique to western Europe and North America; in eastern Europe and non-Western civilizations, the familiar extended family pattern was much more typical.

It is interesting that family patterns in preindustrial Europe bore a close relationship to the spread of capitalism (Table 15.4). Those areas where core capitalism had penetrated most significantly were overwhelmingly characterized by nuclear family arrangements. Other areas of western Europe, such as southern France and parts of Germany and Austria, tended to have a type of extended family known as the **stem family** as the dominant type (Shorter, 1975). In the stem family, the farmer and his wife passed their farm to one of their sons. The son and his wife took over farming the land and lived with the son's parents until their death. With the birth of the son's children, there would for a time be three generations living together in extended family style. In eastern Europe, an even more elaborate extended family system was the norm. In Serbia the main family unit was known as the *zadruga* (Shorter, 1975). The *zadruga* was a household of perhaps three or four nuclear families who submitted to the authority of a patriarch and who constituted a single economic unit. The average *zadruga* contained anywhere from 10 to 30 members. In parts of Russia a similar type of extended family called the *Gesind* prevailed. This was a household averaging about 14 members (Shorter, 1975).

It thus seems that the rise of the nuclear family in the West was more closely linked to the development of capitalism than to industrialization. In fact, as the above clearly suggests, and as Table 15.4 indicates even more dramatically, there seems to have been a very close relationship between European household patterns and the hierarchical structuring of the capitalist

Table 15.4 HOUSEHOLD COMPOSITION IN SELECTED PREINDUSTRIAL COUNTRIES

Country	Community/Region	Date	% Simple Family Households	% Complex Family Households
1. Colonial America	Rhode Island	1689	97	3
2. Belgium	Lampernisse	1814	69	20
3. Belgium	Lisswege	1739	85	12
4. Northern France	Villages around Valenciennes	1693	86	11
5. Northern France	Brueil-en-Vexin	1625	84	7
6. England	30 reliably recorded villages	1622–1821	72	15
7. Russia	Kurland (Spahren estate)	1797	43	51
8. Russia	Mishino estate	1814	8	85
9. Serbia	Belgrade	1733	55	32
10. Estonia	Vandra	1683	45	52
11. Hungary	Alsónyék	1792	44	54
12. Italy	Molise, Isernia	1753	63	37
13. Italy	Fiesole, Tuscany	1790	40	51
14. Southern France	Montplaisant	1644	51	37
15. Southern France	Mirabeau	1745	51	42
16. Austria	Heidenreichstein manor	1763	——	25
17. Germany	Grossenmeer	1785	68	30

Note: Simple family households consist of a married couple, or a married couple (or widow) with children. Complex family households are extended families of one type or another.

Sources: 1. Laslett (1977); 2. Danhieux (1983); 3. Laslett (1977); 4. Flandrin (1979); 5. Lions and Lachiver (1967); 6. Laslett (1977); 7. Plakans (1982); 8. Czap (1983); 9. Laslett (1977); 10. Palli (1974); 11. Andorka and Farago (1983); 12. Douglass (1980); 13. Laslett (1977); 14. Biraben (1970); 15. Flandrin (1979); 16. Berkner (1972); 17. Laslett (1983).

world-economy during its early stages (Alderson and Sanderson, 1991). It was in the capitalist core that the nuclear family household first became established as the norm; the more economically dissimilar a region was to the core the less likely it was to contain nuclear family households. Thus, household patterns were more likely to be complex in semiperipheral regions than in the core, but peripheral regions were even more likely to have complex households (and, when they had them, to have complex households of greater size and elaborateness).

The reason for this association between household structure and types of capitalist production has to do with the way in which households respond to labor needs (Alderson and Sanderson, 1991). In the core, the nuclear family household was economically adaptive for the capitalist farmers who were increasingly coming to characterize this zone. The existence of a capitalist labor market made it more efficient for farmers to hire agricultural workers than to produce them themselves. The economic demands faced by semiperipheral sharecroppers and peripheral peasants, however, were very different. Such workers were under strong pressures to keep their levels of economic production very high, for they were producing for some type of overlord, and not just for themselves. This created a need for extensive labor teams, and such teams had to be created largely by relying on family members. In the case of peripheral peasants, the absence of a capitalist labor market offered no choice in the matter. Semiperipheral sharecroppers could often draw on a capitalist labor market to hire some of the labor they needed, and sometimes did so. However, this strategy was usually too economically costly and thus tended to be avoided (Berkner and Shaffer, 1978).

What then remains of the thesis that industrialization has caused the nuclear family? Although the thesis must obviously be highly qualified, it need not be abandoned entirely. Clearly industrialization has accelerated the move toward the nuclear family even in those regions where such a family form preceded industrialization. Moreover, in those parts of the world where the nuclear family was not the dominant form before industrialization, industrialization has produced a marked movement toward the dominance of the nuclear family (Goode, 1970). In Japan from the seventeenth century to the middle of the nineteenth century, for example, the extended family was widespread (Laslett, 1977). Yet in modern Japan the nuclear family is clearly the norm (Kumagai, 1986). Because of the demands for geographic mobility produced by a modern industrial economy, the extended family would be a major encumbrance in the lives of most individuals, and thus the nuclear family is really the only suitable type.

In addition, once the extended family is no longer economically adaptive, the emphasis on the nuclear family may well be encouraged by the desire of individuals in the West for greater freedom from control by the older generation. This notion is suggested by a comparison of the West with Japan. In Japan the emphasis on the nuclear family has not gone as far as it has in the West (Kumagai, 1986), and Japan is notable for its antagonism to Western-style individualism and freedom.

The Evolution of the Modern Family System

The story of the emergence of the modern family is a fascinating one, and has been told especially well by two contemporary social historians, Edward Shorter in his book *The Making of the Modern Family* (1975) and Lawrence Stone in *The Family, Sex and Marriage in England, 1500–1800*

(1979). Shorter's study concentrates on France, but he believes his analysis to be applicable to most of western Europe. He believes that the transition to the modern family in most of western Europe began around the middle of the eighteenth century. Stone's book deals with England, and he dates the beginning of the transition toward modernism there about a century earlier. Both writers are basically agreed that this family transition began in the middle and upper classes and diffused later to the lower classes.

The Traditional European Family The premodern European family bears little resemblance to the modern family in terms of the whole tone and texture of familial relationships. There is, first of all, little evidence that the relationship between husband and wife was typically one based upon strong mutual affection and a sense of companionship. Although romantic love as we know it today existed, it was uncommon and was not considered an appropriate basis for marriage. Marriages were arranged by the families of the respective spouses, and economic considerations determined the choice of a spouse, and even the decision to marry at all. Clearly marital unions were fundamentally economic rather than affective relationships. As Shorter has noted in this connection (1975:57):

> The prospect of death seemed to arouse no deep sentiments between spouses. Among rustics to the east of Paris (Seine-et-Marne), special testamentary provisions were seldom made for spouses in a will. And so much more firmly did economics rather than emotion bind together the peasant couple that when the wife fell ill, her husband commonly spared the expense of a doctor, though prepared to "cascade gold" upon the veterinarian who came to attend a sick cow or bull. That was because, in the last analysis, a cow was worth much more than a wife.

Of course a wife was valuable—and precisely in economic terms. Her domestic labor was essential, and she played a crucial role as a producer of offspring. Yet her value to her husband went little beyond this, and social and economic conditions in premodern Europe really did not permit the development of strong affection within the marital relationship.

The premodern parent-child relationship was also vastly different from its modern counterpart. There seems to have been little in the way of sentimental ties between parents and their children. Mothers infrequently nursed their own children. Children were commonly fostered out right after birth to paid wet nurses who cared for them for perhaps a year or more. Moreover, children were frequently treated in ways that today would be regarded as extreme forms of child abuse. They were left unattended for long periods of time, often were hung by their clothing on hooks to keep them out of the way, and, as Shorter has remarked, were frequently left to "stew in their own excrement" for long hours. In addition, they were commonly subjected to all manner of violence from which they frequently died or suffered great injury. There is also the fact that children in the same family were often given the same first name. A newborn infant might be given the name of an older sibling who had recently died, or two living children might have the very same name. This suggests no conception of the child as a unique individual with whom a parent can have a special relationship.

This view of premodern parent-child relations has won wide acceptance, but it has also been strongly challenged (Pollock, 1983; Shahar, 1990). Linda Pollock asserts that it is both logically flawed and empirically false. On the logical side, she notes that sociobiological studies of parental care in other species show that good parenting is a basic attribute of mammals and nonhuman primates. By extension, she says, this should be true of humans as well. Pollock also points out that anthropological studies of childrearing in other societies show that good parental care is a widespread human characteristic; throughout the world parents give adequate care to their children. Pollock musters empirical data showing, she claims, that prior to the eighteenth century parents grieved for their dead children just as they did in later times, and that children were not typically brutally treated. She believes that parents were, on the whole, emotionally attached to their children and quite concerned about their welfare.

Although Pollock is certainly right in what she says about sociobiological studies of parental care in other animals, as well as about anthropological studies of parental behavior in other societies, her conclusions may well be wrong. What she fails to consider is the extent to which extreme social and economic conditions can distort typical parental behavior. Recall the Ik of Uganda, mentioned in Chapter 3 as an example of a society whose social cohesion was destroyed as a result of their loss of most of their means of subsistence. Colin Turnbull (1972) has observed not only that the Ik lost their social cohesion, but also that Ik parents became particularly callous toward their own children; even the most elementary aspects of parental care disappeared. Moreover, consider infanticide. This widespread social practice has been observed to occur under very specific conditions, especially economic stress. It is a highly predictable behavior in circumstances in which parents find it difficult to support a child (Daly and Wilson, 1988). Finally, consider the recent reports of child abuse in modern societies. There is no doubt that this is a much more widespread phenomenon than we have imagined; if it is not uncommon in the modern world, then how much more common must it have been in the premod-

ern world's much more trying economic circumstances?

Thus, extreme forms of parental behavior can and do occur when social and economic conditions put pressure on typical parent-child interaction. And this is precisely what we have observed in premodern Europe. As Stone has pointed out, the rate of infant and child death was so high in premodern Europe that it would have been unthinkable for a mother to invest considerable emotion in her children. To become emotionally attached to them, and then watch them die in such high proportions, would be too traumatic an experience to bear. The basic lack of parental affection, then, was not something parents voluntarily chose, but rather something that was imposed on them by external conditions. Parental indifference was a predictable (and psychologically adaptive) response to debilitating economic conditions and a high rate of infant and child death. A basic reason why parents in industrial societies of the late twentieth century invest so much emotion in their children is the extremely high rate of survivorship of the modern child.

A final characteristic of the traditional family was its fundamental lack of privacy or "separateness" from the rest of society. The family form that most of us live in today—a private social unit relatively isolated from the rest of society—scarcely existed. As Shorter has remarked, the traditional family was "pierced full of holes." Outsiders interacted freely with members of the household, and the relations between family members and outsiders were just as close as those among the family members themselves. There was, in other words, no real boundary between the family and the rest of society.

The Rise of the Modern Family   The traditional family was basically an economic subsystem of the larger society, "much more a productive and reproductive unit than an emotional unit" (Shorter, 1975:5). It was most vitally concerned with transmitting property between the generations and with reproduction. Its crucial role as a transmitter of property explains the powerful role of family elders in the arrangement of marriage. But in the seventeenth and eighteenth centuries this mode of family life began to decay and give way to the kind of family unit familiar to us in the late twentieth century. Lawrence Stone has suggested that the rise of the modern family involved the emergence of four fundamental characteristics: increasing ties of affection between family members, a growing concern with the right to individual freedom and happiness in marriage, growing concern with sexual pleasure and an increasing tendency to separate it from sin and guilt, and a growing desire for a private family life.

One of the most important aspects of the transition to the modern family was the emergence of romantic love as the basis for marriage. Romantic love has no doubt existed since the earliest human societies, but in no society before the seventeenth or eighteenth century has it played a significant role in the selection of marriage partners. The rise of romantic love as the basis for marriage was a revolutionary phenomenon.

There were really two aspects of this phenomenon. First, young people began to reject parental interference in the choice of marriage partners and increasingly demanded the right to choose for themselves. Second, the marriage itself came increasingly to be seen as an affective rather than an economic unit, one held together by the sentimental attachment of the spouses rather than by considerations of property ownership. The tie between the spouses thus shifted from an emotionally weak or indifferent one to one in which affection was of paramount significance. They were becoming companions sharing a long life together. Spouses (and courting partners) began to idealize their loved ones and to prefer their company to that of everyone else. They spent countless hours with each other, called each other by special names of endearment, and expressed their attachment in poetry, literature, and song. One of the most interesting features of eighteenth- and nineteenth-century literature, for instance, is the rise of the romantic novel, a magnificent symbolic expression of the great family change that was occurring.

The sentimental revolution in the family also transformed the relations between parents and their children; a growing concern of parents (mothers in particular) for the welfare of their children became manifest. Mothers began to breast-feed their children rather than send them out to wet nurses, and to concern themselves with childrearing practices that would produce healthy personalities. There was a dramatic decline in the neglect and physical abuse of children, and methods of punishment were progressively liberalized. An era of permissiveness in childrearing was clearly dawning.

Sexual behavior also began to change in major ways. In premodern Europe there was, of course, a sexual urge present in both sexes, and both men and women sought out sex for pleasure to some extent. Yet marital and nonmarital sex were both infrequent and relatively insignificant by modern standards. The relations between the sexes were, as Shorter has suggested, "resolutely unerotic." It is likely that premarital sexual behavior was uncommon, especially for women, and extramarital affairs were in all probability very infrequent (for women they must have been extremely rare). There is also little evidence of much autoerotic behavior.

The seventeenth and eighteenth centuries witnessed a major change in these traditional sexual patterns. A great increase in premarital sex seems to have occurred in these times, for we see a marked rise in rates of illegitimacy. Marital sex also seemed to become more common and to be given more erotic significance. Social life was becoming, at least relative to the past, highly eroticized, and the idea of sexual pleasure as an end in itself was becoming significant.

Hardly less important than these changes was the corresponding change in relations between the family and the outside world, what Shorter has called "the rise of domesticity." The modern family was becoming more and more private, and the boundaries between it and the rest of society more and more closely drawn. In the premodern family the relations between family members and outsiders were as close as those among the members of the family itself, but in the seventeenth, eighteenth, and nineteenth centuries all that changed. By the middle of the nineteenth century the family had become a unit insisting upon its private existence and its separation (or even isolation) from the outside world. Shorter provides a clear understanding of what the rise of domesticity was really all about (1975:227–228):

> Domesticity, or the family's awareness of itself as a precious emotional unit that must be protected with privacy and isolation from outside intrusion, was the third great spearhead of the great onrush of sentiment in modern times. Romantic love detached the couple from communal sexual supervision and turned them towards affection. Maternal love created a sentimental nest within which the modern family would ensconce itself, and it removed many women from involvement with community life. Domesticity, beyond that, sealed off the family as a whole from its traditional interaction with the surrounding world. The members of the family came to feel far more solidarity with one another than they did with their various age and sex peer groups.

We know in practical terms when domesticity is present if, like the French, people begin removing their names from the front doors to insure that no one will knock; if, as in Germany, long Sunday walks through the woods begin to tear Papa from his card games; and if, as happens everywhere, people begin spending greater proportions of their time at home.

Explaining the Transition to the Modern Family The evolution of the modern family was largely a product of the vast changes that were taking place during these centuries toward a highly commercialized capitalist civilization (Shorter, 1975; Stone, 1979; Zaretsky, 1976; Lasch, 1977). Shorter links the rise of capitalism to the modern family revolution through the rise of economic individualism (1975:258–259):

> Laissez-faire marketplace organization, capitalist production, and the beginnings of proletarianization among the work force were more important than any other factors in the spread of sentiment.
>
> . . . How did capitalism help cause that powerful thrust of sentiment among the unmarried that I have called the romance revolution? . . . The logic of the marketplace positively demands individualism: the system will succeed only if each participant ruthlessly pursues his own self-interest, buying cheap, selling dear, and enhancing his own interests at the cost of his competitors (i.e., his fellow citizens). Only if this variety of economic egoism is internalized will the free market come up to the high expectations of its apologists, for if people let humanitarian or communitarian considerations influence their economic behavior, the market becomes inefficient; the weak cease to be weeded out. Thus, the free market engraves upon all who are caught up in it the attitude: "Look out for number one."
>
> . . . Egoism that was learned in the marketplace became transferred to community obligations and standards, to ties to the fam-

ily and lineage—in short, to the whole domain of cultural rules that regulated familial and sexual behavior.

. . . So capitalism exerted its impact upon romantic love through involvement in the market labor force: economic individualism leads to cultural egoism; private gratification becomes more important than fitting into the common weal; the wish to be free produces the illegitimacy explosion.

Although Shorter offers this explanation for the rise of romantic love and the liberalization of sexual behavior, his explanation of the emergence of greater parental involvement in children is slightly different. This, he claims, was linked to the rising standard of living. Maternal indifference in premodern Europe was the unfortunate consequence of the low standard of living and the extremely high childhood mortality rate. But with a notable improvement in the standard of living in the eighteenth and nineteenth centuries and a consequent reduction of infant and child death rates, mothers could begin to invest greater emotion in their children.

What about the rise of domesticity, the increasing seclusion of the family from the outside world? Christopher Lasch (1977) has suggested that the private family of the eighteenth and nineteenth centuries emerged as a kind of shelter into which people could escape from the increasingly harsh realities of the outside world. The family became, in Lasch's memorable phrase, a "haven in a heartless world." The heartless world that Lasch has in mind is the competitive capitalist marketplace. The intensely competitive character of the work environment created the need for a refuge in which people could recover from the slings and arrows of the work world so as to be able to enter it again. As Lasch (1977:xix) has put it, "As business, politics, and diplomacy grow more savage and warlike, men seek a haven in private life, in personal relations, above all in the family—the last refuge of love and decency."

THE CONTEMPORARY FAMILY REVOLUTION

Lasch has also suggested, however, that in the past several decades the family has been under so much stress that it is having greater and greater difficulty fulfilling its role as a refuge from the capitalist workplace. Whether this is actually true or not, the Western family since the early 1960s has suffered from enormous strains and has undergone profound changes. These involve both the relations between husbands and wives and those between parents and their adolescent children.

Recent Changes in Marital Relationships

One of the more widely discussed changes in family life since the 1960s has been the marked increase in cohabitation—couples living together without marriage. Increased cohabitation has been a notable occurrence in all Western industrial societies, although it has been considerably more common in some than in others. In the United States, for example, there was a large increase in the rate of cohabitation during the 1970s. Only 11 percent of persons who married in the period from 1965 to 1974 cohabited, but the figure rose to 32 percent of persons marrying between 1975 and 1979, and to 44 percent of those marrying between 1980 and 1984 (Cherlin, 1992). Living together has also become common in France. A 1977 survey found that 31 percent of married couples between 18 and 29 years of age had lived together before they were married (Cherlin, 1981). Cohabiting relationships last longer in France than in the United States. Only 10 percent of American cohabiting relationships last at least five years, but 30 percent of French relationships last that long (Cherlin, 1992). The country that leads the modern industrial world in the rate of cohabitation is Sweden, and by a large distance. Fully 96 percent of Swedish women who had married by the late 1970s had first cohabited, and cohabitation in Sweden is today a virtually universal practice. In fact, cohabitation is so pervasive in Sweden that having one's first child in a cohabiting relationship has become the norm. The Scandinavian countries actually have a long tradition of cohabitation and out-of-wedlock births, one that dates back several centuries (Cherlin, 1992).

The current high rate of cohabitation does not appear to pose a significant threat to marriage. As Cherlin (1992) suggests, cohabitation seems to be more a preparatory stage for marriage than a permanent substitute for it; most cohabitors plan to marry the person they are living with. That cohabitation has become so common, however, surely suggests that marital and family life has become decidedly different in the past

quarter century, and that people have very different expectations of it.

Another major change in family life in the past quarter century has been the marked decline in fertility, or women's childbearing activities. The fertility rate rose significantly after World War II, and women whose prime childbearing years fell in the mid- to late 1950s were producing an average of 3.2 children apiece (these were, of course, the years of the famous "baby boom"). But since the early 1960s the fertility rate has declined markedly, all the way down to 1.9 children per woman for women whose prime childbearing years fell in the 1970s. Since the middle of the 1970s the fertility rate seems to have leveled off at this current all-time low figure (U.S. Bureau of the Census, 1992).

Last, but hardly least, is the trend in divorce. As Figure 15.1 shows, the divorce rate has in general been rising since the mid-nineteenth century. It took a sudden spurt during World War II (because of the disruptive effects of the war upon married

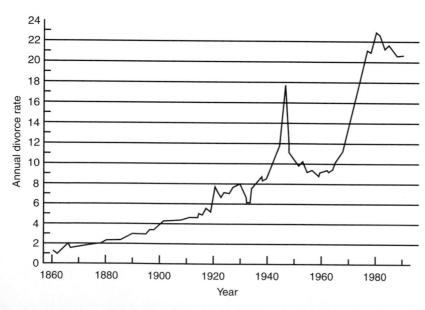

FIGURE 15.1
Divorce rates in the United States, 1860–1985. The divorce rate shown here is the number of divorces per 1000 married women age 15 and over (1920–1985), or the number of divorces per 1000 existing marriages (1860–1920). (*Source:* Andrew J. Cherlin, *Marriage, Divorce, Remarriage,* revised and enlarged edition. Cambridge, Mass.: Harvard University Press, 1992, Figure 1–5.)

life), then returned to its prewar level and remained stable from the late 1940s until the early 1960s. Since then it has increased very sharply, from about 9 divorces per 1000 married women in 1960 to 23 divorces per 1000 married women in 1979. Since its peak year in 1979, the divorce rate has declined slightly, reaching 21 divorces per 1000 married women in the mid-1980s. Although it has levelled off since then, it is still very high, and if it remains near this level then approximately half of all marriages undertaken since 1985 will end in divorce (Cherlin, 1992).

These recent trends in marital relationships are exemplified most strikingly by Sweden (Popenoe, 1988). At the present time Sweden has the lowest marriage rate of any industrial society and one of the highest average ages of first marriage. Since about 1960 marriage has been increasingly replaced by nonmarital cohabitation. For example, in 1960 only about 1 percent of all couples residing together were unmarried, but the number escalated to about 21 percent by 1983 (Popenoe, 1988), and, as noted above, today cohabitation is almost universally practiced as a substitute for or prelude to marriage. Sweden also leads the industrialized world in the percentage of families that are headed by a single parent and in the percentage of all households that are single-person households. In addition, it has the smallest average household size of any industrial society.

Explaining the Recent Family Changes

What accounts for the current upheaval in marital relationships? Why are young people living together frequently before marriage, having fewer children, and divorcing at alarming rates? It has often been said that the current family changes are attributable to changing values and attitudes in regard to family life. This explanation, though, has little to commend it. Even if true, it would

be trivial, for we would still be faced with the problem of explaining why attitudes and values in regard to marriage and family life have changed. But the explanation does not even appear to be true. Recent survey and opinion-poll evidence suggests that familial attitudes and values did not begin to change until the late 1960s or early 1970s, whereas the recent behavioral changes in question really began during the early 1960s. It thus seems that changes in values and attitudes have actually followed rather than generated behavioral changes (Cherlin, 1992).

Cherlin's survey of the available evidence suggests to him that these recent trends are due to fundamental economic changes involving the participation of women in the labor force. These trends correspond very closely to the dramatic increase in the proportion of married women with dependent children who work full-time outside the household. As women have entered the labor force in much larger numbers, their economic power has been substantially amplified, and this has reduced their dependence on their husbands. They are therefore much less likely to stay in an unpleasant marriage. In the past women often felt they had little chance to end an unsatisfactory marriage because they would have had great difficulty supporting themselves and their children on their own. But this has now changed dramatically, and with these changes in the balance of power women's expectations of marriage have changed. They expect much more from it and are likely to end it quickly when it does not live up to their hopes. Men's expectations have changed correspondingly, and with both men and women now heavily involved in their careers it is difficult for children to be as important as they once were. Hence young couples are having fewer of them. Finally, cohabitation is a logical response to a higher rate of marital failure. Because they understand how risky marriage has become, young people want to go into it with the feeling that they have a good chance of making theirs work. Cohabitation, then, becomes a kind of trial period for a possible marriage.

Recent Changes in Parent-Child Relations

The current family revolution involves not only a change in marital relations, but just as important a change in the whole character of relations between parents and their children, especially adolescent children. These relations have been changing for a very long time, but in the past two or three decades the changes have accelerated markedly. The changes are in the direction of an increasing loss of parental control over children and an increasing separation of parents and children into two distinct worlds. As Shorter (1975) suggests, children are now caught up in an elaborate youth subculture that has at least as much role in shaping their basic values as do the teachings of their parents. Parents seem to be increasingly irrelevant as educators and teachers of the young, and many youth seem to view their parents (and members of the older generation generally) as having little of value to transmit to them. According to Shorter (1975:276–277), we are witnessing

> a fundamental shift in the willingness of adolescents to learn from their parents. In the 1960s, relations between the generations started to undergo the same evolution that kinship had earlier undertaken: from function to friendship. In the heyday of the modern nuclear family, the prime burden of transmitting values and attitudes to teenage children fell upon the parents, and the rules of the game were learned in the cloistered intimacy of countless evenings about the hearth. But as the post-modern family rushes down upon us, parents are losing their role as educators. The task passes instead to the peers, and with its transfer passes as well a sense of the family as an institution continuing over time, a chain of links across

the generations. The parents become friends (an affective relationship), not representatives of the lineage (a functional relationship). If this is so, we are dealing with an unprecedented pattern.

As Shorter has himself noted, this revolution in parent-child relations seems to be a kind of "push-pull" phenomenon. The children have been pulled away by the massive development of an independent youth culture, but they also seem to have been pushed out of the family as a result of the fundamental changes it has undergone. Putting it baldly, parents simply do not have the time for their children that they once did. Given that the dual-career family has become a significant form of family life, it is difficult for either parent to have the time that was once available for intensive socialization and upbringing. Hence the closeness between parents and their children so characteristic of days gone by is more and more missing now, and that makes the pull of the adolescent subculture all the more enticing.

The Current Crisis of the Family

Despite the increased rate of cohabitation and divorce, people still want to marry. At least 90 percent of people are still opting for marriage, and the rate of remarriage after divorce is very high (Cherlin, 1992). So the family is not falling apart as an institution, even though it is very different from what it once was (see the Special Topic at the end of the chapter).

Perhaps the real crisis of the family is not that people are living together more often without marriage or getting divorced more often. Perhaps the real crisis is the increasing inability of the family to function, in Lasch's terms, as a haven or refuge, a development that Shorter refers to as the "destruction of the nest." The family seems to be increasingly losing its capacity to shelter the young and the adult males from the extreme pressures of competition in an advanced capitalist civilization, and it is exposing the women more and more to these pressures. In a recent book dealing with the work and family lives of employees in a modern American corporation, Arlie Russell Hochschild (1997) found, much to her dismay, that people's work lives and family lives are in a sense the reverse of what they were decades ago. Work life has become the refuge and stress is concentrated in the family. Both parents put in workdays of ten hours or longer and often indicate that they prefer work life to family life. As a result, the pace of family life has accelerated markedly. Parents have less and less time to devote to the emotional needs of children. Hochschild relates the appalling story of a young boy whose parents were scheduled to give presentations at work on a day in which a medical emergency developed and the boy had to be taken to the hospital. The parents chose to give their presentations rather than be with their son! Surely all of this has major implications for the psychological well-being of individuals in modern society, as well as for the whole tone and character of human relationships.

MARRIAGE, FAMILY, AND KINSHIP IN EVOLUTIONARY PERSPECTIVE

Unlike the evolution of such phenomena as technology, economy, and political organization, the evolution of family and kinship systems reveals no overall linear direction. On the contrary, the evolution of family systems reveals a *curvilinear* pattern (Blumberg and Winch, 1977); small-scale nuclear families coupled with bilateral descent predominate at the hunting and gathering and industrial ends of the evolutionary spectrum, while more elaborate unilineal corporate descent groupings are concentrated in societies found closer to the middle ranges

of the spectrum (i.e., in horticultural and many agrarian societies). Furthermore, it is not possible to view different forms of unilocal residence and unilineal descent as representing different "stages" in sociocultural evolution. Patrilocality and matrilocality, for example, as well as patriliny and matriliny, are different adaptations to different underlying conditions; none of these can be placed as "lower" or "higher" (or as "earlier" or "later") developments in sociocultural evolution (i.e., they are forms of specific rather than general evolution [cf. Aberle, 1961]). Nevertheless, marriage, family, and kinship systems are general evolutionary phenomena, for they display regular variations along the entire course of evolutionary transformation.

Based on a sample of 90 hunter-gatherer societies. Martin and Voorhies (1975) found that 62 percent were bilateral, 26 percent were patrilineal, and only 12 percent had either double or matrilineal descent. Residence is typically patrilocal or bilocal, and the nuclear family unit is given great emphasis. Hunting and gathering societies therefore tend to have very flexible family systems that are highly adaptive under the migratory conditions of a foraging existence. Despite the similarity of hunting and gathering family patterns to those found in industrial societies, there is a crucial difference. Among hunter-gatherers, kinship represents the whole fabric of social life, and virtually everyone is a kinsman. Thus kinship dominates the social lives of hunter-gatherers to an extent that would be inconceivable to the members of industrial societies.

Marriage in hunter-gatherer societies is frequently polygynous, but polygyny occurs less often here than among horticulturalists. Exogamy rules are invariably applied to the nuclear family, and are often extended to larger categories of kin. Sometimes they apply to the entire band.

Horticultural societies are overwhelmingly characterized by the existence of corporate descent groups, generally of the unilineal variety. Patriliny is the most frequent descent type. Martin and Voorhies (1975), using a sample of 104 horticultural societies, report that patriliny occurs in 56 percent of them, matriliny in 24 percent, double descent in 3 percent, and bilateral descent in 16 percent. In most such societies, the nuclear family becomes highly subordinate to these larger groups of kin. Such large-scale kin groups dominate the fabric of social life, and they define for each individual his or her proper place in the world. Individuals relate to one another on the basis of their membership in these corporate groups—as members of the same or different groups and as particular kinds of relatives in the same group. All social activities are carried out within the framework of kinship.

Such groups become so prominent at this stage of sociocultural evolution because they arise to regulate the access of individuals to land and the products of that land. Unilineal descent has the great advantage of allowing the formation of discrete, mutually exclusive, nonoverlapping groups of kins people. This permits each person to be a member of one and only one distinct group. Membership in such a group defines one's rights in land and other property and, additionally, establishes a distinct set of relatives who may provide aid and assistance when required.

Corporate descent groups play vital roles in the regulation of marriage. They are typically exogamous, and this forces persons to seek mates among groups other than their own. Marriage in horticultural societies is frequently polygynous, and the vast majority of horticulturalists clearly prefer this form of plural marriage.

With the rise of intensive social stratification and the state in agrarian societies, kin groups begin to decline in significance. Classes, castes, and estates become key elements in social organization and begin to displace some of the former functions of kinship groups. The state replaces kinship as the prime integrator of society. While kinship remains of durable significance in the lives of most individuals, its structure changes. Unilineal descent declines in favor of a rise in bilateral descent, and both descent types are about equally represented in agrarian societies. A sample of 53 agrarian societies shows 45 percent of them to be patrilineal, another 45 percent to be bilateral, and only 9 percent to be matrilineal (Martin and Voorhies, 1975). Thus, while many agrarian societies continue to have corporate descent groups, almost as many have large bilateral extended families.

Although most agrarian societies have permitted polygyny, monogamy is overwhelmingly the marriage practice of most people. Furthermore, **endogamy**—the tendency of people to marry into their own social groups or categories—is probably more important than exogamy. Marriage thus becomes highly restricted to the members of one's own class, caste, religion, or ethnic group.

Industrial societies are integrated by complex economies and states, not by kinship. Kinship and family life come to be greatly reduced in significance. The nuclear family emerges as the predominant family unit, and bilaterally extended kin networks, though still in existence, play a much smaller role in social life. The family in industrial societies is a much less functional unit than in preindustrial societies, many of its former functions having been usurped by other institutions. It is, for example, no longer a unit of economic production, but is relegated to a consumptive role in the economy.

Marriage in industrial societies is universally monogamous, with polygamy legally prohibited. In addition, it is strongly regulated by endogamous considerations. People tend to marry within their own social class and racial, ethnic, and religious groupings. Within this context, marriage is largely a matter of mutual free choice unconstrained by the larger interests of kin groups.

SUMMARY

1. The most basic types of kin groups in human societies are nuclear families, extended families, and corporate descent groups. Nuclear families consist of a husband, a wife, and their offspring living together and maintaining a common household. Extended families are larger networks of related nuclear families. Corporate descent groups are especially large extended family groupings found in many preindustrial societies.

2. All societies have means for organizing residence and descent groups. Residence groups are groups of kinspeople who maintain a common household. They may be patrilocal, matrilocal, avunculocal, bilocal, ambilocal, natolocal, or neolocal. Descent groups are groups of individuals who organize themselves according to certain principles of kinship connection. These principles may be patrilineal, matrilineal, double, ambilineal, or bilateral in nature.

3. Patrilineal descent is the most common descent type in the world's societies. It traces descent through the father, and descent groups are formed around the relationship between father and son. Patrilineal groups are almost always patrilocal. Matrilineal descent is a less common type that traces descent through the mother's line. The core of a matrilineal descent group consists of a set of sisters and their brothers, the latter being managers of the descent group's affairs. Matrilineal descent systems are unique in their establishment of "sociological fatherhood," an arrangement in which children are reared primarily by their maternal uncles rather than by their biological fathers. Matrilineal descent groups are most commonly matrilocal or avunculocal, but they also employ other residence arrangements.

4. Most social scientists believe that residence systems are established first and give rise to descent arrangements. Patrilocality and patriliny seem to be found under a wide range of infrastructural and structural conditions, but especially where there is high population pressure, frequent warfare with neighboring societies, and the concentration of wealth. The most generally accepted theory of matrilocality is that it arises from conditions requiring men to be frequently absent from their home territories for long periods of time. Warfare conducted at long distances from home seems to be the most common reason for such absence. Once matrilocality has developed, matriliny seems to arise naturally from it. Some matrilocal and matrilineal societies tend to evolve in the direction of preserving their matrilineal institutions but adopting avunculocality, possibly due to the need to reunite male kinsmen to manage new forms of wealth.

5. The three basic forms of marriage throughout the world are monogamy, polygyny, and polyandry. Polygyny is the preferred marriage form in most of the world's societies, but most people, even in polygynous societies, marry monogamously. The extremely widespread preference for polygyny seems to reflect men's interests in sexual variety, and perhaps secondarily their interest in increasing their wealth. Monogamy in agrarian societies generally results from the inability of most men to support more than one wife. In industrial societies, though, monogamy may have become the norm because of the radical incompatibility of polygyny with companionate marriage. Polyandry is a rare practice and is still very imperfectly understood. In some polyandrous societies, at least, polyandry may reflect the need to keep family property together so that individuals have sufficient land to support themselves.

6. Social scientists have revised their earlier view that industrialization created the modern nuclear family. Recent evidence shows that the nuclear family preceded industrialization in western Europe and North America. The nuclear family arose first in those regions most deeply penetrated by core capitalism.

7. The traditional European family was basically an economic rather than a sentimental institution. Affection was not a significant part of the marital tie, and most parents invested little emotion in their children. In many ways the relations between nonfamily members were as close as those between members of the same family.

8. In the seventeenth and eighteenth centuries the Western family began to evolve in the direction of greater sentimentality. Relations between spouses came to be based increasingly on affection, and romantic love became a common basis for marriage. Parental indifference toward children declined sharply, and parents began to pay much more attention to the personality development of their children. The family was also becoming an increasingly private group sealed off from the outside world.

9. These marked changes in family behavior occurred earliest and most extensively in England and France. They clearly were associated with the rise of modern capitalism. The economic individualism so basic to capitalism seemed to spill over into the organization of marriage and family life, as people grew increasingly concerned with their own individual needs in regard to sex and love. The increasing separation of the family from the outside world, though, seems to be an adaptation to the extreme competitiveness of the capitalist marketplace. The family was becoming a refuge from this competition.

10. In the past three or four decades there has been a revolution in family life in modern industrial societies. The divorce rate has skyrocketed, and people live together more frequently without benefit of marriage. Women are also tending to have fewer children and to delay their first pregnancy. These changes seem to be most closely linked to the dramatic increase in the rate at which married women with young children have been entering the labor force. Parent-child relations have also been changing markedly, and in the direction of decreasing parental control over children.

11. Marriage, family, and kinship are evolutionary phenomena, although not in any simple way. The relationship between kinship and a society's technological stage of development is curvilinear. Bilateral descent and emphasis on the nuclear family tend to be found at the least and most advanced ends of the evolutionary spectrum, that is, among hunter-gatherers and industrialists. Horticultural societies commonly have unilineal corporate descent groups. These groups play important roles in the management of land. Agrarian societies also tend to emphasize unilineal corporate descent groups, although not so strikingly as horticultural societies.

SPECIAL TOPIC: IS THE FAMILY IN DECLINE?

For decades social scientists and ordinary laypersons have debated whether the family in modern industrial societies is in a state of decline. Indeed, the debate seems to be renewed in each new generation. David Popenoe (1988) notes that sociologists throughout much of this century have generally argued that the notion that the family is in a state of decline is a myth. The family has been changing to adapt to new circumstances, they have tended to argue, but this does not mean that it is weakening or declining in importance. Popenoe himself, however, challenges this view and claims that the family in the late twentieth century is in fact in a rather profound state of decline. By decline Popenoe means that "the institution of the family is growing weaker; it is losing social power and functions, losing influence over behavior and opinion, and generally becoming less important in life" (1988:xii). One can find no fewer than 10 dimensions of family decline discussed in Popenoe's book *Disturbing the Nest: Family Change and Decline in Modern Societies* (1988):

- The modern family is less cohesive and less capable of controlling the behavior of its individual members; it has lost power to other social groups, such as the state, the mass media, schools, and peer groups.
- Families have become smaller, with fewer children and more single-parent families.

- Families today engage in fewer joint activities; they do fewer things as a unit.
- Meaningful contact time between parents and children has diminished (parents often rationalize this by claiming that they spend "quality time" with their children).
- Families today have less time for the development and maintenance of family-centered routines and activities, such as those that revolve around mealtime, bedtime, birthdays, and holidays.
- Children have entered an era of less regular contact with relatives outside the nuclear family.
- Marriages break up more easily and are far less durable and stable.
- As a result of the greater degree of marital breakup, children suffer increasing anxiety about the possibility of a breakup, and increased anxiety when a breakup does occur.
- At one time children had a close association with the work of their parents and could develop mental models of the occupational roles of adulthood; this is less true today, and children live increasingly in their own separate world.
- Familism—the emphasis on the family as an important social institution—has weakened and has been increasingly replaced by values relating to individual self-fulfillment and egalitarianism.

The majority of sociologists would agree with most or perhaps all of the points above in the sense that they accurately describe the situation of the family in the late twentieth century. However, although Popenoe evaluates these facts negatively, most sociologists would probably evaluate them in a much more positive sense. For example, in his family textbook Randall Collins (1985:473) has said that "the family is not fundamentally weakening under all this change" and in "some respects it is even stronger than before." He adds (1985:473–474):

> Individuals now form families predominantly as a matter of personal preference for marriage. Love has become more important, not less. People make their marriages more for love, now that they are less coerced into depending upon a family economically. . . . Children, too, are apparently recipients of more love than before. There are fewer children per family, and their births are more carefully chosen. This actually makes children more important to their parents, not less. . . .
> . . . Although it lives with strains, nevertheless the family seems to be in better shape than ever.

Why do Popenoe and Collins end up drawing such different conclusions from basically the same set of facts? The only conceivable answer, I believe, is that they approach these facts from different political perspectives. Popenoe has a rather conservative outlook, unusual for a sociologist, whereas Collins has the liberal outlook that is much more typical of sociologists. As Andrew Cherlin (1992:138) has remarked, when they examine the various dimensions of family change "liberal defenders of family change focus on the emotionally enhanced relationships between adults and on the increased autonomy of women, [whereas] conservatives focus on instability and on children." In other words, Collins concludes that the family is not weakening because he approves of many of the changes it has undergone, whereas Popenoe concludes that the family is under siege because he wants to see families exert stronger control over their members.

I would argue that both Popenoe and Collins have captured significant portions of the truth. Certainly many aspects of family change in recent decades, such as skyrocketing divorce rates and the alarming rise in the number of female-headed households among blacks, are cause for concern, but other aspects of family change, such as greater individual autonomy and increasing opportunities given to women, seem very positive. On this matter, as on others, we cannot have our cake and eat it too. In the not-too-distant past of the societies of the West the family was a powerful and highly coercive institution, dictating the lives of its individual members, and the relations between husbands and wives and between parents and children were much colder and more formal. Indeed, it still functions in this way across much of the world, as it did throughout a good deal of social evolution. If we value the increased autonomy and possibilities for individual self-fulfillment that family change brings, as well as the greater warmth between husbands and wives and parents and children—and most members of Western societies do—then we have to be willing to acknowledge that for many of us there will be losses as well as gains.

So, in the end the answer to the question, Is the family in a state of decline? is that there is no answer, at least not any single unambiguous answer. In some senses the family has indeed declined and is likely to decline even further, but in other senses it seems quite reasonable to say, with Collins, that "the family seems to be in better shape than ever."

FOR FURTHER READING

Anderson, Michael. *Approaches to the History of the Western Family, 1500–1914.* London: Macmillan Press, 1980. A brief and illuminating introduction to three contrasting theoretical approaches to the study of European family history since the sixteenth century.

Berger, Brigitte, and Peter L. Berger. *The War over the Family: Capturing the Middle Ground.* Garden City, N.Y.: Doubleday (Anchor Books), 1983. A defense of the family as a crucial social institution and a plea for its strengthening in the face of the tremendous recent pressures undermining its effectiveness.

Cherlin, Andrew J. *Marriage, Divorce, Remarriage.* Revised and enlarged edition. Cambridge, Mass.: Harvard University Press, 1992. One of the best recent studies of the contemporary upheaval in marital and family relationships. Contains much useful statistical information and pays considerable attention to various theoretical interpretations of recent family trends.

Collins, Randall, and Scott Coltrane. *Sociology of Marriage and the Family: Gender, Love, and Property.* Fourth edition. Chicago: Nelson Hall, 1995. Perhaps the best textbook on the sociology of the family in several decades. Unusually comparative and historical for family texts. Provocative reading on a range of historical and contemporary issues.

Fox, Robin. *Kinship and Marriage.* Baltimore: Penguin Books, 1967. An extremely well-written and highly informative introduction to the comparative study of marriage and kinship systems. Excellent chapters on incest avoidance, residence, descent, and marital exchange systems.

Goody, Jack. *Production and Reproduction: A Comparative Study of the Domestic Domain.* New York: Cambridge University Press, 1976. A valuable discussion of how the organization of economic production shapes many features of family structure. Focuses upon the ways in which Eurasian agrarian family systems diverge from those found in African horticultural societies.

Pasternak, Burton, Carol R. Ember, and Melvin Ember. *Sex, Gender, and Kinship: A Cross-Cultural Perspective.* Upper Saddle River, N.J.: Prentice Hall, 1996. An excellent succinct treatment of family and kinship from a very wide-ranging comparative perspective.

Popenoe, David. *Disturbing the Nest: Family Change and Decline in Modern Societies.* New York: Aldine de Gruyter, 1988. A study of the contemporary family revolution with an emphasis on Sweden. Claims that the family in modern industrial societies is in a state of serious decline.

Shorter, Edward. *The Making of the Modern Family.* New York: Basic Books, 1975. Shows that a "sentimental revolution" occurred in western European family relations in the eighteenth and nineteenth centuries and attempts to identify its causes. Makes an important contribution to our understanding of the development of the Western family despite having a tendency to romanticize the modern nuclear family.

Stone, Lawrence. *The Family, Sex and Marriage in England, 1500–1800.* Abridged edition. New York: Harper & Row, 1979. Another first-rate historical study of the western European family revolution of the seventeenth through the nineteenth centuries. The arguments are much the same as Shorter's, although with considerably more attention to historical detail.

van den Berghe, Pierre L. *Human Family Systems: An Evolutionary View.* New York: Elsevier, 1979. Contains many useful discussions of a wide range of kinship phenomena and attempts to show how both biological and sociocultural factors are intertwined in shaping these behavioral patterns.

Chapter
16

The Rise and Expansion of Mass Education

This chapter discusses education as a social phenomenon. **Education** is any sort of formalized or semiformalized system of cultural or intellectual instruction. While in this sense education is a universal feature of human societies, the concern here is primarily with those highly formalized systems of education characteristic of the Western world in the past century or two. The discussion focuses on describing and trying to explain the emergence of systems of mass education and their expansion, both in industrial societies and in the Third World. As in the other chapters in this book, a comparative and historical perspective is adopted.

THE NATURE AND TYPES OF EDUCATIONAL SYSTEMS

Education in Comparative and Historical Perspective

Education is a cultural universal, but its specific nature differs sharply from one society to another. Randall Collins (1977) has pointed to three basic types of education found throughout the world's societies: education in practical skills, education for status-group membership, and bureaucratic education.

Practical-skill education is designed to impart certain technical skills and capacities deemed to be important in performing occupational or other activities. It is typically based on a master-apprentice form of teaching. This kind of education is essentially the only kind of education in primitive societies. It is also found in agrarian societies (where, for example, craftsmen teach their skills to new recruits) and, to some extent, in modern industrial societies.

In primitive societies important crafts like metalworking and important social roles like that of the shaman are generally learned by apprenticeship. In agrarian civilizations, apprenticeship has also been the basis for transmitting the content of such occupational roles as physician, construction engineer, and architect. One of the most important skills to be taught formally has been literacy. Formal literacy training began in ancient Mesopotamia and Egypt, where specialized schools were established to train children for careers as scribes (R. Collins, 1977).

Practical-skill education is notable for its lack of the sorts of ritual accompaniments so characteristic of status-group and bureaucratic education. There are no attendance, examination, grade, or degree requirements since the only feasible test of the effectiveness of this type of education is its success in practice (R. Collins, 1977).

Status-group education is conducted for the purpose of symbolizing and reinforcing the prestige and privilege of elite groups in highly stratified societies. It is generally designed to be impractical in any technical sense and is often given over to the learning and discussion of esoteric bodies of knowledge. It has been widely found in agrarian and industrial societies. As Collins comments (1977:9–11):

In historical perspective, education has been used more often for organizing status groups than for other purposes. Since the defining locus of status-group activity is leisure and consumption, status-group education has been sharply distinguished from practical education by the exclusion of materially productive skills. Because status groups have used a common culture as a mark of group membership, status-group education has taken the form of a club and has included much ceremony to demonstrate group solidarity and to publicly distinguish members from nonmembers. This club aspect characterized the activities of Chinese gentlemen who met for genteel conversation and poetry writing, as well as the periodic festivals put on for the Greek public by students, an elite sector of the population.

Status-group education, then, has been ceremonial, aesthetic, and detached from practical activities. Its rituals rarely have dramatized rankings within the group; formal grades, competitive examinations, and degrees usually have been absent. . . . The main distinctions have been between insiders and outsiders, not among members of the group. Frequently, there have been no formal attendance requirements, and the absence of formal degrees has reflected the fact that acquisition of the status group's culture is the object of education. . . .

. . . In China, the first educated men were diviners or sages, who read oracles for the court and probably passed their skills along through apprenticeship. . . . [In later eras the] leisure pursuits of Chinese gentlemen . . . centered on poetry writing and painting; the prestigious form of sociability was the "literary gathering" where literature was read and discussed. . . .

. . . In India, from the beginnings of literacy, education was closely associated with status-group prestige. Brahmin priests monopolized knowledge of the Vedic traditions and thereby helped not only to close off entry to their caste but also to legitimate the caste system. . . .

Similarly, in the Heian court of early Japanese civilization (A.D. 1000), men and women courtiers developed an elaborate culture of poetry writing and art appreciation and even produced the first great Japanese works of prose fiction, largely through informal family education. In the Islamic world, education developed from religious training in the holy scriptures and laws to a form of culture that, in the cosmopolitan cities of prosperous periods, provided entertainment and status for the wealthy. . . .

In Europe, informal education as the basis of status emulation was most prominent during the Renaissance, especially in the wealthy commercial cities of Italy, but also in Germany, the Netherlands, France, and England. Poetry writing and allusions to the classics were marks of prestige in everyday social life.

Bureaucratic education is created by governments to serve either or both of two purposes: the recruitment of individuals to governmental or other positions, or the socialization and disciplining of the masses in order to win their political compliance. This type of education has generally placed great emphasis on examinations, attendance requirements, grades, and degrees. It has been common in several of the great historic civilizations, especially in those with centralized bureaucratic states. In classical China, for example, an elaborate form of bureaucratic education existed, the core of which was its examination system. Rigorous examinations had to be passed in order for individuals to gain entry into the important positions in the government bureaucracy. The higher the position, the more elaborate the series of examinations a candidate had to pass. Usually only a tiny fraction of degree candidates was allowed to pass each examination (R. Collins, 1977).

Bureaucratic education has also been characteristic of more contemporary societies. The creation of modern school systems clearly had a great deal to do with the emergence and consolidation of strong bureaucratic states in Europe (R. Collins, 1977). As Collins (1977:19) notes, "The militarily expansive and rigidly bureaucratized Prussian state led the way in the seventeenth and eighteenth centuries in building a public school system at the elementary and university levels and in drawing state officials from among holders of university degrees."

These different types of education are frequently combined in the same society. Agrarian societies, for example, often combined all three types, although one might very well have been given emphasis over the others. Modern industrial societies have educational systems that are primarily combinations of status-group and bureaucratic education, with the bureaucratic element taking priority. Although such systems also engage in the teaching of practical skills, this aspect is distinctly subordinate to the others.

There is also an important distinction between two different types of contemporary bureaucratic education that should not be overlooked. These two types are known respectively as sponsored-mobility and contest-mobility systems (R. H. Turner, 1960). Throughout most of Western Europe there developed **sponsored-mobility educational systems.** Sponsored-mobility systems place students into one or the other of two educational channels early in their educational careers. At approximately age 11 students take qualifying exams, and those who pass, who are usually a small minority, are placed in the channel that leads to a university education and the occupational opportunities it affords. Those failing the exam, usually a large majority, end up in the channel that terminates with a vocational education. This type of system tends to be highly class-segregated, inasmuch as the exam passers tend to be disproportionately middle, upper-middle, or upper class, and the exam failers tend to be disproportionately working class. The classic sponsored-mobility systems were once found in England, Germany, and France, but England has now moved substantially in the direction of the contest-mobility system, and thus is somewhat intermediate between the two.

Contest-mobility educational systems do no official channeling (although a subtle, informal kind of channeling or "tracking" generally exists) and there is a more open competition for the pursuit of advanced education. In this system students do not take qualifying exams whose results determine their educational and occupational chances once and for all. Essentially they can go as far as their abilities and inclinations will take them. The United States has the quintessential contest-mobility system, a system also found to some extent in Japan and the old Soviet Union. Contest-mobility systems tend to be much more egalitarian than sponsored-mobility systems, giving working-class students more opportunity and a chance to fail repeatedly before finally succeeding.

The Emergence of Modern Educational Systems

Modern systems of formal mass education arose mainly during the nineteenth century and became consolidated in the twentieth, emerging first in the more industrialized countries but eventually being carried throughout the world. Formal education of long duration is now the normal experience of youth in all industrial societies and is increasingly so in the Third World. Table 16.1 gives some idea of the size of enrollments at different educational levels in both modern industrial and less-developed societies. It is clear that primary education is universal throughout the industrialized world. Many Third World countries have reached universal primary education, and most of the others, at least outside Africa, have come very close to it. Secondary education is also universal, or nearly so, in industrial societies. It has not achieved universality in less-developed countries, but still has developed extensively, especially in Latin America. It is little developed in Africa.

Table 16.1 shows that tertiary education, which includes not only colleges and universities, but also business schools and other postsecondary technical schools, has also become a major part of the educational systems of industrial societies. Tertiary enrollments are now extensive throughout the industrialized world and beginning to move in that direction in some Third World countries. However, the tertiary enrollment ratios in Table 16.1 must be interpreted cautiously. Several of these figures are inflated, some probably considerably so, as a result of the manner in which they were calculated. The figures are gross enrollment ratios, which means that the number of tertiary students in a society, *of whatever age*, was divided by the number in the population *of the appropriate age group*, which would normally be 18–22 or 19–23. Since a growing number of tertiary students come from older age groups, there is a clear tendency for gross enrollment ratios to be artificially inflated over time. Undoubtedly the figures for Canada and the United States are the most inflated. However, Table 16.1 also reports the number of students per 100,000 population. Here it can be seen that, even though the enrollment ratios for Canada and the United States are substantially inflated, these countries still have the world's largest and second-largest number of tertiary students, respectively, per 100,000 population.

Now that we have looked at the size and significance of educational systems at all levels throughout the world, we need to consider how these systems got started and how they have expanded over time. The first Western society to introduce compulsory primary education was Germany (Prussia), which did so in 1763. Germany was followed by Denmark (1814), Sweden (1842), Norway (1848), Italy (1859), Switzerland (1874), England and Wales (1880), France

Table 16.1   EDUCATIONAL ENROLLMENTS FOR SELECTED NATIONS

Nation	Primary Education	Secondary Education	Tertiary Education		Number of Tertiary Students per 100,000 Population
			All	Coll./Univ. Only	
Developed nations					
United Kingdom	113	94	37	15	2,788
Netherlands	97	123	45	21	3,352
France	106	106	50	33	3,623
Germany	97	101	36	—	2,319
Denmark	99	115	41	35	3,284
Sweden	100	99	38	—	2,697
Canada	103	106	103	45	6,980
United States	107	97	80	50	5,546
Australia	108	84	42	25	3,267
Japan	102	96	30	24	---
Soviet Union	106	99	21	—	---
Russia	107	88	45	19	3,104
Czech Republic	99	86	16	8	1,484
Hungary	95	81	17	11	1,312
Poland	98	84	26	22	1,952
Underdeveloped nations					
Ethiopia	27	11	1	1	68
Nepal	109	36	3	3	490
Tanzania	70	1	1	1	---
India	102	49	—	—	---
China	118	55	4	3	377
Ghana	76	37	2	—	---
Senegal	60	16	3	3	298
Indonesia	115	45	10	9	951
Nigeria	90	29	—	—	---
Egypt	97	76	17	14	1,542
Thailand	88	44	19	12	2,029
Peru	119	65	40	25	3,264
Turkey	97	64	16	14	1,918
Colombia	119	62	16	14	---
Chile	98	67	27	21	2,369
Brazil	112	44	12	12	1,080
Mexico	112	58	14	14	1,509
Argentina	107	62	39	30	3,206
South Korea	101	93	48	38	4,756

The figures are gross enrollment ratios and are for 1993. The figures for the Soviet Union are for 1989. The gross enrollment ratio is the number of students, of whatever age, enrolled at a given educational level divided by the total population in the age bracket normally representing that level. In the case of primary and secondary education, ratios often exceed 100 percent because of the presence of students outside the normal age bracket for that educational level. This means that the figures are artificially inflated to some degree.

Tertiary education is defined as all postsecondary education; it includes all students in colleges, universities, and various types of technical schools. Enrollment ratios are reported for all tertiary education as well as that portion of it that pertains to colleges and universities only. It is likely that the ratios for this level are also artificially inflated, and for the same reason that ratios are inflated for primary and secondary education.

Sources: World Bank, *World Development Report*, New York: Oxford University Press, 1996, Table 7; UNESCO, *Statistical Yearbook 1996*, Paris: UNESCO, Tables 3.2 , 3.9, and 3.10.

(1882), the Netherlands (1900), and Belgium (1914) (Flora, 1983; Johansen, Collins, and Johnson, 1986). In the United States, the first state to establish compulsory education was Massachusetts, which did so in 1852, and by 1900 32 states had established compulsory education (Flora, 1983). Japan first began compulsory education in 1872 (Hane, 1992). By the end of the nineteenth century compulsory primary education had become well established throughout the Western world and enrollments were high (Benavot and Riddle, 1988).

Secondary education existed in the nineteenth century but did not experience significant expansion in most Western societies until the middle third of the twentieth century (Flora, 1983). Even as late as 1950 secondary education in most Western societies was still very limited, with less than 20 percent of the age group 10–19 attending a secondary school (Flora, 1983). Tertiary education, as would be expected, developed even later than secondary education. Enrollment levels in tertiary institutions were low even as late as 1965, including more than 18 percent of the relevant age group only in Canada and the United States. It was not until the 1960s that tertiary education began to expand on a major scale on its way to becoming the major social force that it is today.

Although educational systems have been expanding since the nineteenth century, the single greatest period of educational expansion on a world level was after World War II, especially between 1950 and 1970. John Meyer and his colleagues (Meyer, Ramirez, Rubinson, and Boli-Bennett, 1977) have referred to this period as witnessing a "world educational revolution." Table 16.2 depicts this period of major educational expansion. Although compulsory primary

Table 16.2   WORLD EDUCATIONAL ENROLLMENT, 1950–1993

Educational Level/ Type of Country	Percentages			Number of Countries	
	1950	1970	1993	1950 & 1970	1993
Primary students					
All countries	58	83	92.5	117	113
Richer countries	90	102	101.8	51	59
Poorer countries	37	72	82.3	56	54
Secondary students					
All countries	12.7	30.5	59.3	102	107
Richer countries	21.3	46.4	81.9	49	55
Poorer countries	5.3	17.0	35.3	46	52
Tertiary students					
All countries	1.4	5.3	22.7	109	101
Richer countries	2.6	9.2	29.2	46	61
Poorer countries	0.6	2.6	12.7	55	40

The figures are gross enrollment ratios. The gross enrollment ratio is the number of students, of whatever age, enrolled at a given educational level divided by the total population in the age bracket normally representing that level. In the case of primary education, some numbers exceed 100 percent because of the presence of students outside the normal age bracket for that educational level. This means that the figures are artificially inflated to some degree.

Tertiary education is defined as all postsecondary education, including but not limited to students in colleges and universities. It is likely that the ratios for this level, as well as for the secondary level, are also artifically inflated, especially the 1993 ratios.

Richer countries are defined as those above the median in per capita GNP, poorer countries as those below the median.

Sources: The data for 1950 and 1970 are from John W. Meyer, Francisco O. Ramirez, Richard Rubinson, and John Boli-Bennett, "The World Educational Revolution, 1950–1970," *Sociology of Education* 50:242–258, 1977, Table 1. The data for 1993 are from World Bank, *World Development Report*, New York: Oxford University Press, 1996, Table 7.

education had essentially become universal throughout the industrialized world by the beginning of this period, it had also moved extensively in this direction in the less-developed world by the end of the period. Secondary education also expanded greatly during this time, especially in the richer countries. And, of course, this was the period during which tertiary education underwent its first major phase of dramatic expansion, at least in the industrialized world. I have extended Meyer et al.'s data to 1993, and it can be seen that major educational expansion has still been occurring at a world level. Secondary enrollments nearly doubled between 1970 and 1993, and tertiary enrollments more than quadrupled during this period. (Again, it must be borne in mind that some of the 1993 enrollment ratios are artificially inflated, especially the tertiary ratios, so the numbers must be interpreted cautiously.)

EXPLAINING THE RISE AND EXPANSION OF EDUCATIONAL SYSTEMS

The Functionalist Theory

The functionalist theory (Clark, 1962; Trow, 1966) has until recently dominated sociological thinking about education. This theory attempts to explain the nature of education and its expansion over the past century or so as a consequence of the functional requirements of an industrial society, particularly the requirements arising from technological and economic change. Education is seen as having taken its particular form because of the positive contributions it makes to the proper functioning of industrial society. The main principles of the theory are summarized by Collins (1979) as follows:

1. The educational requirements of jobs in industrial society are constantly increas-

ing as a result of technological change. There are two aspects of this:
   a. The proportion of jobs requiring low skill declines while the proportion requiring high skill increases.
   b. The same jobs are continually upgraded in their skill requirements.
2. Formal education provides the training necessary for persons to undertake the more highly skilled jobs.
3. As a result of the above, educational requirements for employment continually rise, and more and more people are required to spend longer and longer periods in school.

Collins (1979) argues that the available evidence strongly contradicts this interpretation of education and educational change. Regarding the proposition that educational requirements increase because of a decrease in the proportion of jobs requiring low skill and an increase in the proportion requiring high skill, Collins suggests that such a process accounts for only a small amount of educational upgrading. For example, one well-known study has found that only 15 percent of educational expansion during the twentieth century could be attributed to shifts in the occupational structure (Folger and Nam, 1964). The assertions that educational requirements rise because the same jobs are upgraded in skill requirements and that formal education provides necessary job skills are also held to be contradicted by available evidence. Collins approaches a test of these ideas by asking, "Are better-educated employees more productive than less-educated ones?" and "Are vocational skills learned in school or elsewhere?" His answer to the first question is "no," to the second "elsewhere." Regarding the first question, he points to a major study (Berg, 1971) that shows that better-educated employees are typically not more productive than less-educated ones, and in some cases are even less productive. In terms of the second question, Collins sets forth evidence indicating that most of what students learn in schools has little or no relevance to the acquisition of job skills, and that most such skills are acquired much more quickly and easily on the job (cf. D. Brown, 1995).

The functionalist theory's assumption that there has been an overall increase in the skill levels of jobs throughout the twentieth century can also be seriously questioned (Braverman, 1974; D. Brown, 1995). In fact, this is likely true for only a minority of jobs, perhaps not more than 20 percent. In his book *Labor and Monopoly Capital: The Degradation of Work in the Twentieth Century* (1974), Harry Braverman has shown fairly convincingly that there has been an actual *deskilling* of many jobs since the late nineteenth century.

A Marxian Interpretation

A Marxian theory of the origins and expansion of education in the United States has been presented by Samuel Bowles and Herbert Gintis in their book *Schooling in Capitalist America* (1976). Bowles and Gintis argue that American education has been greatly shaped by the capitalist economy. Capitalists, they argue, have had a major influence in shaping the educational system at all levels so that it would turn out committed and productive workers who would help capitalists maximize their profits. Instead of developing autonomously, American education has been held hostage by the capitalist economy and bent to the service of its aims.

Bowles and Gintis give explicit attention to how capitalism has shaped the historical evolution of American education. They note that the rise of mass public education in the middle of the nineteenth century corresponded to the beginnings of industrialization and the emergence of the factory system. The introduction of mass public education, they claim, was a response on the part of capitalists to the increased need for socializing and disciplining a new kind of working population. They argue that capitalists were the strongest proponents of a system of public education, and that schools most frequently arose in those areas with the largest concentrations of factory workers. The conversion of the high school from an elite to a mass institution corresponded closely to the rise of corporate monopoly capitalism. By this time a very large proportion of the workforce consisted of factory wage laborers, and many of these were recent immigrants. Bowles and Gintis hold that the expansion of the educational system to a new level was required as a stronger means of disciplining a larger, more ethnically varied, and more recalcitrant labor force.

Bowles and Gintis see the major expansion of higher education since World War II as a result of such factors as the greatly increased demand on the part of employers for technical, clerical, and other white-collar skills and the increased demand by minority and working-class youth for access to higher education. But other major changes in higher education have occurred as well in recent years. These have mainly involved increasing diversification and vocationalization. One of the most prominent of the recent changes is the massive growth of community colleges, institutions that are strongly vocational in nature and that draw a large proportion of their students from working-class backgrounds. Bowles and Gintis see the rise of community colleges as a way of facilitating the increased demand for higher education without posing a threat to the status of the more elite colleges and universities.

Although Bowles and Gintis are concerned only with the American educational system, their theory has generally been assumed to be relevant to Western educational systems in general. But once these other educational systems are examined, it quickly becomes clear that this theory does not hold up well. In many Western European countries and in Japan, mass education appeared before the beginnings of industrialization (Boli, Ramirez, and Meyer, 1985), and in England mass schooling began a good century after the onset of industrialization. Moreover, in the United States it appears that mass schooling began first as a rural phenomenon, and thus was hardly prompted by capitalist industrialization (Meyer, Tyack, Nagel, and Gordon, 1979).

However, even though the specifics of Bowles and Gintis's theory cannot be accepted, it is nonetheless the case that modern education is in general tied in to the economic system, and to some extent changes and expands because of economic changes. Capitalist culture penetrates significantly into the workings of the educational system, especially at the level of higher education. In his famous *The Higher Learning in America* (1965; orig. 1918), Thorstein Veblen noted long ago the domination of American universities by businessmen. In the more than three-quarters of a century since Veblen wrote, American universities have become far more dominated by businessmen and their ethos. Indeed, these universities increasingly resemble capitalist corporations in their overall character and functioning. And European universities appear to be traveling the same evolutionary path, although they have proceeded less far along it. Throughout the industrialized world, education has become increasingly characterized by the advancing commodification that is such an important trend in the evolution of capitalism.

Education as Nation-Building

A politically oriented theory of the development and expansion of mass educational systems has been developed by John Meyer and his colleagues (Meyer, Ramirez, Rubinson, and Boli-Bennett, 1977; Meyer, Tyack,

Nagel, and Gordon, 1979; Boli, Ramirez, and Meyer, 1985). For lack of a better name, I will call this *theory the theory of education as nation-building.* The authors of this theory generally reject the main assumptions of all competing theories, arguing in particular that none of them can satisfactorily explain the specific features of modern mass educational systems. These features, they claim, are primarily the following:

- Mass educational systems are intended to be universal, standardized, and highly rationalized. They apply to everyone in the same fashion, cutting across the class, ethnic, racial, religious, and gender cleavages of a society.
- Mass educational systems are highly institutionalized at a world level. They are extraordinarily similar in very different societies throughout the world, and have become increasingly similar over time.
- Mass educational systems are specifically directed toward the socialization of the individual as the primary social unit. This is seen, for example, in the extent to which educational rituals celebrate individual choice and responsibility rather than the imbeddedness of individuals in such corporate groups as social classes, castes, or extended families.

The nation-building theory proposes that mass education arose in the modern world specifically as a device for the intensive socialization of the individual into the values and aspirations of the modern, rational nation-state. As John Boli, Francisco Ramirez, and John Meyer put it (1985:158), "In the broadest sense, mass education arises as a purposive project to construct the modern polity, reconstructing individuals in accordance with collective religious, political, and economic goods and purposes."

John Meyer, David Tyack, Joane Nagel, and Audri Gordon (1979) have applied this line of thinking in order to under-

stand the development of American education between 1870 and 1930. Contrary to
Bowles and Gintis, they stress that mass education during this time was not primarily
an urban, industrial phenomenon. They
claim that it was at least as characteristic of
rural as of urban areas, and quite likely was
even more prominent in the former. As
such, it was motivated by the desire of
important segments of American society to
socialize their children into the new national culture that was emerging. This culture was capitalistic, rationalistic, and
highly individualistic. As the authors explain (1979:601):

> One critical factor to understand in this
> whole process is the role of the American
> *farmer*, an important carrier of capitalistic
> culture, involved in rational calculations in
> a world market, and eager to maintain free
> action in a free society. . . .
>
> A political economy or moral polity
> based upon free individuals—freed from both
> traditional forms of community and from an
> old-world statism—requires great effort and
> constant vigilance: to educate these individ-
> uals (freedom from ignorance), to reform
> their souls (freedom from sin), to save them
> from political subordination (freedom from
> aristocracy), and to save them from sloth
> (freedom from old-world customs). To liber-
> ate such individuals and to link them by ed-
> ucation and salvation to a millennial Amer-
> ica seemed within the reach of a responsible
> citizenry. . . .
>
> The major educational agents of this in-
> dividualistic political culture of capitalism—
> rational and universalistic in premises but
> almost stateless in structure—were actors
> whose authority was more moral than offi-
> cial. They combined in associations that
> look to 20th-century eyes like social move-
> ments—religious and other voluntary groups
> rather than organizations clothed with the
> authority of a bureaucratic state. . . . These
> groups acted not simply to protect the status
> of their own children but to build a millen-
> nial society for all children. Their modes of

thought and action were at once political,
economic, and religious. That these school
promoters were often in fact ethnocentric
and served their own religious, political, and
economic interests is quite clear; but they
were doing so in a very broad way by constructing an enlarged national society.

To my mind, this theory has much to
recommend it and seems to make very good
sense of those specific features of modern
educational systems that Meyer and his colleagues see as most crucial. It can certainly
help us understand not only the origins of
mass education, but the reasons why primary education, and to some extent secondary education, have become so prominent in so many societies around the world.
However, the theory seems inadequate as a
means of understanding many of the developments in higher education, especially
why it has expanded so rapidly and so substantially in some societies. Moreover, the
nation-building theory may not be fully adequate even in explaining a good deal of the
expansion of secondary education. To explain these things I think we have to draw
on the last theory of educational expansion
to be discussed, the credential inflation argument of Randall Collins and Ronald Dore.

The Theory of Credential Inflation

The best-known version of the theory of
credential inflation is the one developed by
Randall Collins in his book *The Credential
Society* (1979). This book focuses on the
American educational system and why it
has become one of the world's largest and
most comprehensive systems, but an important part of Collins's overall theory can be
extended to other modern educational systems. Collins uses a Weberian version of
conflict theory as the general foundation for
his theory. He makes particular use of
Weber's concept of status group and sees
status groups as being more important than
classes in shaping the American educational

system. Collins believes that the most important status groups in American society are ethnic groups.

Collins views the character of American education and its dramatic expansion throughout the past century as rooted in the great ethnic diversity of American society. Such diversity has resulted in major struggles among ethnic groups for privilege and prestige. These struggles began mainly in the late nineteenth century and continued well into the twentieth. Education, Collins holds, became the major weapon used in such struggles. Dominant groups used the educational system as a means of maintaining their cultural and economic dominance. For them it was a mechanism for transmitting their dominant cultural values to new immigrant groups of workers, as well as a resource to be used to reinforce their economic dominance. But subordinate groups also saw it as a resource they could use in their attempts to improve their economic status. The possession of a certain amount of education came to be viewed as establishing a set of *credentials* that would provide access to certain desired occupational positions. Education thus became an arena in which different groups struggled for economic success. As these struggles progressed, education began to increase in size and importance.

As more and more persons began to obtain educational credentials, however, an unexpected and unwanted thing happened: these credentials declined in value. Drawing an analogy to monetary inflation, Collins calls this process **credential inflation.** Just as money inflates when there is more of it in circulation, educational credentials inflate when more people possess more of them. Credential inflation in the educational sphere means that the same amount of education no longer "purchases" what it once did. One must acquire more of it just to keep even in the struggle for economic suc-

cess. Collins argues that this is exactly what has been happening in the American educational system over the past century. The struggle over education has caused continual educational inflation, resulting in the massive expansion of the educational system (and educational requirements for jobs) over time. Since it now takes a college degree to "purchase" a job that could have been obtained with a high school diploma 30 or 40 years ago, a greater number of young people are going to college. Most of them go not because of a desire for learning, Collins insists, but because they seek credentials that they hope will pay off in economic success.*

Collins also makes special note of the fact that, as American education expanded, educational institutions were forced to make major changes in their curricula and in their overall character in order to appeal to an increasingly mass clientele. The most prominent changes involved the watering down of the classical liberal arts curriculum and the introduction of a host of extracurricular activities. The transformation of the high school into a mass institution, for instance, was accompanied by the so-called progressive movement in education. Two of progressivism's major innovations were the introduction of athletics and other extracurricular activities and the attempt "to substitute a rather vague 'life-adjustment' training for the classical curriculum" (R. Collins,

---

*The massive expansion of education has had essentially no effect on economic inequality, a fact pointed out both by Collins and by Bowles and Gintis. In view of Collins's argument, this should not be surprising. Educational credentials have expanded at all levels, and therefore status groups that had an educational head start many years ago have been able to maintain their lead. As some groups moved over time from high school completion to college completion, others simply moved from getting college degrees to doing postgraduate work, and so on.

1979:115–116) Similar changes occurred when colleges and universities started to be attended by a larger clientele, most of whom were seeking educational credentials rather than intellectual stimulation. As Collins points out (1979:124–125):

> The main appeal of the revitalized university for large groups of students was not the training it offered but the social experience of attending it. The older elite was being perpetuated in a new, more easy-going form. . . . Through football games colleges for the first time became prominent in the public eye, and alumni and state legislators found renewed loyalty to their schools. At the same time, fraternities and sororities became widespread, and with them came college traditions of drinking, parties, parades, dances, and "school spirit." It is little exaggeration to say that the replacement of the pious, unreformed college by the sociable culture of the university was crucial in the growth of enrollments, or that football rather than science was the salvation of American higher education.
>
> . . . The rise of the undergraduate culture indicates first of all that college education had come to be treated as consumption by the new industrial upper classes, although it also attracted growing numbers of the intellectually oriented and those seeking careers in teaching. College attendance had become an interlude of fun in the lives of upper-class and upper-middle-class young Americans. . . .
>
> . . . [An attempt] to put training back as the central function of the college was a failure. Students did not want to disturb the rituals of freshman and sophomore class rivalries, junior dances, and senior privileges. . . . Most students found the essence of college education to be the enjoyable and status-conferring rituals and social life of college rather than the content of classroom learning.

Collins (1977) notes that there are significant differences among the educational systems of industrial societies. As mentioned earlier, England, Germany, and France, have much smaller educational systems of the sponsored-mobility type, whereas industrial societies such as the United States and the Soviet Union have large contest-mobility systems. Collins believes that less inflationary sponsored-mobility systems develop in societies where the level of class segregation is high. The class-segregated character of the educational system reflects the class-segregated character of the larger society. Competition for advanced education is strictly regulated, and as a result the system of tertiary education tends to remain relatively small. By contrast, highly inflationary contest-mobility systems tend to emerge in societies in which the level of class segregation is low. Low class segregation is associated with a strong egalitarian ideology, and the educational system becomes the focus for the implementation of this ideology. As a result, a more open competition for advanced education occurs, which in turn leads to a larger and more rapidly inflating educational system.

Collins's theory is a major improvement on both the functionalist and the Marxian interpretations. However, one difficulty with the theory concerns Collins's argument that ethnic diversity is at the root of educational expansion. This assertion is contradicted by empirical research (Boli, Ramirez, and Meyer, 1985). Indeed, even casual observation would suggest considerable skepticism on this count. For example, the world's most ethnically heterogeneous society, the Soviet Union, has undergone less educational expansion than the world's most ethnically homogeneous society, Japan. Fortunately, there is a simple way of explaining credential inflation and educational expansion that does not rely on the factor of ethnic heterogeneity, so the most important part of Collins's theory can be saved.

Ronald Dore (1976) has developed a similar argument that he has applied to several Western industrial societies and, in particular, to the educational systems of Third World countries. What Collins calls credentialism—the process whereby educational systems come to be built around the pursuit of educational certificates for their occupational value rather than around learning as valuable for its own sake—Dore refers to by the term *qualificationism*. He suggests that it is a significant phenomenon in all or most major industrial societies. Moreover, the underdeveloped nations appear to be involved in imitating the educational patterns of the industrial countries and thus building strong elements of qualificationism into their own educational systems. All (or at least most) contemporary nations have thus become infected with what Dore calls "the diploma disease." The diploma disease is a type of vicious circle in which individuals become obsessed with the acquisition of diplomas or degrees because employers increasingly emphasize such educational certificates in their statements of job qualifications. The two sides feed off each other, and educational certificates inflate as a result.

Although qualificationism seems to be a more prominent characteristic of the United States and Canada than of other advanced industrial societies, it has certainly become a significant feature of the educational systems of virtually all other industrial societies in the twentieth century. England and Japan, for example, have experienced very significant growth of qualificationism throughout this century. (See the Special Topic at the end of the chapter for an analysis of the growth of qualificationism in Japan.) Historic changes in the career preparation of engineers and librarians are excellent indicators of the rise of qualificationism in the English educational system (Dore, 1976). In the late nineteenth century, civil engineers took no formal examinations and gained entry into their profession by an apprenticeship system. By the middle of the twentieth century this had changed markedly, so that educational certificates had become very important for entry into the profession. Furthermore, by 1970 formal educational preparation had become an absolute necessity. Librarians have followed a similar course. At the beginning of the twentieth century, no formal degrees were necessary for librarianship. Yet by the 1930s an educational certificate was becoming very useful, by 1950 it had become a minimal requirement, and by 1970 the period of formal educational preparation minimally necessary for librarianship had been lengthened. Moreover, the prospects were clearly in sight for lengthening it even more.

Many underdeveloped countries in recent decades seem to be experiencing an especially acute form of qualificationism. They are victims of what Dore calls the "late-development effect": the later development starts, the more rapidly school enrollments increase. In such countries, educational certificates have been made necessary requirements for individuals to gain entry into modern-sector jobs (e.g., civil service posts, office jobs). These jobs are highly attractive because they promise a level of economic reward far beyond that experienced by the average person. Therefore, the demand for them is very high, producing substantial credential inflation.

There are a number of serious consequences of the growth of qualificationism. Among these, two seem perhaps most important. One is the "overeducation" problem (Freeman, 1976). As an increasing number of persons hold educational certificates of a certain level, and as the number of jobs requiring that educational level does not increase proportionately, many of the certificate holders are unable to gain employment at that level. They either take jobs for which they have more education than necessary, or they go on to gain more education, hoping that this extra amount of education will secure for them the kinds of jobs they desire. Thus the overeducation problem is both the result of qualificationism and a cause of accelerated qualificationism.

A second serious consequence of the growth of qualificationism involves the quality of education itself. As Dore has remarked, when qualificationism gains the upper hand in an educational system, examinations begin to dominate the curriculum, learning becomes ritualized, curiosity and creativity are deemphasized, and students not only fail to develop an interest in what they are learning, but even lose concern for its relevance. Education comes to be oriented around passing examinations and receiving chits, rather than around the expansion of the mind and the stimulation and satisfaction of intellectual curiosity. Classrooms become sterile places characterized by a kind of ritualized boredom. When students begin to grow aware of the real nature and functions of the educational system, and when credential inflation has reached very high levels, a "credential crisis" may occur. Collins believes that this has happened within the past three decades in the United States. As he remarks (1979:191–192):

> As of the 1960s, the credential system went into a state of explicit crisis. . . . There was tremendous pressure from subordinated ethnic groups, especially blacks and Latin Americans, for integration into the dominant educational and occupational institutions. The result has been a multifaceted crisis in confidence in the system and a variety of reactions and criticisms.
>
> . . . [Students began] to demand revision of traditional curricular requirements. Such demands were usually put in the form of a shift to greater "relevance," or toward the cultures of the ethnic minorities themselves. But in fact, the alternatives lacked substance; their principal appeal was negative, a reaction against the traditional requirements that were now recognized as purely procedural formalities of the process

of gaining a credential. More recently, the idealistic rhetoric of curricular alternatives has been replaced by a manipulative cynicism. Students electing to remain within the system have adopted the goal of high grades, irrespective of content and by any means whatsoever, producing an inflation in college grades, while at the same time achievement levels have been steadily dropping.

Although qualificationism produces these negative effects in both the developed and the underdeveloped countries, the effects seem to be worse in the underdeveloped world. Unemployment of credential holders has reached very high levels in some underdeveloped nations, producing tremendous frustrations for these persons. Moreover, as Dore remarks (1976:81):

> In the later developers the birth of a school system and the development of a qualification-based occupational system are likely to be simultaneous. The very concept of "school" and of formal education entered the society in recent times as part of the package of "modernity" brought by the imperialist powers. By contrast, most of the older industrial countries have formal pedagogical traditions (and some educational institutes) dating back to pre-industrial times *before* educational certificates acquired bread-and-butter value—dating back, in other words, to the time when learning was thought to be about getting *knowledge* or wisdom, to make a man respected or holy or righteous or rich. These older traditions still persist in the older countries. They serve to maintain the fiction that education is about moral and intellectual uplift and enrichment. And such fictions *are* important. What men define as real is real in its consequences. The fictions *do* serve as a countervailing force to weaken tendencies towards qualification-orientation, particularly when they are boldly reasserted by rebellious students demanding the end of examinations, and urging that universities should stop prostituting themselves by subserviently acting as graders of human material for the capitalist system (even if they do

falter and fall into confusion when any university teacher offers to take them at their word and abolish all degree *certificates* as well as examinations). In later-developing societies, where all except the very first generation of purely soul-saving mission schools (and even some of those) had selection/credentialling functions, these useful countervailing fictions, having no roots in any local past, are harder to establish and sustain. The pursuit of certificates can be even more naked and unashamed.

Conclusions: Explaining the Birth and Expansion of Mass Education

How, then, can we account for the emergence of modern systems of mass education and their long-term expansion throughout the world in the twentieth century? I suggest combining the nation-building and credential inflation theories (minus the ethnic conflict argument). John Meyer and his colleagues present a convincing and well-supported argument that modern educational systems have originated primarily as devices to create the modern citizen. However, creating the modern citizen requires much less education than people are receiving today, especially in the more industrialized countries. This is where we need to turn to the credential inflation argument. Remember that credential inflation is a self-perpetuating process. Once it gets started, it tends to continue of its own accord and is difficult to stop. The process is, in essence, a quite simple one: The logic of the "market" for educational credentials causes continuous qualification expansion. As more people gain credentials, the worth of these credentials declines in terms of the kinds of jobs for which their holders can qualify. Therefore, unless people are willing to lower their occupational aspirations, they must stay in school longer in order to achieve a higher credential. Moreover, educational certificates that were once desirable as a basis for

acquiring a certain job eventually end up becoming minimal requirements. As Dore explains (1976:5):

> The way the qualification-escalation ratchet works is roughly like this. A bus company may "normally" require a junior secondary leaving certificate for £5-a-week bus conductors and a senior secondary leaving certificate for its £7-a-week clerks. But as the number of senior certificate leavers grows far larger than the number of clerkships that are available, some of them decide that £5 a week as a bus conductor is better than nothing at all. The bus company gives them preference. Soon all the available conductor slots are filled by senior certificate holders: a senior certificate has become a necessary qualification for the job.
>
> It is not entirely clear why employers allow qualifications to escalate in this way. The chief reason seems to be that they are simply unquestioning victims of the widespread myth that education "improves" people, and that they are therefore getting more for their money if they get a senior certificate for £5 a week rather than a junior certificate. . . . Or it might just be that, faced with fifty applicants for five bus conducting jobs, all of whom could do the job equally well, it just simplifies the whole process to consider only the ten people with senior certificates—and provides a clear objective and legitimate reason for saying no to the other forty. . . .
>
> Whatever the reason, it happens. Senior certificates get the bus conducting jobs: BAs pre-empt the clerkships. The pressure to get on higher up the school ladder is intensified: so is the pressure on the government to build more schools to *allow* more children to get higher up. And it is hard to see a limit to the process.

SUMMARY

1. Three major types of educational systems are found in the world's societies. Practical-skill education functions to transmit socially use-

ful knowledge and skills to members of the younger generation. Status-group educational systems serve to signify the social status of high-ranking groups. They are generally highly impractical and are devoted to the transmission and discussion of esoteric bodies of knowledge. Bureaucratic educational systems function either to win the political compliance of the masses or to recruit personnel to jobs. They stress attendance requirements, grades, and diplomas.

2. Educational systems in modern industrial societies are combinations of status-group and bureaucratic education, but have been evolving increasingly in the bureaucratic direction in the past several decades. In some industrial societies sponsored-mobility educational systems prevail, in which case considerable educational tracking at an early age exists. In other industrial societies contest-mobility systems are found. These systems are more openly competitive and are not formally based on a tracking mechanism.

3. Most modern systems of mass education began in the nineteenth century and became consolidated in the twentieth. By the end of the nineteenth century most Western societies had established compulsory primary education and enrollments in primary schools were high. Several decades ago primary education became universal in the industrialized world, and has now become universal or virtually so throughout most of the Third World.

4. Secondary education has developed more recently. Public secondary education got going around 1870 in the United States, but at that time it was an alternative to a college education rather than preparation for it. In the early decades of the twentieth century public secondary education expanded greatly and by 1930 was becoming a mass institution with a mainly college-preparatory role. Secondary education expanded more slowly in Europe. It did not begin its first major expansion in most European countries until about the time of World War II. Secondary education is now universal or nearly so throughout the industrialized world and has penetrated significantly into the most developed parts of the Third World. In many Third World countries a majority of the relevant age group is enrolled in secondary schools.

5. The period between 1950 and 1970 was perhaps the greatest period of educational expansion on a world level since the beginnings of mass educational institutions. Educational expansion was so great during this period that some sociologists have spoken of the period as undergoing a "world educational revolution." Since 1970 educational systems have continued to expand substantially, although perhaps somewhat less rapidly than between 1950 and 1970.

6. The result of all this educational expansion is that most people throughout the world now spend many years passing through one or another formal educational institution. Education has become an extremely prominent part of the lives of most people everywhere, especially those in the highly-industrialized countries.

7. Four major theories of the rise and expansion of modern educational systems have been developed by sociologists. These are the functionalist theory, the Marxian theory, the nation-building theory, and the theory of credential inflation. The main arguments of these theories are laid out and critically evaluated in Table 16.3.

Table 16.3   THEORIES OF MODERN EDUCATIONAL SYSTEMS

Theory	Characteristics	Evaluation
Functionalist theory	Modern educational systems have originated and expanded as a result of the changing functional needs accompanying industrialization. Industrialization has increased the skill level of work, and education has had to expand in order to provide people with the training they need to function effectively in the occupational realm.	Although a widely accepted theory, it is contradicted by some important facts. Most of what people learn in school has little relationship to specific job skills, and most of these skills can be (and are) learned rather quickly on the job.
Marxian theory	In the well-known version of Bowles and Gintis, modern educational systems arose as systems of labor discipline for the emerging working class, as well as legitimizing ideologies for the class inequalities of capitalist society. The needs of the capitalist class have shaped the content and character of education, and educational systems have expanded in conjunction with the evolution of industrial capitalism.	Although capitalism penetrates modern educational systems in various ways, the specific arguments of Bowles and Gintis and most other Marxian theorists falter in the face of considerable evidence. The onset of mass schooling and industrialization often do not correspond.
Education as nation-building	Modern mass educational systems originate and expand in order to provide the intensive socialization individuals need to become proper citizens in modern, rationalistic, technologically advanced industrial (or industrializing) societies. Education becomes a vast tool tying individuals to the aims of modern political systems in promoting economic development and overall societal modernization.	Seems to identify some of the critical forces underlying the birth of modern mass education, and also may successfully explain why modern educational systems are so alike. But cannot explain much of the expansion that educational systems have undergone, especially at the level of higher education.
Credential inflation theory	As developed by Collins and Dore, proposes that education is a highly valued commodity sought by individuals as a means of economic success and upward mobility. The educational system becomes a focus of struggle for diplomas and degrees. Once set in motion, this struggle undergoes a type of inflationary spiral, and thus education expands at all levels as individuals run faster educationally just to keep even in the struggle for success.	Identifies a crucial aspect of the process of educational expansion in the modern world. However, it is weak in accounting for the origin of mass education.

SPECIAL TOPIC: THE JAPANESE EDUCATIONAL SYSTEM

Because Japan was a relatively late developer among contemporary industrial societies, it has created what is perhaps the most qualification-oriented educational system in the industrialized world (Dore, 1976). As Ronald Dore (1976) remarks, almost from the very beginning of its industrialization Japan was building qualificationism into its career preparation. Even as early as 1910 many Japanese business firms were attempting to recruit only university graduates. University degrees were also becoming increasingly necessary at this time for entry into the technical professions and government administrative positions.

Japan has undergone enormous educational expansion throughout the twentieth century. In 1918 private colleges were given the right to call themselves universities, and two decades later 26 such universities had been established. At the same time there were also 19 state universities and 2 municipal universities (Dore, 1976). By 1950 the total number of institutions of higher education had exploded to 350. The number swelled to 525 institutions (245 universities and 280 junior colleges) by 1960, to 861 (382 universities and 479 junior colleges) by 1971, and to 963 (446 universities and 517 junior colleges) by 1980. By 1987 there were over 2.3 million students enrolled in 474 universities and 561 junior colleges (Kitamura, 1991). This obviously represents an extremely high rate of educational expansion, and there doesn't appear to be an end in sight. As Kazuyuki Kitamura notes (1991:310):

> Despite the prediction of a declining college-age population in the 1990s, there was a great "rush" to establish new institutions, new departments, and new programs in 1987 and 1988. During the 1987 academic year, nine new universities (one public and eight private) and fifteen junior colleges (one national, one public, and thirteen private) were established, and during the 1988 academic year, seventeen new universities (one national, one public, and fifteen private) and eleven new junior colleges (one national, two public, and eight private) were created.

And the number of spaces available for student enrollment at Japanese colleges and universities still does not appear to be sufficient to satisfy student demand, as many Japanese students are now enrolling in colleges and universities in Western societies. It is hard to know just when or how this process of educational expansion will come to an end, or at least markedly slow down.

But this tells only part of the story of Japan's educational system. A look at its nature and content reveals the great extent to which it is a highly qualification-oriented system. There is enormous pressure on students in primary and secondary schools to achieve high grades so they can get into the best universities. Many students spend most of their after-school time studying, often until late each night. Parents, especially the notorious "education mamas," drive their children relentlessly. As if this is not enough, many students enroll in the famous *juku,* or "cram schools," which are designed to give them extra preparation for the examinations on which they must achieve high marks in order to get into the university of their choice (Frost, 1991). And the examinations themselves put an emphasis on rote learning, stressing largely the memorization of facts that most Westerners would consider to be very trivial (Frost, 1991). This whole process is referred to by the Japanese as "examination hell," and it is a process they dislike and constantly complain about. As Peter Frost (1991:291–292) has said, "At least since the 1920s there have been repeated complaints in the Japanese press that examination hell has prevented Japanese students from having a healthy childhood, has blunted intellectual curiosity, has discouraged females from applying to universities, has overlooked less academic leadership skills, and has encouraged those students who finally do get admitted to do almost no academic work while in college." This last point may appear startling: *It has encouraged those students who finally do get admitted to do almost no academic work while in college!* Yes, that statement does read correctly. On the surface it appears to make no sense whatsoever, but on closer inspection it makes perfect sense. What it shows virtually beyond doubt is that Japanese education is a system of highly ritualized learning, the content of which is essentially irrelevant. The fact that much of what Japanese students learn consists of trivial facts learned by rote, and that Japanese university students often need do little real academic work at all, demonstrates that the Japanese educational system is a pure occupational recruitment or filtering device that has little to do with the acquisition of valuable knowledge. What is important is not that students acquire what they "need to know" in order to perform certain jobs, but that they can survive an extremely competitive and psychologically demanding process. And that surely is the hallmark of qualification-oriented education.

FOR FURTHER READING

Beauchamp, Edward R. (ed.). *Windows on Japanese Education.* Westport, Conn.: Greenwood Press, 1991. A collection of essays on various aspects of the Japanese educational system.

Boli, John, Francisco O. Ramirez, and John W. Meyer. "Explaining the origins and expansion of mass education." *Comparative Education Review* 29:145–170, 1985. An approach to modern educational systems emphasizing the role of mass education in the building of modern rational states.

Bourdieu, Pierre, and Jean-Claude Passeron. *Reproduction: In Education, Society, and Culture.* Beverly Hills, Calif.: Sage, 1977. A famous book by two French social scientists that develops an argument about the social role of education similar to that of Bowles and Gintis.

Bowles, Samuel, and Herbert Gintis. *Schooling in Capitalist America.* New York: Basic Books, 1976. An argument for the shaping of American education by the capitalist economy.

Brown, David K. *Degrees of Control: A Sociology of Educational Expansion and Occupational Credentialism.* New York: Teachers College Press, 1995. An insightful study of the beginnings of credentialism and the expansion of higher education in the United States around the turn of the twentieth century.

Collins, Randall. "Some comparative principles of educational stratification." *Harvard Educational Review* 47:1–27, 1977. A look at the major types of education in human societies. Emphasis is given to developing a theory of divergent educational systems in industrial societies. Provides an excellent comparative and historical baseline for understanding the nature of education in the United States and other contemporary industrial societies.

Collins, Randall. *The Credential Society: An Historical Sociology of Education and Stratification.* New York: Academic Press, 1979. A brilliant analysis of the American educational system and its monumental expansion over the past century.

Dore, Ronald. *The Diploma Disease: Education, Qualification, and Development.* Berkeley: University of California Press, 1976. A provocative analysis of the growth of qualification-oriented education on a worldwide scale throughout the twentieth century, with special attention to the growth of qualificationism in the Third World.

Halsey, A. H., A. F. Heath, and J. M. Ridge. *Origins and Destinations: Family, Class, and Education in Modern Britain.* Oxford: Clarendon Press, 1980. A major study of the role of education in the class structure of contemporary Britain.

Karabel, Jerome, and A. H. Halsey. *Power and Ideology in Education.* New York: Oxford University Press, 1977. An excellent collection of articles on various aspects of the sociology of education from a variety of theoretical perspectives.

Chapter
17

The Forms and Functions of Religious Belief and Action

The truth of religion comes from its symbolic rendering of man's moral experience; it proceeds intuitively and imaginatively. Its falsehood comes from its attempt to substitute itself for science and to pretend that its poetic statements are information about reality.

—*Eugene Genovese*

Religion is a universal feature of human social life in the sense that all societies have modes of thought and patterns of behavior that qualify to be labeled "religious." Much of what goes under the heading of religion belongs to the superstructure: It consists of specific types of symbols, images, beliefs, and values whereby human beings interpret their existence. However, since religion also embodies a ritualistic component, a part of religion belongs as well to the social structure. In this chapter we will explore how the structural and superstructural features of human religious life emerge in conjunction with the material infrastructure and other aspects of the social structure. As in other chapters, concern lies in both the sociocultural similarities and differences revealed by the phenomenon in question. Our concern is necessarily of a scientific nature. We wish to determine what religion is, what various forms it has taken across time and space, and how it varies in accordance with material and social arrangements. Questions regarding the empirical reality of supernatural phenomena (whether or not God or other supernatural beings or forces actually exist) lie outside the bounds of scientific discourse. We shall therefore leave it to philosophers and theologians to speculate about the existence and possible nature of supernatural powers. But whether or not supernatural powers really exist, they become socially real and sociologically meaningful when people believe in them and act accordingly. It is the social reality of these beliefs and actions that is under investigation in this chapter.

Of course, many people will still insist that a scientific approach to the study of religious phenomena is inappropriate, if not logically impossible; they will claim that such an approach can yield no valid insights and can only serve to distort the proper spiritual meaning of such phenomena. However, social scientists have been systematically studying religious phenomena for over a century, and the results have been profoundly revealing.

THE NATURE OF RELIGION

Social scientists have had considerable difficulty in defining religion with any degree of precision. The main problem in arriving at a good definition has been to determine where the boundaries of the phenomenon should be placed. As Roland Robertson (1970) points out, two main kinds of definitions of religion have been proposed by social scientists: *inclusive* and *exclusive*. Inclusive definitions define religion in the broadest possible terms, conceiving of it as any system of belief and ritual that is imbued with "sacredness" or is oriented to "ultimate human concerns." Those who favor the inclusive view generally regard as religions not only theistic systems organized around the concept of a supernatural power or powers, but also various nontheistic belief systems such as communism, nationalism, or humanism. By contrast, exclusive definitions restrict the term *religion* to those belief systems that postulate the existence of supernatural beings, powers, or forces. Nontheistic belief systems such as communism or humanism, since they do not involve a supernatural realm, are automatically excluded, even though it may be

granted that such nontheistic belief systems may share elements in common with religious systems. The following are good examples of inclusive definitions of religion:

> A religion is a unified system of beliefs and practices relative to sacred things, that is to say, things set apart and forbidden—beliefs and practices which unite into one single moral community called a Church, all those who adhere to them (Durkheim, 1965:62; orig. 1912).

> Let me define religion as a set of symbolic forms and acts which relate man to the ultimate conditions of his existence (Bellah, 1964:359).

> Religion, then, can be defined as a system of beliefs and practices by means of which a group of people struggles with these ultimate problems of human life (Yinger, 1970:7).

The first definition given above is very famous and has been cited repeatedly throughout the years by a host of sociologists. For Durkheim, the crucial characteristic of religion was that it was oriented toward a realm defined by human beings as *sacred*, that is, the object of special reverence, respect, and even awe. This realm stood in sharp contrast to the realm of the *profane*, or the world of ordinary, everyday existence. The second and third definitions cited above emphasize that religion is, above all else, oriented toward the "ultimate concerns" of humankind. What are these ultimate concerns? According to Yinger (1970), whose own definition makes them the essence of religion, they have to do with the fact of death; the need to cope with frustration, suffering, and tragedy; the need to bring hostility and egocentrism under control; and the need to "deal with the forces that press in upon us, endangering our livelihood, our health, and the survival and smooth operation of the groups in which we live—forces that our empirical knowledge cannot handle adequately" (Yinger, 1970:6).

At first sight, these definitions seem quite unobjectionable. Religion is, after all, generally associated with a realm postulated by human beings to be of sacred significance. Furthermore, it is generally true that religious belief and action have a special concern for the ultimate problems of human existence given emphasis by Bellah and Yinger. Yet these definitions of religion are problematic. The difficulty lies not in what they say, but rather in what they fail to say. In none of these definitions is religion restricted to systems of human thought and action that postulate the existence of supernatural powers or forces. All of the inclusive definitions allow anything to be called religion so long as it identifies a realm of sacred concern or relates to questions of ultimate meaning. Indeed, Yinger himself has stated that "some nontheistic systems of belief and action share so much in common with theistic ones that we do well to call them religions" (1970:13). Granted that some nontheistic systems share important elements in common with theistic ones, it is still an intellectual distortion to lump theistic and nontheistic systems together as if they were essentially the same kind of thing. It is of crucial significance whether or not a belief system postulates the existence of a supernatural realm.

It is clear that this book adopts an exclusive definition of religion. Others also prefer such restriction. Roland Robertson stresses the importance of an exclusive definition and holds that religion "is that set of beliefs and symbols (and values deriving directly therefrom) pertaining to a distinction between an empirical and a superempirical, transcendent reality; the affairs of the empirical being subordinated in significance to the non-empirical" (1970:47). Similarly, Anthony Wallace has defined religion as

"that kind of behavior which can be classified as belief and ritual concerned with supernatural beings, powers, and forces" (1966:5). Along these same lines, we shall define **religion** as *an organized system of beliefs and practices, resting on unproved faith, that postulates the existence of supernatural beings, powers, or forces that act upon the physical and social world.*

There are three main elements in this definition. First, religion always involves both a set of rituals or practices and a set of beliefs, and these beliefs and rituals are socially organized and enacted by the members of a society or some segment of a society. The private thoughts of some individuals do not constitute religion so long as they remain personal and unincorporated into some larger body of doctrine and ritual (i.e., these thoughts may be *religious* in nature, but by themselves they do not constitute *a religion*). Second, the beliefs in question are taken to be true on the basis of faith alone, there generally being no felt need to validate them in any empirical sense. Religious beliefs therefore lie outside the realm of scientific validation, and many of them as well lie outside the realm of scientific invalidation. In short, the criterion for the acceptance of religious beliefs has nothing to do with the standards of scientific evidence and proof or disproof. Finally, and most important, religion always involves the concept of a supernatural realm of existence that lies above and beyond the everyday, knowable, natural world. In the definition presented here, a system of belief and practice may be called religious only if it meets all three of the criteria stated above.

In addition to specifying what religion is, it is also desirable to indicate what it is not. In the first place, religion should not be seen as equivalent to a belief in a god or gods. While many religious systems postulate the existence of a god or gods who rule over humankind and to whom respect or reverence is due, many do not. Throughout Melanesia and Polynesia, for example, a central religious concept is that of *mana*. There is nothing godlike about *mana*; rather, *mana* is an abstract supernatural force that floats around and instills itself into people and things. People who have especially good fortune are said to be filled with *mana*, while those with bad fortune are said to have lost their *mana*. *Mana* can be controlled and used for beneficial consequences, but it is only an impersonal force, not a godlike or spiritlike being.

In addition, it is inappropriate to equate religion with a system of morality. Religious systems are often closely connected with systems of secular morality, but the two are hardly the same. There are many societies in which the religious system and the system of secular morality are quite independent of each other.

Many scholars have drawn a sharp distinction between religion and magic. The distinction usually made is that religion is based on "supplication," while magic depends on "manipulation"; that is, in religion human beings request, beg, or beseech things of the supernatural powers, who are free to deny such requests, while in magic human beings attempt to compel the supernatural forces to serve their ends (de Waal Malefijt, 1968). Some modern anthropologists, however, do not accept such a distinction, arguing that religion and magic are often intimately intertwined and that the distinction between them often gets lost in practice (R. Robertson, 1970).

A few words should be said about the differences between religion and science and about their relationship. Religion deals with the supernatural or "supraempirical" and bases its claims about the existence and nature of this realm on faith, divine revelation, or intuitive or imaginative experience. Science, by contrast, confines its claims to the natural or empirical world and demands

that its claims be subject to agreed-upon standards of evidence and proof and disproof. There is a huge gulf separating these two modes of knowledge and understanding; they are based on radically different, indeed incommensurable, conceptions of what constitutes knowledge and truth. This means that there is a conflict between religion and science that is logically inevitable. Furthermore, where the claims that religion might make about empirical reality come into conflict with established principles of scientific knowledge, the claims of religion must give way to those of science, since the latter is a demonstrably superior mode of acquiring knowledge about the empirical world. Indeed, it has historically been the case that science has won out over religion where their claims about empirical reality have clashed. However, this does not mean that science can or should replace religion as a mode of understanding all aspects of human existence. As long as religion confines itself to the supernatural or supraempirical realm, it ceases to conflict with scientific principles, since no scientist can ever formulate tests to determine the nature or existence of such a realm. Religion therefore retains, and is likely to retain indefinitely, exclusive control over a realm of human understanding that is totally unapproachable by science.

THE EVOLUTION OF RELIGION

Scholarly work on the evolution of religion has lagged behind work on the evolution of many other features of sociocultural life. Nonetheless, some valuable schemes of religious evolution have been presented, perhaps the best of which is that of Anthony Wallace (1966). Wallace considers the religion of any society to be a conglomeration of **cult institutions.** A cult institution is "a set of rituals all having the same general goal, all explicitly rationalized by a set of similar or related beliefs, and all supported by the same social group" (1966:75). Four main types of cult institutions are identified by Wallace. **Individualistic cult institutions** exist when there are no shamans, priests, or other religious specialists available to perform rituals; rather, each person acts as his or her own specialist, performing specific rituals as the need arises. In **shamanic cult institutions** there exists a part-time religious specialist—a shaman—deemed to have special religious qualifications and powers. For a fee, shamans intervene with the supernatural powers on behalf of their clients. In contrast to individualistic cult institutions, shamanic cult institutions maintain a religious division of labor in which there is a distinction between religious specialists possessing special skills and powers and laymen who lack such special attributes. A third level of cult institution is the communal. **Communal cult institutions** are characterized by groups of laymen who "are responsible for calendrical or occasional performance of rituals of importance to various social groups ranging in scope from the members of special categories—such as age grades, the sexes, members of secret societies, particular kinship groups, and sufferers from particular diseases—to the whole community" (1966:86–87). Communal cult institutions include the agricultural rituals of the Iroquois, the ancestor ceremonies of the Chinese and some African tribes, and totemic and puberty rituals among the Australian aborigines. While communal cult institutions are characterized by a specific type of religious specialization, there is no full-time priesthood or extensive religious hierarchy. The latter are found, however, among **ecclesiastical cult institutions.** These cult institutions are based upon the existence of professional priesthoods organized in bureaucratic fashion. Members of the priesthood are full-time religious specialists elected or appointed to permanent religious offices. A sharp demarcation exists between priests and religious laymen; the former monopolize religious knowledge and the direction of religious rituals, while the latter are typically passive recipients of knowledge and ritual.

Wallace identifies four evolutionary types of religion based on combinations of cult institutions:

- **Shamanic religions,** which contain only individualistic and shamanic cult institutions.
- **Communal religions,** which contain individualistic, shamanic, and communal cult institutions.
- **Olympian religions,** which contain individualistic, shamanic, and communal cult institutions, as well as ecclesiastical cult institutions organized around polytheistic pantheons of high gods.
- **Monotheistic religions,** which contain individualistic, shamanic, and communal cult institutions, along with ecclesiastical cult institutions organized around the concept of a single high god.

Wallace believes that shamanic religions prevail primarily among hunting and gathering societies. The Eskimos have a shamanic religion. They populate the world with a variety of greater and lesser spirits, the most important of which is Sedna the Keeper of the Sea Animals. A major cult institution is the Shamanic Cult. The most important activity performed by the shaman is his annual trip to the bottom of the sea, a trip in which he attempts to persuade Sedna the Keeper of the Sea Animals to release the game she controls in order that the Eskimos can live through another year. Eskimo shamans are also frequently called upon for the diagnosis of illness. The Eskimos also maintain two individualistic cults, the Spirit Helper Cult and the Game Animal Cult. Religious activity in these cults involves the individual enactment of certain ritual performances as well as the individual avoidance of certain taboos.

Communal religions are most characteristic of horticultural societies. Wallace indicates that such religions have been found among many North American Indian societies, among African societies (excepting Muslim North Africa and the centralized African kingdoms), and among a number of Melanesian and Polynesian peoples. The Trobriand Islanders of Melanesia are organized along the lines of a communal religion. The major cult institution is what Wallace terms the Technological Magic Cult. In this cult, public magicians preside over communal rituals involving garden magic, canoe magic, and fishing magic. These rituals are calendrical in nature, being tied to the cycle of the seasons. In addition to this communal cult, the Trobriand Islanders have one other communal cult, shamanic services, and they engage in a variety of individualistic religious practices.

Olympian religions are most commonly found among intensive horticultural and early agrarian societies. Olympian religions have been found among the early civilizations of the New World, such as the Mayas, Aztecs, and Incas; among many of the centralized chiefdoms or kingdoms of Africa; among east Asian societies on the edges of China and India, such as the kingdoms of Myanmar (formerly Burma), Indonesia, and Korea; and among the ancient Greeks and Romans. The African kingdom of Dahomey possesses an Olympian religion. In addition to individualistic, shamanic, and communal cults, the Dahomeans have a Great Gods Cult. This cult has many of the features of an established church, as it actively supports and legitimizes the Dahomean ruling class. This cult possesses a priesthood and many temples. The pantheon of gods is divided into four subpantheons, and each of these is associated with

a separate religious order. Each religious order contains its own priesthood, temples, and rituals. As is typical in Olympian religions, each deity is associated with a particular aspect of nature over which it exercises control.

The great world religions, such as Judaism, Christianity, Islam, and Hinduism, are, of course, monotheistic religions. Such religions arose in the context of complex agrarian societies and have continued right into the modern industrial era. Although there are a number of fundamental differences among these great monotheistic religions, all share in common the conception of a single high god to whom great reverence and obedience is due.

THE AXIAL AGE AND THE RISE OF CHRISTIANITY

In the first millennium B.C., and especially around the sixth century B.C., there occurred an extraordinary revolution in human consciousness. This revolution involved major achievements in philosophy among the Greeks, and, more importantly for our purposes here, the rise of most of the major world religions. This period has been called the Axial Age (Jaspers, 1953; Eisenstadt, 1986). Its nature and significance is summarized well by Karl Jaspers (1953:2):

> The most extraordinary events are concentrated in this period. Confucius and Lao-tse were living in China, all the schools of Chinese philosophy came into being...; India produced the Upanishads and Buddha and, like China, ran the whole gamut of philosophical possibilities down to scepticism, to materialism, sophism and nihilism; in Iran Zarathustra taught a challenging view of the world as a struggle between good and evil; in Palestine the prophets made their appearance, from Elijah, by way of Isaiah and Jeremiah to Deutero-Isaiah; Greece witnessed

the appearance of Homer, of the philosophers—Parmenides, Heraclitus and Plato—of the tragedians, Thucydides and Archimedes. Everything implied by these names developed during these few centuries almost simultaneously in China, India, and the West. . . .

In this age were born the fundamental categories within which we still think today, and the beginnings of the world religions, by which human beings still live, were created. The step into universality was taken in every sense.

Little research has been done on the causes of the Axial Age phenomena, but we do know that the Axial Age corresponds very closely to two major social developments, one economic and the other political. On the economic side, the period between 650 B.C. and 430 B.C. was witness to a major spurt in world urbanization (Chandler, 1987). During this period the number of large cities nearly tripled, and the total population represented by these cities increased more than threefold.

This period was also associated with a major increase in the size and scope of political empires (Taagepera, 1978; Eckhardt, 1992). Near the end of the Axial Age, specifically between 430 B.C. and A.D. 100, there was another spurt in world urbanization and there also emerged the first truly worldwide trade axis between east Asia and the Mediterranean (McNeill, 1982; Curtin, 1984). Were these political and economic developments driving the ideological developments of the Axial Age? It would be hard to argue against such a view, to which we shall return shortly.

At the very end of the Axial Age was born the major world religion that has come to be the overwhelmingly dominant religion of the entire Western world: Christianity. Early Christianity, which began as a sect of Judaism in the first century B.C., in due time became one of the most successful religious movements of all time (if not *the* most successful). In a recent highly celebrated book, *The Rise of Christianity* (1996), the

Table 17.1 RELIGION IN SOCIOCULTURAL EVOLUTION

Type of Religion	Typical Technological Level of Society	Examples
Shamanic: only individualistic and shamanic cult institutions present	Hunting and gathering	Eskimos, !Kung San, Mbuti of central Africa
Communal: individualistic, shamanic, and communal cult institutions present	Simple horticultural	Trobriand Islanders, many North American Indian tribes
Olympian: individualistic, shamanic, and communal polytheistic ecclesiastical cult institutions present	Intensive horticultural and early agrarian	Mayas, Aztecs, Incas, ancient Greeks and Romans, African kingdoms
Monotheistic: individualistic, shamanic, and communal monotheistic ecclesiastical cult institutions present	Complex agrarian and contemporary industrial	Ancient China and India, medieval Europe, contemporary Western capitalism, contemporary Japan

sociologist Rodney Stark has traced the development of Christianity in its first few centuries and attempted to account for its expansion. As Stark notes, Christianity grew extremely rapidly, probably on the order of 40 percent per decade. Starting with the assumption that there were 1,000 Christians in A.D. 40, Stark estimates that the number grew to 7,530 by A.D. 100, to 217,795 by A.D. 200, to 6,299,832 by A.D. 300, and to 33,882,008 by A.D. 350. In A.D. 316 the Roman emperor Constantine converted to Christianity and declared it to be the official religion of the Roman empire. Stark argues that this was not because of some new, deeply-held belief in Christian doctrines, but rather because Christianity had grown so significantly that it had become a political force to be reckoned with. Constantine's actions were thus those of an astute politician rather than a committed believer.

In trying to account for the great appeal of Christianity in its first three centuries Stark emphasizes a variety of factors, but central to his analysis is the presence of urban misery and disease. Life in the cities of ancient Rome—and it was in the cities that Christianity found most of its adherents—was one of misery and chaos for most people. Cities were severely crowded, and most people lived in extremely cramped quarters under squalid conditions. Crime and social disorder were rampant. Cities contained a great mixture of ethnic groups, and ethnic hatred and conflict were commonplace. Christianity, Stark argues, was of great help in allowing people to deal with the suffering associated with these problems.

Of greatest significance to the appeal of Christianity, however, was the everpresent illness and disease, particularly the epidemics that regularly swept through the cities. The epidemics, Stark argues, overwhelmed the explanatory and comforting capacities of the other major explanatory systems of the Greco-Roman world, paganism and the Hellenic philosophies. Within this context, Christianity was able to offer a much more acceptable and comforting account of why so many people were living in such misery. Stark puts it well (1996:161):

> Christianity served as a revitalization movement that arose in response to the misery, chaos, fear, and brutality of life in the urban Greco-Roman world. . . . Christianity revitalized life in Greco-Roman cities by providing new norms and new kinds of social relationships able to cope with many urgent urban problems. To cities filled with the homeless and impoverished, Christianity offered charity as well as hope. To cities filled with newcomers and strangers, Christianity offered an immediate basis for attachments. To cities filled with orphans and widows, Christianity provided a new and expanded sense of family. To cities torn by violent ethnic strife, Christianity offered a new basis for social solidarity. . . . And to cities faced with epidemics, fires, and earthquakes, Christianity offered effective nursing services.

Christianity was thus a highly materially adaptive religion. It promised people not only relief from suffering in an afterlife, but rewards in the here and now. As Stark points out, "because Christians were expected to aid the less fortunate, many of them received such aid, and all could feel greater security against bad times. Because they were asked to nurse the sick and dying, many of them received such nursing. Because they were asked to love others, they in turn were loved" (1996:188). In fact, Christianity was materially adaptive in the rigorous Darwinian sense. When disasters such as epidemics struck, Christians coped better than others and actually were more likely to survive. This, too, helped the spread of Christianity, because when epidemics had passed Christians would have constituted a larger percentage of the population.

Although Stark is certainly no Marxist, his explanation for the rapid growth of Christianity resembles Marx's argument for human attachments to religion in general. Marx called religion the "opium of the people." One of the things he meant by this statement was that people looked to religion as a means of alleviating the suffering and misery they experienced as a result of economic exploitation and political oppression. Stark does not focus on exploitation and oppression as the sources of misery for most people in the Roman empire, but his focus is nonetheless on religion as a response to misery.

But from the perspective of comparative and historical sociology, accounting for the rise and spread of Christianity involves more than just accounting for that religion alone. For Christianity was preceded by, indeed grew out of, Judaism, and Judaism in its turn was preceded, in the late second millennium B.C., by the religion known as Zoroastrianism. These religions had several important things in common that were new in the world. They were all religions that worshiped only one god and that god had great scope. Moreover, they had developed a clear-cut distinction between good and evil, and of God as delivering humans from evil (Cohn, 1993). It was not likely a mere accident that these religions developed at very similar times in world history. And when we add the major Asian religions Confucianism, Buddhism, and Hinduism to the mix, religions that emerged at approximately the same time as the Western religions, then things look even less accidental.

The question really becomes, then, not why Christianity, but why the emergence of most of the major world religions within the time period of approximately a single millennium. And why should this phase of religious evolution have been associated with major economic and political changes? In terms of the economic changes, the answer may be that as urbanization progressed, the greater number of people living in cities of greater size meant a proportionate increase in the amount of misery people were experiencing. In terms of the political changes, an increase in empire size and in the number of large empires would have meant a proportionate increase in the amount of warfare and the damage it inflicted upon ordinary people. In other words, the first millennium B.C. was a time of enormous social change and disruption of the lives of many people, and it seems logical that new forms of religion would have emerged to help people deal with the misery and suffering produced by such change. Another major and essentially new theme of the major world religions was salvation (Bellah, 1964), a notion that corresponds closely to the distinction between good and evil. The world was increasingly seen as an evil place from which people desired to escape. It is likely that the world was increasingly seen as evil because it *really was* becoming more evil—that is, more dangerous, brutal, threatening, insecure, and loathsome.

RELIGION AND THE MODERN WORLD

After Christianity became the official religion of the Roman empire in the fourth century A.D., it went on to become the dominant religion of the Western world in the form of the Roman Catholic Church. Many have said that the Catholic Church was the glue that held Europe together during the long period of feudalism (sometimes called the "Dark Ages"), which lasted from the collapse of Rome in the late fifth century A.D. until approximately the sixteenth century.

Christianity changed during this time, of course, but in western Europe (with a few minor exceptions) Christianity and the Roman Catholic Church were synonomous. With the sixteenth century all that was to change in the form of a revolt against the Church. This revolt came to be known as the Protestant Reformation.

The Protestant Reformation*

The Protestant Reformation can be said to begin in 1517, the year that Martin Luther nailed his famous Ninety-five Theses to the church door. Luther, of course, was the originator of Reformationist ideas and the founder of that major branch of Protestantism known as Lutheranism. Luther's objections to Catholicism centered on what he perceived as widespread abuses and corruption within the Church, as well as on the whole Catholic doctrine of salvation through the absolution by priests of sins. Luther wanted to establish a religion that would return to the original spirit of Christianity as expressed in the Bible, and he declared a doctrine of salvation that was rooted in deep personal faith in God rather than in the actions of religious functionaries representing a religious bureaucracy (the Church).

Luther's ideas had an almost immediate popular appeal and spread quickly and widely. It was not long before they were adopted throughout several of the sovereign states that are now part of modern Germany, and they spread to the Scandinavian countries of Sweden and Denmark (Table 17.2). In England, a very similar form of Protestantism, Anglicanism, became established. Luther was soon followed by other Protestant reformers, the most notable of whom were the Swiss Huldrych Zwingli and the Frenchman Jean Calvin (John

*This discussion is based on Spitz (1985) and Swanson (1967).

Calvin). Calvin was clearly the more important. Although French, Calvin spent most of his time in Geneva, Switzerland, and thus that city became the birthplace of Calvinism. Calvin's ideas were similar to Luther's and showed Luther's influence. There were, of course, many different features to Calvin's theology. Perhaps the most important of these was his famous doctrine of predestination, which held that God had from all eternity predestined some persons for salvation and others for damnation. This was a modification of Luther's notion of salvation through faith, and of course a marked departure from the Catholic Church's approach to salvation. Like Lutheranism, Calvinism spread quickly and widely (Table 17.2). It was adopted in many Swiss cantons, in the Netherlands, in several German states, in Lowland Scotland, and even for a time in parts of Poland and Hungary.

Many areas of Europe were highly resistant to the Reformation (Table 17.2). In the leading countries of Mediterranean Europe—Italy, Spain, and Portugal—Protestant ideas had little influence, and Catholicism remained overwhelmingly dominant. The Catholic Church also remained secure in several Swiss cantons, in several sovereign German states, and in Austria, Ireland, Highland Scotland, and most of eastern Europe. France also remained Catholic, although Protestant ideas spread there quickly after their initial formulation. A significant minority of the French population did convert to Protestantism, but the Protestant movement in France was violently crushed and the number of persons still embracing Protestantism dwindled to a tiny few.

Explaining the Reformation

To understand the causes of the Reformation—why it began and why its ideas were adopted when and where they were—it is

Table 17.2 PROTESTANT AND CATHOLIC STATES IN SIXTEENTH-CENTURY EUROPE

States Adopting Lutheranism or Anglicanism

- The German states of Prussia (1525), Württemberg (1535), Saxony (1539), Brandenburg (1539), and Hesse (1605)[a]
- England (1553)

- Sweden (1536)
- Denmark (1536)

States Adopting Zwinglianism or Calvinism

- The Swiss cantons of Geneva (1536), Basel (1528), Schaffhausen (1530), Bern (1528), Zurich (1525), Glarus (1531), and Appenzell (1523)
- The German states of Cleves (1569) and Mark (1569)
- Bohemia (1593)

- United Provinces (Netherlands) (1579)
- Hungary (1540)
- Transylvania (1557)
- Lowland Scotland (1560)

States Remaining Catholic

- The Italian states of Venice and Florence
- The Swiss cantons of Schwyz, Unterwalden, Uri, Zug, Fribourg, Lucerne, and Solothurn
- Poland
- France
- Austria

- The German states of Bavaria, Jülich, and Berg
- Portugal
- Spain
- Ireland
- Highland Scotland

[a]The dates in parentheses refer to the year in which a state formally adopted Protestantism or by which a majority of the citizens had become Protestant. The religious situation in a few of these states changed in later years, usually as a result of political conquest.

Source: Guy E. Swanson, *Religion and Regime: A Sociological Account of the Reformation.* Ann Arbor: University of Michigan Press, 1967.

vital to understand the most important doctrinal differences between Catholicism and Protestantism. Max Weber (1958; orig. 1905) argued, and there is every reason to believe he was correct, that the most important doctrinal innovation of Protestantism lay in its conception of salvation. Protestantism eliminated the Church's role in granting salvation. Rather than gaining their salvation through the mediation of priests, individuals gained salvation by approaching God in a very direct and personal way. Luther's doctrine of salvation by faith and God's grace and Calvin's conception of salvation through predestination both connected God directly with each individual and eliminated the bureaucratic organization of the Church as an agent in salvation. As many sociologists have argued, this meant that, in contrast to Catholicism, Protestantism was a highly *individualistic* religion. This can be especially seen in the seventeenth-century elaboration of Calvinist doctrine. The rigid doctrine of predestination set forth by Calvin in the sixteenth century was gradually modified and made more flexible. It came to be argued by Calvinists that God did indeed predestine each person, but that He had permitted a way for each individual to know, if not to change, His will. Individuals who had achieved worldly success through their own sacrifices and intense efforts could take this as a sign from God that they were among the saved. This was the famous Protestant ethic that figured so prominently in Weber's *The Protestant Ethic and the Spirit of Capitalism* (1958 [orig. 1905]; cf. H. M. Robertson, 1959).

It is a sad fact that sociologists have largely neglected the Reformation. This stems both from the ahistorical outlook of most sociologists, and from the still highly underdeveloped status of the sociology of religion. Even Weber's famous work linking Protestantism and capitalism was devoted only to explaining the rise of capitalism, and Weber offered no systematic explanation for the rise of Protestantism itself. One of the most thorough sociological analyses of the Reformation is that of Guy Swanson (1967), who sets forth a political theory. Swanson argues that the Reformation was adopted in those European states that had come to have an organization devoted to serving various kinds of external interests, such as bodies of merchants, artisans, or nobles. This idea is rooted in Swanson's more general claim that religion's basic importance is as a mechanism designed to symbolize and legitimize political structures. Swanson's analysis of 41 sovereign European states shows that there was, indeed, a striking correlation between the form of government (as conceptualized and categorized by Swanson) and the adoption or rejection of Protestantism. However, it is very likely that the correlations to which Swanson points actually disguise another factor that was at work. This factor was economic. To a great extent, the modes of government that Swanson sees as associated with the adoption of Protestantism were *governments in which capitalist economic interests and ideals played a major role.*

To the extent that they concern themselves with questions of causation at all, many theologians and historians are inclined to argue that the Reformation was primarily devoted to the correction of major abuses of the Church, or that it was a kind of logical working out of theological doctrines—a kind of internal development of the logic of religious ideas (cf. Lortz, 1972). There is no doubt that the leaders of the Reformation were concerned with many activities of the Church that they regarded as abuses, and that they were highly motivated to correct these problems. However, abuses had been going on for a very long time. Why did a major attempt to correct them arise at the particular time it did, and why was the effort successful in some places but not in others? Furthermore, if Protestantism involved simply the internal development of religious ideas, why did the ideas take the particular form they did? The answers to these questions, I believe, most properly center on the close historical relationship between the Reformation and the emergence of modern capitalism (cf. Engels, 1978 [orig. 1850]; Walker, 1972; Wuthnow, 1980). Weber was right in pointing to a close historical connection between Protestantism and capitalism, but he had the causal relationship backwards. Protestantism emerged in, or spread to, largely those parts of Europe that were in the forefront of capitalist advance. This was because Protestant ideas greatly helped to legitimate and express the capitalist worldview, as well as because of certain practical economic benefits that Protestantism could convey. As Robert Wuthnow has written (1980:63–64):

> The Protestant Reformation occurred in the context of rapid population growth, a long-term rise in grain prices, great expansion in the volume and circulation of money due to the importation of bullion from America, naval and military innovations, and an intensification and broadening of trade. This expansion greatly benefited the German and Polish nobility, the Swiss city magistrates, and the Dutch and English merchants, all of whom prospered from the expanding trade

between the Baltic and the Mediterranean. It was [in these areas] that the Reformation first became institutionalized. The reformers' attacks against the Church implicitly desacralized the Hapsburg empire, whose legitimacy rested heavily in the defense of universal faith, and broadened access to legitimate authority. . . . [T]he Reformation prompted the secularization of church lands, giving elites revenues independent of church and other taxes, and encouraging land reform beneficial to commercial agriculture. . . . After the middle of the sixteenth century, owing significantly to the financial burdens which Spain incurred in combating the Protestant heresies, the core of the European economy shifted increasingly to the north, and with it the Reformation became firmly established.

In a more recent work, Wuthnow (1989) has suggested a more complex relationship between capitalism and the Reformation. In what is essentially a type of neo-Weberian argument, Wuthnow claims that capitalism was linked to the Reformation indirectly rather than directly. The spread of capitalism led to political support for the reformers' ideas when the state came to be freed from the control of the landed nobility. Under such circumstances, governments were enthusiastic about the religious reforms because of the many practical political benefits they could convey. On the other hand, where the landed nobility continued to control the state, the latter crushed efforts at religious reform. The nobility and the Church were closely linked, especially in terms of the strong social legitimation that the Church provided for the nobility's dominant position. Thus the nobility had every reason to resist all efforts at undermining the Church's authority and continued influence.

Wuthnow's theory has a certain appeal. It seems particularly relevant, for instance, in explaining the deviant case of France, the one core capitalist society in which Protestantism made little headway. As Wuthnow suggests, in France "the nobility were too much in control of the state for the Reformation to succeed" (1989:91). However, as suggestive as it is, Wuthnow's argument is by no means proven. His analysis is unbalanced in the sense that he considers only whether or not the state was controlled by the nobility. He does not consider the fact that, in those early capitalist areas in which the state had been freed from the nobility's control, the state had fallen under the control of other economic groups, namely merchants and capitalist landlords. Because he ignores the strategic importance of such groups, Wuthnow is unable to prove that it was politics rather than economics that really counted. The role of economics is also strongly suggested by the fact that, as Wuthnow himself notes time and again, the reformers' ideas were most prominently taken up and promoted by urban classes— merchants and craftsmen—and were strongly resisted by rural classes—landlords and peasants.

Types of Religious Organization in Modern Industrial Societies

Substantially as a result of the Protestant Reformation, modern industrial societies are characterized by great religious diversity, containing within their boundaries a large number of different religious groups. Nevertheless, all of these diverse religious groups can be classified into a limited number of organizational types.

An early student of the subject who was concerned with the problem of types of religious organization was Ernst Troeltsch (1931). Troeltsch identified two polar types of religious organization, which he called **church** and **sect.** His conceptualization of the church identified it as a religious organization having the following characteristics: it was large, literally coextensive with society as a whole; individuals were born into it and baptized as infants; it had an official ecclesiastical structure in which priests were earthly extensions of God; it placed great emphasis on established doctrines and dogmas; and it accepted the secular world as it was, even identifying itself quite closely with the ruling secular powers. The Roman Catholic Church of the Middle Ages was held to be the example *par excellence* of this type of religious organization.

The sect stood at the opposite extreme from the church. It was small, membership in it being limited to a select number of individuals; individuals joined the group as adults; its members constituted a "community of believers" who thought of themselves as religiously distinct from the members of other religious groups; it had no official ecclesiastical structure, its ministry being lay; it placed great emphasis on "living the right kind of life"; and it was hostile toward the secular world, which it generally perceived to be corrupt and decadent.

Sociologists have generally found Troeltsch's concepts useful, but only as a starting point. Most have felt the need to distinguish an additional number of types in order to capture fully the variety of religious organization in industrial societies. J. Milton Yinger (1970) has distinguished five basic types of religious groups: ecclesiae, denominations, established sects, sects, and cults.

Yinger identifies the **ecclesia** in terms quite similar to Troeltsch's conception of the church. However, he views the ecclesia as being even more aligned with society's dominant segments than was the medieval Roman Catholic Church. Hence the ecclesia fails to serve the needs of many of its members, particularly those from lower social strata. For this reason, Yinger refers to the ecclesia as "a universal church in a state of rigidification." The Lutheran Church in Scandinavia and the Anglican Church in England are among the better examples of the ecclesia.

The **denomination** is a conventional and respectable type of religious organization that is in substantial harmony with the secular powers. Unlike Troeltsch's church or the ecclesia, however, the denomination is not coextensive with society as a whole; rather, it is limited by such boundaries as class, race, and region. Contemporary denominations are typically former established sects, or sects that have evolved into more conventional and respectable organizations. In the United States, such groups as Presbyterians, Methodists, and Baptists are good examples of denominations.

The **established sect** is viewed by Yinger as a sect (in Troeltsch's sense) that has retained many of its sectlike characteristics while at the same time having evolved some distance in the direction of conventionality and respectability. In this sense, established sects lie partway between denominations and sects, having some of the characteristics of each. Yinger cites the modern-day Quakers as an example of this type of religious group. Yinger's conception of the sect is essentially the same as Troeltsch's. However, he distinguishes among several different types of sects. *Acceptance sects* generally do not seek to change the world, and they live in harmony with it; their sectlike quality is based on their adherence to religious doctrines that are esoteric and mystical in nature. *Aggressive sects* reject the world and seek to alter it, often on the basis of eschatological fantasies. Jehovah's Witnesses belong to this type of sect. A third type is the *avoidance sect*. These sects reject the secular world, but make no particular effort to alter its nature; rather, the members of such groups withdraw from the world and seek special religious knowledge and insight of a personal nature. Some of these groups, such as the Pentecostals, "seek trances, visions, and the 'gift of tongues'—temporary escapes into a world where their standards rule" (Yinger, 1970:277–278).

Cults are religious groups standing at the farthest extreme from ecclesiae. They are typically very small, short-lived, and built around a charismatic leader. Although similar to sects, they are more extreme in their religious doctrines, frequently representing a radical break with the dominant religious tradition or traditions of a society. As Yinger indicates, they are "religious mutants." Examples include the Church of Satan and the Krishna Consciousness organization in the United States.

These types of religious organization illustrate quite well how diverse religious forms are adapted to the needs of different individuals and groups within industrial societies. As Yinger has made clear, the ecclesia is almost wholly centered around the needs and interests of the dominant segments of society. Denominations are groups that embrace a wide variety of members, but still tend to be oriented toward individuals and groups from particular social backgrounds. In American society, for example, upper-middle-class individuals tend to be Episcopalians, Congregationalists, or Presbyterians; however, the Baptist Church tends to draw its members disproportionately from the lower socioeconomic strata. It is generally agreed that sectarian groups are responses to various kinds of deprivation. Most commonly it is economic deprivation that pushes people toward sects, but other kinds of deprivation may also be responsible for sect formation; various kinds of psychological deprivation are sometimes prime motives leading individuals to join particular sects. Cults typically arise under conditions of very rapid social change; such change leaves many people confused and befuddled about the nature of the world and predisposes them to seek solutions to their confusion in extremist religious groups. In the 1960s and 1970s, for example, many new cults sprang up in the United States. These cults were direct responses to the disorienting changes that were taking place during those years (cf. Glock and Bellah, 1976; M. Harris, 1981). Religion is a prime means of providing answers to the fundamental problems of human existence; as those problems differ, so will the kinds of religious responses called forth to deal with them.

SECULARIZATION AND THE FUTURE OF RELIGION

The Controversy over Secularization

The concept of **secularization** refers to the process by which religion's influence over many spheres of social life has been steadily reduced. Many sociologists have subscribed to the view that secularization has been a major trend in Western societies in the past few centuries, or at least since the onset of industrialization. They have held that the forces of scientific advance, industrialization, urbanization, and the overall rationalization and modernization of society have caused religion to recede more and more from the arenas of social life that it traditionally occupied. The stronger versions of this *secularization thesis* claim that the process of secularization is an inexorable force that will culminate in the extinction of organized religion. Weaker versions claim only that secularization has historically been a significant trend and do not necessarily postulate the ultimate end of institutionalized religious activity.

Jeffrey Hadden (1987) has claimed that the secularization thesis has been so widely embraced by sociologists that it has become virtually an unchallenged, taken-for-granted truth. Hadden's point is not likely far off the mark. In recent years, however, a variety of challenges to the secularization thesis have emerged. Hadden himself claims that the thesis is empirically false, and that it has been sustained more by sociologists' antagonism to organized religion than by any systematic examination of the evidence. Against the secularization thesis Hadden places the following lines of evidence:

- Since the end of the Second World War there has been a general religious revival, at least in the United States.
- In recent years there has been major growth in the more conservative religious traditions, such as the evangelicals and the fundamentalists.
- The beliefs and behaviors of American Catholics have been dramatically affected by the Second Vatican Council, with the result that the authority of the Church is now stronger than at any point in American history.
- The overwhelming majority of Americans still report a belief in God.
- Church membership statistics in the United States have fluctuated only slightly in the past 40 years, and even church attendance has remained remarkably stable.
- The presence of religious devotion (e.g., prayer) has also remained very stable in recent decades.

Timothy Crippen (1988) also attacks the secularization thesis. He pursues a line of thinking that has become common among many opponents of the thesis, arguing that religion in modern society is undergoing *transformation* but not *decline* (cf. Bellah, 1970; Glock and Bellah, 1976; Wuthnow, 1976; Stark and Bainbridge, 1985). "Traditional religions may be waning," he suggests, but "even so, religious conscious-

ness remains powerful and manifests itself in new beliefs and rituals corresponding to modern organizational forms of dominance and exchange" (1988:325). Crippen holds that "new gods" are arising to replace the "old gods," and that these new gods have much to do with "new sacred beliefs and rituals that symbolize the sovereignty of the nation-state and the moral integrity of the individual" (1988:331). The new kind of "religion" that Crippen is talking about is what Robert Bellah (1967) once called "civil religion."

Crippen's position is untenable, in my view, because it relies entirely on a classically inclusivist definition of religion. Although Crippen explicitly favors such a definition, he readily concedes that from the exclusivist's viewpoint there has indeed been an extensive secularization of social life in recent centuries. What then of Hadden's argument? Although the religious trends he points to are more or less accurately identified, the problem is that his argument is lacking in both a historical perspective and a comparative foundation. Hadden is really discussing only one society, the United States, and his analysis of it covers a very brief period of time. This obviously will not suffice. It is well known that the United States is in many respects the most religious of all contemporary Western industrial societies, and many sociologists have spoken of "American exceptionalism" (Zeitlin, 1984). One cannot legitimately use a single society, let alone a highly unusual one, to disprove a general theory that is intended to apply to many societies.

The counterarguments of Hadden and Crippen, and of those sociologists who largely agree with them, therefore do not do much damage to the secularization thesis, at least in its weaker form. A staunch defender of the thesis is the well-known British sociologist of religion Bryan Wilson (1982). Wilson points out that the secularization thesis depends on the notion that earlier forms of human society generally gave a marked social significance to religion. This is generally true, Wilson says, arguing that "simpler cultures, traditional societies, and past communities . . . appear to have been profoundly preoccupied with the supernatural" (1982:150). Compared to these past societies and communities, Wilson asserts (1982:149), contemporary industrial societies have experienced

> the sequestration by political powers of the property and facilities of religious agencies; the shift from religious to secular control of various of the erstwhile activities and functions of religion; the decline in the proportion of their time, energy, and resources which men devote to super-empirical concerns; the decay of religious institutions; the supplanting, in matters of behavior, of religious precepts by demands that accord with strictly technical criteria; and the gradual replacement of a specifically religious consciousness (which might range from dependence on charms, rites, spells, or prayers, to a broadly spiritually-inspired ethical concern) by an empirical, rational, instrumental orientation; the abandonment of mythical, poetic, and artistic interpretations of nature and society in favour of matter-of-fact description and, with it, the rigorous separation of evaluative and emotive dispositions from cognitive . . . orientations.

It is impossible to deny that Wilson's characterization of religious change is an accurate one, and there is thus every reason to sustain the secularization thesis as it concerns the recent past. However, we still need to evaluate the version of this thesis that applies to the future of religion.

The Future of Religion

Given the secularizing trends of recent centuries, what can reasonably be expected regarding the future of religion? Will secularization continue and intensify, to the point that religion eventually will be eliminated from sociocultural life altogether? Or will some fundamental core of religious belief and activity remain, no matter how scientifically and technologically sophisticated human societies become? Social scientists are highly divided in the answers they give to such questions. Many hold that modern science and technology will eventually destroy religion as a social institution. Others maintain that, even though its significance may be reduced still further, religion will remain as a persistent and permanent feature of sociocultural systems. Anthony Wallace takes the former view, claiming that (1966:264–265)

> the evolutionary future of religion is extinction. Belief in supernatural beings and in supernatural forces that affect nature without obeying nature's laws will erode and become only an interesting historical memory. To be sure, this event is not likely to occur in the next generation; the process will very likely take several hundred years, and there will probably always remain individuals, or even occasional small cult groups, who respond to hallucination, trance, and obsession with a supernaturalist interpretation. But as a cultural trait, belief in supernatural powers is doomed to die out, all over the world, as a result of the increasing adequacy and diffusion of scientific knowledge and of the realization by secular faiths that supernatural belief is not necessary to the effective use of ritual. The question of whether such a denouement will be good or bad for humanity is irrelevant to the prediction; the process is inevitable.

An opposing view is held by J. Milton Yinger. Yinger conceives religion to be a "residual" institution, by which he means that it is "that which always remains." Religion is a means of providing answers to ultimate questions; since ultimate questions will always be with us, and since it is impossible for science to attempt answers to some of these questions, religion will always remain in order to reduce uncertainty. Yinger states his case as follows (1970:9):

> Is there no core of functions that seems likely to be a continuing source of religious activity? Or are science, philosophy, art, government, medicine, and the like chiseling away at religion so steadily that it has become a "suicidal institution," as Dunlap calls it? I myself find it difficult to envisage a society in which no major problems of the ultimate variety we have discussed remain unresolved. We reduce the amount of premature death only to discover the tragedies of senescence. We begin to conquer poverty only to realize that the knowledge behind that achievement is part of a larger knowledge that brought the hydrogen bomb. I suspect . . . that the belief that man can devise secular processes for performing the functions now served by religion is itself a "citadel of hope," and not an empirically validated proposition. . . .
> . . . What evidence we have inclines me toward the view that religion as I have defined it is a permanent aspect of human society, which is no more likely to disappear than the family (however much it may change) or government (despite the enormous range of variation).

Wallace's scenario has much to recommend it. Science has already eroded religious belief, and we know that when people acquire highly developed intellectual outlooks (especially scientific ones) their religious beliefs tend to dissipate (Glock and Stark, 1965). Hence, if future societies are permeated by the mass dissemination of advanced forms of learning (and it seems reasonable to expect that they will be), religion might well collapse or be greatly reduced in significance. On the other hand, Yinger's scenario also has its attractions. The most ultimate of all the ultimate concerns is that regarding human finitude—the fact that humans die. All cultures everywhere have shown some degree of preoccupation with questions relating to this concern. Humans have never wanted to accept their own finitude and have repeatedly created conceptions of an afterlife in order to disavow that things must end. Religion has been the only institutionalized means whereby human beings have grappled with the issue of finitude. The issue is completely off-limits for science; no matter how successful science becomes in explaining and controlling the empirical world, it is powerless in the face of a nonempirical concern such as this one. On the basis of these considerations, there is good reason to believe that some essential core of religious belief and ritual will continue indefinitely. Although the scope of religion's influence will no doubt be increasingly reduced in the future, it may well be unwise to predict that its influence will disappear altogether.

SUMMARY

1. Two fundamentally different types of definitions of religion have been offered by social scientists. Inclusive definitions stress that religion is a system of beliefs and practices organized around things said to be sacred, or oriented toward ultimate human concerns. Exclusive definitions are more restrictive and limit the notion of religion to beliefs and practices postulating supernatural forces that act in the world. This book favors an exclusive definition.

2. Religion is an evolutionary phenomenon in much the same sense that the other components of human societies are. A useful scheme of religious evolution has been offered by Anthony Wallace, who distinguishes four stages: shamanic, communal, Olympian, and monotheistic religions. These stages correspond reasonably well to stages in the evolution of technology, economics, and politics.

3. A revolution in human thought known as the Axial Age occurred throughout much of the world in the first millennium B.C. This revolution was associated with the emer-

gence of most of the major world religions, which were monotheistic and visualized a sharp contrast between good and evil. The Axial Age corresponded closely to a major increase in world urbanization and in the size and scope of trade networks. There was also a major increase in the size of political empires during this time, and in the extent of warfare between them. The disruptive changes associated with these economic and political developments were very likely causal conditions in the development of new forms of religion.

4. Christianity was one of the major world religions to arise during the Axial Age. Christianity had enormous popular appeal and went on to become one of the most successful religious movements of all time. Its spread was so rapid that it moved from being a tiny sect of Judaism to the official religion of the Roman empire within only three centuries. The tremendous appeal of Christianity may have been its capacity to offer comfort to people living in the squalid cities of the Greco-Roman world, with their extreme crowdedness, disease, crime, disorder, and ethnic hatreds.

5. Modern forms of religious organization essentially began with the Protestant Reformation of the sixteenth century. This was a great religious transformation that challenged the authority of the Catholic Church and its doctrine of salvation. It corresponded historically to the beginnings of the capitalist world-economy, and it is likely that Protestantism was a religious manifestation of this great economic change.

6. Various types of religious organization exist in modern industrial societies. Yinger has identified five basic types of religious groups: ecclesiae, denominations, established sects, sects, and cults. These types of religious organization closely correspond to such social groups as classes, racial and ethnic groups, and regional groupings. This indicates the adaptiveness of religion to a variety of human needs.

7. In recent centuries increasing economic rationalization, industrialization, urbanization, and scientific advance have led to the extensive secularization of modern industrial societies. However, the extent to which secularization will continue is very much an open question. Some social scientists suggest that the evolutionary future of religion is extinction, while others hold that, because of religion's function as a "residual" institution, some minimal core of religious belief and practice is likely to persist indefinitely.

SPECIAL TOPIC: REVITALIZATION AND MILLENARIAN MOVEMENTS

Is religion a conservative or a liberal force in society? Does it act so as to preserve the status quo, or is it an agent of change? Perhaps the most famous answer ever given to this question was given by Marx in connection with his "opium of the people" thesis. When people looked to religion to alleviate misery and suffering, he said, the result was that religion merely placated them. It allowed them to tolerate the social conditions in which they lived and thus discouraged them from trying to change those conditions. This worked greatly to the advantage of the ruling elites of societies. For them, religion helped preserve their position in society by announcing that the established social order is an expression and embodiment of supernatural will, and therefore should be accepted just as it is. The Marxian view is therefore that religion is a profoundly conservative social force.

The evidence in support of Marx's claims is very strong. With the emergence of social stratification the supernatural powers develop a significant concern with secular morality and are commonly invoked as a means of regulating earthly social arrangements (Swanson, 1960). The evolution of powerful centralized political systems—chiefdoms and states—is highly correlated with the evolution of powerful priesthoods and ecclesiastical religious institutions. Priests typically share heavily in the exercise of political power. Early chiefdoms or kingdoms, in fact, tended to be theocracies, forms of government carried out by religious functionaries. As chiefdoms evolved into states, government came to be lodged primarily in the hands of secular political officials rather than priest-chiefs or priest-kings; nevertheless, these secular officials still retained close ties with priests and actively used the priesthood as a means of bolstering their own power. Most chiefs and kings throughout history have justified their rule in religious terms, claiming either direct descent from the gods or to be God's principal representative on Earth. And even in the modern world religion and conservative politics are usually strong allies. Established governments and the stratified orders of modern societies are generally strongly supported by orthodox religion, and the most traditionally religious segments of modern societies tend to be the most politically conservative (Glock and Stark, 1965; G. Marx, 1967; Sanderson, 1973).

Yet to leave matters here would be to give a one-sided picture of the role of religion in human society. Although religion most commonly acts to preserve established social arrangements, there have been numerous instances in which religion has served as an important catalyst for attempts to change the world. At many points in history and in a great many places, people have formed themselves into religiously inspired movements devoted to basic alterations in the established social order. These movements are generally known as **revitalization** or **millenarian movements.** The term *revitalization* implies an attempt to create a new or "revitalized" mode of existence that would be highly preferable to the current state of affairs. The term *millenarian* is most frequently applied to socioreligious movements that anticipate the coming of a millennium —a new age of peace, harmony, and prosperity, a literal paradise on Earth—and that are often led by charismatic leaders held to be messiahs.

Revitalization or millenarian movements typically occur under conditions of extreme social stress or crisis: in periods of rapid social change when people are uprooted and disoriented from their traditional patterns of life; when native cultures are severely altered by colonialism, warfare, or the invasion of an alien culture; or when oppression and exploitation have reached extreme proportions. Under such conditions, millenarian movements are likely when people are confused or befuddled as to what is really happening to them, and when more strictly secular means of dealing with this stress are unavailable (M. Harris, 1974). Virtually all millenarian movements contain both religious and political elements in their ideologies and in their strategies for change; however, the particular mixture of the religious and the political varies widely from one movement to another.

These socioreligious movements have occurred at many points in history and virtually throughout the world. They have been found in classical antiquity, medieval and modern Europe, Melanesia, Polynesia, Africa, South America, North America, and Indonesia, among other places. Many are still found today, even in the industrialized West. The vast majority of these movements have ended in failure, but a few have been successful to one extent or another. Christianity, for example, was originally an outgrowth of Jewish millenarianism. The best-known revitalization and millenarian movements (in addition to the early Jewish ones) are those that have occurred in Melanesia and medieval Europe, and among the Indians of North America.

Marvin Harris (1974) has discussed Jewish military messianism as it existed around the time of Christ and has attempted to show how it gave birth to Christianity. The ancient nation of Palestine had long been subject to colonial rule by a host of powerful empires. Under Roman rule most of the Jews who inhabited Palestine were subject to enormous oppression and exploitation. The vast majority of the population consisted of landless peasants, poorly paid artisans, servants, and slaves. Apart from them were tiny elites of priests, landowners, and merchants who lived in magnificent luxury.

It was during the period of Roman rule that the tradition of Jewish military messianism developed into a potent religious and political force. Many men came forward and claimed to be messiahs who would deliver Palestine from the clutches of Roman oppression and establish the Kingdom of God on Earth. In addition to enunciating religious proclamations about the coming of the Kingdom of God, they were actively engaged in military operations designed to bring it about. Many messiahs organized armies and fought against the Roman legions. At least two major wars were fought against the Roman armies, one in A.D. 68–73 and the other in A.D. 132–136. Jesus was one of many Jewish messiahs who arose in Palestine to fight against Roman oppression and exploitation. It is widely believed that Jesus' teachings were strictly of a peaceful nature, that he was opposed to violence and vengeance. Harris sharply disputes this image of Jesus, however, and claims that his activities were actually highly consistent with the whole tradition of Jewish military messianism. He presents a good deal of evidence to support his view.

Just as Christianity arose out of millenarian activity, new forms of millenarian activity were soon to arise out of Christianity, at least after it became a highly established religion. By the later Middle Ages, millenarian movements directed against the ruling religious, economic, and political powers were becoming quite common (Cohn, 1970). Most of these movements were guided by eschatological fantasies, that is, by doctrines espousing that the end of the world was near at hand and that a messiah was coming to install a heavenly paradise on Earth. In many cases, men claiming to be messiahs advocated and actually carried out militant actions against both secular and religious authorities. A European millenarian movement that was especially militant was the Anabaptist movement (Cohn, 1970).

Most Anabaptists were peasants and artisans who believed in the communal holding of property, regarded the state with suspicion, and tended to reject society at large. Many of them were obsessed by the belief in the coming of a day of reckoning on which the mighty would be cast down and Christ would return to establish a millennium on Earth. In the early 1530s they took over the town of Münster in Germany and proclaimed it to be the New Jerusalem. Under their leader, Jan Matthys, they felt that they were inaugurating a social revolution. After Matthys died he was replaced by a man named Jan Bockelson. Bockelson established a new government in Münster that was given authority over all public, private, spiritual, and material concerns. He also established a new moral code that was so strict that it made such things as quarreling and lying capital offenses. Eventually, Bockelson declared himself to be a king—King of the New Jerusalem—and he began to dress in magnificent robes and to wear rings and chains made of the finest metal. At the same time, he imposed a life of severe austerity on his followers.

The Anabaptist occupation of Münster ended in complete disaster. Famine eventually struck the town, and it became so severe that people were actually forced to eat grass, moss, old shoes, the whitewash on walls, and even the bodies of the dead. Death from starvation became such a common occurrence that large communal graves had to be dug. When people tried to leave the town, Bockelson had them beheaded; often the body was quartered and its sections nailed up for public display as a warning to others. Such atrocities eventually became an almost everyday occurrence. The troops that had been besieging the town for some time eventually overwhelmed it and brought the New Jerusalem to an end.

The Anabaptist movement may seem like a particularly extreme occurrence, and in some ways it was. Nevertheless, medieval Europe was witness to many other millenarian movements in which extremes of behavior were typical. In the thirteenth and fourteenth centuries, for example, groups of flagellants engaged in religious rituals in which they beat themselves with spikes until chunks of flesh were torn from their bodies.

Around the end of the nineteenth century, many areas of Melanesia fell under European colonial domination, resulting in severe dislocations in the lives of native inhabitants of the region. Under these conditions, revitalization movements known as **cargo cults** developed (Worsley, 1968). The most persistent ideological element in these cults was the belief that shiploads of modern Western industrial goods (cargo) would be arriving at any moment for the complete use and enjoyment of the natives. These goods were being sent and accompanied by the natives' dead ancestors, who had come back to life. When the goods arrived, a new age of joy and prosperity would commence. In earlier times, the cargo was believed to be arriving by ship, and the natives busied themselves building ports where the ships could dock. But with the arrival of the airplane, the cargo was said to be coming by plane; this prompted many cult members to build runways on which the planes could land. The cults also perpetuated doctrines regarding the reorganization of native society. Above all, the Europeans would be thrown out and native society returned to the control of the natives themselves. Some of these cults can still be found today.

Revitalization movements also arose among a number of North American Indian tribes in the nineteenth century as a response to the encroachment of the whites and the destruction of traditional cultures. The most famous of these was the Ghost Dance, which appeared in two waves, the first in 1870 and the second in 1890 (Lanternari, 1963; cf. Thornton, 1981). The first wave of the Ghost Dance occurred among the Paviotsos, Indians living in Nevada and California. The Paviotsos were led by a prophet named Wodziwob, who founded the movement after receiving a vision in 1869. In his vision, Wodziwob saw a railroad train carrying the Indians' ancestors. He held that these travelers were going to announce their return to Earth with a great explosion: "Wodziwob's revelation occurred at the top of a mountain: the Great Spirit announced that a major cataclysm would soon shake the entire world, in the course of which the white man would vanish from the Indian land. The earth would open up to swallow the whites, while all their buildings, goods, and tools would remain for the use of the Indians" (Lanternari, 1963:132). Wodziwob's revelations began to spread, and soon they had reached tribes all over the western part of the United States. The Ghost Dance of 1890 was started by a Paiute Indian named Wovoka. Wovoka preached a strict moral code to his people: They were not to fight, lie, steal, or drink whiskey, and they were to work hard and love one another. He prophesied that the whites would be blown away by high winds, but that all their possessions would be left to the Indians (de Waal Malefijt, 1968). Like the earlier version of the Ghost Dance, this one spread widely and rapidly to other tribes, among them the Shoshoni, Arapaho, Cheyenne, Kiowa, and Sioux.

Millenarian movements have by no means been limited in their occurrence to primitive, ancient, or medieval societies. On the contrary, they have continued to be found even in Western industrialized societies. One of the most recent examples of a millenarian movement is the People's Temple, organized under the leadership of the Reverend Jim Jones. This cult flourished in the United States during the 1960s and 1970s. It bears a striking resemblance to many other millenarian movements of the past. Jones thought of himself as a messiah who had come to deliver his followers from the wickedness of the world. In 1974 Jones and several hundred members of the People's Temple established a communitarian settlement known as Jonestown in the jungles of Guyana. Like the Anabaptists, Jonestown ended in total disaster. As a result of an investigation planned by the U.S. government in 1978, Jones persuaded his followers to consume poisoned drinks in a ritual of mass suicide, while at the same time putting a bullet through his own head.

Although the radical nature of revitalization and milleniarian movements belies Marx's claim that religion is by nature an inherently conservative force, these movements actually offer strong support for one major dimension of Marx's sociological theory of religion—the notion that people adopt religion to relieve intense misery and suffering. Thus, although religion is more often a conservative than a radical force, even radical religious movements show that religion frequently is an "opium of the people."

FOR FURTHER READING

Cohn, Norman. *The Pursuit of the Millennium: Revolutionary Millenarians and Mystical Anarchists of the Middle Ages.* Revised edition. New York: Oxford University Press, 1970. A scintillating discussion of millenarian movements in medieval Europe.

Cohn, Norman. *Chaos, Cosmos, and the World to Come: The Ancient Roots of Apocalyptic Faith.* New Haven, Conn.: Yale University Press, 1993. A study of the millenarian dimensions of three major world religions: Zoroastrianism, Judaism, and Christianity.

Harris, Marvin. *Cows, Pigs, Wars, and Witches: The Riddles of Culture.* New York: Random House, 1974. Provocative discussions of Jewish military messianism, early Christianity, and the "great witch craze" of early modern Europe.

Spitz, Lewis W. *The Protestant Reformation, 1517–1559.* New York: Harper & Row, 1985. Although utterly lacking in theory, a useful contemporary exposition of the basic character of the Reformation.

Stark, Rodney. *The Rise of Christianity: A Sociologist Reconsiders History.* Princeton, N.J.: Princeton University Press, 1996. One of the best sociological analyses of the development of early Christianity ever undertaken. The author is especially concerned to understand the rational reasons why so many people converted to Christianity so quickly.

Swanson, Guy. *The Birth of the Gods.* Ann Arbor: University of Michigan Press, 1960. A detailed study of 50 primitive and ancient societies that attempts to uncover the basic social conditions giving rise to various forms of religious belief.

Thomas, Keith. *Religion and the Decline of Magic.* New York: Scribners, 1971. A provocative study of widespread beliefs in such things as astrology, witchcraft, and magical healing in sixteenth- and seventeenth-century England and their ultimate decline.

Turner, Bryan S. *Religion and Social Theory: A Materialist Perspective.* London: Heinemann, 1983. One of the few efforts by a sociologist to develop a materialist (basically Marxian) analysis of religion.

Wallace, Anthony F. C. *Religion: An Anthropological View.* New York: Random House, 1966. The leading textbook on religion from an anthropological slant.

Wilson, Bryan. *Religion in Sociological Perspective.* New York: Oxford University Press, 1982. An overview of some major concerns in the sociology of religion by a noted British specialist.

Wuthnow, Robert. *Communities of Discourse: Ideology and Social Structure in the Reformation, the Enlightenment, and European Socialism.* Cambridge, Mass.: Harvard University Press, 1989. The first major section is perhaps the best systematic sociological treatment of the Reformation to date.

Yinger, J. Milton. *The Scientific Study of Religion.* New York: Macmillan, 1970. The leading textbook on religion from a sociological slant.

Chapter

18

Retrospect and Prospect: The Past 10,000 Years and the Next 100

In this final chapter we take a long look backwards and a short look forwards. Our look backwards attempts to summarize the broadest changes in human societies over the past 10,000 years and their significance for the human condition and the quality of human life. The key question concerns the extent to which human societies have been, as popularly believed, making steady progress in the quality of human life. Our look ahead attempts to use our understanding of sociocultural evolution over the past 10,000 years to project the human future over the next century or so. This look is necessarily highly selective and focuses on the crucial issues of environmental deterioration and the likelihood of nuclear warfare. The chapter and the book conclude by briefly considering the importance of a general theory of world history as a reliable guide to thinking about the future.

THE PAST 10,000 YEARS: HUMAN PROGRESS?

The most important evolutionary trends of the past 10,000 years in relation to the overall quality of human life concern the *standard of living,* the *quantity and quality of work, equality,* and *democracy and freedom.* To discuss these evolutionary trends in a meaningful way, an abstract concept known as the

average world citizen is employed, and the implications of major evolutionary changes are judged from the perspective of this hypothetical individual. The average world citizen is the typical member of the typical type of human society prevailing in any given historical era. For example, 15,000 years ago all humans lived in hunter-gatherer societies, and thus the average world citizen was a hunter or a gatherer. By contrast, some 3,000 years ago the agrarian way of life had basically become the predominant form of social life on Earth, and thus the average world citizen was a peasant farmer. Since most of the world's population currently lives in the underdeveloped nations, today's average world citizen is a Third World peasant or urban worker. It must be remembered that the employment of the concept of the average world citizen is a purely methodological device designed to simplify the discussion about the nature and meaning of broad evolutionary trends. To talk about an average world citizen is to talk about how evolutionary trends affect the majority of the world's population, if not all individuals, groups, and societies.

The Standard of Living

To be able to talk at all about evolutionary trends in the standard of living, the highly subjective nature of this concept must be neutralized. Societies have different conceptions of the kinds of material things that are needed or desired. In the advanced industrial capitalist societies of today, for instance, people have come to depend on such things as fast cars, stereo systems, microwave ovens, and personal computers, and they feel deprived if these things are taken away. Hunter-gatherers, on the other hand, have no need or desire for such material items, and they certainly do *not* feel deprived because they lack them. Since the desire for such things is an artificially derived rather than a basic human need, it is not

meaningful to compare hunter-gatherers and modern industrialists (or the members of any other type of society) in terms of whether or not they possess such goods.

The only meaningful comparison of societies' standards of living is in terms of a universally desired good or state of affairs, something all humans need and desire and whose absence produces a feeling of deprivation. The *quality of the diet* is proposed as such a universal measure of the standard of living. Using this measure, there has been an overall decline in the standard of living over the past 10,000 years, at least when judged from the perspective of our average world citizen. The most recent evidence suggests that ancient hunter-gatherers probably enjoyed diets that were abundant in calories, fully adequate in animal proteins, and highly nutritious. As argued in Chapter 4, hunter-gatherers probably constituted an "original affluent society"—a type of society in which people are able to satisfy all their basic needs with a minimum of effort.

The decline in the standard of living began with the transition to the first agricultural (horticultural) communities (see the Special Topic in Chapter 4). The real decline in the living standard, though, was brought about several thousand years later at about the time people were greatly intensifying their agricultural methods. By the time the average world citizen had become a peasant, the standard of living had dropped very sharply. The average peasant in the average agrarian society of the past had a diet markedly inferior to that of the average hunter-gatherer of earlier times. Peasant diets were notoriously deficient in calories, proteins, and nutrients, and they probably also had a stultifying monotony. As Lenski has noted in regard to medieval England (1966:270–271), "The diet of the average peasant consisted of little more than the following: a hunk of bread and a mug of ale in the morning; a lump of cheese and bread with perhaps an onion or two to flavor it, and more ale at noon; a thick soup or pottage followed by bread and cheese at the main meal in the evening. Meat was rare, and the ale was usually thin." Things were just as bad or worse outside Europe (at least in the past few centuries). In China and Japan little meat was eaten by the average peasant, and in India virtually the entire population had been reduced to a state of obligatory vegetarianism. In China, even the rich mandarins ate little meat (Braudel, 1981).

While the quality of the diet has improved today for the members of industrial societies, these persons do not make up a majority of the world's population. Most people alive on Earth today live in the Third World and are poor peasants or urban workers. It is doubtful whether the average member of a contemporary Third World country is dramatically better off than the average peasant of past agrarian societies.

If evolutionary trends in the standard of living were measured by the level of health and the incidence of disease, a similar picture would emerge. Hunter-gatherers were far healthier and freer from disease than commonly thought (M. Harris, 1977; Cohen and Armelagos, 1984; Cohen, 1989), and their life expectancies, though short, were comparable to those of peasants. Moreover, the great killer contagious diseases familiar to humankind were products of the high-density urban life of agrarian societies (McNeill, 1976). Modern medicine has made great strides in the advanced industrial countries, of course, and in recent decades infant mortality rates have dropped significantly and longevity has increased appreciably throughout the Third World. However, most of this improvement is a product of only the last century or so—the average life span in the United States in 1900, for example, was only 49 years—and so for the vast majority of human history the trend either has been downward or has remained steady.

There are two basic reasons for the overall decline in the standard of living. One of these is population growth. An increasing pressure of numbers compels people to adopt more intensive methods of production. Yet the adoption of such methods does not allow people to increase their living standard or even to maintain it, for the pressure of numbers drives the living standard ever downward. By intensifying their production methods, people are simply keeping their living standards from dropping to drastically low levels. The other basic cause of the decline in living standards is the rise of class stratification, itself due in part to the growth of population. As some individuals and groups gain control over productive resources, they are able to compel other individuals and groups to produce economic surpluses that the members of the dominant group may live off. In the preindustrial world this process reached its peak in agrarian societies and contributed very heavily to the low living standard of the peasantry. In modern capitalism, the world stratification system dominated by the core capitalists is one of the most important causes of the low living standard of Third World peoples.

The Quantity and Quality of Work

There is little doubt that the quantity of work has increased and its quality has deteriorated over the past 10,000 years. Hunter-gatherers seem to work less and enjoy more leisure time than the members of all other types of societies. Evidence from contemporary hunter-gatherer societies indicates that they strongly resist advancing their technology because they realize this will bring increases in their workload. The members of horticultural societies do indeed appear to work somewhat harder and longer than people in hunting and gathering societies. But, as with the standard of living, the truly marked change seems to be associated with the emergence of agrarian societies. The workload in agrarian societies is markedly greater than in all previous forms of preindustrial society. In the modern world, work levels are still very high in both the industrialized countries and the Third World nations (Minge-Klevana, 1980). The average member of an industrial society may spend on the order of 60 hours a week in subsistence activities, if we add to the 40 hours per week spent earning a living the time spent shopping for food and preparing it, as well as the time spent maintaining a household. This is about three to four times the average weekly workload of many hunter-gatherers. The average Third World worker probably spends considerably more time than this in all subsistence activities.

A basic assumption of the preceding discussion is that people seem to obey what has been called a "Law of Least Effort" (Zipf, 1965; Harris, 1979). This law holds that, other things being equal, people prefer to accomplish activities with a minimum amount of energy expenditure. This seems to be a basic feature of human nature. Thus, increasing the workload is something people normally wish to avoid. Under what conditions will people work harder and longer than would otherwise be the case? There are perhaps three basic reasons why people will increase their energy expenditure: political compulsion, economic necessity, and psychological conditioning. People will work harder and longer when other people gain power over them and force them to increase their workload. They will also increase their work activities if compelled by a declining standard of living to intensify their productive efforts. Finally, people can be conditioned to believe that hard work is a moral virtue, laziness a moral defect (this idea has been basic to the Protestant work ethic of Western civilization in recent centuries). The first two of these have been the leading causes of the intensification of the workload over the past several millennia.

What, then, of the quality of work? Marx argued that work is the primary means of human self-realization. Humans realize their humanity and achieve meaning in life when they manipulate the world according to their own purposes and designs. The primitive hunter and the agrarian craftsman were classic examples of self-fulfilled workers. To a large extent the same was true even of agrarian peasants. Despite their exploitation and low standard of living, they had considerable control over their work activities and worked in harmony with nature and the seasons. In precapitalist and preindustrial societies, then, work was not primarily alienated labor (Thomas, 1964). The real emergence of alienated labor began with the transition to modern industrial capitalism. Here workers came to be reduced to instruments of production who performed routinized and fragmented tasks. They lost control over the means of production, had little control over their work activities, and had little sense of identification with the final product they produced. In the Third World, much work is also alienated labor, especially to the extent that capitalist methods of production and worker control have penetrated underdeveloped societies. Thus the trend in the quality of human work—one of the most basic of all human needs—has been negative.

Equality

There is no mistaking the overall trend in social and economic equality. It has been decidedly in the direction of greater *inequalities*, particularly those based on access to economic resources. Band and tribal societies are egalitarian societies in which the only real inequalities are those of status and influence. These inequalities are generally not socially inherited, and they are unrelated to control over economic resources or to political power. Influential and prestigious leaders in band and tribal societies have no greater wealth than others, nor do they have any capacity to compel the actions of others. In other words, in such societies class stratification does not exist.

Class stratification tends to emerge in more intensive horticultural societies, where population pressure has already reached significant levels. It is here that societies first come to be divided into groups possessing unequal levels of power and wealth, although the first forms of stratification usually do not impose severe economic penalties on the members of subordinate classes. But in high-density agrarian societies class stratification becomes so extreme that the members of subordinate classes generally suffer from marked economic deprivations. It is in such societies that a great social and economic gap between rich and poor emerges. Although contemporary industrial societies may have reduced some of the extremes of stratification compared to agrarian societies of the past, the economic inequalities among nations within the world-capitalist economy are probably greater today than ever before in human history.

The overall direction of the past 10,000 years of human history has been toward greater and greater exploitation in human affairs. Band and tribal societies display communal patterns of ownership, intensive cooperation and sharing, and a general absence of exploitation. With the growth of numbers and the emergence of scarcity in resources, people act more and more selfishly, and some groups begin to exploit others. More numbers produce more scarcity, more scarcity produces greater conflict over resources, and this in turn produces greater inequalities in power or control over resources. Furthermore, power begets power: groups that end up on top want to stay there and even work to increase the favorableness of the view from the top. And thus stratification tends to feed on itself.

With the emergence of modern industrial capitalist and socialist societies, exploitation does not disappear but takes new forms that are more severe under capitalism. As capitalism has penetrated the globe, it has opened up huge economic gaps among the nations of the world. These gaps are growing rather than shrinking and have time and again led to explosive political conflict.

Democracy and Freedom

Although there is a strong tendency in Western capitalist society to use the concepts of democracy and freedom more or less interchangeably, the terms, though related, should really carry different meanings. Democracy is a process of self-government, one whereby people decide their own affairs through open discussion and debate and in the absence of any individuals or groups who can command their actions.

Given this definition, human societies over the past ten millennia have moved more and more away from democracy. Band and tribal societies are fundamentally democratic in that they lack elite groups capable of commanding the actions of others. Headmen and big men are leaders of some influence and respect, but they have no genuine power. People are under no obligation to obey their wishes, and such leaders have no possibility of imposing penalties on those who ignore their suggestions. Democracy is undermined at the same basic point in sociocultural evolution at which class stratification emerges. With the growth of large-scale agrarian societies and their elaborate stratification systems, democracy drops to a very low point. In such societies tiny elites rule the actions of others and have the capacity to impose severe penalties on them for disobedience.

In the modern world a form of democracy, parliamentary democracy, has been created. Under this political arrangement people gain a great deal of protection from the arbitrary exercise of power that is so common in agrarian societies. However, democracy conceived as the direct participation of the populace in the affairs of government is more an illusion than a reality. (In the totalitarian Communist states, of course, it is not even an illusion.) Modern Western parliamentary democracies are governed by elite groups whose actions are self-serving and to a very great extent beyond significant control by the masses.

But what of **freedom?** Assessing the evolutionary history of freedom depends crucially on what is meant by the concept, which has been subject to rather diverse definitions. In the Western tradition of thought freedom has usually been conceptualized as *individual autonomy*. Freedom in this sense involves the absence of external constraints on individual thought and action. Autonomous individuals are those who follow their own courses of action relatively unimpeded by others. Alexandra Maryanski and Jonathan Turner (1992) assert that there is a curvilinear relationship between individual autonomy and sociocultural evolution. Greatest freedom occurs at the ends of the evolutionary spectrum—in hunter-gatherer and industrial societies—whereas people in horticultural and agrarian societies have the least freedom. Maryanski and Turner claim that the main external constraint on individual autonomy in horticultural societies is the web of kinship, whereas in agrarian societies the leading constraint is that of power. They argue, in addition, that the constraints of kinship are more severe than those of power. I agree with Maryanski and Turner's overall argument, but I would question their claim that it is in horticultural societies that individuals are subjected to the most severe constraints. I would nominate agrarian societies for that dubious honor. In these societies people are subjected not only to

the constraints of kinship ties and obligations, but also to severe class domination and the overwhelming power of the state.

Another difficulty with Maryanski and Turner's argument is that they overlook the constraining influence of custom and tradition. Individuals in hunter-gatherer societies have a great deal of freedom from direct coercion by others, and individual autonomy is highly prized (Gardner, 1991), but they are hardly free to set their own normative standards of behavior. People are, in fact, highly coerced by what the French sociologist Emile Durkheim called the *collective conscience*—the will of the group. There is extremely strong group pressure to conform to the norms and values of the group, and the penalties for failure to conform are often severe, including either death or banishment from the group. What is true of hunter-gatherers is also true of people in horticultural and agrarian societies. In fact, concerning this dimension of freedom, what might be called *individuality*, it is clear that people in all forms of preindustrial societies are relatively unfree, and that it is modern capitalism and industrialism that have generated the highest levels of human freedom. In modern industrial capitalist societies there is government protection of individual rights and liberties and strong encouragement of individual self-expression. This individualistic conception of freedom pervades all of the basic social arrangements of modern Western capitalist societies (but not yet non-Western capitalist Japan).

There is yet a third form of freedom, one that might be called freedom as *human species-realization*. This conception of freedom is associated with the Marxian tradition of thought (cf. Elster, 1985). Freedom in this sense involves the equal capacity of all individuals to realize their basic nature as members of the human species. For Marx, freedom existed when everyone had the full opportunity to achieve meaning and purpose in life, especially in so far as this could be achieved through work. Marx thought that freedom could only be achieved in a classless society with a very advanced level of technology—in the future socialist society. He believed that modern Western capitalist societies, even though they granted certain political freedoms to individuals, failed to achieve true human freedom because most of the population was exploited by the capitalist class and had no genuine opportunity for the realization of their human nature. If we follow this tradition of conceptualizing freedom, we can see that freedom has not been increasing in human history, and in a sense has been decreasing inasmuch as the members of precapitalist societies generally do have considerable opportunity to realize themselves through their labor.

Associated with this conception of freedom is another important dimension. If freedom is human species-realization, and if humans are fundamentally social animals, then freedom can only be achieved in and through society. That is, people can only be considered free when they participate with their fellow humans in social relationships that are intrinsically meaningful. This means that freedom is more likely to exist in societies in which individuals place definite limitations on their own individual self-expression in favor of sharing a common set of values and standards with others. And since individual self-expression has become an increasingly common feature of Western societies, freedom in the Marxian sense is actually decreasing in such societies.

The Concept of Progress Revisited

The preceding discussion suggests once again what was asserted early in the book: that we must be extremely wary of using the concept of progress to characterize the major changes of the past 10,000 years. Indeed, it seems apparent that much of what

has been happening over this period has actually been a form of cultural *regression*. How else are we to regard a general decline in the standard of living, an increase in the quantity of and a deterioration in the quality of work, the emergence of marked social and economic inequalities, and the undermining of democracy? Of course, not all of these changes apply to all persons and groups in all societies. For some individuals and groups the standard of living has increased; work has become lighter, easier, and more gratifying; and the emergence of economic inequality and the undermining of democracy have actually been beneficial rather than detrimental. Yet for the majority of the world's population—for our average world citizen—things have been going downhill.

On the other hand, to suggest a general deterioration in the quality of life in these respects does not mean that improvements have not been occurring in other areas of social life. Humans have made enormous artistic, intellectual, literary, scientific, and technological achievements. Such achievements—those of Picasso, Mozart, Shakespeare, Einstein, Darwin, da Vinci, et al.—cannot be swept aside as insignificant. It is possible to say, then, that humans have actually been making certain forms of progress over the past 10,000 years in spite of the very significant regressions that have been occurring.

A LOOK AT THE FUTURE: ENVIRONMENTAL DEPLETION

We now turn away from what the past has produced to take a look into the future. The first part of the discussion is oriented around what I believe are the two most serious threats that the human species faces in the immediate years ahead: major ecological and demographic problems resulting from an extremely advanced technology and the serious world maldistribution of resources, and the possibility of world-annihilating war resulting from the extremely competitive interstate system of modern capitalism.

Ecological and Demographic Catastrophe?

In his book *An Inquiry into the Human Prospect* (1980), Robert Heilbroner issues a deeply pessimistic judgment in regard to the future. As he puts it (1980:20), "The outlook for man, I believe, is painful, difficult, perhaps desperate, and the hope that can be held out for his future prospect seems to be very slim indeed. . . . The answer to whether we can conceive of the future other than as a continuation of the darkness, cruelty, and disorder of the past seems to me to be no; and to the question of whether worse impends, yes."

Heilbroner sees three fundamental reasons why the future looks so grim. One of these is the current rate of population growth on a world scale. He argues that total population in the Third World will reach approximately 40 billion within a century, compared to only about 1.4 to 1.7 billion for the industrialized world. In the nearly 20 years since Heilbroner's book was written, fertility rates have fallen somewhat in some Third World countries, and so the projection of 40 billion people living in that part of the world by the late twenty-first century is too high. Nonetheless, even if this number were to be cut in half, 20 billion people living in the Third World is still an enormous number with extremely serious consequences. The most obvious consequence of such a population glut would be a marked deterioration in the economic conditions of the Third World countries. This deterioration would undoubtedly be accompanied by rising social disorder and the intensification of the dictatorial character of governments in order to control it. As Heilbroner notes, "This condition could continue for a considerable period, effectively removing these areas from the concern of the rest of the world and consigning the billions of their inhabitants to a human state comparable to that which we now glimpse in the worst regions of India or Pakistan" (1980:38).

It is possible, of course, that some of the Third World countries will attempt to head off such problems before they become so critical. But this will require, Heilbroner argues, the emergence of "iron" governments devoted to establishing very strict birth control policies, such as are now in effect in China. Moreover, as Heilbroner points out, such governments are not likely to limit their authoritarian techniques to the regulation of the birth rate. They are likely to extend their power into many other sectors of social life as well, and thus the attempt to control population growth in many Third World countries will be accompanied by a general rise in political repression.

Heilbroner concludes his discussion of the likely effects of current population growth rates by arguing (1980:43–44):

> If current projections of population growth rates are even roughly accurate, and if the environmental limitations on the growth of output . . . begin to exert their negative influences within the next two generations, massive human deterioration in the backward areas can be avoided only by a redistribution of the world's output and energies on a scale immensely larger than anything that has hitherto been seriously contemplated. Under the best of circumstances such a redistribution would be exceedingly difficult to achieve. . . . Such an unprecedented international transfer seems impossible to imagine except under some kind of threat. The possibility must then be faced that the underdeveloped nations which have "nothing" to lose will point their nuclear pistols at the heads of the passengers in the first-class coaches who have everything to lose.

Heilbroner is also pessimistic about the future because of the current rate at which the industrial nations are using up natural resources. He believes we are now moving toward the finite limits of the earth's ability to support the industrial form of technology. In order to avoid an ecological catastrophe in the near future, the industrial countries must begin placing sharp limits on their rate of resource utilization. Heilbroner thinks that this, like population control, can only be accomplished through the rise of authoritarian governments, because private individuals and groups would not voluntarily restrict their rate of resource use. Here, then, is another serious threat to our basic democratic institutions. Undoubtedly a markedly reduced standard of living would also accompany reduced industrial activity.

There is yet a third possible threat to humankind looming in the future. This involves the heat generated as a by-product of industrial activity (Heilbroner, 1980:50):

> Even if we make the heroic assumption that all these difficulties will be overcome, so that another century of uninterrupted industrial growth, with its thousandfold increase in required inputs, will face no constraints from resource shortages, there remains one barrier that confronts us with all the force of an ultimatum from nature. It is that all industrial production, including, of course, the extraction of resources, requires the use of energy, and that all energy, including that generated from natural processes such as wind power or solar radiation, is inextricably involved with the emission of heat.
>
> The limit on industrial growth therefore depends in the end on the tolerance of the ecosphere for the absorption of heat. . . . The emission of man-made heat is . . . growing exponentially, as both cause and consequence of industrial growth.

Heilbroner believes that at the current rate of energy use we have perhaps a century in which to solve the problem of "heat pollution." Failing that, the future is one of extinction of the human species.

Heilbroner's pessimistic conclusions are strongly reinforced by a recent study by Donella Meadows, Dennis Meadows, and Jørgen Randers (1992). They ran a series of 13 computer simulations designed to determine what controls would need to be placed on resource use and population growth in order to allow for a sustainable world throughout the twenty-first century. Of their 13 simulations, only two produced a sustainable world. All of the others led to ecological collapse. The authors show that a sustainable world is possible only if all of the following conditions are implemented simultaneously:

- Pollution controls.
- Land yield enhancement.
- Land erosion protection.
- The development of more resource-efficient technology.
- Faster development of new technology.
- Every couple in the world limiting itself to two children.
- Every nation in the world limiting its industrial output to the level of contemporary South Korea.

Moreover, all of these conditions must be implemented very soon, probably within 20 years. Assuming that Meadows, Meadows, and Randers are correct, is it realistic to assume that all of these things will be done? Not especially. Finding the means to persuade every couple in the world to limit itself to two children would be extremely difficult, but so would persuading capitalists to reduce their industrial output dramatically. In fact, capitalists would never voluntarily restrict their output because they see that it would be economically suicidal to do so. The ceaseless accumulation of capital is the driving engine of the world capitalist system, and capitalists would only voluntarily restrict output under the most extreme conditions, that is, when disaster is staring them in the face. But by then it will be too late. Once again we return to the theme of highly authoritarian governments being necessary to achieve ecological sustainability. But given the extraordinary influence that capitalists have over the actions of states, could such governments even emerge?

A Critique of the Pessimistic View

The "gloom and doom" outlook on the future we have been discussing has been severely criticized by the economist Julian Simon (1981). Simon argues strongly against the view that we are rapidly running out of crucial resources. He suggests that our natural resources are not finite in any meaningful sense of that term, since technological breakthroughs are highly likely in the future and will probably head off any serious problems generated by resource depletion.

Simon believes that the doomsaying forecasters have gone wrong in a very fundamental methodological way: they have based their forecasts on the concept of "known reserves" of natural resources. Simon claims that this concept is essentially worthless for making future predictions inasmuch as the "known reserves" of any natural resource are limited to how diligently scientists and engineers have searched for it. Simon believes that our natural resources probably exist in vastly greater abundance than the "known reserves" concept allows for. According to Simon, this kind of forecasting should be replaced with a method in which the price trends of resources are used to determine their scarcity. Price-trend data, he claims, clearly show that our resources are getting

less rather than more scarce, since the historical trend of prices for these resources has been downward. In short, Simon believes there is no cause for alarm about the availability of crucial natural resources in either the near or the distant future.

Simon is also highly critical of those who predict dire social consequences for the future as the result of rapid population growth. He believes the historical record shows that population growth does not necessarily produce negative social consequences; indeed, he claims that in many instances population growth is actually beneficial rather than harmful. For example, it is frequently a stimulus to technological advance. Thus there is no particular cause for worry about continuing population growth, either in the developed or the underdeveloped countries.

While it is difficult to evaluate Simon's claims about the availability of natural resources, there is good reason to be highly suspicious of his argument in regard to population. Simon claims that, although in the 1960s demographers were concerned that fertility rates would not fall in less-developed countries, in the 1970s fertility did begin to fall in some of these countries. He concludes from this that it is reasonably certain that the Third World as a whole will sooner or later (probably sooner) undergo the same pattern of demographic transition experienced by the First World countries.

This is dubious reasoning. While fertility rates have fallen in some less-developed countries (China being the best example), they remain very high in the vast majority of the underdeveloped nations. It is illogical to assert, as Simon does, that there is reasonable certainty that the underdeveloped countries will soon be following the demographic path of the developed countries. In fact, nothing seems less certain. Most underdeveloped countries are thus far not following the historical demographic path of the developed countries any more than they are following their historical economic path.

To point out this basic logical flaw in Simon's argument, though, is not to suggest that he is clearly wrong and the pessimists are therefore correct. Rather, it is to suggest that Simon's dismissive attitude toward the kind of argument that the pessimists are making is unwarranted. What can only be regarded as an uncritically optimistic view of both the past and the future is very characteristic of Simon's book. He appears to have fallen victim to the view that humans have steadily been making progress over the millennia. For example, he asserts that "the standard of living has risen along with the size of the world's population since the beginning of recorded time" (1981:345). This is simply untrue. As seen throughout this book, and as noted earlier in this chapter, from the Neolithic Revolution to the present major technological changes seem to have been associated with declines in the standard of living for the majority of the world's population. Thus, although Simon continually argues that the doomsayers have not been learning the proper lessons from history, neither, it seems, has he.

As is fairly obvious, then, I am more sympathetic to the view of the pessimists than to that of Simon. The compelling feature of the pessimists' analysis is its hardheaded realism: its recognition of the genuinely excruciating problems now presented by several hundred years of expansion of capitalism and industrialism. Heilbroner's position perhaps goes too far in its near fatalism. Yet the more moderated position advocated by Meadows, Meadows, and Randers must be taken with the utmost seriousness. I fear that they may very well be correct in their assertion that major changes must be made, and made very soon, if world civilization is not to experience an ecological and economic collapse sometime during the twenty-first century.

A LOOK AT THE FUTURE: WAR AND POLITICS

War and the Capitalist World-Economy

A number of scholars from several of the social sciences have noticed that over much of its history capitalism has been characterized by a highly regularized cyclical pattern of economic boom and bust (Goldstein, 1988; Wallerstein, 1984c). It has been observed that periods of economic upturn are invariably followed by periods of downturn, and that there is an amazingly regular rhythm to these oscillations. The first major scholar to identify this feature of capitalism was the Russian economist Nikolai Kondratieff (1984; orig. 1928), who identified economic cycles of approximately 50 years duration. Once an upturn began it took about 25 years to reach its crest, and then a downturn began. The downturn itself lasted approximately 25 years, and after it reached bottom a new upturn would begin. The waves or cycles that Kondratieff identified have subsequently been named *Kondratieff waves*. However, since many other scholars have identified similar waves, these waves need not be associated exclusively with Kondratieff (Goldstein, 1988). For this reason I shall call them simply *long waves*.

Several scholars have also been struck by the association between long waves in the history of capitalism and the incidence of war. In a major study of this problem, Joshua Goldstein (1988) has shown that long waves since 1495 have been remarkably correlated with the outbreak of major wars (Table 18.1). Goldstein identifies ten long waves since 1495 and finds that a major war between powerful states has almost always occurred in the second half of the upturn phase of the cycle. The only exception to this striking regularity is World War II, which occurs at the beginning of an upturn. However, World War II may not be a genuine exception. Some social scientists re-

Table 18.1   LONG WAVES AND MAJOR WARS IN THE HISTORY OF CAPITALISM, 1495–1975

Cycle	Starting Date of War Cycle	Peak War Years	Length (Years)	Ending Date of Corresponding Long Wave Phase Period
1	(1495)	1521–1529	(35)	1528
2	1530	1552–1556	28	1558
3	1558	1593–1604	47	1594
4	1605	1635–1648	44	1649
5	1649	1701–1713	65	1719
6	1714	1755–1763	50	1761
7	1764	1803–1815	52	1813
8	1816	1870–1871	56	1871
9	1872	1914–1918	47	1917
10	1919	1939–1945?	(27)	(1968/80?)

Cycle	Peak Wars	Annual Fatality Rate at Peak
1	First and Second Wars of Charles V; (Ottoman War vs. Hapsburgs)[a]	13,000
2	Fifth War of Charles V; (Ottoman War vs. Hapsburgs)[a]	22,000
3	War of the Armada; (Austro-Turkish War)[a]	11,000
4	Thirty Years' War: Swedish/French Phase	88,000
5	War of the Spanish Succession	107,000
6	Seven Years' War	124,000
7	Napoleonic Wars	156,000
8	Franco-Prussian War	90,000
9	World War I	1,934,000
10	World War II	2,158,000

[a]The dating of war peaks in cycles 1–3 is based primarily on intra-European wars rather than those against Turkey. Wars against Turkey are included in the statistics, however, and are shown above in parentheses.

Source: Joshua S. Goldstein, *Long Cycles: Prosperity and War in the Modern Age.* New Haven, Conn.: Yale University Press, 1988, p. 241, Table 11.3.

gard World Wars I and II as really being two phases of one great war, not as two separate wars. If this is a valid interpretation, then the pattern identified by Goldstein is perfect.

It needs to be stressed that Goldstein's data do not relate to the overall frequency of war, nor to the duration of wars. Rather, they are concerned only with wars of great magnitude. These wars have always occurred near the end of an economic upswing. Although there are several possible ways of interpreting this empirical finding, Goldstein theorizes that powerful states fight truly major wars with one another only when they can bear the expense of doing so. Major wars occur near the end of

an upswing, then, because it is only at that time that states are financially capable of undertaking such military efforts.

Implications for the Next Major War

On the basis of his findings, Goldstein goes on to predict the timing of the next major war. The world-economy has been in a downturn phase since about 1970, and the next upturn is expected to begin around 2000. If it does, this upturn will crest in approximately 2025, which would mean that the next major war can be expected to occur during the decade between 2015 and 2025.

Actually, Goldstein regards the entire period from 2000 to 2030 as a serious "danger period" for the outbreak of war, although he expects that the danger is greater toward the end of the period.

Goldstein's predictions are contingent upon the validity of the assumption that the basic features of the world political system will not change appreciably in the years ahead. Some world-system theorists, however, think that this assumption is not likely to hold (Wallerstein, 1982; Arrighi, 1982; cf. Chase-Dunn and O'Reilly, 1989). They think that the presence of nuclear weapons changes everything. Since core states now have these weapons, war becomes unthinkable because it is recognized by all parties as unwinnable. But not all world-system theorists take such an optimistic position. Christopher Chase-Dunn and Kenneth O'Reilly (1989) have examined a number of factors that they believe strongly bear on the likelihood of a major war in the near future, what they call a "core war." These factors include the long wave, intensifying ecological problems, the declining position of the United States in the world-economy, efforts at nuclear disarmament, and the emergence of new international organizations designed to reduce the threat of war. They conclude that "developments that lower the probability of core war are not great enough to offset those factors that will increase the chance of war in the coming decades. The probability of serious war among core states over the next four decades may be as much as fifty-fifty" (1989:61).

Averting Catastrophic War: The Possibility of a Future World State

If a major core war were to break out early in the next century, it would not necessarily have to be a nuclear war, but in all probability nuclear weapons would be involved. There is therefore a distinct possibility in the near future of a war that would devastate civilization and perhaps threaten the very existence of human life. What might be done to avert such an unprecedented catastrophe? Chase-Dunn (1989b, 1990; Bornschier and Chase-Dunn, 1985) has argued that the answer lies in the creation of a *world state*. This would be an overarching political system that would centralize political and economic decision making on a world scale. It would eliminate the system of competing and conflicting nation-states—the interstate system—that has characterized the capitalist world-economy for approximately 500 years. As such, the threat of world-destroying war would be enormously reduced if not eliminated altogether. In addition, such a state could be an extremely effective tool in eliminating gross inequalities in the worldwide distribution of economic resources, and thus could do much toward rectifying the massive problems of economic underdevelopment in the Third World.

Chase-Dunn suggests that a future world state ought to combine the best features of both capitalism and socialism. It should contain a centralized system of political and economic decision making, but at the same time be sufficiently decentralized to allow for local and national preferences and for important cultural differences. What Chase-Dunn really has in mind is a kind of federation that eliminates the worst and most dangerous forms of struggle between nation-states while simultaneously permitting them to retain a good deal of their identity. Thus, the world state is not a single political society, but an artificially imposed structure that oversees the political and economic functioning of various individual societies.

To his credit, Chase-Dunn recognizes that there are grave dangers inherent in the creation of a world state. The distinct possibility exists that such a state could become a kind of Orwellian monster, a state so powerful that it would constitute an extreme threat to individual freedoms of all sorts. He believes, however, that the risk is worth taking because the alternative risk—complete destruction of the human species—is just as great and so much more appalling. Moreover, if we know in advance the risks to freedom that a world state can pose, then we can take strong steps to try to avert this eventuality.

I am in strong agreement with Chase-Dunn's proposals, but serious questions can be raised about their workability, at least in the short term. If the next major war will be a nuclear war, and if it is no more than 15 to 25 years away, then very little time remains for the creation of the kind of political structure that Chase-Dunn has in mind. It is doubtful that the highly ethnocentric species known as *Homo sapiens* can exchange its intensely nationalistic ideologies for much more panhuman ones in such a short time. Over the longer term Chase-Dunn's proposals gain a much greater measure of realism. The big question is, though, will the longer term ever arrive?

CONCLUSIONS: THE FUTURE FROM THE PERSPECTIVE OF A GENERAL THEORY OF HISTORY

No one really knows what the future, even the very near future, has in store, and even the most brilliant social analysts have seldom been able to make reliable predictions about what is to come. But one thing is certain: If we do not have a good general theory of the past, then we have absolutely no hope of speculating intelligently about what is ahead. This book has offered a materialist and evolutionary perspective in order to understand the past, and it may be suggested that such a perspective is our most reliable guide to the future. I do not know whether the predictions of Heilbroner, Goldstein, and Chase-Dunn are good ones, but I do believe that, to some extent, they come to grips with the factors that are likely to be most centrally involved in shaping the fu-

ture. Today we live in a capitalist world-economy that has been expanding and evolving for half a millennium. This world-economy is closely intertwined with an interstate system, and both of these interact with (now largely defunct) socialist states in major ways. The world-system of capitalism has created massive technological advance that now threatens our species, both in an ecological sense (through continuing environmental degradation) and in a political sense (through the threat of nuclear war). We are thus poised on the brink. It will do no good to put our heads in the sand and deny these realities. They exist, and they have a special kind of urgency about them. As intelligent citizens, we have an obligation to learn about them and to do whatever we can to avoid their leading us into the abyss. After all, what is the alternative?

SUMMARY

1. Over the past 10,000 years many of the fundamental changes in human social life seem to be more indicative of cultural regression than of progress. For most of the world's population the standard of living has declined, the quantity of work has increased and its quality has declined, inequalities in wealth and power have become increasingly prominent, and democracy has been steadily replaced by elite domination of the many by the few.

2. Robert Heilbroner is a modern thinker who takes a deeply pessimistic view of the human prospect in the years ahead. He believes that world overpopulation and the overuse of natural resources spell potentially disastrous consequences for the quality of human life in both the short and the long run.

3. Computer simulations run by Meadows, Meadows, and Randers suggest that major limitations must be placed very soon on population growth, industrial output, and resource use if the world is to remain ecologically and economically unsustainable over the next century.

4. The economist Julian Simon has been severely critical of this view, holding that the future is far rosier than doomsayers believe. Simon believes that available natural resources are far greater than pessimists like Heilbroner and Meadows, Meadows, and Randers claim. He also believes that population growth is declining throughout the Third World and will soon reach the relatively low levels characteristic of the highly industrialized countries.

5. War has been an extremely common activity throughout the history of capitalism, but the most devastating wars have almost invariably occurred late in phases of economic upturn. Extrapolations from this historical trend suggest that the next major war is likely to break out sometime during the next 15 to 25 years. There is every reason to expect that such a war would involve the use of nuclear weapons. Alarmed by this horrible prospect, some social scientists have begun to propose the construction of a world state that could take major steps to prevent such an occurrence.

6. The general theory of human history presented throughout this book suggests that the future will be shaped most significantly by changes in the material conditions of social life. In order to understand the future we must pay closest attention to the world capitalist system and its international economic inequalities and political and military tensions. This world capitalist organization of production has both politico-military and ecological effects of vast significance.

SPECIAL TOPIC: THE POSTMODERN CONDITION

In recent years intellectuals and artists of all sorts have increasingly spoken of a phenomenon variously known as "postmodernism," "postmodernity," or "the postmodern condition." Postmodernism is, in essence, a broad cultural and intellectual movement that began in the late 1960s or early 1970s and that has embraced philosophy, the social sciences, art, architecture, literature, and film. Postmodernists see themselves as reacting against modernism or modernity, which came into existence in the second half of the eighteenth century with the cultural and intellectual movement known as the Enlightenment. Modernism or modernity is associated with beliefs in linear human progress, the search for objective knowledge or truth, and the use of social-scientific knowledge for rational planning and the reconstruction of society. It is associated with a sense that the world is coherent and definite and can be represented as such by intellectual and artistic forms (Harvey, 1989).

Postmodernism, by contrast, repudiates the notion of a coherent, objectively knowable world that can be rationally analyzed and improved (Harvey, 1989). The key words to describe postmodernist thinking are fragmentation, indeterminacy, pluralism, ephemerality, discontinuity, chaos, and relativism. In philosophy and social theory postmodernism involves the notion that no interpretation of the world can lay a claim to objective validity. All interpretations are subjective and spring from the social and historical circumstances of the interpreters. No path to knowledge is better than any other, and all have to be given their due. Science is not considered to be a superior form of acquiring knowledge, as its technological applications have led to domination and oppression rather than human liberation. Science is just another "language game." Since no theoretical argument can lay claim to objective validity or intellectual superiority, all we can do is "deconstruct" it, or critically examine its fundamental elements, grounding assumptions, and social and historical context (Lyotard, 1985; Derrida, 1978).

Postmodern art and architecture are characterized by the combination or juxtaposition of elements that previously had been kept separate. In postmodern art the artistic form known as collage abounds; in postmodern architecture the guiding theme is a mixing of premodern and modern styles within the same structure. This combination of seeming incommensurables is also witnessed in postmodern film. As David Harvey (1989:48) has said, "We find, in a film like *Blue Velvet*, the central character revolving between two quite incongruous worlds—that of a conventional 1950s small-town America with its high school, drugstore culture, and a bizarre, violent, sex-crazed underworld of drugs, dementia, and sexual perversion." Postmodernism is also associated with the idea that there is no proper hierarchy of aesthetic values, and that mass taste is just as virtuous as highbrow taste. The aesthetic world, like the intellectual world, is characterized by a great pluralism of values, and relativism is the only proper stance to take with respect to this pluralism. This extreme relativism has been negatively judged by many. For example, David Harvey (1989:116) says that postmodernism, with its

> *penchant for deconstruction bordering on nihilism, its preference for aesthetics over ethics, takes matters too far. . . . Postmodernist philosophers tell us not only to accept but even to revel in the fragmentations and the cacophony of voices through which the dilemmas of the modern world are understood. Obsessed with deconstructing and delegitimating every form of argument they encounter, they can end only in condemning their own validity claims to the point where nothing remains of any basis for reasoned action.*

Indeed, taken to its logical extreme postmodernism completely self-destructs. A little scrutiny and it is gone in a puff of smoke. If no perspective can lay claim to objective validity, and if postmodernism is a perspective (which it obviously is), then what reason could anyone ever have for taking it seriously?

What accounts for this postmodern attack on human reason? Various answers have been proposed, but to my mind the most plausible answer has been offered by David Harvey, a Marxian geographer. In his superb book *The Condition of Postmodernity* (1989), Harvey argues that the dynamic character of capitalism as a mode of economic production has led to continual increases in what he calls *time-space compression*. This is a shrinking of the psychological experience of time and space that results from the increasingly global character of capitalist production. Harvey argues that in the history of capitalism there have been several surges of time-space compression. The latest episode began in the early 1970s, Harvey declares, and this episode, like the earlier ones, has psychologically disturbed and destabilized the individuals who have been experiencing it. Periods of such psychological destabilization are accompanied by dramatic shifts in systems of cultural and intellectual representation, and postmodernism is the form of representation that has accompanied the most recent compression episode. What is perhaps most characteristic of the last 30 years is an enormous acceleration in the pace of capitalist production, as well as in the pace of social life more generally. I quote at length from Harvey, who expresses the matter so well (1989:284–286):

> *I want to suggest that we have been experiencing, these last two decades, an intense phase of time-space compression that has had a disorienting and disruptive impact upon . . . cultural and social life. . . .*
>
> *. . . Speed-up was achieved in production by organizational shifts towards vertical disintegration—sub-contracting, outsourcing, etc.—that reversed the . . . tendency towards vertical integration and produced an increasing roundaboutness in production even in the face of increasing financial centralization. Other organizational shifts—such as the "just-in-time" delivery system that reduces stock inventories—when coupled with the new technologies of electronic control, small-batch production, etc., all reduced turnover times in many sectors of production.*

... For the labourers this all implied an intensification (speed-up) in labour processes and an acceleration in the de-skilling and re-skilling required to meet new labour needs. ...

Accelerating turnover time in production entails parallel accelerations in exchange and consumption. Improved systems of communication and information flow, coupled with rationalizations in techniques of distribution ..., made it possible to circulate commodities through the market system with greater speed. ... Financial services (aided by computerized trading) likewise speeded up. ...

Of the many developments in the arena of consumption, two stand out as being of particular importance. The mobilization of fashion in mass (as opposed to elite) markets provided a means to accelerate the pace of consumption. ... A second trend was a shift away from the consumption of goods and into the consumption of services—not only personal, business, educational, and health services, but also into entertainments, spectacles, happenings, and distractions. ...

Of the innumerable consequences that have flowed from this general speed-up in the turnover times of capital, I shall focus on those that have particular bearing on postmodern ways of thinking, feeling, and doing.

The first major consequence has been to accentuate volatility and ephemerality of fashions, products, production techniques, labour processes, ideas and ideologies, values and established practices. The sense that "all that is solid melts into air" has rarely been more pervasive. ...

In the realm of commodity production, the primary effect has been to emphasize the values and virtues of instantaneity (instant and fast foods, meals, and other satisfactions) and of disposability (cups, plates, cutlery, packaging, napkins, clothing, etc.). ... It meant more than just throwing away produced goods (creating a monumental waste-disposal problem), but also being able to throw away values, life-styles, stable relationships, and attachments to things, buildings, places, people, and received ways of doing and being. ... [I]ndividuals were forced to cope with disposability, novelty, and the prospects for instant obsolescence. ... [A]nd this implies profound changes in human psychology. ... The bombardment of stimuli, simply on the commodity front, creates problems of sensory overload.

If Harvey's theory is correct, then the implications for the future are ominous. Time-space compression is built into the very logic of capitalist development, and the pace of production and social life constantly increase. Future waves of time-space compression would be expected to be even more intense, and as such would likely produce even more severe forms of psychological destabilization. If this were to occur, then the postmodernism of the late twentieth century may turn out in retrospect to seem relatively mild. As hardly needs to be said, that is not an enticing prospect.

FOR FURTHER READING

Cohen, Mark N. *Health and the Rise of Civilization.* New Haven: Yale University Press, 1989. An extremely detailed analysis of health, nutrition, and disease among many different evolutionary types of society. Using extensive empirical data, Cohen makes a persuasive case for the relatively good health and nutrition of hunter-gatherer societies as compared to those that evolved later.

Galtung, Johan, Tore Heiestad, and Erik Rudeng. "On the decline and fall of empires: The Roman Empire and Western imperialism compared." *Review* 4:91–153, 1980. A comparison of the current state of the capitalist world-economy with that of the Roman Empire during the beginning of its decline. A provocative comparison, perhaps with considerable merit, but one that must be approached with caution.

Gendron, Bernard. *Technology and the Human Condition*. New York: St. Martin's Press, 1977. A good overview of various optimistic and pessimistic views regarding the future. Examines what the author calls the utopian, dystopian, and socialist views.

Giddens, Anthony. *The Consequences of Modernity*. Stanford: Stanford University Press, 1990. This work by a major sociologist argues that we are living in an age of "high modernity" rather than postmodernity and explores the nature of high modernity and its effects on the psychological existence and daily life of individuals.

Goldstein, Joshua S. *Long Cycles: Prosperity and War in the Modern Age*. New Haven: Yale University Press, 1988. An exhaustive analysis of economic cycles of upturn and downturn in the history of capitalism, with a special application of those cycles to war. Contains important predictions about the future.

Harvey, David. *The Condition of Postmodernity*. Oxford: Blackwell, 1989. An analysis of the emergence of a "postmodern" cultural sensibility since the early 1970s, especially as it is revealed in contemporary art, architecture, and intellectual life. Also sets forth an extremely provocative materialist interpretation of the postmodern condition, as well as a critique of it.

Heilbroner, Robert. *An Inquiry into the Human Prospect*. New York: Norton, 1980. One of the best-known of the recent spate of books taking a deeply pessimistic view of the human future. A new edition "updated for the 1990s" is available, but it is little changed and Heilbroner's pessimism remains.

Kennedy, Paul. *Preparing for the Twenty-first Century*. New York: Random House, 1993. One of the most recent pessimistic and concerned projections of the human future.

Meadows, Donella H., Dennis L. Meadows, and Jørgen Randers. *Beyond the Limits: Confronting Global Collapse, Envisioning a Sustainable Future*. Post Mills, Vt.: Chelsea Green, 1992. Through the use of computer simulations, the authors show the restraints that must be put on population growth, resource use, and industrial output if the world is to be ecologically and economically sustainable throughout the twenty-first century.

Sanderson, Stephen K. *Social Transformations: A General Theory of Historical Development*. Oxford: Blackwell, 1995. Chapters 8 and 9 offer much more detailed treatments of the question of progress and predicting the future than available here.

Sennett, Richard. *The Fall of Public Man*. New York: Random House (Vintage Books), 1976. Offers some important insights into the individualizing tendencies of capitalism over the past two centuries.

Simon, Julian. *The Ultimate Resource*. Princeton, N.J.: Princeton University Press, 1981. A strong critique of the "gloom and doom" vision of the future and an argument for believing that there is every reason to anticipate a sunny future for humankind.

Wagar, W. Warren. *A Short History of the Future*. Second edition. Chicago: University of Chicago Press, 1992. World-system theory provides the context for this extraordinary work of fiction in which a historian from the twenty-third century narrates world history from the late twentieth century to his own time. By 2015 the world has fallen under the control of 12 megacorporations. Devastating nuclear war in 2044 leads to the creation of a socialist world commonwealth that regulates world affairs for the better part of a century, only to yield to the formation of thousands of tiny statelets and the reestablishment of some elements of capitalism.

Glossary

absolute immiseration, thesis of The view that the overall quality of human life in the capitalist periphery is deteriorating with the continuing evolution of the capitalist world-economy. Compare *relative immiseration, thesis of.*

absolutism See *absolutist monarchy.*

absolutist monarchy A type of state found in late medieval and early modern Europe in which a centralized bureaucracy developed around the king. This bureaucratic centralization was associated with the general intensification of state power. Compare *national states.*

accumulation The process whereby surplus value earned from capitalist activity is reinvested in that activity, thus causing an expansion of the overall scale of economic production and exchange.

accumulationist See *accumulation.*

adaptation Biologically, the process whereby organisms acquire the genetic materials that promote their survival in a particular environment. Socioculturally, the process whereby various features of social life develop because they meet certain needs and desires of particular individuals or social groups.

adaptive See *adaptation.*

affinity The existence of kinship ties based on marriage.

agrarian society A society whose members make a living by using intensive and advanced agricultural methods, such as plows and animal energy for plowing.

agriculture As distinguished from horticulture, a form of farming in which large plots of land (fields) are carefully prepared and then cultivated with the use of plows and traction animals.

agrobureaucratic state A type of agrarian state in which enormous power is concentrated in the hands of a ruler and the bureaucracy with which he or she is surrounded. Such a state centralizes its control over large territories and usually has extensive involvement in public works projects.

alienation In Marxian theory, that process under capitalism whereby the worker ceases to regard work as an intrinsically enjoyable activity, regarding it instead as stultifying and dehumanizing. In a more general sociological vein, a process by which people feel estranged from other people and from the basic character of their society.

ambilocality Residence of a newly married couple with the husband's or the wife's kinship group.

ancestor-focus Tracing descent relationships from some real or mythical ancestor.

antagonistic cooperation Cooperative behavior resulting from people's attempts to serve their long-run selfish interests. Also known as *enlightened self-interest*.

anthropological linguistics The study of human languages, their relationship to sociocultural patterns, and their changes through time.

anthropology The study of humankind.

archaeology The study of the past through examination of artifacts left by earlier peoples. *Prehistoric archaeology* studies peoples who left no written records, while *historic archaeology* studies societies which developed writing.

articulated economy One whose multiple economic sectors are highly interconnected so that changes in one sector contribute significantly to changes in other sectors. Such an economy has balance and diversification.

Asiatic mode of production As conceived by Marx and earlier historians, a type of agrarian society characterized by an absence of private property in land and a highly oppressive centralized state brought into existence by a need to manage complex irrigation works.

authority The socially legitimated right to command the actions of others.

average world citizen A high-level abstraction referring to the typical member of the typical form of human society prevailing in any given historical era.

avunculocality Residence of a newly married couple in the household of the husband's mother's brother.

balanced reciprocity See *reciprocity*.

band A stage of political evolution in which the primary political leader is a headman who has no capacity to compel the actions of others. Also, the group in a hunter-gatherer society that forages and resides together.

basic class locations In Wright's Marxian class scheme, class positions that are consistent with respect to the dimensions of ownership and authority.

beliefs Ideas shared among the members of a group or society about what is true and what is false.

big men Men of considerable prestige and renown who perform important political and economic leadership roles in many horticultural societies, especially those of Melanesia.

bilateral descent The formation of personal kindreds by tracing one's relatives through both males and females simultaneously.

bilocality Alternating residence of a newly married couple between the husband's and wife's kinship groups.

biological anthropology The study of human biological characteristics, especially as these involve the evolution of humankind over the past several million years.

biological evolution The genetic changes that occur over time within populations of organisms, most commonly as the result of the retention of favorable genetic mutations through environmental selection.

bourgeoisie In Marxian theory, the class owning capital.

bureaucracy A form of social organization in which rationalization, or deliberate calculation of the most efficient ways to achieve goals, is a supreme characteristic. Bureaucracies generally have highly formalized modes of organization, elaborate hierarchies of command, and a strong reliance upon elaborate written forms of communication.

bureaucratic See *bureaucracy.*

bureaucratic education A type of educational system designed as a recruitment device for personnel to occupational positions, or as a means of socializing the masses in order to gain their political compliance.

capitalism An economic system devoted to the production and sale of commodities on a market, with the objective of earning the maximum profit and accumulating profit over time.

cargo cult A type of revitalization movement occurring in the twentieth century in parts of Melanesia in which native populations organize themselves for what they believe will be the future return of their dead ancestors bringing with them large supplies of Western goods.

caste A highly rigid stratification system, generally limited to southern Asia, in which endogamous and highly impermeable social strata crystallize around distinct occupations.

chiefdom A centralized political system organized into a hierarchy of chiefs and subchiefs.

chiefly ownership A form of property rights characterized by the (at least theoretical) ownership of land by a ruling chief and his royal family.

church In Troeltsch's formulation, a type of religious organization coextensive with society as a whole, having an official ecclesiastical structure, placing great emphasis on established religious doctrines, and accepting the basic character of the secular world as it is.

clan A corporate descent group whose members cannot precisely identify their genealogical connections to one another but assume such connections nonetheless.

class See *social class.*

class structuration The degree of cultural distinctiveness of a social class and the level of impermeability among the classes in a class structure.

cognatic descent Descent in which both males and females are used to establish descent groupings.

commodification The process whereby economic production is increasingly governed by considerations of exchange-value.

commodity An object produced by humans that contains both use-value and exchange-value.

communal cult institution One characterized by groups of laymen who perform religious rites that are important to such groups as age grades, secret societies, the sexes, and kinship groups.

communal religion One containing communal, shamanic, and individualistic cult institutions.

competitive race relations A form of race relations characteristic of industrial societies in which the members of historically dominant and subordinate racial groups engage in extreme competition and conflict over access to economic and other social positions.

conflict An opposition of interests between and among various individuals and social groups, which may or may not be overtly observable, and which may or may not break out into open dispute or physical violence. For example, the opposition of interests between capitalists and workers to which Marx pointed.

Conflict Principle The notion that social conflict is a fundamental feature of human relationships and a major determinant of the organization of society.

conflict theory A theoretical strategy that attempts to understand social phenomena as the result of the antagonistic interests and aims of individuals and social groups.

consanguinity The existence of kinship ties based on genetic relatedness.

contest-mobility educational system One in which no official tracking or channeling of students exists, and in which students are in principle free to compete for as much education as their talents and inclinations allow.

contradictory class locations In Wright's Marxian class scheme, class positions that are inconsistent or ambiguous with respect to the dimensions of ownership and authority.

convergent evolution Changes in two or more originally dissimilar societies that make them increasingly alike.

core Those societies within the capitalist world-economy that are the most technologically and economically advanced, that concentrate on the production of the most advanced commodities, and that usually contain the most powerful governments and military structures.

corporate descent group A network of kinspeople who trace descent from a common ancestor and who function as a single, discrete group.

corvée A system whereby the elite groups of highly stratified agrarian societies recruit large teams of laborers for special work projects.

cottage industry See *putting-out system.*

counterculture A smaller culture contained within a larger culture, but one that generally rejects much of the larger culture.

credential inflation A process whereby educational credentials (diplomas and degrees) decline in value over time because of the increasing number of people who possess them. See also *qualificationism.*

cult A small and generally short-lived religious group whose doctrines and practices represent an extreme departure from the established religious traditions of a society.

cult institution A set of religious rituals having the same goal, rationalized by a set of similar beliefs, and supported by the same social group.

cultural anthropology The study of patterns of social life, with an emphasis on primitive and contemporary peasant societies.

cultural relativism The doctrine that cultural patterns can be evaluated only on their own terms, not in terms of any other patterns. Cultural relativism in the strict sense assumes that all cultural patterns are "equally valid," and that the culture itself makes anything right or wrong, good or bad, etc.

culture The total lifeways characteristic of the members of a society that are socially learned and shared, including technology, knowledge, and organized patterns of action and thought.

demesne The "home-farm" of the feudal manor, or the land held directly by the landlord and cultivated exclusively for his own use.

demographic See *demography*.

demographic transition A process of demographic change associated with large-scale industrialization in which mortality and fertility rates drop sharply and family size declines markedly.

demography Features of a human population, such as its size, density, and age and sex distributions.

denomination A conventional and respectable religious organization limited in its membership to individuals drawn from certain classes, races, or regions.

dependency theory An approach to the problem of economic underdevelopment that holds that underdevelopment results from the economic dependency to which many nations have been historically subjected. See *economic dependency*.

devolution Social change resulting in the emergence of characteristics typical of an earlier stage of sociocultural evolution.

dialectical materialism See *historical materialism*.

differential access to resources The existence of unequal levels of control over the means of production by different segments of a sociocultural system.

diffusion The spread of cultural elements from one society to another.

disarticulated economy One whose multiple sectors do not significantly interrelate such that growth in one sector contributes little or nothing to the growth of other sectors. Such an economy is characterized by a lack of diversification and by exaggerated specialization, typically of the raw-materials-production-for-export sector.

discrimination Unequal and unfair treatment of one social group (race, ethnic group, sex, etc.) by another.

distribution See *economic distribution*.

divergent evolution Changes in two or more originally similar societies that make them increasingly different.

ecclesia A religious organization similar to the church but less successfully meeting the needs of many of its members.

ecclesiastical cult institution One containing a specialized professional priesthood holding full-time bureaucratic offices.

ecology The natural environment to which human societies must adjust, as well as the relationships between this environment and social patterns.

economic dependency A process whereby one society's economy falls under the domination of a foreign society.

economic distribution The set of social relationships through which people allocate the goods and services they produce.

economic exchange The social relationships through which people transfer valuables between and among one another.

economic production The set of social relationships through which people create valuables.

economic surplus A quantity of economic valuables above and beyond that necessary for the subsistence of the members who produce such valuables.

economy The set of social relationships through which people organize the production, distribution, and exchange of valuables.

education Any formalized or semiformalized system of cultural or intellectual instruction.

ego-focus Tracing descent relationships from the point of view of some living individual.

empirical Referring to the making of systematic observations and the collection of data in order to test the value of proposed ideas.

endogamy The tendency for persons to marry members of their own social group, especially their own race, ethnic group, religious group, or social class.

enlightened self-interest See *antagonistic cooperation*.

established sect A religious sect having evolved somewhat in the direction of conventionality and respectability.

ethnic group A social group or category having a socially meaningful distinctiveness that rests on cultural criteria.

ethnocentrism A universal social doctrine holding that one's own culture or society is superior to all others. Literally, "my group is the center."

ethnography A detailed written account of a culture by a foreign observer.

ethnomethodology A theoretical strategy in microsociology that resembles symbolic interactionism but is even more extreme in its emphasis on shared definitions of reality. Ethnomethodologists attempt to study, often in great detail, the ways in which people construct their definitions of social reality.

evolution See *biological evolution* and *sociocultural evolution*.

evolutionary theory A theoretical strategy that attempts to describe and explain directional sequences of long-term social change. *Functionalist evolutionary* theories tend to view long-term changes as increases in social complexity that produce increasingly well-adapted societies. *Materialist evolutionary* theories explain the major transformations that occur in human social life as responses to changing material conditions.

exchange See *economic exchange*.

exchange-value The value a good will fetch when it is exchanged for other goods.

exogamy The prohibition against marriage within a kinship group, usually a corporate descent group.

exploitation An economic process that occurs when one party compels another to give up more than it receives in return.

extended family A number of related nuclear families bound together and functioning as a definite social unit.

feudalism An economic and political system found in some agrarian societies in which a private landlord class holds land in the form of fiefs. See also *fief* and *vassalage*.

feudal state An agrarian state characterized by the fragmentation of power, that is, its dispersal among a range of political leaders, each of whom has control of a limited territory.

fief A grant of land given by an overlord to a vassal (lesser lord) in return for the performance of such obligations as military service and personal protection.

forced labor Any labor system in which workers are not free to negotiate the kind and amount of labor they will perform and their level of compensation.

freedom In the Western individualist tradition, a relative absence of constraints on the individual's capacity to act and think according to his or her own personal standards. In the Marxian tradition, the full opportunity for persons to realize their basic nature as members of the human species.

functional analysis A viewpoint that assumes that social phenomena can be understood in terms of their usefulness in fulfilling the aims of individuals or groups. Not to be confused with *functionalism*.

functionalism A contemporary theoretical strategy that analyzes social phenomena in terms of the functions they perform in maintaining the existence or stability of society. Functionalists usually assume that societies have needs much as organisms do, and that they must develop particular structures to satisfy these needs.

gender The socially and culturally constructed beliefs and practices associated with the biological differentiation between males and females. Compare *sex*.

gender inequality The presence of unequal levels of power and privilege between men and women, including unequal evaluations of men's and women's worth.

generalized reciprocity See *reciprocity*.

geopolitics The intersection of politics and geography. Geopolitical considerations are those that involve the territorial and diplomatic relations among states, either regionally or worldwide. See *interstate system*.

goal displacement A phenomenon that occurs in modern bureaucracies when the means people develop to achieve certain goals end up becoming the goals themselves.

Herrenvolk democracy A parliamentary democracy that limits the application of its democratic principles to a dominant racial group.

historical materialism The original theoretical strategy of Marx and Engels, which was the first systematic form of sociological materialism. Also called *dialectical materialism*. See also *materialism*.

history The study of the past, both descriptively and theoretically.

horticulture A simple form of agriculture in which small plots of land (gardens) are crudely prepared and cultivated through the use of hand tools.

human nature Those psychological and biological qualities universally characteristic of the human species.

hunter-gatherer society One whose members make a living primarily or exclusively through the hunting of wild animals and the collection of wild vegetable matter.

hypergyny The marriage of a woman to a man of higher social rank.

idealism In social science, the doctrine that the basic features of human social life result from the nature of human thought and ideas.

idealist See *idealism*.

ideological superstructure The organized set of beliefs, values, feelings, and symbols shared by the members of a sociocultural system.

inclusive fitness The sum total of an individual organism's own fitness and the fitness that organism has represented in the genes it shares with related organisms. Also known as *kin selection*.

individualism As conceived by the French sociologist Emile Durkheim, a social and moral doctrine that treats the individual person as the principal object of moral concern. Under this social philosophy the individual's rights, needs, aims, etc. are promoted through the very organization of society itself.

individualistic cult institution One in which each individual performs his or her own religious rites as the need arises.

industrial capitalism The form of economic activity that emerged in Europe with the Industrial Revolution and that today characterizes most of the societies of Western Europe, North America, Australia, and Japan. In Marx's formulation, it involves the making of profits through the exploitation of labor power in the very process of production itself.

industrialization The process by which a society comes to be characterized by an economic system and a mode of social life based around machinery and the factory system of manufacturing. See *mechanization*.

industrial society One having acquired a level of technology based upon the use of machines to replace hand labor and the widespread use of these machines in the process of economic production.

influence The process whereby the thoughts and actions of one party produce modifications in the thoughts and actions of other parties.

intensification of production An increase in the expenditure of energy involved in carrying out economic production. This may occur through greater work inputs, use of more natural resources, advancement of the level of technology, or any combination of these.

intensive horticultural society A horticultural society whose members have adopted more energy-intensive means of cultivation, such as shortening the fallow period of land or using more advanced tools and techniques of production.

interstate system The complex system of competing and conflicting nation-states that is closely intertwined with the capitalist world-economy.

kindred A small-scale personal kin group generally activated only at special times, such as ritual occasions or the need for assistance.

kin selection See *inclusive fitness*.

labor power In Marxian theory, the capacity of the worker to work.

Law of Least Effort The principle that, other things being equal, people prefer to carry out activities with a minimum amount of energy expenditure.

legitimacy See *legitimation*.

legitimation The process whereby certain social relationships are deemed to be morally right and proper.

lineage A corporate descent group whose members can actually identify their genealogical connections to one another.

lineage ownership Communal ownership of land by large-scale kinship groups.

macrosociology That type of sociology that studies large-scale forms of social organization, especially entire societies and the world network of societies. Macrosociology is in general comparatively and historically focused.

manor The lands and the labor force controlled by a feudal landlord.

market An economic institution that involves the buying and selling of goods and services in a socially organized manner.

market-dominated society A society having both markets and marketplaces and in which market principles govern economic activity.

marketless society A society having neither markets nor marketplaces.

marketplace A physical site where market activities occur.

material infrastructure The raw materials and social forms used by the members of a sociocultural system to meet their needs in regard to economic production and biological reproduction.

materialism In social science, the viewpoint that the basic features of human social life derive from the "material conditions of social life," such as the economy, the physical environment, and the level of technology.

materialist See *materialism*.

matrilineal descent See *matriliny*.

matriliny Descent traced only through females.

matrilocality Residence of a newly married couple in the household of the wife's mother.

mechanization The process whereby machinery and other advanced forms of technology are increasingly applied to economic production. See *industrialization*.

mercantilism An economic practice in the seventeenth and early eighteenth centuries whereby governments granted monopolies to European trading companies so that these companies could make large profits from their trade with foreign colonies.

merchant capitalism In Marx's formulation, an early form of capitalism, prevailing approximately in the years 1450–1750, in which trading companies made profits throughout the world by capitalizing on favorable terms of trade.

microsociology That type of sociology that investigates patterns of social behavior that occur in small groups and face-to-face social relationships.

millenarian movement See *revitalization movement*.

mode of production A concept used by Marx and Engels to refer to a society's level of technological development combined with the overall organization of its economy (especially in terms of the ownership of property).

modernization theory An approach to the problem of economic underdevelopment that postulates that contemporary underdeveloped nations remain in a "traditional" state because they contain certain internal deficiences that constitute obstacles to development.

monogamy The marriage of one man to one woman.

monopoly capitalism That stage of capitalism, generally beginning in the last quarter of the nineteenth century, characterized by the rise of the giant corporation as the basic economic unit and the emergence of extensive foreign investment of core nations in the capitalist periphery.

monotheistic religion One containing individualistic, shamanic, and communal cult institutions in addition to ecclesiastical cult institutions organized around the concept of a single high god.

national states Those highly centralized, bureaucratically organized, and militarily powerful states that arose in Europe between the sixteenth and nineteenth centuries. Compare *absolutist monarchy*.

natolocality Residence of husband and wife in the separate households in which they resided before marriage.

natural selection The process whereby favorable genetic materials are retained because they have high survival value and unfavorable genetic materials are eliminated because they have low survival value. The retention and proliferation of new genetic materials amounts to *evolution*.

Neolithic Revolution That major technological transformation, beginning about 10,000 years ago, most importantly associated with the beginnings of agriculture.

neolocality Residence of a newly married couple in an independent household of its own.

norms Socially shared rules defining forms of behavior that are prohibited and forms that are desirable or essential.

nuclear family A kinship unit consisting of the married spouses and their immediate offspring who maintain a common household and act together as a distinct group.

Olympian religion One containing individualistic, shamanic, and communal cult institutions in addition to ecclesiastical cult institutions of the polytheistic type.

Oriental despotism As formulated by Karl Wittfogel, a type of agrarian state characterized by massive centralization of power, extensive involvement in public works projects, and brutal tyrannization of the mass of the subject population. See also *Asiatic mode of production.*

parallel evolution Changes in two or more societies that are similar in form and in the rate of change.

parliamentary democracy A type of government resting on the existence of a parliamentary or congressional body to which other segments of government must be responsible; the regular, free, and fair election of government officials; and the granting of individual rights and freedoms to the mass of the population.

partial redistribution See *redistribution.*

party A social group whose members aim to exert a certain degree and type of power in the political realm of society.

pastoralism See *pastoral society.*

pastoral society A society whose members survive primarily through the tending of animal herds.

paternalistic race relations A form of race relations characteristic of preindustrial societies in which the members of one racial group relegate members of another racial group to a subordinate social status, regarding them essentially as childlike beings needing the "fatherly" protection and guidance of the dominant racial group.

patrilineal descent See *patriliny.*

patriliny Descent traced only through males.

patrilocality Residence of the newly married couple in the household of the husband's father.

patrimonial ownership A form of seigneurial ownership in which land is privately owned by a landlord class and inherited in family lines.

peasant A farmer, ordinarily found in an agrarian or contemporary underdeveloped society, who typically exists in an economically and politically subordinate relationship to the principal owner or controller of the land from which he or she gains his or her subsistence.

peripheral market society A society having marketplaces, but in which market principles are not the primary organizers of economic life.

periphery The least economically developed part of the capitalist world-economy, extensively subjected to high levels of surplus expropriation by the core.

polity The socially organized means whereby a society maintains internal law and order and carries out relationships with other societies.

polyandry The marriage of one woman to two or more men.

polygyny The marriage of one man to two or more women.

population pressure A level of population density that, for any given society at a given level of technology, produces a deterioration in the economic standard of living.

postsocialism A term characterizing the economic and political situation of those Eastern European societies (including the former Soviet Union) that after 1989 experienced profound economic and political changes involving the delegitimation of the Communist party and the shift toward private ownership in the economy.

postsocialist societies See *postsocialism.*

potlatch An elaborate giveaway feast prominent among many of the Indian tribes of the Northwest Coast of North America in recent centuries.

power The capacity of one party to compel the actions of other parties even against their will.

practical-skill education A type of educational system primarily designed to teach certain technical skills.

prebendal ownership A form of seigneurial ownership in which land is owned by a powerful government that assigns officials to oversee its cultivation and make their living from it.

precapitalist economy See *precapitalist society.*

precapitalist society One existing before the emergence of modern capitalism, or not yet significantly characterized by capitalist economic features.

preindustrial society One existing prior to the Industrial Revolution, or not yet having acquired an industrial level of technology.

prejudice An attitude of dislike or hostility on the part of a member of one racial or ethnic group toward the members of some other racial or ethnic group.

prestige The social honor or respect accorded individuals or groups.

primitive communism A form of economic ownership in which all individuals and groups have equal access to the resources of nature that sustain life.

primitive society One that has not yet developed writing, that has a relatively simple level of hunting-gathering, pastoral, or agricultural technology, and that is strongly organized according to patterns of kinship.

primordialism In regard to the study of ethnicity, the view that ethnic identities are first-order human concerns that are difficult if not impossible to eradicate.

Principle of Infrastructural Determinism The notion that the material infrastructure has a logical priority in the creation of social life, and that the character of this component of society has a major influence on the character of the other societal components.

Principle of Sociocultural Adaptation The notion that the features of social life are created by people as rational responses to the basic problems they face and the needs and wants they have.

Principle of Sociocultural Integration The notion that the various components of society form together into an overall system.

pristine state A state that arises under conditions in which no preexisting state is to be found.

private property The ownership and control of important productive resources by a small part of a group or society.

privilege The material benefits accruing to individuals or groups, or the opportunity to acquire such material benefits.

production See *economic production.*

production-for-exchange A type of economic production in which the aim of the producers is to create goods that will generate value when they are exchanged for other valuables, especially money.

production-for-use A type of economic production in which the aim of the producers is to create goods that have direct or indirect consumption value.

profit That portion of surplus value that remains once capitalists have met additional expenses of production, such as the payment of rent and taxes. See also *surplus value.*

progress A betterment or improvement in social life and its various features.

proletarianization The process whereby the contractual form of labor known as wage labor increasingly becomes the dominant form of labor organization. See *wage labor.*

proletariat In Marxian theory, the class that must sell its labor power to capitalists in order to earn a living.

protoculture The capacity of some infrahuman animals to engage in limited forms of tool use and limited symbol manipulation.

pure redistribution See *redistribution*.

putting-out system An early type of capitalist industry in which workers remained in their homes to produce goods destined to be sold by capitalist entrepreneurs. The entrepreneurs did not affect the production process except to advance raw materials and partial wages with their orders for goods. Also known as *cottage industry*.

qualificationism The process whereby an educational system comes to be oriented around the pursuit of education for its credential value rather than for its intrinsic merits. Also, the expansion of the credentializing character of an educational system over time. See also *credential inflation*.

race A category of persons who are identified by themselves and by others as having a socially meaningful distinctiveness that rests on biological criteria.

racism An elaborate ideology holding that one race is biologically superior and that all others are biologically inferior to it. This doctrine regards the unequal economic and social positions of different races as the outcome of their genetic differences.

rank society An unstratified society in which there is a limited number of high-status social positions for which individuals vigorously compete.

rationalization Weber's concept referring to the tendency of modern Western society to become increasingly subject to social relationships guided by the deliberate calculation of the most efficient ways to achieve stated goals.

reciprocity The obligation to repay others for what they have given to us, as well as the act of repayment itself. *Balanced reciprocity* occurs when the obligation to reciprocate is specific as to time and amount. *Generalized reciprocity* occurs when the obligation for repayment is vague and non-specific.

redistribution A process of economic distribution in which goods are brought to a central source (person or group) and then returned in some manner to the points from which they originated. *Pure redistribution* occurs when all that is funneled in one direction is re-funneled in the other. *Partial redistribution* occurs when only some of what is received is returned to the original parties.

relative immiseration, thesis of The view that the economic gap between core and periphery in the capitalist world-economy is widening, and thus that the overall quality of human life in the periphery is deteriorating relative to the core (rather than absolutely). Compare *absolute immiseration, thesis of*.

religion An organized set of beliefs and practices resting on unproved faith and postulating the existence of supernatural beings, powers, or forces that act upon the physical and social world.

repression Any action by a state that forcefully prevents individuals from taking actions perceived as harmful to that state.

revitalization movement A socioreligious movement in which people attempt to bring about basic changes in the structure of society and establish a more meaningful and rewarding existence. Also known as *millenarian movement*.

revolution A rapid, basic transformation of a society's state and class structures that is accompanied and carried through by class-based revolts from below (Skocpol).

rule of hypo-descent A principle of racial classification, common especially in the United States, which assigns all offspring of racially heterogeneous parents to the socially subordinate racial group.

rules of descent The means by which the members of a society organize networks of kinspeople and specify the rights and duties of these kinspeople toward each other.

rules of residence The means by which the members of a society organize themselves into households or domestic residential groups.

scarcity An insufficient quantity of material resources relative to the technological level, the degree of population pressure, and the standard of living experienced by any group or society.

science A mode of intellectual inquiry seeking a coherent theoretical understanding of the world by reliance upon empirical procedures, that is, upon systematic observation and data collection. Also, the accumulated results of such intellectual activity.

scientific See *science*.

secondary state A state that has arisen as the result of the presence of one or more preexisting states.

sect A small religious organization identifying itself as a community of select believers, having no official ecclesiastical structure, and generally maintaining a hostile stance toward the secular world as well as toward established religious organizations.

secularization The process whereby the influence of religion in social life is steadily reduced.

seigneurial ownership Ownership of land by a class of landlords having the power to impose severe penalties on other persons for the use of the land.

semiperiphery That segment of the capitalist world-economy that is neither as highly exploitative as the core nor as

exploited as the periphery. This intermediate zone of the world-economy contains a mixture of core-like and periphery-like economic activities.

sex The biological differentiation between males and females. Compare *gender*.

shamanic cult institution One in which part-time religious specialists known as shamans perform religious rites in return for a fee.

shamanic religion A type of religion containing only individualistic and shamanic cult institutions.

sign An element of animal communication whose meaning is determined by biological inheritance.

simple commodity production A precapitalist form of economic activity in which producers generate commodities designed to be exchanged for other commodities of equal value.

simple horticultural society One whose members earn a living through reliance upon the simplest agricultural techniques. Normally this involves long-fallow cultivation of small garden plots using hand tools.

slavery A form of labor organization in which some persons are legally owned as a form of human property, are compelled to work by their owners, and are deprived of most or all political rights.

social class In conventional sociology, a category of persons sharing a similar level of privilege and social status by virtue of their occupational roles. In Marxian sociology, a social group whose members share the same relationship to the ownership of productive resources, and who also share similar levels of control over their own or others' work. Compare *social stratum*.

social closure The tendency for social groups to use certain social criteria as marks of distinction whereby they can monopolize resources, such monopolization being thought essential to the acquisition of privilege and prestige.

social differentiation The increasing social complexity that frequently accompanies social change.

social inequality The existence of unequal levels of social influence or prestige among individual members of a society.

social influence See *influence*.

social institution Any part of a sociocultural system that involves established and regularized patterns of social behavior and consciousness, e.g., the economy, the polity, kinship, religion.

socialism In Marx's original works, a form of society in which private property and social classes do not exist, in which work is no longer treated as a commodity, and in which people have the genuine possibility of achieving human freedom. See also *state socialism*.

socialization The process whereby the members of a society transmit the content of their culture to new generations through various forms of child training and other instruction.

social mobility The upward or downward movement of individuals between positions in the class structure of a society.

social stratification The existence within a society (or world-system) of social groups that possess unequal levels of social power, privilege, and prestige.

social stratum A category of persons occupying the same approximate level of power, privilege, and prestige within a society. Compare *social class*.

social structure The organized patterns of social behavior common to the members of a sociocultural system.

societal needs A concept fundamental to functionalism that assumes that societies have basic requirements in much the same way that organisms or human individuals do.

sociobiology A theoretical strategy that attempts to explain various features of human social life as the result of certain universal biological characteristics of humankind. The basic concept of this theory is *inclusive fitness*. Sociobiology holds that much of the behavior of organisms, humans included, derives from their strivings to maximize their inclusive fitness, or the reepresentation of their genes in future generations.

sociocultural adaptation See *adaptation*.

sociocultural continuity The preservation of the basic features of a society over time.

sociocultural evolution Qualitative structural transformations within a sociocultural system (or one or more of its parts) that exhibit a directional pattern.

sociocultural extinction The elimination of a sociocultural system, either through the death of its members or through its absorption into another sociocultural system.

sociocultural system A social collectivity having organized its social life culturally.

sociology The scientific study of human social life in all its aspects.

sponsored-mobility educational system A type of educational system in which students are channeled into different educational tracks early in their careers based on their performance on standardized examinations.

state A political system claiming a monopoly over the use of the means of violence within a specified territory.

state breakdown A crisis within a government so severe that it cripples its capacity to govern.

state socialism A form of economy in which the government is the principal owner and manager of the means of production.

state socialist See *state socialism*.

status group A social group whose members share a similar lifestyle or cultural outlook and a similar level of social status or prestige.

status-group education A type of educational system whose primary aim is to disseminate knowledge and styles of behavior, the possession of which serves to symbolize and reinforce the prestige and privilege of elite groups in highly stratified societies.

stem family A type of extended family in which an older couple live together with one of their sons and his wife and children.

subculture A smaller culture contained within a larger culture that generally accepts the broader patterns of the larger culture.

surplus expropriation The siphoning off of the economic surplus produced by one group into the hands of another group by means of one or another form of compulsion.

surplus value In Marxian theory, the increment in value that the capitalist generates over and above the original capital investment. See also *profit*.

symbol In communication, an element of speech that is arbitrary, or whose meaning is determined by social definition rather than by biological inheritance. Otherwise, any physical or social invention that signifies a socially shared meaning.

symbolic interactionism A major theoretical strategy in microsociology that stresses the definitional and subjective elements of social life. Symbolic interactionists place great emphasis on how people use symbols to construct shared definitions of reality and on how these shared definitions shape their social actions.

technology The material means, which include tools, techniques, and knowledge, whereby humans meet their needs and desires.

teleological explanation An attempt to explain the existence of a phenomenon by uncovering the alleged purposes it seeks to fulfill or some goal or end state it is seeking to attain.

teleology See *teleological explanation.*

theoretical strategy A highly generalized set of concepts, assumptions, and principles designed to explain phenomena in the broadest sense.

theory A statement (or interrelated set of statements) designed to explain some particular phenomenon or category of related phenomena.

theory of kin selection The basic premise of the sociobiological theoretical strategy that holds that many forms of human social behavior represent the efforts of individuals to maximize their inclusive fitness. See also *inclusive fitness.*

theory of surplus value Marx's theory holding that capitalist profits derive from paying workers less than the full value of the commodities they produce. See also *surplus value.*

thesis of absolute immiseration See *absolute immiseration, thesis of.*

thesis of relative immiseration See *relative immiseration, thesis of.*

totalitarian dictatorship A type of government, generally associated with modern state socialist societies, in which all power is concentrated in the hands of a governmental elite that rules the people without regard to any concept of "popular sentiment" or individual rights and liberties.

transnational corporation A company that has branches of production in several countries.

tribe A network of bands or villages sharing a common culture and speaking the same language. Also, a level of political evolution characterized by the absence of centralized authority and political leaders with the power to compel the actions of others.

underdeveloped society One of the least technologically and economically advanced members of the capitalist world-economy.

undeveloped society A society outside the framework of a capitalist world-economy, which thus remains in a precapitalist and preindustrial state.

unilineal descent Descent traced only through a single line, that is, through males or through females.

unilineal descent groups See *unilineal descent.*

use-value The utilitarian value of a good, or the benefit it confers when it is consumed.

values Standards of worth held in common by the members of a society or any of its subgroups.

vassalage The personal tie between lords in a feudal society created by the granting of a fief from an overlord to a lesser lord (vassal), who in turn takes an oath to serve and protect his overlord. See also *fief.*

wage labor A labor relationship in which workers are legally free to bargain with employers for a specified rate of compensation for their work and the conditions under which they will perform that work.

world-economy A world-system lacking political centralization and that therefore contains within it a plurality of competing states. A world-economy is characterized by economic relations of production and exchange that serve to integrate it. See also *core, periphery,* and *semiperiphery.*

world-empire A world-system that is politically and militarily centralized or unified.

world-system Any relatively large social system having a high degree of autonomy, an extensive division of labor, and a plurality of cultural groups.

world-system theory A theoretical approach designed to explain many features of the evolution of capitalism since the sixteenth century. It holds that capitalism has evolved as a hierarchical arrangement of exploiting and exploited nations, each of which can be properly understood only as part of the entire system. As applied specifically to the underdeveloped nations of the contemporary world, it predicts that stagnation or deterioration will continue to be the lot of most. However, it does identify certain conditions that allow a few nations to improve their status at critical historical junctures.

Bibliography

Aberle, David F. 1961. "Matrilineal descent in cross-cultural perspective." In David M. Schneider and Kathleen Gough (eds.), *Matrilineal Kinship.* Berkeley: University of California Press.

Abonyi, Arpad. 1982. "Eastern Europe's reintegration." In Christopher Chase-Dunn (ed.), *Socialist States in the World-System.* Beverly Hills, Calif.: Sage.

Abu-Lughod, Janet. 1988. "The shape of the world system in the thirteenth century." *Studies in Comparative International Development* 22 (4):3–24.

——. 1989. *Before European Hegemony: The World-System A.D. 1250–1350.* New York: Oxford University Press.

Adams, Robert McC. 1966. *The Evolution of Urban Society.* Chicago: Aldine.

——. 1972. "Demography and the 'Urban Revolution' in lowland Mesopotamia." In Brian Spooner (ed.), *Population Growth: Anthropological Implications.* Cambridge, Mass.: MIT Press.

Aganbegyan, Abel. 1988. "New directions in Soviet economics." *New Left Review* 169:87–93.

——. 1989. *Inside Perestroika: The Future of the Soviet Economy.* Translated by Helen Szamuely. New York: Harper & Row.

Alderson, Arthur S. 1997. "Globalization, deindustrialization, and the great u-turn: The growth of direct investment in 18 OECD nations, 1967–1990." Ph.D. dissertation, University of North Carolina at Chapel Hill.

Alderson, Arthur S., and Stephen K. Sanderson. 1991. "Historic European household structures and the capitalist world-economy." *Journal of Family History* 16:419–432.

Alexander, Jeffrey C. 1982. *Theoretical Logic in Sociology. Volume 1: Positivism, Presuppositions, and Current Controversies.* Berkeley: University of California Press.

———. 1984. *Theoretical Logic in Sociology. Volume 4. The Modern Reconstruction of Classical Thought: Talcott Parsons.* Berkeley: University of California Press.

Alexander, Jeffrey C. (ed.). 1985. *Neofunctionalism.* Beverly Hills, Calif: Sage.

Alexander, Richard D. 1987. *The Biology of Moral Systems.* Hawthorne, N.Y.: Aldine de Gruyter.

Amin, Samir. 1974. *Accumulation on a World Scale.* New York: Monthly Review Press.

———. 1991. "The ancient world-systems versus the modern capitalist world-system." *Review* 14:349–385.

Anderson, Charles H., and Jeffrey Gibson. 1978. *Toward a New Sociology.* Third edition. Homewood, Ill.: Dorsey Press.

Anderson, Michael. 1980. *Approaches to the History of the Western Family, 1500–1914.* London: Macmillan Press.

Anderson, Perry. 1974a. *Passages from Antiquity to Feudalism.* London: New Left Books.

———. 1974b. *Lineages of the Absolutist State.* London: New Left Books.

Andorka, Rudolf, and Tamas Farago. 1983. "Preindustrial household structure in Hungary." In Richard Wall, Jean Rodin, and Peter Laslett (eds.), *Family Forms in Historic Europe.* Cambridge: Cambridge University Press.

Angel, J. Lawrence. 1975. "Paleoecology, paleodemography, and health." In Steven Polgar (ed.), *Population, Ecology, and Social Evolution.* The Hague: Mouton.

Apter, David E. 1987. *Rethinking Development: Modernization, Dependency, and Post-Modern Politics.* Beverly Hills, Calif.: Sage.

Arizpe, Lourdes. 1977. "Women in the informal labor sector: The case of Mexico City." *Signs: Journal of Women in Culture and Society* 3:25–37.

Armstrong, et al. 1993. "Uncovering reality: Excavating women's rights in African family law." *International Journal of Law and the Family* 7:314–369.

Arrighi, Giovanni. 1982. "A crisis of hegemony." In Samir Amin et al., *Dynamics of Global Crisis.* New York: Monthly Review Press.

Aseniero, George. 1994. "South Korean and Taiwanese development: The transnational context." *Review* 17:275–336.

Aston, T. H., and C. H. E. Philpin (eds.). 1985. *The Brenner Debate: Agrarian Class Structure and Economic Development in Pre-Industrial Europe.* Cambridge: Cambridge University Press.

Atkinson, A. B. 1983. *The Economics of Inequality.* Second edition. Oxford: Oxford University Press.

Baca-Zinn, Maxine, and D. Stanley Eitzen. 1993. *Diversity in American Families.* Third edition. New York: Harper Collins.

Baran, Paul, and E. J. Hobsbawm. 1973. "The stages of economic growth: A review." In Charles K. Wilber (ed.), *The Political Economy of Development and Underdevelopment.* New York: Random House.

Barash, David P. 1977. *Sociobiology and Behavior.* New York: Elsevier.

Barfield, Thomas J. 1989. *The Perilous Frontier: Nomadic Empires and China*. Oxford: Basil Blackwell.

Barnet, Richard J., and Ronald E. Müller. 1974. *Global Reach: The Power of the Multinational Corporations*. New York: Simon & Schuster (Touchstone).

Barrett, Richard E., and Martin King Whyte. 1982. "Dependency theory and Taiwan: Analysis of a deviant case." *American Journal of Sociology* 87:1064–1089.

Barth, Fredrik. 1961. *Nomads of South Persia*. New York: Humanities Press.

Bates, Daniel G., and Fred Plog. 1991. *Human Adaptive Strategies*. New York: McGraw-Hill.

Beals, Ralph L., and Harry Hoijer. 1971. *An Introduction to Anthropology*. Fourth edition. New York: Macmillan.

Beard, Charles. 1962. *An Economic Interpretation of the Constitution of the United States*. New York: Macmillan. (Originally published 1913.)

Beauchamp, Edward R. (ed.). 1991. *Windows on Japanese Education*. Westport, Conn.: Greenwood Press.

Beaud, Michel. 1983. *A History of Capitalism, 1500–1980*. New York: Monthly Review Press.

Becker, Howard S. 1963. *Outsiders: Studies in the Sociology of Deviance*. New York: Free Press.

Bell, Daniel. 1973. *The Coming of Post-Industrial Society*. New York: Basic Books.

Bellah, Robert N. 1964. "Religious evolution." *American Sociological Review* 29:358–374.

———. 1970. *Beyond Belief: Essays on Religion in a Post-Traditional World*. New York: Harper & Row.

Benavot, Aaron, and Phyllis Riddle. 1988. "The expansion of primary education, 1870–1940: Trends and issues." *Sociology of Education* 61:191–210.

Benedict, Ruth. 1934. *Patterns of Culture*. Boston: Houghton Mifflin.

Bennett, H. S. 1937. *Life on the English Manor: A Study of Peasant Conditions, 1150–1400*. Cambridge: Cambridge University Press.

Berg, Ivar. 1971. *Education and Jobs: The Great Training Robbery*. Boston: Beacon Press.

Berger, Brigitte, and Peter L. Berger. 1983. *The War over the Family: Capturing the Middle Ground*. Garden City, N.Y.: Doubleday (Anchor Books).

Berger, Peter L. 1986. *The Capitalist Revolution*. New York: Basic Books.

Berger, Peter L., and Thomas Luckmann. 1966. *The Social Construction of Reality*. Garden City, N.Y.: Doubleday (Anchor Books).

Berger, Stephen D. 1974. "Review of Daniel Bell, *The Coming of Post-Industrial Society*." *Contemporary Sociology* 3:101–105.

Berkner, Lutz K. 1972. "The stem family and the developmental cycle of the peasant household: An eighteenth-century Austrian example." *American Historical Review* 77:398–418.

Berkner, Lutz K., and John W. Shaffer. 1978. "The joint family in the Nivernais." *Journal of Family History* 3:150–162.

Berreman, Gerald D. (ed.). 1981. *Social Inequality: Comparative and Developmental Approaches*. New York: Academic Press.

Bettinger, Robert L. 1991. *Hunter-Gatherers: Archaeological and Evolutionary Theory*. New York: Plenum.

Betzig, Laura L. 1986. *Despotism and Differential Reproduction*. Hawthorne, N.Y.: Aldine de Gruyter.

Bickerton, Derek. 1990. *Language and Species*. Chicago: University of Chicago Press.

Bienefeld, Manfred. 1981. "Dependency and the newly industrialising countries (NICs): Towards a reappraisal." In Dudley Seers (ed.), *Dependency Theory: A Critical Assessment*. London: Frances Pinter.

Binford, Lewis R. 1968. "Post-Pleistocene adaptations." In S. R. Binford and L. R. Binford (eds.), *New Perspectives in Archaeology*. Chicago: Aldine.

Biraben, J. N. 1970. "Document." *Annales de démographie historique,* pp. 441–462.

Bischof, Norbert. 1975. "Comparative ethology of incest avoidance." In Robin Fox (ed.), *Biosocial Anthropology*. London: Malaby Press.

Blackburn, Robin. 1988. *The Overthrow of Colonial Slavery, 1776–1848.* London: Verso.

———. 1991. "Fin de siècle: Socialism after the crash." In Robin Blackburn (ed.), *After the Fall: The Failure of Communism and the Future of Socialism.* London: Verso.

Blau, Peter, and Otis Dudley Duncan. 1967. *The American Occupational Structure.* New York: Free Press.

Bluestone, Barry, and Bennett Harrison. 1982. *The Deindustrialization of America.* New York: Basic Books.

Blomstrom, Magnus, and Bjorn Hettne. 1984. *Development Theory in Transition.* London: Zed Books.

Blumberg, Rae Lesser. 1978. *Stratification: Socioeconomic and Sexual Inequality.* Dubuque, Iowa: Brown.

———. 1984. "A general theory of gender stratification." In Randall Collins (ed.), *Sociological Theory 1984.* San Francisco: Jossey-Bass.

Blumberg, Rae Lesser, and Robert F. Winch. 1977. "The curvilinear relation between societal complexity and familial complexity." In Robert F. Winch, *Familial Organization.* New York: Free Press.

Blumer, Herbert, 1969. *Symbolic Interactionism.* Englewood Cliffs, N.J.: Prentice-Hall.

Bohannan, Paul, and George Dalton (eds.). 1962. *Markets in Africa.* Evanston, Ill.:

Northwestern University Press.

Boli, John, Francisco O. Ramirez, and John W. Meyer. 1985. "Explaining the origins and expansion of mass education." *Comparative Education Review* 29:145–170.

Bollen, Kenneth. 1983. "World system position, dependency, and democracy: The cross-national evidence." *American Sociological Review* 48:468–479.

Bonacich, Edna. 1972. "A theory of ethnic antagonism: The split labor market." *American Sociological Review* 37:547–559.

———. 1979. "The past, present, and future of split labor market theory." In Cora B. Marrett and Cheryl Leggon (eds.), *Research in Race and Ethnic Relations.* Volume 1. Greenwich, Conn.: JAI Press.

———. 1981. "Capitalism and race relations in South Africa: A split labor market analysis." In Maurice Zeitlin (ed.), *Political Power and Social Theory.* Volume 2. Greenwich, Conn.: JAI Press.

Bornschier, Volker, and Christopher Chase-Dunn. 1985. *Transnational Corporations and Underdevelopment.* New York: Praeger.

Bornschier, Volker, Christopher Chase-Dunn, and Richard Rubinson. 1978. "Cross-national evidence of the effects of foreign investment and aid on economic growth and inequality: A survey of findings and a reanalysis." *American Journal of Sociology* 84:651–683.

Boserup, Ester. 1965. *The Conditions of Agricultural Growth.* Chicago: Aldine.

———. 1981. *Population and Technological Change.* Chicago: University of Chicago Press.

Boswell, Terry E. 1986. "A split labor market analysis of discrimination against Chinese immigrants, 1850–1882." *American Sociological Review* 51:352–371.

Bourdieu, Pierre, and Jean-Claude Passeron. 1977. *Reproduction: In Education, Society and Culture.* Beverly Hills, Calif.: Sage.

Bowler, Peter J. 1983. *The Eclipse of Darwinism.* Baltimore: Johns Hopkins University Press.

———. 1988. *The Non-Darwinian Revolution.* Baltimore: Johns Hopkins University Press.

Bowles, Samuel, and Herbert Gintis. 1976. *Schooling in Capitalist America.* New York: Basic Books.

Bradshaw, York W., and Michael Wallace. 1996. *Global Inequalities.* Thousand Oaks, Calif.: Pine Forge Press.

Braudel, Fernand. 1981. *The Structures of Everyday Life.* (Volume 1 of *Civilization and Capitalism, 15th–18th Century.*) New York: Harper & Row.

———. 1982. *The Wheels of Commerce.* (Volume 2 of *Civilization and Capitalism, 15th–18th Century.*) New York: Harper & Row.

———. 1984. *The Perspective of the World.* (Volume 3 of *Civilization and Capitalism, 15th–18th Century.*) New York: Harper & Row.

Braverman, Harry. 1974. *Labor and Monopoly Capital: The Degradation of Work in the Twentieth Century.* New York: Monthly Review Press.

Brenner, Robert. 1976. "Agrarian class structure and economic development in pre-industrial Europe." *Past and Present* 70:30–75.

———. 1977. "The origins of capitalist development: A critique of neo-Smithian Marxism." *New Left Review* 104:25–92.

Bronson, Bennet. 1972. "Farm labor and the evolution of food production." In Brian Spooner (ed.), *Population Growth: Anthropological Implications.* Cambridge, Mass.: MIT Press.

Brown, David K. 1995. *Degrees of Control: A Sociology of Educational Expansion and Occupational Credentialism.* New York: Teachers College Press.

Brown, Judith K. 1975. "Iroquois women: An ethnohistoric note." In Rayna R. Reiter (ed.), *Toward an Anthropology of Women.* New York: Monthly Review Press.

Burch, Ernest S., and Linda J. Ellanna (eds.). 1994. *Key Issues in Hunter-Gatherer Research.* Oxford: Berg.

Burns, Edward McNall. 1973. *Western Civilizations.* Volume 2. Eighth edition. New York: Norton.

Cameron, Kenneth Neill. 1973. *Humanity and Society: A World History.* New York: Monthly Review Press.

Cammack, Paul. 1986. "Resurgent democracy: Threat and promise." *New Left Review* 157:121–128.

Campbell, Donald T. 1965. "Variation and selective retention in sociocultural evolution." In Herbert R. Barringer, George I. Blanksten, and Raymond W. Mack (eds.), *Social Change in Developing Areas: A Reinterpretation of Evolutionary Theory.* Cambridge, Mass.: Schenkman.

Cann, R. L. 1987. "In Search of Eve." *The Sciences* 27:30–37.

Cann, R. L., M. Stoneking, and A. C. Wilson. 1987. "Mitochondrial DNA and human evolution." *Nature* 325:31–36.

Cardoso, Fernando Henrique. 1982. "Dependency and development in Latin America." In Hamza Alavi and Teodor Shanin (eds.), *Introduction to the Sociology of "Developing Societies."* London: Macmillan Press.

———. 1986. "Democracy in Latin America." *Politics and Society* 15:23–41.

Cardoso, Fernando Henrique, and Enzo Faletto. 1979. *Dependency and Development in Latin America.* Berkeley: University of California Press.

Carneiro, Robert L. 1968. "Slash-and-burn cultivation among the Kuikuru and its implications for cultural development in the Amazon Basin." In Yehudi A. Cohen (ed.), *Man in Adaptation: The Cultural Present.* Chicago: Aldine.

———. 1970. "A theory of the origin of the state." *Science* 169:733–738.

———. 1972. "The devolution of evolution." *Social Biology* 19:248–258.

———. 1973. "The four faces of evolution." In J. J. Honigmann (ed.), *Handbook of Social and Cultural Anthropology.* Chicago: Rand McNally.

———. 1978. "Political expansion as an expression of the principle of competitive exclusion." In Ronald Cohen and Elman R. Service (eds.), *Origins of the State.* Philadelphia: Institute for the Study of Human Issues.

———. 1981. "The chiefdom: Precursor of the state." In Grant D. Jones and Robert R. Kautz (eds.), *The Transition to Statehood in the New World.* New York: Cambridge University Press.

———. 1985. "The role of natural selection in the evolution of culture." Unpublished manuscript. New York: American Museum of Natural History.

———. 1987. "Further reflections on resource concentration and its role in the rise of the state." In Linda Manzanilla (ed.), *Studies in the Neolithic and Urban Revolutions.* Oxford: British Archaeological Reports. International Series, No. 349.

———. 1988. "The circumscription theory: Challenge and response." *American Behavioral Scientist* 31:497–511.

Carnoy, Martin. 1984. *The State and Political Theory.* Princeton, N.J.: Princeton University Press.

Cashdan, Elizabeth A. 1980. "Egalitarianism among hunters and gatherers." *American Anthropologist* 82:116–120.

———. 1985. "Coping with risk: Reciprocity among the Basarwa of northern Botswana." *Man* 20:454–474.

———. 1989. "Hunters and gatherers: Economic behavior in bands." In Stuart Plattner (ed.), *Economic Anthropology.* Stanford, Calif., Stanford University Press.

Castells, Manuel. 1996. *The Information Age: Economy, Society, and Culture. Volume 1: The Rise of the Network Society.* Oxford: Blackwell.

Cavalli-Sforza, L. L., and M. W. Feldman. 1981. *Cultural Transmission and Evolution.* Princeton, N.J.: Princeton University Press.

Chafetz, Janet Saltzman. 1984. *Sex and Advantage: A Comparative, Macro-Structural Theory of Sex Stratification.* Totowa, N.J.: Rowman and Allanheld.

Chagnon, Napoleon A. 1983. *Yanomamö: The Fierce People.* Third edition. New York: Holt, Rinehart and Winston.

———. 1992. *Yanomamö: The Last Days of Eden.* San Diego: Harcourt Brace Jovanovich.

Chambliss, William J., and Thomas E. Ryther. 1975. *Sociology: The Discipline and Its Direction.* New York: McGraw-Hill.

Champion, Timothy, Clive Gamble, Stephen Shennan, and Alasdair Whittle. 1984. *Prehistoric Europe.* New York: Academic Press.

Chandler, Tertius. 1987. *Four Thousand Years of Urban Growth.* Lewiston, N.Y.: St. David's University Press.

Chang, Kwang-chih. 1986. *The Archaeology of Ancient China.* Fourth edition. New Haven: Yale University Press.

Chase-Dunn, Christopher. 1975. "The effects of international economic dependence on development and inequality: A cross-national study." *American Sociological Review* 40:720–738.

———. 1982. "Socialist states in the capitalist world-economy." In Christopher Chase-Dunn (ed.), *Socialist States in the World-System.* Beverly Hills, Calif.: Sage.

————. 1989a. *Global Formation: Structures of the World-Economy*. Oxford: Blackwell.

————. 1989b. "Is a world state necessary?" Paper presented at the joint meetings of the British and American International Studies Associations, London, March 24.

————. 1990. "World-state formation: Historical processes and emergent necessity." *Political Geography Quarterly* 9:108–130.

Chase-Dunn, Christopher, and Kenneth O'Reilly. 1989. "Core wars of the future." In Robert K. Schaeffer (ed.), *War in the World-System*. Westport, Conn.: Greenwood Press.

Chase-Dunn, Christopher (ed.). 1982. *Socialist States in the World-System*. Beverly Hills, Calif.: Sage.

Chaudhuri, K. N. 1985. *Trade and Civilisation in the Indian Ocean*. Cambridge: Cambridge University Press.

Cherlin, Andrew J. 1981. *Marriage, Divorce, Remarriage*. Cambridge, Mass.: Harvard University Press.

————. 1992. *Marriage, Divorce, Remarriage*. Second edition. Cambridge, Mass.: Harvard University Press.

Childe, V. Gordon. 1936. *Man Makes Himself*. London: Watts & Co.

Chinchilla, Norma S. 1977. "Industrialization, monopoly capitalism, and women's work in Guatemala." *Signs: Journal of Women in Culture and Society* 3:38–56.

Chirot, Daniel. 1977. *Social Change in the Twentieth Century*. New York: Harcourt Brace Jovanovich.

————. 1985. "The rise of the West." *American Sociological Review* 50:181–195.

————. 1986. *Social Change in the Modern Era*. San Diego: Harcourt Brace Jovanovich.

————. 1991. "What happened in Eastern Europe in 1989?" In Daniel Chirot (ed.), *The Crisis of Leninism and the Decline of the Left*. Seattle: University of Washington Press.

Chirot, Daniel (ed.). 1989. *The Origins of Backwardness in Eastern Europe*. Berkeley: University of California Press.

Clark, Burton R. 1962. *Educating the Expert Society*. San Francisco: Chandler.

Clarke, William C. 1966. "From extensive to intensive shifting cultivation: A succession from New Guinea." *Ethnology* 5:347–359.

Cohen, G. A. 1978. *Karl Marx's Theory of History: A Defence*. Princeton, N.J.: Princeton University Press.

Cohen, Jere. 1980. "Rational capitalism in Renaissance Italy." *American Journal of Sociology* 85:1340–1355.

Cohen, Mark N. 1977. *The Food Crisis in Prehistory*. New Haven: Yale University Press.

————. 1984. "An introduction to the symposium." In Mark N. Cohen and George J. Armelagos (eds.). *Paleopathology at the Origins of Agriculture*. New York: Academic Press.

————. 1985. "Prehistoric hunter-gatherers: The meaning of social complexity." In T. Douglas Price and James A. Brown (eds.), *Prehistoric Hunter-Gatherers*. New York: Academic Press.

————. 1989. *Health and the Rise of Civilization*. New Haven: Yale University Press.

Cohen, Mark N., and George J. Armelagos. 1984. "Paleopathology at the origins of agriculture: Editors' summation." In Mark N. Cohen and George J. Armelagos (eds.), *Paleopathology at the Origins of Agriculture*. New York: Academic Press.

Cohen, Mark N., Roy S. Malpass, and Harold G. Klein (eds.). 1980. *Biosocial Mechanisms of Population Regulation*. New Haven: Yale University Press.

Cohen, Percy. 1968. *Modern Social Theory*. New York: Basic Books.

Cohen, Ronald, and Elman R. Service (eds.). 1978. *Origins of the State.* Philadelphia: Institute for the study of Human Issues.

Cohn, Norman. 1970. *The Pursuit of the Millennium: Revolutionary Millenarians and Mystical Anarchists of the Middle Ages.* Revised edition. New York: Oxford University Press.

———. 1993. *Cosmos, Chaos, and the World to Come: The Ancient Roots of Apocalyptic Faith.* New Haven, Conn.: Yale University Press.

Colchester, Marcus. 1984. "Rethinking Stone Age economics: Some speculations concerning the pre-Columbian Yanoama economy." *Human Ecology* 12:291–314.

Collins, Randall. 1975. *Conflict Sociology: Toward an Explanatory Science.* New York: Academic Press.

———. 1977. "Some comparative principles of educational stratification." *Harvard Educational Review* 47:1–27.

———. 1979. *The Credential Society: An Historical Sociology of Education and Stratification.* New York: Academic Press.

———. 1980. "Weber's last theory of capitalism: A systematization." *American Sociological Review* 45:925–942.

———. 1985. *Sociology of Marriage and the Family: Gender, Love, and Property.* Chicago: Nelson-Hall.

———. 1986a. "Is 1980s sociology in the doldrums?" *American Journal of Sociology* 91:1336–1355.

———. 1986b. *Weberian Sociological Theory.* New York: Cambridge University Press.

———. 1988. *Theoretical Sociology.* San Diego: Harcourt Brace Jovanovich.

———. 1994. *Four Sociological Traditions.* New York: Oxford University Press.

Collins, Randall, and Scott Coltrane. 1995. *Sociology of Marriage and the Family: Gender, Love, and Property.* Fourth edition. Chicago: Nelson-Hall.

Collins, Randall, and David Waller. 1992. "What theories predicted the state breakdowns and revolutions of the Soviet bloc?" In Louis Kriesberg (ed.), *Research in Social Movements, Conflicts and Change.* Volume 14. Greenwich, Conn.: JAI Press.

Connah, Graham. 1987. *African Civilizations.* Cambridge: Cambridge University Press.

Conelly, W. Thomas. 1992. "Agricultural intensification in a Philippine frontier community: Impact on labor efficiency and farm diversity." *Human Ecology* 20:1–21.

Cowgill, George L. 1975. "On causes and consequences of ancient and modern population changes." *American Anthropologist* 77:505–525.

Cox, Oliver C. 1948. *Caste, Class, and Race.* New York: Monthly Review Press.

Crane, George T. 1982. "The Taiwanese ascent: System, state, and movement in the world-economy." In Edward Friedman (ed.), *Ascent and Decline in the World-System.* Beverly Hills, Calif.: Sage.

Cribb, Roger. 1991. *Nomads in Archaeology.* Cambridge: Cambridge University Press.

Crippen, Timothy. 1988. "Old and new gods in the modern world: Toward a theory of religious transformation." *Social Forces* 67:316–336.

Cumings, Bruce, 1984. "The origins and development of the northeast Asian political economy: Industrial sectors, production cycles, and political consequences." *International Organization* 38:1–40.

———. 1989. "The abortive abertura: South Korea in the light of Latin American experience." *New Left Review* 173:5–32.

Curtin, Philip D. 1984. *Cross-Cultural Trade in World History*. New York: Cambridge University Press.

Czap, Peter. 1983. "A large family: The peasants' greatest wealth: Serf households in Mishino, Russia, 1814–1858." In Richard Wall, Jean Rodin, and Peter Laslett (eds.), *Family Forms in Historic Europe*. Cambridge: Cambridge University Press.

Dahrendorf, Ralf. 1958. "Out of utopia: Toward a reorientation of sociological analysis." *American Journal of Sociology* 64:115–127.

Dalton, George. 1972. "Peasantries in anthropology and history." *Current Anthropology* 13:385–416.

———. 1974. "How exactly are peasants exploited?" *American Anthropologist* 76:553–561.

Daly, Martin, and Margo Wilson. 1978. *Sex, Evolution and Behavior*. North Scituate, Mass: Duxbury Press.

———. 1988. *Homicide*. Hawthorne, N.Y.: Aldine de Gruyter.

Danhieux, Luc. 1983. "The evolving household: The case of Lampernisse, West Flanders." In Richard Wall, Jean Rodin, and Peter Laslett (eds.), *Family Forms in Historic Europe*. Cambridge: Cambridge University Press.

Davis, Howard, and Richard Scase. 1985. *Western Capitalism and State Socialism: An Introduction*. Oxford: Blackwell.

Davis, Kingsley, and Wilbert E. Moore. 1945. "Some principles of stratification." *American Sociological Review* 10:242–249.

Dawkins, Richard. 1976. *The Selfish Gene*. New York: Oxford University Press.

———. 1986. *The Blind Watchmaker*. New York: Norton.

de Ste. Croix, G. E. M. 1981. *The Class Struggle in the Ancient Greek World*. Ithaca, N.Y.: Cornell University Press.

Degler, Carl N. 1972. "Slavery and the genesis of American race prejudice." In Donald L. Noel (ed.), *The Origins of American Slavery and Racism*. Columbus, Ohio: Merrill.

———. 1991. *In Search of Human Nature: The Decline and Revival of Darwinism in American Social Thought*. New York: Oxford University Press.

Delacroix, Jacques, and Charles C. Ragin. 1981. "Structural blockage: A cross-national study of economic dependency, state efficacy, and underdevelopment." *American Journal of Sociology* 86:1311–1347.

Derrida, Jacques. 1978. *Writing and Difference*. Translated by A. Bass. Chicago: University of Chicago Press.

de Waal Malefijt, Annemarie. 1968. *Religion and Culture: An Introduction to Anthropology of Religion*. New York: Macmillan.

Divale, William Tulio, and Marvin Harris. 1976. "Population, warfare, and the male supremacist complex." *American Anthropologist* 78:521–538.

Dixon, William J., and Terry Boswell. 1996a. "Dependency, disarticulation, and denominator effects: Another look at foreign capital penetration." *American Journal of Sociology* 102:543–562.

———. 1996b. "Differential productivity, negative externalities, and foreign capital: Reply to Firebaugh." *American Journal of Sociology* 102:576–584.

Djilas, Milovan. 1957. *The New Class*. New York: Praeger.

Dobb, Maurice. 1963. *Studies in the Development of Capitalism*. Revised edition. New York: International Publishers.

Dobzhansky, Theodosius. 1962. *Mankind Evolving*. New Haven: Yale University Press.

Domhoff, G. William. 1990. *The Power Elite and the State: How Policy Is Made in America.* Hawthorne, N.Y.: Aldine de Gruyter.

Dore, Ronald. 1976. *The Diploma Disease: Education, Qualification, and Development.* Berkeley: University of California Press.

Dos Santos, Theotonio. 1970. "The structure of dependence." *American Economic Review* 60:231–236.

Douglass, William A. 1980. "The south Italian family: A critique." *Journal of Family History* 5:338–359.

Dubrow, Joshua, and Stephen K. Sanderson. 1997. "Was there racial antagonism in the ancient world?" Paper presented at the annual meetings of the American Sociological Association, Toronto, August.

Duby, Georges. 1968. *Rural Economy and Country Life in the Medieval West.* Translated by Cynthia Postan. Columbia: University of South Carolina Press.

Durham, William H. 1991. *Coevolution: Genes, Culture, and Human Diversity.* Stanford, Calif.: Stanford University Press.

Durkheim, Emile. 1965. *The Elementary Forms of the Religious Life.* New York: Free Press. (Originally published 1912.)

Earle, Timothy. 1991. "Property rights and the evolution of chiefdoms." In Timothy Earle (ed.), *Chiefdoms: Power, Economy, and Ideology.* New York: Cambridge University Press.

Earle, Timothy (ed.). 1991. *Chiefdoms: Power, Economy, and Ideology.* New York: Cambridge University Press.

Eckhardt, William. 1992. *Civilizations, Empires, and Wars: A Quantitative History of War.* Jefferson, N.C.: McFarland.

Eckstein, Susan. 1986. "The impact of the Cuban revolution: A comparative perspective." *Comparative Studies in Society and History* 28:502–534.

Eisenstadt, S.N. (ed.). 1986. *The Origin and Diversity of Axial Age Civilizations.* Albany: State University of New York Press.

Ekholm, Kajsa. 1981. "On the structure and dynamics of global systems." In J. S. Kahn and J. R. Llobera (eds.), *The Anthropology of Precapitalist Societies.* London: Macmillan Press.

Ekholm, Kajsa, and Jonathan Friedman. 1982. "'Capital' imperialism and exploitation in ancient world-systems." *Review* 4:87–109.

Eldredge, Niles, and Stephen Jay Gould. 1972. "Punctuated equilibria: An alternative to phyletic gradualism." In Thomas J. M. Schopf (ed.), *Models in Paleobiology.* San Francisco: Freeman, Cooper.

Ellis, Lee, and M. Ashley Ames. 1987. "Neurohormonal functioning and sexual orientation: A theory of homosexuality-heterosexuality." *Psychological Bulletin* 101:233–258.

Elster, Jon. 1985. *Making Sense of Marx.* Cambridge: Cambridge University Press.

Elvin, Mark. 1973. *The Pattern of the Chinese Past.* Stanford, Calif.: Stanford University Press.

Ember, Carol R. 1974. "An evaluation of alternative theories of matrilocal versus patrilocal residence." *Behavior Science Research* 9:135–149.

———. 1978. "Myths about hunter-gatherers." *Ethnology* 17:439–448.

———. 1983. "The relative decline in women's contribution to agriculture with intensification." *American Anthropologist* 85:285–304.

Ember, Melvin, and Carol Ember. 1971. "The conditions favoring matrilocal versus patrilocal residence." *American Anthropologist* 73:571–594.

Engels, Frederick. 1963. "Speech at the graveside of Karl Marx." In Howard Selsam and Harry Martel (eds.), *Reader in Marxist Philosophy.* New York: International Publishers. (Originally given 1883.)

———. 1970. *The Origin of the Family, Private Property, and the State.* Edited by Eleanor Burke Leacock. New York: International Publishers. (Originally published 1884.)

———. 1973. *The Condition of the Working Class in England.* Moscow: Progress Publishers. (Originally published 1845.)

———. 1978. "The peasant war in Germany." In Karl Marx and Frederick Engels, *Collected Works.* Volume 10. New York: International Publishers. (Originally published 1850.)

Ericson, Richard E. 1995. "The Russian economy since independence." In Gail W. Lapidus (ed.), *The New Russia: Troubled Transformation.* Boulder, Colo.: Westview.

Erikson, Robert, and John H. Goldthorpe. 1993. *The Constant Flux: A Study of Class Mobility in Industrial Societies.* Oxford: Oxford University Press (Clarendon Press).

Erikson, Robert, John H. Goldthorpe, and Lucienne Portocarero, 1982. "Social fluidity in industrial nations: England, France and Sweden." *British Journal of Sociology* 33:1–34.

Esping-Andersen, Gosta. 1990. *The Three Worlds of Welfare Capitalism.* Princeton, N.J.: Princeton University Press.

Evans, Peter B. 1979. *Dependent Development: The Alliance of Multinational, State, and Local Capital in Brazil.* Princeton, N.J.: Princeton University Press.

———. 1987. "Class, state, and dependence in east Asia: Lessons for Latin Americanists." In Frederic C. Deyo (ed.), *The Political Economy of the New Asian Industrialism.* Ithaca, N.Y.: Cornell University Press.

Evans, Peter B., Dietrich Rueschemeyer, and Theda Skocpol (eds.). 1985. *Bringing the State Back In.* New York: Cambridge University Press.

Fagan, Brian M. 1989. *People of the Earth: An Introduction to World Prehistory.* Sixth edition. Glenview, Ill.: Scott, Foresman.

Farb, Peter. 1978. *Man's Rise to Civilization.* Revised edition. New York: Bantam Books.

Farley, Reynolds. 1984. *Blacks and Whites: Narrowing the Gap?* Cambridge, Mass.: Harvard University Press.

Farley, Reynolds, and Walter R. Allen. 1987. *The Color Line and the Quality of Life in America.* New York: Russell Sage Foundation.

Fernandez-Kelly, Maria Patricia. 1983. *For We Are Sold, I and My People: Women and Industry in Mexico's Frontier.* Albany: State University of New York Press.

Fiedel, Stuart J. 1987. *Prehistory of the Americas.* New York: Cambridge University Press.

Firebaugh, Glenn. 1992. "Growth effects of foreign and domestic investment." *American Journal of Sociology* 98:105–130.

———. 1996. "Does foreign capital harm poor nations? New estimates based on Dixon and Boswell's measures of capital penetration." *American Journal of Sociology* 102:563–575.

Flandrin, Jean-Louis. 1979. *Families in Former Times: Kinship, Household, and Sexuality in Early Modern France.* Cambridge: Cambridge University Press.

Flannery, Kent V. 1973. "The origins of agriculture." *Annual Review of Anthropology* 2:271–310.

Flora, Peter. 1983. *State, Economy, and Society in Western Europe, 1815–1975.* Volume 1. Frankfurt: Campus Verlag.

Fogel, Robert William. 1989. *Without Consent or Contract: The Rise and Fall of American Slavery.* New York: Norton.

Fogel, Robert William, and Stanley L. Engerman. 1974. *Time on the Cross: The Economics of American Negro Slavery.* Boston: Little, Brown.

Folger, J. K., and C. B. Nam. 1964. "Trends in education in relation to the occupational structure." *Sociology of Education* 38:19–33.

Foner, Philip S. 1975. *A History of Black Americans.* Westport, Conn.: Greenwood Press.

Fox, Robin. 1967. *Kinship and Marriage.* Baltimore: Penguin Books.

Frank, Andre Gunder. 1966. "The development of underdevelopment." *Monthly Review* 18(4):17–31.

———. 1967. "Sociology of development and underdevelopment of sociology." *Catalyst* 3:20–73.

———. 1969. *Capitalism and Underdevelopment in Latin America.* New York: Monthly Review Press.

———. 1979. *Dependent Accumulation and Underdevelopment.* New York: Monthly Review Press.

———. 1980. *Crisis: in the World Economy.* New York: Holmes & Meier.

———. 1981. *Crisis: in the Third World.* New York: Holmes & Meier.

———. 1992a. "Economic ironies in Europe: A world economic interpretation of East-West European politics." *International Social Science Journal* 13:41–56.

———. 1992b. "Nothing new in the East: No new world order." *Social Justice* 19:34–61.

Frayer, David W., Milford H. Wolpoff, Alan G. Thorne, Fred H. Smith, and Geoffrey G. Pope. 1993. "Theories of modern human origins: The paleontological test." *American Anthropologist* 95:14–50.

Fredrickson, George M. 1971. "Toward a social interpretation of the development of American racism." In Nathan I. Huggins, Martin Kilson, and Daniel M. Fox (eds.), *Key Issues in the Afro-American Experience.* New York: Harcourt Brace Jovanovich.

———. 1981. *White Supremacy: A Comparative Study in American and South African History.* New York: Oxford University Press.

Freeman, Richard B. 1976. *The Overeducated American.* New York: Academic Press.

Fried, Morton H. 1957. "The classification of corporate unilineal descent groups." *Journal of the Royal Anthropological Institute* 87:1–29.

———. 1967. *The Evolution of Political Society.* New York: Random House.

———. 1978. "The state, the chicken, and the egg: Or, what came first?" In Ronald Cohen and Elman R. Service (eds.), *Origins of the State.* Philadelphia: Institute for the Study of Human Issues.

Friedan, Betty. 1963. *The Feminine Mystique.* New York: Dell.

Friedl, Ernestine. 1975. *Women and Men: An Anthropologist's View.* New York: Holt, Rinehart and Winston.

Fröbel, Folker, Jürgen Heinrichs, and Otto Kreye. 1980. *The New International Division of Labour.* Cambridge: Cambridge University Press.

Frost, Peter. 1991. "'Examination hell.'" In Edward R. Beauchamp (ed.), *Windows on Japanese Education.* Westport, Conn.: Greenwood Press.

Fryer, Peter. 1984. *Staying Power: The History of Black People in Britain.* London: Pluto Press.

Fuentes, Annette, and Barbara Ehrenreich. 1983. *Women in the Global Factory.* INC Pamphlet No. 2. New York: Institute for New Communications.

Furstenburg, Frank F., Jr. 1966. "Industrialization and the American family: A look backward." *American Sociological Review* 31:326–337.

Futuyma, Douglas J. 1986. *Evolutionary Biology.* Second edition. Sunderland, Mass.: Sinauer.

Galtung, Johan, Tore Heiestad, and Erik Rudeng. 1980. "On the decline and fall of empires: The Roman Empire and

Western imperialism compared." *Review* 4:91–153.

Gardner, Peter. 1991. "Foragers' pursuit of individual autonomy." *Current Anthropology* 32:543–572.

Gardner, R. A., and B. T. Gardner. 1969. "Teaching sign language to a chimpanzee." *Science* 165:664–672.

Gazzaniga, Michael S. 1992. *Nature's Mind.* New York: Basic Books.

Geertz, Clifford. 1963. *Agricultural Involution: The Processes of Ecological Change in Indonesia.* Berkeley: University of California Press.

Gendron, Bernard. 1977. *Technology and the Human Condition.* New York: St. Martin's Press.

Genovese, Eugene D. 1965. *The Political Economy of Slavery.* New York: Random House (Vintage Books).

———. 1969. *The World the Slaveholders Made.* New York: Random House (Vintage Books).

———. 1974. *Roll, Jordan, Roll: The World the Slaves Made.* New York: Random House (Vintage Books).

Gereffi, Gary, and Donald L. Wyman (eds.). 1990. *Manufacturing Miracles: Paths of Industrialization in Latin America and East Asia.* Princeton, N.J.: Princeton University Press.

Gershenkron, Alexander. 1962. *Economic Backwardness in Historical Perspective.* Cambridge, Mass.: Harvard University Press.

Gibbs, James L., Jr. 1965. "The Kpelle of Liberia." In James L. Gibbs, Jr. (ed.), *Peoples of Africa.* New York: Holt, Rinehart and Winston.

Giddens, Anthony. 1973. *The Class Structure of the Advanced Societies.* New York: Harper & Row.

———. 1980. *The Class Structure of the Advanced Societies.* Second edition. London: Hutchinson.

———. 1981. *A Contemporary Critique of Historical Materialism.* Berkeley: University of California Press.

———. 1985. *The Nation-State and Violence.* Berkeley: University of California Press.

———. 1990. *The Consequences of Modernity.* Stanford, Calif.: Stanford University Press.

Giddens, Anthony, and David Held (eds.). 1982. *Classes, Power, and Conflict: Classical and Contemporary Debates.* Berkeley: University of California Press.

Giele, Janet Zollinger. 1977. "Introduction: Comparative perspectives on women." In Janet Zollinger Giele and Audrey Chapman Smock (eds.), *Women: Roles and Status in Eight Countries.* New York: Wiley.

Gills, Barry K., and Andre Gunder Frank. 1992. "World system cycles, crises, and hegemonial shifts, 1700 B.C. to 1700 A.D." *Review* 15:621–687.

Glock, Charles Y., and Robert N. Bellah (eds.). 1976. *The New Religious Consciousness.* Berkeley: University of California Press.

Glock, Charles Y., and Rodney Stark. 1965. *Religion and Society in Tension.* Chicago: Rand McNally.

Goldberg, Steven. 1993. *Why Men Rule: A Theory of Male Dominance.* Chicago: Open Court.

Goldstein, Joshua S. 1988. *Long Cycles: Prosperity and War in the Modern Age.* New Haven: Yale University Press.

Goldstone, Jack A. 1991. *Revolution and Rebellion in the Early Modern World.* Berkeley: University of California Press.

Goldthorpe, John H. 1980. *Social Mobility and Class Structure in Modern Britain.* Oxford: Clarendon Press.

Good, Kenneth R. 1987. "Limiting factors in Amazonian ecology." In Marvin Harris and Eric B. Ross (eds.), *Food and Evolution.* Philadelphia: Temple University Press.

———. 1993. "Foraging and farming among the Yanomami: Can you have one without the other?" Paper presented at the 7th International Conference on Hunting and Gathering Societies, Moscow.

Goode, William J. 1970. *World Revolution and Family Patterns.* New York: Free Press.

Goodenough, Ward. 1969. "Frontiers of cultural anthropology: Social organization." *Proceedings of the American Philosophical Society* 113:329–335.

Goody, Jack. 1976. *Production and Reproduction: A Comparative Study of the Domestic Domain.* Cambridge: Cambridge University Press.

Gorin, Zeev. 1985. "Socialist societies and world system theory: A critical survey." *Science and Society* 49:332–366.

Gossett, Thomas F. 1963. *Race: The History of an Idea in America.* Dallas, Tex.: Southern Methodist University Press.

Gould, Stephen Jay, and Niles Eldredge. 1977. "Punctuated equilibria: The tempo and mode of evolution reconsidered." *Paleobiology* 3:115–151.

Graber, Robert B., and Paul B. Roscoe. 1988. "Introduction: Circumscription and the evolution of society." *American Behavioral Scientist* 31:405–415.

Granovetter, Mark. 1979. "The idea of 'advancement' in theories of social evolution and development." *American Journal of Sociology* 85:489–515.

Greenfield, Sidney M. 1961. "Industrialization and the family in sociological theory." *American Journal of Sociology* 67:312–322.

Haas, Jonathan. 1982. *The Evolution of the Prehistoric State.* New York: Columbia University Press.

Hadden, Jeffrey K. 1987. "Toward desacralizing secularization theory." *Social Forces* 65:587–611.

Hall, John A. 1985. *Powers and Liberties: The Causes and Consequences of the Rise of the West.* Berkeley: University of California Press.

Hall, John Whitney. 1970. *Japan: From Prehistory to Modern Times.* New York: Delacorte Press.

Halliday, Fred. 1991. "The ends of cold war." In Robin Blackburn (ed.), *After the Fall: The Failure of Communism and the Future of Socialism.* London: Verso.

Hallpike, C. R. 1986. *The Principles of Social Evolution.* Oxford: Clarendon Press.

Halsey, A. H., A. F. Heath, and J. M. Ridge. 1980. *Origins and Destinations: Family, Class, and Education in Modern Britain.* Oxford: Clarendon Press.

Hamilton, William D. 1964. "The genetical evolution of social behavior, parts 1 and 2." *Journal of Theoretical Biology* 7:1–51.

Handwerker, W. Penn. 1986. "The modern demographic transition: An analysis of subsistence choices and reproductive consequences." *American Anthropologist* 88:400–417.

Hane, Mikiso. 1992. *Modern Japan: A Historical Survey.* Second edition. Boulder, Colo.: Westview Press.

Hardin, Garrett. 1968. "The tragedy of the commons." *Science* 162:1243–1248.

Harner, Michael J. 1970. "Population pressure and the social evolution of agriculturalists." *Southwestern Journal of Anthropology* 26:67–86.

———. 1975. "Scarcity, the factors of production, and social evolution." In Steven Polgar (ed.), *Population, Ecology, and Social Evolution.* The Hague: Mouton.

Harris, David R. 1977. "Alternative pathways toward agriculture." In Charles A. Reed (ed.), *Origins of Agriculture.* The Hague: Mouton.

Harris, Marvin. 1964. *Patterns of Race in the Americas.* New York: Norton.

———. 1968. *The Rise of Anthropological Theory.* New York: Crowell.

———. 1971. *Culture, Man, and Nature. An Introduction to General Anthropology.* New York: Crowell.

———. 1974. *Cows, Pigs, Wars, and Witches: The Riddles of Culture.* New York: Random House.

———. 1975. *Culture, People, Nature: An Introduction to General Anthropology.* Second edition. New York: Crowell.

———. 1977. *Cannibals and Kings: The Origins of Cultures.* New York: Random House.

———. 1979. *Cultural Materialism: The Struggle for a Science of Culture.* New York: Random House.

———. 1980. *Culture, People, Nature: An Introduction to General Anthropology.* Third edition. New York: Harper & Row.

———. 1981. *America Now: The Anthropology of a Changing Culture.* New York: Simon and Schuster.

———. 1985a. *Good to Eat: Riddles of Food and Culture.* New York: Simon and Schuster.

———. 1985b. *Culture, People, Nature: An Introduction to General Anthropology.* Fourth editon. New York: Harper & Row.

Harris, Marvin, and Eric B. Ross. 1978. "How beef became king." *Psychology Today* 12(5):88–94.

———. 1987. *Death, Sex and Fertility: Population Regulation in Preindustrial and Developing Societies.* New York: Columbia University Press.

Hartung, John. 1982. "Polygyny and inheritance of wealth." *Current Anthropology* 23:1–12.

Harvey, David. 1989. *The Condition of Postmodernity.* Oxford: Blackwell.

Hassig, Ross. 1985. *Trade, Tribute, and Transportation: The Sixteenth-Century Political Economy of the Valley of Mexico.* Norman: University of Oklahoma Press.

Hatch, Elvin. 1983. *Culture and Morality: The Relativity of Values in Anthropology.* New York: Columbia University Press.

Hayden, Brian. 1981. "Research and development in the Stone Age: Technological transitions among hunter-gatherers." *Current Anthropology* 22:519–48.

Hechter, Michael. 1975. *Internal Colonialism: The Celtic Fringe in British National Development, 1536–1966.* Berkeley: University of California Press.

———. 1976. "Ethnicity and industrialization: On the proliferation of the cultural division of labor." *Ethnicity* 3:214–224.

Heilbroner, Robert L. 1963. *The Great Ascent: The Struggle for Economic Development in Our Time.* New York: Harper & Row.

———. 1972. *The Making of Economic Society.* Fourth edition. Englewood Cliffs, N.J.: Prentice-Hall.

———. 1980. *An Inquiry into the Human Prospect.* New York: Norton.

———. 1985. *The Making of Economic Society.* Seventh edition. Englewood Cliffs, N.J.: Prentice-Hall.

Hendrix, Lewellyn, and Zakir Hossain. 1988. "Women's status and mode of production: A cross-cultural test." *Signs: Journal of Women in Culture and Society* 13:437–453.

Henry, Donald O. 1989. *From Foraging to Agriculture: The Levant at the End of the Ice Age.* Philadelphia: University of Pennsylvania Press.

Herman, Edward, and James Petras. 1985. "Resurgent democracy: Rhetoric and reality." *New Left Review* 154:83–98.

Hill, Christopher. 1953. "The transition from feudalism to capitalism." *Science and Society* 17:348–351.

Hill, J. H. 1978. "Apes and language." *Annual Review of Anthropology* 7:89–112.

Hill, Kim, Hillard Kaplan, Kristen Hawkes, and Ana Magdelena Hurtado. 1985.

"Men's time allocation to subsistence work among the Aché of eastern Paraguay." *Human Ecology* 13:29–47.

Hilton, Rodney (ed.). 1976. *The Transition from Feudalism to Capitalism.* London: New Left Books.

Hobsbawm, Eric J. 1968. *Industry and Empire.* New York: Pantheon.

———. 1991a. "Goodbye to all that." In Robin Blackburn (ed.), *After the Fall: The Failure of Communism and the Future of Socialism.* London: Verso.

———. 1991b. "Out of the ashes." In Robin Blackburn (ed.), *After the Fall: The Failure of Communism and the Future of Socialism.* London: Verso.

Hochschild, Arlie R. 1997. *The Time Bind: When Work Becomes Home and Home Becomes Work.* New York: Henry Holt.

Hockett, Charles F., and Robert Ascher. 1964. "The human revolution." *Current Anthropology* 5:135–168.

Hodges, Richard. 1988. *Primitive and Peasant Markets.* Oxford: Blackwell.

Hogbin, H. Ian. 1964. *A Guadalcanal Society: The Kaoka Speakers.* New York: Holt, Rinehart and Winston.

Hole, Frank. 1977. *Studies in the Archaeological History of the Deh Luran Plain.* Ann Arbor: University of Michigan Museum of Anthropology, Memoir No. 9.

Holton, Robert J. 1985. *The Transition from Feudalism to Capitalism.* New York: St. Martin's Press.

Hoogvelt, Ankie M. M. 1982. *The Third World in Global Development.* London: Macmillan Press.

Hraba, Joseph. 1979. *American Ethnicity.* Itasca, Ill.: F. E. Peacock.

Huaco, George A. 1963. "A logical analysis of the Davis-Moore theory of stratification." *American Sociological Review* 28:801–804.

———. 1986. "Ideology and general theory: The case of sociological functionalism." *Comparative Studies in Society and History* 28:34–54.

Huxley, Julian. 1942. *Evolution: The Modern Synthesis.* New York: Harper & Brothers.

Ingold, Tim. 1986. *Evolution and Social Life.* Cambridge: Cambridge University Press.

Jaspers, Karl. 1953. *The Origin and Goal of History.* New Haven, Conn.: Yale University Press.

Johansen, J. H., H. W. Collins, and J. A. Johnson. 1986. *American Education.* Fifth edition. Dubuque, Iowa: Wm. C. Brown.

Johnson, Allen W., and Timothy Earle. 1987. *The Evolution of Human Societies: From Foraging Group to Agrarian State.* Stanford, Calif.: Stanford University Press.

Jolly, Alison. 1972. *The Evolution of Primate Behavior.* New York: Macmillan.

Jones, E. L. 1988. *Growth Recurring: Economic Change in World History.* Oxford: Clarendon Press.

Jordan, Winthrop D. 1974. *The White Man's Burden.* New York: Oxford University Press.

Jowitt, Kenneth. 1978. *The Leninist Response to National Dependency.* Berkeley: Institute of International Studies.

———. 1992. *New World Disorder: The Leninist Extinction.* Berkeley: University of California Press.

Kaneda, Tatsuo. 1988. "Gorbachev's economic reforms." In P. Juviler and H. Kimura (eds.), *Gorbachev's Reforms.* Hawthorne, N.Y.: Aldine de Gruyter.

Karabel, Jerome, and A. H. Halsey. 1977. *Power and Ideology in Education.* New York: Oxford University Press.

Keesing, Roger M. 1975. *Kin Groups and Social Structure.* New York: Holt, Rinehart and Winston.

Kelly, Robert L. 1995. *The Foraging Spectrum: Diversity in Hunter-Gatherer Lifeways.* Washington, D.C.: Smithsonian Institution Press.

Kennedy, Paul. 1987. *The Rise and Fall of*

the Great Powers. New York: Random House (Vintage Books).

———. 1993. *Preparing for the Twenty-first Century.* New York: Random House.

Kerckhoff, Alan C., Richard T. Campbell, and Idee Winfield-Laird. 1985. "Social mobility in Great Britain and the United States." *American Journal of Sociology* 91:281–308.

Kirch, Patrick Vinton. 1984. *The Evolution of the Polynesian Chiefdoms.* New York: Cambridge University Press.

———. 1988. "Circumscription theory and sociopolitical evolution in Polynesia." *American Behavioral Scientist* 31:416–427.

———. 1994. *The Wet and the Dry: Irrigation and Agricultural Intensification in Polynesia.* Chicago: University of Chicago Press.

Kitamura, Kazuyuki. 1991. "The future of Japanese higher education." In Edward R. Beauchamp (ed.), *Windows on Japanese Education.* Westport, Conn.: Greenwood Press.

Klein, Richard G. 1989. *The Human Career: Human Biological and Cultural Origins.* Chicago: University of Chicago Press.

Kohl, Philip L. 1978. "The balance of trade in southwestern Asia in the mid-third millennium." *Current Anthropology* 19:463–492.

———. 1989. "The use and abuse of world-systems theory: The case of the 'pristine' west Asian state." In C. C. Lamberg-Karlovsky (ed.), *Archaeological Thought in America.* Cambridge: Cambridge University Press.

Kohlberg, Lawrence. 1971. "From is to ought: How to commit the naturalistic fallacy and get away with it in the study of moral development." In Theodore Mischel (ed.), *Cognitive Development and Epistemology.* New York: Academic Press.

Kolko, Gabriel. 1962. *Wealth and Power in America.* New York: Praeger.

Kondratieff, Nikolai. 1984. *The Long Wave Cycle.* New York: Richardson and Snyder. (Originally published 1928.)

Kontorovich, Vladimir. 1987. "Labor problems and the prospects for accelerated economic growth." In Maurice Friedberg and Heyward Isham (eds.), *Soviet Society Under Gorbachev.* Armonk, N.Y.: Sharpe.

Koo, Hagen. 1987. "The interplay of state, social class, and world system in east Asian development: The cases of South Korea and Taiwan." In Frederic C. Deyo (ed.), *The Political Economy of the New Asian Industrialism.* Ithaca, N.Y.: Cornell University Press.

Kornai, János. 1992. *The Socialist System: The Political Economy of Communism.* Princeton, N.J.: Princeton University Press.

Kottak, Conrad Phillip. 1978. *Anthropology: The Exploration of Human Diversity.* Second edition. New York: Random House.

Kovel, Joel. 1984. *White Racism: A Psychohistory.* Second edition. New York: Columbia University Press.

Kriedte, Peter. 1983. *Peasants, Landlords and Merchant Capitalists: Europe and the World Economy, 1500–1800.* Cambridge: Cambridge University Press.

Kumagai, Fumie. 1986. "Modernization and the family in Japan." *Journal of Family History* 11:371–382.

Kumar, Krishan. 1992. "The revolutions of 1989: Socialism, capitalism, and democracy." *Theory and Society* 21:309–356.

———. 1995. *From Post-Industrial to Post-Modern Society: New Theories of the Contemporary World.* Oxford: Blackwell.

Kushnirsky, F. I. 1988. "Soviet economic reform: An analysis and a model." In S. Linz and W. Moskoff (eds.), *Reorganization and Reform in the Soviet Economy.* Armonk, N.Y.: Sharpe.

Landes, David S. 1969. *The Unbound Prometheus: Technological Change and Industrial Development in Western Europe from 1750 to the Present.* New York: Cambridge University Press.

Lane, David. 1971. *The End of Inequality? Stratification Under State Socialism.* London: Penguin Books.

————. 1982. *The End of Social Inequality? Class, Status, and Power Under State Socialism.* London: Allen and Unwin.

————. 1985. *Soviet Economy and Society.* Oxford: Blackwell.

————. 1987. *Soviet Labour and the Ethic of Communism.* Boulder, Colo.: Westview Press.

Langton, John. 1979. "Darwinism and the behavioral theory of sociocultural evolution: An analysis." *American Journal of Sociology* 85:288–309.

Lanternari, Vittorio. 1963. *The Religions of the Oppressed.* New York: Knopf.

Lapidus, Gail W. 1983. "Social trends." In Robert F. Byrnes (ed.), *After Breshnev: Sources of Soviet Conduct in the 1980s.* Bloomington: Indiana University Press.

————. 1988. "Gorbachev's agenda: Domestic reforms and foreign policy reassessments." In P. Juviler and H. Kimura (eds.), *Gorbachev's Reforms.* Hawthorne, N.Y.: Aldine de Gruyter.

Lapidus, Gail W. (ed.). 1995. *The New Russia: Troubled Transformation.* Boulder, Colo.: Westview.

Lasch, Christopher. 1977. *Haven in a Heartless World: The Family Besieged.* New York: Basic Books.

Laslett, Peter. 1977. *Family Life and Illicit Love in Earlier Generations.* Cambridge: Cambridge University Press.

————. 1983. "Family and household as work group and as kin group: Areas of traditional Europe compared." In Richard Wall, Jean Rodin, and Peter Laslett (eds.), *Family Forms in Historic Europe.* Cambridge: Cambridge University Press.

Laslett, Peter, and Richard Wall. 1972. *Household and Family in Past Time.* Cambridge: Cambridge University Press.

Leach, E. R. 1954. *Political Systems of Highland Burma.* Boston: Beacon Press.

Leacock, Eleanor B. 1978. "Women's status in egalitarian society: Implications for social evolution." *Current Anthropology* 19:247–275.

Leacock, Eleanor B., and Helen I. Safa (eds.). 1986. *Women's Work: Development and the Division of Labor by Gender.* South Hadley, Mass.: Bergin and Garvey.

Lee, Richard B. 1968. "What hunters do for a living, or, how to make out on scarce resources." In Richard B. Lee and Irven DeVore (eds.), *Man the Hunter.* Chicago: Aldine.

————. 1972. "The !Kung bushmen of Botswana." In M. G. Bicchieri (ed.), *Hunters and Gatherers Today.* New York: Holt, Rinehart and Winston.

————. 1978. "Politics, sexual and nonsexual, in an egalitarian society." *Social Science Information* 17:871–895.

————. 1979. *The !Kung San: Men, Women, and Work in a Foraging Society.* New York: Cambridge University Press.

————. 1984. *The Dobe !Kung.* New York: Holt, Rinehart and Winston.

————. 1990. "Primitive communism and the origin of social inequality." In Steadman Upham (ed.), *The Evolution of Political Systems: Sociopolitics in Small-Scale Sedentary Societies.* New York: Cambridge University Press.

Lee, Richard B., and Irven DeVore (eds.). 1968. *Man the Hunter.* Chicago: Aldine.

Leggett, Robert E. 1988. "Gorbachev's reform program: 'Radical' or more of the same?" In S. Linz and W. Moskoff (eds.), *Reorganization and Reform in the Soviet Economy.* Armonk, N.Y.: Sharpe.

Lenski, Gerhard E. 1966. *Power and Privilege: A Theory of Social Stratification.* New York: McGraw-Hill.

————. 1970. *Human Societies: A Macrolevel*

Introduction to Sociology. New York: McGraw-Hill.

Lenski, Gerhard E., and Jean Lenski. 1978. *Human Societies: An Introduction to Macrosociology.* Third edition. New York: McGraw-Hill.

———. 1987. *Human Societies: An Introduction to Macrosociology.* Fifth edition. New York: McGraw-Hill.

Lenski, Gerhard, and Patrick Nolan. 1984. "Trajectories of development: A test of ecological-evolutionary theory." *Social Forces* 63:1–23.

Le Roy Ladurie, Emmanuel. 1974. *The Peasants of Languedoc.* Champaign: University of Illinois Press.

Leupp, Gary P. 1992. *Servants, Shophands, and Laborers in the Cities of Tokugawa Japan.* Princeton: Princeton University Press.

Lewis, Bernard. 1971. *Race and Color in Islam.* New York: Oxford University Press.

———. 1990. *Race and Slavery in the Middle East.* New York: Oxford University Press.

Leys, Colin. 1982. "African economic development in theory and practice." *Daedalus* 111(2):99–124.

Lieberman, Leonard. 1989. "A discipline divided: Acceptance of human sociobiological concepts in anthropology." *Current Anthropology* 30:676–682.

Lions, P., and M. Lachiver. 1967. "Dénombrement de la population de Brueil-en-Vexin en 1625." *Annales de démographie historique,* pp. 521–537.

Lord, Jane, and Stephen K. Sanderson. 1997. "Current theoretical and political perspectives of Western sociological theorists." Paper presented at the annual meetings of the American Sociological Association, Toronto, August.

Lortz, Joseph. 1972. "Why did the Reformation happen?" In Lewis W. Spitz (ed.), *The Reformation: Basic Interpretations.* Lexington, Mass.: Heath.

Lyotard, Jean-Francois. 1985. *The Postmodern Condition.* Minneapolis: University of Minnesota Press.

McCord, William, and Arline McCord. 1977. *Power and Equity: An Introduction to Social Stratification.* New York: Praeger.

McCorriston, Joy, and Frank Hole. 1991. "The ecology of seasonal stress and the origins of agriculture in the Near East." *American Anthropologist* 93:46–69.

McNeill, William H. 1976. *Plagues and Peoples.* Garden City, N.Y.: Doubleday (Anchor Books).

———. 1982. *The Pursuit of Power: Technology, Armed Force, and Society Since A.D. 1000.* Chicago: University of Chicago Press.

MacNeish, Richard. 1978. *The Science of Archaeology.* North Scituate, Mass.: Duxbury Press.

Mair, Lucy. 1964. *Primitive Government.* Baltimore: Penguin Books.

Mandel, Ernest. 1989. *Beyond Perestroika: The Future of Gorbachev's USSR.* Translated by Gus Fagan. London: Verso.

Mandelbaum, David G. 1988. *Women's Seclusion and Men's Honor: Sex Roles in North India, Bangladesh, and Pakistan.* Tucson: University of Arizona Press.

Mandle, Joan D. 1979. *Women and Social Change in America.* Princeton, N.J.: Princeton Books.

Mann, Michael. 1986. *The Sources of Social Power. Volume 1: A History of Power from the Beginning to A.D. 1760.* Cambridge: Cambridge University Press.

———. 1988. *States, War and Capitalism.* Oxford: Blackwell.

Martin, M. Kay, and Barbara Voorhies. 1975. *Female of the Species.* New York: Columbia University Press.

Marx, Gary T. 1967. "Religion: Opiate or inspiration of civil rights militancy among Negroes?" *American Sociological Review* 32:64–72.

Marx, Karl. 1963. *Karl Marx: Early Writings.* Edited by Tom Bottomore. New York:

McGraw-Hill. (Originally written 1843–1844.)

———. 1967. *Capital.* Three volumes. New York: International Publishers. (Originally published 1867.)

———. 1978. "The eighteenth brumaire of Louis Bonaparte." In Robert C. Tucker (ed.), *The Marx-Engels Reader.* Second edition. New York: Norton. (Originally published 1852.)

———. 1979. "Letter to Engels." In Saul K. Padover (ed.), *The Letters of Karl Marx.* Englewood Cliffs, N.J.: Prentice-Hall. (Originally written June 18, 1862.)

Marx, Karl, and Friedrich Engels. 1970. *The German Ideology.* Edited by C. J. Arthur. New York: International Publishers. (Originally written 1846.)

Maryanski, Alexandra, and Jonathan H. Turner. 1992. *The Social Cage: Human Nature and the Evolution of Society.* Stanford, Calif.: Stanford University Press.

Matthews, Mervyn. 1978. *Privilege in the Soviet Union.* London: Allen and Unwin.

Mayr, Ernst. 1942. *Systematics and the Origin of Species.* New York: Columbia University Press.

———. 1963. *Animal Species and Evolution.* Cambridge, Mass.: Harvard University Press.

———. 1982. *The Growth of Biological Thought.* Cambridge, Mass.: Harvard University Press (Belknap Press).

———. 1988. *Toward a New Philosophy of Biology.* Cambridge, Mass.: Harvard University Press.

———. 1991. *One Long Argument: Charles Darwin and the Genesis of Modern Evolutionary Thought.* Cambridge, Mass.: Harvard University Press.

Meadows, Donella H., Dennis L. Meadows, and Jørgen Randers. 1992. *Beyond the Limits: Confronting Global Collapse, Envisioning a Sustainable Future.* Post Mills, Vt.: Chelsea Green.

Mellars, Paul A. 1985. "The ecological basis of social complexity in the Upper Paleolithic of southwestern France." In T. Douglas Price and James A. Brown (eds.), *Prehistoric Hunter-Gatherers.* New York: Academic Press.

Mencher, Joan P. 1974. "The caste system upside down: Or the not-so-mysterious East." *Current Anthropology* 15:469–494.

———. 1980. "On being an untouchable in India: A materialist perspective." In Eric B. Ross (ed.), *Beyond the Myths of Culture: Essays in Cultural Materialism.* New York: Academic Press.

Merton, Robert K. 1957. *Social Theory and Social Structure.* New York: Free Press.

———. 1961. "Bureaucratic structure and personality." In Amitai Etzioni (ed.), *Complex Organizations: A Sociological Reader.* New York: Holt, Rinehart and Winston.

Meyer, John W., Francisco O. Ramirez, Richard Rubinson, and John Boli-Bennett. 1977. "The world educational revolution, 1950–1970." *Sociology of Education* 50:242–258.

Meyer, John W., David Tyack, Joane Nagel, and Audri Gordon. 1979. "Public education as nation-building in America: Enrollments and bureaucratization in the American states, 1870–1930." *American Journal of Sociology* 85:591–613.

Milisauskas, Sarunas. 1978. *European Prehistory.* New York: Academic Press.

Minge-Klevana, Wanda. 1980. "Does labor time decrease with industrialization? A survey of time-allocation studies." *Current Anthropology* 21:279–298.

Money, John, and A. A. Ehrhardt. 1972. *Man and Woman, Boy and Girl.* Baltimore: Johns Hopkins University Press.

Moore, Barrington, Jr. 1966. *Social Origins of Dictatorship and Democracy.* Boston: Beacon Press.

Morton, Peggy. 1971. "A woman's work is never done." In Edith Hoshino Altbach (ed.), *From Feminism to Liberation.* Cambridge, Mass.: Schenkman.

Moseley, K. P., and Immanuel Wallerstein. 1978. "Precapitalist social structures." *Annual Review of Sociology* 4:259–290.

Moulder, Frances V. 1977. *Japan, China and the Modern World Economy.* New York: Cambridge University Press.

Murdock, George Peter. 1959. *Africa: Its Peoples and Their Culture History.* New York: McGraw-Hill.

———. 1967. *Ethnographic Atlas.* Pittsburgh: University of Pittsburgh Press.

Murdock, George Peter, and Caterina Provost. 1973. "Factors in the division of labor by sex." *Ethnology* 12:203–225.

Murphy, Raymond. 1988. *Social Closure: The Theory of Monopolization and Exclusion.* Oxford: Clarendon Press.

Murstein, Bernard I. 1974. *Love, Sex, and Marriage Through the Ages.* New York: Springer.

Mutel, Jacques. 1988. "The modernization of Japan: Why has Japan succeeded in its modernization?" In Jean Bacchler, John A. Hall, and Michael Mann (eds.), *Europe and the Rise of Capitalism.* Oxford: Blackwell.

Nasir, Jamal J. 1994. *The Status of Women Under Islamic Law.* Second edition. London: Graham and Trotman.

Nattrass, Jill. 1981. *The South African Economy: Its Growth and Change.* Cape Town: Oxford University Press.

Ndabezitha, Siyabonga W., and Stephen K. Sanderson. 1988. "Racial antagonism and the origins of apartheid in the South African gold mining industry, 1886–1924: A split labor market analysis." In Cora Bagley Marrett and Cheryl Leggon (eds.), *Research in Race and Ethnic Relations.* Volume 5. Greenwich, Conn.: JAI Press.

Nef, John U. 1964. *The Conquest of the Material World.* Chicago: University of Chicago Press.

Noble, William, and Iain Davidson. 1996. *Human Evolution, Language, and Mind.* Cambridge: Cambridge University Press.

Noel, Donald L. 1972a. "Slavery and the rise of racism." In Donald L. Noel (ed.), *The Origins of American Slavery and Racism.* Columbus, Ohio: Merrill.

Noel, Donald L. (ed.). 1972b. *The Origins of American Slavery and Racism.* Columbus, Ohio: Merrill.

North, Douglass C., and Robert Paul Thomas. 1973. *The Rise of the Western World: A New Economic History.* New York: Cambridge University Press.

Nove, Alec. 1989. *Glasnost in Action: Cultural Renaissance in Russia.* London: Unwin Hyman.

Oates, Joan. 1978. "Comment on 'The balance of trade in southwestern Asia in the mid-third millennium.'" *Current Anthropology* 19:480–481.

Office of Management and the Budget. 1973. *Social Indicators 1973.* Washington, D.C.: U.S. Government Printing Office.

Oliver, Douglas. 1955. *A Solomon Island Society: Kinship and Leadership Among the Siuai of Bougainville.* Cambridge, Mass.: Harvard University Press.

Palli, Heldur. 1974. "Perede strukturist ja selle uurimiset." *Proceedings of the Soviet Academy of Estonia* 23:64–76.

Parker, Seymour, and Hilda Parker. 1979. "The myth of male superiority: Rise and demise." *American Anthropologist* 81:289–309.

Parkin, Frank. 1971. *Class Inequality and Political Order: Social Stratification in Capitalist and Communist Societies.* New York: Holt, Rinehart and Winston.

———. 1979. *Marxism and Class Theory: A Bourgeois Critique.* New York: Columbia University Press.

———. 1987. *The Mind and Body Shop.* New York: Atheneum.

Parsons, Talcott. 1937. *The Structure of Social Action.* New York: McGraw-Hill.

———. 1966. *Societies: Evolutionary and*

Comparative Perspectives. Englewood Cliffs, N.J.: Prentice-Hall.

———. 1971. *The System of Modern Societies.* Englewood Cliffs, N.J.: Prentice-Hall.

———. 1977. *The Evolution of Societies.* Edited by Jackson Toby. Englewood Cliffs, N.J.: Prentice-Hall.

Pasternak, Burton, Carol R. Ember, and Melvin Ember. 1996. *Sex, Gender, and Kinship: A Cross-Cultural Perspective.* Upper Saddle River, N.J.: Prentice Hall.

Patterson, Francine G. 1978. "The gestures of a gorilla: Language acquisition by another pongid." *Brain and Language* 12:72–97.

Patterson, Orlando. 1977. *Ethnic Chauvinism: The Reactionary Impulse.* New York: Stein and Day.

———. 1982. *Slavery and Social Death: A Comparative Study.* Cambridge, Mass.: Harvard University Press.

Pearson, M. N. 1991. "Merchants and states." In James D. Tracy (ed.), *The Political Economy of Merchant Empires.* New York: Cambridge University Press.

Petras, James. 1987. "The anatomy of state terror: Chile, El Salvador and Brazil." *Science and Society* 51:314–338.

Phillips, Kevin. 1990. *The Politics of Rich and Poor.* New York: Random House.

Phillipson, David W. 1985. *African Archaeology.* Cambridge: Cambridge University Press.

Piddocke, Stuart. 1965. "The potlatch system of the southern Kwakiutl: a new perspective." *Southwestern Journal of Anthropology* 21:244–264.

Pinker, Steven. 1994. *The Language Instinct: How the Mind Creates Language.* New York: William Morrow.

Pinkney, Alphonso. 1984. *The Myth of Black Progress.* New York: Cambridge University Press.

Pines, Maya. 1978. "Is sociobiology all wet?" *Psychology Today* 11(12):23–24.

Pitshandenge, Iman Ngondo A. 1994. "Marriage law in sub-Saharan Africa." In Caroline Bledsoe and Gilles Pison (eds.), *Nuptiality in Sub-Saharan Africa.* Oxford: Oxford University Press (Clarendon Press).

Piven, Frances Fox, and Richard A. Cloward. 1971. *Regulating the Poor: The Functions of Public Welfare.* New York: Random House (Vintage Books).

Plakans, Andrejs. 1982. "Ties of kinship and kinship roles in an historic eastern European peasant community: A synchronic analysis." *Journal of Family History* 7:52–75.

Plattner, Stuart (ed.). 1989. *Economic Anthropology.* Stanford, Calif.: Stanford University Press.

Polanyi, Karl. 1957. "The economy as instituted process." In Karl Polanyi, Conrad M. Arensberg, and Harry W. Pearson (eds.), *Trade and Market in the Early Empires.* Glencoe, Ill.: Free Press.

Pollock, Linda. 1983. *Forgotten Children: Parent-Child Relations from 1500 to 1900.* New York: Cambridge University Press.

Popenoe, David. 1988. *Disturbing the Nest: Family Change and Decline in Modern Societies.* Hawthorne, N.Y.: Aldine de Gruyter.

Popkin, Samuel L. 1979. *The Rational Peasant.* Berkeley: University of California Press.

Population Reference Bureau. 1989. *World Population Data Sheet.* Washington, D.C.: The Bureau.

Posner, Richard A. 1992. *Sex and Reason.* Cambridge, Mass.: Harvard University Press.

Possehl, Gregory L. 1990. "Revolution in the Urban Revolution: The emergence of Indus urbanization." *Annual Review of Anthropology* 19:261–282.

Postan, Michael M. 1972. *The Medieval Economy and Society.* Berkeley: University of California Press.

Premack, David. 1970. "A functional analysis of language." *Journal of the Experimental Analysis of Behavior* 14:107–125.

Price, T. Douglas, and James A. Brown (eds.), 1985. *Prehistoric Hunter-Gatherers.* San Diego: Academic Press.

Reich, Michael. 1977. "The economics of racism." In David M. Gordon (ed.), *Problems in Political Economy.* Second edition. Lexington, Mass.: Heath.

Reischauer, Edwin O. 1956. "Japanese feudalism." In Rushton Coulborn (ed.), *Feudalism in History.* Princeton, N.J.: Princeton University Press.

Reiter, Rayna R. (ed.). 1975. *Toward an Anthropology of Women.* New York: Monthly Review Press.

Remnick, David. 1997. *Resurrection: The Struggle for a New Russia.* New York: Random House.

Reynolds, Vernon, Vincent Falger, and Ian Vine (eds.). 1986. *The Sociobiology of Ethnocentrism.* Athens: University of Georgia Press.

Riesman, David. 1950. *The Lonely Crowd.* With the assistance of Reuel Denncy and Nathan Glazer. New Haven: Yale University Press.

Ritzer, George. 1992. *Sociological Theory.* Third edition. New York: Knopf.

Robertson, H. M. 1959. "A criticism of Max Weber and his school." In Robert W. Green (ed.), *Protestantism and Capitalism: The Weber Thesis and Its Critics.* Boston: Heath.

Robertson, Roland. 1970. *The Sociological Interpretation of Religion.* New York: Schocken Books.

Roemer, John E. 1982a. "New directions in the Marxian theory of exploitation and class." *Politics and Society* 11:253–287.

———. 1982b. *A General Theory of Exploitation and Class.* Cambridge, Mass.: Harvard University Press.

———. 1994. "A future for socialism." *Politics and Society* 22:451–478.

Rosaldo, Michelle, and Louise Lamphere (ed.). 1974. *Women, Culture, and Society.* Stanford, Calif.: Stanford University Press.

Rosenthal, Bernice Glatzer. 1975. "The role and status of women in the Soviet Union: 1917 to the present." In Ruby Rohrlich-Leavitt (ed.), *Women Cross-Culturally.* The Hague: Mouton.

Ross, Eric B. 1980. "Patterns of diet and forces of production: An economic and ecological history of the ascendancy of beef in the United States diet." In Eric B. Ross (ed.), *Beyond the Myths of Culture: Essays in Cultural Materialism.* New York: Academic Press.

Ross, Robert J. S., and Kent C. Trachte. 1990. *Global Capitalism: The New Leviathan.* Albany: State University of New York Press.

Rossi, Alice S. 1984. "Gender and parenthood." *American Sociological Review* 49:1–19.

Rossides, Daniel. 1976. *The American Class System: An Introduction to Social Stratification.* Boston: Houghton Mifflin.

———. 1990. *Social Stratification: The American Class System in Comparative Perspective.* Englewood Cliffs, N.J.: Prentice Hall.

Rostow, W. W. 1960. *The Stages of Economic Growth: A Non-Communist Manifesto.* New York: Cambridge University Press.

Roxborough, Ian. 1979. *Theories of Underdevelopment.* London: Macmillan Press.

Rubinson, Richard, and Deborah Holtzman. 1981. "Comparative dependence and economic development." *International Journal of Comparative Sociology* 22:86–101.

Rueschemeyer, Dietrich, Evelyne Huber Stephens, and John D. Stephens. 1992. *Capitalist Development and Democracy.* Chicago: University of Chicago Press.

Runciman, W. G. 1989. *A Treatise on Social Theory. Volume II: Substantive Social Theory.* Cambridge: Cambridge University Press.

Ruyle, Eugene E. 1973. "Slavery, surplus, and stratification on the Northwest Coast: The ethnoenergetics of an incipient stratification system." *Current Anthropology* 14:603–631.

Sacks, Karen. 1975. "Engels revisited: Women, the organization of production, and private property." In Rayna R. Reiter (ed.), *Toward an Anthropology of Women.* New York: Monthly Review Press.

———. 1979. *Sisters and Wives: The Past and Future of Sexual Equality.* Westport, Conn.: Greenwood Press.

Safa, Helen I. 1981. "Runaway shops and female employment: The search for cheap labor." *Signs: Journal of Women in Culture and Society* 7:418–433.

Sahlins, Marshall. 1958. *Social Stratification in Polynesia.* Seattle: University of Washington Press.

———. 1960. "Evolution: Specific and general." In Marshall Sahlins and Elman R. Service (eds.), *Evolution and Culture.* Ann Arbor: University of Michigan Press.

———. 1963. "Poor man, rich man, big man, chief: Political types in Melanesia and Polynesia." *Comparative Studies in Society and History* 5:285–303.

———. 1968. *Tribesmen.* Englewood Cliffs, N.J.: Prentice-Hall.

———. 1972. *Stone Age Economics.* Chicago: Aldine.

———. 1976a. *Culture and Practical Reason.* Chicago: University of Chicago Press.

———. 1976b. *The Use and Abuse of Biology: An Anthropological Critique of Sociobiology.* Ann Arbor: University of Michigan Press.

Sanders, William T. 1972. "Population, agricultural history, and societal evolution in Mesoamerica." In Brian Spooner (ed.), *Population Growth: Anthropological Implications.* Cambridge, Mass.: MIT Press.

Sanderson, Stephen K. 1973. "Religion, politics, and morality: A study of religious and political belief systems and their relation through Kohlberg's cognitive-developmental theory of moral judgment." Unpublished Ph.D. dissertation. Lincoln: University of Nebraska.

———. 1985. "The provincialism of introductory sociology." *Teaching Sociology* 12:397–410.

———. 1990. *Social Evolutionism: A Critical History.* Oxford: Blackwell.

———. 1991. "The evolution of societies and world-systems." In Christopher Chase-Dunn and Thomas D. Hall (eds.), *Core/Periphery Relations in Precapitalist Worlds.* Boulder, Colo.: Westview Press.

———. 1994a. "The transition from feudalism to capitalism: The theoretical significance of the Japanese case." *Review* 17:15–55.

———. 1994b. "Expanding world commercialization: The link between world-systems and civilizations." *Comparative Civilizations Review* 30:91–103.

———. 1994c. "Evolutionary materialism: A theoretical strategy for the study of social evolution." *Sociological Perspectives* 37:47–73.

———. 1995. *Social Transformations: A General Theory of Historical Development.* Oxford: Blackwell.

Sanderson, Stephen K., and Lee Ellis. 1992. "Theoretical and political perspectives of American sociologists in the 1990s." *The American Sociologist* 23:26–42.

Sansom, George. 1961. *A History of Japan, 1334–1615.* Stanford, Calif.: Stanford University Press.

Savage-Rumbaugh, E. Sue. 1986. *Ape Language: From Conditioned Response to Symbol.* New York: Columbia University Press.

Savage-Rumbaugh, E. Sue, Duane M. Rumbaugh, and Kelly McDonald. 1985. "Language learning in two species of apes." *Neuroscience and Biobehavioral Reviews* 9:653–665.

Schacht, Robert M. 1988. "Circumscription theory: A critical review." *American Behavioral Scientist* 31:438–448.

Schneider, David M. 1961. "The distinctive features of matrilineal descent groups." In David M. Schneider and Kathleen Gough (eds.), *Matrilineal Kinship.* Berkeley: University of California Press.

———. 1968. *American Kinship: A Cultural Account.* Englewood Cliffs, N.J.: Prentice-Hall.

Schneider, David M., and Kathleen Gough (eds.). 1961. *Matrilineal Kinship.* Berkeley: University of California Press.

Schneider, Jane. 1977. "Was there a precapitalist world-system?" *Peasant Studies* 6:20–29.

Scott, James C. 1976. *The Moral Economy of the Peasant.* New Haven: Yale University Press.

———. 1990. *Domination and the Arts of Resistance.* New Haven: Yale University Press.

See, Katherine O'Sullivan, and William J. Wilson. 1988. "Race and ethnicity." In Neil J. Smelser (ed.), *Handbook of Sociology.* Beverly Hills, Calif.: Sage.

Sennett, Richard. 1976. *The Fall of Public Man.* New York: Random House (Vintage Books).

Service, Elman R. 1963. *Profiles in Ethnology.* New York: Harper & Row.

———. 1966. *The Hunters.* Englewood Cliffs, N.J.: Prentice-Hall.

———. 1971a. *Cultural Evolutionism: Theory in Practice.* New York: Holt, Rinehart and Winston.

———. 1971b. *Primitive Social Organization: An Evolutionary Perspective.* Second edition. New York: Random House.

———. 1975. *Origins of the State and Civilization.* New York: Norton.

———. 1978. "Classical and modern theories of the origins of government." In Ronald Cohen and Elman R. Service (eds.), *Origins of the State.* Philadelphia: Institute for the Study of Human Issues.

Shahar, Shulamith. 1990. *Childhood in the Middle Ages.* New York: Routledge.

Shannon, Thomas Richard. 1996. *An Introduction to the World-System Perspective.* Second edition. Boulder, Colo.: Westview Press.

Shepher, Joseph. 1983. *Incest: A Biosocial View.* New York: Academic Press.

Sherwin-White, A. N. 1967. *Racial Prejudice in Imperial Rome.* Cambridge: Cambridge University Press.

Shorter, Edward. 1975. *The Making of the Modern Family.* New York: Basic Books.

———. 1976. "Women's work: What difference did capitalism make?" *Theory and Society* 3:513–527.

Shreeve, James. 1995. *The Neandertal Enigma: Solving the Mystery of Modern Human Origins.* New York: William Morrow.

Silver, Morris. 1985. *Economic Structures of the Ancient Near East.* London: Croom Helm.

Simon, Herbert A. 1976. *Administrative Behavior.* Third edition. New York: Free Press.

Simon, Julian. 1981. *The Ultimate Resource.* Princeton, N.J.: Princeton University Press.

Simpson, George Gaylord. 1949. *The Meaning of Evolution.* New Haven: Yale University Press.

———. 1953. *The Major Features of Evolution.* New York: Columbia University Press.

Sjoberg, Gideon. 1960. *The Preindustrial City.* New York: Free Press.

Skidmore, Thomas E., and Peter H. Smith. 1989. *Modern Latin America.* Second edition. New York: Oxford University Press.

Skocpol, Theda. 1977. "Wallerstein's world capitalist system: A theoretical and historical critique." *American Journal of Sociology* 82:1075–1090.

———. 1979. *States and Social Revolutions.* New York: Cambridge University Press.

Smedley, Audrey. 1993. *Race in North America: Origin and Evolution of a Worldview.* Boulder, Colo.: Westview Press.

Smith, Alan K. 1991. *Creating a World Economy: Merchant Capital, Colonialism, and World Trade, 1400–1825.* Boulder, Colo.: Westview Press.

Smith, Anthony D. 1973. *The Concept of Social Change.* London: Routledge and Kegan Paul.

———. 1981. *The Ethnic Revival.* Cambridge: Cambridge University Press.

———. 1986. *The Ethnic Origins of Nations.* Oxford: Basil Blackwell.

Smith, Thomas C. 1959. *The Agrarian Origins of Modern Japan.* Stanford, Calif.: Stanford University Press.

Snowden, Frank M. 1983. *Before Color Prejudice.* Cambridge, Mass.: Harvard University Press.

So, Alvin Y. 1990. *Social Change and Development: Modernization, Dependency, and World-System Theories.* Newbury Park, Calif.: Sage.

Sober, Elliott. 1984. *The Nature of Selection: Evolutionary Theory in Philosophical Focus.* Cambridge, Mass.: MIT Press.

Spencer, Daniel Lloyd. 1958. "Japan's pre-Perry preparation for economic growth." *American Journal of Economics and Sociology* 17:195–216.

Spiro, Melford. 1979. *Gender and Culture: Kibbutz Women Revisited.* Durham, N.C.: Duke University Press.

Spitz, Lewis W. 1985. *The Protestant Reformation, 1517–1559.* New York: Harper & Row.

Stampp, Kenneth M. 1956. *The Peculiar Institution: Slavery in the AnteBellum South.* New York: Random House (Vintage Books).

Stark, Barbara L. 1986. "Origins of food production in the New World." In David J. Meltzer, Don D. Fowler, and Jeremy A. Sabloff (eds.), *American Archaeology Past and Future.* Washington, D.C.: Smithsonian Institution Press.

Stark, Rodney. 1996. *The Rise of Christianity: A Sociologist Reconsiders History.* Princeton, N.J.: Princeton University Press.

Stark, Rodney, and William Sims Bainbridge. 1985. *The Future of Religion.* Berkeley: University of California Press.

Starr, Paul. 1982. *The Social Transformation of American Medicine.* New York: Basic Books.

Statesman's Year-Book 1984–85. 1984. New York: St. Martin's Press.

Stavrianos, L. S. 1975. *The World Since 1500: A Global History.* Third edition. Englewood Cliffs, N.J.: Prentice-Hall.

Stebbins, G. Ledyard. 1969. *The Basis of Progressive Evolution.* Chapel Hill: University of North Carolina Press.

———. 1974. "Adaptive shifts and evolutionary novelty: A compositionist approach." In Francisco José Ayala and Theodosius Dobzhansky (eds.), *Studies in the Philosophy of Biology.* Berkeley: University of California Press.

Stebbins, G. Ledyard, and Francisco J. Ayala. 1981. "Is a new evolutionary synthesis necessary?" *Science* 213:967–971.

Steel, Ronald. 1992. "Europe after the superpowers." In Charles W. Kegley, Jr., and Eugene R. Wittkopf (eds.), *The Future of American Foreign Policy.* New York: St. Martin's Press.

Stephens, Evelyne Huber. 1989. "Capitalist development and democracy in South America." *Politics and Society* 17:281–352.

Stephens, William N. 1963. *The Family in*

Cross-Cultural Perspective. New York: Holt, Rinehart and Winston.

Stevenson, Paul. 1974. "Monopoly capital and inequalities in Swedish society." *The Insurgent Sociologist* 5(1):41–58.

———. 1982. "Capitalism and inequality: The negative consequences for humanity." *Contemporary Crises* 6:333–372.

Stone, Lawrence. 1979. *The Family, Sex and Marriage in England, 1500–1800*. Abridged edition. New York: Harper & Row.

Stringer, C. B., and P. Andrews. 1988. "Genetics and the fossil evidence for the origin of modern humans." *Science* 239:1263–1268.

Stringer, Christopher, and Clive Gamble. 1993. *In Search of the Neanderthals*. London: Thames and Hudson.

Swanson, Guy. 1960. *The Birth of the Gods*. Ann Arbor: University of Michigan Press.

———. 1967. *Religion and Regime: A Sociological Account of the Reformation*. Ann Arbor: University of Michigan Press.

Sweezy, Paul. 1976. "A critique." In Rodney Hilton (ed.), *The Transition from Feudalism to Capitalism*. London: New Left Books. (Originally published 1950.)

———. 1980. *Post-Revolutionary Society*. New York: Monthly Review Press.

Symons, Donald. 1979. *The Evolution of Human Sexuality*. New York: Oxford University Press.

Szelenyi, Ivan. 1992. "Social and political landscape, Central Europe, fall 1990." In Ivo Banac (ed.), *Eastern Europe in Revolution*. Ithaca, N.Y.: Cornell University Press.

Szelenyi, Ivan, and Balazs Szelenyi. 1992. "Why socialism failed: Causes of the disintegration of East European state socialism." Paper presented at the annual meetings of the American Sociological Association, Pittsburgh, Pennsylvania, August.

Szymanski, Albert. 1976. "Racial discrimination and white gain." *American Sociological Review* 41:403–413.

———. 1982. "The socialist world-system." In Christopher K. Chase-Dunn (ed.), *Socialist States in the World-System*. Beverly Hills, Calif.: Sage.

———. 1983. *Class Structure: A Critical Perspective*. New York: Praeger.

Tabatabai, Hamid. 1996. *Statistics on Poverty and Income Distribution*. Geneva: International Labour Office.

Taagepera, Rein. 1978. "Size and duration of empires: Systematics of size." *Social Science Research* 7:108–127.

Tainter, Joseph A. 1988. *The Collapse of Complex Societies*. New York: Cambridge University Press.

Templeton, Alan R. 1993. "The 'Eve' hypotheses: A genetic critique and reanalysis." *American Anthropologist* 95:51–72.

Terrace, H. S. 1979. "How Nim Chimpsky changed my mind." *Psychology Today* 12:65–76.

———. 1985. "In the beginning was the 'name.'" *American Psychologist* 40:1011–1028.

Terrace, H. S., L. A. Petitto, R. J. Sanders, and T. G. Bever. 1979. "Can an ape create a sentence?" *Science* 206:891–900.

Testart, Alain. 1982. "The significance of food storage among hunter-gatherers: Residence patterns, population densities, and social inequalities." *Current Anthropology* 23:523–37.

———. 1988. "Some major problems in the social anthropology of hunter-gatherers." *Current Anthropology* 29:1–32.

Therborn, Goran. 1977. "The rule of capital and the rise of democracy." *New Left Review* 103:3–41.

Thomas, Janet. 1988. "Women and capitalism: Oppression or emancipation?"

Comparative Studies in Society and History 30:534–549.

Thomas, Keith. 1964. "Work and leisure in pre-industrial society." *Past and Present* 29:50–66.

———. 1971. *Religion and the Decline of Magic.* New York: Scribners.

Thompson, Lloyd A. 1989. *Romans and Blacks.* London: Routledge.

Thornton, Russell. 1981. "Demographic antecedents of a revitalization movement: Population change, population size, and the 1890 Ghost Dance." *American Sociological Review* 46:88–96.

Tiano, Susan. 1990. "Maquiladora women: A new category of workers?" In Kathryn Ward (ed.), *Women Workers and Global Restructuring.* Ithaca, N.Y.: ILR Press.

Tiger, Lionel, and Robin Fox. 1971. *The Imperial Animal.* New York: Holt, Rinehart and Winston.

Tiger, Lionel, and Joseph Shepher, 1975. *Women in the Kibbutz.* New York: Harcourt Brace Jovanovich.

Tilly, Charles. 1984. "The old new social history and the new old social history." *Review* 7:363–406.

———. 1990. *Coercion, Capital, and European States, A.D. 990–1990.* Oxford: Basil Blackwell.

Tilly, Charles (ed.). 1975. *The Formation of National States in Western Europe.* Princeton, N.J.: Princeton University Press.

Todorov, Tzvetan. 1993. *On Human Diversity: Nationalism, Racism, and Exoticism in French Thought.* Cambridge, Mass.: Harvard University Press.

Tomich, Dale W. 1990. *Slavery in the Circuit of Sugar: Martinique and the World Economy, 1830–1848.* Baltimore: Johns Hopkins University Press.

Toulmin, Stephen. 1972. *Human Understanding.* Princeton, N.J.: Princeton University Press.

Trivers, Robert. 1985. *Social Evolution.*

Menlo Park, Calif.: Benjamin/Cummings.

Troeltsch, Ernst. 1931. *The Social Teaching of the Christian Churches.* Two volumes. New York: Macmillan.

Trow, Martin. 1966. "The second transformation of American secondary education." In Reinhard Bendix and Seymour Martin Lipset (eds.), *Class, Status, and Power.* Second edition. New York: Free Press.

Tumin, Melvin M. 1953. "Some principles of stratification: A critical analysis." *American Sociological Review* 18:387–393.

Turnbull, Colin. 1972. *The Mountain People.* New York: Simon & Schuster (Touchstone).

Turner, Bryan S. 1983. *Religion and Social Theory: A Materialist Perspective.* London: Heinemann.

Turner, Ralph H. 1960. "Modes of social ascent through education: Sponsored and contest mobility." *American Sociological Review* 25:121–139.

United Nations. 1983. *Statistical Yearbook 1981.* New York: United Nations.

———. 1988. *1985/1986 Statistical Yearbook.* New York: United Nations.

———. 1992a. *Human Development Report.* New York: United Nations.

———. 1992b. *Statistical Yearbook.* New York: United Nations.

UNESCO. 1983. *Statistical Yearbook.* Paris: UNESCO.

———. 1996. *Statistical Yearbook.* Paris: UNESCO.

Upham, Steadman (ed.). 1990. *The Evolution of Political Systems: Sociopolitics in Small-Scale Sedentary Societies.* New York: Cambridge University Press.

U.S. Bureau of the Census. 1982. *Statistical Abstract of the United States.* Washington, D.C.: U.S. Government Printing Office.

———. 1984. *Current Population Reports, Series P-60, No. 142. Money Income of*

Households, Families and Persons in the United States: 1982. Washington D.C.: U.S. Government Printing Office.

———. 1985. *Statistical Abstract of the United States.* Washington, D.C.: U.S. Government Printing Office.

———. 1988. *Statistical Abstract of the United States.* Washington, D.C.: U.S. Government Printing Office.

———. 1990. *Statistical Abstract of the United States.* Washington, D.C.: U.S. Government Printing Office.

———. 1991. *Statistical Abstract of the United States.* Washington, D.C.: U.S. Government Printing Office.

———. 1992. *Statistical Abstract of the United States.* Washington, D.C.: U.S. Government Printing Office.

———. 1996. *Statistical Abstract of the United States.* Washington, D.C.: U.S. Government Printing Office.

U.S. Department of Commerce. 1975. *Historical Statistics of the United States.* Washington, D.C.: U.S. Government Printing Office.

van den Berghe, Pierre L. 1967. *Race and Racism: A Comparative Perspective.* New York: Wiley.

———. 1973. *Age and Sex in Human Societies: A Biosocial Perspective.* Belmont, Calif.: Wadsworth.

———. 1978. *Man in Society: A Biosocial View.* Second edition. New York: Elsevier.

———. 1979. *Human Family Systems: An Evolutionary View.* New York: Elsevier.

———. 1981. *The Ethnic Phenomenon.* New York: Elsevier.

———. 1990. "South Africa after thirty years." *Social Dynamics* 16(2):16–37.

———. 1996. "Racism." *Encyclopedia of Cultural Anthropology* 3:1054–1057. New York: Henry Holt.

Vanfossen, Beth. 1979. *The Structure of Social Inequality.* Boston: Little, Brown.

Veblen, Thorstein. 1965. *The Higher Learning in America.* New York: Augustus M. Kelly. (Originally published 1918.)

Vogel, Lise. 1983. *Marxism and the Oppression of Women: Toward a Unitary Theory.* New Brunswick, N.J.: Rutgers University Press.

Wagar, W. Warren. 1992. *A Short History of the Future.* Second edition. Chicago: University of Chicago Press.

Walker, P. C. Gordon. 1972. "Capitalism and the Reformation." In Lewis W. Spitz (ed.), *The Reformation: Basic Interpretations.* Lexington, Mass.: Heath.

Wallace, Anthony F. C. 1966. *Religion: An Anthropological View.* New York: Random House.

Wallerstein, Immanuel. 1974a. *The Modern World-System: Capitalist Agriculture and the Origins of the European World-Economy in the Sixteenth Century.* New York: Academic Press.

———. 1974b. "The rise and future demise of the world capitalist system: Concepts for comparative analysis." *Comparative Studies in Society and History* 16:387–415.

———. 1979a. "American slavery and the capitalist world-economy." In Immanuel Wallerstein, *The Capitalist World-Economy.* New York: Cambridge University Press.

———. 1979b. "Dependence in an interdependent world: The limited possibilities of transformation within the capitalist world-economy." In Immanuel Wallerstein, *The Capitalist World-Economy.* New York: Cambridge University Press.

———. 1980. *The Modern World-System II: Mercantilism and the Consolidation of the European World-Economy, 1600–1750.* New York: Academic Press.

———. 1982. "Crisis as transition." In Samir Amin et al., *Dynamics of Global Crisis.* New York: Monthly Review Press.

———. 1983. *Historical Capitalism.* London: Verso.

———. 1984a. "Marx and history: Fruitful and unfruitful emphases." *Contemporary Marxism* 9:35–43.

———. 1984b. "The quality of life in different social systems: The model and the reality." In Immanuel Wallerstein, *The Politics of the World-Economy.* New York: Cambridge University Press.

———. 1984c. "Long waves as capitalist process." *Review* 7:559–575.

———. 1984d. "Patterns and prospectives of the capitalist world-economy." In Immanuel Wallerstein, *The Politics of the World-Economy.* New York: Cambridge University Press.

———. 1989. *The Modern World-System III: The Second Era of Great Expansion of the Capitalist World-Economy, 1730–1840s.* San Diego: Academic Press.

Ward, Kathryn (ed.). 1990. *Women Workers and Global Restructuring.* Ithaca, N.Y.: ILR Press.

Ware, Helen. 1979. "Polygyny: Women's views in a transitional society, Nigeria 1975." *Journal of Marriage and the Family* 41:185–195.

Weber, Max. 1927. *General Economic History.* With an introduction by Ira J. Cohen. New Brunswick, N.J.: Transaction Books.

———. 1958. *The Protestant Ethic and the Spirit of Capitalism.* New York: Charles Scribner's Sons. (Originally published 1905.)

———. 1978. *Economy and Society.* Two volumes. Edited by Guenther Roth and Claus Wittich. Berkeley: University of California Press. (Originally published 1923.)

Weissner, Polly. 1982. "Risk, reciprocity, and social influence on !Kung San economies." In Eleanor Leacock and

Richard B. Lee (eds.), *Politics and History in Band Societies.* Cambridge: Cambridge University Press.

Welch, Charles E. III, and Paul C. Glick. 1981. "The incidence of polygamy in contemporary Africa: A research note." *Journal of Marriage and the Family* 43:191–193.

Wenke, Robert J. 1984. *Patterns in Prehistory: Mankind's First Three Million Years.* Second edition. New York: Oxford University Press.

———. 1990. *Patterns in Prehistory: Mankind's First Three Million Years.* Third edition. New York: Oxford University Press.

Westergaard, John, and Henrietta Resler. 1975. *Class in a Capitalist Society: A Study of Contemporary Britain.* New York: Basic Books.

White, Benjamin. 1976. "Population, involution and employment in rural Java." *Development and Change* 7:267–290.

———. 1982. "Child labour and population growth in rural Asia." *Development and Change* 13:587–610.

White, Douglas R., and Michael L. Burton. 1988. "Causes of polygyny: Ecology, economy, kinship, and warfare." *American Anthropologist* 90:871–887.

White, Leslie. 1945. "History, evolutionism, and functionalism." *Southwestern Journal of Anthropology* 1:221–248.

———. 1949. *The Science of Culture.* New York: Grove Press.

———. 1959. *The Evolution of Culture.* New York: McGraw-Hill.

Whiting, Beatrice. 1950. *Paiute Sorcery.* New York: Viking Fund Publications in Anthropology, No. 15.

Wickham-Crowley, Timothy P. 1992. *Guerrillas and Revolution in Latin America: A Comparative Study of Insurgents and Regimes Since 1956.* Princeton, N.J.: Princeton University Press.

Wilber, Charles K. (ed.) 1973. *The Political Economy of Development and Under-development.* New York: Random House.

Wilkinson, David. 1992. "Cities, civilizations, and oikumenes: I." *Comparative Civilizations Review* 27:51–87.

———. 1993. "Cities, civilizations, and oikumenes: II." *Comparative Civilizations Review* 28:41–72.

Wilkinson, Richard G. 1973. *Poverty and Progress: An Ecological Perspective on Economic Development.* New York: Praeger.

Williams, Eric. 1966. *Capitalism and Slavery.* New York: G. P. Putnam's Sons. (Originally published 1944.)

Wilson, Bryan. 1982. *Religion in Sociological Perspective.* New York: Oxford University Press.

Wilson, Carter A. 1996. *Racism: From Slavery to Advanced Capitalism.* Thousand Oaks, Calif.: Sage.

Wilson, Edward O. 1975. *Sociobiology: The New Synthesis.* Cambridge, Mass.: Harvard University Press.

———. 1977. "Foreword." In David P. Barash, *Sociobiology and Behavior.* New York: Elsevier.

Wilson, William J. 1973. *Power, Racism, and Privilege.* New York: Free Press.

———. 1978. *The Declining Significance of Race.* Chicago: University of Chicago Press.

———. 1987. *The Truly Disadvantaged: The Inner City, the Underclass, and Public Policy.* Chicago: University of Chicago Press.

Winch, Robert F. 1977. *Familial Organization.* New York: Free Press.

Winterhalder, Bruce. 1993. "Work, resources, and population in foraging societies." *Man* 28:321–340.

Winterhalder, Bruce, and Eric Alden Smith (eds.). 1981. *Hunter-Gatherer Foraging Strategies: Ethnographic and Archaeological Analyses.* Chicago: University of Chicago Press.

Wittfogel, Karl. 1957. *Oriental Despotism.* New Haven: Yale University Press.

Wolf, Eric. 1966. *Peasants.* Englewood Cliffs, N.J.: Prentice-Hall.

———. 1982. *Europe and the People Without History.* Berkeley: University of California Press.

Wolpoff, Milford H. 1989. "Multiregional evolution: The fossil alternative to Eden." In P. Mellars and C. B. Stringer (eds.), *The Human Revolution.* Edinburgh: Edinburgh University Press.

Woodburn, James. 1968. "An introduction to Hadza ecology." In Richard B. Lee and Irven DeVore (eds.), *Man the Hunter.* Chicago: Aldine.

———. 1982. "Egalitarian societies." *Man* 27:431–451.

Woolfson, Charles. 1982. *The Labour Theory of Culture.* London: Routledge & Kegan Paul.

World Bank. 1984. *World Development Report.* New York: Oxford University Press.

———. 1986. *World Development Report.* New York: Oxford University Press.

———. 1988. *World Development Report.* New York: Oxford University Press.

———. 1992. *World Development Report.* New York: Oxford University Press.

———. 1996. *World Development Report.* New York: Oxford University Press.

———. 1997. *World Development Report.* New York: Oxford University Press.

Worsley, Peter. 1968. *The Trumpet Shall Sound: A Study of "Cargo" Cults in Melanesia.* New York: Schocken Books.

Wright, Erik Olin. 1978. *Class, Crisis and the State.* London: New Left Books.

———. 1979. *Class Structure and Income Determination.* New York: Academic Press.

——. 1983. "Giddens's critique of Marxism." *New Left Review* 138:11–35.

——. 1985. *Classes.* London: Verso.

Wright, Erik Olin, David Hachen, Cynthia Costello, and Joey Sprague. 1982. "The American class structure." *American Sociological Review* 47:709–726.

Wuthnow, Robert. 1976. *The Consciousness Reformation.* Berkeley: University of California Press.

——. 1980. "World order and religious movements." In Albert Bergesen (ed.), *Studies of the Modern World-System.* New York: Academic Press.

——. 1989. *Communities of Discourse: Ideology and Social Structure in the Reformation, the Enlightenment, and European Socialism.* Cambridge, Mass.: Harvard University Press.

Yanowitch, Murray. 1977. *Social and Economic Inequality in the Soviet Union.* White Plains, N.Y.: Sharpe.

Yellen, J. E. 1977. *Archaeological Approaches to the Present: Models for Reconstructing the Past.* New York: Academic Press.

Yesner, David R. 1994. "Seasonality and resource 'stress' among hunter-gatherers: Archaeological signatures." In Ernest S. Burch, Jr., and Linda J. Ellanna (eds.), *Key Issues in Hunter-Gatherer Research.* Oxford: Berg.

Yinger, J. Milton. 1970. *The Scientific Study of Religion.* New York: Macmillan.

Yoshihara, Kunio. 1986. *Japanese Economic Development.* Second edition. Tokyo: Oxford University Press.

Zaretsky, Eli. 1976. *Capitalism, the Family, and Personal Life.* New York: Harper & Row.

Zaslavsky, Victor. 1995. "From redistribution to marketization: Social and attitudal change in post-Soviet Russia." In Gail W. Lapidus (ed.), *The New Russia: Troubled Transformation.* Boulder, Colo.: Westview.

Zeitlin, Irving. 1973. *Rethinking Sociology: A Critique of Contemporary Theory.* Englewood Cliffs, N.J.: Prentice-Hall.

——. 1984. *The Social Condition of Humanity.* Second edition. New York: Oxford University Press.

Zelditch, Morris, Jr. 1964. "Cross-cultural analyses of family structure." In H. T. Christensen (ed.), *Handbook of Marriage and the Family.* Chicago: Rand McNally.

Zeman, Z. A. B. 1991. *The Making and Breaking of Communist Europe.* Oxford: Blackwell.

Zemtsov, Ilya, and John Farrar. 1989. *Gorbachev: The Man and the System.* New Brunswick, N.J.: Transaction Books.

Zipf, George Kingsley, 1965. *Human Behavior and the Principle of Least Effort.* New York: Hafner. (Originally published 1949.)

Zolberg, Aristide R. 1981. "Origins of the modern world system: A missing link." *World Politics* 33:253–281.

Credits

Name Index

Subject Index